Designing for Cisco Network Service Architectures (ARCH) Foundation Learning Guide, Fourth Edition
CCDP ARCH 300-320

Marwan Al-shawi, CCDE No. 20130066
André Laurent, CCDE No. 20120024, CCIE No. 21840

Cisco Press

800 East 96th Street

Indianapolis, Indiana 46240 USA

Designing for Cisco Network Service Architectures (ARCH) Foundation Learning Guide, Fourth Edition

Marwan Al-shawi and André Laurent

Copyright © 2017 Cisco Systems, Inc.

Published by:
Cisco Press
800 East 96th Street
Indianapolis, IN 46240 USA

All rights reserved. No part of this book may be reproduced or transmitted in any form or by any means, electronic or mechanical, including photocopying, recording, or by any information storage and retrieval system, without written permission from the publisher, except for the inclusion of brief quotations in a review.

Printed in the United States of America

2   17

Library of Congress Control Number: 2016958010

ISBN-13: 978-1-58714-462-2

ISBN-10: 1-58714-462-x

Warning and Disclaimer

This book is designed to provide information about designing Cisco Network Service Architectures. Every effort has been made to make this book as complete and as accurate as possible, but no warranty or fitness is implied.

The information is provided on an "as is" basis. The authors, Cisco Press, and Cisco Systems, Inc. shall have neither liability nor responsibility to any person or entity with respect to any loss or damages arising from the information contained in this book or from the use of the discs or programs that may accompany it.

The opinions expressed in this book belong to the author and are not necessarily those of Cisco Systems, Inc.

Trademark Acknowledgments

All terms mentioned in this book that are known to be trademarks or service marks have been appropriately capitalized. Cisco Press or Cisco Systems, Inc., cannot attest to the accuracy of this information. Use of a term in this book should not be regarded as affecting the validity of any trademark or service mark.

Special Sales

For information about buying this title in bulk quantities, or for special sales opportunities (which may include electronic versions; custom cover designs; and content particular to your business, training goals, marketing focus, or branding interests), please contact our corporate sales department at corpsales@pearsoned.com or (800) 382-3419.

For government sales inquiries, please contact governmentsales@pearsoned.com.

For questions about sales outside the U.S., please contact intlcs@pearson.com.

Feedback Information

At Cisco Press, our goal is to create in-depth technical books of the highest quality and value. Each book is crafted with care and precision, undergoing rigorous development that involves the unique expertise of members from the professional technical community.

Readers' feedback is a natural continuation of this process. If you have any comments regarding how we could improve the quality of this book, or otherwise alter it to better suit your needs, you can contact us through email at feedback@ciscopress.com. Please make sure to include the book title and ISBN in your message.

We greatly appreciate your assistance.

Editor-in-Chief: Mark Taub	**Copy Editor:** Chuck Hutchinson
Alliances Manager, Cisco Press: Ron Fligge	**Technical Editors:** Denise Fishburne, Orhan Ergun
Product Line Manager: Brett Bartow	**Editorial Assistant:** Vanessa Evans
Acquisitions Editor: Michelle Newcomb	**Cover Designer:** Chuti Prasertsith
Managing Editor: Sandra Schroeder	**Composition:** codeMantra
Development Editor: Ginny Munroe	**Indexer:** Lisa Stumpf
Senior Project Editor: Tonya Simpson	**Proofreader:** Deepa Ramesh

Americas Headquarters
Cisco Systems, Inc.
San Jose, CA

Asia Pacific Headquarters
Cisco Systems (USA) Pte. Ltd.
Singapore

Europe Headquarters
Cisco Systems International BV
Amsterdam, The Netherlands

Cisco has more than 200 offices worldwide. Addresses, phone numbers, and fax numbers are listed on the Cisco Website at www.cisco.com/go/offices.

CCDE, CCENT, Cisco Eos, Cisco HealthPresence, the Cisco logo, Cisco Lumin, Cisco Nexus, Cisco StadiumVision, Cisco TelePresence, Cisco WebEx, DCE, and Welcome to the Human Network are trademarks; Changing the Way We Work, Live, Play, and Learn and Cisco Store are service marks; and Access Registrar, Aironet, AsyncOS, Bringing the Meeting To You, Catalyst, CCDA, CCDP, CCIE, CCIP, CCNA, CCNP, CCSP, CCVP, Cisco, the Cisco Certified Internetwork Expert logo, Cisco IOS, Cisco Press, Cisco Systems, Cisco Systems Capital, the Cisco Systems logo, Cisco Unity, Collaboration Without Limitation, EtherFast, EtherSwitch, Event Center, Fast Step, Follow Me Browsing, FormShare, GigaDrive, HomeLink, Internet Quotient, IOS, iPhone, iQuick Study, IronPort, the IronPort logo, LightStream, Linksys, MediaTone, MeetingPlace, MeetingPlace Chime Sound, MGX, Networkers, Networking Academy, Network Registrar, PCNow, PIX, PowerPanels, ProConnect, ScriptShare, SenderBase, SMARTnet, Spectrum Expert, StackWise, The Fastest Way to Increase Your Internet Quotient, TransPath, WebEx, and the WebEx logo are registered trademarks of Cisco Systems, Inc. and/or its affiliates in the United States and certain other countries.

All other trademarks mentioned in this document or website are the property of their respective owners. The use of the word partner does not imply a partnership relationship between Cisco and any other company. (0812R)

About the Authors

Marwan Al-shawi, CCDE No. 20130066, is a Cisco Press author whose titles include the top Cisco certification design books *CCDE Study Guide* and *Designing for Cisco Network Service Architectures (ARCH) Foundation Learning Guide*, Fourth Edition. He also is an experienced technical architect. Marwan has been in the networking industry for more than 12 years and has been involved in architecting, designing, and implementing various large-scale networks, some of which are global service provider–grade networks. Marwan holds a Master of Science degree in internetworking from the University of Technology, Sydney. He enjoys helping and assessing network designs and architectures; therefore, he was selected as a Cisco Designated VIP by the Cisco Support Community (CSC) (official Cisco Systems forums) in 2012 and by the Solutions and Architectures subcommunity in 2014. In addition, Marwan was selected as a member of the Cisco Champions program in 2015 and 2016. In his spare time, Marwan provides CCDP- and CCDE-related training and blogs at netdesignarena.com.

André Laurent, 3xCCIE No. 21840, CCDE No. 20120024, is the worldwide director of engineering for enterprise networking sales at Cisco Systems and a Cisco Press author. Outside his own personal development, André has an equal passion for helping others develop their systems and assisting them with the certification process. André is recognized in the industry as a subject matter expert in the areas of routing, switching, security, and design. Although he wears a Cisco badge, André takes a neutral approach in helping clients establish a long-term business and technology vision covering necessary strategy, execution, and metrics for measuring impact.

About the Technical Reviewers

Denise "Fish" Fishburne, CCDE No. 20090014, CCIE No. 2639 (R&S, SNA), is an engineer and team lead with the Customer Proof of Concept Lab (CPOC) in North Carolina. Fish is a geek who absolutely adores learning and passing it on. She works on many technologies in the CPOC, but her primary technical strength is troubleshooting. Fish has been with Cisco since 1996 and CPOC since 2001, and has been a regular speaker at Networkers/Cisco Live since 2006. Cisco Live is a huge passion for Fish! As such, in 2009, she got even more deeply involved with it by becoming a Cisco Live session group manager. Look for Fish swimming in the bits and bytes all around you, or just go to www.NetworkingWithFish.com.

Orhan Ergun, CCDE No. 2014:0017, CCIE No. 2014:0017 (CCNP, CCDP, JNCIS, and JNCIP), is a network architect who focuses on service providers, data centers, virtualization, cloud, and network security. He has more than 13 years of IT experience and has worked on many medium- and large-scale network design and deployment projects. He teaches Cisco network design concepts and writes exam questions for Cisco Systems.

Dedications

I would like to dedicate this book to my wonderful mother for her continued support, love, encouragement, guidance, and wisdom, as well as to the people in my life who always support and encourage me.

And most importantly, I would like to thank God for all blessings in my life.

—*Marwan*

I would like to dedicate this book to the women in my life. My mother, for her unconditional dedication and love. My sister, for rescuing me from the drifter life and setting me up with my first job in the industry. My beautiful wife, who continues to stand by my side while encouraging me through all the new challenges, opportunities, and experiences life brings.

—*André*

Acknowledgments

A special thank you goes to the Pearson Cisco Press team for their support in making this book possible.

A big thank you goes to André for being part of this publication and adding his expert perspective. It's always a pleasure to work with an experienced and extremely helpful person like André.

We would like to give special recognition to the wonderful technical reviewers Denise Fishburne and Orhan Ergun for their valuable contributions in editing the book. Both Denise and Orhan are very experienced network designers and CCDE certified; therefore, their suggestions and feedback helped shape and optimize the quality of the contents on multiple areas.

In addition, a special thank you to Maurizio Portolani (Cisco Press author and distinguished system engineer at Cisco Systems) and John Weston (systems engineer at Cisco) for their help and support with the technical review and optimization of the ACI chapter.

Also, we want to thank Adrian Arumugam (network engineer for a major content provider) for his technical review and valuable comments of certain chapters.

Contents at a Glance

Introduction xxix

Part I **Designing Reliable and Resilient Enterprise Layer 2 and Layer 3 Networks**

Chapter 1 Optimal Enterprise Campus Design **1**

Chapter 2 EIGRP Design **49**

Chapter 3 OSPF Design **75**

Chapter 4 IS-IS Design **101**

Chapter 5 Border Gateway Protocol Design **145**

Part II **Enterprise IPv6 Design Considerations and Challenges**

Chapter 6 IPv6 Design Considerations in the Enterprise **193**

Chapter 7 Challenges of the Transition to IPv6 **219**

Part III **Modern Enterprise Wide-Area Networks Design**

Chapter 8 Service Provider–Managed VPNs **229**

Chapter 9 Enterprise-Managed WANs **271**

Chapter 10 Enterprise WAN Resiliency Design **323**

Part IV **Enterprise Data Center Designs**

Chapter 11 Multitier Enterprise Data Center Designs **375**

Chapter 12 New Trends and Techniques to Design Modern Data Centers **397**

Chapter 13 Cisco Application-Centric Infrastructure **431**

Chapter 14 Data Center Connections **477**

Part V **Design QoS for Optimized User Experience**

Chapter 15 QoS Overview **513**

Chapter 16 QoS Design Principles and Best Practices **553**

Chapter 17   Campus, WAN, and Data Center QoS Design   **567**

Chapter 18   MPLS VPN QoS Design   **605**

Chapter 19   IPsec VPN QoS Design   **619**

Part VI   IP Multicast Design

Chapter 20   Enterprise IP Multicast Design   **633**

Chapter 21   Rendezvous Point Distribution Solutions   **665**

Part VII   Designing Optimum Enterprise Network Security

Chapter 22   Designing Security Services and Infrastructure Protection   **689**

Chapter 23   Designing Firewall and IPS Solutions   **709**

Chapter 24   IP Multicast Security   **743**

Chapter 25   Designing Network Access Control Solutions   **759**

Part VIII   Design Scenarios

Chapter 26   Design Case Studies   **777**

Appendix A   Answers to Review Questions   **843**

Appendix B   References   **855**

Index   **857**

Contents

Introduction xxix

Part I **Designing Reliable and Resilient Enterprise Layer 2 and Layer 3 Networks**

Chapter 1 **Optimal Enterprise Campus Design 1**

Enterprise Campus Design Principles 2

Hierarchy 3

  Access Layer 4

  Distribution Layer 5

  Core Layer 6

  Enterprise Campus Two-Tier Layer Model 8

  Enterprise Campus Three-Tier Layer Model 9

Modularity 10

  Modular Enterprise Campus Architecture and Modular Enterprise Campus with OSPF 10

  Access-Distribution Block 13

Flexibility 15

  Campus Network Virtualization 16

  Campus Network Virtualization Technologies and Techniques 17

  VLAN Assignment 17

  Virtual Routing and Forwarding 18

  Path Isolation Techniques 19

Resiliency 23

  Enterprise Campus High-Availability Design Considerations 23

  VLANs, Trunking, and Link Aggregation Design Recommendations 24

  VLAN Design 24

  Trunking 27

  Link Aggregation 28

  First-Hop Redundancy Protocol (FHRP) 31

  IP Gateway Redundancy Optimization with VSS 35

  Layer 2 to Layer 3 Boundary Design Options and Considerations 36

  Distribution-to-Distribution Link Design Considerations 36

  A Summary of Enterprise Campus HA Designs 44

Summary 46

Review Questions 46

References 48

Chapter 2   EIGRP Design   49

Scalable EIGRP Design Overview   50
EIGRP with Multiple Autonomous Systems   50
    EIGRP Queries   52
    Multiple EIGRP Autonomous System Drivers   53
EIGRP Multilayer Architectures   53
    EIGRP Two-Layer Hierarchy Architecture   56
    EIGRP Three-Layer Hierarchy Architecture   57
EIGRP Hub-and-Spoke Design   60
    Summarization Challenges   61
    Route Summarization Black Holes   61
    Route Summarization and Suboptimal Routing   63
    EIGRP Hub-and-Spoke Scalability Optimization   65
    EIGRP Stub Leaking   67
    EIGRP DMVPN Scaling   69
EIGRP Fast Convergence Design Considerations   70
    Bidirectional Forwarding Detection   70
EIGRP Graceful Restart/NSF Considerations   71
Summary   72
Review Questions   72

Chapter 3   OSPF Design   75

OSPF Scalability Design Considerations   76
    Adjacent Neighbors   76
    Routing Information in the Area and the Routed Domain   78
    Numbers of Routers in an Area   80
    Number of Areas per ABR   81
OSPF Area Design Considerations   82
    OSPF Hierarchy   84
    Area and Domain Summarization   85
OSPF Full-Mesh Design   87
OSPF Hub-and-Spoke Design   88
    OSPF ABR Placement in Hub-and-Spoke Design   89
    Number of Areas in OSPF Hub-and-Spoke Design   91
    OSPF Network Types in Hub-and-Spoke Design   92

OSPF Convergence Design Considerations and Optimization
   Techniques   93
  Event Detection   94
  OSPF Event Propagation   94
  OSPF Event Processing   96
  OSPF Flooding Reduction   97
  OSPF Database Overload Protection   97
Summary   98
Review Questions   99

Chapter 4 IS-IS Design   101

Protocol Overview   102
  IS-IS Characteristics   103
  Integrated IS-IS Routing   104
IS-IS Hierarchical Architecture Overview   105
  IS-IS Router and Link Types   106
  IS-IS Adjacencies   108
IS-IS Versus OSPF   110
  Similarities Between IS-IS and OSPF   110
  OSPF and IS-IS Characteristics   110
  Integrated IS-IS and OSPF Area Designs   112
  OSPF Area Design   112
  Integrated IS-IS Area Design   113
IS-IS Technical Deep Dive   114
  IS-IS Addressing   114
  IS-IS Packets   117
  IS-IS Information Data Flow   118
  IS-IS Network Types   119
  IS-IS Protocol Operations   119
  Level 1 and Level 2 LSPs and IIHs   121
  IS-IS Link-State Packets Flooding   122
  IS-IS LSDB Synchronization   123
IS-IS Design Considerations   124
  IS-IS Routing Logic Overview   125
  Advanced IS-IS Routing   126
  Route Leaking   126
  Asymmetric Versus Symmetric IS-IS Routing   129

IS-IS Routing over NBMA Hub-and-Spoke   132
IS-IS Routing over a Full-Mesh Network   133
Flat IS-IS Routing Design   134
Hierarchal IS-IS Design   135
IS-IS Routes Summarization   136
Integrated IS-IS for IPv6   138
IS-IS Single-Topology Restrictions   138
Multitopology IS-IS for IPv6   140
Final Thoughts on IS-IS Routing Design   141
Summary   142
Review Questions   142

Chapter 5   Border Gateway Protocol Design   145

BGP Overview   146
   BGP Speaker Types   147
   BGP Loop Prevention and Split-Horizon Rule   148
   BGP Path Attributes and Path Selection (Review)   149
   BGP Path Attributes   150
   How BGP Selects Paths   150
Designing Scalable iBGP Networks   152
   iBGP Scalability Limitations   152
   IBGP Scalability Solutions   152
   BGP Route Reflectors   153
   BGP Confederations   155
   BGP Confederations Versus BGP Route Reflectors   157
BGP Route Reflector Design   158
   Route Reflector Split-Horizon Rule   158
   BGP Route Reflectors Redundancy Design Options and
      Considerations   159
   Route Reflector Clusters   160
   Loop-Prevention Mechanisms   162
   Congruence of Physical and Logical Networks   165
   Hierarchical Route Reflector Design   167
   Route Reflector Potential Network Design Issues   169
Enhancing the Design of BGP Policies with BGP Communities   169
   BGP Community Attribute Overview   169
   Well-Known BGP Communities   170

BGP Named Community List   171
Planning for the Use of BGP Communities   171
Case Study: Designing Enterprise wide BGP Policies Using BGP Communities   172
Enterprise BGP Policy Requirements   173
BGP Community Solution Design   174
Solution Detailed Design and Traffic Flow   175
BGP Load-Sharing Design   177
Single-Homing Versus Multihoming   177
Dual-Homing and Multihoming Design Considerations   178
Single-Homed, Multiple Links   178
Dual-Homed to One ISP Using a Single Local Edge Router   180
Dual-Homed to One ISP Using Multiple Edge Routers   182
Multihoming with Two ISPs Using a Single Local Edge Router   183
Multihoming with Two ISPs Using Multiple Local Edge Routers   186
Summary   189
Review Questions   189

Part II   Enterprise IPv6 Design Considerations and Challenges

Chapter 6   IPv6 Design Considerations in the Enterprise   193

IPv6 Deployment and Design Considerations   194
Business and Network Discovery Phase   196
Assessment Phase   196
Planning and Design Phase   196
Implementation and Optimization Phases   197
Considerations for Migration to IPv6 Design   197
Acquiring IPv6 Prefixes   197
Provider Independent Versus Provider Assigned   198
Where to Start the Migration   199
Migration Models and Design Considerations   200
IPv6 Island   200
IPv6 WAN   201
IPv6 Transition Mechanisms   203
Dual Stack   205
NAT64 and DNS64   206
Manual Tunnels   208
Tunnel Brokers   209

6 Rapid Deployment   210
Dual-Stack Lite (DS-Lite)   211
Locator/ID Separation Protocol (LISP)   212
LISP Site Edge Devices   213
LISP Infrastructure Devices   213
Final Thoughts on IPv6 Transition Mechanisms   216
Summary   217
Review Questions   217

Chapter 7   Challenges of the Transition to IPv6   219
IPv6 Services   219
Name Services   220
Implementation Recommendations   220
Addressing Services   220
Implementation Recommendations   221
Security Services   221
Link Layer Security Considerations   221
Application Support   222
Application Adaptation   223
Application Workarounds   223
Control Plane Security   224
Dual-Stack Security Considerations   225
Tunneling Security Considerations   225
Multihoming   226
Summary   226
Review Questions   227

Part III   Modern Enterprise Wide-Area Networks Design

Chapter 8   Service Provider–Managed VPNs   229
Choosing Your WAN Connection   230
Layer 3 MPLS VPNs   233
MPLS VPN Architecture   234
Enterprise Routing Considerations   236
Provider Edge (PE) Router Architecture   237
Route Distinguishers   238
Route Target (RT)   240
PE-CE Routing Protocol   241
Using EIGRP as the PE-CE Routing Protocol   241

Using OSPF as the PE-CE Routing Protocol 247
Using BGP as the PE-CE Routing Protocol 252
Case Study: MPLS VPN Routing Propagation 255
Forwarding in MPLS VPN 258
Layer 2 MPLS VPN Services 259
Virtual Private Wire Service (VPWS) 259
Virtual Private LAN Service (VPLS) 261
VPLS Scalability Considerations 263
VPLS Resiliency Considerations 265
VPLS Versus VPWS 266
Summary 267
Review Questions 268

Chapter 9 Enterprise-Managed WANs 271
Enterprise-Managed VPN Overview 272
GRE Overview 273
Multipoint GRE Overview 275
Point-to-Point and Multipoint GRE Comparison 276
IPsec Overview 278
IPsec and GRE 280
IPsec and Virtual Tunnel Interface 281
IPsec and Dynamic VTI 283
DMVPN Overview 283
DMVPN Phase 1 287
DMVPN Phase 2 289
DMVPN Phase 3 292
Case Study: EIGRP DMVPN 295
EIGRP over DMVPN Phase 1 295
EIGRP over DMVPN Phase 2 297
EIGRP over DMVPN Phase 3 299
DMVPN Phase 1–3 Summary 302
DMVPN and Redundancy 302
Case Study: MPLS/VPN over GRE/DMVPN 304
SSL VPN Overview 312

FlexVPN Overview   314
   FlexVPN Architecture   315
   FlexVPN Capabilities   315
   FlexVPN Configuration Blocks   315
GETVPN   317
Summary   320
Review Questions   321

Chapter 10   Enterprise WAN Resiliency Design   323
WAN Remote-Site Overview   324
MPLS Layer 3 WAN Design Models   326
Common Layer 2 WAN Design Models   329
Common VPN WAN Design Models   331
3G/4G VPN Design Models   335
Remote Site Using Local Internet   337
Remote-Site LAN   339
Case Study: Redundancy and Connectivity   343
   ATM WAN Design   344
   Remote-Site (Branch Office) WAN Design   346
   Regional Offices WAN Design   348
   Basic Traffic Engineering Techniques   351
NGWAN, SDWAN, and IWAN Solution Overview   354
   Transport-Independent Design   356
   Intelligent Path Control   356
   Application Optimization   356
   Secure Connectivity   357
   Management   357
IWAN Design Overview   358
   IWAN Hybrid Design Model   359
Cisco PfR Overview   361
   Cisco PfR Operations   362
   Cisco IWAN and PfRv3   363
   Cisco PfRv3 Design and Deployment Considerations   366
Enterprise WAN and Access Management   367
   APIC-EM   368
   Design of APIC-EM   370
Summary   371
Review Questions   372

Part IV   Enterprise Data Center Designs

Chapter 11   Multitier Enterprise Data Center Designs   375

    Case Study 1: Small Data Centers (Connecting Servers to an Enterprise LAN)   376

    Case Study 2: Two-Tier Data Center Network Architecture   378

    Case Study 3: Three-Tier Data Center Network Architecture   380

        Data Center Inter-VLAN Routing   381

        End of Row Versus Top of Rack Design   383

        Fabric Extenders   385

        Data Center High Availability   388

        Network Interface Controller Teaming   392

    Summary   394

    Review Questions   394

Chapter 12   New Trends and Techniques to Design Modern Data Centers   397

    The Need for a New Network Architecture   397

    Limitations of Current Networking Technology   398

    Modern Data Center Design Techniques and Architectures   400

        Spine-Leaf Data Center Design   400

        Network Overlays   402

        Cisco Fabric Path   402

        Virtual Extensible LAN (VXLAN)   407

        VXLAN Tunnel Endpoint   408

        Remote VTEP Discovery and Tenant Address Learning   411

        VXLAN Control-Plane Optimization   413

        Software-Defined Networking   414

        How SDN Can Help   416

        Selection Criteria of SDN Solutions   417

        SDN Requirements   419

        SDN Challenges   419

        Direction of Nontraditional SDN   421

    Multitenant Data Center   422

        Secure Tenant Separation   422

        Layer 3 Separation with VRF-Lite   423

        Device-Level Virtualization and Separation   424

Case Study: Multitenant Data Center 425
Microsegmentation with Overlay Networks 427
Summary 428
Review Questions 429
References 430

Chapter 13 Cisco Application-Centric Infrastructure 431

ACI Characteristics 432
How the Cisco ACI Addresses Current Networking Limitations 432
Cisco ACI Architecture Components 434
Cisco Application Policy Infrastructure Controller (APIC) 434
APIC Approach Within the ACI Architecture 436
Cisco ACI Fabric 437
ACI Network Virtualization Overlays 441
Application Design Principles with the Cisco ACI Policy Model 447
What Is an Endpoint Group in Cisco ACI? 450
Design EPGs 451
ACI Fabric Access Polices 454
Building Blocks of a Tenant in the Cisco ACI 456
Crafting Applications Design with the Cisco ACI 459
ACI Interaction with External Layer 2 Connections and Networks 461
Connecting ACI to the Outside Layer 2 Domain 462
ACI Integration with STP-Based Layer LAN 464
ACI Routing 465
First-Hop Layer 3 Default Gateway in ACI 465
Border Leaves 467
Route Propagation inside the ACI Fabric 468
Connecting the ACI Fabric to External Layer 3 Domains 470
Integration and Migration to ACI Connectivity Options 471
Summary 473
Review Questions 475
References 476

Chapter 14 Data Center Connections 477

Data Center Traffic Flows 478
Traffic Flow Directions 478
Traffic Flow Types 479

The Need for DCI 482
IP Address Mobility 484
Case Study: Dark Fiber DCI 490
Pseudowire DCI 495
   Virtual Private LAN Service DCI 496
   Customer-Managed Layer 2 DCI Deployment Models 497
   Any Transport over MPLS over GRE 497
   Customer-Managed Layer 2 DCI Deployment 498
   Layer 2 DCI Caveats 501
   Overlay Transport Virtualization DCI 501
   Overlay Networking DCI 507
   Layer 3 DCI 507
Summary 509
Review Questions 510

Part V   **Design QoS for Optimized User Experience**

Chapter 15   **QoS Overview 513**

QoS Overview 514
IntServ versus DiffServ 514
Classification and Marking 516
   Classifications and Marking Tools 516
      Layer 2 Marking: IEEE 802.1Q/p Class of Service 517
      Layer 3 Marking: IP Type of Service 519
      Layer 3 Marking: DSCP Per-Hop Behaviors 520
      Layer 2.5 Marking: MPLS Experimental Bits 524
      Mapping QoS Markings between OSI Layers 524
      Layer 7 Classification: NBAR/NBAR2 526
Policers and Shapers 527
   Token Bucket Algorithms 529
Policing Tools: Single-Rate Three-Color Marker 532
Policing Tools: Two-Rate Three-Color Marker 533
Queuing Tools 535
  Tx-Ring 536
  Fair Queuing 537
  CBWFQ 538

Dropping Tools   541
    DSCP-Based WRED   541
    IP ECN   547
Summary   550
Review Questions   550

Chapter 16   QoS Design Principles and Best Practices   553

QoS Overview   553
Classification and Marking Design Principles   554
Policing and Remarking Design Principles   556
Queuing Design Principles   557
Dropping Design Principles   557
Per-Hop Behavior Queue Design Principles   558
RFC 4594 QoS Recommendation   559
QoS Strategy Models   560
    4-Class QoS Strategy   561
    8-Class QoS Strategy   562
    12-Class QoS Strategy   564
Summary   565
Review Questions   565

Chapter 17   Campus, WAN, and Data Center QoS Design   567

Campus QoS Overview   568
    VoIP and Video   568
    Buffers and Bursts   569
    Trust States and Boundaries   570
    Trust States and Boundaries Example   571
    Dynamic Trust State   572
    Classification/Marking/Policing QoS Model   573
    Queuing/Dropping Recommendations   574
    Link Aggregation "EtherChannel" QoS Design   575
    Practical Example of Campus QoS Design   576
WAN QoS Overview   588
    Platform Performance Considerations   589
    Latency and Jitter Considerations   590
    Queuing Considerations   591
    Shaping Considerations   592
    Practical Example of WAN and Branch QoS   593

Data Center QoS Overview   594
   High-Performance Trading Architecture   595
   Big Data Architecture   596
   Case Study: Virtualized Multiservice Architectures   596
   Data Center Bridging Toolset   597
   Case Study: DC QoS Application   599
Summary   601
Review Questions   603

Chapter 18 MPLS VPN QoS Design   605

The Need for QoS in MPLS VPN   605
Layer 2 Private WAN QoS Administration   607
Fully Meshed MPLS VPN QoS Administration   608
MPLS DiffServ Tunneling Modes   609
   Uniform Tunneling Mode   612
   Short-Pipe Tunneling Mode   612
   Pipe Tunneling Mode   614
Sample MPLS VPN QoS Roles   615
Summary   617
Review Questions   617

Chapter 19 IPsec VPN QoS Design   619

The Need for QoS in IPsec VPN   619
VPN Use Cases and Their QoS Models   621
IPsec Refresher   621
IOS Encryption and Classification: Order of Operations   623
MTU Considerations   625
DMVPN QoS Considerations   626
GET VPN QoS Considerations   629
Summary   630
Review Questions   631

Part VI IP Multicast Design

Chapter 20 Enterprise IP Multicast Design   633

How Does IP Multicast Work?   634
   Multicast Group   635
   IP Multicast Service Model   636
   Functions of a Multicast Network   638

Multicast Protocols   638
Multicast Forwarding and RPF Check   639
   Case Study 1: RPF Check Fails and Succeeds   641
Multicast Protocol Basics   642
   Multicast Distribution Trees Identification   644
PIM-SM Overview   645
   Receiver Joins PIM-SM Shared Tree   646
   Registered to RP   647
   PIM-SM SPT Switchover   649
Multicast Routing Table   652
Basic SSM Concepts   654
   SSM Scenario   655
Bidirectional PIM   657
   PIM Modifications for Bidirectional Operation   658
   DF Election   658
   DF Election Messages   660
   Case Study 2: DF Election   660
Summary   662
Review Questions   663

Chapter 21   Rendezvous Point Distribution Solutions   665

Rendezvous Point Discovery   665
   Rendezvous Placement   667
   Auto-RP   668
   Auto-RP Candidate RPs   670
   Auto-RP Mapping Agents   670
   Auto-RP and Other Routers   670
   Case Study: Auto-RP Operation   670
   Auto-RP Scope Problem   674
   PIMv2 BSR   676
   PIMv2 BSR: Candidate RPs   677
   PIMv2 BSR: Bootstrap Router   678
   PIMv2 BSR: All PIMv2 Routers   678
   BSR Flooding Problem   678
   IPv6 Embedded Rendezvous Point   679
Anycast RP Features   681
Anycast RP Example   682

MSDP Protocol Overview   683
   MSDP Neighbor Relationship   683
   Case Study: MSDP Operation   684
Summary   686
Review Questions   687

Part VII   Designing Optimum Enterprise Network Security

Chapter 22   Designing Security Services and Infrastructure Protection   689

Network Security Zoning   690
Cisco Modular Network Architecture   691
Cisco Next-Generation Security   696
Designing Infrastructure Protection   696
   Infrastructure Device Access   698
   Routing Infrastructure   699
   Device Resiliency and Survivability   700
   Network Policy Enforcement   701
   Switching Infrastructure   702
   SDN Security Considerations   703
Summary   705
Review Questions   705

Chapter 23   Designing Firewall and IPS Solutions   709

Firewall Architectures   709
Virtualized Firewalls   712
Case Study 1: Separation of Application Tiers   714
   Securing East-West Traffic   716
Case Study 2: Implementing Firewalls in a Data Center   717
Case Study 3: Firewall High Availability   720
IPS Architectures   726
Case Study 4: Building a Secure Campus Edge Design (Internet and Extranet Connectivity)   729
   Campus Edge   730
   Connecting External Partners   737
   Challenges of Connecting External Partners   737
   Extranet Topology: Remote LAN Model   737
   Extranet Topology: Interconnect Model   738
   Extranet: Security and Multitenant Segmentation   739

Summary 740
Review Questions 741

Chapter 24 IP Multicast Security 743
Multicast Security Challenges 744
Problems in the Multicast Network 744
Multicast Network Security Considerations 745
    Network Element Security 746
    Security at the Network Edge 748
    Securing Auto-RP and BSR 749
    MSDP Security 751
    PIM and Internal Multicast Security 752
    Multicast Sender Control 753
    Multicast Receiver Controls 755
    Multicast Admission Controls 757
Summary 757
Review Questions 758

Chapter 25 Designing Network Access Control Solutions 759
IEEE 802.1X Overview 759
Extensible Authentication Protocol 763
802.1X Supplicants 765
IEEE 802.1X Phased Deployment 767
Cisco TrustSec 768
    Profiling Service 768
    Security Group Tag 769
Case Study: Authorization Options 772
Summary 775
Review Questions 775

Part VIII Design Scenarios

Chapter 26 Design Case Studies 777
Case Study 1: Design Enterprise Connectivity 778
    Detailed Requirements and Expectations 778
    Design Analysis and Task List 779
    Selecting a Replacement Routing Protocol 780
    Designing for the New Routing Protocol 780

OSPF Design Optimization   782

Planning and Designing the Migration from the Old to the New Routing   785

Scaling the Design   787

Case Study 2: Design Enterprise BGP Network with Internet Connectivity   788

Detailed Requirements and Expectations   788

Design Analysis and Task List   791

Choosing the Routing Protocol   792

Choosing the Autonomous System Numbers   792

BGP Connectivity   795

BGP Sessions   795

BGP Communities   796

Routing Policy   797

Routing Policy in North American Sites   797

Routing Policy in European and Asian Sites   799

Internet Routing   803

Public IP Space Selection   803

Main HQ Multihoming   804

Default Routing   805

Case Study 3: Design Enterprise IPv6 Network   807

Detailed Requirements and Expectations   808

Design Analysis and Task List   809

Choosing the IP Address Type for the HQ   809

Connecting the Branch Sites   810

Deployment Model   812

Addressing   813

Address Provisioning   814

Communication Between Branches   815

Application and Service Migration   815

Case Study 4: Design Enterprise Data Center Connectivity   816

Detailed Requirements and Expectations   817

Design Analysis and Task List   818

Selecting the Data Center Architecture and Connectivity Model   818

DCN Detailed Connectivity   819

Connecting Network Appliances   821
Data Center Interconnect   822
Data Center Network Virtualization Design   823
Case Study 5: Design Resilient Enterprise WAN   825
Detailed Requirements and Expectations   825
Design Analysis and Task List   826
Selecting WAN Links   828
WAN Overlay   828
Case Study 6: Design Secure Enterprise Network   830
Detailed Requirements and Expectations   831
Security Domains and Zone Design   832
Infrastructure and Network Access Security   833
Layer 2 Security Considerations   834
Main and Remote Location Firewalling   835
Case Study 7: Design QoS in the Enterprise Network   835
Detailed Requirements and Expectations   835
Traffic Discovery and Analysis   836
QoS Design Model   837
QoS Trust Boundary   838
Congestion Management   838
Scavenger Traffic Considerations   839
MPLS WAN DiffServ Tunneling   839

Appendix A   Answers to Review Questions   843

Appendix B   References   855

Index   857

Icons Used in This Book

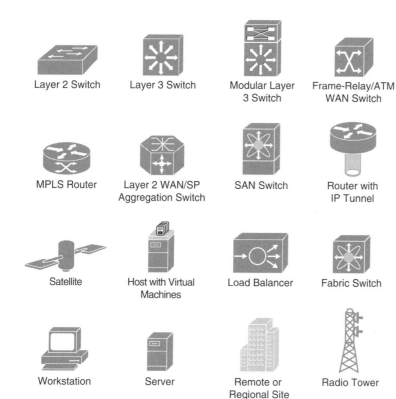

Command Syntax Conventions

The conventions used to present command syntax in this book are the same conventions used in the IOS Command Reference. The Command Reference describes these conventions as follows:

- **Boldface** indicates commands and keywords that are entered literally as shown. In actual configuration examples and output (not general command syntax), boldface indicates commands that are manually input by the user (such as a **show** command).

- *Italic* indicates arguments for which you supply actual values.

- Vertical bars (|) separate alternative, mutually exclusive elements.

- Square brackets ([ ]) indicate an optional element.

- Braces ({ }) indicate a required choice.

- Braces within brackets ([{ }]) indicate a required choice within an optional element.

Reader Services

Register your copy at www.ciscopress.com/title/9781587144622 for convenient access to downloads, updates, and corrections as they become available. To start the registration process, go to www.ciscopress.com/register and log in or create an account*. Enter the product ISBN 9781587144622 and click Submit. When the process is complete, you will find any available bonus content under Registered Products.

*Be sure to check the box that you would like to hear from us to receive exclusive discounts on future editions of this product.

Introduction

Enterprise environments require networks designed for performance, availability, and scalability to achieve outcomes. Seasoned IT professionals with progressive end-to-end network design expertise are crucial in ensuring networks deliver to meet today's requirements while future-proofing investments. For senior network design engineers, principal system engineers, network/solution architects, and CCDA professionals looking to build on your fundamental Cisco network design expertise, the Cisco CCDP certification program focuses on advanced addressing and routing protocols, WANs, service virtualization, and integration strategies for multilayered enterprise architectures.

This exam tests a candidate's knowledge and skills needed to design or help in designing an enterprise network. Successful candidates will be able to design and understand the inner workings of all elements within the common enterprise network, including internal routing, BGP routing, modern WAN connectivity, modern data center and data center interconnect, basic network security considerations, advanced quality-of-service design, transition to IPv6, and multicast routing design.

Goals of This Book

Designing Cisco Network Service Architectures (ARCH) enables network designers, engineers, architects, and CCDP candidates to perform the conceptual, intermediate, and detailed design of a network infrastructure that supports desired network solutions over intelligent network services to achieve effective performance, scalability, and availability. By applying solid Cisco network solution models and recommended design practices, ARCH enables learners to provide viable, stable enterprise internetworking solutions. This book presents concepts and examples necessary to design converged enterprise networks. Also, this new edition has content addressing software-defined networks (SDNs). You will learn additional aspects of modular campus design, advanced routing designs, WAN service designs, enterprise data center design, and security design.

Who Should Read This Book

Besides those who are planning or studying for the CCDP certification, this book is for

- Network designers, architects, consultants, or engineers seeking a thorough understanding of enterprise network design

- Network engineers or architects who are studying for the CCDE certification and need to improve their foundational knowledge of modern enterprise network design

- Anyone wanting to understand basic and advanced network design with an intermediate to advanced level of experience

How This Book Is Organized

This book is organized into eight distinct sections.

Part I of the book explains briefly the various design approaches, requirements, and principles required to design an optimum enterprise campus network. Also, it focuses on enterprise routing design, covering the different design options, considerations, and design implications with regard to business and other design requirements.

- **Chapter 1, "Optimal Enterprise Campus Design":** This chapter discusses how to design a scalable and reliable enterprise campus taking into account applications and business requirements.

- **Chapter 2, "EIGRP Design":** This chapter highlights, analyzes, and discusses different design options and considerations of EIGRP that any network designer must be aware of.

- **Chapter 3, "OSPF Design":** This chapter looks at the different design options and considerations of OSPF that any network designer must be aware of, such as OSPF area design.

- **Chapter 4, "IS-IS Design":** This chapter discusses IS-IS level design. It also compares the key functionalities of IS-IS and OSPF as link-state routing protocols.

- **Chapter 5, "Border Gateway Protocol Design":** This chapter highlights, analyzes, and discusses different design options and considerations of BGP that any network designer must be aware of. It also provides some advanced BGP design approaches to address enterprise design needs.

Part II of the book focuses on IPv6 and how to plan and migrate your network to be IPv6 enabled along with the different design considerations and implications.

- **Chapter 6, "IPv6 Design Considerations in the Enterprise":** This chapter highlights and explains the different design considerations and approaches of migrating IPv4 networks to IPV6.

- **Chapter 7, "Challenges of the Transition to IPv6":** This chapter discusses the different challenges associated with migration to IPv6 that you need to take into account.

Part III of the book focuses on the different models of modern enterprise wide-area network design.

- **Chapter 8, "Service Provider–Managed VPNs":** This chapter highlights and discusses the MPLS Layer 3 and Layer 2 VPN-based WAN modes along with the different design considerations and aspects that you need to be aware of.

- **Chapter 9, "Enterprise-Managed WAN":** This chapter discusses the different enterprise-controlled VPN-based WAN models that can be used in today's enterprise networks.

- **Chapter 10, "Enterprise WAN Resiliency Design":** This chapter explains how to optimize the enterprise-managed WAN model to design a resilient overlay WAN model.

Part IV of the book focuses on the design options and technologies required to design an enterprise data center network.

- **Chapter 11, "Multitier Enterprise Data Center Designs":** This chapter analyzes, explains, and compares the different data center design options and where each should be used.
- **Chapter 12, "New Trends and Techniques to Design Modern Data Centers":** This chapter analyzes, explains, and compares the different modern data center design options and technologies and the drivers of each. It also introduces you to the data center overlay and SDN concepts.
- **Chapter 13, "Cisco Application-Centric Infrastructure":** This chapter analyzes and explains the foundations of the Cisco ACI and the design concepts and terms that are ACI-specific, along with the different migration options from a traditional data center network to an ACI-based data center network.
- **Chapter 14, "Data Center Connections":** This chapter analyzes, explains, and compares the different data center interconnect design options and considerations.

Part V of the book focuses on designing quality of service (QoS) for an optimized user experience and dives deeper, discussing QoS design for the different places in the network.

- **Chapter 15, "QoS Overview":** This chapter explains the different QoS design concepts, techniques, and tools that any design engineer needs to be fully aware of its foundations.
- **Chapter 16, "QoS Design Principles and Best Practices":** This chapter explains the different QoS design principles and strategies required to design a reliable QoS-enabled network.
- **Chapter 17, "Campus, WAN, and Data Center QoS Design":** This chapter explains the best-practice design principles for enabling QoS in campus, WAN, and data center networks.
- **Chapter 18, "MPLS VPN QoS Design":** This chapter covers the basics of designing QoS for MPLS VPN networks.
- **Chapter 19, "IPsec VPN QoS Design":** This chapter reviews QoS-related considerations for IPsec VPNs.

Part VI of the book is an entry point to IP multicast services. It presents the functional model of IP multicast and gives an overview of technologies that are present in IP multicasting. The part is composed of an introduction to IP multicast concepts as well as a discussion of distribution trees and protocols.

- **Chapter 20, "Enterprise IP Multicast Design":** This chapter reviews the foundations of IP multicast and how a multicast-enabled network delivers traffic from a source to a receiver. Also, it explains the most current scalable IP multicast routing protocol.

- **Chapter 21, "Rendezvous Point Distribution Solutions":** This chapter offers an overview of RP distribution solutions. It explains the drawbacks of manual RP configuration and describes the Auto-RP and the BSR mechanisms. The chapter also introduces the concept of Anycast RP, which works in combination with the MSDP.

Part VII of the book focuses on how to design security services and what solutions are available today to implement network-level security.

- **Chapter 22, "Designing Security Services and Infrastructure Protection":** This chapter explains how to secure the network infrastructure as it is a critical business asset.

- **Chapter 23, "Designing Firewall and IPS Solutions":** This chapter explains the common firewall and IPS architectures, high-availability modes, and firewall virtualization along with design recommendations.

- **Chapter 24, "IP Multicast Security":** This chapter describes the challenges with IP multicast security along with recommendations of how to secure a multicast network edge, Auto-RP, BSR, and MSDP.

- **Chapter 25, "Designing Network Access Control Solutions":** This chapter discusses the different access control design approaches, including IEEE 802.1X–based access control and Cisco TrustSec technology.

Part VIII of the book offers some design scenarios that help you, as design engineer, practice designing technology solutions based on business and technical requirements.

- **Chapter 26, "Design Case Studies":** This chapter provides different design scenarios that cover the design of IGP, BGP, WAN, data center networks, security, IPv6, and QoS.

Chapter 1

Optimal Enterprise Campus Design

Upon completing this chapter, you will be able to

- Describe the hierarchal model of enterprise campus design
- Explain the role and attributes of the campus layers (access, distribution, and core)
- Describe modularity
- Describe flexibility
- Explain spanning-tree design options and optimization
- Explain Multichassis EtherChannel (MEC) design
- Describe network virtualization
- Describe campus network virtualization design options
- Describe Layer 3 gateway design options
- Describe campus high-availability design considerations

An enterprise campus is usually that portion of a computing infrastructure that provides access to network communication services and resources to end users and devices spread over a single geographic location. It might span a single floor, building, or even a large group of buildings spread over an extended geographic area. Some networks have a single campus that also acts as the core or backbone of the network and provides inter-connectivity between other portions of the overall network. The campus core can often interconnect the campus access, the data center, and WAN portions of the network. The largest enterprises might have multiple campus sites distributed worldwide with each providing end-user access and local backbone connectivity. From a technical or network engineering perspective, the concept of a campus has also been understood to mean the high-speed Layer 2 and Layer 3 Ethernet switching portions of the network outside the data center. Although all these definitions or concepts of what a campus network is are still valid, they no longer completely describe the set of capabilities and services that comprise the campus network today.

The campus network, as defined for the purposes of enterprise design guides, consists of the integrated elements that comprise the set of services used by a group of users and end-station devices that all share the same high-speed switching communications fabric. They include the packet-transport services (both wired and wireless), traffic identification and control (security and application optimization), traffic monitoring and management, and overall systems management and provisioning. These basic functions are implemented in such a way as to provide and directly support the higher-level services provided by an IT organization for use by the end-user community. These functions include

- Nonstop high-availability services
- Access and mobility services
- Application optimization and protection services
- Virtualization services
- Security services
- Operational and management services

This chapter focuses on the major design criteria and design principles that shape the enterprise campus architecture. You can view the design from many aspects, starting from the physical wiring plant, moving up through the design of the campus topology, and eventually addressing the implementation of campus services. The order or manner in which all these things are tied together to form a cohesive whole is determined by the use of a baseline set of design principles. These principles, when applied correctly, provide for a solid foundation and a framework in which the upper-layer services can be efficiently deployed. Therefore, this chapter first starts by highlighting and discussing the primary design principles of a modern enterprise campus network.

Enterprise Campus Design Principles

Any successful architecture or system is based on a foundation of solid design theory and principles. Much like the construction of a building, if a reliable foundation is engineered and built, the building will stand for years, growing with the owner through alterations and expansions to provide safe and reliable service throughout its life cycle. Similarly, designing any network, including an enterprise campus network, is no different than building a design concept or designing any large, complex system—such as a piece of software or even something as sophisticated as a space shuttle. The use of a guiding set of fundamental engineering principles ensures that the campus design provides for the balance of availability, security, flexibility, and manageability required to meet current and future business and technological needs.[1] This section discusses the primary design principles that, in turn, leverage a common set of engineering and architectural principles:

- Hierarchy
- Modularity

- Flexibility
- Resiliency

Each of these principles is summarized in subsequent sections. It important to be aware that these are not independent principles. The successful design and implementation of an enterprise campus network require an understanding of how each applies to the overall design and how each principle fits in the context of the others.

Hierarchy

The hierarchical design principle aims to break down the design into modular groups or layers. Breaking the design into layers allows each layer to implement specific functions, which makes the network design simple. This also makes the deployment and management of the network simpler. In addition, designing the enterprise campus network in a hierarchical approach creates a flexible and resilient network foundation that enables network architects to overlay the security, mobility, and unified communication features that are essential for today's modern businesses. The two proven, time-tested hierarchical design architectures for campus networks are the three-tier layer and the two-tier layer models, as shown in Figure 1-1.[2]

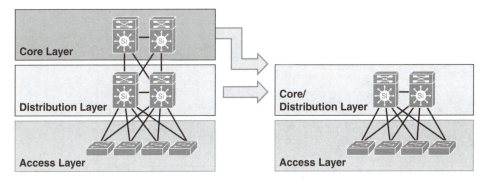

Figure 1-1 *Hierarchical Design Architectures*

Note Later in this chapter, you will learn more about when and why you should consider the three-tier versus the two-tier hierarchical design architecture.

As noted, the key design principle of the hierarchical design is that each element in the hierarchy has a specific set of functions and services that each layer offers and a specific role to play in each design. The following sections discuss the design attributes of each of these layers.

Access Layer

The access layer is the first layer, or edge, of the campus network. As shown in Figure 1-2, it's the place where endpoints (PCs, printers, cameras, and so on) attach to the wired or wireless portion of the campus network. It is also the place where devices that extend the network out one more level are attached. Such devices include IP phones and wireless access points (APs), which are the two prime examples of devices that extend the connectivity out one more layer from the actual campus access switch. In addition, the access layer is the first layer of defense in the network security architecture and the first point of negotiation between end devices and the network infrastructure.

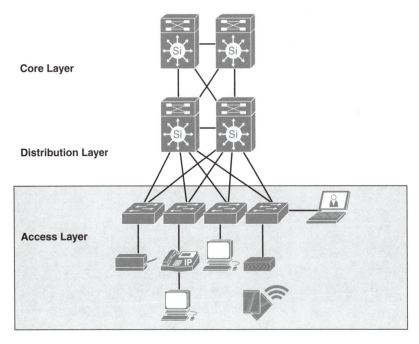

Figure 1-2 *Enterprise Campus: Access Layer*

Furthermore, the various possible types of devices that can connect and the different services and configuration requirements that are necessary make the access layer one of the most feature-rich parts of the campus network. Consequently, the access layer is almost always expected to provide security, quality of service (QoS), and policy trust boundary functions (see Table 1-1). As a result, these wide-ranging needs sometimes introduce a challenge for the network architect to determine how to generate a design that meets a wide variety of requirements. This is a key element in enabling multiple campus services (such as the need for various levels of mobility; unified voice, video, and data access; the need for a cost-effective and flexible operations environment), while being able to provide the appropriate balance of security and availability expected in more traditional, fixed-configuration environments. The next-generation Cisco Catalyst switching portfolio includes a wide range of fixed and modular switching platforms, each designed with unique hardware and software capabilities to function in a specific role.

Table 1-1 lists examples of the various typical services and capabilities that access layer switches are required to support.[3]

Table 1-1 *Typical Access Layer Switches Capabilities and Services*

Service Requirements	Service Features
Discovery and Configuration Services	802.1AF, CDP, LLDP
Security Services and Network Identity and Access	IBNS (802.1X), port security, DHCP snooping, DAI, IPSG, 802.1X, Web-Auth
Application Recognition Services	QoS marking, policing, queuing, deep packet inspection NBAR, and so on
Intelligent Network Control Services	PVST+, Rapid PVST+, EIGRP, OSPF, DTP, PAgP/LACP, UDLD, FlexLink, Portfast, UplinkFast, BackboneFast, LoopGuard, BPDUGuard, Port Security, RootGuard
Physical Infrastructure Services	Power over Ethernet (PoE)

Distribution Layer

The distribution layer in the campus design has a unique role in that it acts as a services and control boundary between the access and the core. Both the access and the core are essentially dedicated special-purpose layers. The access layer is dedicated to meeting the functions of end-device connectivity, and the core layer is dedicated to providing non-stop connectivity across the entire campus network.[4] In contrast, the distribution layer (see Figure 1-3) serves multiple purposes, such as the following:

- Acting as an aggregation point for all the access nodes (performing both physical link aggregations and traffic aggregation toward the core layer)

- Providing connectivity and policy services for traffic flows within a single access-distribution block for traffic between access nodes (east-west traffic flows)

- Providing the aggregation, policy control, and isolation demarcation point between the campus distribution building block and the rest of the network (north-south traffic flows)

- Routing at the distribution layer, which is considered an element in the core because it participates in the core routing

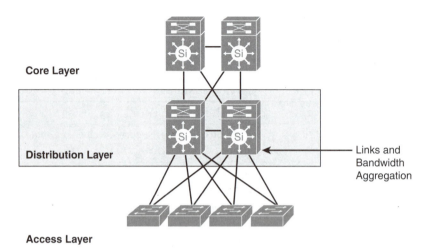

Figure 1-3 *Enterprise Campus: Distribution Layer*

Therefore, the configuration choices for features in the distribution layer are often determined by the requirements of the access layer (for example, are the access layer nodes intended to provide typical user access switches, or are the access layer nodes intended to be WAN routers?). Configuration choices for features in the distribution layer are also determined by the requirements of the core layer or by the need to act as an interface to both the access layer and the core layer.

Later in this chapter, the different design considerations of the distribution layer are covered in more detail from different angles, such as Layer 2 and Layer 3 demarcation point placement and high-availability considerations.

Core Layer

The campus core is in some ways the simplest yet most critical part of the campus network. It provides a limited set of services and must be designed to be highly available and operate in an *always-on* mode. In today's modern businesses, the core of the network must operate as a nonstop 7×24×365 service. The key design objectives for the campus core are based on providing the appropriate level of redundancy to allow for near-immediate data-flow recovery in the event of any component (switch, supervisor, line card, or fiber) failure. The core of the network should not implement any complex policy services, nor should it have any directly attached endpoint connections.[5]

The core should also have minimal control plane configuration combined with highly available devices configured with the correct amount of physical redundancy to provide for this nonstop service capability. In other words, the core layer serves as the aggregator for all the other campus blocks and ties together the campus with the rest of the network.

The core layer offers flexibility to the design of large campus networks to meet physical cabling and geographic challenges. For instance, consider a core layer in a campus network with multiple buildings (distribution blocks) like the one shown in Figure 1-4.

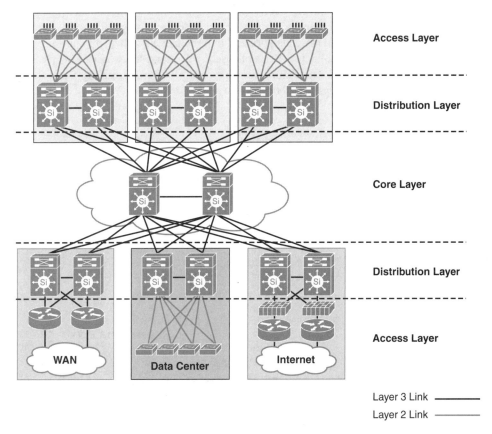

Figure 1-4 *Large Campus Network with a Core Layer*

This design offers a solution that is scalable and flexible enough to introduce new buildings to the network, each with its own distribution layer, without adding any complexity to network cabling or routing. As result, there is no impact on the distribution layers of the existing buildings. Nonetheless, some smaller network campus sites consisting of a single building with a smaller number of users (such as 300 users) do not require a separate core layer (assuming there is no future plan for this network to grow significantly in size, such as merging with another company).

Consequently, based on the current network size (taking into consideration future plans of the business), you can choose one of the two common design models of the hierarchal enterprise campus design: the two-tier or the three-tier layer model. The following sections discuss the attributes of each of these models and the recommended uses.

Enterprise Campus Two-Tier Layer Model

As discussed previously, smaller campus networks, such as a small remote campus location, may have several departments working on various floors within a building. In these environments, network designers can consider collapsing the core function into the distribution layer switch for such a small campus where there may be only a single distribution block without compromising basic network design principles, as shown in Figure 1-5. However, prior to deploying the two-tier "collapsed" core and distribution layers, network architects must consider the future scale, expansion, and manageability factors that may reduce overall operational efficiency.

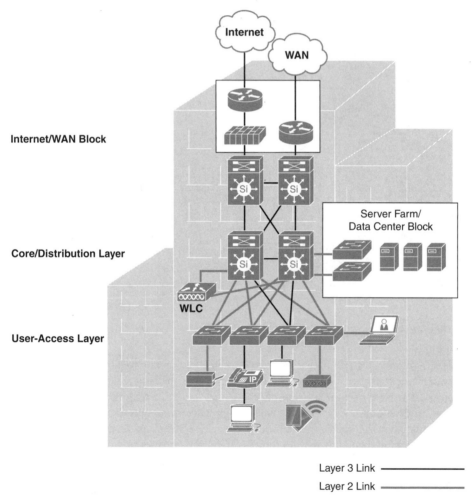

Figure 1-5 *Enterprise Campus Two-Tier Layer Model (Collapsed)*

This design model offers a cost-effective solution (fewer tiers means fewer devices—specifically, core devices) without sacrificing most of the benefits of the three-tier hierarchical model for small campus networks.

As shown in Figure 1-5, the distribution layer provides connectivity to network-based services, such as WAN edge devices, and to the Internet edge. These network-based services can include and are not limited to Wide Area Application Services (WAAS) and wireless LAN controllers. Depending on the size of the LAN and nature of the network (such as retail, manufacturing, or financial services), these services and their connectivity to the WAN and Internet edge might be terminated at the distribution layer switch that also provides LAN aggregation to the users' access-layer connectivity.

With this design model, the distribution layer and core layer functions will be combined in a single layer/device, so the collapsed core/distribution device should offer the following functions and capabilities:

- High-capacity interconnections
- Layer 2 aggregation and a demarcation point between Layer 2 and Layer 3
- Defined routing and network access policies
- Intelligent network services such as QoS and network virtualization

Enterprise Campus Three-Tier Layer Model

Designing large enterprise campus networks requires a dedicated distribution layer for each building (distribution block). The main campus network is typically constructed of multiple buildings. Therefore, implementing the three-tier layer model is a highly recommended and feasible design model, especially if the network is expected to grow significantly over time.

Furthermore, in large-scale enterprise campus networks, when the density of WAN routers, WAAS controllers, Internet edge devices, and wireless LAN controllers grows, it is not feasible and not advised to connect these nodes to a single distribution layer switch. This way, you avoid design and operational complexities as well as a single point of failure, which will make it an inflexible, nonresilient, and nonscalable design.

Therefore, you should consider a separate distribution layer for the network-based services. As a result, there will be more distribution blocks to be interconnected, and the more distribution blocks in the network, the more you need to consider a separate core block (layer). As a rule, when you have three or more distribution blocks, you should consider a separate core layer/block to interconnect these distribution blocks, as illustrated in Figure 1-6, where multiple distribution switches must be interconnected.

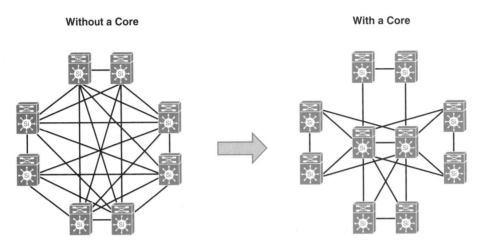

Figure 1-6 *Enterprise Core Block (Layer)*

Modularity

The modules of the system are the building blocks that are assembled into the larger campus. The advantage of the modular approach is largely due to the isolation that it can provide. Failures that occur within a module can be isolated from the remainder of the network, providing for both simpler problem detection and higher overall system availability. Also, considering modularity in your design will provide an optimized operation, as network changes, upgrades, or the introduction of new services can be made in a controlled and staged fashion, allowing greater flexibility in the maintenance and less complex operation of the campus network.

In addition, a modular design offers repeatable design standards; for instance, when a specific module no longer has sufficient capacity or is missing a new function or service, it can be updated or replaced by another module that has the same structural role in the overall hierarchical design without impacting other modules in the network due to the fact that the building blocks of modular networks are easy to replicate, redesign, and expand. There should be no need to redesign the whole network each time a module is added or removed. Therefore, introducing modularity to the enterprise campus design makes the network easy to scale, understand, and troubleshoot by promoting deterministic traffic patterns.

Modular Enterprise Campus Architecture and Modular Enterprise Campus with OSPF

Normally, large-scale enterprise campus network architecture can have multiple different specialized modules, also referred to as "building blocks" or "places in the network PINs," as illustrated in Figure 1-7.

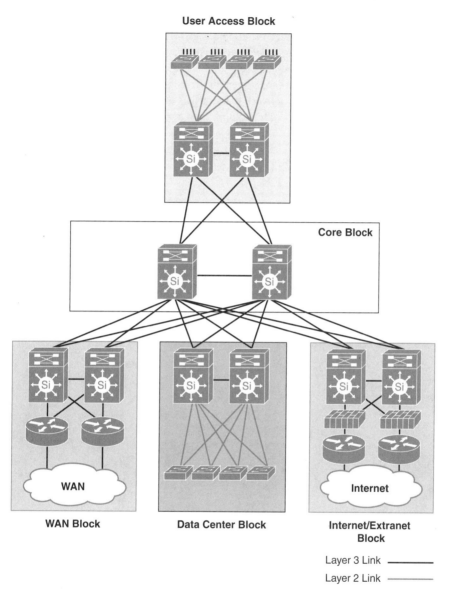

Figure 1-7 *Modular Enterprise Campus Architecture*

However, each of the enterprise campus building blocks still needs to use the hierarchal design model, such as the access-distribution block and its connectivity to the enterprise core block. The following section describes in more detail the design options and considerations of the enterprise campus access-distribution block. The specific detailed designs of other blocks such as the WAN edge and the data center block are covered in more detail later in this book.

Furthermore, introducing modularity into large campus networks with multiple distribution blocks will promote more optimized routing design so that you can have better fault isolation per block/module and more efficient route summarization (assuming there is a structured IP addressing scheme in which each block has its own IP range). For instance, Figure 1-8 illustrates a modular multi-area Open Shortest Path First (OSPF) routing design of a large enterprise campus network that consists of multiple blocks. The modular campus architecture here will facilitate building such a structured routing design.

Note Subsequent chapters analyze and discuss routing designs in more detail.

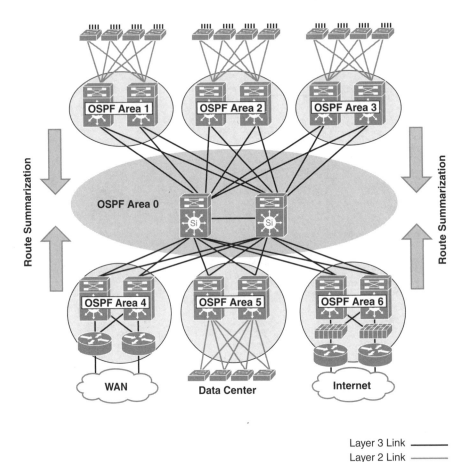

Figure 1-8 *Modular Enterprise Campus with OSPF*

Access-Distribution Block

The access-distribution block of the modular enterprise campus architecture (also referred to as the distribution block) is probably one of the most familiar element of the campus architecture to network engineers. It is a fundamental component of the campus design. Properly designing the distribution block goes a long way toward ensuring the success and stability of the overall campus architecture. The access-distribution block consists of two of the three hierarchical tiers within the multilayer campus architecture: the access and distribution layers.

There are three common and proven design choices for configuring the access-distribution block and the associated control plane protocols (routing, Spanning-Tree, and so on): multitier, virtual switch (switch clustering), and routed access. Even though these designs relatively use the same basic physical topology and cabling structure, some key differences exist between each design option (you must be aware of these differences to be able to design an optimal campus network architecture), such as where the Layer 2 and Layer 3 boundaries exist, how the network topology redundancy is implemented, and how traffic distribution works. Following are descriptions of each:

- **Multitier:** This design model is primarily based on the traditional Layer 2 designs that rely on the Spanning-Tree Protocol (STP) to prevent Layer 2 loops and control traffic-forwarding topology from a Layer 2 perspective (for which the link is active). In general, this design option provides the least flexibility and fewest convergence capabilities compared to the other options. Typically, there are different topologies in this design, such as the looped and loop free. Considering any one of these options can influence the level of design flexibility and convergence time. Therefore, the actual level of flexibility and fast convergence capability depends on the topology used. The subsequent section in this chapter discusses the different topologies and considerations of a resilient Layer 2 design in more detail.

- **Virtual switch (switch clustering):** This model offers an optimized, flexible, resilient, and easy-to-manage design for the access-distribution connectivity; with this model, there is no need to rely on other protocols such as Spanning-Tree Protocol (STP) and First-Hop Redundancy Protocol (FHRP); see Figure 1-9. In addition, the concept of multichassis link aggregation (mLAG) with the clustered upstream distribution switches (virtual switching) makes this model more flexible when spanning Layer 2 VLANs between different access switches is required. Also, having both uplinks from the access to the distribution clustered switches in forwarding state helps maximize the available bandwidth for the endpoints connected to the access layer switches and significantly optimizes the convergence time following a node or link failure event.

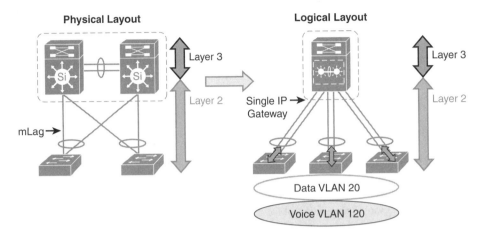

Figure 1-9 *Virtual Switch Model*

In addition, considering this design approach across all the campus blocks (when possible) will provide an optimized architecture that is easy to manage, resilient, and more flexible with higher aggregated uplink bandwidth capacity. Figure 1-10 shows how the end-to-end campus will look when the Cisco virtual switching system (VSS) is used across the different blocks and layers.

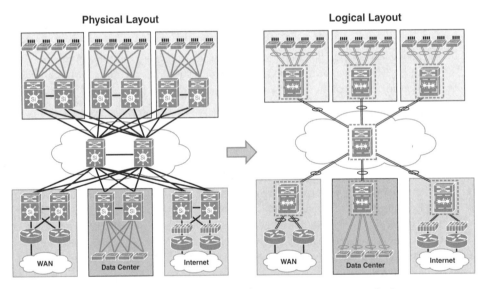

Figure 1-10 *Apply the Virtual Switch Model Across the Campus Blocks*

- **Routed access:** This is a proven reliable and fast-converging access-distribution connectivity model. In modern enterprise campus networks, routed access is used sometimes as an alternative configuration to the traditional distribution block model, in which the access switch acts as a full Layer 3 routed node (providing both Layer 2 and Layer 3 switching), and the access-to-distribution Layer 2 uplink trunks are replaced with Layer 3 point-to-point routed links. Consequently, the Layer 2/3 demarcation point is moved from the distribution switch to the access switch, as illustrated in Figure 1-11. The routed access-distribution block design has a number of advantages over the multitier design with its use of Layer 2 access to distribution uplinks. It offers common end-to-end troubleshooting tools (such as ping and traceroute), it uses a single control protocol (either Enhanced Interior Gateway Routing Protocol [EIGRP] or Open Shortest Path First [OSPF]), and it removes the need for features such as Hot Standby Router Protocol (HSRP). While it is the appropriate design for many environments, it is not suitable for all environments because it does not natively support spanning VLANs across multiple access switches; also it can sometimes be an expensive option because the access layer switches with Layer 3 routing capability cost more than Layer 2–only switches.

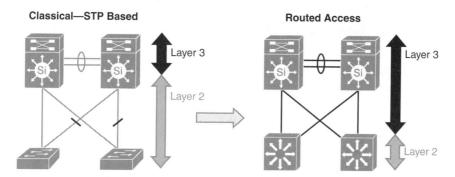

Figure 1-11 *Routed Access Model*

Flexibility

The rapidly evolving requirements of today's modern business, such as the convergence of different communications networks such as voice, video, data, and mobility (bring your own devices, or BYOD), require a flexible enterprise campus network design that is capable of facilitating the addition and integration of these requirements and can support business growth in seamless manner. The design principle *flexibility* refers to the capability to modify portions of the network, add new services, or increase capacity without going through a major *fork-lift* (major) upgrade.[6]

The structured hierarchical design inherently provides for a high degree of flexibility because it allows staged or gradual changes to each module in the network fairly independently of the others. Changes in the core transport can be made independently of the distribution blocks. Changes in the design or capacity of the distribution layer can be implemented in a phased or incremental manner.

As a network designer, you need to consider a number of key areas when designing a modern enterprise campus network that can evolve over the next few years. Existing designs should be adapted to incorporate the appropriate level of flexibility to accommodate these potential changes. Key areas to consider include the following:[7]

- **Control plane flexibility:** The capability to support and allow migration between multiple routing, spanning-tree, and other control protocols.

- **Forwarding plane flexibility:** The capability to support the introduction and use of IPv6 as a parallel requirement alongside IPv4.

- **User group flexibility:** The capability to virtualize the network-forwarding capabilities and services in the campus fabric to support changes in the administrative structure of the enterprise. This can involve acquisition, partnering, or outsourcing of business functions.

- **Traffic management and control flexibility:** Unified communications, collaborative business approaches, and software models continue to evolve—along with a trend toward increased growth in peer-to-peer traffic flows. These fundamental changes require campus designs that allow the deployment of security, monitoring, and troubleshooting tools available to support these new traffic patterns.

- **Flexibility to support multitenancy and traffic isolation requirements:** The capability to support these requirements is necessary in today's modern networks (the following section covers this point in more detail).

Campus Network Virtualization

If we look back to the 1990s, campus LANs were characterized mainly by broad deployments of Layer 2 switches. In the past two decades since the introduction of Ethernet switching, campus LAN design has significantly changed and evolved to accommodate requirements changes. In today's enterprise network, the growth of campus LANs drives the need to partition the network more effectively by users, location, or function. Everyone needs to retain privacy while sharing the same physical network. For end users on the network, the experience should be that of using totally separate physical networks that can be securely interconnected.[8]

In today's campus networks, it is vital to provide a great degree of flexibility to accommodate various connectivity options while keeping *closed user groups* (groups of users and resources isolated from nongroup members). Conceding network virtualization offers the flexibility to the design to provision different logical networks and translates to different access groups over a single physical network while keeping them logically separated; this is a solution that has challenged network operators.

One of the network virtualization approaches aims to enable a single physical entity to act in multiple physical instances in which it can be used by different user groups.

From a design point of view, to provide the desired level of flexibility and efficiency with network virtualization, the design solution needs to consider the following aspects (see Figure 1-12):

- **Access control:** Also referred to as edge control, which helps ensure that legitimate users and devices are recognized, classified, and authorized to enter their assigned portions of the network. One such technology that can be used here is IEEE 802.1X, which is the standard for port authentication (refer to Chapter 25, "Designing Network Access Control Solutions," for more details).

- **Path isolation:** Helps ensure that the substantiated user or device is effectively mapped to the correct secure set of available resources, such as the relevant tenant network (virtual network) in a multitenant environment.

- **Services edge:** Also referred to as services virtualization, which helps ensure that the right services are accessible to the legitimate set or sets of users and devices (for example, a multitenant data center).

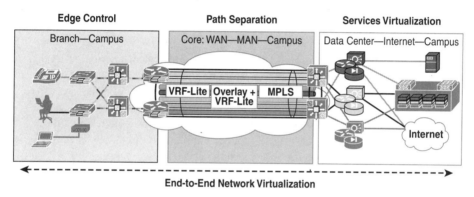

Figure 1-12 *Campus Network Virtualization Functional Architecture*

Campus Network Virtualization Technologies and Techniques

This section discusses the foundational technology requirements to achieve network virtualization in a campus network and the different techniques that can be used to achieve end-to-end path isolation across the network per virtual network (VN).

VLAN Assignment

As mentioned earlier, the first point to assign a user or a device to a given network is at the access layer, which is the first entry point to the campus network. The simplest and most common approach here is to assign a different VLAN per user group or virtual network at the access layer. In the past, the typical approach to VLAN assignment would be to manually assign a port to be a member of a specific VLAN. Another method that is becoming much more common today is through the enhanced security capabilities of Flexible Authentication Sequencing using 802.1X, MAC Authentication and Bypass (MAB), or Webauth as alternate means to first authenticate a user against a Radius Server or a Policy Enforcement Server, such as the Cisco Identity Services Engine (ISE), for network access. Once authenticated, by using Radius attributes communicated between the

Radius Server and access switch, the switchport is dynamically changed to the appropriate VLAN and, optionally, an ACL can be pushed down to the switch, enforcing specific access to the network.

Virtual Routing and Forwarding

As you know from the previous section, the VLANs are the most basic path isolation technique for Layer 2, typically at the access or entry level of the user or endpoint. However, as the goal of every solid network design is to minimize the extent of the broadcast domain and exposure to spanning-tree loops, a method to translate the Layer 2 VLAN to a Layer 3 virtual network or virtual private network (VPN) is required. This Layer 3 VN must be capable of supporting its own unique control plane, complete with its own addressing structure and routing tables for data forwarding completely isolated from any other Layer 3 VPN on that device and in the network. The technology enabling this type of functionality is known as the virtual routing and forwarding (VRF) instance. Figure 1-13 illustrates how the Layer 2 VLAN mapping to the corresponding VRF at Layer 3 offers an integrated solution where you can allocate a virtual network (VN) per user group or any logical group. Moreover, based on the campus design model (multitier versus routed access) used, the VRFs are defined where the Layer 2 VLANs border the Layer 3 network. Therefore, if the access layer is connected to aggregation via Layer 2, the VRFs are defined on the distribution or collapsed core switches aggregating the access layer. If, however, the access layer is connected to Layer 3 (the routed access model), the VRFs are defined on the access switch itself.

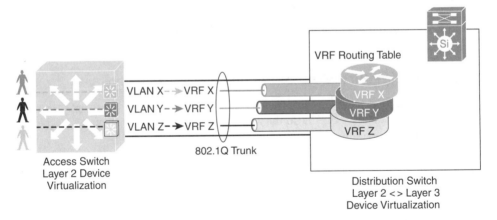

Figure 1-13 *Device Virtualization and VLAN-to-VRF Mapping*

The question here is how to extend these virtual networks across the campus network to communicate with other users within the same virtual network or to use other services such the Internet or an application in the data center without compromising the path separation requirements. The following section discusses the different techniques to achieve path isolation across the campus network.

Path Isolation Techniques

The VRF instance on a networking device is an isolated object that must be linked to other instances of the same VRF on other devices throughout the network. There are several means by which this is accomplished today. Following are the most common methods to achieve path isolation across the campus network:

- **Hop-by-hop VRF-Lite based:** As shown in Figure 1-14, VRF-Lite deployed on a hop-by-hop basis in a campus uses 802.1Q trunks to interconnect the devices configured for VRFs. Once the VLAN-to-VRF mapping has been completed at either the access or distribution networking hardware, the core-facing interfaces must then be configured. These interfaces can potentially be configured in two different ways. The first approach is to use a VLAN and its associated SVI, which would then be assigned to the appropriate VRF. The second is to use subinterfaces on the core-facing interface with each subinterface assigned to the appropriate VRF. Although the use of subinterfaces is preferred, it must be noted that some switching platforms do not support routed subinterfaces and thus require the use of SVIs. Typically, for each VRF, a unique VLAN ID must be used for every physical link interconnecting network devices because each is considered a routed hop.

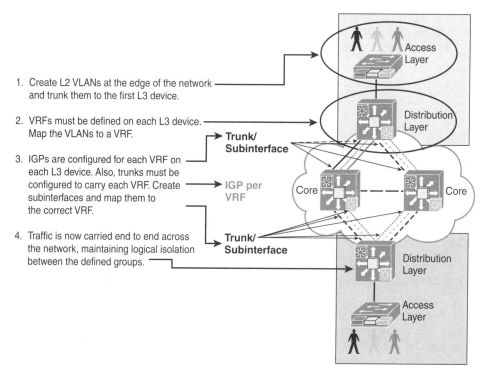

Figure 1-14 *Hop-by-Hop VRF-Lite Path Isolation*

- **Hop-by-hop easy virtual network (EVN) based:** Hop-by-hop VRF-lite is manageable for networks with fewer numbers of virtual networks and fewer numbers of hops in a virtual network path. However, when the number of logical networks (virtual/tenants) increases, there will be a high degree of operational complexity to create and configure the interface or subinterface per VN. EVN provides the same benefits for guaranteeing traffic separation with more simplified operations. In other words, EVN builds on VRF-Lite concepts and capabilities and provides additional benefits, including the following:

  - EVN offers better end-to-end VN scalability compared to the classic hop-by-hop 802.1Q-based solution.
  - EVN offers simplified configuration and management.
  - EVN offers the capability to provision shared services among different logical groups.

As illustrated in Figure 1-15, with the EVN path, you can achieve isolation by using a unique tag for each VN. This tag is referred to as VNET tag. Each VN carries over a virtual network the same tag value that was assigned by a network administrator. Based on that, EVN-capable devices along the path will use these tags to ensure end-to-end traffic isolation among different VNs. With this approach, the dependency on the classical (802.1Q based) physical or logical interfaces to provide traffic separation is eliminated.

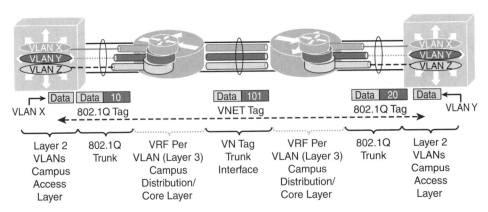

Figure 1-15 *Hop-by-Hop VRF-Lite Path Isolation*

In other words, you do not need to create an end-to-end subinterface per VN/VRF (EVN automatically generates subinterfaces for each EVN). Also, instead of identifying a unique 802.1Q for each VN on a per-hop basis, now with Cisco EVN technology, the administrator can define a network-wide unique VNET Tag ID and carry it among the different EVN-capable devices over VNET trunk (see Figure 1-16).

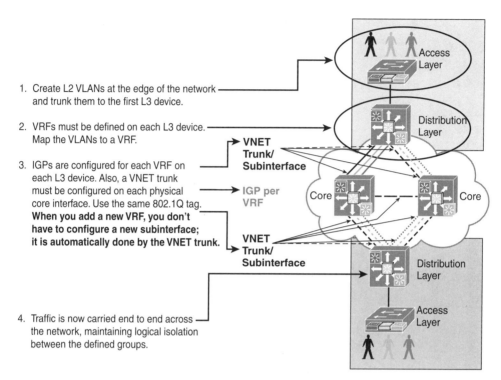

Figure 1-16 *Hop-by-Hop EVN End-to-End Path Isolation*

- **Multihop GRE tunneling based:** If not all devices in the path support VRF-Lite, the VRF can be transported using generic routing encapsulation (GRE) tunnels so that each VRF can be mapped to a specific tunnel interface, as shown in Figure 1-17. Depending on the topology, point-to-point or point-to-multipoint tunnels can be used. (Refer to Chapter 8, "Service Provider Managed WAN," and Chapter 9, "Enterprise Managed WAN," for more information about tunneling design and its considerations. Although these chapters cover this topic from the WAN design point of view, the actual design concepts and considerations are still applicable when GRE tunneling is used between the different distribution blocks across the campus network.) In addition, GRE may add some processing overhead on the switches (platform dependent); therefore, this approach is not always recommended unless it is used as an interim solution.

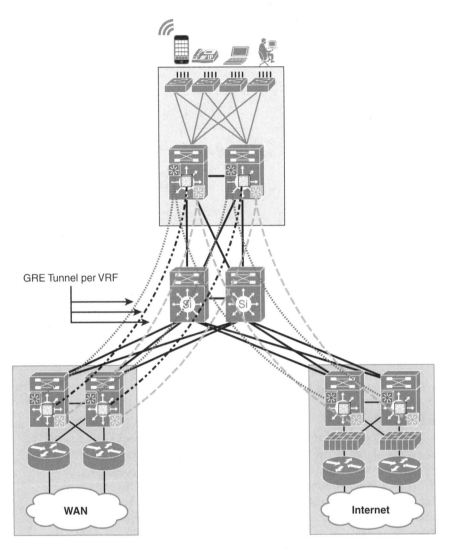

Figure 1-17 *Multihop Path Isolation: GRE Tunneling*

- **Multihop MPLS core based:** One of the primary benefits of deploying an MPLS infrastructure is the capability to provide dynamic any-to-any mesh connectivity per virtual private network (VPN) through the use of Multiprotocol BGP and the Label Distribution Protocol (LDP). The concept of building such a network is covered in more detail in Chapter 8. Although Chapter 8 discusses the design from the service provider design point of view, the actual design and principles are still the same. In such a design, you can think of the campus core like the provider router (P) and the distribution layer node as the provider edge (PE) nodes. In fact, MPLS should not be viewed as a solution intended for WANs alone. Many enterprise organizations have successfully deployed MPLS throughout the distribution and core of campus networks as well as data center, WAN, and Internet edges. For instance, many organizations take advantage of MPLS and multiprotocol BGP to build multitenant campus networks and to provide other connectivity models such as guest access or peering with the WAN edge, traffic isolation for PCI/Point of Sale applications, and even SCADA control traffic found in the utilities.

Resiliency

The increased need of a higher "up time," or the availability of technology services, in today's modern businesses is a key to facilitate achieving business goals. This makes the enterprise campus network an integral part of business success, due to the fact that most of the critical business communications within a location (voice, video, and data) are carried over the campus network. In other words, a network failure may lead to business communication interruption or a complete service outage. Therefore, the availability of the underlying network transport is critical in today's modern enterprises. As a result, one of the primary design principles that network designers need to consider is *resiliency*. Resiliency refers to a system's capability to remain available for use under both normal and abnormal conditions. Normal conditions (also referred to as planned outages) include such events as change windows and normal or expected traffic flows and traffic patterns. Abnormal conditions (also referred to as unplanned outages) include hardware or software failures, extreme traffic loads, unusual traffic patterns, denial of service (DoS) events whether intentional or unintentional, and any other unplanned events.[9]

Resilient design is not a feature, nor is there a specific thing that you do to achieve it. As with hierarchy and modularity, resiliency is a basic principle that is made real through the use of many related features and design choices. The following section discusses the general design considerations to achieve a resilient (highly available) enterprise campus network.

Enterprise Campus High-Availability Design Considerations

Campus network stability and reliability are challenged during most common path failures caused by fiber cuts, faulty hardware, or Layer 1 link errors. Such fault conditions destabilize the network and result in service disruptions and degraded application performance. Therefore, building a resilient Layer 2 and Layer 3 foundational design maintains the availability of all upper-layer network services and applications.[10]

This section covers the key design considerations and recommendations to achieve a resilient enterprise campus LAN design.

In general, the following three key resiliency requirements encompass most of the common types of failure conditions; depending on the LAN design tier, the resiliency option appropriate to the role and network service type must be deployed:[11]

- **Network resiliency:** Provides redundancy during physical link failures, such as fiber cut, bad transceivers, incorrect cabling, and so on. To achieve this type of resiliency, you should always aim to have redundant uplinks between any two network layers in the campus network.

- **Device resiliency:** Protects the network during abnormal node failure triggered by hardware or software, such as software crashes, a nonresponsive supervisor, and so on. For instance, considering the virtual switch concept such as VSS or Stackwise technology will help achieve device-level resiliency.

- **Operational resiliency:** Enables resiliency capabilities to the next level, providing complete network availability even during planned network outages using in-service software upgrade (ISSU) features.

VLANs, Trunking, and Link Aggregation Design Recommendations

This section provides the best practice recommendations with regard to VLANs, trunking, and link aggregation to achieve a design that supports a highly available campus network.

VLAN Design

The fundamental use of VLANs is to provide separation at Layer 2 between different broadcast/collision domains. A VLAN design is also often used to provide network partitioning at Layer 2 to support network virtualization and separation between different logical domains, such as different user groups. One common traditional design of VLANs is to be configured across multiple access switches that connect to the same upstream distribution layer switch. Although this deployment model is technically valid, it has a few disadvantages that ultimately can introduce scalability and stability limitations to the network. For example, when you use a topology in which VLANs are spanned across multiple access layer switches, you may introduce asymmetrical routing and unicast flooding, in which traffic returning through the standby HSRP, VRRP, or alternate/nonforwarding GLBP peer can be flooded to all ports in the target VLAN. This can have a significant impact on performance and service availability and stability. Figure 1-18 illustrates a redundant topology in which a common VLAN is shared across the access layer switches.

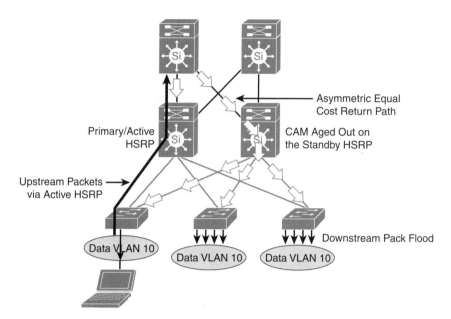

Figure 1-18 *Unicast Flooding with Spanned VLAN Across Access Switches*

In this topology, the CAM table entry ages out on the standby HSRP router. This occurs because the ARP and CAM aging timers are different (for most platforms). The CAM timer expires because no traffic is sent upstream toward the standby HSRP peer after the endpoint initially sends address resolution protocols (ARP) for its default gateway. When the Content Addressable Memory (CAM) entry has aged out and is removed, the standby HSRP peer must forward the return path traffic to all ports in the common VLAN.[12]

The corresponding access layer switches also do not have a CAM entry for the target MAC, and they also broadcast the return traffic on all ports in the common VLAN. This traffic flooding can have a performance impact on the connected end stations because they may receive a large amount of traffic that is not intended for them.

If you must implement a topology in which VLANs span more than one access layer switch, the recommended workaround is to tune the ARP timer to be equal to or less than the CAM aging timer. A shorter ARP cache timer causes the standby HSRP peer to ARP for the target IP address before the CAM entry timer expires and the MAC entry is removed. The subsequent ARP response repopulates the CAM table before the CAM entry is aged out and removed. This removes the possibility of flooding asymmetrically routed return path traffic to all ports.

As noted, this issue may occur only in a scenario in which the same VLANs are defined across multiple access layer switches in a large Layer 2 domain that connects to the same distribution layer switches. This is not an issue when the same VLANs are not present across access layer switches because the flooding occurs only to switches where the traffic normally would have been switched. In addition, larger Layer 2 domains have a greater potential for impact on end-station performance because the volume of potentially flooded traffic increases in larger Layer 2 environments.[13]

To mitigate or eliminate the impact of this issue, you need to consider a design in which VLANs are local to individual access layer switches. This type of problem is therefore inconsequential because traffic is flooded on only one interface (the only interface in the VLAN) on the standby HSRP, VRRP, or nonforwarding GLBP peer. Traffic is flooded out the same interface that would be used normally, so the end result is the same. Additionally, the access layer switch receiving the flooded traffic has a CAM table entry for the host because it is directly attached, so traffic is switched only to the intended host.[14] As a result, no additional end stations are affected by the flooded traffic, as shown in Figure 1-19.

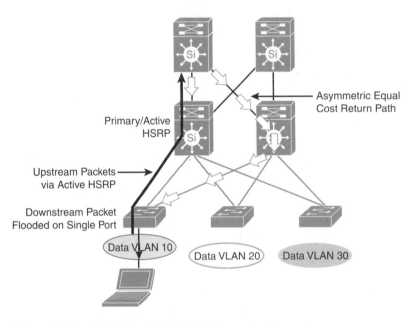

Figure 1-19 *Optimized VLANs Design at the Access Layer*

However, if the design requirements mandate that some VLANs must span multiple access switches, you may need to consider the switch clustering (virtual switching) design model at the distribution layer to optimize the overall solution performance and stability. For example, with the VSS, there is no STP and no FHRP. In addition, the use of MEC collectivity still provides a significantly optimized and reliable design model, regardless of whether or not you are spanning Layer 2 VLANs across the access layer switches. That being said, in general, the larger the Layer 2 domain, the larger the fault domain will be in the network. Therefore, you should always aim to avoid spanning Layer 2 VLANs across the access layer switches, unless it is required for certain VLANs for certain applications. In this case, you should span these specific VLANs only and not all the VLANs.

Trunking

As mentioned previously, VLANs provide the broadcast isolation, policy implementation, and fault isolation benefits at Layer 2 that are required in highly available networks.

Trunking protocols allow the links between network devices to carry multiple VLANs through a single physical or logical (EtherChannel) link.[15]

Two types of trunks are currently available:

- **802.1Q:** The Institute of Electrical and Electronics Engineers (IEEE) standard implementation.

- **Inter-Switch Link (ISL):** Cisco Proprietary trunk; in fact, Cisco developed ISL trunking before the standard was established.

The following are best practices to use when deploying multiple VLANs on a single switch-to-switch interconnection or trunk:

- Deploy VLANs on the interconnection between access and distribution layers.

- Use the VLAN Trunking Protocol (VTP) in transparent mode to reduce the potential for operational error. Otherwise, it is not recommended today because its concerns outweigh its benefits.

- Hard set the trunk mode to on and the encapsulation negotiate to off for optimal convergence. When the Dynamic Trucking Protocol (DTP) and 802.1Q or ISL negotiation are enabled, considerable time can be spent negotiating trunk settings when a node or interface is restored. While this negotiation is happening, traffic is dropped because the link is up from a Layer 2 perspective (see Figure 1-20).

- Assign the native VLAN to an unused ID or use the Tagged Native VLAN option to avoid VLAN hopping.

- Manually prune all VLANS except those needed.

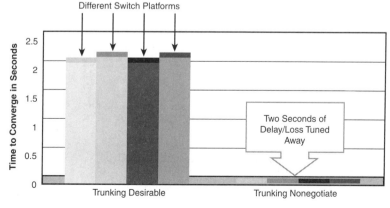

Figure 1-20 *Optimized Trunk Convergence*

Note As mentioned, setting the trunk mode to On/On and without negotiation of configuration is faster from a link-up (restoration) perspective than setting both ends of the trunk to the Desirable/Desirable alternative. However, in this configuration, DTP is not actively monitoring the state of the trunk, and a misconfigured trunk is not easily identified. Therefore, it's really a balance between fast convergence and your ability to manage configuration and change control.

Link Aggregation

The logical grouping of multiple redundant links into a single logical entity is called *link aggregation*. There are two variants: the prestandard Cisco EtherChannel implementation that uses Port Aggregation Protocol (PAgP) as a control mechanism and the IEEE 802.3ad standards-based implementation that uses Link Aggregation Control Protocol (LACP) as its control mechanism.[16]

Typically, link aggregation is used to eliminate single points of failure (that is, link or port) dependencies from a topology. Therefore, it is commonly deployed between the network tiers' access-to-distribution, distribution-to-core, and core-to-core interconnections, where increased availability and scaled bandwidth are required.

The convergence time following an EtherChannel member link failure is faster than routed interface convergence time. Figure 1-21 summarizes the process of EtherChannel convergence following a member link failure.

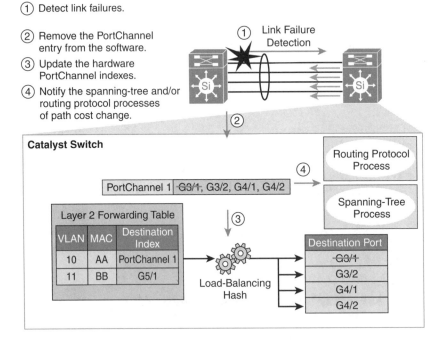

① Detect link failures.
② Remove the PortChannel entry from the software.
③ Update the hardware PortChannel indexes.
④ Notify the spanning-tree and/or routing protocol processes of path cost change.

Figure 1-21 *EtherChannel Convergence*

You can create channels containing up to eight parallel links between switches. You can also create these channels on interfaces that are on different physical line cards, which provides increased availability because the failure of a single line card does not cause a complete loss of connectivity. In some Cisco switches that support stackable channels such as the 3750, 2960, or 380 switch families, you can create a cross-stack channel where members of the EtherChannel exist on different members of the stack, yielding very high availability, as shown in Figure 1-22.

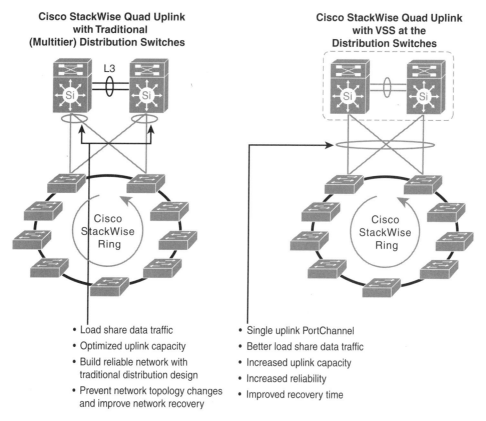

Figure 1-22 *Optimized Link Aggregation with Stackwise Technology at the Access Layer*

The following are best-practices recommendations to consider when deploying link aggregation:

- For Layer 2 EtherChannels, Desirable/Desirable is the recommended configuration so that PAgP is running across all members of the bundle, ensuring that an individual link failure will not result in an STP failure.

- For Layer 3 EtherChannels, consider a configuration that uses On/On. There is a trade-off between performance/high-availability impact and maintenance and operations implications.

- An On/On configuration is faster from a link-up (restoration) perspective than a Desirable/Desirable alternative. However, in this configuration, PAgP is not actively monitoring the state of the bundle members, and a misconfigured bundle is not easily identified.

- Routing protocols may not have visibility into the state of an individual member of a bundle. You can use LACP and the minimum links option to bring down the entire bundle when the capacity is diminished.

- You should disable PAgP negotiation if EtherChannel tunnels are not required. If you do not disable EtherChannel negotiation, the mismatch between the states (one side could be desirable and the other off) can cause as much as 7 seconds of loss during link negotiation (see Figure 1-23).

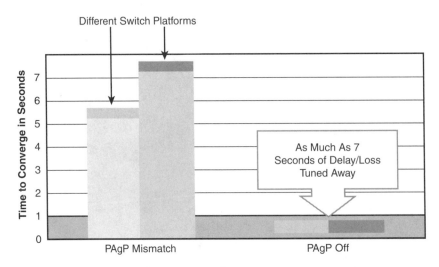

Figure 1-23 *PAgP Performance Results Layer*

On the other hand, Multichassis EtherChannel (MEC) offers the best high availability, performance, and fastest convergence design. As shown in Figure 1-24, in the case of an MEC member unlink failure toward a VSS distribution switch, from the upstream traffic point of view, the convergence is determined by the access device link failure detection. In such a scenario, the EtherChannel convergence is about 200 ms, and only the flows on the failed link at that moment are affected. Similarly, from a downstream traffic point of view, the convergence is determined by the VSS node, and VSS EtherChannel convergence will typically take about 200 ms, and only the flows on the failed link are affected.

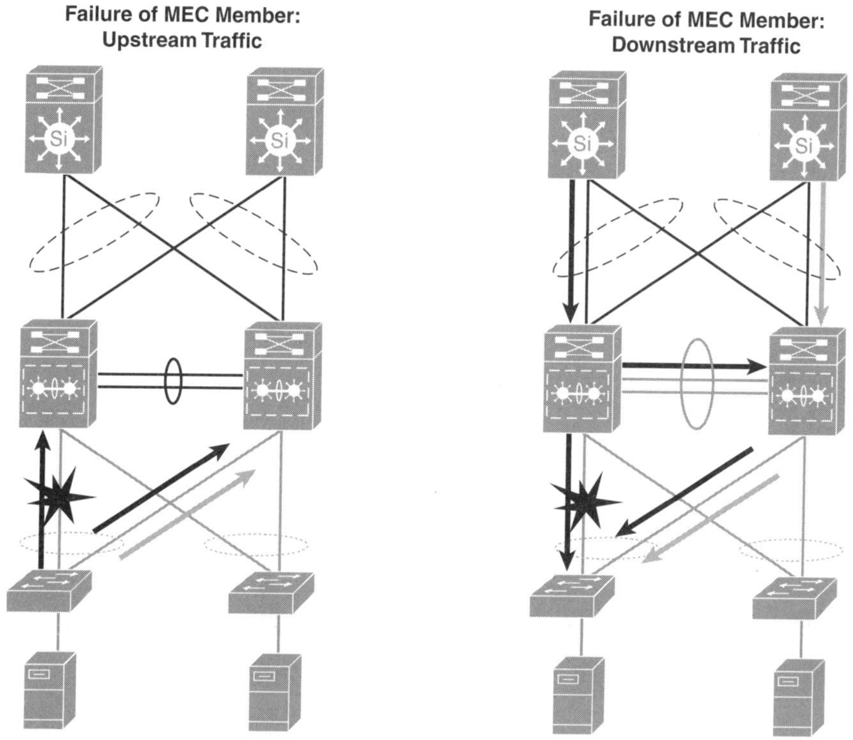

Figure 1-24 *MEC Member Link Failure Convergence*

First-Hop Redundancy Protocol (FHRP)

Default gateway redundancy (also known as first-hop redundancy) allows a highly available network to recover from the failure of the device acting as the default gateway for the end stations on a physical segment.

In a campus hierarchical design that uses a multitier access model, the distribution switches are the Layer 2/Layer 3 boundary, and they typically provide Layer 3 default gateway service for the corresponding Layer 2 domain. To maintain the availability of such key functions, you must consider FHRP redundancy to avoid any outage that could occur if the device acting as default gateway failed.[17]

For this purpose, Cisco has developed the Hot Standby Router Protocol (HSRP) to address this need, and the Internet Engineering Task Force (IETF) subsequently ratified the Virtual Router Redundancy Protocol (VRRP) as the standards-based method of providing default gateway redundancy.[18]

The Gateway Load Balancing Protocol (GLBP), on the other hand, protects data traffic from a failed router or circuit, like HSRP and VRRP, while allowing packet load sharing between a group of redundant routers.[19]

When HSRP or VRRP is used to provide default gateway redundancy, the backup members of the peer relationship are idle, waiting for a failure event to occur for them to take over and actively forward traffic, as illustrated in Figure 1-25.

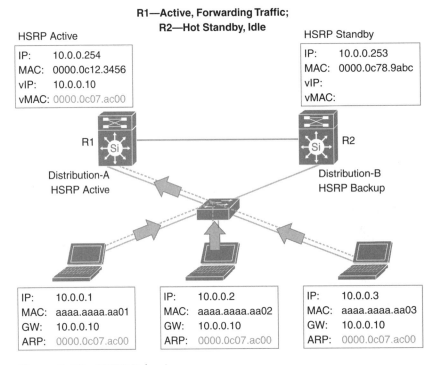

Figure 1-25 *HSRP Behavior*

Prior to the development of GLBP, some workarounds utilized uplinks more efficiently. For example, one of the common techniques used with HSRP is to ensure that the STP/RSTP root roles are alternated between distribution node peers, with the even VLANs homed on one peer and the odd VLANs homed on the alternate. Another technique used multiple HSRP groups on a single interface and used DHCP to alternate between the multiple default gateways. Although these techniques worked, they were not optimal from a configuration, maintenance, or management perspective.

GLBP offers all the benefits of HSRP plus load balancing the default gateway so that you can more efficiently utilize all available bandwidth. With the GLBP, a group of routers function as one virtual router by sharing one virtual IP address but using multiple virtual MAC addresses for traffic forwarding (see Figure 1-26). Consequently, traffic from a single common subnet can go through multiple redundant gateways using a single virtual IP address.[20]

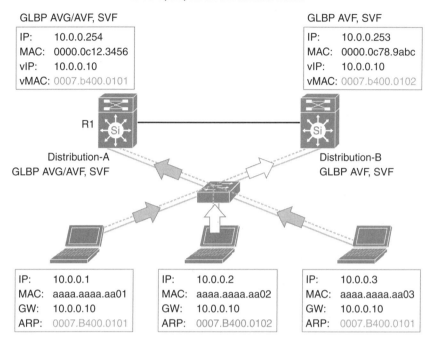

Figure 1-26 *GLBP Behavior*

Nevertheless, GLBP leads to asymmetrical routing because it will send outbound traffic flows over the available upstream paths, and most probably the return traffic of these distributed flows will come back over a single return path. This outcome can lead to some design issues if a stateful security device such as a firewall is in the path, as illustrated in Figure 1-27. The solution to this issue is to consider HSRP and align the subnet advertisement to the outside networks to ensure return traffic comes back over the same path (because HSRP also, by default, leads to asymmetrical routing if the routing advertisement is not aligned with the active HSRP node). Alternatively, you can use the firewall clustering capability that is offered by Cisco ASA firewalls (covered in Chapter 24, "IP Multicast Security").

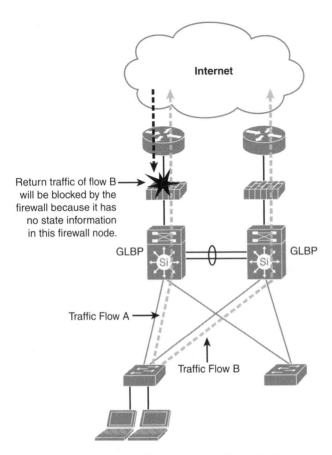

Figure 1-27 *GLBP and Asymmetrical Routing Issue*

Furthermore, you must ensure that the inter-distribution switch link is always in the STP blocking state if it is deployed as Layer 2. You also must ensure that the uplinks from the access layer switches are in a forwarding state (for example, by changing the port cost on the interface between the distribution layer switches on the STP secondary root switch to high value) to allow traffic to flow up both uplinks from the access layer switches to both GLBP Virtual MAC addresses and avoid a two-hop path at Layer 2 for upstream traffic, as illustrated in Figure 1-28.

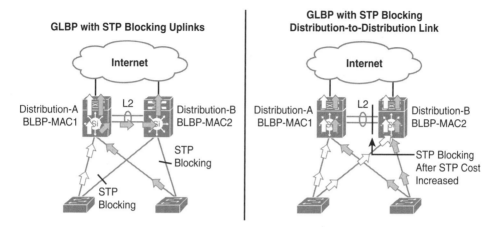

Figure 1-28 *GLBP with STP Blocking Links*

For more optimized FHRP operations in environments that rely on STP, preemption is important to provide a fast and reliable convergence. For instance, HSRP preemption will allow HSRP to follow a spanning-tree topology. With the preemption, the primary HSRP peer reassumes the primary role when it comes back online after a failure or maintenance event. However, it needs to be aware of the switch boot time and connectivity to the rest of the network because an HSRP neighbor relationship may form and preemption will occur before the primary switch has Layer 3 connectivity to the core. If this happens, traffic will probably be dropped until full connectivity is established.

Therefore, the recommended best practice is to measure the system boot time and set the HSRP preempt delay statement to 50 percent greater than this value. Doing so ensures that the HSRP primary distribution node has established full connectivity to all parts of the network before HSRP preemption is allowed to occur.

IP Gateway Redundancy Optimization with VSS

Because the virtual switching system (VSS) clusters two physical chasses into single logical systems, there is no need to deploy a protocol such as HSRP to provide IP gateway redundancy for endpoints. Instead, the gateway redundancy at the aggregation layer is now offered with built-in interchassis stateful switchover (SSO) architecture rather than building any virtual gateway configuration. Hence, VSS eliminates the need of implementing FHRP for each VLAN, which significantly improves the CPU performance in a large-scale Layer 2 network design (see Figure 1-29). It also reduces operational and troubleshooting complexity with simple network configuration to implement networks. In addition, VSS eliminates the need to implement FHRP protocols completely; as a result, you do not need to tune this protocol for the rapid recovery process anymore. This is add-on advantage to improve CPU performance and bring more stability in the system.

- Single logical Layer 3 gateway. Eliminates complete need of implementing FHRP protocols.
- Removes FHRP dependencies and increases Layer 3 network scalability.

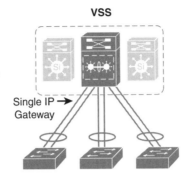

Figure 1-29 *GLBP with STP Blocking Links*

Layer 2 to Layer 3 Boundary Design Options and Considerations

This section first highlights and analyzes the critical role of the interconnection link between the distribution layer switches to achieve a resilient Layer 2 design; then it discusses the different design options that you can use to provide the demarcation point for Layer 2 and Layer 3 as part of the hierarchal campus network architecture.

Distribution-to-Distribution Link Design Considerations

Sometimes network engineers underestimate the importance of the interconnection link between the distribution layer switches at the distribution block of the enterprise campus network. However, when you remove a direct path of communication for the distribution layer switches, you then become dependent on the access layer for connectivity. In a traditional (STP-based) environment, this can introduce unexpected behavior in the event of a failure, such as the following (see Figure 1-30):

- Traffic is dropped until HSRP becomes active.
- Traffic is dropped until the link transitions to the forwarding state, taking as long as 50 seconds.
- Traffic is dropped until the MaxAge timer expires and until the listening and learning states are completed.
- STP could cause nondeterministic traffic flows/link load engineering.
- Unexpected Layer 3 convergence and reconvergence could occur.

Resiliency 37

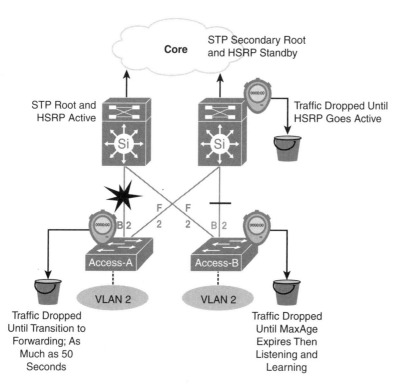

Figure 1-30 *Impact of Not Connecting the Distribution Layer Switches*

Note In Figure 1-30, B refers to a blocking link, and F refers to a forwarding link.

Also, there is a major impact on the overall campus network high availability and performance if you do not interconnect the distribution layer switches when using routed access and the virtual switch model. The following sections discuss the attributes of the possible design options of the distribution-to-distribution link on each of the access-distribution design models.

Distribution-to-Distribution Interconnect with the Multitier Access Model

As highlighted in the previous section, the removal of the distribution-to-distribution link can significantly impact the resiliency and performance of the campus network design. You can add an interconnect link between the distribution layer switches of a campus network based on the multitier access model discussed earlier in this chapter (STP-based) by using one of the following two main design models:

- Looped model
- Loop-free model

The looped model has the following attributes:

- VLANs can be extended between aggregation switches, creating the looped topology.
- Spanning tree is used to prevent Layer 2 loops.
- Redundant paths are available through a second path that is in the STP blocking state.
- VLANs can be load-balanced across the available access to distribution layer uplinks.
- Two possible topologies can be achieved with this model: triangle and square looped topologies.

Figure 1-31 illustrates each of the two possible looped topologies along with its attributes.

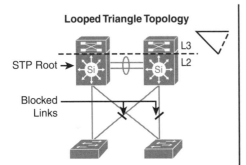
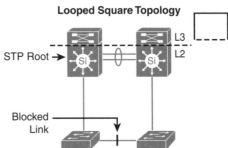

Figure 1-31 *Access-Distribution Looped Design Model*

Ideally, as a network designer, you must build your design based on the requirements of the applications. Therefore, if the requirements of certain critical applications require VLANs to span across multiple access layer switches and using STP is an integral part of your convergence plan, you should consider the following steps to ensure you can obtain the best of this suboptimal situation:

- Consider Rapid PVST+ as the version of STP. When spanning-tree convergence is required, Rapid PVST+ is superior to PVST+ or plain 802.1d.

- Ensure that you provision a Layer 2 link between the two distribution switches with the right sizing of this link (for example, 10/40 Gbps) to avoid unexpected traffic paths and multiple convergence events.

- If you choose to load-balance VLANs across uplinks, be sure to place the HSRP primary and the STP primary on the same distribution layer switch. The HSRP and Rapid PVST+ root should be co-located on the same distribution switches to minimize using the inter-distribution link for transit.

- Because STP plays a vital role in such topology, ensure that you enable the STP enhanced feature to harden the STP operation, as shown in Figure 1-32.

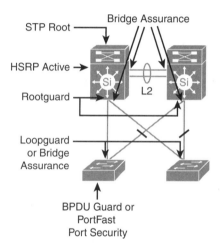

Figure 1-32 *Recommended STP Configurations with Looped Model*

In contrast, the loop-free model has the following attributes:

- As implied from this design model name, it is loop free. Therefore, even though spanning tree is enabled in such a topology, there will be no uplinks in the blocking state (all ports are forwarding).

- Two possible topologies can be achieved with this model: the U and Invert-U topologies.

- It offers a more protective solution because there will be less chance of a loop condition due to misconfiguration.

- Unlike the looped model, in the loop-free model, the Layer 2 and Layer 3 boundary varies depending on whether the U or Invert-U topology is used.

Figure 1-33 illustrates each of the two possible loop-free topologies along with its attributes.

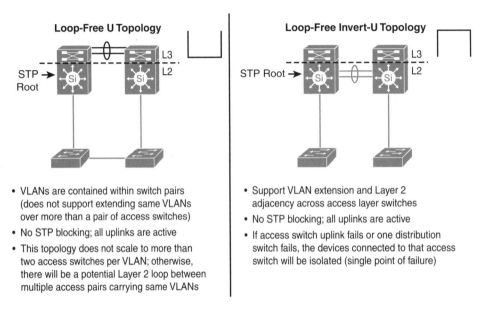

Figure 1-33 *Access-Distribution Loop-Free Design Model*

Consequently, if you have a traditional campus LAN (STP-based) and you cannot upgrade it to the routed access design model or use the virtual switch concept (such as Cisco VSS), it is recommended that you consider the topology shown in Figure 1-34. The reason is that it's a time-proven topology that provides the best availability and does not require STP/RSTP convergence. However, this design does not support spanning VLANs across access layer switches. In this topology, the distribution layer interconnection is a Layer 3 point-to-point link. From an STP perspective, both access layer uplinks are forwarding, so the only convergence dependencies are the default gateway and return path route selection across the distribution-to-distribution link. Nevertheless, you can achieve reliable default gateway failover from the HSRP primary to the HSRP standby within 1 second or less, by tuning the HSRP timers, as described earlier in this chapter.

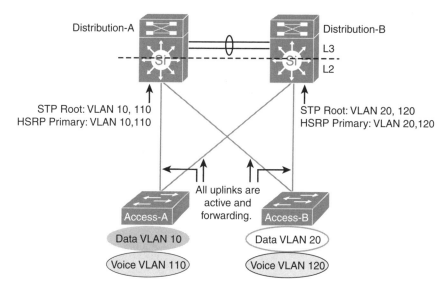

Figure 1-34 *Recommended Loop-Free Topology*

Distribution-to-Distribution Interconnect with the Routed Access Model

When you are implementing a routed access campus, it is important to understand both how the campus routing design fits into the overall network routing hierarchy and how to best configure the campus switches to achieve the following:

- Rapid convergence because of link and/or switch failures
- Deterministic traffic recovery
- Scalable and manageable routing hierarchy

One of the key design considerations to achieve rapid convergence and more deterministic traffic recovery is the physical layout of the routed links between the different tiers, specifically between the distribution layer nodes. As illustrated in Figure 1-35, the scenario on the left side shows that without having an inter-switch link between the distribution layer switches, there is high potential for 50 percent of the traffic to be dropped when the link from Distribution-A to the Access-A switch fails, and this will continue until the routing protocols converge (in this scenario, after Distribution-A detects the link failure, it has to process and update its routing table and notify the core switch about the routing change to update its routing table). In today's modern campus networks, this can lead to a major impact, especially for delay-sensitive traffic such as voice over IP (VoIP) or video. By introducing a routed link between the distribution switches, you can significantly optimize this issue (in this scenario, after Distribution-A detects the link failure, its routing protocol can converge and reroute traffic using the existing routed path over the inter-switch link to reach the Access-A switch), as shown on the right side of Figure 1-35.

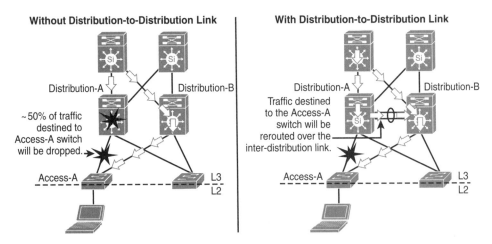

Figure 1-35 *Impact of Distribution-to-Distribution Link in the Routed Access Design*

Note In both cases, the failure must be detected and the routing protocol needs to converge; however, when there is an inter-switch link between the distribution layer switches, the convergence will be quicker. For the upstream traffic, the access switch should have two equal-cost multipath routes (ECMP) to the two upstream distribution switches. In this case, when the link between the access and distribution fails, the access switch will immediately update the next-hop entries in hardware, thereby reducing the possibility of blackholing the traffic. With this design, the failover operation takes place in the hardware (based on the information available in the forwarding information–based FIB) and therefore offers faster rerouting of traffic at the distribution node.

Note Although the basic topology of the routed campus is similar to the WAN environment, it is not exactly the same. Therefore, you should keep in mind the following differences between the two environments when optimizing the campus routing design for fast routing convergence:

- Unlike in the WAN, the abundance of bandwidth in campus networks allows for more aggressive tuning of control plane traffic (for example, hello packet intervals).
- Hierarchical campus networks typically have lower neighbor counts than the WAN and thus have a reduced control plane load.
- Direct fiber interconnects simplify neighbor failure detection.
- The ease and lower cost of provisioning redundancy in the campus network allow for use of optimal redundant design.
- Hardware Layer 3 switching ensures dedicated CPU resources for control plane processing.

Distribution-to-Distribution Interconnect with the Virtual Switch Model

The virtual switch system operates differently at different planes. From a control plane point of view, the VSS peers (switches) operate in active standby redundancy mode. The switch in active redundancy mode will maintain the single configuration file for the VSS and sync it to the standby switch, and only the console interface on the active switch is accessible (see Figure 1-36).

Both VSS nodes are active from a data-forwarding perspective.

```
vss# show switch virtual redundancy
My Switch Id = 1
Peer Switch Id = 2
<snip>
Switch 1 Slot 5 Processor Information :
-----------------------------------------
  Current Software state = ACTIVE
<snip>
           Fabric State = ACTIVE
      Control Plane State = ACTIVE
Switch 2 Slot 5 Processor Information :
-----------------------------------------
  Current Software state = STANDBY HOT (switchover
    target)
<snip>
           Fabric State = ACTIVE
      Control Plane State = STANDBY
```

Figure 1-36 *VSS Control*

From a data and forwarding plane perspective, both data and forwarding planes are active. The standby supervisor and all line cards are actively forwarding (see Figure 1-37).

Switch 1 Console (Active)

```
vss#
vss#
vss#
vss#
vss# show switch virtual
Switch mode                          : Virtual Switch
Virtual switch domain number         : 10
Local switch number                  : 1
Local switch operational role        : Virtual Switch Active
Peer switch number                   : 2
Peer switch operational role         : Virtual Switch Standby
vss#
```

Switch 2 Console (Standby Hot)

```
vss-sdby> enable
Standby console disabled

vss-sdby>
```

Figure 1-37 *Data Plane*

The interconnection link between the two virtual switch members of VSS peers is called a virtual switch link (VSL). This link is key because in addition to regular data traffic, it carries the control plane communication between the two virtual switch members (see Figure 1-38).

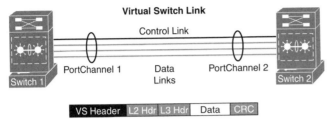

All traffic traversing the VSL link is encapsulated with a 32-byte "Virtual Switch Header" containing ingress and egress switchport indexes, class of service (COS), VLAN number, and other important information from the Layer 2 and Layer 3 header.

Figure 1-38 *VSS VSL*

VSLs can be configured with up to eight links between the two switches across any combination of line cards or supervisor ports to provide a high level of redundancy. If, for some rare reason, all VSL connections are lost between the virtual switch members, leaving both the virtual switch members up, the VSS will transition to the dual-active recovery mode.

The dual-active state is detected rapidly (subsecond) by any of the following three methods:

- Enhancement to PAgP used in MEC with connecting Cisco switches
- Layer 3 Bidirectional Forwarding Detection (BFD) configuration on a directly connected link (besides VSL) between virtual switch members or through a Layer 2 link through an access layer switch
- Layer 2 Fast-Hello dual-active detection configuration on a directly connected link (besides VSL) between virtual switch members

In the dual-active recovery mode, all interfaces except the VSL interfaces are in an operationally shutdown state in the formerly active virtual switch member. The new active virtual switch continues to forward traffic on all links.

A Summary of Enterprise Campus HA Designs

Applying hierarchy and modularity design principles will promote a highly available enterprise campus design architecture. Also, as discussed in this chapter, there are three primary design models for access to distribution layer connectivity: the multitier access, routed access, and virtual switch models.

In general, the least resilient and reliable in modern campus networks is the multitier access model because it relies on STP and FHRP timers in most of its topologies. If the topology does not rely on STP, flexibility is limited. For example, VLAN cannot span more than a pair of access switches. The routed access model, on the other hand, offers more reliable, scalable, and optimized resiliency in terms of failover time. Also, because there is no need to configure any STP or FHRP, this model tends to be more simple to design and operate than the multitier model. However, with the routed access design, if you want to have shared VLAN, such as management VLAN across the access switches, you cannot span a Layer 2 domain (VLAN) unless you use an overlay technology such as VxLAN. Last but not least, the virtual switch model is the most resilient, flexible, and easy-to-manage model to be considered; it offers more optimized performance from a data and forwarding plane perspective.

Table 1-2 compares the different design options of the enterprise campus distribution blocks from different technical aspects.[21]

Table 1-2 *Comparison of Enterprise Campus Access-Distribution Design Models*

	Multitier Access	**Routed Access**	**Virtual Switch**
Access-Distribution Control Plane Protocols	Spanning Tree (PVST+, Rapid PVST+, or MST)	EIGRP or OSPF	PAgP, LACP
Spanning Tree	STP required for network redundancy and to prevent Layer 2 loops	No*	No*
Network Recovery Mechanisms	Spanning Tree and FHRP (HSRP, GLBP, VRRP)	EIGRP or OSPF	Multichassis EtherChannel (MEC)
VLAN-Spanning Access Switches	Supported in some topologies (looped topologies)	No***	Supported
Layer 2/3 Demarcation	Distribution	Access	Distribution**
First-Hop Redundancy Protocol	HSRP, GLBP, VRRP required	Not Required	Not Required****
Access to Distribution Per Flow Load Balancing	No	Yes, ECMP	Yes, MEC
Convergence	Moderate to fast (Dependent on STP topology and FHRP tuning)	Very fast with tuned IGP timers	Very fast
Scalability	Limited	High	High
Change Control	Dual distribution switch design requires manual configuration synchronization but allows for independent code upgrades and changes	Dual distribution switch design requires manual configuration synchronization but allows for independent code upgrades and changes	Single virtual switch auto-syncs the configuration between redundant hardware but does not currently allow independent code upgrades for individual member switches

* Neither the routed access nor virtual switch designs require STP configured to maintain the network topology. It is still recommended and required to allow the use of features such as BPDU Guard on access ports.

** With a virtual switch design, it is possible to configure a routed access layer, but this will affect the capability to span VLANs across wiring closets.

*** Requires an overly (tunneling) technology to be achieved (for example, VxLAN).

**** FHRP is required when you are using Cisco virtual switch port-channel vPC (from a data plane perspective, both FHRP nodes will be active and forwarding).

> **Note** The selection and design of the routing protocol with the campus network have a major impact on the level of resiliency and convergence time. Subsequent chapters cover the design considerations and options of each routing protocol in more details.

Summary

Although the design options and recommendations discussed in this chapter are best practices intended to achieve the best convergence possible, each network is unique; and constraints such as cost, physical plant limitations, or application requirements may limit full implementation of these recommendations.

The hierarchical network model is essential for achieving high availability. In a hierarchical design, the capacity, features, and functionality of a specific device are optimized for its position in the network and the role that it plays. As a result, you can achieve more optimized scalability and stability. If the foundation is not rock solid, the performance of applications that depend on network services such as IP telephony, IP video, and wireless communications will eventually suffer.

In addition, in today's evolved networking environments, typical campus network designs use a mix of switching (Layer 2) technologies at the network edge (access) and routing (Layer 3) technologies at the network core (distribution and core layers). Thus, based on the design model used in the campus network, network virtualization can be achieved either at the network access layer (Layer 2) by means of VLANs or at the network core (Layer 3) by using GRE tunnels, VRF-Lite, and/or MPLS-based Layer 3 VPNs to partition the routed domain and thus achieve scalable end-to-end virtualization.

Review Questions

After answering the following questions, please refer to Appendix A, "Answers to Review Questions," for the answers.

1. Which is the recommended access-distribution design model when you need to span Layer 2 VLANs across access layer switches?
    a. Routed access model
    b. Loop-free Invert-U topology
    c. Virtual switch model
    d. Multitier access model

2. Large enterprises with several departments need to have the flexibility to restrict users' communication from different departments across the campus and to the data center applications based on the department they belong to. Which one of the following design approaches or mechanisms would you suggest using without introducing operational complexity or cost increases?
   a. Provision a separate physical network per department.
   b. Place a pair of firewalls at the data center and require users to use VPN to log in and access the required applications per department.
   c. Use lists end to end across the network to achieve the required communication restriction between the users who belong to different departments.
   d. Use network virtualization, in which each department will be assigned its own virtual network to achieve end-to-end traffic separation.

3. Which statements are true of hierarchal campus design? (Select two.)
   a. It increases operational complexity.
   b. It increases design flexibility.
   c. It requires more physical cabling.
   d. It leads to more manageable networks.
   e. It is not recommended in today's campus network designs.

4. Which two design models offer the fastest convergence time following a distribution switch failure? (Select two.)
   a. Loop-free U topology
   b. Loop-free Invert-U topology
   c. Virtual switch model
   d. Routed access model
   e. Multitier triangle access model with Layer 3 distribution-to-distribution link

5. Which statement about hierarchal campus design is true?
   a. The core layer is always recommended.
   b. Collapsed core/distribution is the most recommended design model.
   c. The core layer is recommended when you have three or more distribution blocks.
   d. The core layer is recommended when you have five or more distribution blocks.

6. Which one of the following design approaches or mechanisms would you suggest an organization using the routed access design model would need to deploy path isolation?
   a. Configure Layer 2 VLANs per virtual network at the access layer and configure a VRF per VLAN at the distribution layer.
   b. Use GRE tunneling per virtual network. The tunnels should be built between the distribution switches.
   c. Configure MPLS at the core and VRFs at the distribution layer.
   d. Configure Layer 2 VLANs per virtual network at the access layer and map each VLAN to a VRF at the access layer. VRFs need to be defined across the path end to end with a subinterface per VRF.

7. Which statement is true about the virtual switch design model?
   a. It is always recommended to be used at the core only.
   b. It is complex to manage.
   c. It eliminates the need to implement any FHRP such as HSRP.
   d. It is easy to manage but increases convergence time.

8. Which statements are true about FHRP? (Select two.)
   a. It is always recommended to be used with the routed access design.
   b. GLBP offers better load distribution.
   c. GLBP may lead to asymmetrical routing.
   d. HSRP does not support subsecond convergence time.

References

1. "Enterprise Campus 3.0 Architecture: Overview and Framework," http://www.cisco.com
2. See note 1 above.
3. See note 1 above.
4. See note 1 above
5. See note 1 above.
6. See note 1 above.
7. See note 1 above.
8. "Network Virtualization for the Campus," http://www.cisco.com
9. "Enterprise Campus 3.0 Architecture: Overview and Framework," http://www.cisco.com
10. "Borderless Campus 1.0 Design Guide," http://www.cisco.com
11. See note 10 above.
12. "Campus Network for High Availability Design Guide," http://www.cisco.com
13. See note 12 above.
14. See note 12 above.
15. See note 12 above.
16. See note 12 above.
17. See note 12 above.
18. See note 12 above.
19. See note 12 above.
20. See note 12 above.
21. "Enterprise Campus 3.0 Architecture: Overview and Framework," http://www.cisco.com

Chapter 2

EIGRP Design

Upon completing this chapter, you will be able to

- Describe the issues that have to be taken into consideration when designing the Enhanced Interior Gateway Routing Protocol (EIGRP) topology
- Describe the EIGRP with multiple autonomous systems
- Explain the reasons for multiple EIGRP autonomous systems
- Describe the basics of EIGRP hierarchical design
- Describe the EIGRP choke point creation
- Describe the EIGRP two-layer hierarchy
- Describe the EIGRP three-layer hierarchy
- Describe the EIGRP hub-and-spoke design
- Describe how summarization can lead to routing black holes
- Describe how summarization can lead to suboptimal routing
- Describe how EIGRP hub-and-spoke topologies scale
- Describe the EIGRP stub and stub leaking
- Describe how EIGRP scales in a Dynamic Multipoint Virtual Private Network (DMVPN) network
- Describe the bidirectional forwarding detection
- Describe the EIGRP graceful restart/nonstop forwarding (NSF) fundamentals

Enhanced Interior Gateway Routing Protocol (EIGRP) is the advanced version of Interior Gateway Routing Protocol (IGRP) developed by Cisco. It provides superior convergence properties and operating efficiency, and it combines the advantages of link-state protocols with those of distance vector protocols. This chapter discusses how to scale and optimize EIGRP designs with a focus on EIGRP over hub-and-spoke topology, as it's commonly used in today's enterprise grade networks. In addition, this chapter helps you learn how to design multilayer EIGRP topologies, logical zones, and choke points; properly implement summarization; and avoid summarization caveats.

Scalable EIGRP Design Overview

Although EIGRP design is considered flexible and tolerant of arbitrary topologies for small and medium networks, this tolerance can be seen as both a strength and a weakness. The reason this can be seen as either a strength or a weakness is that EIGRP can be deployed without restructuring the network (flat). However, as the scale of the network increases, the risk of instability or long convergence times becomes greater. Consequently, when the network scales beyond a couple of hundred routers, without a structured hierarchy, you will face EIGRP performance issues. As you increase the size of the network, you also need to make your network design more structured and strict. In other words, considering flat EIGRP with an arbitrary topology would be similar to an Open Shortest Path First (OSPF) design that puts everything into OSPF area 0. That design works with limited scalability and stability (for small and medium networks, up to around 300 OSPF routers; Chapter 3, "OSPF Design," and Chapter 4, "IS-IS Design," cover this point in more detail).

Therefore, to design a scalable and stable EIGRP, you should use a structured hierarchical topology in conjunction with route summarization, to break a single flooding domain into multiple domains that offer more structured, manageable, and scalable design.

Technically, one of the most significant stability and convergence issues with EIGRP is the propagation of EIGRP queries. When EIGRP does not have a feasible successor, it sends queries to its neighbors. The query tells the neighbor: "I do not have a route to this destination anymore; do not route through me. Let me know if you hear of a viable alternative route." The router has to wait for replies to all the queries that it sends out. Queries can flood through many routers in a portion of the network and increase convergence time. Summarization points, EIGRP stub routing, and route filtering limit the EIGRP query scope (propagation) and minimize convergence time. The subsequent sections cover these aspects in more detail.

Note The examples used throughout this book focus on IPv4; however, the concepts equally apply to both IPv4 and IPv6.

EIGRP with Multiple Autonomous Systems

Some network designers consider using multiple EIGRP autonomous systems (AS), and redistributing partially or fully between the two, as a scaling technique. The usual rationale is to reduce the volume of EIGRP queries by limiting them to one EIGRP autonomous system. However, some issues are associated with this design approach (multiple EIGRP ASs and distribution between the two).

Technically, the "external route redistribution" brings up a potential issue. As shown in Figure 2-1, a route is redistributed from the Routing Information Protocol (RIP) domain into EIGRP AS200. Router A redistributes it into AS100. Router B hears about the route prefix in advertisements from both AS200 and AS100. The administrative distance is the same because the route is external to both autonomous systems. Based on that, the route that is installed into the EIGRP topology database first gets placed into the routing table. This placement may lead to a potential suboptimal routing in which packets destined to the RIP domain may take a longer path that may impact some delay sensitive applications such as Voice over IP (VoIP).

Note In this section, we assume that the design of EIGRP with the multiple autonomous systems redistributes between each other either in a single direction or both directions.

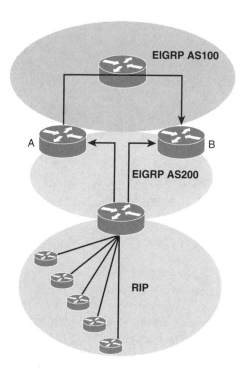

Figure 2-1 *EIGRP with Multiple Autonomous Systems*

The question here is, "Does this design approach (multiple EIGRP autonomous systems and redistribution between them) help to optimize EIGRP queries propagation?" The following section analyzes this issue in more detail.

EIGRP Queries

Let's consider the same scenario used in Figure 2-1 and see whether designing EIGRP with multiple autonomous systems will help contain and limit EIGRP queries or not. In Figure 2-2, when router C sends an EIGRP query to router A, router A needs to query its neighbors. Router A sends a reply to router C because it has no other neighbors in AS200. However, router A must also query all its neighbors in AS100 for the missing route. These routers may have to query their neighbors. Also, we must not forget that if this prefix is being redistributed into EIGRP AS100, router A is now missing this prefix in EIGRP AS100. Because router A is missing this redistributed prefix in EIGRP AS100, it now must send out a query for this missing prefix into EIGRP AS100.

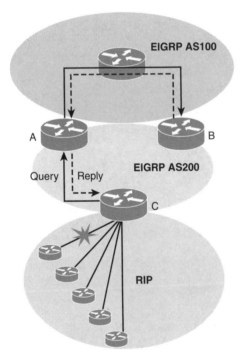

Figure 2-2 *EIGRP with Multiple Autonomous Systems and Query Scope*

Also, this issue may lead to an EIGRP stuck in active (SIA) condition, where an EIGRP router has not received a reply to a query from one or more neighbors within a defined time (approximately 3 minutes).

The query from router C is answered promptly by router A, but router A still needs to wait for a response to its query in AS100. As a result, having multiple autonomous systems and redistributing between them does not really stop queries; it just delays them on the way.

Therefore, consider this design approach (EIGRP with multiple autonomous systems and redistributing between them) as an EIGRP query-limiting design attempt is not an optimal or recommended solution in this case. To contain queries, it is recommended you use general scaling methods such as summarization, filtering (distribution lists), and EIGRP stubs.

Multiple EIGRP Autonomous System Drivers

As discussed in the preceding section, considering EIGRP with multiple autonomous systems and redistributing between them does not help limit the volume of EIGRP queries in the topology. That said, there could be several valid reasons for having multiple EIGRP autonomous systems, including the following (careful attention must be paid to limiting EIGRP queries):

- **Migration strategy after a merger or acquisition:** Although this use case scenario is not permanent, multiple autonomous systems are appropriate for merging two networks over time.

- **Different groups manage different EIGRP autonomous systems:** This scenario adds complexity to the network design, but it might be used for different domains of trust or administrative control.

- **Organizations with very large networks may use multiple EIGRP autonomous systems as a way to divide their networks:** Generally, such a design approach uses summary routes at the AS boundaries to contain summarizable blocks of IP prefixes in very large networks and to address the EIGRP query propagation issue.

EIGRP Multilayer Architectures

EIGRP doesn't technically have "areas" like OSPF because topology information is hidden at each hop by design. EIGRP offers the flexibility to be designed with multiple tiers (layers) in hierarchal network topologies. This flexibility is driven by the fact that network designers can define as many tiers as needed. What technically defines a tier or layer boundary in EIGRP design is the place where you define route summarization or filtering. In other words, in an EIGRP network, hierarchy is created through summarization or filtering. EIGRP has no imposed limit on the number of levels of hierarchy, which is a key design advantage. When you are designing multilayer logical routing domains, as a network designer, you should be aware of two main concepts: zones and choke points, as illustrated in Figure 2-3.

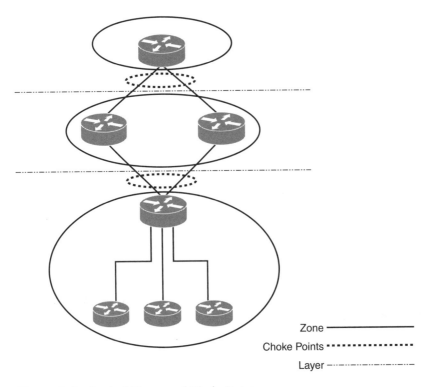

Figure 2-3 *Logical Zones and Choke Points*

Zones are topologically defined parts of the network. Zones represent a failure domain; link and device failures within a zone should have little or no impact outside of that specific zone.

Choke points represent the places where zones are interconnected. Choke points provide a place where you aggregate reachability and topology information. Choke points are a place where you apply summarization. They are also a place where you aggregate traffic flows and apply traffic policies.

When you are designing an EIGRP network, the main question is how many layers you should have. Although EIGRP is not limited with several layers, typical EIGRP designs implement either two or three layers. Geographical dispersion of the network has a great effect on the number of layers. You should strive to use two layers for small, contained networks. Use three layers for networks with a greater reach.

Topology depths, that is, the maximum number of hops from one edge to another, also dictate the number of layers. Normally, splitting large routed domains into smaller ones helps to provide more controlled and stable routing design. Therefore, in large and complex networks with greater depth, it is better to divide the network into more manageable logical layers and zones.

It is important to understand that the ideal logical design of choke points requires adjustment not only to the existent topology but also to addressing. Choke points should be created at points where you can do efficient summarization, as shown in Figure 2-4.

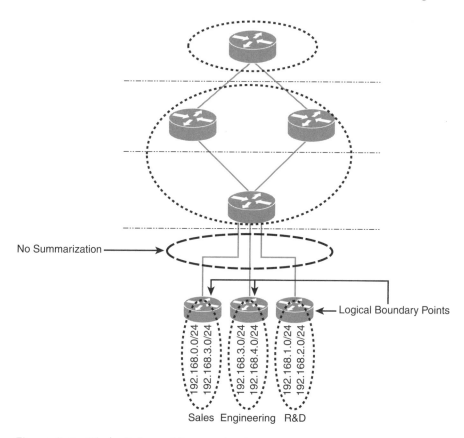

Figure 2-4 *Choke Point and Summarization*

However, sometimes it is not easy or practically possible to redesign the existing IP addressing scheme that is already used in the production network. For example, the scenario in Figure 2-4, *considering choke points to be positioned too low* in the topology, is not a feasible choice because it does not have a place to summarize all the existing subnets optimally because you cannot summarize the Engineering subnets on the lowest tier of routers. The reason is that the summarized route would also include subnets from Sales.

Therefore, by having a structured IP scheme and moving the choke points a layer higher, you are able to summarize all underlying addresses, creating an efficient choke point that aggregates reachability information, as shown in Figure 2-5.

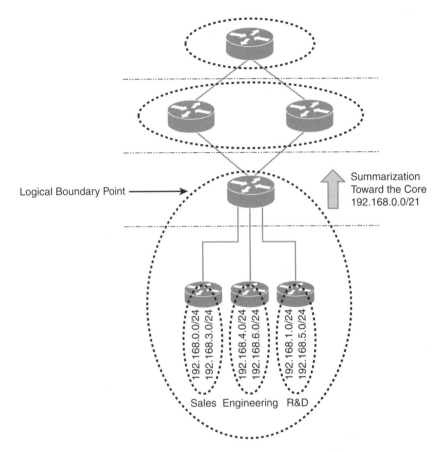

Figure 2-5 *Design Optimization Using Choke Points and Summarization*

Is using a two-layer or three-layer EIGRP hierarchy better? Technically, it is easier to do efficient traffic engineering with a two-layer design. However, resource restriction policies prefer three-layer designs. In the end, you have to decide on a design that balances simplicity, optimal routing, and functional separation.

The following sections discuss the two common multitier/multilayer EIGRP designs used in enterprise networks (two layer and three layer).

EIGRP Two-Layer Hierarchy Architecture

The two-layer hierarchy architecture is mainly based on two primary layers or EIGRP logical boundaries: core and distribution. This is shown in Figure 2-6.

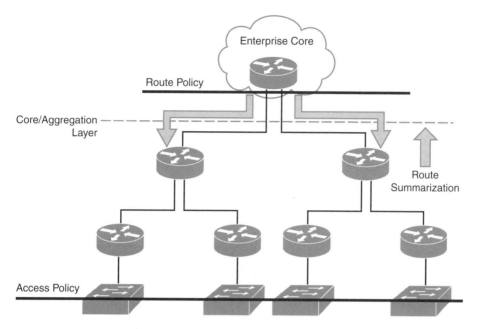

Figure 2-6 *EIGRP Two-layer Hierarchy Architecture*

In this architecture, the primary function of the core layer is to get traffic from one topological area of the network to another and perform high-speed switching of packets, so you should avoid the application of complex policies in the core. Also, you should avoid reachability and topology aggregation inside the core itself. However, the core routers must summarize routing information toward the aggregation layer to define a logical boundary from the core to the distribution layer: the fewer routes that are advertised toward the edge, the better. In addition, you can implement routing policies to control how many and which routes should be accepted from the aggregation areas to protect the core from being flooded by unnecessary or malicious routes that may impact the entire network.

The aggregation layer typically provides access layer attachment points. Information about the edge should be hidden from the core using summarization and topology-hiding techniques and to define the logical boundary of the aggregation layer, as shown in Figure 2-6.

Ideally, traffic acceptance and security policies should be defined at the edge of the network using Layer 2 and Layer 3 filtering techniques to enforce the policies as close to the source as possible.

EIGRP Three-Layer Hierarchy Architecture

The three-layer hierarchy architecture is based on using the classic three layers: access, aggregation, and core. As in the two-layer hierarchy, the core layer gets traffic from one topological area of the network to another. It performs high-speed switching of packets, so you should avoid the application of complex policies in the core. Also, inside the core layer itself, reachability and topology aggregation should be avoided.

Address summarization occurs at choke points between the aggregation and core layers and between the distribution and access layers, as shown in Figure 2-7.

> **Note** Throughout this book, the terms *aggregation* and *distribution* are used interchangeable.

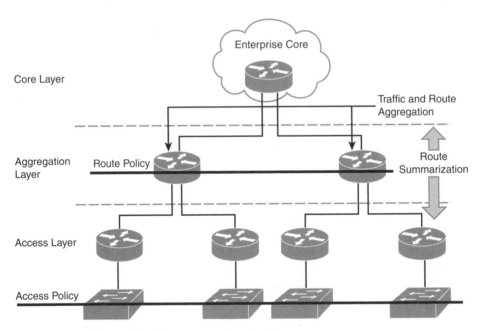

Figure 2-7 *EIGRP Three-layer Hierarchy Architecture*

To avoid unexpected traffic black-holing or suboptimal routing in some failure scenarios, do not summarize inside the distribution layer itself (between the distribution layer routers). From a routing design optimization and control point of view, a network designer can consider the following:

- Implement routing policies to control how many routes and which routes get accepted from the access areas and which of the routes will be passed to the core.

- Aggregate traffic in the aggregation layer as much as possible.

- Perform traffic engineering by directing traffic to the best core entry points by either sending more specific routes (nonsummarized) or using traffic filtering.

Typically, the access layer provides access ports for users or endpoints, and this layer should be used to place traffic acceptance and security policies and to filter unwanted Layer 2 and Layer 3 traffic. Ideally, the access layer routers should be configured as EIGRP stubs.

Defining route summarization or filtering at the different layers of the network will minimize the EIGRP query scope, which eventually will offer more stability to the EIGRP routed network following any network failure event. In this type of architecture, it is recommended that route summarization to be performed up and down the layers, and summarization between the interconnected nodes within the same layer should be avoided.

A deeper hierarchy does not change fundamental three-layer design concepts. Use the distribution layer as a blocking point from queries and provide minimal information toward the core and toward the access layer.

Furthermore, for both architectures discussed in this section (two tier and three tier), if the network designer decides to add a separate interface per LAN segment at the access layer (whether using physical interfaces or subinterfaces), technically, EIGRP will peer over these links (over each link in the query path). This will lead to reduced convergence time as well as increased control plane complexity (see Figure 2-8). A simple and proven solution to avoid this issue is to consider using the "passive-interface" command for the LAN interfaces to avoid forming any neighbor relationship over these links, as well as to stop sending and receiving routing updates in both directions.

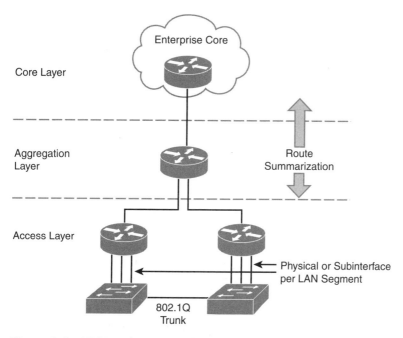

Figure 2-8 *EIGRP Alternate Paths at the Access Layer*

EIGRP Hub-and-Spoke Design

Hub and spoke is one of the most common topologies used to interconnect multiple branches to a single (or dual) headquarter site or data center over a wide area network (WAN) transport. Typically, spokes (branches) communicate with other spokes through the hub (headquarter); commonly, this is due to security requirements having centralized policy enforcement. The hub is thus an ideal choke point where you aggregate reachability and topology information, as illustrated in Figure 2-9.

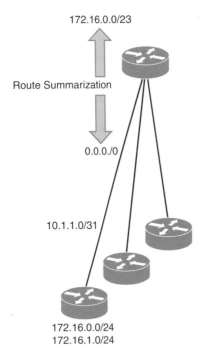

Figure 2-9 *EIGRP: Hub and Spoke*

Because the hub is the only point through which spokes can reach the other networks, advertise only the default route from the hub to the spokes.

As discussed earlier in this chapter, it is recommended that you summarize spoke networks on the hub toward the core; this way, you minimize the number of routes and create a logical layer (boundary) to limit EIGRP queries propagation from the remote sites to the core to achieve more stable routing design. In addition, when building topology with point-to-point links, consider using /31 subnets for the links to conserve address space when possible. Address the links out of the address space that is available on the spoke to allow for simple summarization. If this action is not possible, consider using distribute-lists to filter link subnets from being advertised back into the core of the network.

> **Note** RFC 3021 describes the use of 31-bit prefixes on IPv4 point-to-point links. The simplest way to explain it is to say that the use of a 31-bit prefix (created by applying a 31-bit subnet mask to an IP address) allows the all-0s and all-1s IP addresses to be assigned as host addresses on point-to-point networks. Prior to RFC 3021 the longest prefix in common use on point-to-point links was 30 bits, which meant that the all-0s and all-1s IP addresses were wasted.

Designing EIGRP over a hub-and-spoke topology has some design concerns and limitations that network designers must be aware of to produce a reliable and scalable EIGRP design. The following sections discuss these points in more detail.

Summarization Challenges

Although EIGRP route summarization offers a more scalable and stable routing design, in some scenarios it will introduce some limitation to the design that you must take into consideration to avoid producing a nonreliable design that does not meet application and business requirements. The typical challenges route summarization introduces are

- Routing black holes
- Suboptimal routing

The following sections analyze each of these challenges along with the possible mitigation techniques.

> **Note** Routing black holes toward downstream networks and suboptimal routing toward upstream networks caused by route summarization are common concerns across different topologies.

Route Summarization Black Holes

In a typical redundant hub-and-spoke network, each spoke is dual-homed to two hub routers, along with route summarization toward the network core. This design normally has a high potential for route black holes (see Figure 2-10).

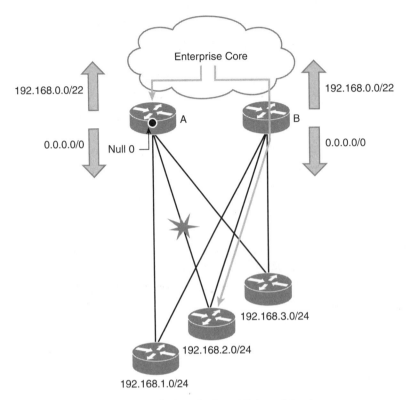

Figure 2-10 *Summary Black Hole Over Hub and Spoke*

In the scenario depicted in Figure 2-10, when spoke networks are summarized toward the core from a pair of hub routers, both hub routers advertise the 192.168.0.0/22 summary. When the hub A router loses connection with one of the spokes, the 192.168.2.0/24 gets removed from its routing table, while the summary route is still being advertised toward the core and default (0.0.0.0/0) toward the spokes. Therefore, incoming packets, which are destined to 192.168.2.0/24, are now discarded due to the 192.168.0.0/22 summary *discard route* that points to the Null0 interface. The local discard route gets created when you configure summarization to prevent routing loops. Hence, you have created a *black hole*.

To overcome this design limitation and avoid the potential of route black hole, you need to interconnect the two hub routers. Doing so will help steer the traffic over the interhub link to reach the hub that has a working connection with the spoke, as shown in Figure 2-11.

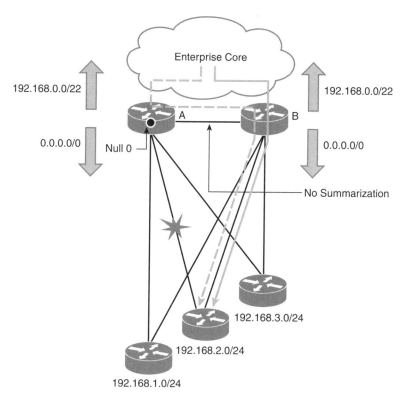

Figure 2-11 *Optimized Hub-and-Spoke Design to Avoid Summary Black Holing*

However, you must be careful not to enable summarization over the interconnection between the hub routers. The reason is that, technically, the discard route of the EIGRP summary route gets installed with an administrative distance (AD) of 5. Should one of the hub routers receive a summarized network advertisement of the same prefix length from the other hub router, the discard route will always take precedence before the received route, due to its lower AD, and will eliminate the benefit of the added interhub link.

> **Note** Technically, you can configure a higher EIGRP summary route AD when configuring summarization; however, this will complicate the design and will remove the basic purpose of the discard route, which is loop prevention. Thus, you should use this approach with great care.

Route Summarization and Suboptimal Routing

Ideally, to achieve a stable and scalable routing design, when the network design requires more than just a default route to be advertised from the hub to the spokes, you should summarize the routes that you advertise from the hub toward the spokes as much as possible. However, in dual-hub and some other complex hub-and-spoke scenarios, this situation may lead to *suboptimal routing in which the traffic will take a longer (indirect) path*.

In Figure 2-12, although all hub and core networks could be easily summarized with only the 10.1.0.0/16 summary that is advertised down to a dual-homed spoke, this summary may result in suboptimal routing. Packets that are destined to 10.1.1.0/24 can be forwarded directly through hub A or hub B. Based on that, practically, packets sent over hub B (the suboptimal path) may result in an increased latency that can impact delay-sensitive applications such as VoIP.

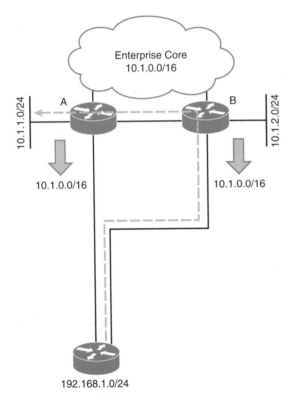

Figure 2-12 *EIGRP Suboptimal Routing*

With EIGRP, you optimize this design by leaking more specific routes through a summary, enabling you to still summarize all core networks on hub routers, while leaking more specific routes through a summary. (In the example shown in Figure 2-13, the LAN 10.1.1.0/24 hosts delay sensitive applications, and optimal routing is an important requirement here. Therefore, the more specific route is leaked through hub A.) Technically, you can do that on Cisco IOS devices while configuring summarization using the **leak-map** CLI argument.

EIGRP Hub-and-Spoke Design 65

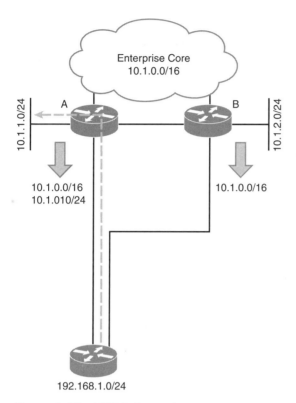

Figure 2-13 *EIGRP Optimal Routing*

EIGRP Hub-and-Spoke Scalability Optimization

Technically, the scalability of EIGRP in hub-and-spoke topologies relies on several factors, including the following:

- When spokes are connected to the hub over multiple interfaces, the processor is the primary limiting factor.
- With point-to-multipoint topology over a single interface, the primary limiting factor is the queue congestion. EIGRP has a theoretical limitation of 4000 peers per interface, when they are in the same prefix.

EIGRP is used in production environments, where over 800 EIGRP neighbors are seen from one point. Topologies with over 1400 EIGRP neighbors have been successfully run in the lab. These numbers, however, can be achieved only with a careful design.

To achieve a scalable EIGRP design that is capable of supporting a large number of spokes without sacrificing network stability and its ability to converge fast, you need to consider EIGRP stub at the spoke sites.

Stubs are a must in an EIGRP hub-and-spoke topology if you want to achieve a resilient, scalable, and reliable design. With the EIGRP stub routing feature, the routers (typically the spokes) configured as a stub will send a special peer information packet to all neighboring devices to report its status as a stub router. In turn, any EIGRP neighbor that receives a packet informing it of the stub status will not query the stub device for any routes (see Figure 2-14), and a router that has a stub peer will not query that peer. Therefore, the stub device will depend on the hub router(s) to send proper updates to all other spokes. Also, when an EIGRP stub is configured at the spokes routers, they will not be used as transit routers by the other spokes or hub routers.

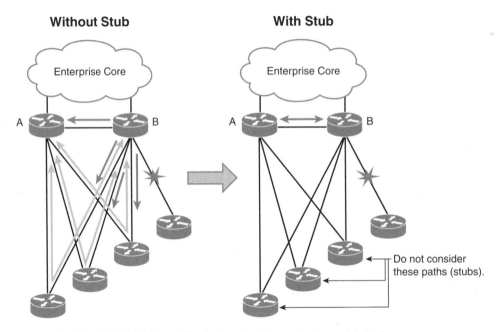

Figure 2-14 *EIGRP Hub-and-Spoke Design Optimization with Stub*

Furthermore, the other key scalability consideration in this design is summarization. Bandwidth and memory can be conserved by summarizing advertisements to spokes. Advertise either the default route or a carefully selected group of summarized networks. However, if EIGRP stub routing at the spokes is not enabled, even after routes that are sent from the hub router to the spokes have been filtered or summarized, there is still a potential of network instability or slower convergence time following a network failure event. For example, if a router or a link fails in one of the other remote spokes in the corporate network, EIGRP could send a query to the hub device, which in turn would send a query to the other spokes, even if routes are being summarized. If a communication problem (over the WAN link) occurs between the hub and the spoke, an EIGRP stuck in active (SIA) condition could occur and cause instability elsewhere in the network.

The EIGRP stub routing feature enables a network operator to prevent queries from being sent to the remote device (limiting query scope). As a result, the network will be more stable, capable of converging faster and scaling to large number of spokes. In fact, if spokes are not configured as stubs, you will not be able to build a reliable network of over 100 EIGRP neighbors that will converge fast. The blue line with the steep slope shows the rate at which the failover convergence time increases as EIGRP neighbors are added to a single hub router. Figure 2-15 presents the outcomes of LAB tests that show a significant difference in the amount of convergence time and number of neighbors network designers can achieve when the stubs concept is considered in dual-hub EIGRP design model.

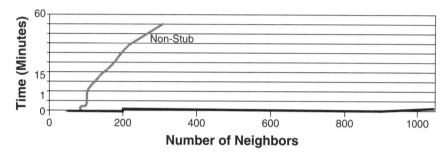

Figure 2-15 *Stub Influence on Design Scalability and Convergence Time*

EIGRP Stub Leaking

Let's examine a scenario in which two remote sites (spokes) are interconnected directly to each other (backdoor link) and each site is single-homed to the same hub site but connected to a different hub router, as shown in Figure 2-16. With this design, both spoke routers are configured as stub routers, and they advertise connected and summary networks, but they do not advertise the routes that they learn from their neighbors as per the typical stub route advertisement behavior. Then what happens when the link between routers RTR-Y and RTR-B fails?

68 Chapter 2: EIGRP Design

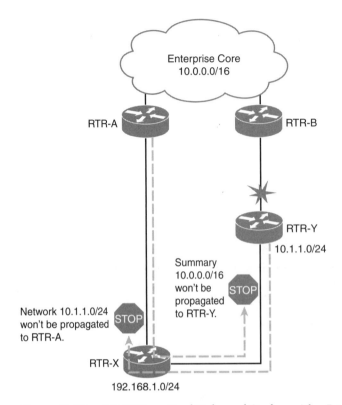

Figure 2-16 *EIGRP Over Dual Hubs and Spokes with a Backdoor Link*

Router RTR-X receives the 10.1.1.0/24 route from router RTR-Y, but it does not advertise it to router RTR-A because stub routers do not advertise learned routes. Network 10.1.1.0/24 is now not reachable from the hub, even though one of the redundant connections between the hub and the spoke is alive.

A similar problem occurs in the opposite direction. Router RTR-X is a stub, so it does not advertise the summary route of the core network (10.0.0.0/16) to router RTR-Y. As a result, router RTR-Y has no connectivity with the other hub; therefore, RTR-Y will be isolated, and it can only reach RTR-X subnets.

To solve the issue and offer a more resilient design by allowing the stub routers to advertise a subset of their learned routes, you need to consider EIGRP stub leaking. With stub leaking, you can permit stub router RTR-X to advertise the learned 10.1.1.0/24 route toward hub router RTR-A, as well as the core network summary route to be advertised toward router RTR-Y. With this "EIGRP stub leaking" feature, you can establish a fully redundant solution in a topology like this, while keeping the hub router queries out of the stub.

EIGRP DMVPN Scaling

Although EIGRP offers scalable network design over Dynamic Multipoint VPN (DMVPN), the actual scalability over DMVPN networks depends on several factors: topology, number of peers, number of advertised prefixes, and DMVPN phase.

> **Note** For more details about DMVPN and EIGRP over a DMVPN design scenario, refer to Chapter 9, "Enterprise Managed WAN."

The EIGRP behavior varies depending on the DMVPN phase used. Newer phases yield lower convergence times when the same EIGRP topology is used. DMVPN Phase 3 offers not only optimal routing but also the fastest EIGRP convergence times.

Production deployments show that a practical maximum of EIGRP peers in a DMVPN Phase 2 network is around 600. This number does not differ for single-hub and dual-hub deployments. After that number, convergence times start to rise significantly. Scaling the DMVPN network beyond that number typically requires multiple hubs, each terminating up to 600 spokes. Figure 2-17 shows the impact of peer count on convergence time (with ~5K spokes' prefixes).

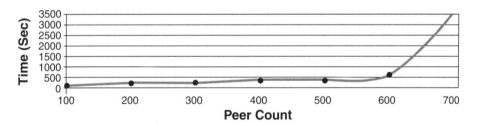

Figure 2-17 *The Peer Count Effect on EIGRP Convergence Time over DMVPN*

The increase in the number of advertised prefixes linearly increases convergence times. Convergence times can be easily hedged by using summarization, especially in DMVPN Phase 3 networks. Figure 2-18 shows the impact of the number of prefixes on convergence time (with 500 peers).

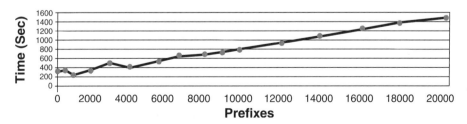

Figure 2-18 *The Prefix Count Effect on EIGRP Convergence Time over DMVPN*

EIGRP Fast Convergence Design Considerations

Although EIGRP was designed to achieve subsecond convergence, the key factor for this EIGRP fast convergence capability is the presence of a feasible successor. When there is no feasible successor, EIGRP uses queries to EIGRP peers and has to wait for responses, and these queries typically will slow down the overall convergence time.

To achieve fast EIGRP convergence, you need to design your network properly, taking into account the different design considerations discussed in this chapter. For example, route summarization helps limit the scope of EIGRP queries, which will indirectly speed up the convergence time. Summarization also shrinks the number of entries in the routing table, which speeds up various CPU operations. The effect of CPU operation on convergence is far less significant than the presence or absence of a feasible successor. Therefore, it is always recommended to ensure that a feasible successor is present. Also, having multiple paths in the routing table (equal-cost or unequal-cost routing) offers faster convergence times because an existing path is already available in the routing table if one of them failed.

In addition, from a design point of view, it is difficult to put an exact boundary on the number of EIGRP neighbors that a router can support because this approach depends on the proper use of summarization, route filtering, and stub routing. A properly designed network with 500 peers can converge quickly, whereas a poorly designed EIGRP network with 20 peers might experience severe routing instability.

Furthermore, one of the key elements to achieve a fast converging network is its capability to detect the failure and report it to the routing protocol in a fast and reliable manner. The bidirectional forwarding detection (BFD) is one of the most recommended protocols for this task. The following section covers it in more detail.

Bidirectional Forwarding Detection

The process of network convergence relies on the speed with which a device on the network can detect and react to a failure of one of its own components, or the failure of a component in a routing protocol peer. Layer 2 failure detection times can vary widely, depending on the physical media. Intervening devices (for example, the Ethernet switch) can hide Layer 2 failures from routing protocol peers. BFD can provide fast failure detection times for all media types, encapsulations, topologies, and routing protocols. In the best-case scenario, it can provide fast failure detection in ~50 milliseconds. BFD verifies connectivity between two systems. BFD control packets are always sent as unicast packets to the BFD peer. Cisco's BFD implementation encapsulated BFD control packets in User Datagram Protocol (UDP) packets, using destination port 3784. EIGRP informs the BFD process of the IP address of the neighbor that it needs to monitor. BFD does not discover its peers dynamically. It relies on the configured routing protocols to tell it which IP addresses to use and which peer relationships to form.

BFD on each router forms a BFD control packet. These packets are sent at a minimum of one-second intervals until a BFD session is established. After the remote router receives a BFD control packet during the session initiation phase, it copies the value of the My Discriminator field into its own Your Discriminator field and sets the H (I Hear You) bit for any subsequent BFD control packets it transmits. When both systems see their own Discriminators in each other's control packets, the session is established. Both systems continue to send at (at least) one-second intervals until they see the appropriate Discriminators in each other's BFD control packets.

When the BFD session is established, BFD timers are negotiated. These timers can be renegotiated at any time during the session without causing a session reset. BFD timers can be negotiated asynchronously. One peer may be sending BFD control packets at 50 ms intervals in one direction while the other peer is sending its BFD control packets every 150 ms in the other direction.

As long as each BFD peer receives a BFD control packet within the detect-timer period, the BFD session remains up, and any routing protocol that is associated with BFD maintains its adjacencies. If a BFD peer does not receive a control packet within the detect interval, it will inform any routing protocol of that BFD session about the failure. It is up to the routing protocol to determine the appropriate response to that information. The typical response will be to terminate the routing protocol peering session and reconverge, bypassing the failed peer.

In a BFD mode called *BFD echo*, the local device sends echo packets from the forwarding engine to the remote BFD neighbor. The BFD neighbor forwards the echo packet back along the same path to perform detection; the BFD neighbor does not participate in the actual forwarding of the echo packets. This is still a light process without adding on the CPU. With this mode, you can have either both or only one end sending the BFD echo.

EIGRP Graceful Restart/NSF Considerations

Traditionally, when a networking device restarts, all routing peers that are associated with that device detect that the device has gone down and routes from that peer are removed. The session is reestablished when the device completes the restart. This transition results in the removal and reinsertion of routes, which could spread across multiple routing domains.

Dual processor systems that support stateful switchover (SSO) or in-service software upgrade (ISSU) can continue to forward traffic while restarting the control plane on the second processor. In this case, route removal and insertion caused by routing protocol restarts are no longer necessary because they create unnecessary routing instabilities, which are detrimental to the overall network performance. Graceful restart (GR), also known as nonstop forwarding (NSF), suppresses routing changes on peers to SSO-enabled devices during processor switchover events (SSO or ISSU), reducing network instability and downtime.

Unlike the typical routing convergence approach that aims to route traffic around the failure, GR allows the forwarding of data packets to continue along known routes (through the same router with a route processor failure) while the routing protocol information is being restored, following a processor switchover.

When GR is used, peer networking devices are informed via protocol extensions before the event of the SSO-capable routers' capability to perform a graceful restart. The peer device must have the capability to understand this messaging. When a switchover occurs, the peer will continue to forward to the switching over the router as instructed by the GR process for each particular protocol, even though in most cases the peer relationship needs to be rebuilt. Essentially, the peer router will give switching over the router a "grace" period to reestablish the neighbor relationship, while continuing to forward to the routes from that peer.

> **Note** Graceful restart is available today for OSPF, IS-IS, EIGRP, LDP, and BGP. Standards are defined for OSPF, IS-IS, BGP, and LDP to ensure vendor interoperability.

Summary

- EIGRP tolerates arbitrary topologies better than OSPF.
- You must always summarize, filter, and limit EIGRP queries where possible.
- Multiple EIGRP AS is not an optimal scaling technique.
- Zones are parts of networks separated by choke points. Multiple zones that are equally distant from the core form layers.
- You should summarize at choke points, but beware of holes and suboptimal routing.
- EIGRP allows multiple layers, but you typically employ two- or three-layer topologies.
- Use should stubs. They are key to optimize the operation and convergence time of hub-and-spoke topologies.
- Even though EIGRP offers scalable network design over DMVPN, the targeted topology, number of peers, number of advertised prefixes, and DMVPN phase must be taken into consideration in large-scale networks to avoid creating a complex design that is hard to scale with slow convergence time.

Review Questions

After answering the following questions, please refer to Appendix A, "Answers to Review Questions," for the answers.

1. Which of the following do you need to take into account when creating choke points? (Choose two.)
    a. EIGRP Areas
    b. Addressing

    c. Topology
    d. EIGRP zones
    e. Router choke point support
 2. Which EIGRP stub-related statement is correct?
    a. Routers configured as stubs automatically summarize all connected routes.
    b. When remote sites employ two stub routers, each connected to one of the hub routers, remote site routers exchange locally connected routes by default.
    c. You should always configure spoke routers as stubs in hub-and-spoke topology.
    d. You should avoid configuring spoke routers as stubs in hub-and-spoke topology to avoid routing black holes.
 3. Which of the following is correct when creating route summarization from the hub sites (a dual-hub scenario) to the spokes? (Choose three.)
    a. Decrease the routing table of the spokes.
    b. Decrease the routing table of the hubs.
    c. Increase the routing table of the spokes.
    d. Increase the routing table of the spoke.
    e. Provide more optimal routing.
    f. May introduce suboptimal routing.
    g. Optimize convergence time.
 4. Which of the following is a valid driver to consider a design with multiple EIGRP autonomous systems?
    a. To limit EIGRP query scope
    b. To simplify the design
    c. Different administrative authorities manage the network
    d. To achieve more optimal routing
 5. What are the influencing factors that can impact EIGRP scalability over DMVPN? (Choose two.)
    a. Number of peers
    b. DMVPN encryption type
    c. Number of prefixes
    d. Number of users
    e. Available WAN bandwidth at the spoke sites

Chapter 3

OSPF Design

Upon completing this chapter, you will be able to

- Name factors that influence OSPF scalability
- Describe the impact of adjacent neighbors on OSPF scalability
- Describe routing information in the area and domain
- Explain the optimal number of routers in an area
- Explain the optimal number of areas an ABR can be part of
- Explain design areas
- Describe OSPF hierarchy
- Describe area and domain summarization
- Explain OSPF full-mesh design challenges
- Explain OSPF hub-and-spoke design
- Describe the ABR placement dilemma with a hub-and-spoke design
- Explain the number of areas in a hub-and-spoke design
- List OSPF hub-and-spoke network types
- Describe OSPF flood reduction
- Describe OSPF database overload protection

Open Shortest Path First (OSPF) is a link-state routing protocol derived from an early version of the IS-IS protocol. Being able to achieve a scalable OSPF design depends, to large extent, on your overall network structure and address scheme. The most important factors in determining the scalability of your internetwork are adopting a hierarchical address environment and a structured address assignment.

This chapter discusses designing advanced routing solutions using OSPF. It describes how to scale OSPF designs and which factors can influence convergence, stability, and scalability of OSPF in a large network.

OSPF Scalability Design Considerations

Utilization of a router's hardware resources—its memory and CPU—and its interface bandwidth are the primary influencing factors on OSPF scalability. The workload that OSPF imposes on a router depends on several factors:

- **Number of prefixes:** The number of prefixes that OSPF carries is arguably the most important factor in determining OSPF stability and its scalability.

- **Stability of connections:** OSPF sees unstable connections as flapping links. These flapping links introduce recalculation into the routing process and, thus, instabilities.

- **Number of adjacent neighbors for any one router:** OSPF floods all link-state changes to all routers in an area. Routers with many neighbors have the most work to do when link-state changes occur.

- **Number of adjacent routers in an area:** OSPF uses a CPU-intensive algorithm. The number of calculations that must be performed given n link-state packets is proportional to $n \log n$. As a result, the larger and more unstable the area, the greater the likelihood for performance problems that are associated with routing protocol recalculation.

- **Number of areas any one router can support:** A router must run the link-state algorithm for each link-state change that occurs for every area in which the router resides. Every area border router (ABR) typically belongs to at least two areas—the backbone and one adjacent area.

Subsequent sections in this chapter discuss each of these factors in more detail. From a design perspective, the first and most important decision when developing an OSPF network design, or evaluating an existing one, is to determine which routers and links should be included in the backbone area and which routers and links should be included in each adjacent area (nonbackbone).

Adjacent Neighbors

In OSPF, adjacency is the next step after the neighboring process. Adjacent routers are routers that go beyond the simple Hello exchange and proceed into the database exchange process. To minimize the amount of information exchange on a particular segment, OSPF elects one router to be a designated router (DR) and one router to be a backup designated router (BDR) on each multiaccess segment. The BDR is elected as a backup mechanism in case the DR goes down. The idea behind this is that routers have a central point of contact for information exchange. Instead of each router exchanging updates with every other router on the segment, every router exchanges information with the DR and BDR. The DR and BDR relay the information to everybody else (the BDR starts relaying information when the DR is down).

From a design viewpoint, OSPF scalability is influenced by the number of adjacent neighbors. Either neighbor routers are connected to the same segment, or each router uses its own connection segment. Typically, each segment has a DR and BDR that build adjacencies with all other routers, as shown in Figure 3-1. Put simply, the fewer neighbors that exist on a segment, the smaller the number of adjacencies a DR or BDR has to build and communicate with.

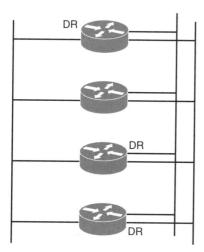

Figure 3-1 *OSPF Adjacencies per LAN Segment*

Note There is no concept of DR and BDR over the OSPF point-to-point network interface type.

Each OSPF adjacency represents another router, whose resources are expended to support these activities:

- Exchanging hellos
- Synchronizing link-state databases (LSDB)
- Reliably flooding OSPF link-state advertisement (LSA) changes
- Advertising the router and network LSA

Therefore, considering hierarchical design and load distribution (spreading the branch connections to multiple hub routers) can help to reduce the number of OSPF adjacencies. Volatility, amount of change, and other workload need to be considered when determining how many peers a central hub router can support in a hub-and-spoke topology. When you are testing a future production environment, take into account the worst-case situations: simultaneous restarts on all peers or flapping connections.

Routing Information in the Area and the Routed Domain

The amount of routing information that exists within an OSPF area or a single routing domain has a direct impact on the router's workload. This issue can be noticeable when a router needs to converge following a node or link failure and a large number of routes need to be processed.

Therefore, the number of routers and links to adjacent routers in an area determine how much information is in the LSA database or how much routing information is in the area. The type of area and the amount of summarization also are factors that influence the amount of routing information. The number of areas and types of areas that are supported by each router also influence how much routing information is in a domain.

Techniques and tools are available to reduce this information. Stub and totally stubby areas import less information about destinations outside the routing domain, or the area, than normal areas do (see Figure 3-2). Therefore, using stub and totally stubby areas further reduces the workload on an OSPF router. Technically, OSPF stub areas suppress external routing information, whereas the totally stubby areas suppress both external and interarea routing information. On the other hand, the not-so-stubby areas (NSSA) and totally NSSAs use the same concept of the "stub and totally stub area" except that both allow external routing information to be injected into the area as LSA Type-7. To maintain full reachability for these areas, information that is suppressed is replaced by IPv4 default route (0.0.0.0/0) or IPv6 default route (::/0), depending on the IP version used.

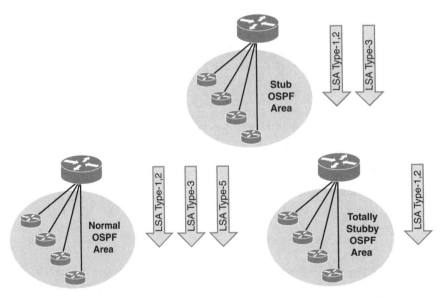

Figure 3-2 *Output from the SIMPLE Program*

Interarea routes and costs are advertised into an area by each ABR. As mentioned previously, the totally stubby areas keep not only external routes but also this interarea information from having to be flooded into and within an area.

Also, it is recommended that you exclude IP prefixes of connected networks (IPs of transit transport links) from LSA in large OSPF networks. This is important because these IPs limits the number of IP prefixes that are carried in the OSPF LSAs to speed up OSPF convergence. In Cisco IOS software, the CLI argument **prefix-suppression** helps simplify the filtering of these IP prefixes by preventing OSPF from advertising all IP prefixes of the connected interfaces—except prefixes that are associated with loopbacks, secondary IP addresses, and passive interfaces—because typical network designs require those to remain reachable.

Another technique to reduce the number of prefixes that are exchanged between areas is interarea filtering using prefix lists. You can use this method instead of totally stubby areas if specific routing information is needed for some prefixes but not for others. This approach, however, may increase the complexity of maintaining a large number of prefix lists in large networks.

On the other hand, area/autonomous system border routers (ASBR) in OSPF provide a distance-vector-like list of external destinations and costs. The more external prefixes and the more ASBRs there are, the higher the workload for type 5 or 7 LSAs. Stub areas keep all this information from being flooded within an area. Similarly, the more ABRs between any two areas exist, the more OSPF summary LSAs are generated to each area. For example, if there are four ABRs between area 0 and area 1, and area 1 has five IP prefixes to advertise to area 0, in turn each ABR advertises each of these IP prefixes into area 0. This means, with four ABRs, there could be 20 summary LSAs generated from these four ABRs, as illustrated in Figure 3-3.

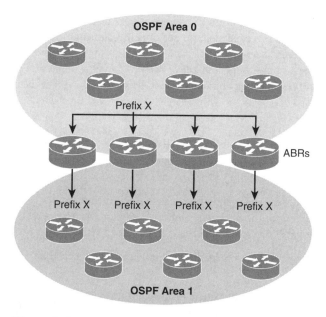

Figure 3-3 *OSPF with Multiple ABRs*

The conclusion is that area size and layout design, area types, route types, number of ABRs/ASBRs, redistribution, and summarization all affect the size of the LSA database in any single area. Therefore, use this general advice to achieve a simple-to-manage and easy-to-scale OSPF design:

- Keep it simple (for example, avoid multiple redistributions points, large numbers of prefix lists, and routing polices).
- Keep it stubby (or keep it totally stubby, especially for remote sites).
- Limit the number of ABR/ASBR routers to the minimum per area.
- Keep it summarized (using a structure IP addressing scheme is key to achieving optimal route summarization design).

Numbers of Routers in an Area

Although the impact of the number of adjacent neighbors on scalability is far more critical than the total number of routers in a single area, the amount of information that has to be flooded within an area is still an important factor to take into consideration when designing a large OSPF network. For instance, one network might have 30 routers with one Fast Ethernet subnet in one area. Another network might have fewer routers and more subnets. In both cases, there will be more information/LSAs to be flooded (the more nodes or subnets/interfaces in an area, the more information to be flooded).

The amount of information in the LSA increases the size of an LSA. Therefore, in general, it's a good design practice to keep the OSPF router's LSAs under the IP maximum transmission unit (MTU) size. When the MTU is exceeded, the result is IP fragmentation, a problem that is, under the best circumstances, a less efficient way to transmit information that also requires extra router processing. A large number of router LSAs also implies that there are many interfaces (and perhaps neighbors); it is an indirect indication that the area may have become too large.

> **Note** MTU represents the maximum packet size, in bytes, that a particular interface can handle.

Targeting to achieve only scalable design is not enough, because stability and redundancy are the most important criteria for the backbone and other areas in the network. Typically, keeping the size of the backbone reasonable leads to increased stability.

If link quality is high and the number of routes is small, the number of routers can be increased.

Practically, due to several complexity factors, it is difficult to specify a maximum number of routers per area. A well-designed area 0, with the latest Cisco hardware, should nevertheless have no more than about 300 routers.

OSPF Scalability Design Considerations   81

Note This number is intended as an approximate indication that an OSPF design is getting into trouble and should be reconsidered, focusing on a smaller area 0.

Number of Areas per ABR

As highlighted earlier in this chapter, each ABR maintains a copy of an LSDB for each area this ABR services. In other words, if a router is connected to ten areas, for example, it has to keep a list of ten different LSDBs (see Figure 3-4). That said, different factors can influence the number of areas per ABR, such as type of area (normal, stub, not-so-stubby area [NSSA]), ABR hardware resources power (CPU, memory), number of routes per area, and number of external routes per area.

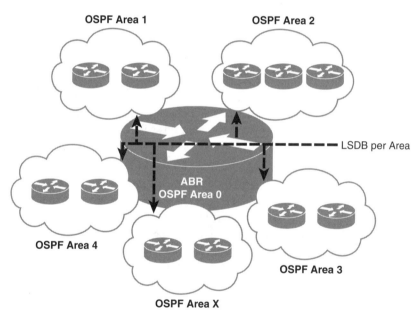

Figure 3-4 *ABR with Multiple OSPF Areas*

Therefore, it is commonly recommended to try to avoid overloading an ABR and instead spread the areas over several routers (previously, it was recommended to have up to three areas per ABR). However, practical designs require only a few routers to serve as multi-area ABRs, and these routers can be upgraded to the latest hardware to support 50 and more areas per ABR. Therefore, with today's next-generation routers, with large memory capacity and high CPU processing capabilities, placing an ABR in tens of areas simultaneously is no longer an issue, especially if area topologies are simple. In some cases, lower performance can be tolerated. For this reason, a specific number of areas per ABR cannot be recommended. Carefully monitor your ABRs and add extra ABRs to distribute the load if needed. For example, if you have an ABR using an old hardware platform with limited hardware resources, you should not consider more than three areas (assuming these areas are not flooded with a large number of LSAs).

> **Note** Consider three areas per ABR as a general rule of thumb (best practice). However, you can use more than three areas per ABR if it is required and the ABR platform you are using has enough hardware resources.

OSPF Area Design Considerations

A structured OSPF area's design helps to reduce the amount of routing information in an area, which leads to a more stable and scalable OSPF routed network. However, a practically structured OSPF design is not always a simple goal to achieve because OSPF area design depends to a large degree on the network topology and IP addressing scheme.

Ideally, the network topology and addressing should be designed with division of areas in mind. Although Enhanced Interior Gateway Routing Protocol (EIGRP) tolerates more arbitrary network topologies, OSPF requires a cleaner hierarchy with a clearer backbone and area topology.

In addition, in large networks the geographic and functional boundaries should be considered when determining OSPF area placement, because this will influence the information flooding boundary.

As discussed previously, a scalable and stable OSPF design aims to minimize the amount of routing information that is advertised into and out of areas, taking into consideration that anything in the LSDB must be propagated to all routers within a single area. In particular, changes need to be propagated, consuming bandwidth and CPU for links and routers within the area. Rapid changes or flapping requires the most effort because the routers have to repeatedly propagate changes. Therefore, considering stub areas, totally stubby areas, and summary routes helps reduce the size of the LSDB and impose a more stable OSPF network by isolating the area from propagating external changes.

Experience shows that you should be conservative about adding routers to the backbone area 0. Some organizations have found that, over time, too many routers may end up in area 0, which may lead to reduced stability, longer convergence time, and higher CPU utilization. A commonly recommended practice is to put only the essential backbone and ABRs into area 0.

Also, redundancy is important in the backbone to prevent a partitioned backbone area when a link fails. Good backbones are designed so that no single link failure can cause a partition, which can lead either to broken communication between areas or suboptimal routing. For instance, in the scenario illustrated in Figure 3-5, if the link between the two ABR routers went down, the communication between the routers in area 0 would be broken, which would lead to isolated networks. Therefore, for this design, you must consider adding a redundant link in area 0 to avoid situations like this.

OSPF Area Design Considerations   83

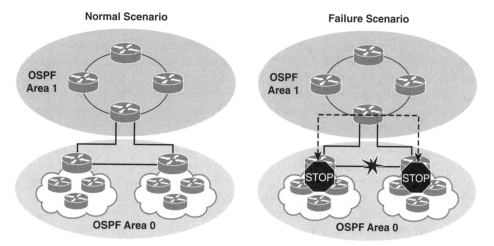

Figure 3-5 *Partitioned Backbone Area*

> **Note** Considering OSPF virtual link is not a recommended practice. It's better to redesign the physical topology or OSPF area's layout.

From an optimal routing point of view, network designers must be aware of the following when designing OSPF areas:

- As discussed earlier in this chapter, the totally stubby areas receive only a default route from the ABR; therefore, the totally stubby area cannot distinguish one ABR from another, in terms of the best route to destinations outside the area because it won't have visibility to the more specific routes. This leads to suboptimal routing in some scenarios. Unless the ABRs are geographically far apart, in general it should not matter.

- Similarly, because stub areas do not have visibility to external routes, this may lead to suboptimal routing to reach external networks, as the stub area cannot distinguish among ABRs for destinations that are external to the OSPF domain (redistributed routes). Unless the ABRs are geographically far apart, in general it should not matter.

Consequently, if optimal routing to external prefixes is an important requirement for certain applications, the benefit of considering a normal OSPF area in such a scenario, from an applications point of view, outweighs the benefits of considering a stub or totally stubby area. Therefore, as a network designer or architect, you must always look at the big picture to achieve the optimum design.

OSPF Hierarchy

The most typical architecture used in large enterprise networks is the three-layer hierarchal architecture that consists of the core, distribution, and access layers. The nature of the OSPF protocol, however, allows for only two levels of hierarchy: the backbone, or area 0, and all other areas that are connected to the backbone via ABRs. That said, you can still use OSPF in hierarchal networks with three layers with some challenges around optimal routing and summarization boundaries.

Therefore, almost always, OSPF naturally fits better when there is a backbone area 0 and areas off the backbone with one router, or even a few routers, interconnecting the other areas to area 0. If you must have three levels of hierarchy for a large network, when possible, you should consider using the Border Gateway Protocol (BGP) as a core routing protocol to interconnect different OSPF routing domains to achieve more flexible and scalable design for large-scale enterprise networks.

A difficult question in the OSPF design is where to put the ABRs. Should they be put in the core or in the distribution layer? The general design advice is to separate complexity from complexity, and to put complex parts of the network into separate areas. A part of the network might be considered complex when it has considerable routing information, such as a full-mesh, a large hub-and-spoke, or a highly redundant topology such as a redundant campus or data center, as shown in Figure 3-6.

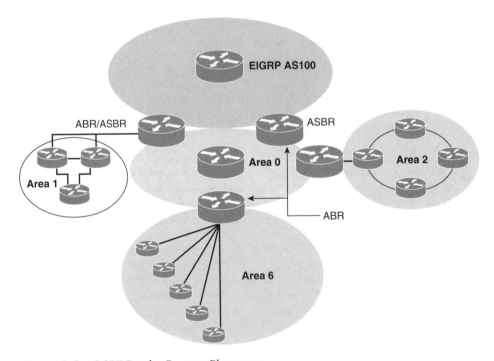

Figure 3-6 *OSPF Border Routers Placement*

As discussed earlier in this chapter, to maintain a reliable and scalable OSPF, you should consider network route summarization where possible. Typically, ABRs provide opportunities to support route summarization or create stub or totally stubby areas. However, to achieve optimum effective route summarization, a structured IP addressing scheme is required to align with the area's layout. One of the simplest ways to allocate addresses in OSPF is to assign a separate network number for each area.

Note OSPFv2 for IPv4 and OSPFv3 for IPv6 are implemented as two entirely independent protocols. This independence means that, theoretically, the area structure and ABRs could be entirely different for each of these protocols. However, from design and operational standpoints, it is often best to align the area structure and ABRs for both protocols to reduce operational complexity and ease troubleshooting and to simplify the design when the network grows in size. This approach implies that the IPv6 and IPv4 address blocks that are assigned to the areas should also be aligned to support summarization for both protocols.

Area and Domain Summarization

In OSPF, summarization is supported in and out of areas at the ABR or ASBR, and there are different possible ways to summarize routes in OSPF. However, the basic fundamental requirement to achieve effective route summarization is to have a structured IP addressing scheme, as illustrated in Figure 3-7.

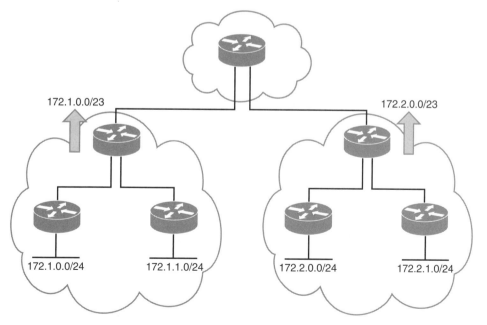

Figure 3-7 *Structured Summarizable IP Addressing Scheme*

To minimize route information that is inserted into the area, consider the following guidelines when planning your OSPF internetwork:

- Configure the network addressing scheme so that the range of subnets that are assigned within an area is contiguous.
- Create an address space that easily splits areas as the network grows. If possible, assign subnets according to simple octet boundaries.
- Plan ahead for the addition of new routers to the OSPF environment. Ensure that new routers are inserted appropriately as area, backbone, or border routers.

Following are some of the approaches to summarize routes and otherwise reduce the LSDB size and flooding in OSPF (see Figure 3-8):

- Area ranges per the OSPF RFCs
- Area filtering
- Summary address filtering
- Originating default
- Filtering for NSSA routes

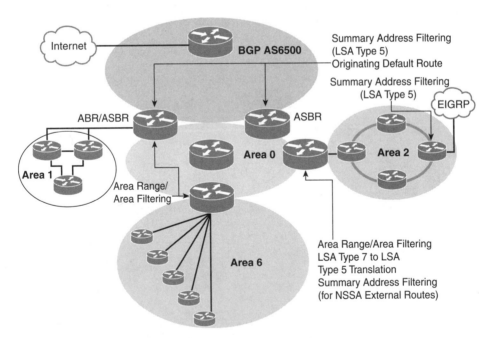

Figure 3-8 *Approaches to Summarize Routes in OSPF*

OSPF Full-Mesh Design

Full- and partial-mesh topologies are typically implemented in networks that demand high throughput and optimal routing, such as core networks. However, full-mesh networks are expensive and complex because they experience quadratic growth of interconnecting links as you add the number of routers and, thus, pose a specific scaling challenge for OSPF. For instance, a network that consists of two routers requires a single interconnection, a full mesh of 6 routers requires 15 interconnections, and so on. You can calculate the number of interconnections required by following this formula, where n routers require $((n)(n - 1))/2$ interconnections.

From a control plane point of view, flooding routing information through a full-mesh topology is the main concern. Technically, each router receives at least one copy of new information from each neighbor. The concern with this behavior is that, in a large-scale full-mesh domain, or even partial-mesh OSPF domains, a significant amount of routing information flooding can impact overall network performance and convergence time. Therefore, if any of these topologies is used, you should deploy techniques to reduce the amount of routing information flooding.

Intermediate System–to–Intermediate System (IS-IS) provides a simple mechanism to counter full-mesh flooding, called mesh groups. OSPF uses a technique similar to the mesh groups in concept, by reducing the flooding in a full-mesh network by manual *database-filter* configuration using the logic listed here (see Figure 3-9):

- Pick a subset of two or more routers in a mesh network that will flood the LSAs to all other routers.

- Configure all other routers to filter out their LSA for all but the selected subset of routers.

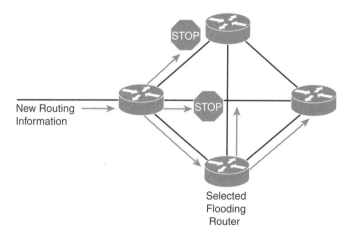

Figure 3-9 *OSPF over Full-Mesh Topology*

As a result, the chosen flooding routers behave similarly to the way a DR behaves in a shared LAN. This eventually helps reduce the amount of routing information flooding with the mesh or partial-mesh network. Also, it is important to consider at least two routers to perform the flooding "DR-like behavior" to avoid a single point of failure in this type of scenario.

> **Note** From an operations point of view, database filtering is a manual technique, and it can be very error prone. Be careful not to block LSAs on the wrong adjacencies.

Furthermore, network designers also can consider OSPF flood reduction mechanism (RFC 4136) in full-mesh networks to eliminate periodic refresh of unchanged LSAs, which leads to a more stable and scalable OSPF mesh design.

> **Note** Periodic refresh provides recovery from bugs and glitches in the OSPF implementation. Flood reduction removes this benefit. Therefore, you need to evaluate and prioritize which one is more critical in your network before enabling a flood reduction feature.

OSPF Hub-and-Spoke Design

Although OSPF over hub and spoke is one of the most commonly deployed WAN designs, it has several technical limitations that you, as a network designer, must be aware of and avoid to be able to provide a reliable and scalable-enough design. For example, when OSPF is used as the control plane over hub-and-spoke topology, any change at one spoke site is passed up across the link to the hub and is then replicated to each of the other spoke sites (if a single area is used between the hub and spokes). Another common example, one that causes frequent changes in small periods of time, is a link flapping that might be due to a physical issue. As a result, in large networks, these frequent changes can place a great burden on the hub router as well as on the spokes, when the flooding propagates to other spokes.

One of the primary mitigation techniques to the preceding issues is to reduce the amount of routing information to be flooded. Therefore, it's always recommended, in hub-and-spoke topology, to place the spokes in a stub area to minimize the amount of information within the area. In fact, you should aim to configure the areas as stubby as possible. That's why totally stubby areas are considered even better in this case. However, if a spoke site needs to redistribute routes into OSPF, you should make it an NSSA or totally NSSA to minimize the number of routing information.

Furthermore, limiting the number of spokes per area reduces the flooding at the hub. However, keep in mind that smaller areas allow for less summarization into the backbone. Also, each spoke may require a separate subinterface on the hub router.

> **Note** Typical hub-and-spoke topologies have a single or redundant hub-spoke connection, with one or multiple hubs serving as go-through points. Many network engineers prefer the use of distance-vector routing protocols such as EIGRP or RIPv2 in hub-and-spoke networks, as distance-vector protocols feature natural topology hiding behind the hub.

OSPF ABR Placement in Hub-and-Spoke Design

Commonly, hub-and-spoke topologies are deployed in scenarios in which multiple remote sites are connected to a center headquarter HQ or a regional HQ. As shown in Figure 3-10, although both topologies are hub and spoke, the depth of the topology and IP addressing scheme can influence the placement of ABR or OSPF area boundary.

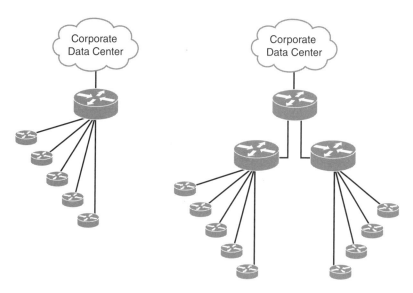

Figure 3-10 *Hub-and-Spoke Topologies*

In general, the connections between a hub and spoke are WAN connections, which typically have lower bandwidth capacity and are less reliable compared to LAN connections, and thus a common source of routing changes that need to be propagated through the network.

From an OSPF design point of view, the backbone area is extremely important. Therefore, it is always recommended to design area 0 to be as small and stable as possible. Taking this into consideration, network designers need to stop any WAN instability (such as routing changes due to WAN link flapping) from affecting the network core stability. To achieve this in OSPF, you typically need to use a hub router as an ABR between core area 0 and one or multiple spoke areas. With this design, you may need to employ a high-end hub router, which can serve as an ABR for multiple areas, as shown in Figure 3-11. With this design approach, the hub ABR, along with route summarization, can provide topology and routing information hiding between the backbone (area 0) and the WAN area(s), which ultimately will offer more stable and scalable design.

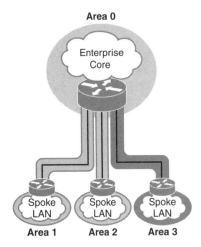

Figure 3-11 *OSPF over Hub and Spoke (Hub as ABR)*

In addition, you may extend area 0 down to the spoke routers, in which the spokes now serve as ABRs between the hub-and-spoke WAN and their branch LANs, as shown in Figure 3-12. With this design approach, you reduce the pressure on the hub router. However, the caveat is that all the WAN links are now part of the backbone area. As a result, any WAN link flapping produces many routing updates, which can destabilize the core. This design is viable for topologies with a small core with reliable WAN links, or a small network in general, with a small number of spokes. Also, this design model can be used in some multitier hub-and-spoke topologies, in which the backbone area can be extended to the first spoke's tier; each tier then acts as a hub for the second spoke's tier routers, as shown in Figure 3-12.

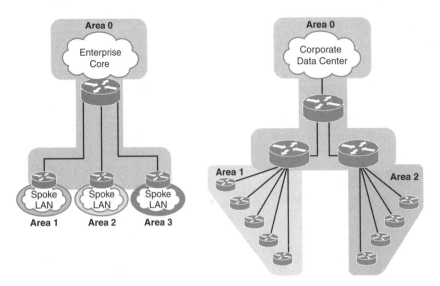

Figure 3-12 *OSPF over Hub and Spoke (Spokes as ABR)*

Number of Areas in OSPF Hub-and-Spoke Design

As discussed earlier in this chapter, designing OSPF with multiple areas, along with summarization at each area boundary, helps optimize the design and make it more stable and scalable. Therefore, in a hub-and-spoke topology, when the number of remote sites goes up, you need to start breaking the network into multiple OSPF areas. However, the number of routers per area depends on a couple of factors. For example, say the number of remote sites is small. Practically, you can place the hub and its spokes within a single area. In contrast, if you have a large number of remote sites, you should make the hub an ABR, as discussed in the preceding section. From there, you can split off the spokes in one or more areas. In other words, the larger the hub-and-spoke network size, the more OSPF areas will be required to optimize the flooding domains' design, as shown in Figure 3-13.

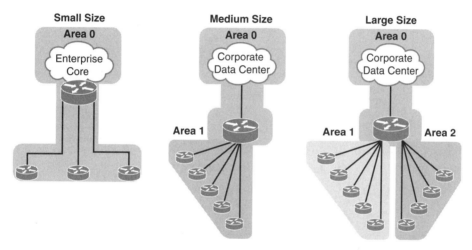

Figure 3-13 *Number of OSPF Areas in Hub-and-Spoke Topology*

Furthermore, keeping each spoke in a separate area will contain branch routing changes and WAN link flapping, not only from the core, but also from the other branches. However, this approach increases the number of areas on the hub ABR, which means increases in the number of LSDBs that the ABR needs to hold and maintain. As discussed before, this solution might not be a big issue if the hub router is using a next-generation router with high hardware resource capabilities (memory, CPU).

Note You must take into consideration any anticipated growth in the network and the addition of routers, if you start with the area 0 model on the left in Figure 3-13, you will have to take a change window as your network grows to move to the other OSPF areas' model design.

OSPF Network Types in Hub-and-Spoke Design

OSPF over hub-and-spoke networks offers flexible choices to deploy the OSPF network type. However, each of the available network types has its advantages and disadvantages, as summarized in Table 3-1.

Table 3-1 *OSPF Network Types: Advantages and Disadvantages*

Network Type	Advantages	Disadvantages
Single interface at the hub treated as an OSPF broadcast or non-broadcast multiaccess (NBMA) network	Single IP subnet Fewer host routes in routing table	Manual configuration of each spoke, with the correct OSPF priority for DR and BDR No reachability between spokes, or labor-intensive Layer 2 configuration
Single interface at the hub treated as an OSPF point-to-multipoint network	Single IP subnet Less configuration per spoke	Extra host routes inserted in the routing table Longer hello and dead timer intervals
Individual point-to-point interface at the hub for each spoke	Can take advantage of end-to-end signaling for down state Shorter hello and dead timer intervals	Lost IP address space More routes in the routing table Overhead of subinterfaces

To achieve the desired outcome of the OSPF design over a hub-and-spoke topology, you must consider the right combination of network types for OSPF hub and spoke to work well. Generally, as summarized in Table 3-1, although it is wisest to use either the point-to-multipoint OSPF network type at the hub site, or configure the hub site with point-to-point subinterfaces, some design considerations and limitations are associated with each, as explained in the following text.

Although the point-to-multipoint is a simple option, the disadvantage of a point-to-multipoint design is that additional host routes are added to the routing table, and the default OSPF hello and dead timer interval is longer. That being said, consider that the point-to-multipoint OSPF network type offers simplified configuration, as compared to broadcast or NBMA implementations, and it conserves IP address space as compared to point-to-point implementations.

However, from a network operation point of view, the configuration of point-to-point subinterfaces takes more initial work—perhaps a few more hours—and this may lead to longer operational efforts in large-scale hub-and-spoke networks. In addition, each such subinterface adds a route to the routing table, making this option about equal to point-to-multipoint in terms of routing table impact. Furthermore, point-to-point typically consumes more address space, even with /30 or /31 subnetting for the point-to-point links. Nonetheless, considering point-to-point subinterfaces offer higher stability, with everything working well in this environment, including management.

On the other hand, broadcast or NBMA network types are best avoided over hub-and-spoke networks. Although, technically they can be made to work with some configuration effort, they lead to less stable networks, or networks where certain failure modes have odd consequences.

OSPF Convergence Design Considerations and Optimization Techniques

Practically, what should drive the required convergence time is application requirements—in particular, mission-critical applications that have a direct impact on the business functions. However, it is common that in some networks, the default reaction time of the routing protocol is not fast enough to meet application requirements. Therefore, a good understanding of what influences OSPF convergence will help you improve it (at least to a large extent).

Network convergence is the time that is needed for the network to respond to events. It is the time that it takes for traffic to be rerouted onto an alternative path when a node or link fails, or onto a more optimal path when a new link or node appears. Traffic is not rerouted until the data plane "data structures," such as the forwarding information base (FIB) and adjacency tables of all devices, have been adjusted to reflect the new state of the network. For that to happen, all network devices need to go through the following steps:

1. **Detect the event:** Loss or addition of a link or neighbor needs to be detected. It can be done through a combination of Layer 1, Layer 2, and Layer 3 detection mechanisms, such as carrier detection (carrier delay timers), routing protocol hello timers, and BFD.

2. **Propagate the event:** Routing protocol update mechanisms are used to forward the information about the topology change from neighbor to neighbor.

3. **Process the event:** The information needs to be entered into the appropriate routing protocol data structures, and the routing algorithm needs to be invoked to calculate updated best paths for the new topology.

4. **Update forwarding data structures:** The results of the routing algorithm calculations need to be entered into the data plane's packet forwarding data structures.

At this point, the network has converged. The first step is dependent on the type of failure and the combination of Layer 1, Layer 2, and Layer 3 protocols that are deployed. Second and third steps are most specific to OSPF, and tuning the associated parameters can greatly improve OSPF convergence times. The fourth step is not routing protocol-specific but depends on the hardware platform and the mechanisms that are involved in programming the data plane data structures.

Event Detection

One of the more significant factors in routing convergence is the detection of link or node failure. In scenarios in which routers are connected over intermediate nodes of a system, such as a Layer 2 switch, an indirect link failure typically takes time to be detected. As a result, convergence time will be longer. In addition, the detection of a link or a node failure in a scenario like this is primarily based on protocol rather than a hardware detection mechanism, which is normally slower and less deterministic.

In environments where routers running OSPF need to detect network changes rapidly, you should rely on external protocols like BFD to achieve subsecond failure detection, without impacting OSPF and network performance.

BFD is a technology that uses fast Layer 2 link hellos to detect failed or one-way links and enables subsecond event detection. The CPU impact of BFD is less than the CPU impact of routing protocol fast hellos because some of the processing is shifted to the data plane rather than the control plane. On nondistributed platforms, Cisco testing has shown a minor 2 percent CPU increase above baseline when supporting 100 concurrent BFD sessions.

BFD is an independent protocol, and you need to tie it to the selected routing protocol. You can configure BFD support for OSPF either globally under routing protocol configuration or per specific interface.

OSPF Event Propagation

Network convergence requires all affected routers to process network events. Understanding OSPF event propagation enables you to optimize protocol behavior and improve convergence time.

OSPF topology changes are advertised with LSA flooding. OSPF propagation delay equals the sum of the LSA generation delay, LSA arrival delay, and LSA processing delay.

Original OSPF specifications required that the generation of similar LSAs, with same link-state ID, type, and origin Router ID but possibly updated content, is delayed for a fixed interval. This interval defaults to 1 second. To optimize this behavior, Cisco implemented an exponential backoff algorithm to dynamically calculate the delay, before generating similar LSAs.

The initial backoff timers are low, which enables quicker convergence. If successive events are generated for the same LSA, the backoff timers increase. Three configurable timers control the delay:

- **Start-interval:** Defines the initial delay to generate an LSA. This timer can be set at a very low value, such as 1 ms or even 0 ms. Setting this timer to a low value helps improve convergence because initial LSAs for new events are generated as quickly as possible. The default value is 0 ms.

- **Hold-interval:** Defines the minimum time to elapse before flooding an updated instance of an LSA. This is an incremental value. Initially, the "hold time" between successive LSAs is set to be equal to this configured value. Each time a new version of an LSA is generated, the hold time between LSAs is doubled, until the max-interval value is reached, at which point that value is used until the network stabilizes. The default value is 5000 ms.

- **Max-interval:** Defines the maximum time that can elapse before flooding an updated instance of an LSA. Once the exponential backoff algorithm reaches this value, it stops increasing the hold time and instead uses the max-interval timer as a fixed interval between newly generated LSAs. The default value is 5000 ms.

Determining optimal values depends on the network. Tuning the timers too aggressively could result in excessive CPU load during network reconvergence, especially when the network is unstable for a period. Lower the values gradually from their defaults and observe router behavior to determine what the optimal values are for your network.

When you adjust the OSPF LSA throttling timers, you may also need to adjust the LSA arrival timer. Any LSAs that are received at a higher frequency than the value of this timer will be discarded. To prevent routers from dropping valid LSAs, you should make sure that the LSA arrival timer is configured to be lower or equal to the hold-interval timer. Otherwise, a neighbor would be allowed to send an updated LSA sooner than this router would be willing to accept it.

Figure 3-14 illustrates the OSPF exponential backoff algorithm. It is assumed that every second an event happens, it generates a new version of an LSA. With the default timers, the initial LSA is generated after 0 ms. After that, there is a 5-second wait between successive LSAs.

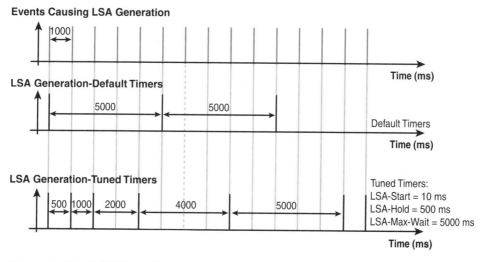

Figure 3-14 *OSPF Event Propagation—Exponential Backoff Algorithm*

With the OSPF LSA throttle timers set at 10 ms for LSA start-interval, 500 ms for LSA hold-interval, and 5000 ms for LSA max-interval, the initial LSA is generated after 10 ms. The next LSA is generated after the LSA hold-interval time of 500 ms. The next LSA is generated after 2 × 500, or 1000 ms. The next LSA is generated after 4 × 500 (2000 ms) and then 8 × 500 (4000 ms). The next one would be generated after 16 × 500, or 8000 ms, but because the max-interval is set at 5000 ms, the LSA is generated after 5000 ms. From this point onward, a 5000-ms wait is applied to successive LSAs, until the network stabilizes and the timers are reset.

OSPF Event Processing

The timing of successive OSPF SPF calculations is throttled in the same manner as LSA generation, using an exponential backoff algorithm.

After a router receives an updated LSA, it needs to schedule its SPF to process the update. Because a topology change often affects multiple routers, it is prudent to wait some time for more updated LSAs to arrive and then run the SPF only after this waiting period is over. This action allows the SPF to process multiple updates in a single run. However, if the topology change is caused by a repetitive fault, such as a flapping link because of faulty connectors, frequently running SPF puts unnecessary burden on the router. Therefore, if a router continuously keeps receiving updated LSAs, the delay before the upcoming SPF run should progressively grow to dampen the negative impact of the flapping in the network.

The timers that are involved in OSPF SPF throttling are similar to the LSA throttling timers. The three tunable timers are

- **SPF-Start:** This is the initial delay to schedule an SFP calculation after a change.
- **SPF-Hold:** This is the minimum hold time between two consecutive SPF calculations. Similar to the LSA-Hold timer, this timer is used as an incremental value in an exponential backoff algorithm.
- **SPF-Max-Wait:** This is the maximum wait time between two consecutive SPF calculations.

By default, Cisco routers will schedule an SPF run 5 seconds after receiving an updated LSA, and if an updated LSA arrives after this SPF run, the subsequent delay grows up to 10 seconds.

Considerations in adjusting these timers are similar to the LSA throttling timers. Another factor that needs to be considered is the time that it takes for an SPF calculation to complete on the implemented router platform. You cannot schedule a new SPF run before the previous calculation completes; therefore, you should ensure that the SPF-Hold timer is higher than the time it takes to run a complete SPF. When estimating SPF run times, you should account for future network growth.

> **Note** The default timers are code version dependent. For example, you may notice that NXOS and XR have default timers different than IOS and IOS XE. Therefore, you should refer to the release notice of the platform software you are using. Considering the default timers will be more critical when you have different software versions in your environment and you want to standardize the timers' settings across the entire network.

OSPF Flooding Reduction

By design, OSPF requires unchanged LSAs to be refreshed every 1800 seconds, before they expire after 3600 seconds. Periodically refreshed LSAs can introduce unnecessary overhead in large stable networks.

The OSPF flooding reduction feature works by reducing unnecessary refreshing and flooding of already known and unchanged information. As defined in RFC 4136, an interface that is configured with flood reduction advertises LSAs with the DoNotAge bit set. As a result, LSAs do not need to be refreshed unless a network change is detected. The highest impact is achieved in full-meshed topologies, where the highest number of regenerated LSAs is reduced.

You can configure OSPF flooding reduction only on a per-interface basis, but make sure that you enable OSPF flooding reduction only in stable environments. A periodic refresh of LSAs enables the OSPF mechanism to recover from bugs and glitches, which ensures robustness of the protocol.

OSPF Database Overload Protection

The OSPF Link-State Database Overload Protection feature enables you to limit the number of non-self-generated LSAs and protect the OSPF process. Excessive LSAs that are generated by other routers in the OSPF domain can substantially drain the CPU and memory resources of the router.

When other OSPF routers in the network have been misconfigured, they may generate a high volume of LSAs, for instance, to redistribute large numbers of prefixes. This protection mechanism prevents routers from receiving many LSAs and therefore experiencing CPU and memory shortages (see Figure 3-15).

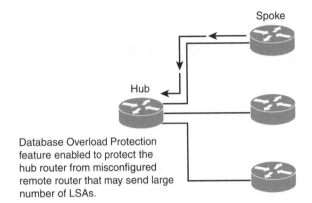

Figure 3-15 *OSPF Link-State Database Overload Protection*

When the OSPF Link-State Database Overload Protection feature is enabled, the router keeps a count of the number of LSAs it receives. When it reaches the configured threshold number of LSAs, it logs an error message. When it exceeds the configured maximum number of LSAs, the router sends a notification. If the count of received LSAs is still higher than the configured maximum after one minute, the OSPF process takes down all adjacencies and clears the OSPF database.

In this ignore state, all OSPF packets received on any interface that belong to this OSPF process are ignored, and no OSPF packets are generated on any of these interfaces. The OSPF process remains in the ignore state for the time that is configured by the ignore-time keyword of the **max-lsa** command. Each time the OSPF process gets into an ignore state, it increments a counter. If this counter exceeds the number counts, as configured in the ignore-count keyword, the OSPF process stays permanently in the same ignore state, and manual intervention is required to get the OSPF process out of the ignore state. The ignore state counter is reset to zero when the OSPF process remains in the normal state of operation for the amount of time specified by the reset-time keyword.

Summary

- OSPF scalability is influenced by the stability of connections, number of prefixes, number of adjacent neighbors, number of routers in an area, and number of areas supported by an ABR.

- You should always keep it simple, keep it as stubby as possible, and keep it summarized.

- Place the area borders so that you maintain a stable backbone and divide complexity from complexity.

- You must use the mesh groups technique to counter flooding in a mesh network.

- You need to balance between the number of areas on an ABR and a WAN link's stability when you position ABRs in a hub-and-spoke network.

- You may adjust the timer to improve convergence if the design mandates meeting certain levels of convergence time.
- You should protect the OSPF routers from flooding and database overload.

Review Questions

After answering the following questions, please refer to Appendix A, "Answers to Review Questions," for the answers.

1. Which statements are true about BFD? (Select two.)
   a. BFD provides very fast link error detection but uses more resources than routing protocol fast hellos.
   b. BFD can be configured only over Ethernet links.
   c. BFD not only detects link failures but also speeds up routing event propagation between neighbors by using fast hellos.
   d. BFD is resource efficient, as some function can be supported directly in the hardware.
   e. BFD is routing protocol independent and can work with all modern routing protocols.
   f. BFD can be enabled either globally or per interface.

2. A router running OSPF simultaneously receives three different LSAs from its neighbors. How will the router process LSAs?
   a. The first LSA will be processed immediately; second and third LSA processing will be delayed due to the exponential backoff algorithm.
   b. The first and second LSAs will be processed immediately; third LSA processing will be delayed due to the exponential backoff algorithm.
   c. The first LSA will be processed right away; the second and third LSA will be dropped due to a minimal LSA arrival timer.
   d. All three LSAs will be processed immediately.

3. Which of the following do you need to take into account when designing OSPF areas? (Choose three.)
   a. Topology
   b. Number of users
   c. Summarization points
   d. Business functions of the targeted network
   e. The routers' hardware resources of all routers
   f. The routers' hardware resources of ABRs

4. Which statements about OSPF optimal design are true? (Choose two.)
   a. Summarization depends on the IP addressing scheme structure.
   b. In hub-and-spoke topology, the hub must be the ABR.
   c. Multiarea OSPF design offers more scalable design.
   d. Multiarea OSPF design adds increased operational complexity.

5. Which statements about OSPF stub areas are true? (Choose two.)
   a. OSPF stub areas such as stubby or totally stubby, when used at the spokes sites in a dual-hub topology, help optimize network convergence time for spoke sites.
   b. OSPF stub areas such as stubby or totally stubby, when used at the spoke's sites in dual-hub topology, add operational complexity.
   c. OSPF stub areas such as totally stubby, when used at the spoke's sites in dual-hub topology, may lead to suboptimal routing to external prefixes.
   d. OSPF stub areas such as totally stubby, when used at the spoke's sites in dual-hub topology, ensure optimal routing is always achieved to eternal prefixes.

6. Which of the following OSPF area types can be used at a remote spoke site with a connection to an external network? (Choose two.)
   a. Normal area
   b. Stubby area
   c. Totally stubby
   d. NSSA

Chapter 4

IS-IS Design

Upon completing this chapter, you will be able to

- Describe the basics of IS-IS
- Describe IS-IS hierarchical design
- Describe IS-IS characteristics
- Identify IS-IS router and link types
- Describe IS-IS adjacencies
- Explain integrated IS-IS routing
- Describe similarities between IS-IS and OSPF
- Compare IS-IS and OSPF area designs
- Compare OSPF and IS-IS characteristics
- Explain IS-IS addressing on a case study
- Describe IS-IS packets
- Describe IS-IS information data flow
- Explain IS-IS routing logic on a case study
- Describe IS-IS route leaking
- Describe the differences between asymmetric and symmetric IS-IS routing
- Identify IS-IS network types
- Describe IS-IS operations

- Describe IS-IS topologies
- Identify IS-IS single-topology restrictions
- Describe multitopology IS-IS for IPv6

Intermediate System–to–Intermediate System (IS-IS) is an OSI link-state hierarchical routing protocol based on DECnet Phase V routing, whereby ISs (routers) exchange routing information based on a single metric to determine network topology. IS-IS is a proven and extensible IP routing protocol that converges quickly and supports variable-length subnet mask (VLSM). IS-IS is a public standard, which is published as ISO 9542 and republished as RFC 995. Integrated IS-IS is specified in RFC 1195 and offers support for IP and OSI protocols. In this chapter, you learn the operational and design aspects of Integrated IS-IS in enterprise networks

Protocol Overview

The International Organization for Standardization (ISO) developed a complete suite of routing protocols for use in the Open Systems Interconnection (OSI) protocol suite, which includes IS-IS, End System-to-Intermediate System (ES-IS), and Interdomain Routing Protocol (IDRP). This chapter focuses on the design and operation of the *IS-IS Protocol*, which is an intradomain OSI dynamic routing protocol that is specified in ISO 10589. IS-IS was originally developed to route in ISO Connectionless Network Protocol (CLNP) networks; however, a version has since been created that supports both CLNP and IP networks. This version is usually referred to as Integrated or dual IS-IS.

ISO specifications refer to routers as intermediate systems. Thus, IS-IS is a protocol that allows routers to communicate with other routers. The OSI suite uses CLNS to provide connectionless delivery of data, and the actual Layer 3 protocol is CLNP. Also, IS-IS uses Connectionless Network Service (CLNS) addresses to identify the routers and to build the link-state database (LSDB). The *CLNS addresses*, which are known as network service access points (NSAPs), are made up of three components:

- An area identifier (area ID) prefix
- A system identifier (sysID)
- An N-selector

The N-selector refers to the network service user, such as a transport protocol or the routing layer. It has a similar interpretation as the application port number that is used in the IP Transmission Control Protocol (TCP).

Note The CLNP addressing scheme is covered later in this chapter.

In addition, the type, length, value (TLV) mechanism makes the IS-IS flexible protocol easy to extend. The TLV strings, which are called *tuples*, are present in all IS-IS updates. IS-IS today supports IPv6; it can easily grow to support any other protocol because extending IS-IS consists of simply creating new TLVs. Therefore, introducing new features to the protocol is easy and more flexible with the use of the TLVs.

The intermediate systems communicate between each other by using Layer 2 of the OSI model directly. This means there is no technical need for IP or any other higher layer protocol. The interfacing with the data link layer (Layer 2) primarily involves operations for detecting, forming, and maintaining routing adjacencies with neighboring routers over various types of interconnecting network media or links. This also makes IS-IS relatively more secure than other routing protocols that run over IP.

The ISO Connectionless Network Protocol is specified for transfer of data between two main categories of network devices:

- **End systems:** Workstations or network hosts with limited routing capability.
- **Intermediate systems:** Network devices, such as routers, with extensive packet-forwarding capabilities. The word *intermediate* refers to the capabilities of routers as intermediate forwarding or relay devices. These devices, and the application of IS-IS on them, are the primary focus of this chapter.

IS-IS Characteristics

IS-IS is the dynamic link-state routing protocol for the OSI protocol stack. As mentioned earlier, it distributes routing information for routing CLNP data for the ISO CLNS environment.

Like OSPF, IS-IS is also a link-state protocol using Dijkstra's algorithm, in which each router has topology information for its area. IS-IS is part of the OSI standard protocol suite and was originally used with CLNS. Each router is identified using a unique NSAP address, which is part of the CLNS protocol. IS-IS still uses CLNS to maintain adjacencies and build SPF trees, but the integrated version of IS-IS can be used for other protocols, such as IP, and can also have extensions for Multiprotocol Label Switching Traffic Engineering (MPLS TE).

From a high-level design point of view, IS-IS operates similarly to OSPF. IS-IS allows the routing domain to be partitioned into areas. Typically, IS-IS routers establish adjacencies using a "Hello" protocol and exchange link-state information, using link-state packets (LSP) throughout an area to build the LSDB. Each router then runs the Dijkstra shortest path first (SPF) algorithm against its LSDB to pick the best paths. A minimal amount of information is communicated between areas, thus reducing the burden on routers supporting the protocol. IS-IS routing takes place at two levels within a routed autonomous system (AS): Level 1 and Level 2. These levels in IS-IS are similar to OSPF areas in concept (each has its own routed flooding domain and offers the capability to hide topology and reachability information at the area/level boundary).

The original IS-IS specification defines four different types of metrics. Cost, the default metric, is supported by all routers. Delay, expense, and error are optional metrics. The delay metric measures transit delay, the expense metric measures the monetary cost of link utilization, and the error metric measures the residual error probability associated with a link.

The Cisco implementation uses only the cost metric. If the optional metrics were implemented, there would be a link-state database for each metric and SPF would run for each link-state database.

The wide-style metric should be used for large, high-speed service provider networks (24-bit link metric, 32-bit path metric). The link cost defaults to 10 and can be modified to reflect the desired cost. The narrow-style metric can accommodate only 64 metric values, which is typically insufficient in modern networks and may not even be compatible with IS-IS extensions, such as those for Cisco MPLS TE.

Cisco Software addresses this issue with the support of the 24-bit link metric, 32-bit path metric (the so-called "wide metric"). Therefore, deploying IS-IS in the IP network with wide metrics is recommended (especially in large, high-speed service provider grade networks) to enable finer granularity and to support future applications, such as route tagging, route leaking, and traffic engineering.

Integrated IS-IS Routing

Integrated IS-IS, or dual IS-IS, is an implementation of the IS-IS protocol for routing multiple network protocols; IP and CLNS Integrated IS-IS are specified in RFC 1195 and ISO 10589.

Integrated IS-IS tags CLNP routes with information about IP networks and subnets. As an alternative to OSPF, Integrated IS-IS combines ISO CLNS and IP routing in one protocol. Integrated IS-IS can be used for IP routing, CLNS routing, or a combination of the two. Integrated IS-IS uses its own packet data units (PDU), including IP reachability information, to transport information between routers. IS-IS information is not carried within a network layer protocol, but instead is carried directly within data link layer frames.

This protocol independence makes IS-IS easily extensible; there is also a version of Integrated IS-IS that supports IPv6, as described in RFC 5308. Because IS-IS uses CLNS addresses to identify the routers and to build the LSDB, an understanding of CLNS addresses is required to configure and troubleshoot IS-IS, even when it is used only for routing IP.

The following implementation options for IS-IS domains are specified by RFC 1195:

- **Pure IP domain:** Routes only IP traffic but supports forwarding and processing of OSI packets that are required for IS-IS operation.
- **Pure ISO domain:** Carries only ISO traffic, including communication that is required for IS-IS operation.
- **A dual domain:** Routes both IP and OSI CLNP traffic simultaneously.

It is also possible to design a dual domain so that some areas route IP only, whereas others route CLNP only, and yet others route both IP and CLNP. The goal is to achieve consistent routing information within an area by having identical Level 1 link-state databases on all routers in that area. In other words, this means that you should have consistency of router configurations within one area by configuring all routers in an area the same way. If it is an IP-only area, all routers should be configured for IP only and so on. On the domain level, you can mix different types of areas and attach them to the backbone. The concept and structure of IS-IS areas and levels are described in the following section.

IS-IS Hierarchical Architecture Overview

Like OSPF, IS-IS as a link-state routing protocol has built-in support for structured logical routed network design. However, the layout and terms used in IS-IS are slightly different than they are in OSPF. The following are the primary IS-IS OSI networking terms that collectively can construct an IS-IS hierarchal architecture (see Figure 4-1):

- An *area* is a group of contiguous networks and attached hosts that is specified to be an area by a network administrator or manager.

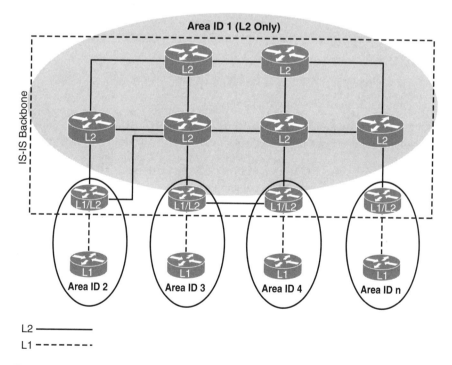

Figure 4-1 *Typical IS-IS Hierarchal Architecture*

- A *domain* is a collection of connected areas. Routing domains provide full connectivity to all end systems within them. In other words, an IS-IS routing domain is a network in which all the routers run the Integrated IS-IS routing protocol to support intradomain exchange of routing information.

- *Level 1 routing* is routing within an area. A Level 1 router knows only the topology of its own area and can have Level 1 or Level 1/Level 2 neighbors only in its own area. It has a Level 1 link-state database with all the information for intra-area routing. It uses the closest L1/L2 router in its own area to send packets out of the area.

- *Level 2 routing* is routing between different areas. A Level 2-capable router (L2 or L1/L2) may have L2 neighbors in the same or in different areas, and it has a Level 2 link-state database with all information for interarea routing. The router can also serve as an L1/L2 system, in which case it has both L1 and L2 link-state databases.

- The *IS-IS Backbone* is a contiguous chain of L2-capable routers (L2 or L1/L2) that hold the information for complete interarea routing. The backbone will span multiple areas with member routers in every area. The backbone must not be interrupted; therefore, you have to design your network with redundant L2 links in mind. This will make the backbone more resilient to faults in links or routers along the way.

Figure 4-1 illustrates a typical hierarchical IS-IS architecture with the following attributes:

- Area ID 1 has Level 2-only routers in the core.
- Areas ID "2 to N" has Level 1 and Level 1/Level 2 routers connecting areas to the backbone.
- All L2-capable routers constitute the backbone of this network.
- All interarea traffic must cross the backbone.
- IS-IS L2 adjacencies are shown as dotted lines, while IS-IS L1 adjacencies are shown as dashed lines/connections between the routers.

The figure shows a generic representation of how IS-IS can be designed. Unlike OSPF, in IS-IS all areas do not have to connect to a common backbone area. To demonstrate this, you could have an L2 connection between areas just like the one between Areas ID 3 and 4 in Figure 4-1. This means that traffic between Areas ID 3 and 4 can go directly over the L2 link between them, with no need to go through Area ID 1. On the other hand, traffic between Areas 2 and 3 must go through Area 1. However, both OSPF and IS-IS are link-state routing protocols, and they have some similarities in the way they work and can be designed to certain extent. For example, like OSPF, IS-IS can also be designed in a simpler model with fewer areas or simply in a flat manner, using a single area with one level.

IS-IS Router and Link Types

As discussed previously, IS-IS can be divided into multiple areas and levels in which different router and link types are required to form and maintain IS-IS adjacencies and communication. This section highlights the different IS-IS router types and links required in a typical multilevel IS-IS design. The following are the IS-IS router types you need to consider in a multilevel (hierarchal) IS-IS design (see Figure 4-2):

- **Level 1 router:** This router knows the topology only of its own area and has Level 1 or Level 1/Level 2 neighbors in this area. It has a Level 1 link-state database with all the information for intra-area routing. It uses the closest Level 1/Level 2 router in its own area to send packets out of the area.

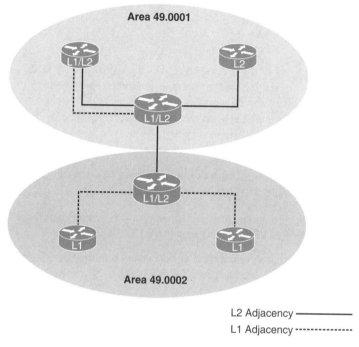

Figure 4-2 *IS-IS Router and Link Types*

- **Level 2 router:** This router may have neighbors in the same or in different areas, and it has a Level 2 link-state database with all information for interarea routing. Level 2 routers know about other areas but will not have Level 1 information from its own area. If the traffic in an area is IP-only, all the routers can be configured as Level 2.
- **Level 1/Level 2 router:** This router may have neighbors in any area. It has two link-state databases: a Level 1 link-state database for intra-area routing and a Level 2 link-state database for interarea routing. A Level 1/Level 2 router runs two SPFs and may require more memory and processing power.

IS-IS link types play a key role for forming neighbor adjacencies, taking into consideration the type of router to be interconnected and the IS-IS area layout. All of these factors come into play when determining whether an IS-IS adjacency can be formed or not, as summarized here:

- Level 1 adjacencies can be formed only between routers in the same area. It is not possible to have an L1 adjacency between routers in different areas.

- Only Level 2 adjacencies can be formed between routers in different areas. Level 2 adjacency can also be formed between routers in the same area if they are both L2 capable (by configuration).

- Both Level 1 and 2 adjacencies between a pair of routers can be formed only if they exist within the same area.

IS-IS Adjacencies

The subnetwork-dependent functions of the routing layer, which are provided by IS-IS, are responsible for discovering, establishing, and maintaining adjacencies between the routers in an IS-IS domain. As with any dynamic routing protocol, typically the successful formation of an IS-IS adjacency between two nodes is a prerequisite for the exchange of IS-IS routing information. This happens using LSPs and sequence number packets (SNP).

In IS-IS, for any two routers to become neighbors and build an IS-IS adjacency between them, the following parameters must be satisfied (agreed upon):

- **Level 1:** Two routers sharing a common network segment must have their interfaces configured to be in the same area to be able to establish a Level 1 adjacency.

- **Level 2:** If two routers are sharing a common network segment and they belong to different areas, they must be configured as Level 2 if they need to become neighbors.

- **Authentication:** IS-IS allows for configuration of a password for a specified link, for an area, or for an entire domain. For an adjacency to form, the passwords must match.

Note It is valid for two routers to have both an L1 and an L2 adjacency between them. This behavior is the default IS-IS behavior on Cisco IOS routers.

Figure 4-3 shows some common examples of different router types and IS-IS adjacencies that can be formed between them. In these examples, the topology layout differences are considered a primary influencing factor to the formation of adjacencies.

IS-IS Hierarchical Architecture Overview   109

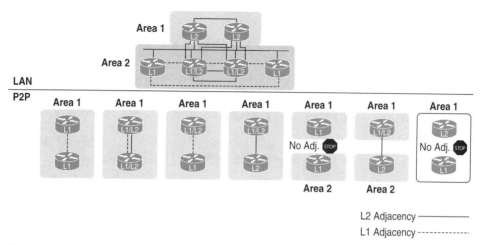

Figure 4-3 *IS-IS Adjacencies*

For LAN topologies, an example is

- The routers from one area accept Level 1 IS-IS Hellos IIH packet data units (PDU) only from their own area and therefore establish Level 1 adjacencies only with their own area Level 1 routers.

- The routers from a second area similarly accept Level 1 IIH PDUs only from their own area.

- The Level 2 routers (or the Level 2 process within any Level 1–2 router) accept only Level 2 IIH PDUs and establish only Level 2 adjacencies.

For point-to-point topologies, the IIH PDUs are common for L1 and L2; however, within the same hello packet, the actual level (L1, L2, or L1/L2) is announced as follows:

- Level 1 routers in the same area exchange IIH PDUs that specify Level 1 and establish a Level 1 adjacency.

- Level 2 routers exchange IIH PDUs that specify Level 2 and establish a Level 2 adjacency.

- Two Level 1–2 routers in the same area establish both Level 1 and Level 2 adjacencies and maintain these adjacencies with a common IIH PDU that specifies the Level 1 and Level 2 information.

- Two Level 1 routers that are physically connected, but that are not in the same area, can exchange IIHs, but they do not establish adjacency because the area addresses do not match.

IS-IS Versus OSPF

This section highlights and explains the similarities and differences between IS-IS and OSPF in order to simplify the job for network designers when they have to select a link-state routing protocol.

Similarities Between IS-IS and OSPF

Because both IS-IS and OSPF are link-state routing protocols, they share several similarities. In general, both routing protocols have the following characteristics:

- They are open-standard link-state interior routing protocols.
- They support VLSM.
- They use similar mechanisms, such as LSAs/LSPs, link-state aging timers, and LSDB synchronization, to maintain the health of the LSDB.
- They use the Dijkstra SPF algorithm, with similar update, decision, and flooding processes.
- They both use the concept of areas.
- Although IS-IS is most commonly deployed in service provider networks, they are equally successful in small enterprise and the largest and most demanding deployments (service provider networks).
- They support MPLS-TE.
- They are scalable and converge quickly after network changes.

OSPF and IS-IS Characteristics

As discussed earlier, OSPF relies on LSAs to send updates; however, it produces many small LSAs. In contrast, IS-IS updates are grouped by the router and are sent as one LSP, as illustrated in Figure 4-4. Thus, as network complexity increases, the number of IS-IS updates is not an issue. Each update packet must be routed, though, and routing takes network resources, so more packets represent a larger impact on the network.

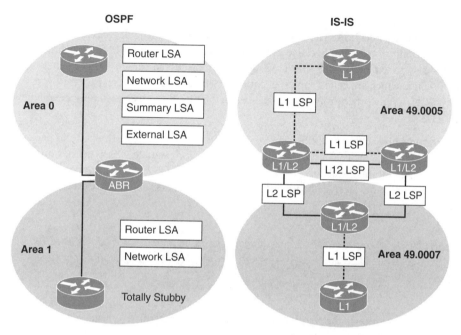

Figure 4-4 *Protocol Updates (OSPF Versus IS-IS)*

Because IS-IS uses significantly fewer LSPs, more routers, at least 1000, can reside in a single area, making IS-IS more scalable than OSPF. That said, in a typical medium-to-large enterprise network, one with modern routers, both OSPF and IS-IS are perfectly valid choices. As a matter of practicality, enterprise networks with structured areas/level design, it is very rare that you need an extremely large number of routers in a single area. In addition, OSPF runs over IP, whereas IS-IS runs through CLNS, which may give preference to OSPF in designs where it needs to run over IP, such as over a GRE or mGRE tunnel. In addition, unlike OSPF, IS-IS has no concept of NBMA networks, which may be required by some legacy WANs, such as Frame Relay.

Furthermore, IS-IS is also more efficient than OSPF in the use of CPU resources and in the way it processes routing updates. Not only are there fewer LSPs to process (LSAs, in OSPF terminology), but also the mechanism by which IS-IS installs and withdraws prefixes is less intensive. IS-IS uses network entity title (NET) addresses, which are already summarized. Practically, in enterprise-grade networks with next-generation routers that have high hardware capabilities, this point is not a big concern.

Both OSPF and IS-IS are link-state protocols, so they provide fast convergence. The convergence time depends on several factors, such as timers, number of nodes, and the type of router. Based on the default timers, IS-IS detects a failure faster than OSPF does; therefore, convergence occurs more rapidly. If there are many neighboring routers and adjacencies, the convergence time may also depend on the processing power of the router. IS-IS is less CPU intensive than OSPF.

Unlike in IS-IS, in OSPF packets, new features are not easily implemented; they require the creation of a new LSA. The OSPF description schema is difficult to extend, because of compatibility issues and because it was developed exclusively for IPv4. In contrast, IS-IS is easy to extend through the TLVs mechanism discussed earlier in this chapter. *TLV strings*, which are called tuples, encode all IS-IS updates. IS-IS can easily grow to cover IPV6, or any other protocol, because extending IS-IS consists of simply creating new TLVs.

An enterprise may choose OSPF over IS-IS because OSPF is more optimized and because it was designed exclusively as an IP routing protocol. For example, OSPF defines different area types (normal, stub, and NSSA). Also, the default OSPF metric is more flexible as it is related to the interface bandwidth, while IS-IS defaults to a metric of ten on all interfaces.

Note In OSPF, the interface default metric reference value must be altered when traffic is sent over high-speed links such as 10 Gbps to provide differentiation from lower-speed links such as 1 Gbps.

From implementation and operation points of view, if an enterprise considers OSPF as the core routing protocol, typically it requires networking equipment that supports OSPF, along with network engineers that are familiar with OSPF theory and operation. It is relatively easy to find both equipment and personnel to support an OSPF infrastructure. Furthermore, OSPF documentation is much more readily available than documentation for IS-IS.

Integrated IS-IS and OSPF Area Designs

This section focuses on the differences between OSPF and Integrated IS-IS area design.

OSPF Area Design

As shown in Figure 4-5, with OSPF, network design is constrained by the fact that OSPF is based on a central backbone, Area 0, with all other areas being physically attached to Area 0. The border between areas is inside the ABRs; each link is in only one area. When you use this type of hierarchical model, a consistent IP Addressing structure is necessary to allow for an effective route summarization toward the backbone. This reduces the amount of information that is carried in the backbone and advertised across the network.

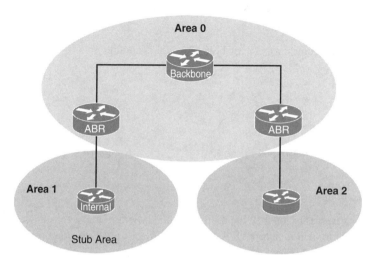

Figure 4-5 *OSPF Multiarea Design*

Integrated IS-IS Area Design

Unlike OSPF, IS-IS has a hierarchy of Level 1 and Level 2, or Level 1–2 routers, and the area borders lie on links. The ability of IS-IS to support overlapping between Level 1 and Level 2 at the ABR offers a more flexible approach to extending the backbone, as well as facilitate achieving more optimal routing in complex networks. As shown in Figure 4-6, you can extend the backbone by simply adding more Level 2 and Level 1–2 routers, a less complex process than with OSPF.

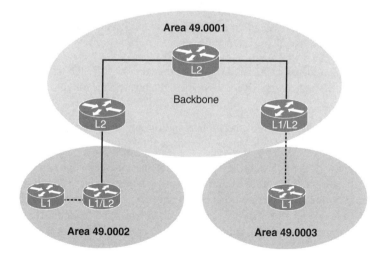

Figure 4-6 *IS-IS Area Design*

IS-IS Technical Deep Dive

This section covers several technical aspects of IS-IS protocol, including

- IS-IS addressing
- IS-IS packs and data flow
- IS-IS network types and operation
- IS-IS LSP flooding and LSDB synchronization

IS-IS Addressing

IS-IS LSPs use NSAP addresses to identify the router and build the topology table and the underlying IS-IS routing tree; therefore, IS-IS requires NSAP addresses to function properly, even if it is used only for routing IP.

NSAP addresses contain the following:

- OSI address of the device
- Link to the higher-layer process

The NSAP address is equivalent to the combination of the IP address and upper-layer protocol in an IP header. NSAP addresses have a minimum size of 8 bytes and a maximum size of 20 bytes. The high-order bits identify the interarea structure, and the low-order bits identify unique systems within an area. There are various NSAP address formats.

The Cisco implementation of Integrated IS-IS divides the NSAP address into three fields: the area address, the system ID, and the NSAP selector NSEL.

Cisco routers routing CLNS use addressing that conforms to the ISO10589 standard. ISO NSAP addresses consist of these elements (see Figure 4-7):

- The authority and format identifier AFI and the initial domain identifier IDI make up the initial domain part IDP of the NSAP address. The IDP corresponds roughly to an IP classful major network:
    - The AFI byte specifies the format of the address and the authority that is assigned to that address. Some valid values are shown in the figure.
    - Addresses starting with the AFI value of 49 are private addresses, analogous to RFC 1918 for IP address IS-IS routes to these addresses; however, this group of addresses should not be advertised to other CLNS networks because they are ad hoc addresses. Other companies that use the value of 49 may have created different numbering schemes that, when used together, could create confusion.
    - The IDI identifies a subdomain under the AFI.

IS-IS Technical Deep Dive

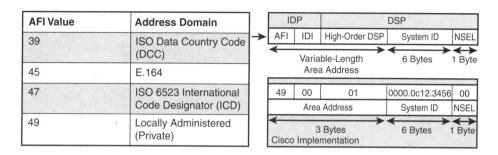

Figure 4-7 *IS-IS Addressing*

- The Domain specific part contributes to routing within an IS-IS routing domain. The DSP is composed of the high-order DSP HO-DSP, the system ID, and the NSEL.

  - The HO-DSP subdivides the domain into areas. The HO-DSP is approximately the OSI equivalent of a subnet in IP.

  - The system ID identifies an individual OSI device. In OSI, a device has an address, just as it does in DECnet, whereas in IP, each interface has an address.

  - The NSEL (NSAP selector) identifies a process on the device and corresponds roughly to a port or socket in IP. The NSEL is not used in routing decisions.

The simplest NSAP format, used by most companies that are running IS-IS as their IGP, is composed of the following:

- **Area address:** It must be at least 1 byte, separated into two parts:

  - The AFI, set to 49, which signifies that the AFI is locally administered, and thus, individual addresses can be assigned by the company.

  - The area ID, the octets of the area address, follows the AFI.

- **System ID:** A 6-byte system ID.

- **NSEL:** NSEL must always be set to 0 for a router. NET is an NSAP address with an NSEL of 0.

Routers use the NET to identify themselves in the IS-IS PDUs. For example, you might assign 49.0001.0000.0c12.3456.00, which represents the following (see Figure 4-8):

- AFI of 49
- Area ID of 0001
- System ID of 0000.0c11.3456, the MAC address of a LAN interface
- NSEL of 0

The area address is also referred to as the prefix.

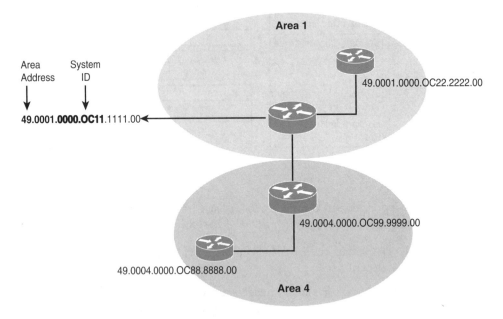

Figure 4-8 *IS-IS Addressing Breakdown*

The area address uniquely identifies the routing area, and the system ID identifies each node. The first part of an NSAP is the area address, and it is associated with the IS-IS routing process. Unlike OSPF, an IS-IS router can be a member of only one area. All routers in an area must use the same area address, which defines the area. The area address is used in Level 2 (interarea) routing.

The 6-byte NSAP system ID must be unique within an area. It is customary to use a MAC address from the router or, for Integrated IS-IS, to encode an IP address into the system ID. All system IDs in a domain must be of equal length and unique. Cisco enforces this OSI directive by fixing the length of the system ID at 6 bytes.

When designing IS-IS addressing, you must take the following into account:

- All routers within an area must use the same area address.
- The area address is used in Level 1 and 2 routing.
- The system ID identifies the intermediate system.
- The system ID for L1 routers must be unique within an area.
- The system ID for L2 routers must be unique within the whole domain.
- A domainwide unique system ID is usually used.

IS-IS Packets

The first eight octets of all IS-IS PDUs are header fields that are common to all PDU types. The TLV information is stored at the end of the PDU. Different types of PDUs have a set of currently defined TLV codes. Any TLV codes a router doesn't recognize should be ignored and passed through unchanged.

IS-IS PDUs are encapsulated directly into an OSI data link frame. IS-IS defines four general types of PDUs, and each type can be Level 1 or Level 2:

- **IS-IS Hello IIH:** Enables the intermediate systems to detect IS-IS neighbors and form adjacencies. There are two types of IIH:
    - **LAN IIH:** Routers send separate LAN IIH packets for Level 1 and Level 2 adjacencies.
    - **Point-to-point IIH:** Routers send a single packet for L1, L2, or L1/L2, depending on the nature of the adjacency.
- **LSP PDU:** Used to distribute link-state information.
- **Partial sequence number PDU PSNP:** Used to acknowledge and request missing pieces of link-state information.
- **Complete sequence number PDU CSNP:** Used to describe the complete list of LSPs in the LSDB of a router. CSNPs are used to inform other routers of LSPs that may be outdated or missing from their own database. This ensures that all routers have the same information and are synchronized. The packets are similar to an OSPF database description packet.

The following information is included in IIH PDUs:

- Whether the PDU is a point-to-point (WAN) PDU or a LAN PDU.
- Source ID, or the system ID of the sending router.
- Holding time, or the time period to wait to hear a "hello" before declaring the neighbor dead. Similar to the OSPF dead interval, the default value is three times the hello interval but can be changed with the IS-IS **hello-multiplier** command.
- Circuit type indicating whether the interface on which the PDU was sent is Level 1, Level 2, or Level 1/Level 2.
- PDU length.
- Local circuit ID on the sending interface (in point-to-point hello PDUs).
- LAN ID, which is the system ID of the Designated Intermediate System (DIS) plus the pseudonode ID (circuit ID) to differentiate LAN IDs on the same DIS.
- Priority. Higher is better; it is used in DIS election.

> **Note** The source address of IS-IS messages is always the data link layer address of the local end of the adjacency. The destination address on broadcast media such as Ethernet is one of two reserved multicast MAC addresses: 0180:c200:0014 or 0180:c200:0015.

IS-IS Information Data Flow

As illustrated in Figure 4-9, the flow of information within the IS-IS routing function consists of four processes along with routing and forwarding information bases. The routing information–based RIB consists of the link-state database, and the forwarding information base FIB holds the forwarding database. This is where Cisco Express Forwarding (CEF) plays a vital role to speed up a packet's switching. The four processes in the IS-IS data-flow diagram are:

- Receive
- Update
- Decision
- Forward

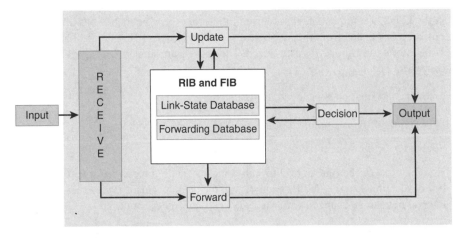

Figure 4-9 *IS-IS Data Flow Processes*

The *receive process* is the entry point for all data, including user data, error reports, routing information, and control packets. It passes user data and error reports to the forward process and passes routing information and control packets (hellos, LSPs, and sequence number packets) to the update process.

The *update process* generates local link information that is flooded to adjacent routers. In addition, the update process receives, processes, and forwards link information that is received from adjacent routers. This process manages the Level 1 and Level 2 link-state databases and floods Level 1 and Level 2 LSPs throughout an area.

The *decision process* runs an SPF algorithm on the link-state database and creates the forwarding database. It computes next-hop information and computes sets of equal-cost paths, creating an adjacency set that is used for load balancing. On a Cisco router, IS-IS supports load balancing over and up to six equal-cost paths.

The *forward process* gets its input from the receive process and uses the forwarding database to forward data packets toward their destination. It also redirects load sharing and generates error reports.

IS-IS Network Types

In general, physical links can be placed in these two groups:

- **Broadcast:** Multiaccess subnetworks that support the addressing of a group of attached systems.
- **Point-to-point:** Permanent or dynamically established links.

In contrast, IS-IS supports two media representations for its link states:

- Broadcast for LANs and multipoint WAN links
- Point-to-point for all other media

In addition, it is important that network designers be aware that IS-IS has no concept of NBMA networks. Therefore, it is recommended that you use point-to-point links, such as point-to-point subinterfaces, over NBMA networks, when possible, as an alternative approach.

Table 4-1 summarizes the differences between broadcast and point-to-point links.

Table 4-1 *Differences Between IS-IS Broadcast and Point-to-Point Links*

	Broadcast	**Point-to-Point**
Usage	LAN, full-mesh WAN	PPP, HDLC, partial-mesh WAN
Hello timer	3.3 sec for DIS, else 10 sec	10 sec
Adjacencies	$n*(n-1)/2$	$n-1$
Uses DIS	Yes	No
LSP and IIH	Sent as multicast	Sent as unicast
IIH type	Level 1 IIH, Level 2 IIH	Point-to-point IIH

IS-IS Protocol Operations

Typically, routers on a LAN establish adjacencies with all other routers on the LAN. IS-IS routers on a LAN establish the two adjacencies with specific Level 1 and Level 2 IIH PDUs. The IIH PDUs announce the area address, where separate IIH packets announce the Level 1 and Level 2 neighbors.

Adjacencies are formed and are based on the area address that is communicated in the incoming IIH and the type of router (Level 1 or Level 2). Level 1 routers accept Level 1 IIH PDUs from their own area and establish adjacencies with other routers in their own area. Level 2 routers accept only Level 2 IIH PDUs and establish only Level 2 adjacencies.

On broadcast multiaccess media (LAN), a Designated Intermediate System (DIS) is elected and conducts the flooding over the media. The DIS is analogous to the designated router in OSPF Protocol. Dijkstra's algorithm requires a virtual router (a pseudonode), which is represented by the DIS, to build a directed graph for broadcast media, as shown in Figure 4-10. The DIS is responsible for two primary tasks:

- Creating and updating pseudonode LSP
- Flooding LSPs over the LAN

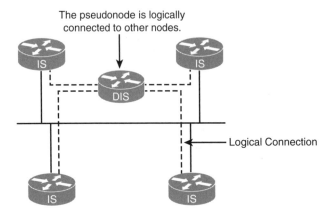

Figure 4-10 *IS-IS Operation*

For IS-IS nodes to select a DIS, it must satisfy the following selection criteria:

- The highest priority; the priority value is configurable.
- The highest subnetwork point-of-attachment SNPA; on LANs, the SNPA is the MAC address. The SNPA for a WAN interface is the virtual circuit identifier.

Cisco router interfaces have the default Level 1 and Level 2 priority of 64. You can configure the priority from 0 to 127. The Level 1 DIS and the Level 2 DIS on a LAN may or may not be the same router because an interface can have different Level 1 and Level 2 priorities.

A selected router is not guaranteed to remain the DIS. Any adjacent intermediate system with a higher priority automatically takes over the DIS role. This behavior is called preemptive. Because the IS-IS LSDB is synchronized frequently on a LAN, giving priority to another intermediate system over the DIS is not a significant issue. IS-IS does not use a backup DIS, and routers on a LAN establish adjacencies both with the DIS and with all other routers.

Level 1 and Level 2 LSPs and IIHs

The two-level nature of IS-IS requires separate types of LSPs: Level 1 and Level 2. The following list explains these types:

- **Level 1 and Level 2 LSP:** IS-IS uses a two-level area hierarchy. The link-state information for these two levels is distributed separately, which results in Level 1 LSPs and Level 2 LSPs. Each intermediate system originates its own LSPs (one for Level 1 and one for Level 2).

On a LAN:

- One router (the DIS) sends out LSP information on behalf of the LAN.
- The DIS represents a pseudonode.
- The DIS sends out the separate Level 1 or Level 2 LSPs for the pseudonode.
- The Level 1 DIS and the Level 2 DIS on a LAN may or may not be the same router because an interface can have different Level 1 and Level 2 priorities.
- LSPs on point-to-point links are sent as unicast, whereas on broadcast media (LANs) LSPs are sent as multicast.

- **Level 1 and Level 2 IIH:** IIHs are used to establish and maintain neighbor adjacency between intermediate systems. The default hello interval is every 10 seconds; however, the hello interval timer is adjustable.

On a LAN, separate Level 1 and Level 2 IIHs are sent periodically as multicasts to multicast MAC addresses:

- All L1 ISs—**01-80-C2-00-00-14**—The multidestination address "All Level 1 Intermediate Systems"
- All L2 ISs—**01-80-C2-00-00-15**—The multidestination address "All Level 2 Intermediate Systems"

Also, there are two additional MAC addresses that are in use by IS-IS:

- All Intermediate Systems—**09-00-2B-00-00-05**—The multidestination address "All Intermediate Systems" used by ISO 9542
- All End Systems—**09-00-2B-00-00-04**—The multidestination address "All End Systems" used by ISO 9542

The default hello interval for the DIS is three times faster (that is, three times smaller) than the interval for the other routers so that DIS failures can be quickly detected.

A neighbor is declared dead if hellos are not received within the hold time. The hold time is calculated as the product of the hello multiplier and hello time. The default hello time is 10 seconds, and the default multiplier is three; therefore, the default hold time is 30 seconds.

Unlike LAN interfaces with separate Level 1 and Level 2 IIHs, point-to-point links have a common point-to-point IIH format that specifies whether the hello relates to Level 1 or Level 2 or both. Point-to-point hellos are sent to the unicast address of the connected router; therefore, it is relatively more efficient relative to other WAN links.

IS-IS Link-State Packets Flooding

As a link-state routing protocol, IS-IS typically needs to update topology information and propagate the update/change to other IS-IS neighbors. To achieve this, an intermediate system originates its own LSPs (one for Level 1 and one for Level 2). These LSPs are identified by the system ID of the originator and an LSP fragment number starting at 0. If an LSP exceeds the MTU, the LSP is fragmented into several LSPs, numbered 1, 2, 3, and so on.

As shown in Figure 4-11, IS-IS maintains the Level 1 and Level 2 LSPs in separate LSDBs (per flooding domain).

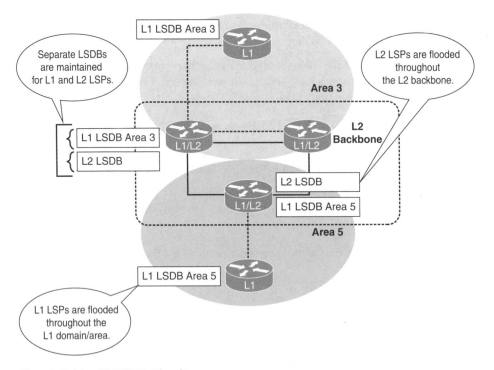

Figure 4-11 *IS-IS LSP Flooding*

However, not every LSP flooded is considered by IS-IS, because when an intermediate system receives an LSP, it examines the checksum and discards any invalid LSPs, flooding them with an expired lifetime age. If the LSP is valid and newer than what is currently in the LSDB, it is retained, acknowledged, and given a lifetime of 1200 seconds. The age is decremented every second until it reaches 0, at which point the LSP is considered to have expired. When the LSP has expired, it is kept for an additional 60 seconds before it is flooded as an expired LSP.

IS-IS LSDB Synchronization

As mentioned earlier, there are two types of sequence number packets (SNPs): complete sequence number (CSNP) PDU and partial sequence number (PSNP) PDU. The use of SNPs differs between point-to-point and broadcast media. CSNPs and PSNPs share the same format; that is, each carries summarized LSP information. However, the primary technical difference is that CSNPs contain summaries of all LSPs in the LSDB "complete SNP," while PSNPs contain only a subset of LSP entries "partial SNP."

Separate CSNPs and PSNPs are used for Level 1 and Level 2 adjacencies. Adjacent IS-IS routers exchange CSNPs to compare their LSDB. In broadcast subnetworks, only the DIS transmits CSNPs. All adjacent neighbors compare the LSP summaries that are received in the CSNP with the contents of their local LSDBs to determine if their LSDBs are synchronized (in other words, whether they have the same copies of LSPs as other routers for the appropriate levels and area of routing).

CSNPs are periodically multicast (every 10 seconds) by the DIS on a LAN to ensure LSDB accuracy. If there are too many LSPs to include in one CSNP, the LSPs are sent in ranges. The CSNP header indicates the starting and ending LSP ID in the range. If all LSPs fit in the CSNP, the range is set to the default values. As illustrated in Figure 4-12, router R1 compares the list of LSPs with its topology table and realizes that it is missing one LSP. Therefore, it sends a PSNP to the DIS (router R2) to request the missing LSP. The DIS reissues only that missing LSP (LSP 77), and router R1 acknowledges it with a PSNP.

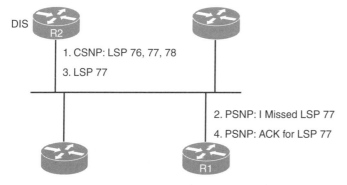

Figure 4-12 *LSDB Sync—LAN*

Adjacent IS-IS routers use PSNPs to acknowledge the receipt of LSPs and to request transmission of missing or newer LSPs. On point-to-point networks, CSNPs are sent only once, when the link comes up to synchronize the LSDBs. After that, LSPs are sent to describe topology changes, and they are acknowledged with a PSNP. Figure 4-13 shows what happens on a point-to-point link when a point-to-point link failure is detected. When this happens, the following occurs in order:

1. A link fails.

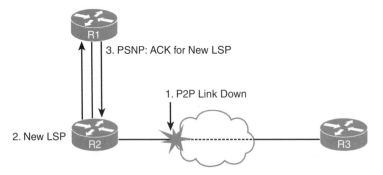

Figure 4-13 *LSDB Sync—WAN Point-to-Point*

2. Router R2 notices this failure and issues a new LSP noting the change.

3. Router R1 receives the LSP, stores it in its topology table, and sends a PSNP back to R2 to acknowledge the receipt of the LSP.

IS-IS Design Considerations

This section discusses various IS-IS routing design considerations over the following topologies:

- Hub-and-spoke over NBMA
- Full mesh
- Flat
- Hierarchal

In addition, some design considerations with regard to IS-IS route summarization and Integrated IS-IS for IPV6 are covered.

This section starts by providing an overview of how routing logic works in IS-IS, along with some advanced routing techniques.

IS-IS Routing Logic Overview

Figure 4-14 refers to the OSI part of the Integrated IS-IS process. This behavior is the same as for pure OSI IS-IS routing without the exchange of IP information within IS-IS.

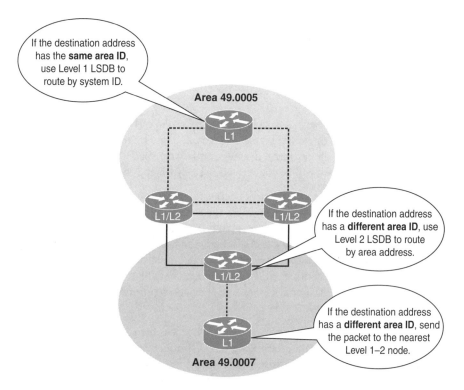

Figure 4-14 *IS-IS Routing Logic Figure*

Routing within an (L1) area involves collecting system IDs and adjacencies for all routers in an area and using Dijkstra's algorithm to compute best paths between the devices. Level 1 routers are aware only of the local area topology. They pass the traffic that is destined to travel outside the area to the closest Level 1–2 router.

Routing between areas is based on the area address. Level 2 routers in different areas exchange area address information and use Dijkstra's algorithm to compute best paths between areas. They pass traffic between areas to the closest Level 1–2 router in the destination area.

ESH and ISH packets are used for routers (intermediate systems) and end systems to detect each other. When a host is required to send a packet to another host, the packet goes to one of the routers on a network that is directly attached to the host. If the destination host is in the same area, the router searches for the destination system ID and forwards the packet appropriately along the best route.

If the destination address is a host in another area, the Level 1 router sends the packet to the nearest Level 1–2 router. Forwarding through Level 2 routers continues until the packet reaches a Level 2 (or Level 1–2) router in the destination area. Within the destination area, routers forward the packet along the best path until the destination host is reached.

In the IP world, when running Integrated IS-IS, IP information is included in the LSPs. IP reachability behaves in IS-IS as if it were end system (ES) information. It is important to note that IP information takes no part in the calculation of the SPF tree; it is simply information about leaf connections to the tree. Therefore, updating the IP reachability is only a partial route calculation (PRC).

IP routes are generated by the partial calculation and placed into the IP routing table. The routes might be accepted to the routing table or rejected, based on the general rules of the routing processes, line administrative distance, or network mask. When the routes do get into the routing table, they will be shown as Level 1 or Level 2 routes, as appropriate.

Based on the logic described, IS-IS is generally considered "to a certain extent" more stable and scalable than OSPF; the reason is that the separation of IP reachability from the core IS-IS network architecture gives Integrated IS-IS better stability and scalability than OSPF. Specifically, OSPFv2 sends LSAs for individual IP subnets. If an IP subnet fails, the LSA is flooded through the network and, in all circumstances, all routers must run a full SPF calculation. In contrast, OSPFv3 has added new LSA types (Type 8 and Type 9) that show similar behavior to IS-IS where reachability information is not carried in router LSA.

In comparison, in an Integrated IS-IS network, the SPF tree is built from CLNS information. If an IP subnet fails in Integrated IS-IS, the LSP is flooded as for OSPF. However, if the failed subnet is a leaf IP subnet (that is, the loss of the subnet has not affected the underlying CLNS architecture), the SPF tree is unaffected and, therefore, only a partial calculation happens, which has significantly less impact on router resources.

Advanced IS-IS Routing

This section covers some advanced routing topics that network designers need to be aware of to be able to achieve optimal and reliable IS-IS routing design in some complex networks.

Route Leaking

Level 1 routers within an IS-IS area, by default, do not carry any routing information external to the area they belong to. Therefore, Level 1 routers, to exit the area and reach any prefix outside the local area, use a default route injected by the L1/L2 border routers, as illustrated in Figure 4-15. (This behavior is described in RFC 1195, in which all the L1 nodes are defined as stub routers.) Although this setup is desirable for scalability reasons, it interferes with BGP routing and MPLS and MPLS-VPN, where all BGP next-hop addresses must be present in the local routing table.

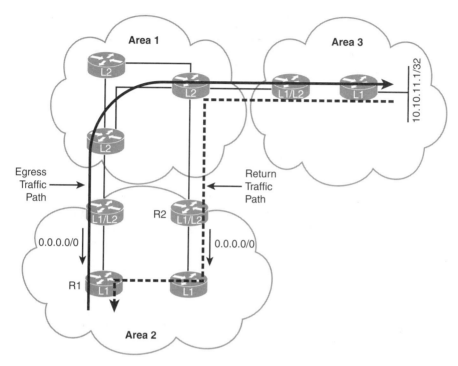

Figure 4-15 *IS-IS Interarea/Level Routing Default Behavior*

In addition, asymmetric routing can cause suboptimal use of network resources as traffic uses different paths from the source to the destination and back. This situation makes troubleshooting potential network-related problems more difficult. It may also impact some delay-sensitive applications such as VoIP.

In the scenario illustrated in this figure, traffic sourced from R1, destined to the host IP (10.10.11.1/32), uses the default route injected by the nearest existing L1/L2 border router and reaches this prefix. The return traffic, on the other hand, enters Area 3 via a different L1/L2 border router. This results in an asymmetric routing situation.

IS-IS supports a feature that is called route leaking, in which selected Level 2 routes can be advertised by a Level 1/Level 2 router into Level 1. Those leaked routes are specially tagged so they are not re-advertised into Level 2 by another Level 1/Level 2 router.

With more detail about interarea routes, a Level 1 router is able to make a better choice about which Level 1–2 router should receive the packet. Leaked routes are referred to as interarea routes in the routing table and the IS-IS database. When you view the routing table, all the leaked routes are marked with an "ia" designation.

Route leaking is defined in RFC 2966, which is a domainwide prefix distribution with two-level IS-IS, for use with the narrow metric TLV types 128 and 130. The IETF has also defined route leaking for use with the wide metric (using TLV type 135).

To implement route leaking at L1/L2 routers, an up/down bit in the TLV indicates whether the route that is identified in the TLV has been leaked. If the up/down bit is set to 0, the route originated within that Level 1 area. If the up/down bit is set to 1, the route has been redistributed into the area from Level 2. The up/down bit is used to prevent routing loops; a Level 1–2 router does not re-advertise, into Level 2, any Level 1 routes that have the up/down bit set to 1. For a route to be leaked, it must already be present in the routing table as a Level 2 route.

Route leaking should be planned and deployed carefully to avoid a situation in which any topology change in one area makes it necessary to recompute multiple routes in all other areas.

By applying the IS-IS route leaking feature to the scenario illustrated in Figure 4-16 (leaking a more specific route via R2), we can steer the egress traffic from R1 to use the R2 border router to exit Area 2 to reach prefix 10.10.11.1/32 and avoid the asymmetrical routing situation.

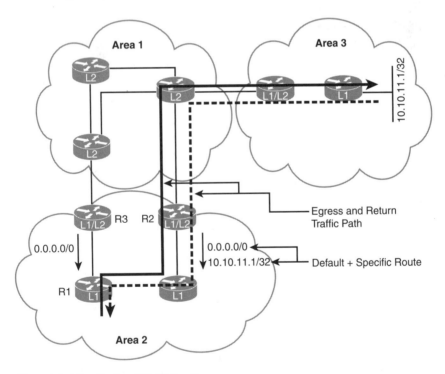

Figure 4-16 *Optimal IS-IS Routing*

The importance of the up/down bit (described previously) in IS-IS loop prevention is demonstrated in the operation of router R3 in Figure 4-17. Because the up/down bit is set by R2, router R3 will not insert the route from the L1 database into its L2 database, and therefore, the route will not be re-advertised into the backbone. This, in turn, prevents possible routing loops for this route because all areas are already getting that route via Level 2 routing.

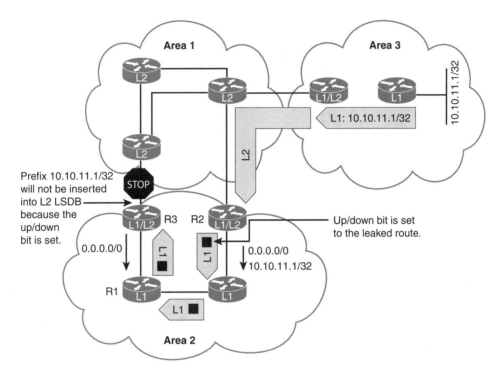

Figure 4-17 *IS-IS Route Leaking and Loop Prevention*

Asymmetric Versus Symmetric IS-IS Routing

As highlighted in the previous section, asymmetric routing (where packets take different paths in different directions) is not detrimental to the network. However, this type of routing can make troubleshooting difficult, and it is sometimes a symptom of a suboptimal design that may impact an application's performance and users' quality of experience.

In the scenario depicted in Figure 4-18, users are complaining about some low video quality and delays when having a point-to-point telepresence video call between two locations. (Telepresence video traffic flows between router X and Y.)

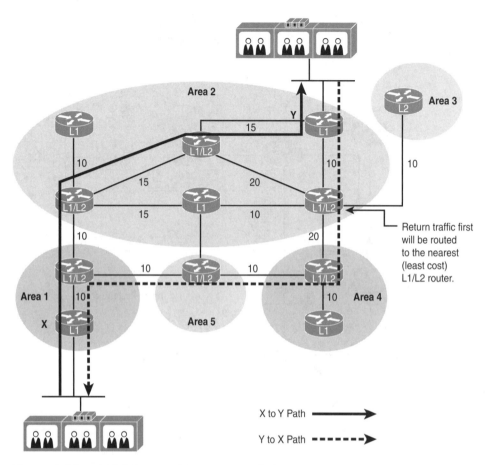

Figure 4-18 *IS-IS Suboptimal (Asymmetrical) Routing*

As shown here, Area 1 contains two routers:

- One router borders Area 2 and is a Level 1–2 intermediate system.
- The other router is contained within the area and is a Level 1 only.

The backbone (Area 2), however, consists of several routers:

- A selection of routers is specified as Level 1. The routers route either internally to that area or to the exit points (the Level 1–2 routers).
- The three Level 1–2 routers form a chain across Area 2, linking to the neighbor Areas 1, 3, and 4. Although the middle router of the three Level 1–2 routers does not link directly to another area, the middle router must support Level 2 routing to ensure that the backbone is contiguous. If the middle router fails, the other Level 1-only routers cannot perform the Level 2 function (despite having a physical path across Area 2), and the backbone is broken (also known as a partitioned backbone).

Area 3 contains one router that borders Areas 2 and 4, yet it has no intra-area neighbors and is performing Level 2 functions only. If you add another router to Area 3, the border router reverts to Level 1–2 functions. In the figure, symmetric routing does not occur because Level 2 details are hidden from Level 1 routers that recognize only a default route to the nearest Level 1–2 router. Traffic from router X to router Y flows from router X to its closest Level 1–2 router. The Level 1–2 router then forwards the traffic along the shortest path to the destination area (Area 2). When the traffic flows into Area 2, the traffic is routed along the shortest intra-area path to router Y.

Router Y routes return packets to router X via its nearest Level 1–2 router. The Level 1–2 router recognizes the best route to Area 1 via Area 4 (over low-bandwidth–capacity links), based on the lowest-cost Level 2 path. Because Level 1 and Level 2 computations are separate, the path that is taken from router Y back to router X is not necessarily the least-cost path from router Y to router X.

Asymmetrical routing can impact sensitive delay traffic such as VoIP and video and, in this particular scenario, it is the primary cause of the quality issues users are facing with the telepresence call because traffic is passing through lower-bandwidth–capacity links. The return traffic takes a longer path, which may lead to delay and delay variation (jitter). Also, using different paths for the egress and ingress traffic flows leads to receiving some out-of-order video RTP packets that ultimately will result in packet loss (because it is real-time traffic).

As a network designer, you need to optimize this design in such a way that traffic between routers X and Y follows the same (symmetrical) path for both egress and ingress traffic flows.

By configuring route leaking on the router in Area 2, bordering Area 1, you can influence the return path selection for traffic from Y to X, while the original path from X to Y stays the same (see Figure 4-19). By performing this action, the L1 router that originates from Y (top right router in Area 2) has a level 1 entry in the routing table for X and will forward traffic via the Level 1 topology (the more specific route) instead of being forced to hand off the traffic to the nearest L2 exit point (refer to Figure 4-18). Now that the traffic follows the same path in both directions, you can control it much better and also potential troubleshooting will be easier.

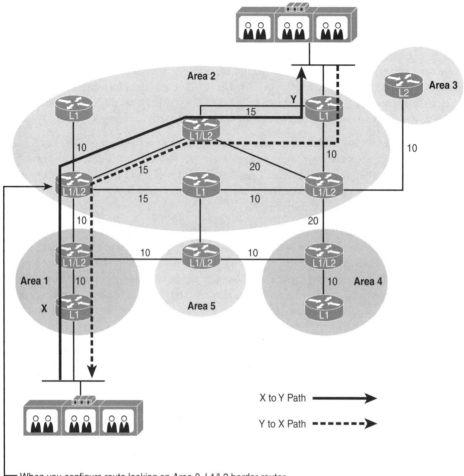

Figure 4-19 *IS-IS Optimal (Symmetrical) Routing*

> **Note** If the same exact route is received as both L1 and L2 route type, the L1 route type is always preferred over the L2 route, based on typical IS-IS route selection preference.

IS-IS Routing over NBMA Hub-and-Spoke

This section uses a sample scenario to explain IS-IS limitation over NBMA hub-and-spoke networks and how to work around the IIH adjacency issues. As shown in Figure 4-20, the hub router RTA's interface is defined as a broadcast interface; therefore, it sends LAN IIH.

The other routers (spokes) are configured as point-to-point subinterfaces and, as such, send the point-to-point IIH packets. As a result, the adjacencies do not form, and no routing information is exchanged in this case.

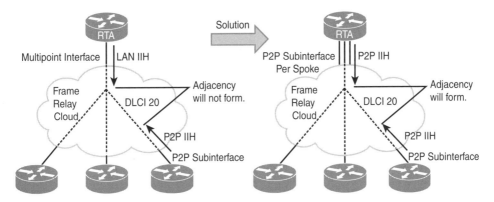

Figure 4-20 *IS-IS over NBMA Hub and Spoke*

To achieve a working solution, you need to have all interfaces configured with the same network type. In this scenario, you can configure multiple point-to-point interfaces on the hub router RTA side and use small subnets for each virtual circuit. As highlighted previously in this book, IS-IS is limited in this type of scenario, and OSPF or EIGRP can offer more flexible design options in a large-scale NBMA hub-and-spoke network.

IS-IS Routing over a Full-Mesh Network

A large NBMA full mesh can result in potential performance and scalability issues. Excessive flooding in such environments can be limited by grouping subinterfaces into mesh groups. Mesh groups are designed for optimizing flooding over large meshed networks including large NBMA clouds with many point-to-point connections. The basic idea behind mesh groups is that each member of the mesh group does not reflood the LSPs, which are received from another member of the group, to other members of the same group because they would have already received copies. However, LSPs that are received from nonmember routers are flooded to all members of the mesh group, and other adjacent nonmembers, as illustrated in Figure 4-21. From a design point of view, full-mesh networks are the most expensive and complex to maintain and scale. Full-mesh topologies are most commonly used in enterprise networks to interconnect a small number of core routers.

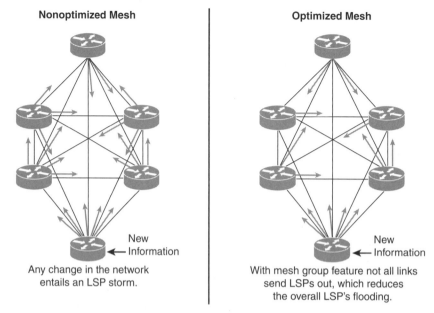

Figure 4-21 *IS-IS Routing over Full-mesh Network*

In addition, in NBMA networks, such as an ATM cloud in which all routers are fully meshed with virtual circuits, the full mesh allows the cloud to be modeled as a broadcast link and configured as such to work with IS-IS. The problem with this model is that the full-mesh ATM cloud does not have the complete broadcast capabilities of a multipoint broadcast technology, such as Ethernet. When any of the virtual circuits (VCs) fail, the any-to-any connectivity is lost, breaking the flooding model.

Flat IS-IS Routing Design

A flat IS-IS design eliminates the ability to reduce the amount of routing information in a single area or level as well as prevent the ability to hide topology information. This may lead to a reduced level of scalability and stability in large-scale networks. However, a small and simple IS-IS network can initially be deployed as a single area (nonhierarchical network). Even then, you most probably want to determine up front when it will be necessary to migrate to a hierarchical topology. Moving to a hierarchical model depends on many factors such as, for example, the number of routers, geographical dispersion of your network, link types, link stability, and so on.

By moving to a hierarchical topology with multiple areas, you can contain the flooding of LSPs within the area. This situation does not prevent you from configuring some areas as L2 only in certain designs, which can save you CPU processing power, if required.

Because having a single area defeats the purpose of having a two-level routing, you can deploy your network as an all-L1 or all-L2 network. The recommended way of deploying such networks is to deploy an L2-only network from the start, which makes future area addition easier and ensures backbone connectivity from the start. Although technically you can start your design with L1–L2 routers, giving them the capability to scale the network in the future without major redesign, all the routers will hold two databases that you won't take advantage of, because they will only put an additional unnecessary load on the routers.

On Cisco routers, the behavior is such that both Level 1 and Level 2 routing are enabled by default. If you want to make your network L1 only or L2 only, additional configuration is needed on per router basis.

Hierarchal IS-IS Design

Like OSPF, IS-IS naturally supports two-layer hierarchal networks. However, network designers can still use it in networks with a three-layer hierarchy. In addition, because IS-IS supports the capability to overlap between IS-IS flooding domains (levels), it offers more flexible design with regards to optimal routing compared to OSPF in network with multiple tiers. Figure 4-22 shows an example of building an IS-IS hierarchical model on top of a classic hierarchal network topology that consists of the core, distribution, and access layers.

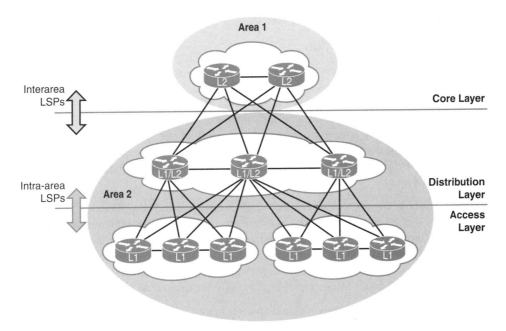

Figure 4-22 *Hierarchal IS-IS Example*

In this design, the core layer consists of L2-only devices, they belong to Area 1. Area 2, on the other hand, is composed of the distribution and access layers. Based on this design, Level 2 LSPs will be only flooded within the core network and between the core and Level 1/Level 2 distribution layer devices. Similarly, access layer devices in the same area as the distribution routers receive and exchange only Level 1 LSPs with the distribution routers. Such a network design has many benefits, one of them being the protection of the core layer from instabilities within the access layer. You do not want link flaps in the access layer to influence IS-IS SPF processes in the core. However, to achieve a reliable hierarchal design with summarization at the areas/levels boundary, the IP addressing scheme needs to be properly structured to allow for the most rational route summarization.

Although you can move the domain boundary of the logical IS-IS L1/L2 one level down, in this particular scenario, moving the boundary to the access devices does not offer any optimized design to support proper route summarization to reduce the amount of routing information in the core. Also, this means any link flap event between the access and distribution devices is propagated to the core, which may introduce instability in the core network.

Note For simplicity, the preceding example covered only one area (Area 2) that is attached to the L2-only Area 1, but in reality, you can attach many more areas in the same manner. The backbone in this scenario is composed of all L2-capable devices, including the L1/L2 ones in Area 2.

IS-IS Routes Summarization

The primary goal of route summarization is to reduce the number of IP prefixes advertised between routing domains. A routing domain could be an OSPF area or an IS-IS Level. In other words, route summarization enables more detailed topology information to be hidden and sets a boundary limit for containing any network changes. By doing so, network designers can achieve a more scalable, stable, and fast-converging routing design because it technically reduces the number of routers that are affected by any topology change. This helps to lower the processing load and network convergence time following any failure event.

However, one of the main factors that determines how well an IGP scales is the addressing layout that is planned into the network architecture. An improper addressing scheme from the summarization perspective, which is used in the design of your network and in the early phases of the implementation, might cause scaling problems later on. As a result, the network may encounter difficulties to scale further, and the devices might end up using more hardware resources (CPU processing, memory) than necessary.

For IP, you can summarize only native IS-IS routes into Level 2 from the Level 1 database. It is not possible to summarize IS-IS internal routes at Level 1, although it is possible to summarize external (redistributed) routes at Level 1.

The key concepts for summarization of IP routes in IS-IS are as follows:

- Internal routes can be redistributed and summarized from Level 1 into Level 2. Summarization should be configured on the Level 1/Level 2 router, which injects the Level 1 routes into Level 2.

- If summarization is being used, all Level 1/Level 2 routers in an area must be summarizing into the backbone. If one of them is advertising more specific routes, all the traffic from the backbone will be sent toward this router because of longest-match routing.

- Internal routes cannot be summarized at Level 1 because this action is not permitted by the protocol.

- It is possible to summarize external (redistributed) routes at Level 1.

For example, the scenario shown in Figure 4-23 illustrates a typical multitier (hierarchal) network. In this scenario, the core is protected by instabilities in the attached areas because only the aggregate route of all the distribution and access networks (10.1.5.0/24) makes its way to the IS-IS databases of the core routers.

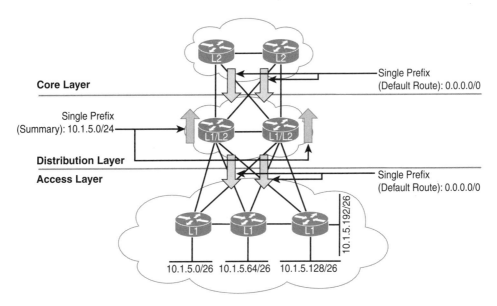

Figure 4-23 *IS-IS Route Summarization Example*

In addition, you can also summarize in the other direction, at the distribution layer from the core downstream toward the access layer. Typically, access devices that attach to a distribution layer (or directly to the core) require only a default route. In other scenarios, such as dual homing, it may be necessary to take appropriate measures to avoid any potential for suboptimal path selection. In this example, you can see that practically all core prefixes are summarized into one advertisement, which is the default route. This is shown as a prefix of all 0s (0.0.0.0/0). This helps to reduce the load on the access nodes (smaller LSDB size) and also facilitates faster network convergence time.

Integrated IS-IS for IPv6

Cisco has added multitopology support to IS-IS to increase flexibility in IS-IS deployment within a dual-stack environment. Two TLVs are added in IS-IS for IPv6 support. These two TLVs are used to describe IPv6 reachability and IPv6 interface addresses:

- IPv6 reachability TLV (0xEC or 236):
    - Describes network reachability (routing prefix, metric, options).
    - Equivalent to IPv4 internal and external reachability TLVs (type code 128 and 130).
- IPv6 interface address TLV (0xE8 or 232):
    - Equivalent to IPv4 interface address TLV (type code 132).
    - For hello PDUs, which must contain the link-local address.
    - For LSPs, which must contain only the non-link–local address.

The protocol-supported TLV (type code 129) lists the supported NLPIDs. All IPv6-enabled IS-IS routers advertise an NLPID value of 0x8E (142). The NLPID of IPv4 is 0xCC (204).

Multitopology IS-IS provides some flexibility when you are transitioning to IPv6. A separate topology is kept for both IPv4 and IPv6 networks; because some links may not be able to carry IPv6, IS-IS specifically keeps track of those links, minimizing the possibility for the traffic to be "black-holed."

Single-topology IS-IS, where there is one SPF instance for both IPv4 and IPv6, also remains a possibility that is even easier to administer, but the network must be homogenous. The same links must carry IPv4 and IPv6 simultaneously.

IS-IS Single-Topology Restrictions

When you migrate from a purely IPv4 environment to a dual-stack environment, a discrepancy in supported protocols would cause adjacencies to fail. The intermediate system performs consistency checks on hello packets and will reject hello packets that do not have the same set of configured address families. For example, a router running IS-IS for both IPv4 and IPv6 does not form an adjacency with a router running IS-IS for IPv4 or IPv6 only. Therefore, in order to facilitate a seamless upgrade, the engineer should consider disabling the consistency checks during the upgrade to maintain adjacencies active even in a heterogeneous environment.

Suppressing adjacency checking on intra-area links (Layer 1 links) is primarily done during transition from single-topology (IPv4) to multitopology (IPv4 and IPv6) IS-IS networks. Imagine that a service provider is integrating IPv6 into a network, and it is not practical to shut down the entire provider router set for a coordinated upgrade. Without disabling the adjacency checking—because routers were enabled for IPv6 and IS-IS for IPv6—adjacencies would drop with IPv4-only routers, and IPv4 routing is severely impacted. With consistent check suppression, IPv6 can be turned up without impacting IPv4 reachability, as illustrated in Figure 4-24.

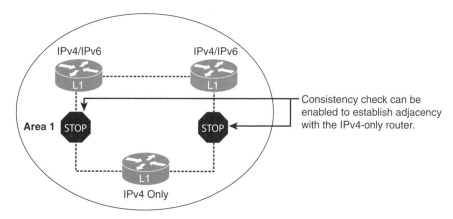

Figure 4-24 *IS-IS Consistency Check Suppression*

As in any IS-IS network design, Level 2 (backbone) routers must be contiguous. IPv6 adjacency checks are not done on Level 2 links. As shown in Figure 4-25, the Level 2 routers are not contiguous for IPv6; therefore, this example shows an incorrect network design. A correct example would have Level 2 routers that are contiguous for both IPv4 and IPv6. This situation is called a "routing hole." In the example in this figure, adjacencies are formed across Layer 2 links between the three areas. However, the IPv6 network is partitioned by the inability of Area 3 to carry IPv6 traffic. Because IS-IS is managing a single topology, the routers will believe that a path for IPv6 exists across Area 3, but all IPv6 traffic that is sent via that path will fail.

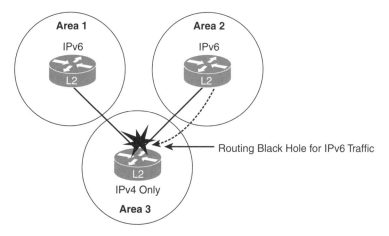

Figure 4-25 *IS-IS IPv6 across Noncontiguous Backbone*

Multitopology IS-IS for IPv6

IS-IS multitopology support for IPv6 allows IS-IS to maintain a set of independent topologies within a single area or domain. This mode removes the restriction that all interfaces on which IS-IS is configured must support the identical set of network address families. It also removes the restriction that all routers in the IS-IS area (for Level 1 routing) or domain (for Level 2 routing) must support the identical set of network layer address families. In addition, with this design approach, a separate SPF is performed for each configured topology. Therefore, it is sufficient that connectivity exists among a subset of the routers in the area or domain for a given network address family to be routable, as exemplified in Figure 4-26.

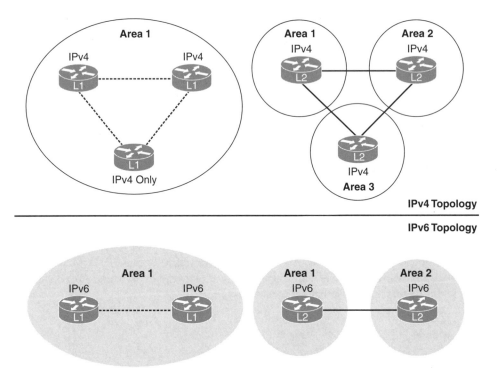

Figure 4-26 *IS-IS Multitopology (IPv4 and IPv6)*

When multitopology support for IPv6 is used, use the wide metric because the TLVs that are used to advertise IPv6 information in LSPs are defined to use only wide metrics.

All routers in the area or domain must use the same type of IPv6 support, either single topology or multitopology. A router that is operating in multitopology mode will not recognize the capability of the single-topology mode router to support IPv6 traffic, which will lead to routing holes in the IPv6 topology. To transition from single-topology support to the more flexible multitopology support, you can deploy a multitopology transition mode.

In migration scenarios where you need to move the design from single to multitopology, you should consider the multitopology transition mode. The multitopology transition mode allows a network that is operating in single-topology IS-IS IPv6 support mode to continue to work while upgrading routers to include multitopology IS-IS IPv6 support. While in transition mode, both types of TLVs (single topology and multitopology) are sent in LSPs for all configured IPv6 addresses, but the router continues to operate in single-topology mode. After all routers in the area or domain have been upgraded to support multitopology IPv6 and are operating in transition mode, transition mode can be removed from the router configurations.

Final Thoughts on IS-IS Routing Design

As highlighted earlier in this chapter, IS-IS does not support NBMA type of networks directly; therefore, you should consider using either a broadcast or point-to-point network model when dealing with NBMA networks, such as frame relay or ATM, depending on the network characteristics, such as the scale of the network, available bandwidth and applications carried over the WAN, and how each network type may impact any of these elements.

In addition, it is technically valid to consider either building flat (nonhierarchical) IS-IS networks or a hierarchical design. However, from a design point of view, the ideal design decision should be driven by different technical and nontechnical variables, such as business direction and future plans (such as expansion plans) to determine the target size of the network. When we talk about a flat IS-IS design, the design involves only one area, so two-level routing is not really required. This is the simplest architecture that facilitates the design of some other network protocols and applications such as MPLS-TE and MPLS-VPN in an MPLS network environments. However, it does not scale as well as the hierarchical design. For this reason, it is always beneficial to design your network with hierarchy in mind. For instance, if there is any projected future growth in network size and it won't break other network services such as MPLS-TE, a hierarchal design should be considered, as it offers more structured, scalable, and flexible design.

In hierarchical IS-IS design, there are multiple areas to consider, as well as the positioning of the backbone within the network to glue the multiple areas together. Therefore, the use of Level 2 routing is crucial in hierarchical networks within the backbone. Also, route summarization toward the core (backbone) is very important in designing a stable and scalable hierarchical IS-IS network; therefore, ideally, it requires a very careful and structured design of the IP addressing scheme within the areas and globally across the entire routing domain. With this approach, route summarization will offer the capability to hide instabilities within a problematic region (area/Level) from the rest of the network.

Although route leaking helps avoid some suboptimal routing issues and overcome troubleshooting complexities, ideally, applications' requirements should drive whether optimal routing is required or not. This, in turn, drives the decision whether you need to consider routing leaking or not.

Furthermore, from the previous section, you know that considering IS-IS multitopology eliminates the restrictions and limitations that you may face when using IS-IS single topology. Therefore, it is recommended to consider IS-IS multitopology if there is any current or future need to use IPv6.

Consequently, when you are designing an IS-IS routing and constructing the network from the ground up, it is very important to have the aforementioned key design points in mind. The reason is that, after the network has been put in operation, it might be hard to make big changes, and you might be forced to make concessions and workarounds. Such concessions make your network needlessly more complex as a result.

Summary

- With IS-IS, asymmetric routing can occur because Level 2 details are hidden from Level 1 routers.
- Route leaking can reduce suboptimal routing by allowing Level 2 routes to be inserted into Level 1.
- IS-IS recognizes two topology types: point-to-point and broadcast.
- IS-IS adjacencies are established based on the area address and the router type.
- Level 1 LSPs are flooded within an area, whereas Level 2 LSPs are flooded throughout the Level 2 backbone.
- Although IS-IS is similar to OSPF in many ways, its backbone is not an area; the backbone is a chain of L2-capable routers.
- Single-topology IS-IS uses a single topology for IPv4 and IPv6. Multitopology IS-IS uses separate topologies for IPv4 and IPv6 and supports different topologies for IPv4 and IPv6.

Review Questions

After answering the following questions, please refer to Appendix A, "Answers to Review Questions," for the answers.

1. Which properties apply to both to OSPF and IS-IS? (Select two.)
   a. Link-state routing protocol
   b. Supports VLSM
   c. Usually deployed in enterprise environment
   d. Uses DUAL algorithm
   e. Uses levels to establish routing hierarchy

2. Which of the following statements are true about IS-IS addressing? (Select two.)
   a. Routers within an area must use unique area addresses.
   b. The area address is used in Level 1 routing.
   c. The system ID identifies the area.

d. The system ID for Level 1 routers must be unique within an area.

e. The system ID for Level 2 routers must be unique within the whole domain.

3. Which of the following statements are true about IS-IS route leaking? (Select two.)

   a. It is done at L1–L2 routers.
   b. For a prefix to be leaked, it must exist in the routing table as IS-IS Level 1 route.
   c. You can use route leaking to solve suboptimal routing.
   d. An up/down bit in the CDP field is used.
   e. You need to disable all loop protection mechanisms.

4. Which of the following do you need to take into account when designing IS-IS over NBMA hub-and-spoke topology? (Select two.)

   a. Hub-and-spoke interfaces must be configured with the same network type.
   b. Hub interfaces can be configured as multipoint, while spokes should be configured as point-to-point.
   c. Only L2 must be used over the NBMA network.
   d. Hubs must be configured as L1/L2, whereas the spokes must be configured as L1 only.
   e. Hub WAN interfaces should be configured with point-to-point subinterfaces, whereas the spokes should be configured as point-to-point interfaces.

5. Which of the following statements are true about IS-IS? (Select two.)

   a. IS-IS supports a larger number of routers per area than OSPF.
   b. Ideally, both IS-IS and OSPF should not be designed with more than 300 routers per area.
   c. IS-IS maintains separate LSDB and LSPs per level.
   d. IS-IS floods the same LSPs to update both L1 and L2 LSDBs.
   e. Optimal routing cannot be achieved when IS-IS is designed with multiple levels over a network with multiple paths.

6. Which of the following do you need to take into account when designing IS-IS for an MPLS-VPN environment? (Select two.)

   a. Route leaking is required from L2 to L1 for MPLS (LDP) to work.
   b. If MPLS-TE is used, it is simpler to use a single area/Level IS-IS design.
   c. If MPLS-TE is used, it is recommended to use a multiarea/Level IS-IS design to achieve more structured architecture.
   d. For MPLS to work over IS-IS, IS-IS wide metric must be enabled.
   e. Route leaking should be avoided when MPLS and MP-BGP is used.

7. Which statements are true about IS-IS routing? (Select two.)

   a. By default, L1-only routers will receive only a default route from the L1/L2 border routers.
   b. By default, L1-only routers can receive only default route + summary from the L1/L2 border routers.
   c. L1-only routers can receive a default route + more specific from the L1/L2 border routers, if route leaking is used.

d. L1-only routers can receive a default route only from the L1/L2 border routers, regardless whether route leaking is used or not.

e. The default route will not be injected into an L1 area from the L1/L2 border routers by default.

8. An enterprise needs to migrate its WAN core from EIGRP to IS-IS, and in the future it wants to enable IS-IS across all other regional networks connected to the WAN core. Which approach do you recommend this enterprise use to enable IS-IS across the WAN core?

    a. Start with L1 across the WAN core and then add the regional networks as L2 each.
    b. Start with L1/L2 across the WAN core and then add the regional networks as L2.
    c. Start with L2 across the WAN core and then add the regional networks as L1.
    d. Start with L1/L2 across the WAN core and then add the regional network as L1/L2 as well.

9. Which of the following statements are true about IS-IS single topology? (Select two.)

    a. A router running IS-IS for both IPv4 and IPv6 will not form an adjacency with a router running IS-IS for IPv4 or IPv6 only.
    b. IPv6 is not supported by IS-IS single topology.
    c. A router running IS-IS for both IPv4 and IPv6 will form an adjacency with a router running IS-IS for IPv4 only.
    d. A router running IS-IS for both IPv4 and IPv6 will form an adjacency with a router running IS-IS for IPv6 only.

10. Which of the following do you need to take into account when designing multitopology IS-IS? (Select two.)

    a. Multitopology IS-IS should be avoided when IPv4 coexists with IPv6 in the same network.
    b. When multitopology for IPv6 is used, IS-IS wide metric should be considered.
    c. In migration scenarios (moving from single to multitopology), you should consider the multitopology transition mode.
    d. All routers must be configured as L1.
    e. All routers must be configured as L2.
    f. Single SPF process will be carried for all the configured topologies.

Chapter 5

Border Gateway Protocol Design

Upon completing this chapter, you will be able to

- Identify IBGP scalability issues
- Describe route reflectors
- Explain BGP route reflector definitions
- Describe confederations
- Compare BGP confederations to BGP route reflectors
- Describe the BGP split-horizon rule
- Describe the route reflector split-horizon rule
- Explain BGP split-horizon rules
- Explain the need for redundant route reflectors
- Describe the need for route reflector clusters
- Describe a cluster ID
- Describe extra BGP loop-prevention mechanisms
- Describe loop prevention, specifically a cluster list
- Describe network design with route reflectors
- Describe hierarchical route reflector design
- Describe potential route reflector network issues
- Design BGP communities
- Use BGP communities
- Design a BGP solution around BGP communities

- Describe BGP named community lists
- Describe the two ways of connecting networks to the Internet with BGP
- Describe dual-homing design considerations
- Describe load sharing when single-homed to one ISP through multiple links
- Describe load sharing when dual-homed to one ISP through a single local router
- Describe load sharing when dual-homed to one ISP through multiple local routers
- Describe load sharing when dual-homed to two ISPs through a single local router
- Describe load sharing when dual-homed to two ISPs through multiple local routers

Border Gateway Protocol (BGP) is commonly used in sites with multiple connections to the Internet. BGP is also frequently used in medium- to large-scale enterprise networks to provide a controlled interconnection between multiple routing domains that are running OSPF or EIGRP. This chapter discusses advanced topics in designing BGP routing solutions. Also, it describes how to identify scaling design issues with interior BGP environments along with the different possible techniques to alleviate these issues.

BGP Overview

BGP, as defined in RFCs 1163 and 1267, is an Exterior Gateway Protocol (EGP). It enables you to set up an interdomain routing system that automatically guarantees the loop-free exchange of routing information between autonomous systems.

Any typical BGP route consists of the following:

- A network number
- A list of autonomous systems that information has passed through (called the autonomous system path)
- A list of other path attributes

Like any dynamic routing protocol, the main goal of BGP is to exchange network reachability information with other BGP systems. Unlike IGP, BGP also passes the information about the list of autonomous system paths of each route; therefore, it is referred to as a path-vector protocol.

BGP can use the list of autonomous systems associated with each route to construct a graph of autonomous system connectivity from which routing loops can be pruned and with which autonomous system-level policy decisions can be enforced.

A next hop router address is used in the NEXT_HOP attribute, regardless of the autonomous system of that router. The Cisco IOS software automatically calculates the value for this attribute.

Any two routers that form a TCP connection to exchange BGP routing information are referred to in BGP terms as *peers* or *neighbors*.

BGP neighbors exchange full routing information when the TCP connection between neighbors is first established. When changes to the routing table are detected, the BGP routers send to their neighbors only those routes that have changed. In addition, by default, each BGP speaker advertises only the optimal path to a destination network from its viewpoint.

BGP Speaker Types

As an intra- and interdomain routing protocol, BGP can offer flexibility to different interconnected autonomous systems (AS), as shown in Figure 5-1. In this scenario, if an AS has multiple BGP speakers and different interconnecting autonomous systems, the AS in the middle can serve as a transit transport service for other autonomous systems. In this figure, AS65001 is a transit AS for AS50 and AS100.

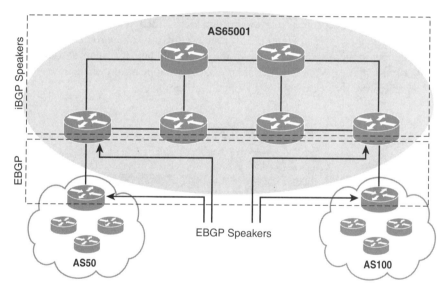

Figure 5-1 *BGP Speaker Types*

To be able to send the information to external ASs, there must be an assurance of the reachability for these networks. To ensure network reachability, BGP uses a different type of BGP speaker and session, and the following processes take place:

- Internal BGP (iBGP) peering between routers inside an AS
- External BGP (EBGP) peering between routers at the edge of the adjacent autonomous systems

When BGP runs between routers that belong to two different ASs, this is called *EBGP*. When BGP runs between routers in the same AS, this is called *iBGP*, as illustrated in Figure 5-1.

In large-scale BGP networks, with large numbers of iBGP speakers, having a full mesh of iBGP sessions between the BGP speakers introduces several design concerns and limitations, such as scalability of the network, operational flexibility, and simplicity. This chapter discusses the different techniques and design options available to you to overcome this design limitation in large-scale BGP networks.

BGP Loop Prevention and Split-Horizon Rule

In interior routing, split-horizon route advertisement is a method of preventing routing loops in distance-vector routing protocols by prohibiting a router from advertising a route back onto the interface from which it was learned. In BGP, split horizon is enforced in a slightly different way, using extra mechanisms.

As highlighted in the preceding section, BGP has two forms of speakers, EBGP and IBGP, and each uses different mechanisms to avoid routing loops. EBGP relies on the AS path to prevent loops. As illustrated in Figure 5-2, if router X (BGP speaking router) detects its own AS number in the AS-Path attribute of the routing update, the route is discarded because it originated in AS 65001. In fact, if an AS number appears anywhere in the AS-Path, it is discarded as a clear sign of a looped routing update.

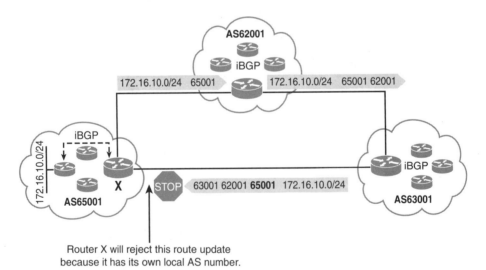

Figure 5-2 *EBGP Loop Prevention*

In contrast, technically there is no way to tell if a route that is advertised through several IBGP speakers is a loop. Because IBGP peers are in the same AS, they do not add anything to the AS path; therefore, they must not re-advertise routes that are learned via IBGP to other IBGP peers.

In IBGP, the split-horizon rule mandates that received updates on EBGP sessions should be forwarded on all IBGP and EBGP sessions, whereas updates that are received on an IBGP session should be forwarded only on all EBGP sessions.

For example, in the scenario shown in Figure 5-3, there are no route reflectors. Router R2 advertises a route that is received from an EBGP peer into the IBGP. The route gets to R3 and R4. However, in this case R3 and R4 do not advertise it to other IBGP peers in this scenario because of the split-horizon rules of IBGP. Therefore, if this route needs to propagate to R4, R2 must form a peering session with R4. Although full mesh requires few IBGP sessions in this scenario, in larger networks, this can reach an unmanageable number of sessions and lead to nonscalable design. Later in this chapter, you will learn how to optimize large iBGP network design to offer more scalable and manageable BGP networks.

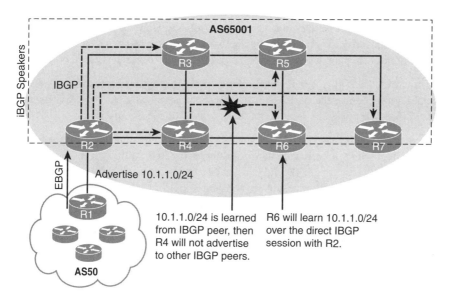

Figure 5-3 *IBGP Split-Horizon Rule*

> **Note** In the scenario in Figure 5-3, the iBGP speakers have full mesh of iBGP sessions among them. For simplicity, only some of these sessions are shown in this figure.

BGP Path Attributes and Path Selection (Review)

This section reviews the BGP path attributes and how these attributes influence BGP path selection.

BGP Path Attributes

Routes learned via BGP have associated properties that are used to determine the best route to a destination when multiple paths exist to a particular destination. These properties are referred to as *BGP path attributes*. In general, BGP path attributes have three categories:

- **Well-known mandatory:** Three specific well-known mandatory attributes must be attached to each update message: Next-hop, AS-PATH, and Origin.

- **Well-known discretionary:** These attributes can be presented, but they are not mandatory; they include BGP Local Preference and Atomic aggregate. In other words, BGP considers these attributes only when their function is required.

- **Optional:** When a BGP speaker receives a BGP update with optional attributes, the BGP speaker will check whether it can recognize the attached optional attribute. If it does, the BGP speaker handles that attribute accordingly. However, if the BGP speaker is not able to identify the attached attribute, it looks into the transitive bit in the attribute. BGP optional path attributes can be categorized into two types based on this bit:

    - **Transitive:** This type of BGP speaker propagates this optional attribute even if it does not recognize the attribute. It does so because the attribute could be useful for other BGP speakers along the path, such as BGP community values.

    - **Nontransitive:** If the type of BGP speaker is unable to recognize the optional attribute, it will not propagate it—for example, the BGP Multi-exit discriminator. Also, the BGP Originator ID and Cluster-List attributes used to prevent looping in BGP routing reflection design are considered optional nontransitive attributes; these attributes are discussed later in this chapter.

Note For more details regarding how each of these attributes work, refer to the "Border Gateway Protocol" guide, which you can find at http://docwiki.cisco.com.

How BGP Selects Paths

From an iBGP point of view, a router running Cisco IOS Release does not select or use an iBGP route unless both of the following conditions are true:

- The router has a route available to the next hop router.

- The router has received synchronization via an IGP (unless IGP synchronization has been disabled; it is disabled by default in the new Cisco software releases).

In general, BGP bases its decision process on the attribute values. When faced with multiple routes to the same destination, BGP chooses the best route for routing traffic toward the destination. The following process summarizes how BGP chooses the best route.

1. If the next hop is inaccessible, do not consider it. This decision is why it is important to have an IGP route to the next hop.

2. If the path is internal, synchronization is enabled, and the route is not in the IGP, do not consider the route.

3. Prefer the path with the largest weight (weight is a Cisco proprietary parameter).

4. If the routes have the same weight, prefer the route with the largest local preference.

5. If the routes have the same local preference, prefer the route that was originated by the local router. For example, a route might be originated by the local router using the **network bgp router** configuration command or through redistribution from an IGP.

6. If the local preference is the same or if no route was originated by the local router, prefer the route with the shortest autonomous system path.

7. If the autonomous system path length is the same, prefer the route with the lowest origin code (IGP < EGP < INCOMPLETE).

8. If the origin codes are the same, prefer the route with the lowest MED metric attribute. This comparison is made only if the neighboring autonomous system is the same for all routes considered, unless the **bgp always-compare-med** router configuration command is enabled.

Note The most recent Internet Engineering Task Force (IETF) decision regarding BGP MED assigns a value of infinity to the missing MED, making the route lacking the MED variable the least preferred. The default behavior of BGP routers running some Cisco IOS software releases is to treat routes without the MED attribute as having a MED of 0, making the route lacking the MED variable the most preferred. To avoid this situation and configure the router to conform with the IETF standard, you can use the **bgp bestpath med missing-as-worst** router configuration command.

9. Prefer the external BGP (eBGP) path over the iBGP path. All confederation paths are considered internal paths.

10. Prefer the route that can be reached through the closest IGP neighbor (the lowest IGP metric). The router will prefer the shortest internal path within the autonomous system to reach the destination (the shortest path to the BGP next hop).

11. If the following conditions are all true, insert the route for this path into the IP routing table:

    a. Both the best route and this route are external.

    b. Both the best route and this route are from the same neighboring autonomous system.

    c. The **maximum-paths** router configuration command is enabled.

Note The eBGP load sharing can occur at this point, which means that multiple paths can be installed in the forwarding table.

12. If multipath is not enabled, prefer the route with the lowest IP address value for the BGP router ID. The router ID is usually the highest IP address on the router or the loopback (virtual) address but might be implementation-specific. Best practice is to manually configure the router ID.

Designing Scalable iBGP Networks

This section highlights the design limitations in large-scale iBGP networks and then discusses the possible solutions to overcome these limitations in detail.

iBGP Scalability Limitations

BGP can provide a controlled interconnection between multiple routing domains that can be running different IGPs and also can support MPLS VPNs. By design, IBGP requires a full mesh of BGP peers to function.

As discussed earlier, the typical BGP protocol behavior is that IBGP speakers do not re-advertise routes that are learned via IBGP peer to other IBGP peers. This is to prevent information from circulating between IBGP speaking routers in a routing information loop or cycle. Therefore, a full mesh of IBGP sessions between routers is needed to propagate all the routing information to all IBGP peers in a BGP AS.

The main concern with the full-mesh IBGP peering sessions approach is that the full-mesh peering can get unmanageable really fast, due to the large administrative overhead of maintaining many peering sessions and BGP polices. Therefore, this approach does not scale well as the network grows.

In general, for n peers in an IBGP full mesh, each router would have $(n - 1)$ peers. There are $n * (n - 1) / 2$ peerings in total, meaning that each peer would need the CPU, memory, and bandwidth to manage updates and peer status for all the other routers. That's why this full mesh "flat and unstructured" design is not cost-effective to scale for large networks.

For example, a router with a BGP AS that contains 50 routers requires $(50 * (50 - 1)) / 2 = 1225$ IBGP sessions. Imagine the number of sessions (and the associated router configuration) that would be required for a single AS containing 1000 routers.

BGP has the following primary approaches to scale IBGP and to overcome the shortcomings of IBGP full-mesh design:

- BGP route reflectors (RR)
- BGP confederations

IBGP Scalability Solutions

This section describes each of the BGP design approaches and then discusses BGP RR in greater detail because it is more applicable to enterprise-grade networks. Although BGP confederation is more commonly used in large-scale service provider types of networks (such as global service providers and service provider networks under different administrative authorities), it is also a valid solution for large-scale enterprise networks. However, as you will see later in this chapter, BGP RR offers a more flexible and simplified solution to enterprise-grade networks to overcome IBGP full-mesh limitations; therefore, it is most commonly used in this type of network.

BGP Route Reflectors

As discussed earlier in this chapter, the natural IBGP behavior is that a regular IBGP speaking router is not allowed to re-advertise any IBGP routes that it learns from its IBGP peers. When a special kind of IBGP node is introduced, this rule can be relaxed; therefore, it is referred to as a route reflector.

The *BGP Route reflector (RR)* is an IBGP speaker that reflects or re-advertises routes that are learned from IBGP peers to some of its other IBGP peers by modifying the classical IBGP split-horizon rule. In other words, the BGP RR facilitates to a particular router (IBGP speaker) to forward incoming IBGP updates to an outgoing IBGP session under certain conditions. This behavior makes the RR router the focal point for IBGP sessions and updates within a BGP AS. Therefore, it is referred to as a route reflector. This, in turn, helps to scale BGP networks to handle large-scale IBGP peers and sessions without adding complexity to the manageability and flexibility of the network (see Figure 5-4)

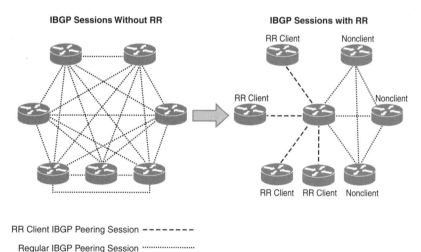

Figure 5-4 *IBGP Design Optimization with BGP RR*

In general, *route reflection* is a process on a route reflector router; it involves re-advertising the received routes from a specific peer to other peers. From a design point view, to properly deploy route reflectors in your BGP network, you need to select the best candidates for the role (in terms of location and hardware resources) to enable the route reflector functionality. Configuration of the route reflector is done on the route reflector itself to identify which IBGP peers are route reflector clients. Therefore, the more centrally located the BGP RR, the better the design will be, such as the advertised optimal path from the BGP RR to its clients. After route reflectors are introduced, the number of peerings in a network with tens of routers drops significantly.

From a configuration point of view, implementing route reflectors is fairly simple and can be done incrementally. Apart from defining route reflectors as peers, no special configuration is needed on the clients themselves. Each client router needs to be configured as a client on the route reflector or on multiple route reflectors. Unnecessary peers can then be removed from the configuration on the client router. Each IBGP speaker can have a mix of direct IBGP sessions with other peers and IBGP sessions with the BGP RRs. In general, though, a well-designed route reflector client should ideally peer only with the route reflectors. That is the case unless there is a special requirement that mandates adding a limited number of direct IBGP sessions between IBGP speakers, such as to avoid a suboptimal path advertised by a BGP RR.

Furthermore, it is important that network designers understand the different terminologies and functions in a BGP environment designed with route reflectors. In general, three different IBGP speakers are used in this environment: RR, RR client, and non-RR client (see Figure 5-5).

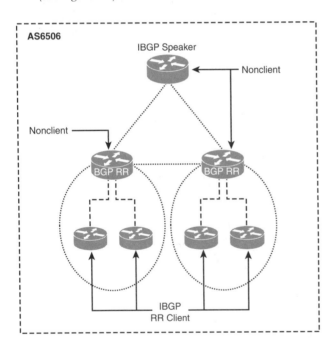

Figure 5-5 *IBGP Speaker Types in an RR Environment*

A *route reflector client* is a peer of a route reflector node. It can send and receive reflected routes from the route reflector routers. To define an IBGP peer as a route reflector client on a route reflector, the peer must specifically be designated as a client by a special BGP configuration option.

On the other hand, a *non-RR client* (also known as a nonclient) is a regular peering definition on a route reflector, with a peer that is not specifically configured as a route reflector client. Because this is a normal IBGP peering session, each route reflector must still be fully IBGP-meshed with nonclients to maintain full IP reachability. Also, as shown in Figure 5-5, the nonclients are normal IBGP speakers; thus, a full-mesh IBGP peering session among them is required to maintain full reachability.

Whether route reflectors can be RR clients or nonclients to the other route reflectors in the BGP network depends on the topology and design requirements.

As a result, route reflectors significantly reduce meshing within clusters. However, all mesh links outside the cluster must be maintained on the route reflector for the route reflector clients to receive IP information from IBGP speakers outside the cluster via the route reflector.

Note The concept of route reflector clusters is discussed later in this chapter.

BGP Confederations

The other possible way to scale your BGP network is to introduce BGP confederations. *BGP confederations* (described in IETF RFC 5065) divide a large BGP autonomous system into multiple smaller autonomous systems within the original AS. With this approach, the small autonomous systems exchange BGP updates between them using a special EBGP session, commonly referred to as *intraconfederation EBGP* sessions. However, the outer or containing AS (known as the confederation AS) is all that is visible to the outside world (peering autonomous systems).

For BGP to avoid any potential loops within an AS, BGP confederations insert information, using the BGP AS path, into BGP routes in which IBGP speakers within a subautonomous system can recognize the full BGP AS path. This recognition includes the subautonomous system AS numbers, so it ignores any route that has the local subautonomous system number (based on the typical IBGP split-horizon loop-prevention mechanism).

For example, as illustrated in Figure 5-6, each of the inner autonomous systems in a smaller sub-AS uses a different AS number, which is typically chosen from the private AS number range 64512 through 65534. Meanwhile, external peering autonomous systems only see the AS number 500 as the peering AS (sub-AS numbers are invisible to the external autonomous systems).

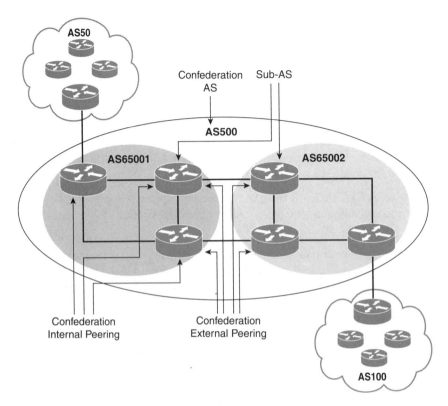

Figure 5-6 *BGP Confederations*

As a result, with this approach BGP confederations limit the full-mesh requirement to be only within a sub-AS rather than between all BGP speakers across the network. This lowers the number of total needed IBGP sessions among BGP speakers within a BGP AS. In addition, in very large BGP networks, you can introduce the concept of route reflectors within each sub-AS to further scale the design and simplify its manageability within each sub-AS.

Commonly, BGP confederations are used when you need to partition your network based on structural or geographic requirements. In addition, because with BGP considerations, each sub-AS can run a completely different IGP, it is suitable for large BGP environments under different administrative authorities. The reason is that each stub-AS can have its own routing policies and IGP without impacting external BGP peering sessions with other autonomous systems.

Another common scenario of using BGP confederations is during companies' mergers, when there is a need to merge two BGP networks. This approach offers easier migration than using BGP RRs typically using private AS numbering, into a consolidated network. The newly created confederation can have a common public AS number when communicating with the rest of the Internet.

BGP Confederations Versus BGP Route Reflectors

From network design point of view, the typical question someone may ask is, "Which design approach is better to scale a BGP network?" To answer this question, you, as a network designer or architect, first need to identify the following nontechnical factors:

- What is the targeted network? Is it an enterprise or service provider? This will help you understand the targeted environment; for example, BGP RR is usually a good fit for enterprise networks but not always.

- What is the current IGP structure of the network? Is it a single IGP domain or multiple IGP domains? If there are multiple IGP domains, BGP may be a good fit if the IGP cannot be restructured.

- Who manages the network? Is it under a single administrative authority or multiple? BGP confederation facilitates maintaining individual sub-BGP domains "AS per domain" under one global BGP ASN.

- What is the impact on the business of any downtime? Is it acceptable or not? For example, migrating a flat IBGP full-mesh network to BGP confederations may introduce some downtime on certain parts of the network during the migration process.

In general, route reflectors are simpler to migrate to and relatively simple to use, while confederations are more flexible about IGP and policy. Table 5-1 compares how confederations and route reflectors provide various IBGP scaling features, and, based on the targeted network and the design requirements, you can select the approach that is a best fit for your design.

Table 5-1 *BGP Confederations Versus BGP Route Reflectors*

	Confederation	**Route Reflector**
Loop prevention	AS confederation set	Originator or cluster ID
Break up a single AS	Subautonomous systems	Clusters
Redundancy	Multiple connections between subautonomous systems	Client connects to several reflectors
External connections	Anywhere in the network	Anywhere in the network
Multilevel hierarchy	Reflectors within subautonomous systems	Hierarchical clusters
May introduce suboptimal routing to other peering ASs	No	Yes
Policy control	Along outside borders and between subautonomous systems	Along outside border
Migration	Very difficult (impossible in some situations)	Moderately easy

BGP Route Reflector Design

This section focuses on the BGP route reflectors design, due its suitability and popularity in enterprise-grade networks. The subsequent sections cover the different BGP RR design considerations and the limitations that BGP RR may introduce and how to avoid them.

Route Reflector Split-Horizon Rule

Split-horizon rules are relaxed in the route reflector design scenario. With these modified rules, the route reflector takes over the communication for the route reflector clients, passing along all the messages that they would normally transmit directly, via a peering session. The route is forwarded according the following rules:

- If a route reflector receives a route from an EBGP peer:
  - It sends the route to all clients and nonclients.
- If a route reflector receives a route from a *client*:
  - It reflects the route to all clients and nonclients and to all EBGP peers.
  - The route is also reflected *back to the sender* (and then discarded at the sender).
- If a route reflector receives a route from a *nonclient*:
  - It reflects the route to *all clients*, but *not to nonclients*.
  - Nonclients are fully mashed.
  - It sends the route to all EBGP peers.

Table 5-2 summarizes the different combinations of peers and the split-horizon rules that apply to each of them.

Table 5-2 *BGP Peer-Forwarding Rules*

Incoming Update From	Is Forwarded To
EBGP peer	All peers (IBGP and EBGP)
Nonclient IBGP peer	EBGP peers and IBGP clients
Client IBGP peer	All peers (including sender)

In addition, as per the typical BGP behavior, the route that is to be reflected must be the best route to a specific destination in the BGP table of the route reflector. If an identical route is received on the route reflector from two or more different clients, under normal circumstances, only one is reflected to other peers. One of the disadvantages of this behavior in a BGP RR environment is that it may introduce suboptimal routing and break traffic load-balancing/sharing requirements over multiple paths.

Note You can modify the default BGP behavior in a BGP RR scenario using some advanced features and techniques such as BGP ADD-PATH feature to overcome the limitations highlighted here. However, if you want to modify the default behavior, you must plan carefully and test to avoid introducing instability and some other unforeseen network issues.

BGP Route Reflectors Redundancy Design Options and Considerations

In a BGP environment designed with BGP route reflectors, the clients may have any number of EBGP peers but typically have IBGP sessions only with their available route reflector within the BGP AS. As a result, if the single-route reflector fails, its clients can no longer send BGP updates to, or receive them from, the rest of the peers within the BGP AS. Therefore, the route reflector is considered as a single point of failure in the design, and typically, to avoid this single point of failure, you need to introduce a redundant route reflector to the network, as shown in Figure 5-7.

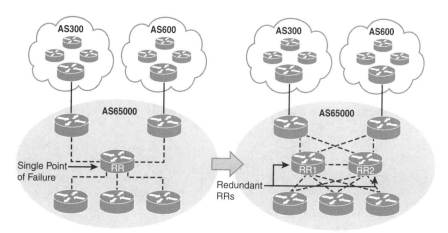

Figure 5-7 *BGP RR Redundancy*

Note In this figure, it is assumed that physical connectivity follows the same layout of the shown IBGP sessions.

As shown here, to achieve a reliable redundant RR design, redundant RR routers must be supported by redundant physical network links and BGP sessions. This allows the BGP RR clients to establish BGP sessions with multiple route reflectors using the available redundant physical paths.

In this type of design (redundant), typically both route reflectors receive the same IBGP update from their clients, and both reflect the update to the rest of the clients. Additionally, both route reflectors receive updates from the full mesh and reflect those updates to their clients. As a result, each client receives two copies of all routes. Under certain circumstances, particularly when you use weights on IBGP sessions to influence BGP route selection, improper route reflection can result in an IBGP routing loop that is impossible to detect. Extra BGP attributes are thus necessary to prevent these routing loops. Consequently, the concept of clusters was introduced to prevent IBGP routing loops when using route reflectors in your network. This concept is covered in the subsequent section in more detail.

Route Reflector Clusters

Route reflector clusters prevent IBGP routing loops in redundant route reflector designs. Therefore, you, as the network designer, need to properly identify which route reflectors and their clients will form a cluster; then you can assign to the cluster a cluster ID number that is unique within the BGP AS. In large-scale networks, a BGP AS can be divided into multiple route reflector clusters, as shown in Figure 5-8.

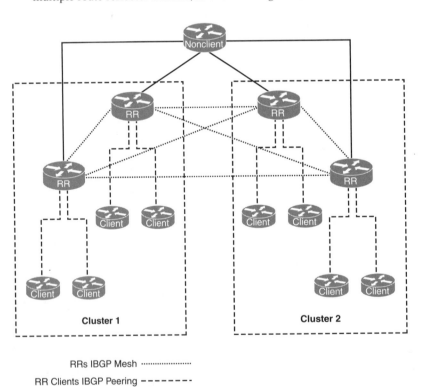

Figure 5-8 *BGP Route Reflector Clusters*

With this design approach, the clients will peer with all route reflectors within the cluster for redundancy. On the other hand, the route reflectors from different clusters need to be fully meshed with each other to maintain full end-to-end reachability across the entire network. However, in some large BGP networks, a BGP route reflector can be defined as a client of another route reflector. This hierarchical design is considered an exception to support very large networks with multiple route reflector clusters. This design approach is discussed later in this chapter.

Note If any router does not support route reflector client functionality, it should be fully meshed with the route reflectors from all clusters as well as with other nonclients, if there are any.

Route Reflector Cluster ID

Technically, in BGP the cluster ID number can be either explicitly configured in the route reflectors or, if it is not explicitly configured, the router ID of the router is used as the cluster ID. The clients, on the other hand, should not be configured with this information.

There are two design approaches to assigning the cluster ID. One approach allocates the same cluster ID to all the route reflectors in a cluster (see Figure 5-9). With this approach, the cluster is called a redundant cluster. Because the cluster ID is identical between the route reflectors in this approach, the routes that are exchanged between route reflectors are discarded because of the cluster-list entry, thus saving resources. (The cluster list and its usability in scenarios like this are discussed in the subsequent section.) However, it can lead to missing routes and suboptimal routing in corner cases where certain BGP sessions go down due to a physical link failure, misconfiguration, or software fault.

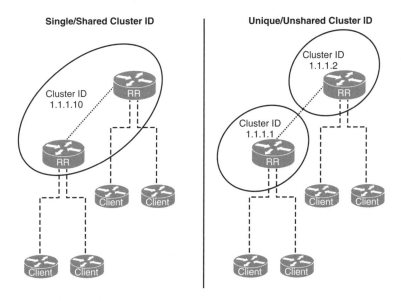

Figure 5-9 *Cluster ID with Single ID (Left) and Multiple IDs (Right)*

The other design approach is to allocate an identical cluster ID to each route reflector, as shown in Figure 5-9. This is also known as overlapping clusters. With this design approach, the clients still connect to two route reflectors for redundancy, but from this perspective each route reflector represents a separate cluster. For the route reflectors to prevent routing information loops, each route reflector adds the router ID of the reflector to the cluster list of routes that it reflects between IBGP speakers. In addition, to further optimize the BGP route selection to accommodate this type of topology, you modify the BGP route selection process so that it includes the criteria of the length of the cluster list. This means routes with a shorter cluster list are preferred to the ones with a longer list.

Loop-Prevention Mechanisms

In a BGP network with multiple route reflectors, to prevent dangerous loops of information, you can use the following nontransitive optional BGP attributes:

- BGP Originator-ID
- BGP Cluster-List

The *BGP Originator-ID attribute* helps prevent loops of routing information in a scenario in which a route is reflected on the route reflector toward other clients. The route reflector sets the Originator-ID attribute of the route to the router ID of the originating router. (The originating router ID is an IBGP peer that injects a route into the BGP AS via an EBGP session or using BGP **network** CLI argument.) As a result, any router that receives a route with its own router ID in the Originator-ID attribute silently ignores that route. For example, in the scenario depicted in Figure 5-10, when RR1 receives the external route advertised by R1, it sets the Originator-ID to the R1 router ID. Therefore, even if the iBGP session from RR1 to RR2 has a higher Local-Preference set (which leads RR1 to prefer the path over the IBGP session with RR2), this situation does not generate any loop. The reason is that when the route is advertised back to R1 with its own Originator-ID, it is discarded by R1.

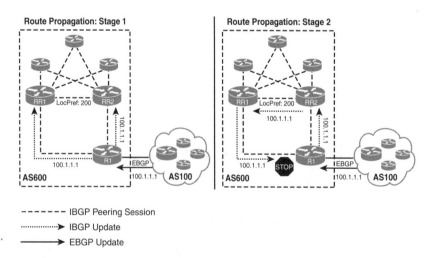

Figure 5-10 *BGP Loop Prevention Using Originator-ID*

> **Note** The scenario in the figure assumes the default behavior in Cisco IOS software, where both RRs are in different clusters; therefore, the prefixes advertised between each other will be accepted.

The *Cluster-List attribute*, on the other hand, offers a loop avoidance mechanism when multiple route reflectors reflect the route in a scenario where there might be many layers of route reflectors in the network. Cluster-List is a sequential list of Cluster IDs, which prepends router IDs (or cluster IDs if configured) of the route reflectors that have reflected the route along the way. You might consider the reflection path that the route has passed. If a route reflector finds its router ID in the Cluster-List, it discards the route as a possible loop.

Therefore, to accommodate these attributes with the typical BGP path selection, you modify the BGP path selection rules to select the best route in scenarios in which a router might receive reflected and nonreflected routes or several reflected routes, as summarized next:

- The traditional BGP path selection parameters, such as weight, local preference, origin, and MED, are compared first.
- If these parameters are equal, the routes that are received from EBGP neighbors are preferred over routes that are received from IBGP neighbors.
- When a router receives two IBGP routes, the nonreflected routes (routes with no originator-ID attribute) are preferred over reflected routes.
- The reflected routes with shorter cluster lists are preferred over routes with longer cluster lists. If the additional route-reflector–oriented selection criteria do not yield a decision, the rest of the traditional BGP path selection criteria will be considered.

From a design point of view, the introduction of the modified path selection rule makes it possible to use route reflectors without setting explicit Cluster IDs. In such a scenario, the Cluster-List attribute relies solely on router IDs of route reflectors. This action adds more resiliency to the network at the expense of slightly higher router resources.

> **Note** For more information, refer to IETF RFC 4456.

Technically, when a route is reflected, the route reflector adds its Cluster ID to the Cluster-List attribute. As already mentioned in this chapter, the Cluster ID value of a route reflector can be derived from one of the following:

- **BGP Cluster ID:** If explicitly configured
- **BGP Router ID:** If Cluster ID is not explicitly configured

The following two examples explain how the Cluster ID works in each of these cases.

As illustrated in Figure 5-11, if you are using a single cluster with two route reflectors that are configured with the identical Cluster ID of 10.10.10.254, when Client A sends a route update to both reflectors, the reflectors reflect the route to other clients and to each other. As soon as RR1 sends the update to RR2, RR2 inspects the Cluster-List of the route and finds its Cluster ID in it; therefore, it must discard the route. The same happens with the route from RR2 to RR1.

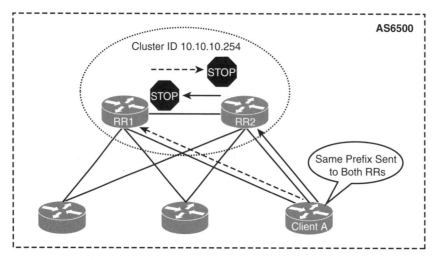

Figure 5-11 *Single Cluster ID*

In contrast, if you are using overlapping clusters, with two route reflectors having their router IDs set as the Cluster IDs as illustrated in Figure 5-12, this approach typically puts them into different clusters yet sharing common clients—hence, overlapping clusters. Based on that, when Client B sends a route update to RR1 and RR2, the route reflectors reflect the routes to their clients and nonclients. The difference is that, for a route from RR1 to RR2, RR2 does not detect its own Cluster ID in the Cluster-List, so it accepts the route. Now RR2 has the same route, which is sent from two sources, Client B and RR1. Because the Cluster-List attribute of the route from Client B (empty) is shorter than the same attribute of the route coming from RR1 (10.10.10.1), the route from Client B is considered the best path for that destination. The clients will end up with multiple copies of routes, but again each client selects the best path that is based on the same selection process.

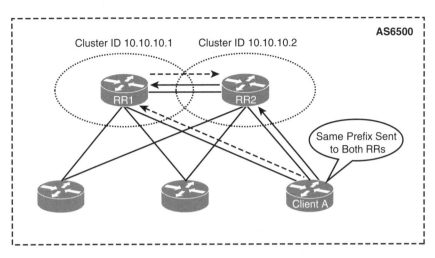

Figure 5-12 *Overlapping Clusters (Unique ID)*

Congruence of Physical and Logical Networks

In some scenarios, the client routers have dual IBGP sessions to two route reflectors; however, there is actually a single physical connection to a single-route reflector router. Therefore, these routers form a nonredundant cluster. Even though the client has dual IBGP sessions to two route reflectors, the router that is designated as the route reflector (physically connected) in the cluster is already a single point of failure in this physical design because a failure of this router prevents the clients in the cluster from reaching the rest of the network. Therefore, there is no actual benefit of introducing another route reflector.

Although the preferred way of designing the route reflector network is by using a redundant cluster, this approach relies on the underlying physical network redundancy. Ideally, when you are considering multiple clusters, the route reflectors should be fully meshed, unless there is a hierarchical route reflector design, which is covered in the following section.

For example, the scenario depicted in Figure 5-13 has two primary physical design issues, which in turn impact the IBGP design. The first issue is that R1 has no physical link to RR2. This means the IBGP session between R1 and RR2 is useless, because if RR1 fails, R1 is fully isolated. The second issue is that the RR1 and RR2 IBGP session between them go over an RR client (R3). This means if there is any issue with R3, the communication in this BGP network is isolated because some RR clients are single-homed to one RR.

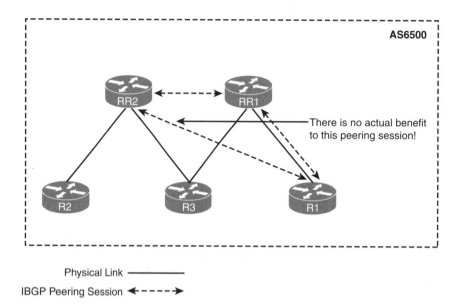

Figure 5-13 *Impact of Physical Links on RR Design*

To fix these two issues, you need to make both the physical and logical (IBGP session) topologies congruent. A simple solution here is to add a physical link between R1 and RR2, as well as a direct physical link between RR1 and RR2, and form the IBGP session between them directly, as shown in Figure 5-14.

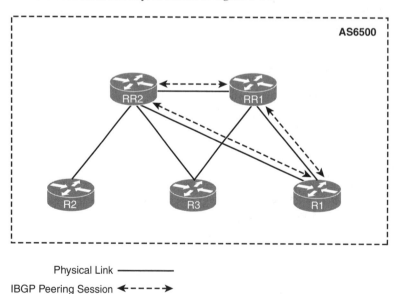

Figure 5-14 *Optimized Physical Network Design to Support Redundant RR Design*

A BGP network can be designed to use dedicated route reflectors that are not actually participating in user data packet processing, but they only deal with route distribution tasks. However, in a non-MPLS environment, this approach may lead to suboptimal routing to external networks.

Hierarchical Route Reflector Design

The typical design of IBGP sessions with route reflectors is that you must use each session to reach a client for the route reflector IBGP split-horizon rules to start working. All other IBGP sessions that are configured on the route reflector are a part of the full mesh. Furthermore, route reflectors must maintain full-mesh IBGP sessions among them to provide an optimal connectivity cross the network. The problem is when this full-mesh portion of the network becomes too large to manage and scale. Therefore, considering a hierarchal route reflector design approach to build route reflector clusters in hierarchies can help reduce the number of full mesh sessions in large networks with a large number of route reflectors. With hierarchies, a router that serves as a route reflector in one cluster can act as a client in another cluster.

In other words, a router that is deployed to be a route reflector still has ordinary IBGP sessions that are part of the full mesh. If these sessions are reduced in number and only a few remain, and the remaining ones reach a second level of route reflectors, a hierarchy of route reflectors is created. Therefore, with this approach, when you build a first level of clusters, the remaining full mesh is smaller than when all routers belonged to a single mesh. In addition, this approach offers the flexibility to introduce multiple levels of hierarchies. For example, if the remaining full mesh is still large in terms of number of router reflectors and IBGP sessions, you may build an extra level of route reflectors to break a large mesh into smaller ones.

As established before, the Cluster-List attribute plays an important role in a hierarchical route reflector BGP network as a key loop-prevention mechanism.

Figure 5-15 shows a sample scenario of hierarchical route reflectors. In this scenario, the first level of hierarchy reduced the original full mesh of 12 routers (all routers in the enterprise network) to a full mesh of 7 routers (the lower three route reflectors, the upper two route reflectors, and two clients). The second level of route reflector clusters was built by creating cluster 27. This second step further reduced the full mesh of 7 routers to a full mesh consisting of only 2 routers (upper route reflectors). Because the RR routers in level 1 are clients of the RRs of level 2, only the two route reflectors in cluster 27 (second level RRs) should be connected in a full mesh.

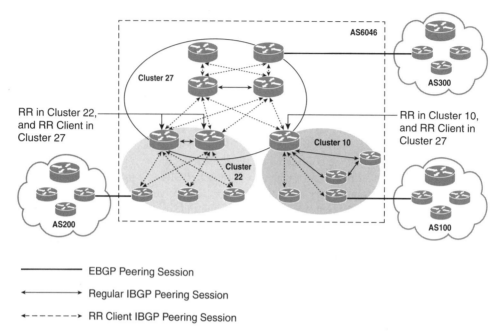

Figure 5-15 *Hierarchal RR Design*

In this scenario, when a client in the lowest level receives an EBGP update,

1. It will forward the update on all configured IBGP sessions to a route reflector.

2. The route reflector (first level) recognizes BGP updates that are received from configured clients and will forward these updates to all other clients and nonclients that use normal IBGP sessions.

3. The update then is sent over an IBGP session to the second-level route reflector.

4. Then, the second-level route reflector recognizes that the update was received from a client, and forwards it to all other clients and into the full mesh to other RR(s) and nonclients.

With this approach, network designers can simplify and overcome the mesh complexity between BGP speakers and RRs by breaking a large mesh domain into smaller ones. Although the network can be divided in to any number of tiers/levels, it is always recommended you keep it simple and aim for two or three levels of hierarchies as a maximum. This is sufficient to optimize very large BGP networks. Nevertheless, hierarchical RR design may lead to suboptimal routing and longer converge time as well as hide additional paths when more than one path exists between any two endpoint RR clients. As mentioned earlier in this chapter, in large-scale networks using some advanced BGP features such as BGP AD-PATH or BGP Diverse Paths, you can optimize this behavior.

Route Reflector Potential Network Design Issues

This section provides a summarized list of some design considerations in BGP environments with route reflectors to avoid any potential or unforeseen issues, especially if network designers deviate from the discussed route reflector network design rules and recommendations in this chapter.

- If route reflectors are not connected with IBGP sessions in a full mesh, some clusters will not have all the routes and will break the full end-to-end reachability requirement.

- In large BGP environments with multiple EBGP exit points, introducing RR to the network may lead to suboptimal routing. Therefore, placing the RR as close to the desired exit point as possible helps optimize this behavior. Alternatively, advanced features such as BGP ADD-PATH can be considered with careful planning.

- If a client has IBGP sessions with some route reflectors in a cluster but not with all of them, the client might miss some BGP routes.

- If a client has IBGP sessions to route reflectors that belong to different clusters, the client will forward the BGP update from the client into the full mesh with different cluster IDs in the Cluster-List attribute. When the BGP update enters the mesh, it will reach the other route reflector, which will, unnecessarily, accept the route as valid and forward it into its cluster. This situation, in turn, causes unnecessary duplication of updates to the clients. However, this approach offers a resilient RR design.

- If a client has IBGP sessions to other clients in the same cluster, those clients will receive unnecessary duplications of updates.

- Modification of route attributes on route reflectors before reflecting the routes can lead to suboptimal routing or even potentially broken networks.

Enhancing the Design of BGP Policies with BGP Communities

BGP communities are designed to give network operators the flexibility to apply complex policies to large numbers of routes alongside built-in mechanisms of routing policy language (RPL) or route maps. This section discusses the structure and some possible application of BGP communities; it also explores ways of implementing reusable policies with the use of BGP community strings.

BGP Community Attribute Overview

A community is a BGP attribute that can be added to any prefix. Communities are transitive optional attributes, which means that BGP implementations do not have to recognize the attribute to pass it on to another AS.

These BGP communities can be applied to any BGP route by using a route map. This communicates to other routers across the network to perform any action based on the tag (community) that is attached to the route. Also, it is technically possible for more than one BGP community to be attached to a single route. However, routers, by default, remove communities in outgoing BGP updates. Therefore, if BGP communities need to be shared with other BGP speakers, this default behavior must be tuned. (In Cisco IOS, you may use the CLI argument **send-community** per BGP neighbor to enable sending *community attributes* to the BGP neighbor.)

BGP communities provide a mechanism to reduce BGP configuration complexity on a router that is controlling the distribution of routing information. It can be read as a 32-bit value or split into two portions. The first two bytes represent an ASN to which the community is intended, and the last two bytes are a value with a predetermined meaning.

The community attribute's value is, in essence, a flat 32-bit integer that can be applied to any set of prefixes. It can be expressed in decimal, hexadecimal, or ordered two 16-bit decimal values that are delimited using a colon. Hexadecimal notation is common in standards, whereas decimal and two-part formats are common in router configurations. Most modern router software displays communities as ASN:VALUE, which is also the easiest human-readable format.

The community ranges are as follows:

- Ranges from 1:0 through 65534:65535 are intended for free use by network administrators; however, there is no inherent meaning to them.

- Ranges from 0:0 to 0:65535 and 65535:0 through 65535:65535 are reserved.

Well-known communities fall into the reserved range group and, as opposed to user-defined communities, they do have a specific meaning.

Well-Known BGP Communities

IETF RFC 1997 and RFC 3765 defined a set of standard well-known community values that help routers in a BGP environment to perform a specific, predefined action when they receive a route marked with a predefined community. The action any given router performs is based on that community setting:

- **no-advertise:** This community instructs a BGP-speaking router not to send the tagged prefix to any other neighbor, including other IBGP routers

- **no-export:** If a router receives an update carrying this community, it does not propagate that update to any external neighbors, except intraconfederation external neighbors. The **no-export** attribute is the most widely used predefined community attribute.

- **no-export-subconfed:** This community has a similar meaning to no-export, but it keeps a route within the local AS (or member AS within the confederation). The route is not sent to external BGP neighbors or to intraconfederation external neighbors. This community is also known as the local-as community.

■ **no-peer:** This community is used in situations in which traffic engineering control over a more specific prefix is required, but to constrain its propagation only to transit providers and not peers. The community does not have good support from major vendors and might require manual implementation.

Cisco devices also recognize the **Internet** community, which is not a standards-based well-known community with a predefined value of 0:0. In Cisco IOS, the **internet** keyword is used to match any community in the community lists. In other words, it is a catchall statement at the end of a community list. These standard communities enable network designers and operators to achieve complex BGP policy requirements in a flexible and easy-to-manage manner across single and different BGP autonomous systems.

BGP Named Community List

The *BGP community lists feature* (Cisco IOS/IOS XE/IOS XR) introduces a new type of community list, the named community list. A named community list can be configured with regular expressions and with numbered community lists. The *BGP named community lists feature* enables the network operator to assign meaningful names to community lists.

All rules of numbered communities apply to named community lists except that there is no limitation on the number of community attributes that can be configured for a named community list. Although both standard and expanded community lists (Cisco IOS/IOS XE) have a limitation of 100 community groups that can be configured within each type of list, a named community list does not have this limitation.

For example, the following sample output is displayed when you enter the **show ip community-list** Cisco IOS command. The output of this command displays the community list name or number and any configured route map clauses:

```
Router# show ip community-list
Named Community standard list COMMUNITY_LIST_NAME
    permit 1234:123 9876:321
    permit 5678:123 9876:321
    permit 1234:123 64984:1
    permit 5678:123 64984:1
Named Community expanded list COMMUNITY_LIST_NAME_TWO
    permit 1
    deny 2
```

Planning for the Use of BGP Communities

In your work as a network designer or operator, considering the use of BGP communities in your network should involve careful planning prior to the deployment in order to avoid breaking any network communication and to ensure that the used BGP communities are in alignment with BGP policy requirements.

To plan effectively, you first must define the routing administrative policy. For example, you need to identify what to filter at what point and how to modify route attributes to influence traffic flows to suit your company's requirements. One of the common deciding factors in creating a routing policy and path section is the cost and reliability of routing traffic over the available WAN links. This decision ideally has to be made during the planning stage.

Next, you have to design the community scheme to fit the individual goals of the policy. When your policy is defined and a community scheme is in place and documented, you deploy the community system by configuring route maps on your devices. This step includes tagging routes and acting on the tags, depending on the position of the router in the network and policy direction. Outbound policy will differ from the inbound policy for a peer or a group of peers.

The community list is an important and flexible tool at your disposal for grouping communities, which is used in the overall process to identify and filter routes by their common attributes.

Also, at this stage, you should plan the design of the BGP communities' scheme and should make the effort to document the values and meaning of your communities in as much detail as possible. Because the subsequent changes might prove difficult after the network is in production, the planning stage is vital for optimal and effective BGP communities and polices design. For example, the community 65000:12345, if tagged at the point of origin, can be used to signal the rest of the BGP network that this route is from area 1 and cities 23 and 45 for some special meaning on which you will base the filtering policy.

You can assign multiple community values to a single route if required, which is a flexible capability because it will appear as a series of communities that are attached to a route. Then, depending on the defined BGP policy, BGP can consider one, some, or all community tags to be processed at peering points.

Case Study: Designing Enterprise wide BGP Policies Using BGP Communities

In this case study, the ABC Corp. enterprise network is composed of the ABC headquarters and two branches that are connected over WAN links. Each location has multiple sites or buildings that are connected with high-speed metro Ethernet links, as shown in Figure 5-16.

Case Study: Designing Enterprise wide BGP Policies Using BGP Communities   173

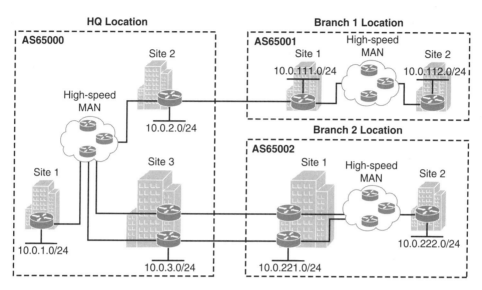

Figure 5-16 *ABC Corp. Enterprise Network*

As shown here, the ABC Corp. headquarter and Branch 1 are connected over single WAN link, while Branch 2 has redundant WAN links to the headquarter site.

To be able to precisely control the routing information exchange between locations, BGP was selected as the routing protocol. The design includes the use of multiple AS numbers and EBGP running between the headquarter and branch locations. Technically, each location is free to use any IGP it deems best fit for the job.

Figures 5-16, 5-17, and 5-18 focus only on the relevant parts for this example. In other words, inside each autonomous system there can be route reflectors or a full-mesh topology. However, it makes no practical difference for the purpose of this case study. Therefore, this information is omitted here because the focus is not on the route exchange within any single AS. Instead, the important part is how the routes tagged with different BGP communities are exchanged between autonomous systems.

For this case study, the emphasis is placed on the edge of each AS, which is the most convenient place to enforce BGP policies. Also, in this case study, you see how BGP communities can help network operators overcome the complexity of managing a large number of ALCs or prefix lists that may induce errors when the network grows in size and makes it difficult to scale.

Enterprise BGP Policy Requirements

ABC Corp. requires all routes to be color coded, depending on the point of origin of the route.

The policy gets a little more restrictive for certain selected routes that should be reachable only from headquarters, but no other branches.

Branch 2, being connected with multiple links to the headquarters, should be able to control both inbound and outbound direction of the traffic on its own, without network administrators from headquarters needing to change any settings on their routers. This capability is implemented by using signaling communities, which indicate the required local preference needs to be set for specifically tagged routes when they arrive on the headquarters' routers. This way, Branch 2 can influence the return path of the traffic and can change primary links based only on its own side router configuration.

BGP Community Solution Design

Structured and standard BGP community values need to be defined in order to meet the requirement described in the preceding section. The following values are used across the ABC BGP network:

- Company headquarters will tag the routes that it originates with
    - 65000:5001 for site 1
    - 65000:5002 for site 2
    - 65000:5003 for site 3
- Branch 1 will tag the routes that it originates with
    - 65001:5101 for site 1
    - 65001:5102 for site 2
- Branch 2 will tag the routes that it originates with
    - 65002:5201 for site 1
    - 65002:5202 for site 2

Additionally, a system is put in place that sets certain attributes on hardware routers in the inbound direction based on the tags set in the branch routers that originate these routes.

If the branch routers tag their routes with

- 65000:99, the headquarters ingress policy will set the no-export community to the router.
- 65000:200, the headquarters ingress policy will set local preference to 200 for this route.
- 65000:300, the headquarters ingress policy will set local preference to 300 for this route.

Figure 5-17 illustrates the allocation of the community values by the relevant routes at their point of origin.

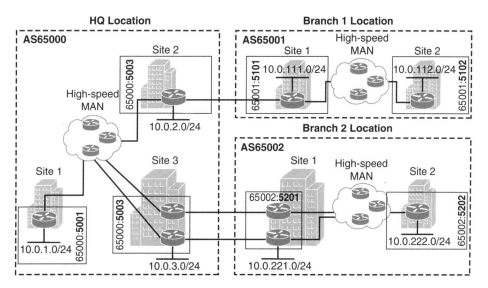

Figure 5-17 *BGP Community Values per Site (Point of Origin)*

At this stage, after BGP community values are defined, it is not difficult to implement a policy that is based on route color filtering, which, for example, would prevent complete traffic blocking between Branch 1 Site 2 and Branch 2 Site 2 (but allow other interbranch traffic). The policy would be implemented at a peering point between ABC headquarters and Branch 1 in the outbound direction, where the headquarters' router would not advertise 65002:5202 tagged routes into Branch 1. On the other side, the two headquarters' routers that peer with Branch 2 would not advertise the routes that are tagged with 65001:5102.

All branch networks would still be completely reachable from the headquarters network.

Solution Detailed Design and Traffic Flow

This section explains in detail the application and outcome of the following points:

- Routes that are tagged at branches with 65000:99 will not be exported out of AS 65000.

- Routes that are tagged at branches with 65000:200 and 65000:300 will be assigned local preference of 200 and 300, respectively, when entering AS 65000.

Figure 5-18 summarizes the whole solution based on BGP community values.

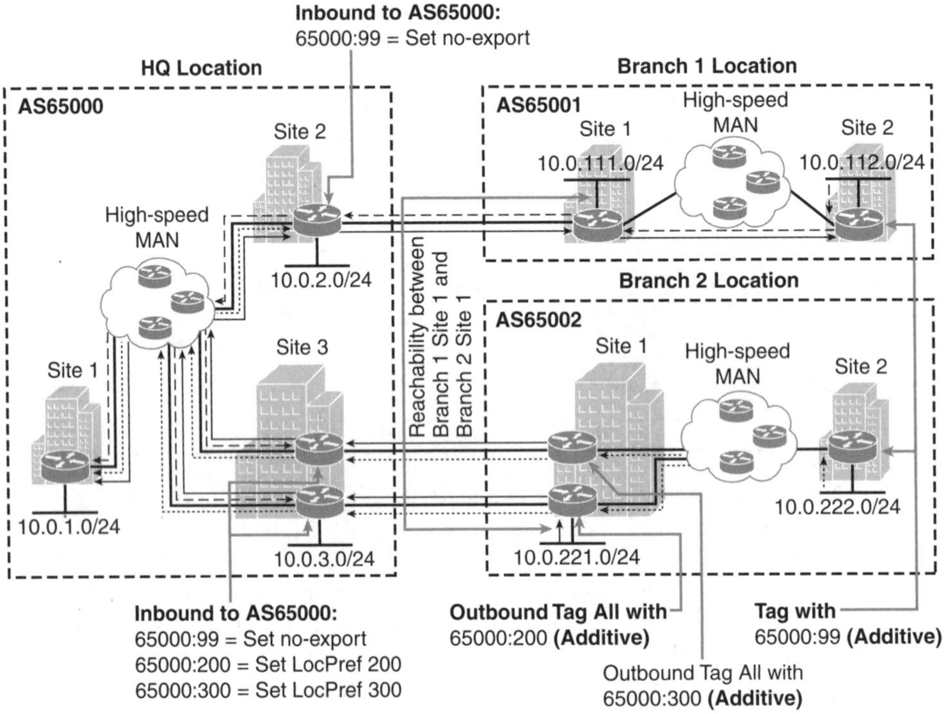

Figure 5-18 *BGP Polices and Route Propagation Based on BGP Community Values*

The following points explain the design depicted in the figure:

- The dotted path/arrow shows the advertisements of the 10.0.222.0/24 through the BGP network. Because it is tagged with the community 65000:99, it will not be advertised beyond AS 65000.

- The dashed path/arrow shows the advertisements of 10.0.112.0/24, which will also be marked as no-export at the entry into AS 65000. As a consequence, it will not be advertised out to AS 65002.

- The straight path/arrow shows the advertisements of network 10.0.221.0/24, which does not have any restrictions, and as such, it will be reached by both headquarters and Branch 1 Site 1. Although this network will be also propagated to Branch 1 Site 2, because the Branch 1 Site 2 route was not advertised toward Branch 2, there will be only one-way communication (broken communication). That's why, in this case only, Branch 1 Site 1 can communicate with Branch 2 Site 1.

- The dotted and straight arrows/routes will be tagged with 65000:300 at the top Branch 2 router and with 65000:200 at the bottom Branch 2 router. As a result, peers of those routers in the headquarters will apply the respective local preferences, thus making the top path better for traffic from headquarters back to Branch 2.

If, in the future, Branch 2 wishes to make the second link more desirable, it could swap the community tags between the top and bottom edge routers. This change requires no changes at the headquarters, if the policy on the headquarters' edge routers is properly set to recognize those communities and apply appropriate local preferences.

> **Note** If you want to preserve the existing communities when applying inbound policies and just append some new ones, always use the **additive** keyword in your router configuration; otherwise, all community values are overwritten.

BGP Load-Sharing Design

Sometimes businesses need to optimize the return on investment of the links they own by utilizing all of them rather than utilizing one link and leaving the other link passive (on cold standby). To achieve this, a mechanism to distribute traffic flows across the available paths is needed; this is also known as load sharing. Load sharing allows a router to distribute the outgoing and incoming traffic among multiple paths. The paths are derived either statically or with dynamic protocols. By default, BGP selects only a single best path and does not perform load balancing. This section explains how to perform load sharing in different scenarios with the use of BGP.

Single-Homing Versus Multihoming

Strictly speaking, *multihoming* is connecting your BGP network to any external network with multiple links. However, depending on the number of ISPs, redundancy requirements, and traffic volume, there can be either a BGP network that is single-homed or multihomed to external networks.

Typically, *single-homed networks* do not provide any redundancy at the ISP level. The address space can be either from the provider-assigned or provider-independent scope; it does not make any difference because the local BGP AS has only one exit point to the Internet.

In contrast, *multihomed networks* provide fully redundant setups, if redundant local routers are used. With this setup, there can be two connectivity models to the outside networks/ISP providers:

- **Single ISP:** With this model, the external ISP may represent a single point of failure if there is any issue within the ISP network. The address space can be either provider-assigned or provider-independent scope; it does not make any difference because the local BGP AS has only one exit AS to the Internet.

■ **Two or more ISPs:** With this model, your enterprise BGP network will connect to at least two ISPs; thus, the use of a provider-independent IP address block is a must. Also, this model offers a higher level of redundancy.

Redundancy is the most notable reason for multihoming. With single-homing, one connection to the Internet means that the network depends on

- Local router (configuration, software, hardware)
- WAN links (physical failure, carrier failure)
- ISP (configuration, software, hardware)

Dual-Homing and Multihoming Design Considerations

To provide a business-driven design that takes into consideration business and applications needs, the design of your multihomed network, policywise, should be derived by the requirements for your traffic flows.

For example, if you need a high-availability–only Internet connection, you may deploy a standard BGP setup where one link acts as the primary link for ingress and egress traffic and the other link operates in standby until the primary fails. If, on the other hand, there is a need for load sharing, as in most cases, you have to use various BGP tools, like local preference, MED, and AS path prepending, to achieve traffic engineering to suit your needs. The use of each tool is different for different scenarios and, as you will learn further on in this section, the way to do it is by implementing different BGP policies. You can do a lot of fine-tuning to get near the desired load-sharing target, but total control over traffic load sharing is difficult to achieve due to the size and unpredictability of traffic flows.

When connecting to multiple exit points from your AS and peering with multiple ISPs, there is a danger that by misconfiguration, you advertise routes that are received from one ISP to the other ISP. Your AS can become a transit area for Internet traffic of other networks, which can cost you money and resources. You can easily avoid this situation by advertising only your assigned address space to all adjacent ISPs (also, you can advertise only your local AS and filter out the other ASs using BGP AS-path filter). The following subsections discuss the design of the different BGP connectivity scenarios to external networks.

Note In this section, the term *dual-homing* refers to the scenario when connecting an enterprise network to a single external ISP, and the term *multihoming* refers to the scenario when connecting an enterprise to two or more external ISPs.

Single-Homed, Multiple Links

The scenario illustrated in Figure 5-19 shows how to achieve load sharing when there are multiple, equal-cost links. In this scenario, the links are terminated in one router at a local AS (corporate network) and in another router at a remote AS (ISP) in a single-homed BGP environment.

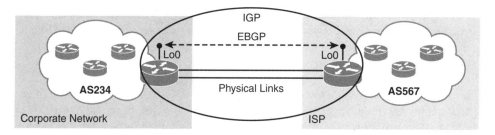

Figure 5-19 *BGP Over Single-Homed Router with Multiple Links*

To facilitate using both links, you must establish the BGP session between loopback interfaces of the EBGP speakers. To achieve this peering, you need to configure the EBGP multihop feature. Without multihop, EBGP sessions can be established only between directly connected devices. Because the two loopback interfaces cannot be directly connected, the multihop feature ensures the session establishment.

Note You may also establish an eBGP session without **ebgp multihop** by disabling the eBGP directly connected check.

In this scenario, an IGP is required (or two static routes with the same administrative distance each point to a different link to reach the remote node loopback IP) between the EBGP speakers over the two links. The reason is that the load sharing in this scenario is implemented on the IGP level, where there can be multiple equal-cost paths between EBGP loopback interfaces, which are serving as the next hop for BGP routes. However, because the loopback interface is not a part of a link between the routers, recursive route lookup is executed on the routers to route traffic across the links.

Multiple equal-cost paths can be utilized by the router on a per packet or per destination basis, depending on the router software and hardware configurations. If you decided to consider per packet load balancing, ensure that this technique does not impact the applications running across the links, because it may lead to some out-of-order packets. And when the packets arrive out of order, the receiving router needs to buffer them and reassemble again, which introduces extra delay.

There are several benefits to the IGP ECMP:

- The underlying physical topology does not affect the EBGP session, meaning only one link has to be active and BGP will work as intended.

- The links can dynamically serve as each other's backup, and IGP will take care of the convergence.

- There is increased bandwidth between EBGP routers for user data traffic with each additional path.

Although static routes can be used in this scenario instead of IGP, if IGP is not used and you opt for static routing between loopbacks, in certain situations, this action can lead to lost traffic because there is no dynamic route exchange and, more importantly, stateful IGP neighbor adjacency. For example, a link can be faulty on the carrier side but still physically operating at the corporate router side, resulting in a healthy static route that leads to a dead end. A static route will exist in the routing table, and the router will route traffic if the physical interface the route is pointing to is up. That being said, this behavior can be optimized if the static route is combined with Cisco IP SLA to ensure that when the remote node is not reachable over a given link (even if the link is physically up), the static route will be taken out from the routing table.

Dual-Homed to One ISP Using a Single Local Edge Router

The scenario depicted in Figure 5-20 shows how to achieve load sharing when multiple links exist between a remote AS and a local AS. These links are terminated in one router at the local AS (corporate network) and on multiple routers at the remote AS (ISP) in a single-homed BGP environment. In this scenario, there are two EBGP sessions between the corporate network and the ISP; each session is established over a separate physical interface.

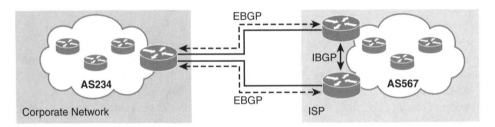

Figure 5-20 *Dual-home Single Router*

In addition, this use case scenario demonstrates the capability to achieve load distribution (ECMP) on the BGP level by using the BGP multipath feature. By default, BGP chooses one best path among the possible equal-cost paths that are learned from one AS. However, you can change the maximum number of parallel equal-cost paths that are allowed.

To make this change, include the **maximum-paths** *paths* command under the BGP configuration with a number between 1 and 6 for the *paths* argument.

The corporate network can fully control the outbound traffic toward the ISP AS, but inbound traffic cannot be controlled completely without the cooperation of the ISP.

For instance, in the scenario depicted in Figure 5-21 (with two separate links going to the ISP), there are several options to consider from a network design point of view.

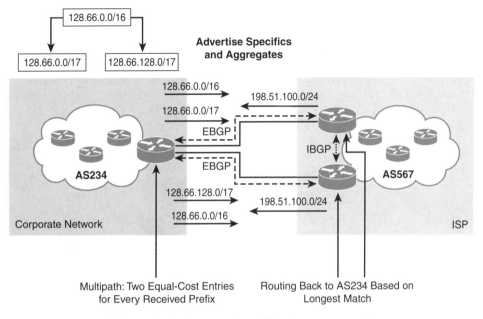

Figure 5-21 *Dual-home Single Router—Load Sharing*

First, you need to identify what is the aim of the multihoming? Is it to achieve redundancy only? This means one link will be active, whereas the other operates in standby. In this case, redundancy can be accomplished by using simple tuning to BGP attributes.

In contrast, if the aim is to achieve load sharing, it can be accomplished in this scenario using several tools, but separately for each direction.

When you are considering the ingress traffic load sharing, you can accomplish it by splitting the corporate network address range in two or more chunks that can be of the same approximate size. In this example, you are splitting the address range in half from 128.66.0.0/16 to get 128.66.0.0/17 and 128.66.128.0/17. Then you will advertise the aggregate prefix and one-half prefix to each EBGP peer, which makes the top link on the figure more preferred for 128.66.0.0/17 and the bottom link more preferred for 128.66.128.0/17. In case the address space is too small to be split, you can use AS path prepending or MED to make one preferred link for all ingress traffic. In this case, note that there is no load sharing because all traffic will use the one selected link; however, you can influence which link is the primary one.

For egress load sharing, you can use the BGP multipath feature on the corporate router side, which then does load balancing of traffic that is based on ECMP. In case you get too many prefixes and the router cannot handle many routes, you can fine-tune load sharing with local preference or weight attributes by setting them for the arriving prefixes. In this way, you can influence that traffic for a prefix that will exit through the desired link. If a router gets two prefixes to the same destination, the one with higher weight or, if weight is not set, higher local preference value will win.

Dual-Homed to One ISP Using Multiple Edge Routers

The scenario depicted in Figure 5-22 shows how to achieve load sharing when there are multiple connections to the same ISP through multiple local routers, where the two ISP EBGP peering sessions are terminated on two separate local routers. Also, in this scenario, an IBGP session between local routers is required to enable BGP route exchange between them.

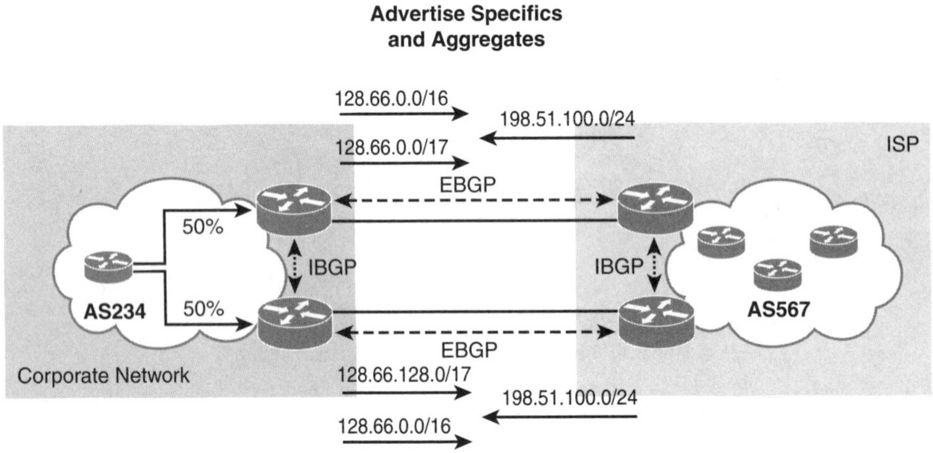

Figure 5-22 *Dual-homing to a Single ISP with Two Edge Routers*

Load balancing for a specific destination (such as a host IP address) over the two external links is not normally possible because BGP chooses the single best path among the networks that is learned from EBGP and IBGP. Load sharing among the multiple paths to AS 456 is the next-best option. With this type of load sharing, traffic to specific networks, which is based on predefined policies, travels through both links. Additionally, each link acts as a backup to the other link in case one link fails.

Furthermore, this scenario still does not make any strict requirements on the type of addressing space that is used by the corporate network. It enables the use of both PA or PI address ranges.

You can achieve load sharing for the ingress direction in this example by splitting the corporate network address range or changing the AS path or MED attribute when sending out routing updates. A similar approach was discussed in a previous scenario in this chapter. In this example (refer to Figure 5-22), you are splitting the address range in half from 128.66.0.0/16 to get 128.66.0.0/17 and 128.66.128.0/17. Then you advertise the aggregate prefix and one-half prefix to each EBGP peer, which will make the top link on the figure more preferred for 128.66.0.0/17 and the bottom link more preferred for 128.66.128.0/17. Again, if AS path or MED is used instead of split address range, load sharing is not an option, just path selection for all traffic.

On the other hand, egress traffic load sharing can be done in two ways: on the edge (BGP) by tuning the BGP Local Preference attribute or internally by relying on FHRP or IGP to distribute the traffic flows to the edge routers.

By manipulating BGP at the edge routers, setting local preference to prefixes as they arrive, you can achieve approximately 50–50 percent distribution of sending traffic across the two links. The prefixes that have higher local preference on the top corporate edge router will have lower local preference on the bottom router and vice versa.

Load balancing of traffic can also be done internally, before it gets to the edge routers. You can distribute the outbound traffic by using an FHRP inside the corporate AS, which would then load balance traffic to the edge routers in approximately equal percentage. Once the traffic hits either of the edge BGP routers, it is routed across the link to the ISP, so it is a matter of how FHRP will distribute the load to get the desired load-sharing ratios. Examples of FHRPs are HSRP and GLBP. Load sharing by using IGP ECMP can be achieved by redistributing 0/0 from BGP into IGP. Then the internal network will have two equal-cost default routes toward the edge BGP routers. However, in both load-sharing approaches, network designers must carefully plan and design BGP polices to avoid asymmetrical routing if it's going to impact the communication of applications running over the network, such as Voice over IP (VoIP).

Multihoming with Two ISPs Using a Single Local Edge Router

Because this design model is based on connecting to two different external ISPs, traffic load balancing to a destination is not an option in a multihomed environment, so again you can only do load sharing. The technical reason behind it is that BGP selects only a single best path to a destination among the BGP routes that are learned from the different ASNs. The idea is to set a better metric for certain routes that are learned from ISP1, and a better metric for other routes that are learned from ISP2.

Note You can alter this default BGP behavior by using the BGP CLI argument **bestpath as-path multipath-relax**, along with the enablement of the BGP multipathing feature in which BGP can treat a route learned from different ASNs the same way to load balance traffic over the available ASNs. However, the other path attributes of the route over the different ASNs must be identical (Weight, Local-Pref, AS-Path length, Origin, and so on) for this capability to work.

To achieve the desired level of flexibility in designing traffic engineering in this design model (multihoming), you, as a network designer, should consider using the PI IP address space because this address space allows the enterprise to advertise it to both ISPs.

From a design point of view, this model requires careful design consideration. For example, to avoid making the enterprise network as a transit AS/path for the two external ISPs (for example, ISP1 and ISP2), it is recommended that you always announce only your PI address space to the ISPs you are directly connected to. If, by mistake, you advertise routes that are received from ISP1 to ISP2, and ISP2's policy is not restrictive enough, your AS will start to participate in the Internet traffic exchange (become a transit AS).

In addition, if AS X, as shown in Figure 5-23, decided that the path to ISP1 from AS X is shorter through your network (via ISP2), it will start sending traffic that is destined for ISP1 to your router. Your router will happily route the traffic to ISP1, but the problem is that this extra traffic might leave your users with no bandwidth for themselves and, as a result, it will impact the overall user experience. Also, this situation raises a high security concern, because external traffic from an unknown network, traffic that could be malicious, will be using your corporate network as a transit path. Therefore, you, as the network designer, need to ensure that only the enterprise-owned PI address range is announced, combined with AS-PATH filtering to permit only routes originating from the enterprise local AS to be advertised.

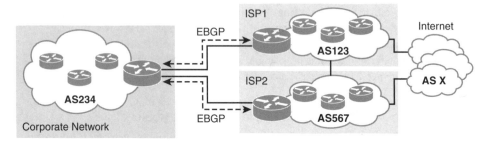

Figure 5-23 *Multihoming: Two ISPs and a Single Local Edge Router*

To achieve load sharing for the ingress direction, you can consider splitting the address space and announcing different chunks to the ISPs. The aggregate is always announced to both ISPs as a best practice because it serves as a backup mechanism if any failure event reaches any of the ISPs. If the address space assigned to you is small (/24 or smaller), the best thing you can do is use active/standby setup by prepending the AS path several times with your ASN. In this way, you achieve redundancy but without load sharing. Figure 5-24 illustrates the possible design to achieve ingress traffic load sharing in this scenario.

Note If the address has a /24 subnet or smaller, it cannot be divided and advertised to both ISPs, because ISPs (and across the Internet) filter small subnets like /24 to avoid propagating a large number of prefixes across the Internet.

Note Using the AS prepending approach, you can achieve active/standby setup to a certain extent, but not 100 percent. The reason is that ISPs usually prefer prefixes that are reachable through their cloud rather than over another inter-ISP link.

BGP Load-Sharing Design   185

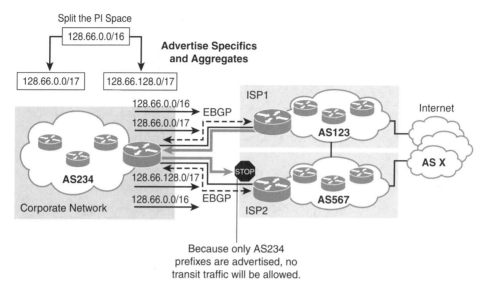

Figure 5-24 *Ingress Traffic: Load Sharing over Multihoming with Two ISPs and a Single Local Edge Router*

To prevent your network from becoming a transit AS, make sure that you advertise only your own PI address space to both ISPs by using outbound route filtering, BGP AS-PATH filtering, or a combination of both.

Note When you are load balancing by splitting the PI space, advertising one-half of the prefixes to one service provider and the other half to the other service provider is usually not the magic solution. You should split the prefixes between the ISPs based on business or policy decisions of ISP connection quality. If you just split the prefixes evenly, you should check if load balancing is unequal and make changes accordingly.

On the other hand, the load sharing for egress traffic when multihomed to two ISPs is possible if you configure local preference of higher values for preferred routes coming from preferred links. In this case, if you are receiving the full Internet routing table from both peers at your corporate router, fine-tuning of egress traffic can be done empirically. Therefore, the distribution of destinations per link (ISP) can be modified until the desired traffic ratios are achieved, by sort of a trial-and-error method. There are many methods of splitting the prefixes. For example, you can split in half based on the first octet, and you can also split them by odd and even principles, and so on.

If you are receiving a default route and a limited set of prefixes from the ISPs, load sharing, while still possible, will not be as precise.

The scenario in Figure 5-25 shows one possible example of how you may achieve load sharing of traffic flows in the egress direction using the following policy design:

- Split incoming prefixes in half and assign local preference.
- Set LocPref = 200 for prefixes 1.x.x.x–128.x.x.x received from ISP1.
- Set LocPref = 200 for prefixes 129.x.x.x–254.x.x.x received from ISP2.
- If traffic distribution is uneven, assign more prefixes to one side.

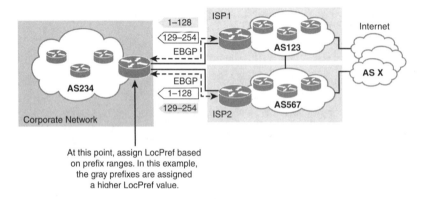

At this point, assign LocPref based on prefix ranges. In this example, the gray prefixes are assigned a higher LocPref value.

Figure 5-25 *Egress Traffic: Load Sharing over Multihoming with Two ISPs and a Single Local Edge Router*

Multihoming with Two ISPs Using Multiple Local Edge Routers

This design model offers the most resilient solution because it's structured of two local routers peering with two different ISPs. Therefore, there will be redundancy at the following elements:

- Local edge routers
- BGP peering sessions
- Physical external links
- ISPs (different providers)

However, this model also has the highest cost; therefore, it's commonly used in large enterprises at their critical and important sites, such as data center Internet edge, that need a high level of service availability.

As shown in Figure 5-26, each edge local router is peering with a router in a different AS/SP, and there is an IBGP session between the local routers. In fact, this IBGP session helps to ensure that both routers are always fully converged in the event one ISP link or an EBGP peering session fails.

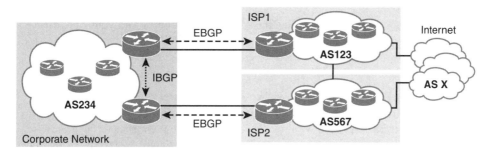

Figure 5-26 *Multihoming: Two ISPs and Two Local Edge Routers*

However, as mentioned in the previous section, you know that one of the design limitations of this model is that load balancing to a destination is not possible in a multihomed environment with two ISPs. BGP selects only the single best path to a destination among the BGP paths that are learned from different ASs, which makes load balancing almost impossible, even with advanced BGP features such as bgp multipath-relax. But load sharing is possible in such multihomed BGP networks. Based on predetermined policies, traffic flow is controlled with different BGP attributes.

As with all multihomed deployments using multiple ISPs, the PI address space is required.

Similar to the multihoming scenario with one local router, in this scenario, again, the load sharing for the ingress traffic is possible by splitting the address space and announcing different chunks to the ISPs. The aggregate is always announced as a best practice because it serves as a backup mechanism if there is a link failure. The primary difference in this model is the IBGP session between the local edge routers is used to assure best convergence in cases of link or router failures, which makes it a highly available setup compared to other scenarios discussed in this section so far (see Figure 5-27).

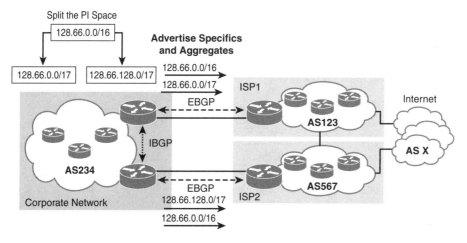

Figure 5-27 *Ingress Traffic: Load Sharing over Multihoming with Two ISPs and Two Local Edge Routers*

If the address space assigned to you is small (/24 or smaller), the best thing you can do is an active/standby setup by prepending the AS path several times with your ASN. Hence, you achieve redundancy without load sharing. Although MED might be considered as a BGP attribute to influence BGP path selection, practically it is not a useful or viable option here as a tool for load sharing because you are dealing with two distinct ISPs.

Load sharing in the egress direction of this scenario, however, is similar to the one with two routers to the same ISP. Local routers need a way to select a proper link for a destination. The goal is accomplished with selectively setting local preference to the routes as they arrive. When there are no failures in the network (see Figure 5-28), traffic flows in this scenario follow the "dotted arrow" routes to reach the network in the range 1–128. This is also applicable to traffic being sent to another edge router. For example, if, on the bottom router, some traffic is received from the inside for a destination that is in-network, in the range 1–128, this traffic is routed to the top router (over the IBGP session between the edge routers) and sent through the top link to ISP1. In the event of the top link or a router or ISP1 failure, the traffic that is destined to 1–128 is instead sent to ISP2.

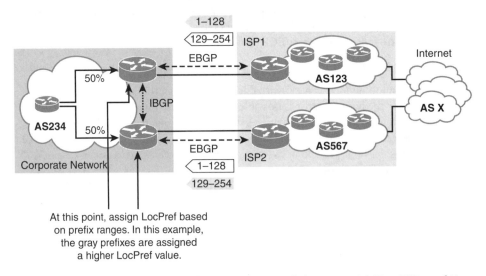

Figure 5-28 *Egress Traffic: Load Sharing over Multihoming with Two ISPs and Two Local Edge Routers*

If you are not using BGP and local preference to distribute the egress traffic, you might consider balancing the traffic internally toward the edge routers, in the same way that was already discussed in a scenario in this section, by using FHRP or redistributing the default route into IGP. In this case, the edge routers should have a simple policy that sends out whatever they receive via the link to their respective ISPs. This policy is, in many cases, the one you get by default in BGP due to the path selection mechanism. If not, you can easily achieve such a policy on corporate edge routers by setting a high weight value for any route that is received from the direct ISP EBGP peering session versus the lower default weight of routes that are received from IBGP (second local edge router connected to the other ISP).

Summary

- Single-homed networks connect to one BGP network (ISP).
- Multihomed networks connect to multiple BGP networks (ISPs).
- Load sharing and redundancy schemes depend on the number of devices and links between the two BGP networks as well as the policy applied to the routers.
- BGP policy on both sides plays a key role in traffic flow patterns.
- IBGP requires full mesh between all BGP-speaking routers. It can be achieved with route reflectors and BGP confederations.
- Route reflectors should be fully meshed. Meshing drives the hierarchical route reflector design on the level of the whole network.
- BGP communities are a means of tagging routes to ensure a consistent filtering or route selection policy.
- Design your community scheme to fit individual goals of route control.
- Load-sharing and redundancy schemes depend on the number of devices and links between the two BGP networks as well as the policy applied to the routers.
- BGP policy on both sides plays a key role in traffic flow patterns.

Review Questions

After answering the following questions, please refer to Appendix A, "Answers to Review Questions," for the answers.

1. Full-mesh BGP is not scalable. Which options loosen the full-mesh requirements? (Select two.)
   a. Route reflectors
   b. IBGP
   c. EBGP
   d. Split horizon
   e. Confederations

2. Which statements are true about confederations? (Select two.)
   a. Confederations can be used with any routing protocol.
   b. Confederations modify the split-horizon rule.
   c. Confederations are IBGP speakers that reflect learned routes from IBGP peers to other IBGP peers.
   d. The AS uses multiple sub-ASs to scale.
   e. Confederations add more information to the AS path.

3. Which two design failures will result in clients receiving duplicate copies of the same route?
   a. Clients not having sessions with all reflectors in a cluster
   b. Clients having sessions with reflectors in several clusters
   c. Clients having IBGP sessions with other clients
   d. Modification of route BGP attributes on route reflectors before reflecting
   e. Having confederations configured in parallel to route reflectors

4. Which statements about BGP communities are true? (Select two.)
   a. The community attribute is a transitive optional attribute.
   b. High-order 16 bits encode the purpose and have local significance.
   c. Low-order 16 bits contain the AS number of the AS that defines the community meaning.
   d. BGP communities are means of tagging routes to ensure a consistent filtering.
   e. The usable scope of communities is 1:0 through 65511:65555.

5. Which statement is true about named community lists?
   a. The limit on the number of named community lists is 255.
   b. The limit on the number of community attributes that you can configure for a named community list is 255.
   c. You cannot use numbered community lists to configure named community lists.
   d. Named community lists can be configured with regular expressions.

6. Match the well-known communities with their descriptions.

   no-advertise   Do not advertise routes to any peer.
   no-export-subconfed   Do not advertise routes to real EBGP peers.
   no-export   Do not advertise routes outside of local AS.
   no-peer   Re-advertise conditionally.

7. Which statement is true about load sharing when you have a multiple-router network connecting to a single ISP?
   a. BGP does load sharing by default.
   b. Load sharing will work only if you have provider-independent space.
   c. Between your local routers, you should have an EBGP session.
   d. Load balancing for a specific destination is normally not possible.

8. Which statement is true about load sharing when you have a single-router network connecting to two ISPs?
   a. You can use BGP multipath.
   b. You can easily use either PA or PI.
   c. For redundancy, advertise routes that you receive from ISP1 to ISP2.
   d. To load share ingress traffic, one option you have is to AS prepend.

9. Which statement is true about load sharing when you have a single router connecting to a single ISP using multiple links?
   a. IGP does the actual load sharing.
   b. You cannot use static routing.
   c. If one link fails, the EBGP session will be lost.
   d. You do not need EBGP multihop configuration.

Chapter 6

IPv6 Design Considerations in the Enterprise

Upon completing this chapter, you will be able to

- Plan IPv6 deployment in an existing enterprise IPv4 network
- Describe the challenges that you might encounter when transitioning to IPv6
- Describe why an organization should consider migrating to IPv6
- Describe the phased approach to deploying IPv6
- Describe the business and network discovery phase in IPv6 deployment
- Describe the assessment phase in IPv6 deployment
- Describe the planning and design phase in IPv6 deployment
- Describe the implementation and optimization phase in IPv6 deployment
- Describe the first steps toward deploying IPv6
- Describe the difference between PI and PA addresses
- Describe where in the network you can start the migration to IPv6
- Describe the migration to IPv6 by using the IPv6 islands concept
- Describe headquarters and branch IPv6 WAN access options
- Describe IPv6 transition mechanisms
- Describe NAT64 and DNS64
- Describe manual tunnels
- Describe tunnel brokers
- Describe 6RD tunneling and 6RD addresses
- Describe DS-Lite

- Describe LISP
- Describe dual-stack
- Describes IPv6 services
- Explain link layer security considerations
- Describe application support
- Describe application adaptation
- Explain application workarounds
- Describe control plane security
- Describe tunneling security considerations
- Explain multihoming

One of the primary drivers to move or transition your network to enable IPv6 is the depletion of IPv4 addresses across the Internet. On September 24, 2015, the American Registry for Internet Numbers (ARIN) issued the final IPv4 addresses in its free pool. This means the need to start considering IPV6 has become a reality and a serious consideration. In addition, IPv6 transition is also driven by continuity and innovation. In other words, continuous growth requires the evolution of architecture to support the growing number of users, new applications, and services such as the Internet of Things (IoT). The transition phase is often long and complex because the main goal is to support both IPv4 and IPv6 protocols in the near future. Translation and tunneling mechanisms can offer intermediate solutions. In any of the deployment methods listed, your goal is to replicate or improve the existing security policies to ensure an uninterrupted business process.

Furthermore, an organization's requirements for IPv6 adoption vary. The fact is that the IPv6 protocol is the future of every network. However, when and how organizations will implement it in their networks is based on a number of factors. Even when implemented, IPv6 will coexist with IPv4 for the foreseeable future, so you should understand the mechanisms that allow that coexistence.

IPv6 Deployment and Design Considerations

Although many organizations find it sufficient to offer their services using their IPv4 allocation, at this moment the next generation of the Internet does not seem possible without IPv6 adoption because the IoT will enable millions, possibly billions of devices to communicate in the near future.

In addition, large content providers already offer their content on both protocol stacks. Service providers have adopted their transport network for IPv6, and large application vendors introduced IPv6 support with a strong road map for the future. Therefore, migrating or transitioning to IPv6 is not an option in modern networks; instead, it's becoming something inevitable. That said, how and when you choose to migrate varies and depends on many factors and variables (technical and nontechnical). This section focuses on the migration or transitioning strategy, along with the different technical approaches you can use to migrate to an IPv6-enabled network.

Note This chapter assumes you have basic knowledge of IPv6 addressing and its structure.

For more information, refer to the following IETF resources:

- RFC 3513, IP Version 6 Addressing Architecture, www.ietf.org
- RFC 2461, Neighbor Discovery for IP version 6 (IPv6), www.ietf.org

When you start any IPv6 design project, following the phased approach depicted in Figure 6-1 will help you establish milestones and mitigate risk.

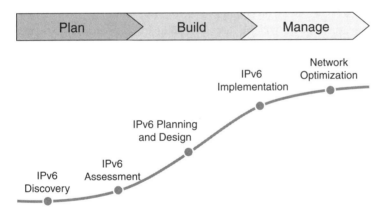

Figure 6-1 *Phased Approach to IPv6 Design*

This approach for IPv6 deployments consists of the following structured phases:

- Discovery
- Assessment
- Planning and design
- Implementation
- Network optimization

Skipping any of the best-practice phases increases the risk of project failure and the associated costs. The following sections define each of these phases.

Business and Network Discovery Phase

At this phase, network architects or designers usually need to identify the business goals and drivers toward the enablement of IPv6 that can be used to build a justified business case. During this phase, you need to take the following factors into account:

- Project time frame
- Government compliance
- Geographic distribution of the sites with regard to IP addressing availability

Often the only companies that are able to provide a business case for IPv6 deployment are service providers, which depend on the increasing customer growth for revenue. When companies are not capable of providing sufficient infrastructure to their customer base, this inability represents a direct hit to their revenue stream.

A company may also look into expanding into regions where IPV4 allocation has been completely depleted and customers or partners have only IPv6 allocation to communicate with the headquarters or other branch offices. Also, some organizations build an IPv6 front end to their customers, because if an end-user device is IPv6 only and cannot access the company's web page, the business will see this as potential lost customers and revenue.

Assessment Phase

Any design project that goes without a thorough assessment of the existing infrastructure incurs a high risk of hitting a showstopper during the project. A showstopper may endanger the entire migration project. Because hardware and OS vendors have already implemented support for IPV6, there is usually a straightforward migration path for which only a software upgrade or a new license is required. You must completely replace equipment that does not support the required feature set and is not capable of processing IPv6 in hardware with a newer platform (forklift).

Note A forklift upgrade or migration is considered a large-scale upgrade in which large parts of the existing infrastructure must be overhauled.

Migrating applications represent the greatest challenge in an IPv6 migration. Well-known application vendors are providing a migration path; however, in-house or custom-built applications can provide a challenge or may force the company to acquire a new solution because the adaptation may consume too many resources.

Planning and Design Phase

The decision over which deployment to choose greatly influences the planning and designing phase. Both dual-stack and hybrid deployment models have strengths and weakness that need to be in line with the business requirements that are defined in the discovery phase.

Although the dual-stack model may be the only long-term strategy and offers end-user transparency, it does introduce higher complexity and a great amount of resources to implement.

Hybrid models utilize tunneling and translation methods for fast IPv6 deployment on the selected network components or during the migration to IPv6.

The result of the design phase has to include a detailed and low-level design that covers addressing, LANs, WANs, security, and other relevant areas. In particular, security issues require crucial consideration because enabling a new protocol stack opens the network to unknown risks.

Implementation and Optimization Phases

Ideally, you should always aim to initially deploy IPv6 in a limited pilot program or within a lab environment that covers a complete set of networking devices, services, and applications (anything included in your production environment). This approach (the pilot program) helps you establish a base from which to test the new protocol stack and gather operational experience before full-scale deployment. Also, if the business requirements include spanning geographies, the pilot program should include validation and testing of the design for each geography.

In addition, you should try to establish an effective feedback process that enables users to inform you about critical issues so that you can fix and optimize the targeted solution.

In comparison with other phases, the network optimization phase is a continuous process. Analysis of operational metrics and user experience can help you establish a list of improvements that you need in the production environment.

Considerations for Migration to IPv6 Design

This section discusses the technical aspects and design approaches that network designers or architects need to consider when migrating a network to be IPv6 enabled.

Acquiring IPv6 Prefixes

The first step, and one of the easier ones, is to acquire an IPv6 prefix. As a network designer, you may choose between Provider-Independent (PI) and Provider-Assigned (PA) prefixes, depending on business requirements and IPv6 availability.

To receive a PI prefix, you need to submit an application to the regional registrar. Based on the application, a larger or a smaller prefix is allocated. For PI, the regional registrars allocate the /48 prefix by default.

If a PI address space is not required, the service provider can allocate a PA prefix for remote locations or branches. If the local service provider does not offer native IPv6, you can acquire a prefix that a tunnel broker allocates to access the IPv6 network.

The following are the different typical IPv6 prefix allocations:

- **/40 prefix:** Is intended for the largest of companies. This prefix offers the capability to span thousands of VLANs and support hundreds of branches in a geographical region.

- **/48 prefix:** Is the default allocation for large companies.
- **/56 prefix:** Offers up to 256 VLANs. This prefix is appropriate for medium and small companies. The /56 prefix is also often allocated for consumer services.

Provider Independent Versus Provider Assigned

Before considering whether PI or PA IPv6 allocation is the best for your design, you need to understand the difference between them from the service provider forwarding point of view. When the service provider offers native IPv6 connectivity, it allocates a prefix from its own /32 segment. In this case, the service provider can advertise only one large prefix to other upstream providers, making the global Internet routing table more efficient and optimized.

However, when planning for a multihomed WAN or Internet connectivity, you will receive multiple different prefixes from the different service providers' segments. In turn, these multiple IPv6 prefixes in your LAN will propagate to host machines, making the autoconfigure work with multiple prefixes. That said, this may lead to high-availability and multihoming issues when one of the prefixes becomes unavailable (you may consider hiding reachability information; that is, "route aggregation"). Therefore, as a designer, you need to evaluate and decide based on the requirements and priorities.

IPv6 PI allocation is accepted as the main multihoming solution. It is similar to the IPv4 multihomed solutions, and it offers high resiliency if one of the service providers fails. PI address allocation can be acquired from the regional registrar, and the allocation can be increased if you present a viable business case. The main downside of PI addressing is that service providers have to advertise a series of PI prefixes besides their own. The increased number of advertised prefixes increases the global routing table out of proportion.

Table 6-1 summarizes the primary differences between IPv6 PI and PA addressing.

Table 6-1 *IPv6 PI versus PA addressing*

Provider Independent (PI)	Provider Assigned (PA)
■ PI is assigned by the Internet registries.	■ PA is assigned by the service provider.
■ It remains assigned as long as the user meets the assignment criteria.	■ In multihoming situations, hosts may have multiple prefixes.
■ It is independent of the service provider.	■ Traditional multihoming issues have to be resolved by using workarounds or protocol evolution.
■ There are concerns about routing table explosion (same as in IPv4).	
■ PI resolves multihoming and load balancing of traffic.	■ The service provider aggregates all PA addresses that it assigned.
■ Some network operators may decide not to route allocation because the prefix cannot be aggregated.	■ It requires readdressing when changing service providers.
	■ PA is effective for small branches with limited connectivity options.

Where to Start the Migration

When approaching a migration or transition to IPv6 project as a network designer or architect, you first should think about where to start the migration. You can define several possible starting points, based on the company's business case for migration. These starting points, which are depicted in Figure 6-2, include the following:

- WAN
- Internet edge (for example, Web services and DMZ)
- Data center
- LAN

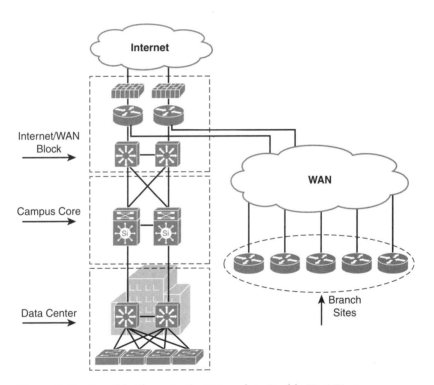

Figure 6-2 *Possible Places in the Network to Enable IPv6 First*

A company may decide to migrate the entire infrastructure. However, due to the complexity, you may suggest starting with smaller islands or non-business–critical infrastructure.

Practically, customers often choose the WAN as the first point of contact because it offers a quick win and requires the least amount of component modification. If DMZ is migrated next, you may already be capable of having an IPV6 presence on the Internet.

From a design point of view, the process of migrating the WAN so that it is IPv6 enabled includes

- Acquiring a prefix
- Assessing the WAN routers
- (Optional) Upgrading the WAN routers
- Configuring dual-stack and peering on the WAN routers

Other network areas may require significantly more resources to migrate to IPv6. Therefore, the part of the network that is most often left as the last piece of the project is the LAN because it may introduce a significant risk to business continuation and many services. This makes it the most demanding project area of any IPv6 migration project.

Migration Models and Design Considerations

The following sections discuss some possible migration approaches that you, as the network designer, can consider when migrating the enterprise network to be IPv6 enabled.

IPv6 Island

One commonly used migration approach is the creation of IPv6 islands. IPv6 islands can represent smaller network segments inside the enterprise network that communicate with each other over the existing IPv4 infrastructure (see Figure 6-3).

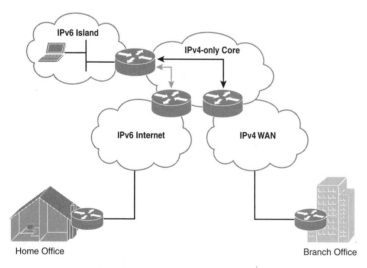

Figure 6-3 *IPv6 Islands*

As you can see, connecting IPv6 islands requires introduction of a tunneling mechanism that can carry IPv6 packets. If the number of IPv6 islands is small, the manual tunneling mechanisms are preferred in the connection of IPv6 islands because they are easy to configure and there is no requirement for a large-scale deployment of tunnels.

Creating IPv6 islands has several benefits. The most important benefits are to test essential services and gather operational experience. When the decision for a large-scale deployment is made, you have already faced and solved most of the technical issues. This lowers the risk of migration.

IPv6 WAN

Often, enterprise headquarters sites includes multiple connections toward the WAN service providers for high availability and multihoming. With IPv6, you can choose from several possible design options to achieve multihoming WAN connectivity. To determine which option is better or more feasible for your design, you must be aware of the capabilities of your local service provider as well as the chosen IP prefix allocation type. The following are the main approaches used to achieve multihomed WAN connectivity with IPv6:

- **Provider-assigned approach:** As already discussed, with this approach each connecting service provider assigns a PA IP allocation to the enterprise, as shown in Figure 6-4.

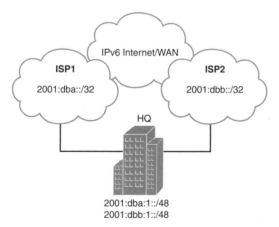

Figure 6-4 *IPv6 WAN: PA Approach*

The concern with this approach is that distributing the prefix of each SP to all network segments will generate multiple IPv6 addresses on hosts. This can cause issues in some failure scenarios. Therefore, as a network designer, you should ask yourself how your applications and services will react once the original prefix is not available due to a failure. Although different possible design options exist for handling link failures, none of them can actually offer a reliable design like the PI design approach (the best practice).

- **Provider-independent approach:** With this design approach, typically the enterprise WAN routers advertise the same PI prefix through BGP to upstream peers that offer a valid and reliable multihoming solution for enterprise customers (see Figure 6-5). In this way, the SPs now carry their own /32 prefix and all /48 PI prefixes of customers.

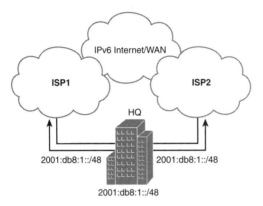

Figure 6-5 *IPv6 WAN: PI Approach*

However, when the PI prefixes of each customer are advertised, the size of the global routing table increases. In addition, PI address allocation does incur some additional costs depending on the regional registrar policy.

- **Tunnel broker approach:** One of the common IPv6 design constraints is that, when IPv6 is a part of your business strategy but the local service providers do not offer native connectivity, either you may deploy your own tunneling solution to overlay IPv6 communication over the IPv6-only WAN/MAN, or you can reach out to tunnel brokers for help. *Tunnel brokers* are, in fact, service providers that offer access to the IPv6 Internet via manual IPv4 tunnels. These tunnels are located at different geographical locations. A tunnel broker may offer both PA or PI connectivity methods. Figure 6-6 shows ample connectivity through two different tunnel brokers with PA IP space allocation.

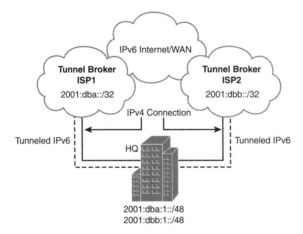

Figure 6-6 *IPv6 Multihoming over Tunnel Broker SPs*

Designing branch office WAN access is a simpler task. Because branch offices are not always meant to be multihomed, requirements for a PI prefix are not dominant. Access methods are often subject to the IPv6 availability of the local service provider that offers connectivity to the branch office.

In general, the following are the common branch office connectivity options (see Figure 6-7):

- **Native IPv6:** The local service provider offers a PA prefix with which the branch communicates to the headquarters.

- **No native IPv6:** The branch LAN uses a subnet that the headquarters assigns. The branch LAN manually configures an IPv4 tunnel to the headquarters without offering a local breakout.

or

The branch LAN uses a PA subnet that a tunnel broker assigns. The branch LAN communicates with the headquarters via the tunnel broker.

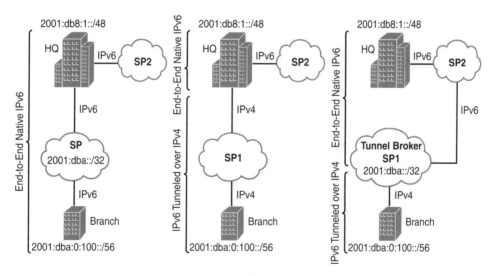

Figure 6-7 *Branch Site IPv6 Connectivity Options*

IPv6 Transition Mechanisms

Although you can select from a number of possible transition mechanisms, you cannot apply all transition mechanisms to a certain network design. Therefore, it is recommended that you choose the mechanisms that closely align with the IPv6 deployment strategy, taking into consideration any design constraints, such as IT staff knowledge or supported features in the hardware and software platforms in use across the network.

Furthermore, many of the transition mechanisms have been deprecated or were not often deployed, such as semiautomatic tunnel mechanisms (ISATAP, 6to4, Teredo, A+P, 464XLAT, 6over4, 4rd, NAT-PT). In fact, these technologies may pose significant security risks based on how they establish tunnels.

From a network design point of view, each approach or transition mechanism has its features, benefits, and limitations. Therefore, understanding these parameters is vital because this understanding facilitates the selection of the most applicable strategy for your situation. As a network designer or architect, you must be aware that the economics might be considerably different depending on the selected design approach, and these approaches are not equal in cost, complexity, or functional capabilities. Understanding the available options and deciding, based on your particular needs, which provides the necessary capabilities will help you select the most appropriate option—both as a transition strategy and as a long-term IPv6 strategy.

As shown in Figure 6-8, the primary options available for migration to IPv6 from the existing network infrastructure can be separated into three categories:

- Dual-stack network
- Tunneling
- Translation

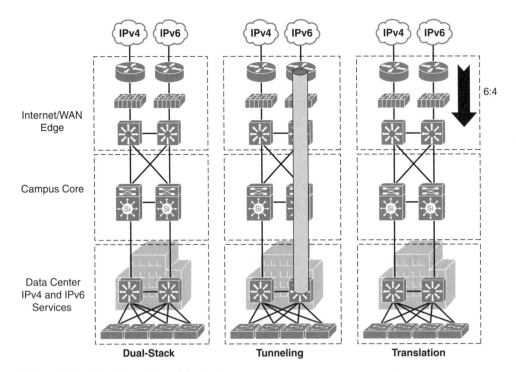

Figure 6-8 *IPv6 Transition Mechanisms*

Each category may include different approaches. For example, tunneling can be achieved using different tunneling technologies, and each has its own characteristics.

The dual-stack deployment model is not always feasible due to complexity, time, or resources. You need to keep these factors in mind when considering a transition mechanism to facilitate IPv6 communication across the network, Therefore, this chapter, in addition to dual stack, also briefly discusses the different common IPv6 transition mechanisms, focusing on the suitable use-case scenario of each mechanism.

Dual Stack

As the primary driver for a long-term strategy for IPv6 adoption, you are faced with considering dual stack at one point or another. Implementing both stacks on hosts, network devices, services, and applications is a difficult task because each layer introduces new challenges.

Although the implementation might be complex, the logic behind the deployment is fairly simple. You create a logically separate network by using the existing resources. Both protocols work completely independently of each other and offer the operator the ability to control each of them without affecting the other. This independence allows the operator to design the new network without legacy considerations as well as implement the best practices and functionalities of the new protocol. The implementation of dual stack is transparent to hosts.

The assessment phase of the IPv6 project is an essential requirement for a dual-stack deployment model, as each network, device, service, and application requires support. The complexity of the network is increased, and the cost and resource allocation of implementing dual stack are extremely high in comparison to a hybrid deployment model.

The complexity of the implementation can lead to several pitfalls, which can slow down or completely stop the dual-stack deployment. You have to consider all the possible pitfalls in the assessment phase to mitigate the risk of failure.

The most common pitfalls include the following:

- Fixed configuration devices can cause resource limitations. A device such as a switch can have a fixed amount of memory or Content-addressable memory (TCAM). When it is being shared between both protocols, these resources may be significantly lower for each protocol. Because this type of device cannot be upgraded, you have to exchange the device.

- Devices cannot handle throughput requirements for IPv6 traffic. An essential requirement is that all hosts, network devices, and applications handle the throughput requirements for IPv6 traffic. If the device is capable of handling IPv6 but does not reach the required processing capacity, it needs to be upgraded or replaced.

- Feature parity of security devices is commonly not equal to IPv4. Your assessment phase must incorporate the capability to mimic your IPv4 security policy to IPv6.

Without the appropriate security mechanisms in place, you open your network to external attacks.

- Legacy or custom applications cannot be ported, or no workaround exists. You have to rewrite the application to become protocol independent because the current application is not capable of supporting IPv6.

- Host devices have no or limited support of IPv6. Low-cost devices have limited software capabilities that require upgrade or replacement.

Table 6-2 summarizes pros and cons of considering a dual-stack model.

Table 6-2 *Dual Stack Pros and Cons*

Pros	Cons
■ There is no encapsulation, which helps to avoid increasing packet overhead.	■ Dual stack increases control plane complexity.
■ This model reduces operational complexity by avoiding or minimizing the need of any overlay technology to transport IPv6 packets.	■ It requires full IPv6 support of all devices.
■ IPv4 and IPv6 services are offered in parallel, and networks are logically separated.	■ There is a high cost and implementation effort.
■ IPv6 network design can incorporate best practices and new technology solutions because it is not burdened by legacy design.	■ Device resources are divided; therefore, higher hardware capabilities are required, such as memory and CPU.
■ It offers end-user transparency.	■ Clients prefer the IPv6 path.

NAT64 and DNS64

Address Family Translation (AFT), or simply "translation," facilitates communication between IPv6-only and IPv4-only hosts and networks (whether in a transit, an access, or an edge network) by performing IP header and address translation between the two address families.

AFT is not a long-term support strategy; it is a medium-term coexistence strategy that can be used to facilitate a long-term program of IPv6 transition by both enterprises and ISPs.

One of the common scenarios of enabling IPV6 is that some organization may require an immediate introduction of IPv6-only hosts, in which you will require a translation mechanism that enables your hosts to communicate with IPv4-only nodes. The following are the most common scenarios that require NAT64:

- An IPv6-only network wants to transparently access both IPv6 and existing IPv4 content.

- Servers in an IPv6-only network want to transparently serve both IPv4 and IPv6 users.

- Servers in an existing IPv4-only network want to serve IPV6 Internet users.
- Both an IPv4 network and an IPv6 network are within the same organization and require reachability between them.

A scenario such as an IPv4 host wanting to access an IPv6-only server is also technically and theoretically possible, but it is unlikely because most content providers prefer to adopt a dual-stack strategy rather than an IPv6-only strategy.

NAT64, in cooperation with DNS64, is a viable option for a scenario in which an IPv6-only host requires access to an IPv4-only server. The scenario, depicted in Figure 6-9, shows you the details about how NAT64 and DNS64 cooperate to allow an IPv6-only host to communicate with an IPv4-only server.

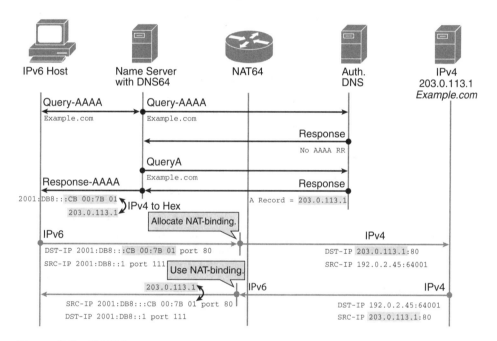

Figure 6-9 *NAT64*

This scenario follows this sequence:

1. The host sends a DNS request for the AAAA record of the IPv4 server to the DNS64.
2. The DNS64 forwards the query to the authoritative DNS.
3. The authoritative DNS does not respond with an AAAA record because it does not exist.
4. The DNS64 node sends out an A query to the authoritative DNS asking for the IPv4 address of the destination server.

5. The authoritative server responds with the appropriate A record.

6. The DNS64 transforms the received A record into an AAAA record that includes the IPv4 destination address and responds to the host's initial request for an AAAA record.

7. The host does not differentiate the received AAAA record and initiates a session.

8. Because the destination IPv6 address does not exist, it needs to be routed to a NAT64 device. A specific IPv6 prefix needs to be designated and always routed to the NAT64 device.

9. The NAT64 establishes the IPv6 session with the host and at the same time initiates the IPv4 session with the destination server.

10. The NAT64 binds both sessions and forwards the traffic from the host to the server.

Manual Tunnels

In some scenarios, you may need to connect several IPv6 islands or dislocated branches, within a small period of time, over an IPv4-only transport network. In this case, the manual tunneling methods are considered a viable option and offer a simplified and scalable enough solution for this type of scenario. (This option is simple to configure with changes only on the edge routers, which have to be dual-stacked.) Tunneling techniques involve transport through encapsulation of one protocol within another protocol (in our case, IPv6 tunneling encapsulates IPv6 packets within IPv4 packets). There are several types of IP tunneling that you can use for this purpose, including the following (see Figure 6-10):

- **Generic routing encapsulation (GRE):** This type of encapsulation supports multicast traffic, offering the capability to use routing protocols and implement multicast. However, the introduced overhead is significant, and it can be difficult to inspect with security devices.

- **IP-in-IP (IPIP):** This is a simple IPv6 encapsulation inside an IPv4 header. It offers a smaller overhead in comparison to GRE but does not support transport of multicast traffic. The same limitations regarding the security inspection apply as for GRE.

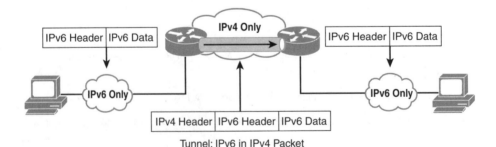

Figure 6-10 *IPv6 Tunneling over IPv4*

Although manual tunnels are easy to implement, some do not scale to many tunnels (specifically the point-to-point tunneling model). Therefore, you should consider this limitation when deciding on the deployment method. Neither method includes any mechanisms for security, and the traffic can be intercepted and inspected by a third party. However, traffic encryption, authentication, and integrity can be achieved by using IPsec. Nevertheless, considering a multipoint GRE (mGRE) tunneling model, such as using Dynamic Multipoint VPN (DMVPN, described in Chapter 8, "Service Provider Managed VPNs"), can offer a more scalable overlay solution to tunnel IPv6 traffic over an IPv4-only network.

Tunnel Brokers

As mentioned previously in this chapter, tunnel brokers refer to those service providers that offer the capability to connect to the IPv6 Internet without the actual native IPv6 connectivity that the local service provider would offer. A tunneling method is used to create an IPv4 tunnel toward the tunnel broker, which de-encapsulates the traffic, and forwards it to the IPv6 Internet, as illustrated in Figure 6-11.

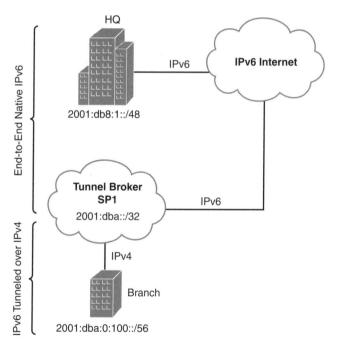

Figure 6-11 *Tunnel Broker*

Also, tunnel brokers can offer several geographical locations for tunnel endpoints, so you can choose the closest available to introduce the smallest possible delay. In addition, the tunnel broker may provide its own PA address allocation or may offer advanced BGP peering and advertisement of allocated customer PI address space.

6 Rapid Deployment

6 Rapid Deployment (or 6RD, described in RFC 5969) is a stateless tunneling mechanism that evolved from the 6-to-4 tunneling mechanism. It offers connecting dual-stacked hosts with IPv6 servers over an IPv4 infrastructure. It also addresses certain problem areas, especially the addressing usage limitation of 6-to-4 tunneling. 6RD was primarily developed to allow service providers a fast deployment rate at which the consumers may quickly transition to a dual-stacked environment without the need to migrate the whole transport infrastructure.

The 6RD solution consists of two network elements (see Figure 6-12):

- **6RD-capable router:** This dual-stack router has the capability to dynamically discover all addresses using the customer premises equipment (CPE), where the border relay router can be defined statically or using a DHCP option. Traffic between 6RD-capable routers is routed directly and does not have to pass any additional network elements. You will possibly have to upgrade or exchange the CPE device to support the 6RD capabilities.

- **6RD border relay:** This stateless border element is designed to de-encapsulate the incoming tunneled traffic and forward it to the destination IPv6 network. Because the operation is stateless, you can implement several border relay elements in your network offering resiliency. The border relay address is often implemented as an Anycast address that enables the routing protocol to compensate for load balancing and high availability.

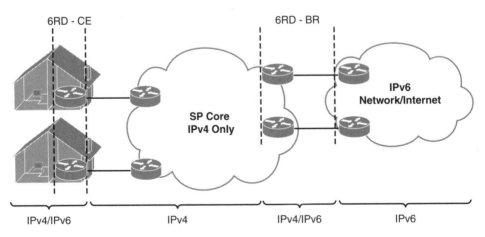

Figure 6-12 *6RD High-level Architecture*

As shown in Figure 6-12, the CE router sits at the edge of the service provider IPv4 access infrastructure and provides IPv6 connectivity to this end user's network. The native IPv6 traffic coming from the end-user host is encapsulated in IPv6 by the CE router and tunneled to the border relay router or directly to the other CE routers in the same 6RD domain. Conversely, encapsulated 6RD traffic received from the Internet through the border relay router, and 6RD traffic from other CE routers, is de-capsulated and forwarded to the end-user nodes. As a result, from a design point of view, 6RD offers the following benefits:

- 6RD enables fast provisioning of IPv6 over the IPv4-only core without forcing re-architecture to the existing service.
- 6RD can be introduced and deployed incrementally.
- IPv6 traffic automatically follows IPv4 routing.
- 6RD offers reduced capital expenditure (CapEx) and investment protection (limited impact on the existing infrastructure).

As an improvement compared to 6-to-4 tunneling, which mandates the use of 2002::/16, 6RD allows an operator to implement its own prefix when addressing the network. Because 6RD was developed to be used in service provider environments, the 6RD prefix is allocated as the first 32 bits. The second 32 bits are used to encapsulate the destination IPv4 address or the border relay address that the CPE will use for relay purposes (see Figure 6-13).

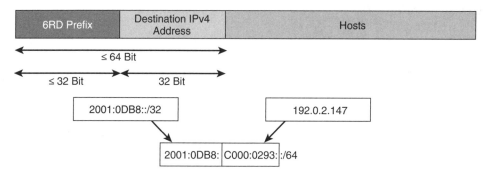

Figure 6-13 *6RD Prefix*

The size of the 6RD prefix and destination IPv4 address may vary, so you can assign 48 bits to the 6RD prefix and 16 bits to the destination IPv4 address. However, in this situation, the first 16 bits of the IPv4 destination must be predefined.

Dual-Stack Lite (DS-Lite)

Dual-Stack Lite (or DS-Lite, described in RFC 6333) allows provisioning of a dual-stacked environment to hosts and facilitates the connectivity of dual-stacked hosts to IPv4 servers that require access across an IPv6 infrastructure. In other words, the transit network in this scenario is based natively on IPv6, and the customer is required to implement backward compatibility with IPv4 (tunnels IPv4 toward the large-scale NAT LSN element; see Figure 6-14).

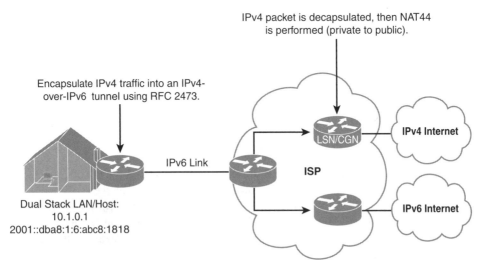

Figure 6-14 *DS-Lite High-level Architecture*

In this approach, the CPE plays a vital role because it is a dual-stacked device and allows

- IPv6 traffic to be transported natively.
- IPv4 traffic to be tunneled and delivered to the LSN or the carrier-grade NAT CGN for translation. Then the IPv6 packet is de-encapsulated, restoring the original IPv4 packet. NAT is performed on the IPv4 packet and is routed to the public IPv4 Internet. The CGN uniquely identifies traffic flows by recording the CPE public IPv6 address, the private IPv4 address, and TCP or UDP port number as a session.

Note LSN or CGN simply is a NAT function performed at the service provider side rather than at the customer side at a large scale.

Locator/ID Separation Protocol (LISP)

The current, and typically used, Internet routing and addressing architecture is based mainly on a single numbering space—the IP address—to simultaneously express two primary functions about a device:

- Device identity
- How the device is attached to the network

The Locator/ID Separation Protocol (LISP), on the other hand, creates a new paradigm by splitting the device identity that is known as an endpoint identifier (EID) and its location, known as its routing locator (RLOC), into two different numbering spaces. Splitting EID and RLOC functions yields several benefits, including

- Simplified and cost-effective multihoming
- More advanced ingress traffic engineering and optimal routing capabilities
- IP address and host mobility
- IPv6 transition simplification, including incremental deployment of IPv6 using the existing IPv4 infrastructure

Using LISP as an IPv6 transition mechanism, in particular, facilitates achieving the following:

- IPv6 multihoming
- Connecting IPv6 islands

The following sections briefly describe the main components of the LISP architecture and the function of each.

LISP Site Edge Devices

The LISP site edge node provides the following functions:

- **Ingress Tunnel Router (ITR):** ITR is deployed as a CE device. It receives packets from site-facing interfaces and either encapsulates packets to remote LISP sites or natively forwards packets to non-LISP sites.
- **Egress Tunnel Router (ETR):** ETR is deployed as a CE device. It receives packets from core-facing interfaces and either de-encapsulates LISP packets or natively delivers non-LISP packets to local EIDs at the site.

It is common for LISP site edge devices (such as CE devices) to implement both ITR and ETR functions. In this case, the device is referred to as an xTR. However, the LISP specification does not require the device to perform both ITR and ETR functions.

For both devices, the EID namespace is used inside the sites for end-site addresses for hosts and routers. EIDs go in DNS records. Generally speaking, the EID namespace is not globally routed in the underlying infrastructure. The RLOC namespace, on the other hand, is used in the core. RLOCs are used as infrastructure addresses for LISP routers and ISP routers, and are globally routed in the underlying infrastructure. Hosts do not know about RLOCs, and RLOCs do not know about hosts.

LISP Infrastructure Devices

The following are the key LISP infrastructure nodes/functions that you need to take into account in your design:

- **Map-Server (MS):** The MS is deployed as a LISP Infrastructure component. It configures the LISP site policy for LISP ETRs that register to it. This includes the EID prefixes, for which the registering ETRs are authoritative, and an authentication key, which must match the one also configured on the ETR. Map-Servers receive Map-Register control packets from ETRs. When the MS is configured with a service interface to the LISP ALT, it injects aggregates for the EID prefixes for the registered ETRs into the ALT. The MS also receives Map-Request control packets from the ALT, which it then encapsulates to the registered ETR that is authoritative for the EID prefix being queried.

- **Map-Resolver (MR):** The MR is deployed as a LISP Infrastructure device. It receives Map-Requests encapsulated by ITRs, and when configured with a service interface to the LISP ALT, forwards Map-Requests to the ALT. Map-Resolvers also send Negative Map-Replies to ITRs in response to queries for non-LISP addresses.

- **Proxy Tunnel Router (PxTR):** The Proxy ITR provides connectivity between non-LISP sites and LISP sites. The Proxy ITR functionality is a special case of ITR functionality whereby the router attracts native packets from non-LISP sites (for example, the Internet) that are destined for LISP sites, and encapsulates and forwards them to the destination LISP site. A Proxy Tunnel Router is ideally placed in the path between LISP and non-LISP sites. The PxTR can either own and be controlled by the enterprise, or this function can be provided by the service provider.

As discussed previously, LISP is not a feature, nor was it invented as an IPv6 transition mechanism like most of the other choices listed in the preceding section. Rather, LISP is a new routing architecture that is designed for a much broader purpose. Because it's designed to transparently accommodate multiple address families, using LISP in IPv6 transition solutions is very natural.

The most common scenario LISP is used to address is the IPv6 transition use case in which an enterprise wants to have phased migration to IPv6 or to gain basic experience with IPv6, but has no urgent needs that would merit significant capital expenditure (CapEx) or operating expenditure (OpEx) outlays or changes to the existing infrastructure. The typical approach used to accomplish this goal is to create several IPv6 islands across the enterprise network (one at headquarters, or HQ, and one at the targeted remote sites). Then LISP can be introduced here to interconnect these IPv6 islands together rapidly and easily over the existing IPv4 network without the need for any changes to the underlying network. This results in a cost-effective solution for this scenario. Figure 6-15 illustrates the application of LISP in this scenario along with the following required LISP functions:

- The HQ LISP router (RTR-A) will be configured to provide LISP mapping services and LISP encapsulation services. Thus, this router will be configured as a Map-Resolver/Map-Server (MR/MS) and as an Ingress Tunnel Router/Egress Tunnel Router (xTR) concurrently.

- The Spoke-1 and Spoke-2 LISP routers (RTR-B and RTR-C) are configured only as LISP xTRs.

IPv6 Transition Mechanisms 215

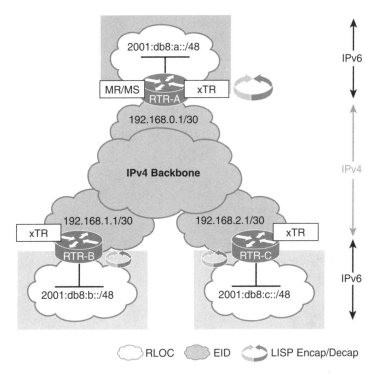

Figure 6-15 *LISP Connecting IPv6 Islands*

Furthermore, one of the other scenarios for which LISP can be used to provide IPv6 transit service occurs when an enterprise or content provider needs to provide access from IPv6 Internet users (non-LISP users/sites) to IPv6-hosted services or contents over the existing IPv4 Internet connectivity. As shown in Figure 6-16, the service provider in this scenario offers PxTR functions and advertises enterprise IPv6 routes toward the IPv6 Internet. In the meantime, the enterprise only needs to deploy xTRs in their data center. With this approach, the enterprise can quickly get IPv6 presence without having direct IPv6 connectivity.

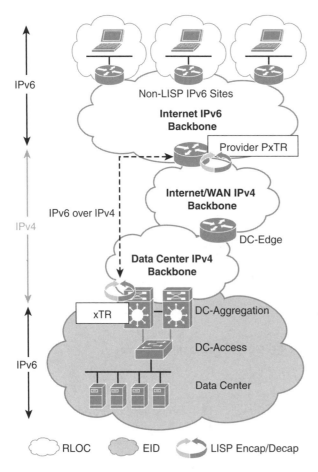

Figure 6-16 *Connecting Non-LISP IPv6 Internet Users to Hosted IPv6 Content over the IPv4 Internet*

Final Thoughts on IPv6 Transition Mechanisms

After discussing the different IPv6 transition mechanisms, we may have to ask the following question: Which mechanism should we consider as a best practice? The simple answer to this question depends on several factors, including the answers to the following questions:

- What is the targeted environment? Service provider, content provider, enterprise network, and so on? Also, the answer to this question could help you understand the scale of the network.

- What is the ultimate business goal with regard to IPv6? Migrate the network to be fully "end-to-end" IPv6 enabled in the future, partially enable IPv6 to run certain services only, and so on.

- Are there any nontechnical design constraints? For example, a limited time frame to enable IPv6, a limited budget to upgrade network comments to be IPv6-ready, and so on.

- Are there any technical design constraints? For example, some applications may not work with NAT, they may have limited support for certain tunneling technologies, IPv6 may not be supported on certain core devices, security devices in the path do not support IPv6, and so on.

- Are there any operational considerations? For example, operation staff knowledge and expertise may prefer to deploy certain technology over others to simplify the solution manageability in the future for them.

After the answers to these questions are identified (ideally during the planning phase), the job for you, as the network designer, will be easier to select the most suitable IPv6 transition mechanism and should take both the current and future state into consideration.

Summary

- The next generation of the Internet will not be possible without IPv6.
- Use a phased approach when implementing IPv6 and follow business requirements.
- Define migration starting points.
- Connect the IPv6 islands.
- Dual-stack is a long-term goal, but transition mechanisms may be required meanwhile:
    - NAT64, DNS64 (binds IPv4 and IPv6 sessions)
    - Manual tunnels (GRE, IP-in-IP)
    - Tunnel brokers (connects local IPv4 with global IPv6)
    - 6RD (transit IPv4, tunnels IPv6)
    - DS-Lite (transit IPv6, tunnels IPv4 to LSN)
    - LISP support for different scenarios to interconnect IPv6 islands

Review Questions

After answering the following questions, please refer to Appendix A, "Answers to Review Questions," for the answers.

1. Which transition mechanisms are considered tunneling mechanisms? (Select two.)
    a. NAT64
    b. Dual Stack
    c. 6RD

d. DS-Lite

e. DHCPv6

2. Which of the statements about NAT64 is correct?
   a. NAT64 translates unique local IPv6 addresses into global IPv6 addresses.
   b. NAT64 is a stateless mechanism and allows end-to-end IPv6 communication.
   c. NAT64 in cooperation with DNS64 is used to allow communication between IPv6-only hosts with IPv4 networks.
   d. Dual-stack hosts require NAT64 to reach IPv4 networks.

3. Which of the statements about dual stack is correct?
   a. Dual stack does not require additional resources on networking devices.
   b. Dual stack improves the latency on hosts.
   c. By default, IPv6 sessions are established only after an IPv4 session request times out.
   d. Dual stack allows the host to communicate both over IPv4 and IPv6 without encapsulation.

4. Which workarounds can be implemented to allow IPv6 communication with applications that do not have IPv6 support? (Select two.)
   a. DNS64
   b. ISATAP
   c. NAT64
   d. SLB64
   e. DS-LITE

5. Which of the statements about LISP is correct?
   a. PxTR is required to enable remote LISP sites to communicate with the hub LISP site.
   b. PxTR is required to enable remote non-LISP sites to communicate with the hub LISP site.
   c. LISP requires DMVPN to be enabled.
   d. LISP requires NAT46 at the Internet edge when connecting to non-LISP sites.

6. An international retailer needs to enable IPv6 communication between the remote spokes' sites and the hub site in a short period of time, but the MPLS WAN provider does not support IPv6. What solution would you, as a network architect, suggest the retailer to consider to achieve its goal?
   a. IPv6 over DMVPN
   b. IPv6 over GRE
   c. NAT64
   d. LISP

Chapter 7

Challenges of the Transition to IPv6

Upon completing this chapter, you will be able to

- Describe IPv6 services
- Explain link layer security considerations
- Describe application support
- Describe application adaptation
- Explain application workarounds
- Describe control plane security
- Describe tunneling security considerations
- Explain multihoming

IPv6 is not a simple replacement for IPv4. Transitioning from IPv4 to IPv6 is a long-term process full of challenges. Application requirements, security, and general IPv6 availability are just some of the challenges you face during the transition period. As a network designer, you must be aware of the challenges and limitations that you can expect in such projects in order to be able to provide optimizations and design alternatives.

IPv6 Services

After a careful assessment of the networking devices, you will have to devise a deployment strategy. It is recommended that you create a list of services to be migrated in the pilot or proof of concept (PoC). Careful planning and testing will help you establish a base of verified services that you can easily extend to the entire production network. This section briefly discusses considerations relative to the following services:

- Name services
- Addressing services
- Security services

Name Services

One of the first services that is instrumental in any IPv6 deployment is the Domain Name System (DNS). To successfully resolve names to addresses, the DNS infrastructure must contain the following resource records, populated either manually or dynamically:

- Address records
- Resource records for the IPv4 addresses
- Quad A (AAAA) resource records for the IPv6 addresses
- Pointer (PTR) resource records, which are required for the IP addresses of the devices that can be reached through the IPv4/6 protocol
  - PTR records in the IN-ADDR.ARPA domain for the IPv4 addresses
  - PTR records in the IP6.ARPA domain for the IPv6 addresses

Implementation Recommendations

To take advantage of the DNS resolution to map between IPv4 and IPv6 services, you need to consider the following:

- Implement DNS transport on IPv4 as a first step, which will enable you to easily troubleshoot any issues and gain operational experience. It will also allow you easier configuration of hosts because they do not require an IPv6 DNS address.
- At a later stage, implement IPv6 transport of AAAA records.
- Implement Dynamic DNS for hosts.

The IPv6 addresses being autoconfigured and having a factor of randomness poses a problem for any DNS configuration, which needs to keep track of both the forward map (name to IP address) and possibly the reverse map (IP address to name).

Addressing Services

Two primary mechanisms are in use for address allocation:

- **DHCPv6:** Dynamic Host Configuration Protocol version 6 DHCPv6 is similar in operation to DHCP; it allows passing of DHCP options alongside the IPv6 address Domain Name System (DNS), Trivial File Transfer Protocol (TFTP), Network Time Protocol (NTP), and so on.

- **Stateless Address Autoconfiguration (SLAAC):** SLAAC uses an IPv6 registration authority (RA) message that passes the network prefix to hosts, which then autoconfigure the IPv6 address. However, it is extremely limited for passing optional information to hosts. SLAAC implements a mechanism to pass DNS information to the hosts through recursive DNS server RDNSS; nevertheless, DNS is the only information that it can pass down.

Implementation Recommendations

Compared to SLAAC, DHCPv6 is the preferred method of implementation because it allows for greater flexibility when handling additional information that needs to be passed to the hosts.

Security Services

When you are implementing IPv6, you are opening up a whole new network that can be exploited. You must plan and prepare a security policy that mimics your existing IPv4 security policy before deploying IPv6 in production.

The challenge that you might be faced with is that many vendors may not provide full feature parity; thus, a detailed assessment is required before deployment. The vendor will provide you with an IPv6 road map that you can use to plan the deployment of firewalls, inspection devices, and remote VPN aggregators. Then you need to validate these road maps and solutions against the road map (intended goal) of the enterprise network you are designing, along with the enterprise security policy and how you can integrate between them.

For instance, Secure Sockets Layer virtual private network (SLL VPN) is the preferred method to allow remote users to access IPv6 services, either natively or tunneling IPv6 across an IPv4 SSL VPN. In some scenarios, the enterprise policy may dictate that within the enterprise internal network, there must be no traffic encapsulation/tunneled. When you take this into consideration, you will need to ensure that the tunneled VPN traffic must be de-capsulated and sent natively before entering the internal network.

Link Layer Security Considerations

Common recommendations in IPv4 include limiting or filtering Internet Control Message Protocol (ICMP) messages. Because ICMP is an error reporting or diagnostic protocol, it can very well be filtered or disabled. However, ICMPv6 has become the main building block of IPv6, and filtering the complete protocol is nearly impossible if you would like to have a fully functional IPv6 network. These functionalities at the link layer should not be filtered:

- Neighbor Discovery (ND)
- Registration authority (RA)
- Duplicate address dedication (DAD)
- Redirections

You can secure the link layer through existing mechanisms that have been ported from IPv4 or by implementing new ones. For example, cryptographically generated access (CGA) is used to authenticate the owner of an actual IPv6 address through the use of PKI. Secure neighbor discovery (SeND) was developed as a security mechanism to secure ND messages and protect against the following:

- Neighbor Solicitation/Advertisement Spoofing
- Neighbor Unreachability Detection Failure
- Duplicate Address Detection DoS attack
- Router Solicitation and Advertisement attacks
- Replay attacks
- Neighbor Discovery DoS attacks

Securing DHCPv6 functions on the same principles as in IPv4, where the Layer 2 devices filter DHCPv6 packets based on the interfaces that are not connected to the DHCPv6 server and limit any rogue DHCPv6 server to assign nonauthorized prefixes to hosts (DHCP Snooping).

On the other hand, ND can be vulnerable to DoS attacks in which a router is forced to perform address resolution for many unassigned addresses. Therefore, you need to filter unused addresses via ACLs and tune the Neighbor Discovery Protocol (NDP) process where possible. Also, RA spoofing is a well-known attack vector for man-in-the-middle (MITM) attacks. RA-Guard resolves the issue of rogue RAs where network segments are designed around switching devices that are capable of identifying invalid RAs and blocking them.

Application Support

At the end of every IPv6 migration project, you will be faced with the most challenging task: migrating business-critical applications. Every business requires a set of common applications supporting the general business process and a set of customized applications pertinent to the area of the business.

Common applications are developed by notable software vendors. Applications have integrated IPv6 support or have a committed road map for the future development and support of the protocol.

Customized applications include software that was contracted and designed for one specific business process. These applications may be critical to the business process and cannot be exchanged for a more common or well-known application. Often the customized applications are built in-house due to in-house knowledge and expertise that is not found on the market. Assessing a customized application is a serious task that includes

- Analysis of the application (collection of capture files and communication)
- Protocol independency (analysis of code)
- Documentation analysis

As a result of the analysis, you may find that the application requires only a minor modification or a complete rewrite. Depending on the result, you may decide to employ a workaround if the adaptation could consume too many resources.

Application Adaptation

After a careful assessment of a customized application, you will gain insight into the level of adaptation required. Adaptation of the application requires access to the source code of the application. You may be faced with a situation in which the company owning the code does not operate any longer. In that case, you will need to commission a full rewrite of the application or implement a workaround.

When you find that a customized application needs adaptation, you may estimate the effort for modification through categorizing the adaptation process into the following:

- **Protocol-independent code:** In most applications, portions of codes deal mainly with logic and algorithmic processing without calling any particular system calls or API to carry out their job. When the application involves only language constructs, it can be easily ported or adopted for IPv6 operation.
- **API adaptation:** The code can be ported by just substituting API and data structures that IPv4 applications use to establish a session.
- **System calls modification:** This category involves part of the code that requires modification of network calls, which may affect other portions of code and relies on system data structures to function.
- **Modification of program logic:** Certain portions of code also affect the logic of the application. Such code is hardest to migrate and cannot be ported automatically.

Protocol-independent code and API adaptation are likely to be ported easily or even automated. However, system calls modification and modification of program logic require detailed analysis and a rewrite of the code to be successfully adopted.

Application Workarounds

If and when you are faced with an application that cannot be ported or one that requires too many resources to adapt, you can choose a workaround that may still allow you to use your customized applications. For instance, to make an IPv4 server in your DMZ available to an IPv6 client, you may use NAT64 for translation purposes. You configure static address mappings and configure both A and AAAA DNS addresses. DNS64 is not needed. The setup is appropriate for situations in which load balancers are not implemented.

Summarily, for data center environments and load balancing, you may use the SLB64 for translation of IPv6 to IPv4. You can configure either automatic or manual rules. The use case is for load balancing of a TCP session.

In addition, "proxying" enables you to maintain your servers on IPv4 and use a proxy server to handle any IPv6 requests (HTTP) to the servers that have yet not been transitioned. Many more proxy server implementations may also function as caching servers and offer fast implementation of IPv6 services

Control Plane Security

When you are implementing control plane protocols, your primary task, next to implementing functionality, is to implement security policies that are associated with the control plane. Neighbor authentication has already been implemented on most of the routing protocols supporting IPv6 and will secure your exchange of information between peers:

- Border Gateway Protocol (BGP)
- Intermediate System to Intermediate System (IS-IS)
- Enhanced Interior Gateway Routing Protocol (EIGRP)
- Open Shortest Path First (OSPF)
- Routing Information Protocol Version 2 (RIPv2)

Route filtering is another import tool to secure the routing infrastructure. Most routing protocols allow the configuration of route filters that prevent specific routes from being propagated throughout the network. In terms of security, these filters are useful because they help ensure that only legitimate networks are advertised:

- **3ffe::/16:** SixBone prefix
- **2001:db8::/32:** Documentation prefix
- **fe00::/9:** Link local and site local prefix

In IPv4, commonly ICMP was referred to as a diagnostic tool that could possibly introduce security risks; thus, many system administrators are encouraged to filter the protocol on networking devices. In IPv6, you have to selectively exclude ICMPv6 functionality as it more deeply intertwines into the new stack itself because Neighbor Discovery and Router Advertisements are ICMPv6 messages. You are also encouraged to allow ICMPv6 error messages on your WAN router to indicate connectivity issues such as MTU problems and Destination Unreachable.

Most protocols have already been adopted for IPv6. Using SSH, Telnet, or SNMP can enable you to utilize your IPv6 connectivity. However, due to the lack of feature parity in many NMS solutions, you are recommended to keep all management of business-critical devices on IPv4 due to it being proven and stable. As development of management software progresses, you may enable it on a smaller base of devices for validation before implementing it in full scale in the production network.

Dual-Stack Security Considerations

Implementing dual stack may provide several benefits, as it includes a logically separate network that can be controlled without impacting the existing IPv4 network. Nevertheless, you must take into account some serious considerations when contemplating dual stack:

- Making sure that the IPv6 security policy is on par with the existing IPv4 security policy will ensure that you have not left any opening in your newly created network to be exploited. When faced with a lack of features or a software defect that might undermine your security, you should consider whether this defect can impose serious security risks and ultimately stop the rollout. The total security of your dual-stacked network is the amount of the least secure network.

- Dual stack lacks translation services like NAT to hide the presence of hosts in your LAN. Each host now possesses at least one globally unique IPv6 address that can be accessed. Host security will become more important as hackers may try to implement attack vectors directly on hosts when the IPv6 address is known. The host security has to include
    - Personal firewall
    - Host intrusion prevention

Although operating systems on hosts prefer the IPv6 stack for outbound communication, it is prudent for you to disable the stack on hosts before production rollout. Also, note that an enabled IPv6 stack might cause excessive timeouts due to fallback mechanisms in situations in which the IPv6 end-to-end connectivity is broken.

Note Be aware that if you disable IPv6 on Windows Vista, Windows Server 2008, or later versions, some components might not function because Windows was designed specifically with IPv6 present.

Tunneling Security Considerations

If you are not capable of implementing a dual stack due to high cost or complexity, you will most likely implement tunneling to interconnect IPv6 islands with the rest of the IPv6 Internet. Several tunneling methods exist, as described earlier, but most of them do not include any security mechanisms. Without these security mechanisms, they can be easily intercepted or the content of the packets spoofed. If confidentiality, integrity, and authentication are prerequisites, you should use IPsec underneath the preferred tunneling method if possible.

Also, note that using tunneling mechanisms may introduce a security risk just in the way they operate or circumvent existing security policies. For example, Teredo will likely be enabled by default and will be encapsulated inside the UDP port 3544, which may pass most security devices if not prohibited explicitly. Also, a tunnel is built in a semiautomatic manner to a third-party tunneling endpoint, which may inspect traffic or spoof content.

Multihoming

As with the IPv4 solution, multiple businesses around the world require a multihoming solution to offer continuity to the business process. Because reliable Internet access is readily available, the design of the WAN is well known in IPv4. The solution is a combination of PI address space announced through BGP to an upstream provider. This solution solves most of the high-availability issues and is elegant to implement for the enterprise customer.

The same design is the best solution also in IPv6. However, it includes its downsides:

- Explosion of global BGP table
- Lack of summarization
- Application and fee for PI at RIR

There have been attempts at solving the multihoming issue with two or more PA allocations through the use of a protocol-based solution. It theoretically looked to be compliant with the requirements of the customer but introduced more problems. The most promising protocol solution is LISP. Its protocol design makes it very natural to be used with IPv6.

There have also been proposals of resolving the multihoming with two PA allocations through alternate design of the WAN routers; however, not one of these solutions fully competes with PI+BGP in network availability, load balancing, and host configuration. You may use policy-based routing, splitting your subnet into regions, or assigning subnet slices to your hosts, but might encounter use cases in which those designs will face issues.

Summary

- Create a list of services that need migration.
- Consider Layer 2 security (IPv6 relies on ICMPv6).
- Are your applications supporting IPv6?
    - Applications might have a dependency that requires a full rewrite.
    - Alternatively, you can provide a workaround (NAT64, SLB64, reverse proxy).
- Consider dual-stack security (have identical security policies for both protocols).
- Consider tunnel security (Teredo is enabled by default).
- IPv6 multihoming is the same as IPv4 multihoming.

Review Questions

After answering the following questions, please refer to Appendix A, "Answers to Review Questions," for the answers.

1. Which workarounds can be implemented to allow IPv6 communication with applications that do not have IPv6 support? (Select two.)
   a. DNS64
   b. ISATAP
   c. NAT64
   d. SLB64
   e. DS-LITE

2. Which mechanisms are present in IPv6 to secure the link layer? (Select two.)
   a. SEND
   b. CGA
   c. RA
   d. PMUTD
   e. PMUTD

3. Which multihoming solution allows for high availability and load sharing of traffic?
   a. Requesting a PA prefix from the connecting service providers and advertising both through BGP
   b. Requesting a PI prefix from the regional registrar and advertising the prefix to connecting service providers
   c. Implementing SHIM6 on WAN routers
   d. Implementing LISP on WAN routers as xTR, which registers with the service providers' Map Server and Map Resolver

4. True or false? If confidentiality, integrity, and authentication are prerequisites, IPsec should be used underneath the preferred tunneling method if possible.
   a. True
   b. False

Chapter 8

Service Provider–Managed VPNs

Upon completing this chapter, you will be able to

- Choose your WAN connection
- Describe the Layer 3 MPLS VPN
- Describe MPLS VPN architecture
- Identify MPLS VPN architecture components
- Describe the PE router architecture
- Describe route distinguishers
- Explain route distinguisher operation in MPLS VPN
- Describe route targets
- Explain route target operation
- Use EIGRP as the PE-CE routing protocol
- Use OSPF as the PE-CE routing protocol
- Use MP-BGP as the PE-CE routing protocol
- Explain MPLS/VPN routing propagation
- Describe packet forwarding through the MPLS/VPN backbone
- Describe VPWS basics
- Design VPWS
- Design VPLS
- Compare VPLS and VPWS

You can connect remote sites to your main site in multiple ways. You can build your own infrastructure, lease a virtual private network (VPN) solution from the service provider, or configure your own VPN solution over the Internet. This chapter focuses on the service provider (SP)-managed-WAN (VPN) solutions.

When using a managed VPN solution, you connect your edge network devices to the service provider wide-area network (WAN). The service provider in turn takes care of traffic routing and forwarding across the WAN, which means that the service provider is responsible for transferring packets from one site to the other. Service providers build networks using different underlying technologies, the most popular being Multiprotocol Label Switching (MPLS). With the Layer 3 MPLS VPN model, businesses can offload their WAN core routing by using a private IP-based service offering from a service provider. Unlike legacy overlay networks (such as ATM or Frame Relay), MPLS VPNs require that the enterprise to peer with the service provider at the IP Layer 3 level. In this case, the SP network is involved in the Layer 3 routing of the IP packets delivered by the enterprise. In addition, modern service providers can offer emulated Layer 2 WAN services that maintain the same Layer 2 legacy WAN model with optimized features and significantly increased bandwidth, commonly referred to as Layer 2 MPLS VPN.

Choosing Your WAN Connection

When it comes to choosing a WAN technology and service provider, you must consider your business needs. There is no single best choice for every organization. The best choice is the provider or providers that best meet your organizational needs and that offer the most transparent service.

As a network designer, you must always assess the different WAN solutions against the different design requirements, which are normally a combination of technical and nontechnical requirements. In other words, there are some major decision points when you are choosing your WAN connection. These decision points may include service availability, along with financial and technical aspects.

When you are designing your WAN, you first need to identify the business continuity and applications' availability requirements (specifically mission-critical business applications). Then you need to check the offered VPN service availability. One of the common concerns here with regard to SP-provided VPN services is that not all services are always available at all customer sites. For instance, in major cities, normally service providers offer a high level of redundancy, whereas in remote locations, this capability can be limited to certain providers, if there are any. Therefore, you might be forced to combine multiple services. If you have different options, there are a couple of major decision points to choose your WAN connection.

Although the financial aspect is not a technical point, it is very important to consider when you choose your WAN connection. This is true especially if cost is one of the primary business-influencing factors to consider a technology or if a limited budget is allocated for the WAN project. Therefore, you must compare the cost of the service, the equipment cost, and the operational cost and ensure that the cost of the selected WAN solution and provider is justifiable to the business. One important aspect to consider with the Layer 3 VPN is whether the service provider will be able to maintain your current customer edge (CE) IP addressing because re-addressing all your CE devices it can be a complicated task. That said, with the Layer 3 VPN, enterprise customers do not need to worry about the WAN core routing redesign or configuration. In contrast, it can be more complicated to change the provider when you choose a Layer 2 VPN because the routing is under your control and all the redesign and configuration will be the customer's responsibility.

In fact, several technical aspects can influence your decision when you are choosing your WAN connection, including the following:

- **Convergence:** With Layer 3 VPNs, the routing is under service provider control, which also includes the convergence time. When you choose a Layer 2 VPN solution, you are responsible for the routing. However, in both scenarios, the provider manages and controls the underlying infrastructure. In the case of link or node failure within the provider's MPLS cloud, the service provider will be responsible to reroute the traffic over a redundant path/component. As a result, this will impact the convergence time. Depending on the time the service provider needs to recover from a failure, it could be as fast as 50 milliseconds, or it could take hours or days in case of a major fiber link failure without efficient redundancy.

- **Scalability:** When you choose a Layer 2 VPN, you will face scalability issues with the full-mesh topologies, in which routing protocols may fail due to having many neighbors and adjacencies. With a Layer 3 VPN solution, each CE device has an adjacency only with the next-hop provider edge (PE) device, and it is therefore much more scalable.

- **Quality of service (QoS):** Almost always, WAN connections have limited bandwidth. Therefore, you often need QoS to prioritize for real-time traffic. Service providers often offer QoS for your traffic, but this solution usually leads to higher costs. Also, the cost and the offered number of classes (class of service, or CoS) vary between different service providers.

- **Service-level agreement (SLA) and reporting:** Some providers may offer some sort of SLA for their services. This SLA should be reviewed to achieve a minimal service level that agrees with the contract. Although the details of an SLA can vary, in general it should meet the specific requirements and network application needs of the customer. The following network performance deliverables might be negotiated:

    - Bandwidth
    - Latencies
    - Jitter
    - Packet drop
    - Network availability
    - SLA reporting

- **Supported traffic:** Often you may need to transfer traffic like multicast. Some service providers support multicast, whereas others do not. For example, you might need Layer 2 VPNs to allow the exchange of routing messages. In general, with a Layer 3 VPN WAN, you may depend on the support routing and forwarding capabilities; in contrast, with a Layer 2 VPN, you have the flexibility to enable capabilities such as multicast or IPv6 as required. The reason is that you (the enterprise) are deploying and controlling the routing while the service provider in a Layer 2 VPN provides only Layer 2 frame forwarding.

- **MTU size:** It is important to reduce fragmentation to a minimum. Therefore, you need to know the MTU size to set the appropriate MTU values on your network. Also, you might need to forward jumbo frames in scenarios in which you send some encapsulated/tunneled packets. Therefore, MTU size also is an important technical aspect to consider.

- **Access coverage and media type:** It is critical to understand the physical access coverage each service provider can provide because some service providers may not be able to connect some remote location as part of your network. When you evaluate an MPLS VPN service offer by a service provider, you should understand the PE access coverage and consider in which cities around the world the PE routers that are used for physical customer connections are located. In some cases, providers have partners that provide local access. It is important to consider the locations where these partners provide PE routers and to make sure this coverage meets your organization's needs. In addition, the access media type is another aspect that you must consider. For example, with a Layer 3 VPN, normally you can have more flexible options, such as classical Copper (Ethernet), 3G, LTE, and DSL, whereas with a Layer 2 VPN, the options are limited.

- **Inter-AS MPLS VPN:** To establish a global-scale footprint, MPLS VPN providers may establish partnerships with other service providers to interconnect MPLS VPNs and have presence in certain countries where they do not have local PEs. This is known as an interprovider MPLS VPN. With this model, the cost can increase significantly when spanning an interprovider link. In addition, inter-AS MPLS VPNs can affect the availability or behavior of services such as QoS and multicast. One provider may support these services in a different manner than another, or a provider might not support a service at all. Therefore, it is important to consider SP inter-AS agreements and whether the implementation supports your network requirements.

- **Managed CE service:** One of the common services offered by today's service providers is the managed CE. With this service, enterprise customers can have immediate access to the benefits of an MPLS network, with network availability and security being managed by the service provider. With this model, enterprises with a limited IT staff or limited knowledge of routing can offload the deployment and management of the CE nodes to the service provider as a paid service. However, with the managed CE service model, it is important to understand the limits of administrative control of the CE device. For instance, you will be limited to the SLA offered by the service provider to perform any change or troubleshooting to the devices, and enterprise customers do not always desire these circumstances.

As a network designer, you must consider the answers to the following questions during planning and before you implement a WAN MPLS VPN:

- Who is responsible for the core WAN routing management? Are there any routing expertise limitations with regard to IT staff?

- Who manages the customer edge WAN devices?

- What is the number of remote sites, and what is the percentage of the projected growth, if any?

- How are the remote sites geographically distributed? Within one city or across different cities or countries?

- Are there any budget constraints?

- What are the required WAN capabilities to transport business applications over the WAN with the desired experience (such as QoS, IP multicast, or IPv6)?

Layer 3 MPLS VPNs

The most common implementation of a Layer 3 VPN is MPLS VPN. MPLS is a technology that is used to forward packets over the core network, by doing forwarding decisions that are based on labels. That is sometimes referred to as label switching. On the other hand, the general VPN concept refers to the technologies that provide a bridge between two network islands such as private networks over a public network (Internet).

Layer 3 MPLS VPN is the technology that is used to connect multiple customer sites. This solution relies mainly on the following core control protocols:

- MPLS is used to forward packets through the service provider core (mainly used for label switching between the network node with the service provider network).

- The Core Interior Gateway Protocol (IGP) is used to exchange internal prefixes only (including the loopback IP address of the PE nodes to form Border Gateway Protocol [BGP] peering sessions among them).

- MP-BGP is used to exchange customer routes between service provider edge routers.

- Customer edge routing is the point where the service provider exchanges routing with the customer edge node. This can be Interior Gateway Protocol (which is different from the core IGP), Exterior Border Gateway Protocol (EBGP), or static route.

Layer 3 MPLS VPN technology is relatively simple from a customer point of view. A customer must connect the equipment directly to the service provider network. If the customer uses dynamic routing to transfer routes to another location, it must configure the IGP on its own routers. This IGP must be deployed in alignment with service provider supported and implemented IGP, and both parties need to agree on the IGP parameters. From an IP routing perspective, when the service provider receives the routes from the IGP, it must transfer these routes to the other locations. In this case, BGP is used to propagate the routes across the SP network (from one PE to another where the customer CE routers are connected). This architecture can easily connect large numbers of sites together because MP-BGP is properly designed to carry a large number of routes.

As a network designer or architect, you need to remember that if you consider Layer 3 MPLS VPN, you must depend on the service provider with regard to introducing network IP services such as multicast or IPv6. It is not easy to change the service provider because complete routing must be reconfigured on the organization edge network.

In addition, when you choose a Layer 3 MPLS VPN solution to connect the sites, the service provider network will be your core WAN that glues the different remote sites together. However, routing scenarios can sometimes be complex, such as in a customer hub-and-spoke topology where traffic to and from each spoke is routed through the hub. However, the most common deployment is an any-to-any topology where any customer site can connect directly to other sites that belong to the same customer over the Layer 3 MPLS VPN core. When IP packets enter the service provider's domain, they will be routed based on the routing information in the VRF table of the corresponding customer's VPN and encapsulated with MPLS labels to ensure proper tunneling and de-multiplexing through the core.

With this routing model, routing convergence and reliability of the WAN core network will not be under your control, so you are mostly dependent on the service provider. Therefore, you need to ensure these aspects are covered and agreed upon as part of the SLA with service providers to meet your business continuity and application requirements.

MPLS VPN Architecture

MPLS, IGP, and MP-BGP form the foundation of the MPLS VPN as control protocols. The main components of MPLS/VPN architecture that use these protocols and perform end-to-end routing and forwarding are as follows (see Figure 8-1):

- **Customer network:** It is a customer-controlled domain.

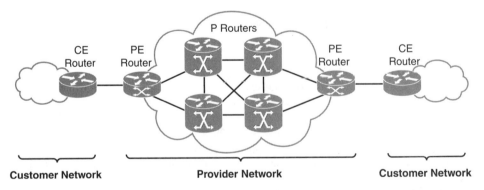

Figure 8-1 *Components of MPLS/VPN Architecture*

- **Customer edge (CE) router:** CE routers are located on the edge of the customer network. These routers have direct connectivity to the service provider network, specifically to the provider edge (PE) router.

- **Provider (P) network:** This provider-controlled domain consists of the PE and core routers. These routers connect the customer sites over a single shared underlying infrastructure. The P router is sometimes referred to as a label switch router (LSR), in reference to its primary role in the core of the network, performing label switching/swapping of MPLS traffic.

- **Provider edge (PE) router:** The PE router is located at the edge of the MPLS service provider cloud. It is connected to the CE and P routers. PE routers provide the capability to terminate links from different customers' CE nodes without compromising the routing separation requirements per customer. The PE is sometimes referred to as a label edge router (LER) or edge label switch router (ELSR) in reference to its role at the edge of the MPLS cloud, performing label imposition and disposition.

- **P router:** P routers are located in the core of the provider network and are connected to either another P router or the PE router. P routers perform fast MPLS label switching to forward packets as fast as possible across the core network.

As in any typical routing design, the customer must push all the routes that will be accessible at the other customer sites to the local CE routers. Thus, the customer is responsible for implementing the proper routing protocol for this task.

Based on the architecture described previously, the CE router peers only with the directly connected PE router outside its own site. The CE router does not peer with any of the CE routers from the other sites across the service provider network.

Consequently, for the customer to advertise the local routes toward the service provider edge (PE) node, the customer and the service provider (CE and PE routers) need to exchange routing information using either a dynamic routing protocol such as OSPF or using static routing. Then the customer must inject all the routes that need to be accessible to the other sites into that routing protocol; this routing protocol (between the CE and PE) can be the same instance as the internal routing protocol at the customer sites or a different one. In fact, the routing protocol selection is a matter of agreement between the customer and the service provider. Also, service providers normally support certain routing protocols to be used with the CE side (most commonly, static, OSPF, and EBGP).

On the other hand, the ingress PE router redistributes the customer routes to the BGP routing protocol. In turn, BGP (specifically MP-iBGP) will propagate these redistributed routes to the other PE routers (egress PEs), which are used to connect to the same customer. These routes are redistributed from MP-BGP into IGP. IGP between the PE and CE routers is then responsible for transferring the routes to the CE router. MP-BGP sessions are established only between the PE routers in the 60920038 network (see Figure 8-2).

236 Chapter 8: Service Provider–Managed VPNs

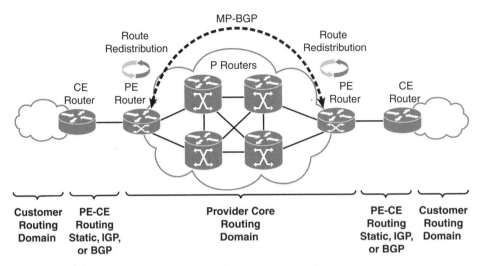

Figure 8-2 *Layer 3 MPLS VPN High-level Routing Architecture*

Enterprise Routing Considerations

When you are designing enterprise WAN routing, and WAN transport is provided by an L3 MPLS VPN service provider, it is important to understand what could impact the enterprise routing design over the WAN. You also need to understand whether any changes are needed to the routing protocol used by the enterprise customer and how this protocol interacts with the SP. The following are some of the primary general considerations:

- **Route limits:** Some Layer 3 MPLS VPN providers impose limits on the number of routes that can be advertised by the customer, in which you may need to consider route summarization where possible to avoid this issue, or the provider may ask for extra charges (which ideally should be part of the agreed-upon SLA).

- **Supported routing protocol and connectivity models:** The used or supported routing protocols as a provider edge–customer edge (PE-CE) routing protocol by the service provider and what is being used by the enterprise internally can lead to major issues if you do not take them into consideration during the planning and design phase. For example, an enterprise might use EIGRP as its IGP and eBGP as the PE-CE protocol. In this scenario, there must be careful consideration of administrative distance, redistribution between EIGRP to/from eBGP, and routing loops that might occur. In addition, as a network designer, you must be aware of the supported connectivity model between the PE and CE side by the service provider and its impact. For example, when backdoor connectivity (connectivity outside the MPLS VPN service to connect two CE routers directly) is used, there is the potential for problems such as routing loops or suboptimal routing. In this case, you need to ensure the routing design from the enterprise takes this into account, and you need to understand what is supported by the service provider in scenarios like this. For instance, are OSPF sham links supported? Does the PE support BGP cost community or site of origin (SoO)?

- **Load balancing:** Normally, when you have a site (CE router) dual-homed to different PEs, you can take advantage of the connectivity model and use all the links to forward traffic. However, CE-to-PE load balancing is controlled by the enterprise, while PE-to-CE load balancing is controlled by the service provider. Therefore, you should find out whether the service provider supports this, and you must coordinate with the SP to achieve proper load balancing.

Provider Edge (PE) Router Architecture

The PE routers are critical components in the MPLS VPN architecture because the routers hold most of the intelligence in the MPLS VPN environment and perform multiple functions.

One of the primary functions of the PE router is to isolate customers' routing instances and traffic. Because the routing should be separate and private for each customer on a PE router, each customer/VPN should have its own routing table. This table is called the *virtual routing and forwarding (VRF) routing table*. Typically, each interface toward a customer CE router belongs to only one VRF. Therefore, each packet that is received on the interface is unambiguously identified as belonging to that VRF. This implementation is similar to having one router for each customer.

The PE router must establish the IGP routing adjacency with the CE routers to get the routes from the customer. These routes are installed in the isolated routing table. Alternatively, the PE router could have a static route in the isolated routing table. It can be an operational burden when you manually need to configure many static routes. Because the routing tables are completely isolated, MPLS Layer 3 VPN offers the flexibility to support overlapping address space among the different customers.

The PE routers exchange routes that are installed in the VRF routing table to the other PE routers with MP-BGP. As mentioned previously, MPLS Layer 3 VPN supports overlapping address space between different customers. When BGP carries IPv4 prefixes across the service provider network, they must be unique. If the customers have overlapping IP addressing, the routing would be wrong. To solve this issue, the concept of route distinguisher (RD) was introduced. The basic idea is that each prefix from each customer receives a unique identifier to distinguish the same prefix from different customers. When a router prepends the RD to the route, the route becomes a VPNv4 prefix in MP-BGP.

In addition, each PE router maintains its own global routing table that is used primarily to establish MP-BGP connections with other PE routers. Also, PE routers use this routing table to define MPLS labels to the other P and PE routers for traffic forwarding over the provider core network (see Figures 8-3 and 8-4).

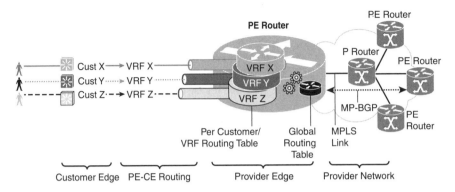

Figure 8-3 *PE Architecture in Layer 3 MPLS VPN Environment*

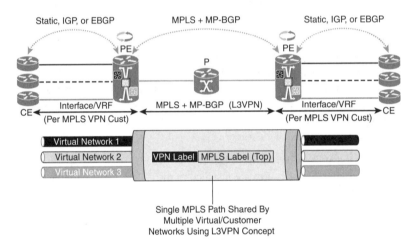

Figure 8-4 *High-level "End-to-End" Path Virtualization in Layer 3 MPLS VPN Environment*

Route Distinguishers

In MPLS VPN, the PE router provides isolation between customers by using VRFs. The prefixes are propagated to the other PE routers with MP-BGP. The problem is that the prefixes need to be unique across the MPLS VPN provider network. For instance, if different customers have overlapping IP addressing (and this is very common and typical for a shared infrastructure providing transit service for many different customers), this situation would cause a serious problem for BGP. As mentioned earlier, to solve this problem, the concept of route distinguisher (RD) was conceived.

The basic idea behind the RD is that every customer receives a unique identifier to distinguish between the same prefix from different customers. To create a unique prefix, you combine the RD with the IPv4 prefix. The combination is called a VPNv4 prefix. MP-BGP needs to carry these VPNv4 prefixes between the PE routers.

An RD is a 64-bit unique identifier prepended to the 32-bit customer prefix learned from the CE router. The combination of the RD and the prefix will generate a unique 96-bit–long IP prefix that can be carried across the MPL-BGP domain as a unique prefix (to overcome customers' overlapping IP addresses). There are two formats for the RD. The first one is ASN:*nn*, where ASN represents the autonomous system number and *nn* represents a number. The second format is IP-address:*nn*. The first format is the most commonly used (see Figure 8-5).

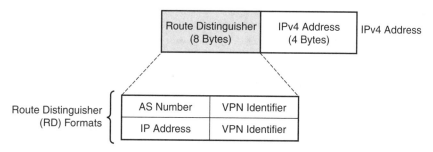

Figure 8-5 *RD Address Format*

VPNv4 addresses are exchanged only between PE routers, whether PE routers are part of the same SP/MP-BGP domain (single autonomous system scenario) or between different SPs/MP-BGP domains (Inter-AS/provider scenario). In contrast, VPNv4 addresses are never used between PE to CE routers.

As illustrated in Figure 8-6, the ingress PE router receives the same IPv4 prefix from two different customers. Then these prefixes are installed into the respective VRF routing table of each customer. When the PE router propagates these two routes to the other PE routers (egress PEs), it prepends a different RD for each customer prefix to make a unique VPNv4 route per customer. When remote egress PE routers receive these routes, they strip the RDs from the VPNv4 prefix and install the routes into the respective VRF routing table for each customer. The IPv4 prefix is then forwarded to the CE routers. The route target (RT) value controls which route to be installed into which VRF table. The subsequent section covers it in more detail.

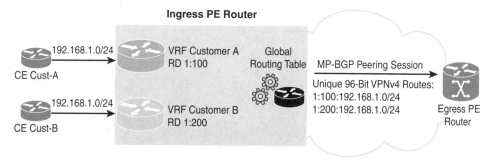

Figure 8-6 *VPNv4 Route Structuring Concept*

Route Target (RT)

RT is considered part of the primary control plane elements of a typical MPLS L3VPN architecture because it facilitates the identification of which VRF can install which VPN routes. Also, it would be hard to achieve more complex VPN scenarios if you are using only the RD. Consider a scenario in which one of the sites has to participate in more than one VPN. To enable more complex scenarios, RTs were introduced into the MPLS VPN architecture.

An RT is a BGP-extended community that identifies the VPN membership of the routes. BGP communities are used to implement RTs. The higher-order 16 bits of the BGP-extended community (64 total bits) are encoded with a value corresponding to the VPN membership of the specific site.

The RTs are attached to a customer route at the moment when the PE router converts the route from an IPv4 route to a VPNv4 route. The RTs attached to the route, called export RTs, are configured separately for each virtual routing table in a PE router. Export RTs identify a set of VPNs in which the sites that are associated with the virtual routing table belong.

When the VPNv4 routes are propagated to other PE routers, those routers need to select the routes to import into their virtual routing tables. This selection is based on import RTs. Each virtual routing table in a PE router can have a number of configured import RTs. They identify the set of VPNs from which the virtual routing table is accepting routes.

In other words, when the PE router receives the VPNv4 route, it checks the export RTs that are attached to the route. This RT is compared to the import RT that is configured on all VRFs. The PE router injects the route into the VRF routing table if there is a match between the RT that was received and the import RT for the specific VRF routing table.

In the example shown in Figure 8-7, the PE router injects routes that are received with RT 1:1 into the VRF routing table for Customer A. The routes with RT 1:2 are injected into the VRF routing table for Customer B. The PE router injects routes with RT 1:100 into both routing tables because both accept routes with RT 1:100. The route with RT 1:100 could be a shared service that different customers require access to, such as a software-based service (software as a service, or SaaS) hosted by the same provider.

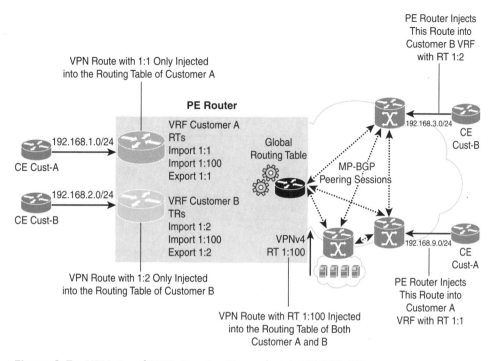

Figure 8-7 *VPNv4 and VRFs Routing Control with MP-BGP RT*

PE-CE Routing Protocol

As we know from the preceding sections, for the enterprise customers and the Layer 3 MPLS VPN to exchange routing information, a form of routing must be enabled between the CE and PE devices. This can be static routing, IGP, or BGP. From a design point of view, apart from static routing, you need to understand the behavior of a routing protocol when it is used as a PE-CE routing protocol, along with the associated implications. This section covers the design considerations when EIGRP, OSPF, or BGP is used as the PE-CE routing protocol.

Using EIGRP as the PE-CE Routing Protocol

When you are designing and deploying EIGRP as the PE-CE routing protocol, it is important to understand how EIGRP behaves and is treated in a Layer 3 MPLS VPN environment. Typically, in a Layer 3 MPLS VPN environment, there will be route redistribution between MP-BGP and EIGRP as the PE-CE routing protocol. Technically, redistributing the routes from BGP into EIGRP makes all the routes external EIGRP routes. This means that some pieces of information are lost during redistribution, and this situation can cause some problems when you have backdoor links between sites. To alleviate these problems, new *extended BGP communities* are introduced. These new communities enable the remote PE routers to reconstruct the EIGRP routes with all their characteristics. These characteristics are metric components, AS, tag and, for external routes, the remote AS number, remote ID, remote protocol, and remote metric.

Table 8-1 describes the extended community attributes that are appended to BGP routes and are used to carry EIGRP information across the service provider backbone.

Table 8-1 *BGP Extended Community Attributes for EIGRP*

Type	Usage	Value
0x8800	EIGRP General Route Information	Route Flag and Tag
0x8801	EIGRP Route Metric Information and Autonomous System	Autonomous System and Delay
0x8802	EIGRP Route Metric Information	Reliability, Next Hop, and Bandwidth
0x8803	EIGRP Route Metric Information	Reserve, Load, and MTU
0x8804	EIGRP External Route Information	Remote Autonomous System and Remote ID
0x8805	EIGRP External Route Information	Remote Protocol and Remote Metric

The following are the most common and possible scenarios when implementing EIGRP as the PE-CE routing protocol:

- The enterprise is running EIGRP at all its sites using the same EIGRP AS number.

- The enterprise is running EIGRP at all its sites using different EIGRP AS numbers.

- The enterprise is running EIGRP at some sites, while others use different routing protocols.

- The enterprise is running EIGRP, and two or more CE routers are connected with a backdoor link as a backup link.

The following section covers each of these scenarios in more detail.

EIGRP as a PE-CE Routing Protocol Using the Same AS Number

As shown in Figure 8-8, the enterprise is running EIGRP at all its sites. The enterprise is also using the same AS number at all its sites. In this case, the following steps are used:

Step 1. The CE1 router advertises a network via EIGRP to the local PE1 router. This network can be internal or external.

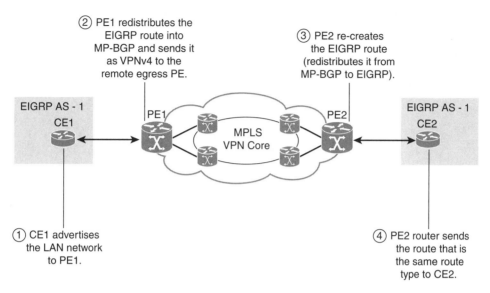

Figure 8-8 *EIGRP PE-CE Routing Using the Same AS*

Step 2. The PE1 router redistributes the network from EIGRP into MP-BGP with encoded route information in the extended community attributes within MP-BGP. It sends the routing updates to other PE routers.

Step 3. The PE2 router receives the MP-BGP update, which includes extended community information for EIGRP as well as a matching EIGRP AS number.

Step 4. The PE2 router re-creates the EIGRP routes and sends them to the CE2 router. These routes have the same route type as the original routes, and they have the same metric as the sending PE1 had for these routes. The backbone appears as zero cost.

EIGRP as the PE-CE Routing Protocol Using Different AS Numbers

As shown in Figure 8-9, the enterprise is running EIGRP at all its sites but is using different EIGRP AS numbers. In this case, the following steps are used:

Step 1. The CE1 router advertises a network via EIGRP to the local PE1 router.

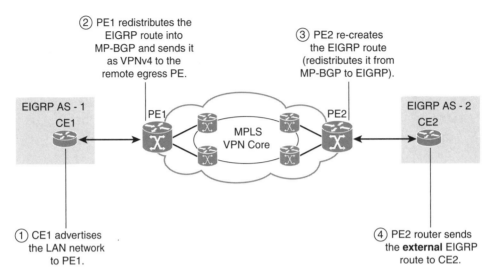

Figure 8-9 *EIGRP PE-CE Routing Using Different AS Numbers*

Step 2. The PE1 router redistributes the network from EIGRP into MP-BGP with route information encoded in the extended community attributes within MP-BGP.

Step 3. The PE2 router receives the MP-BGP update that includes extended community information for EIGRP as well as an EIGRP AS number.

Step 4. The PE2 router re-creates the EIGRP route as an external EIGRP route using the configured default metric and advertises the route to the CE2 router.

EIGRP as the PE-CE Routing Protocol at Some Sites Only

As shown in Figure 8-10, the enterprise is running EIGRP at some sites but not at others. In the example, one of the sites is using OSPF as the routing protocol. In this case, the following steps are used:

Step 1. The CE1 router advertises a network via OSPF to the local PE1 router.

Layer 3 MPLS VPNs   245

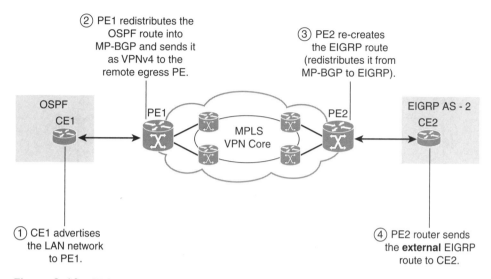

Figure 8-10 *EIGRP PE-CE Routing Using EIGRP at Some Sites*

Step 2. The PE1 router redistributes the network from OSPF into MP-BGP with route information encoded in the extended community attributes within MP-BGP.

Step 3. The PE2 router receives the MP-BGP update, which does not include any extended community information from EIGRP.

Step 4. The PE2 router re-creates the route as an external EIGRP route using the configured default metric and advertises it to the CE2 router. The originated protocol appears to be BGP.

EIGRP as the PE-CE Routing Protocol with a Backdoor Link between Customer Sites

From a network design perspective, this scenario is the most complicated one because it can lead to either suboptimal routing or routing loops if it is not designed properly. As shown in Figure 8-11, CE routers are connected using a backdoor link as a backup link. EIGRP AS-1 runs exchange EIGRP routing between CE1 and PE1 routers and between CE1 and CE2 routers. When the CE1 router advertises a prefix, it is advertised to the PE1 router and the CE2 router. The PE1 router installs this route into VRF, redistributes this EIGRP route into BGP, and passes the route to the PE2 router. Likewise, the CE2 router advertises this route to the PE2 router. At this stage, the PE2 router has two BGP paths available for the prefix:

- The IBGP advertisement from the PE1 router
- The locally redistributed BGP route from the CE2 EIGRP advertisement

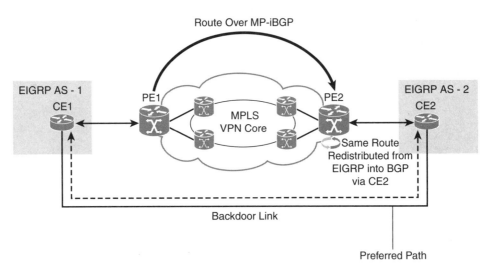

Figure 8-11 *EIGRP with Backdoor Link Suboptimal Routing*

This decision leads to traffic being forwarded over the backdoor link as its primary path. This result may not be what you want to achieve; for example, the backdoor link could be a low-bandwidth–capacity link and you want to use it as a backup path only. As a network designer, you must ensure that the network design always meets the requirements of your business-critical applications. In this case, if the traffic is sent over the backdoor link as the primary path, this will probably impact the quality of the applications and the users' experience because it's a low-bandwidth–capacity link.

The additional attribute that is known as the BGP *cost community* was developed to handle such cases. The BGP cost community is configured on the PE router, which attaches an extended community attribute. The cost community value is compared, and it influences the path determination. When this community is adjusted as needed, traffic can be forwarded to the correct path.

By default, when the PE redistributes the EIGRP path into BGP, the BGP cost community attribute is populated with the EIGRP metric. As shown in Figure 8-12, PE2 has two options: the IBGP path that is learned from PE1 or locally originated BGP path learned through redistribution of the EIGRP route from CE2. The EIGRP metric of the route that is advertised from CE2 includes the added cost of traversing the backdoor link. Therefore, the BGP cost community of the IBGP path is lower and thus preferred and installed.

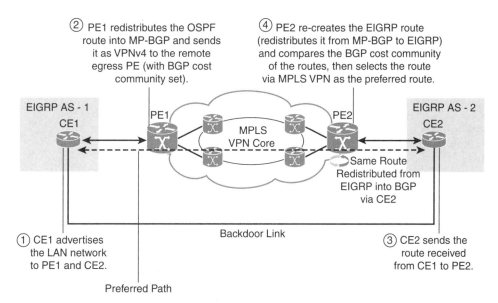

Figure 8-12 *EIGRP with Backdoor Link Optimal Routing*

Using OSPF as the PE-CE Routing Protocol

When you are designing and deploying OSPF as the PE-CE routing protocol, it is important to understand how OSPF behaves and is treated in the Layer 3 MPLS VPN environment.

First of all, the nature of OSPF as a link-state routing protocol and how it selects routes is completely different from EIGRP. As mentioned earlier, as a network designer, you first need to understand how the protocol behaves to be able to optimize the design. That being said, the general concept of route propagation from across the Layer 3 MPLS VPN is the same with slight differences based on the protocol used.

Like EIGRP, OSPF can be designed to use different approaches, such as the same area numbers across all sites, different area numbers, OSPF on at some times only, and CEs with a backdoor link. Also, the design option with a backdoor link between CE routers is always the most complex one and needs to be designed carefully.

As we know from Chapter 3, "OSPF Design," OSPF uses areas to create network hierarchy. Area 0 is the backbone area that connects all other areas. In a PE-CE design with Layer 3 MPLS VPN, the MPLS VPN backbone can be considered as an added hierarchy that is higher than the OSPF backbone area. It can be called the MPLS VPN super backbone. It is actually not an area because it runs IBGP. However, it acts as an area, and PE acts as an ABR when it advertises type 3 LSAs to the CE routers. Or, it acts as an ASBR when it advertises type 5 LSAs to the CE routers. In other words, area 0 is not mandatory when connecting to MPLS VPN service even if the remote sites are using different area numbers.

In fact, CE routers can be in area 0 or any other area. If more than one area exists at the customer site, the PE router must be in area 0 because it is an ABR. If it is not, a virtual link between the PE router and the nearest ABR in the customer site must bring area 0 up to the PE router. Figure 8-13 shows the various possible scenarios.

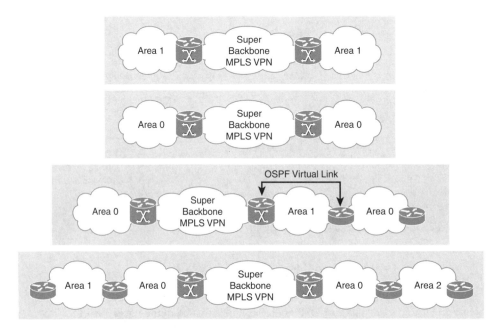

Figure 8-13 *Different OSPF Area Layouts in Layer 2 MPLS VPN Environment*

Also, the same concept is used with EIGRP; several extra BGP-extended communities were defined to transport attributes of the OSPF routes across the MPLS VPN backbone, including

- Route type
- Area number
- OSPF router ID
- Domain ID
- Metric type 1 or 2

The PE router is able to completely reconstruct the OSPF route with these OSPF-specific BGP-extended communities. The route type indicates what kind of route the PE router should advertise in OSPF. The remote PE router will advertise an interarea summary route (LSA type 3) into the OSPF area for route types 1, 2, and 3 (LSA types 1, 2, and 3). The domain ID indicates to the remote PE router how to advertise an external OSPF route. By default, the domain ID is the same as the process ID. If the domain ID of the received route is different from the OSPF process in VRF, the route is advertised as an OSPF external route (LSA type 5) type 2. Otherwise, the route is advertised as an internal route.

To preserve the OSPF metric, the PE router uses the OSPF metric to set the BGP MED attribute. When the route is redistributed again to OSPF on the remote PE router, the PE uses the MED to set the OSPF metric of the OSPF internal or external route.

Consequently, it is important to understand that OSPF as a PE-CE routing protocol over an MPLS VPN behaves slightly different from its normal behavior in a typical routed network. As shown in Figure 8-14, CE2 expects to receive the site-1 prefix 10.11.1.0/24 as the type-3 Summary interarea route from the other site; however, it receives it as External type 5.

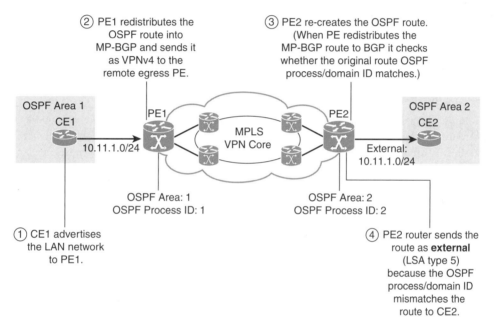

Figure 8-14 *Impact of OSPF Process/Domain ID on the OSPF Route Type in a Layer 3 MPLS VPN Environment*

If you take a closer look at Figure 8-14, you'll find that the OSPF process IDs at PE1 and PE2 are different. Normally, the OSPF process ID is only locally significant; however, in an MPLS VPN setup, the cloud acts as if it's a single OSPF router. Thus, the OSPF process ID should match. Otherwise, external type-5 routes are generated. In other words, when the egress PE router redistributes the MP-BGP route back into the OSPF and the OSPF process ID mismatches the ingress PE router's OSPF process ID, the route will be injected as external type 5.

The downside of this design outcome is that all OSPF routes become external on the remote PE when the routes are redistributed back into the OSPF. When you have a backdoor link between CE routers advertising the same prefix as an interarea route (LSA type 3), by default, this redistribution will make the routes via the MPLS VPN less preferable than the routes that were learned through the backdoor link. Also, in this scenario, the

PE router becomes an ASBR from the CE point of view because it will generate external OSPF routes (LSA type 5).

If this behavior can cause an issue such as suboptimal routing over a backdoor link, you need to ensure that both ingress and egress PE routers have the same OSPF process ID configured, or you need to configure the same domain ID on both PEs to solve the problem.

Both options provide a solution that will prevent the redistributed routes from becoming OSPF external routes. Instead, the routes will become interarea routes. This is different from the typical OSPF behavior because the PE routers are performing redistribution, which would normally generate external OSPF routes (LSA type 5). The PE routers actually become ABR routers instead of ASBR routers. However, all OSPF internal routes become interarea routes after traversing the MPLS/VPN backbone, even if the area number matches on different PE/CE routers.

OSPF as the PE-CE Routing Protocol with a Backdoor Link between Customer Sites

In the normal OSPF operation, intra-area routes are more preferred than interarea OSPF routes. In the MPLS VPN, all internal OSPF routes become interarea routes at the remote sites. When a backdoor link exists between sites, there can be a problem because all intra-area routes remain intra-area routes across the backdoor link. Therefore, the intra-area routes that are advertised across the backdoor link are always preferred. To avoid this situation, you must configure a special link between the PE routers. This link is called the *sham link*.

As shown in Figure 8-15, the sham link is a fake (virtual) link between two PE routers. It has two endpoints, with a /32 IP address. This IP address must be in the VRF routing table for the customer. IBGP must advertise this IP address from one PE to the other. The sham link is a point-to-point link between these two IP addresses.

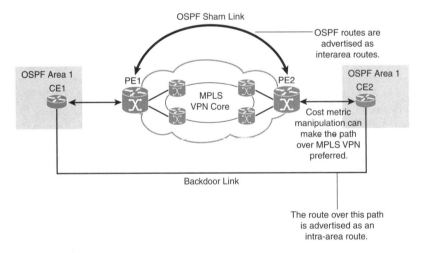

Figure 8-15 *OSPF Sham Link*

The sham link is included in the SPF computation, just as any other link in OSPF. The LSAs are flooded across the sham link, and all OSPF route types are preserved and are not converted to LSA type 3 or 5. If the sham link fails, routing is still possible, but then all the routes become interarea routes, and routes through the backdoor take preference.

Even if the sham link exists and the OSPF routes are flooded across it, the BGP must still advertise the OSPF routes as VPNv4 routes from PE to PE. The reason for this is that BGP must carry MPLS VPN labels for correct forwarding across the MPLS VPN backbone.

OSPF Route Summarization Design Consideration

When you are using OSPF as the PE-CE routing protocol, there will be no backbone area (area 0) in the center to glue all the different areas. Instead, the MPLS VPN cloud will act as a super backbone to provide the transport of OSPF prefixes using MP-BGP. As a result, this architecture will impose a change to the classical OSPF hierarchy or the areas' structure; in turn, this will impact how route summarization can be done. For instance, in the scenario depicted in Figure 8-16, if the HQ site (area 0) needs to send a summary route to all other sites, remote site 4 must receive only a single summary route for other sites.

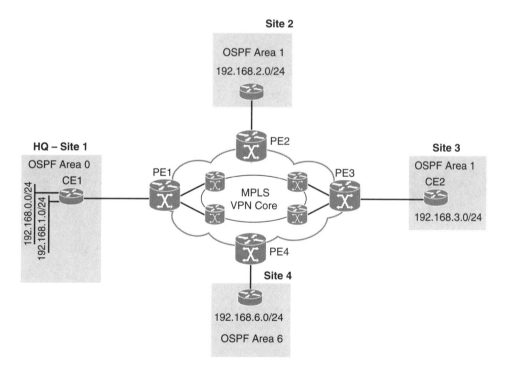

Figure 8-16 *Enterprise with Four Sites Connected over MPLS VPN*

Summarization cannot be performed at any of the CE routers (customer side) because ABR and ASBR do not exist at the customer side. To achieve the summarization requirements described previously, PE1 can send the summary route of the HQ network via BGP and advertise the summarized address to all other sites. In addition, to send a summary route only to site 4, you need to summarize all the other site routes on PE4 (see Figure 8-17).

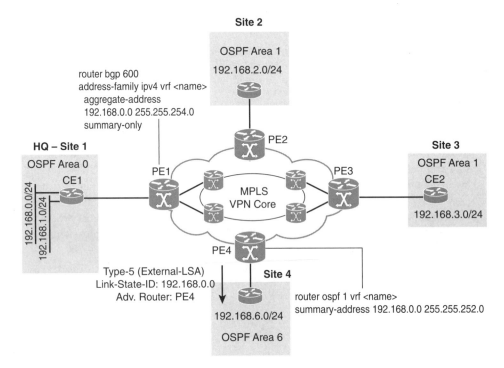

Figure 8-17 *OSPF PE-CE Summarization over Layer 3 MPLS VPN*

Note After the summary route is configured at PE4, this summary route will be propagated to all sites as a result of redistribution from OSPF into BGP; therefore, you must be careful when enabling summarization in such an environment with OSPF. The summary route needs to be filtered while redistributing OSPF into BGP on PE4, unless it is desirable to send the summary to some other PEs.

Using BGP as the PE-CE Routing Protocol

The BGP, specifically EBGP, can be used as the PE-CE routing protocol. In fact, it is one of the most common protocols used for routing between the CE and PE devices because it offers flexible design capabilities to handle all the different PE-CE connectivity models.

After choosing the MP-BGP as your PE-CE protocol, you must next determine the MP-BGP AS allocation scheme. The selection of an MP-BGP AS number for enterprise sites is an important consideration. It affects other aspects of network behavior, such as load balancing, route-loop avoidance, and site characterization over the origin AS.

You have basically two options for BGP AS numbers allocation: you can use the same or a unique MP-BGP AS for every customer site (see Figure 8-18).

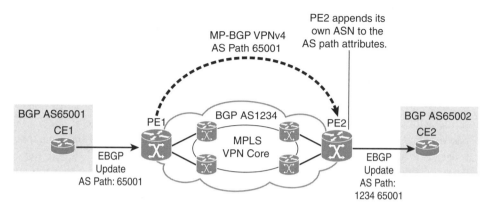

Figure 8-18 *Different BGP AS Number per Site*

One of the main advantages of allocating a unique AS per site is that you identify the originator of the route. You can achieve that by checking the AS path attribute for the origin MP-BGP AS. This identification simplifies troubleshooting. A unique AS per site also allows simple AS path filters to perform MP-BGP route manipulation for a particular site. These advantages are the reasons that using a unique AS per site is the preferred solution. However, this solution may introduce a limitation with regard to the available AS numbers and number of sites per customer (also referred to as AS collisions).

In contrast. one of the advantages of using the same AS for every site is that it reduces the chance of AS collisions. However, the use of the same AS for every customer site also creates some complexity (see Figure 8-19).

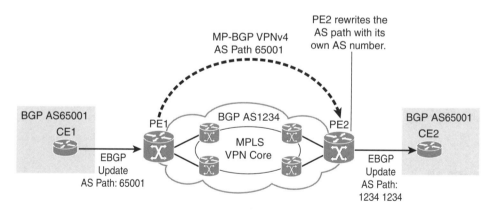

Figure 8-19 *Same BGP AS Number Across All Sites*

An MP-BGP peer performs AS loop prevention by verifying that the AS path attribute in the received update contains its own AS number. If the route meets these conditions, it is discarded. Because the CE router on the other site sees its own AS number in the AS path attribute, it discards the update.

If you want to use the same AS number for every customer site, you must disable AS loop prevention. The service provider uses the **as-override** command to perform this task. When the service provider uses this command, it replaces the customer AS number with its own number in the AS path attribute.

Mechanisms such as **as-override** produce some additional complexity and configuration requirements for the service provider. Another issue when using **as-override** is that none of the MP-BGP routes can be uniquely identified as originating from a specific site that is based on the AS path attribute. If the CE router must identify the origin of the route that is based on some attribute, you must use some other mechanisms, such as MP-BGP standard communities. You need extra configuration on the CE router to support this option.

Rewriting the AS path attribute prevents the CE router from detecting an MP-BGP loop, which can create problems at multihomed sites. You can avoid this situation by using the site of origin (SoO) extended community attribute. This extended community attribute is attached to an MP-BGP route and is used to identify the origin of the route. As shown in Figure 8-20, if the SoO value attached to the prefix is the same as the one attached to the configured SoO for the MP-BGP peering/interface, the route is blocked from being advertised.

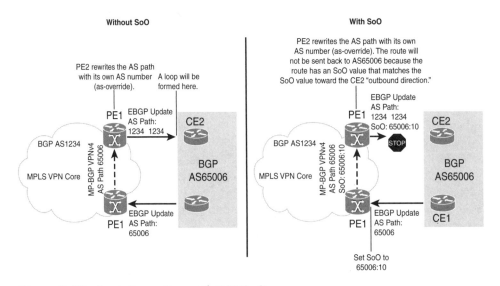

Figure 8-20 *Loop Prevention with BGP SoO*

BGP as the PE-CE Routing Protocol with a Backdoor Link between Customer Sites

When the customer has a backdoor link between sites, the most common scenario is that the same route is advertised over the backdoor link using an IGP and EBGP over the MPLS/VPN backbone. Because you need to redistribute routes from the MP-BGP to the IGP on the CE router, the routes that traverse the MPLS/VPN backbone become external, whereas the routes over the backdoor link are internal. Because an internal route is preferred over the external, in this case the backdoor link will be used to reach the other site instead of the MPLS VPN backbone. This behavior is not always desirable.

One simple way to solve the problem is to summarize the routes over the backdoor link. In this case, the routes over the MPLS/VPN will become more specific, and the routers will therefore use this route (see Figure 8-21).

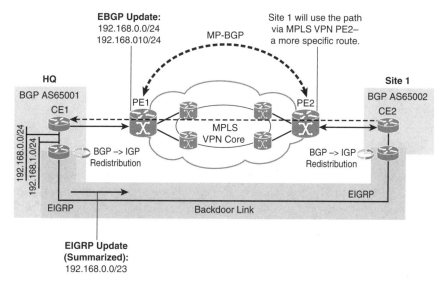

Figure 8-21 *BGP PE-CE and IGP Over the Backdoor*

Case Study: MPLS VPN Routing Propagation

This case study puts together the concepts discussed so far in this chapter and takes you through the end-to-end steps of route propagation between two sites that you decided to use Layer 3 MPLS VPN WAN solution from a local service provider.

In this scenario, you use the following setup (see Figure 8-22):

- Subnet 192.168.1.0/24 at site A and 192.168.2.0/24 at site B.

- You are already using OSPF as an internal routing protocol. Therefore, you agreed with the service provider to use OSPF as the routing protocol between the CE and PE routers.

- You configure OSPF on the interface toward the PE routers, and the service provider configures OSPF on the interface toward the CE routers.

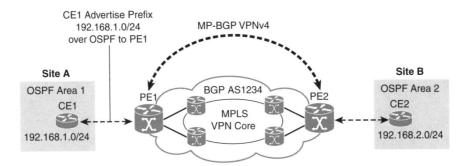

Figure 8-22 *Layer 3 MPLS VPN Scenario*

After the OSPF adjacency is established between the CE and PE routers, the PE1 router injects prefix 192.168.1.0/24 into the respective VRF routing table because it is the ingress PE for this received prefix. At the same time, the service provider has configured the RD with value 1:100 and both RTs (import and export) with the value 1:10. For simplicity, the service provider configured the same RD values on all PE routers. Each remote egress PE needs to advertise this route to a directly connected CE that belongs to the same customer that must configure an import RT value identical to the export value deployed for this customer site (in this example 1:10, see Figure 8-23).

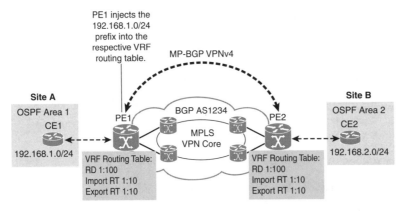

Figure 8-23 *Layer 3 MPLS VPN Scenario: Route Injection into the VRF Routing Table*

As shown in Figure 8-24, the PE1 router appends the RD values to the IPv4 prefix to create a unique 96-bit VPNv4 prefix 1:100:192.168.1.0/24. Then the PE1 router sends this prefix across the MPLS backbone between the PE routers. The PE router also attaches RT to the VPNv4 prefix. It uses the value 1:10, which is configured as the export RT on the PE1 router.

Case Study: MPLS VPN Routing Propagation 257

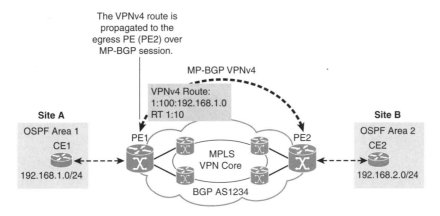

Figure 8-24 *Layer 3 MPLS VPN Scenario: VPNv4 Route Propagation*

When the egress PE router at the other side (PE2) receives the VPNv4 prefix via MP-BGP, it strips the RD tag and imports the IPv4 prefix into the respective VRF routing table. In fact, the PE2 router uses the RT that was received with the prefix to choose the correct VRF. The RT in the received prefix is 1:10, which was configured as the export RT on ingress PE1 router. In turn, the PE2 router checks the VRFs to find the import RT 1:10 and imports the prefix into that VRF routing table, as depicted in Figure 8-25.

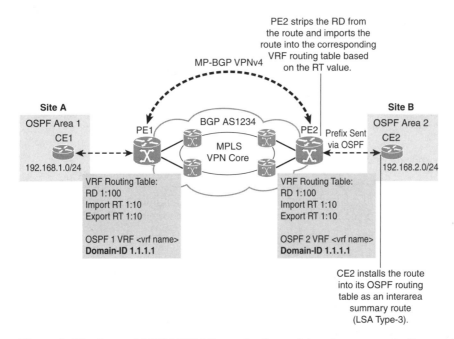

Figure 8-25 *Layer 3 MPLS VPN Scenario: Route Advertisement to the Remote Site*

As mentioned earlier, you have agreed with the service provider to establish OSPF between the PE and the CE at site B. Therefore, the PE2 router will forward prefix 192.168.1.0/24 to the CE router using OSPF. Prefix 192.168.1.0/24 is now in the routing table at the CE2 router, and it is accessible from site B. Also, because this service provider deployed the same OSPF domain ID at both PEs, the site B CE router will receive this prefix as the OSPF interarea summary route (LSA type 3) and not as external (LSA type 5).

The same procedure is repeated for prefix 192.168.2.0/24. When both prefixes are in the routing table at sites A and B, you should have end-to-end connectivity between these two sites.

Forwarding in MPLS VPN

So far we've focused primarily on the control plane aspect and how IP prefixes are injected and propagated between different remote sites across the Layer 3 MPLS VPN backbone. This section covers how packets are forwarded from the data plane perspective.

To forward traffic from one site to another, the IP packet needs to traverse the MPLS core network. Also, P routers use the MPLS protocol to make forwarding decisions. Therefore, MPLS is the core technology in the forwarding process. The following procedures are used to forward packets in such an environment (see Figure 8-26):

- The customer network originates in the IP packet, and it is destined to the other site. The CE router sends the packet to the PE router.

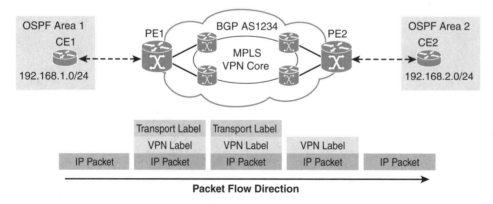

Figure 8-26 *MPLS VPN Forwarding Plane*

- The PE router receives the packet and does a routing lookup according to the VRF table. The PE imposes two labels on the IP packet. The first label is the VPN label. It is used to uniquely identify a customer VPN prefix. The second label is the forwarding label. It is used to tunnel the packet through the provider MPLS network, also commonly referred to as the transport label.

- The labeled packet is forwarded at each hop through the service provider core. Each P router makes a forwarding decision that is based on the top-level label (the transport label). This top-level label is swapped with a new label. The underlying packet and inner label are left undisturbed during this process.

- When the packet arrives at the remote PE router, the router recognizes the inner VPN label as a VPN label for a specific customer prefix. The VPN label is stripped, and a forwarding decision for the IPv4 packet is made based on the VPN label. The forwarding label is usually removed at the last P router in the MPLS network. This process is called penultimate hop popping (PHP).

- The original IP packet is forwarded to the remote CE router.

Layer 2 MPLS VPN Services

With the Layer 3 MPLS VPN, the service provider exchanges routing information with the enterprise customer's WAN edge routers and forwards packets based on Layer 3 information (IP). With the Layer 2 VPN services, on the other hand, the providers typically have no participation in the enterprise Layer 3 WAN routing. The reason is that it is a Layer 2 service; thus, the provider forwards the traffic of any given customer based on its Layer 2 information, such as Ethernet MAC addresses.

The most common Layer 2 WAN connectivity models offered by today's service providers (also referred to as Carrier Ethernet) are the following:

- **Virtual Private Wire Service (VPWS):** Also known as E-Line in Metro Ethernet forum terminologies, which provide a point-to-point connectivity model.

- **Virtual Private LAN Service (VPLS):** Also known as E-LAN in Metro Ethernet forum terminologies, which provide a multipoint or any-to-any connectivity model.

The following sections cover each of these modern Layer 2 WAN services and its connectivity model in more detail.

> **Note** VPLS is commonly referred to as a Layer 2 VPN; however, both VPLS and VPWS are different forms of Layer 2 VPN, each with a different topology model (any-to-any versus point-to-point). Therefore, in this chapter, the term *Layer 2 VPN* refers to both services in general.

Virtual Private Wire Service (VPWS)

From a customer point of view, the Virtual Private Wire Service offers a solution so that the devices see devices at the remote sites as directly connected devices in a point-to-point manner (see Figure 8-27). Because this service provides a Layer 2 transport, the CE devices can be routers or switches.

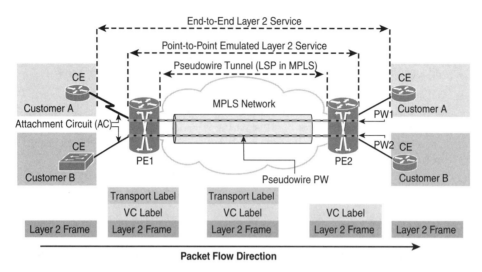

Figure 8-27 *VPWS*

When you connect a router to the VPWS service, you need to deploy routing such as an IGP routing protocol to forward the traffic between the sites. Because it's a Layer 2 service, the network is completely transparent to the CE routers; thus, Layer 3 devices such as routers need to form a direct adjacency. The advantage of this solution is that you gain complete control over your routing in the WAN. You do not need to have any agreement with the service provider. If you have multiple links to the WAN from the CE routers, you can influence which link would be the primary and which would be the secondary by using the desired routing protocol. You also can use the IGP cost metrics to control forwarding.

VPWS offers two operation mode options from the service provider side:

- Port mode, in which 802.1Q frames are tunneled transparently
- VLAN mode

The PE operation mode affects the CE deployment. When the PE is operating in the port mode, the VPWS will act like a pipe between the PE nodes, in which all traffic is tunneled to the remote site. The CE router needs an IP address on the physical interface. It must be in the same subnet as the physical interface on the remote site. You can also use subinterfaces when you want to have multiple Layer 3 connections to the remote site. When you connect a new remote site, you need to physically connect an extra link from the CE to the PE router at the hub. Therefore, this solution is primarily used for a low number of point-to-point connections. On the other hand, when the PE is operating in the VLAN mode, you could configure multiple subinterfaces on the PE router. Each subinterface is connected to a different remote site, where each 802.1Q VLAN tag can be mapped to a different VPWS-emulated circuit (also known as pseudowire, or PW). The solution can be used for hub-and-spoke topologies. In such a deployment, you must also configure different subinterfaces on the CE hub router, as illustrated in Figure 8-28. The VLAN mode is used with a hub router, while the port mode is used with the spokes.

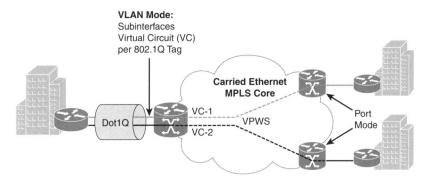

Figure 8-28 *VPWS Modes*

You can also use switches as CE devices to extend the Layer 2 network between remote sites. This solution is usually used to provide a Data Center Interconnect. You must make sure that STP is enabled on the switches and that BPDUs are passing the network to avoid switching loops (within each DC) and filtering out STP/BPDUs across the DCI.

You must consider some other characteristics of the network when choosing the VPWS solution; these characteristics can influence your deployment as a customer. Some of them are the supported maximum transmission unit (MTU) on the WAN, quality of service (QoS) support, and transparency.

Virtual Private LAN Service (VPLS)

Virtual Private LAN Service emulates a LAN segment across the MPLS backbone. It provides multipoint Layer 2 connectivity between remote sites.

As shown in Figure 8-29, the VPLS that runs over MPLS emulates an Ethernet switch where every port is connected to a different customer site. The PE routers are interconnected into a full mesh across the MPLS backbone of the service provider.

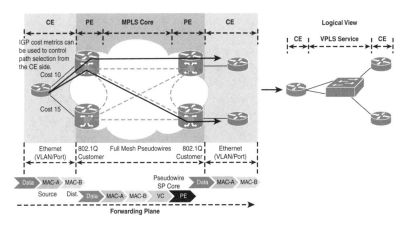

Figure 8-29 *VPLS*

VPLS will self-learn the source MAC address-to-port associations, and frames are forwarded based on the destination MAC address. If the destination address is unknown, or it is a broadcast or multicast address, the frame is flooded to all ports that are associated with the virtual bridge. The VPLS core does not use STP. Instead, it uses split-horizon forwarding so that Ethernet frames are not sent back out the same PW frames received on the same PW or any pseudowires (part of the same customer PW mesh) back to the core, as shown in Figure 8-30. As long as there is a full mesh of PWs, there is no need for any PE to relay any pack back to the core; therefore, the split-horizon rule will not reduce the forwarding efficiency across the core.

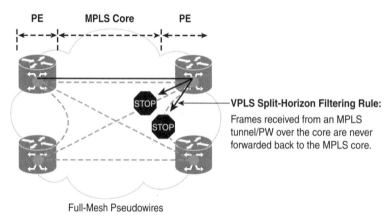

Figure 8-30 *VPLS split horizon in the core*

VPLS acts like an Ethernet switch to the customer and brings the same Layer 2 core issues, including

- **Stability of the network as it grows:** The customer should check if there is an appropriate core network design to support future growth.

- **Impact of network outages:** The customer should ask about what happens to traffic if there is an outage.

- **Multicast and broadcast traffic between sites:** Because the VPLS network acts like a switch, all customer multicasts and broadcasts are sent to all sites. When you design a network that will have significant amounts of multicast traffic, you need to segment your network in such a way to reduce the scope of multicast flooding.

- **IGP peering scalability:** The VPLS network is one broadcast domain, so all the attached routers would typically be routing peers. As the number of routing peers increases, the full mesh of the connections becomes a scaling issue. The only protocol that is designed for a large number of peers is BGP. Therefore, you should consider using BGP as the routing protocol in large VPLS networks.

- **Impact of another customer's STP loop:** Because VPLS uses statistical multiplexing, all customers share the bandwidth. It is reasonable to ask what the impact of a customer with a spanning-tree loop would be on other customers. If the customer is attached via a Layer 2 switch, all the packets from the loop would necessarily be flooded within the links that are interconnecting their VPLS sites. If they connect at 1 Gbps and the provider trunks are 20 Gbps, the impact may not be so bad. If the provider links are 2 Gbps, the impact might be far greater, particularly if EtherChannel is in use.

- **Layer 2 security considerations:** Because the traffic from all customers is traversing the same core network, you should verify that the provider has implemented adequate Layer 2 security measures.

VPLS Scalability Considerations

A service provider VPLS design must address three major scaling factors:

- **Scaling of the full mesh of pseudowires between the PE devices:** As the number of PE devices grows, each edge device must form an adjacency with all other PE devices. This adjacency requires that the edge devices must have the IP address of all remote PEs in its routing table. It also requires that PE routes exchange label information between them. That introduces an N-1 control plane scaling issue.

- **Frame replication and forwarding:** The VPLS forwards Ethernet frames using Layer 2 MAC addresses. The operation of VPLS is the same as the one found within 802.1 bridges. In that case, the switch learns the source MAC address-to-port associations and forwards the frames based on the destination MAC address. If the destination address is unknown, or it is a broadcast or multicast address, the frame is flooded to all ports that are associated with the virtual bridge.

- **MAC address table size:** One of the major considerations in VPLS provider design is MAC address learning. PE devices need to be capable of managing MAC address tables for many customer devices and many customers. That number is far greater than what a typical enterprise campus switch needs to manage today.

Note PE nodes with VPWS do not need to keep customer MAC address information. VPLS, however, has to keep all the customer MAC addresses on the PE.

To address the scaling issues in large VPLS deployments, hierarchical VPLS was introduced. H-VPLS reduces the signaling overhead and packet replication requirements for the provider edge. As shown in Figure 8-31, two types of provider edge devices are defined in this model: a user-facing provider edge called the user provider edge (UPE) and a network provider edge (NPE). Customer edge devices connect to UPEs directly and aggregate VPLS traffic before it reaches the NPE where the VPLS forwarding takes place.

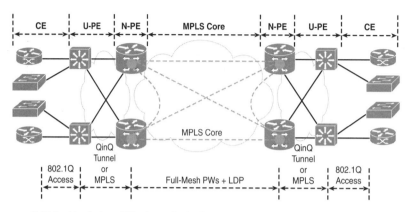

- **U-PE** Provides Customer UNI – Access Service Termination
- **N-PE** Provides VPLS Service Termination – Aggregation Service Termination

Figure 8-31 *H-VPLS Figure*

The H-VPLS addresses some of the scaling factors, including the following (see Figure 8-32):

- **Scaling of the full mesh of pseudowires between the PE devices:** H-VPLS helps address this issue by using UPE devices to spread the edge workload across multiple, less costly devices. A lower number of pseudowires between the NPE devices helps scale the network by reducing the burden on the core for frame replication and forwarding.

- **Frame replication and forwarding:** H-VPLS needs a lower number of pseudowires because only the NPE devices are connected in a full mesh. It helps to reduce the burden on the core for frame replication and forwarding.

- **MAC address table size:** H-VPLS allows MAC tables to be spread across multiple inexpensive devices to scale the edge. UPE devices only need to learn their local NPE devices and therefore do not need large routing table support. Core NPE devices still need to manage very large MAC address tables. Using MPLS in the core removes the MAC learning requirement from the provider devices.

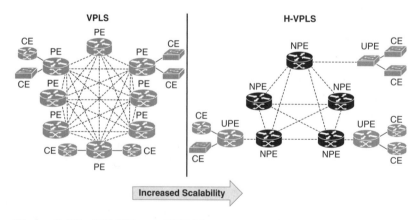

Figure 8-32 *VPLS Versus H-VPLS*

The customer should be interested in how well the provider design manages all these factors. Poor VPLS design can lead to scaling and stability problems as the P-network grows. The customer does not need to be intimately familiar with VPLS designs to evaluate the service. But listening to the answers of the service provider on these topics can provide insight into the qualifications of that provider.

Furthermore, IGP scalability can be an issue over VPLS-emulated networks. All routers that are attached to the VPLS networks see the segment as a broadcast segment. IGP acts as if many routers are connected to the same broadcast segment.

When you are using OSPF as a routing protocol, it is recommended that you use a few neighbors in the same broadcast segment. In general, no router should have more than 60 neighbors. This number can be quickly reached in larger VPLS networks. The problem is that if some sites experience packet loss, OSPF processing may consume more router CPU on all routers in the segment. The same issue can be present when some links are flapping.

Another issue that can cause instability in the VPLS network is the loss of connectivity between the designated router (DR) and backup designated router (BDR). The OSPF routing protocol reduces the number of adjacencies that are needed by using DR/BDR. When routers are connected to VPLS networks, they elect one of the routers as the DR. All routers form adjacency with this router. If connectivity between the DR and the BDR is lost due to a failure with some emulated virtual circuit pseudowires across the VPLS network, the BDR becomes a DR, which will cause problems in the broadcast network because there will be two DRs. These issues make OSPF less preferable for a VPLS network. Therefore, it is more desirable to consider the OSPF point-to-multipoint interface type to avoid this DR and DBR issue.

A similar issue applies to EIGRP. You also should avoid having many peers with EIGRP.

When you have a large VPLS deployment, you can partition your network to reduce the number of adjacencies between routers. Another alternative is to use BGP as the routing protocol because it is designed to have many peers. Or, you may consider using a Layer 3 MPLS VPN if you have a very large number of sites.

VPLS Resiliency Considerations

An advantage of using VPLS is that MPLS is used for the data plane. If a failure occurs in the P network, traffic will automatically be routed along available backup paths in the P network.

There is a cost to this fast failover, however. If redundant pseudowires are used from redundant PE devices, a failure might require aging MAC addresses, followed by unicast flooding. The resulting lost packets, followed by a surge of traffic, would have a negative impact on the customer traffic.

PW rerouting around outages prevents this potential problem. Although PW rerouting increases the availability of the VPLS service inside the provider network, it does not protect against local loop or CE device failure. Implementing redundant CE devices and redundant local loops is challenging because there is no Spanning-Tree Protocol running between the customer and provider to help prevent potential bridging loops.

> **Note** Different technologies and approaches are used in today's networks to overcome the looping issues discussed here. They include the Cisco A-VPLS, Cisco IOS EEM, and N-PE solution. Also, the next-generation VPLS, also referred to as Ethernet VPN (EVPN), overcomes these limitations. For more information, refer to IETF RFC 7432.

VPLS Versus VPWS

Although both VPLS and VPWS are technologies that offer Layer 2 WAN transport between customer sites, they are not identical. As a network designer, you must be aware of the differences between these two technologies so that you can select the right technology when choosing WAN transport and identify the limitations of the one that is currently in use by a customer as WAN technology.

Both VPWS and VPLS offer Layer 2 VPN connectivity between remote sites. However, VPWS is a point-to-point technology in which each PE router has pseudowire connections to the other PE routers. Because it is a point-to-point technology, you would need a pseudowire to each remote site. Clearly, this approach could raise scalability issues when there are many remote sites. VPLS can overcome this issue because it offers a point-to-multipoint connectivity model.

Because VPWS is a point-to-point technology and VPLS is a point-to-multipoint technology, that also means the requirements on the CE devices are different. In VPWS, the CE device must perform switching, which means that the CE must choose which pseudowire it should use to send data to the remote site. The CE router in VPLS simply sends data that is destined for the remote site to the PE router. The PE router must then decide where to send this traffic.

Because the VPLS network acts as the Ethernet switch, it must also provide some of the features that are the core functions of the network switch. Besides forwarding, it must also take care of loop prevention, dynamic MAC learning for correct forwarding to the remote sites, and MAC aging. It is clear that the PE routers must perform more tasks that are not needed with VPWS.

VPWS can be the primary choice when you want to connect a few remote sites. For example, you can use VPWS when you want to bridge your two data centers in the same Layer 2 network. On the other hand, when you have many sites, you would most probably use the VPLS technology. If you want to configure a hub-and-spoke topology, you can configure a point-to-point connection to each site from the hub router. You can also configure point-to-multipoint on the hub and point-to-point on spokes.

In general, today's Carrier Ethernet uses these technologies over a single unified MPLS-based core network to offer the capability to interconnect different Metro Ethernet islands, as illustrated in Figure 8-33.

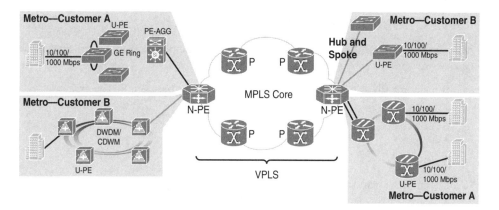

Figure 8-33 *MPLS L2VPN*

Summary

- The major decision points for choosing WAN connections are service availability, cost, and technical decision points.

- Layer 3 MPLS VPN provides Layer 3 connectivity over the MPLS provider core network.

- You can use different routing protocols on the CE-PE link, such as EIGRP, OSPF, or BGP.

- BGP offers more flexible designs that support complex connectivity models when used as a PE-CE routing protocols.

- IBGP is used to transfer customer routes from site to site in Layer 3 MPLS VPN.

- MPLS labels are used for data forwarding in provider networks for Layer 3 MPLS VPN.

- VPWS provides a point-to-point solution, whereas VPLS provides a point-to-multipoint Layer 2 VPN solution.

- Although VPLS offers more scalable Layer 2 WAN design than VPWS, in large networks with a large number of remote sites, VPLS may introduce some design limitations with regard to Layer 3 routing.

Review Questions

After answering the following questions, please refer to Appendix A, "Answers to Review Questions," for the correct answers.

1. Which protocol is used for transferring VPNv4 routes between PE routers?
   a. OSPF
   b. EIGRP
   c. BGP
   d. RIP

2. Match each component of MPLS VPN architecture with its description.

Component	Description
Provider network	Customer-controlled domain
Customer network	Router on the edge of the customer network
PE router	MPLS forwarding backbone
P router	Router on the edge of the provider cloud
CE router	Router in the core of the provider network

3. Which are the main characteristics of a route distinguisher? (Select three.)
   a. It does not allow overlapping addresses from different customers.
   b. It allows overlapping addresses from different customers.
   c. It is a 64-bit unique identifier.
   d. It is a 32-bit unique identifier.
   e. It is prepended to the IPv4 prefixes.
   f. It is a BGP-extended community.

4. Which answer about PE-CE routing is correct in a Layer 3 MPLS VPN environment?
   a. EIGRP cannot be used as a PE-CE routing protocol.
   b. OSPF offers simplified route summarization when used as a PE-CE routing protocol.
   c. BGP provides the most flexible PE-CE routing design.
   d. OSPF provides the most flexible PE-CE routing design.

5. Which answer about PE-CE routing design is correct in a Layer 3 MPLS VPN environment?
   a. EIGRP has the built-in capability to stop a routing loop when there is a backdoor link between the CE routers.
   b. BGP, along with SoO, can stop the routing loop when there is a backdoor link between the CE routers.
   c. OSPF does not support a PE-CE design when there is a backdoor link between the CE routers.

d. EIGRP does not support a PE-CE design when there is a backdoor link between the CE routers.

6. Which of the following can be used to provide scalable WAN connectivity that supports a very large number of remote sites (over 500 sites)?
   a. Layer 3 MPLS VPN
   b. VPLS
   c. VPWS
   d. Point-to-point GRE tunnels

7. Which of the following offers high bandwidth and scalable Layer 2 WAN connectivity?
   a. VPWS
   b. Frame Relay
   c. VPLS
   d. L2TPv3

8. From a service provider point of view, which of the following offers higher bandwidth and a more scalable Layer 2 WAN solution?
   a. VPWS
   b. VPLS
   c. H-VPLS
   d. L2TPv3

9. In a scenario in which a backdoor link is used to connect two CE routers using EIGRP between them and the Layer 3 MPLS VPN provider as a PE-CE routing protocol, which BGP attribute can be used to avoid using the backdoor link as the preferred path?
   a. AS path
   b. Origin
   c. Cost community
   d. Extent community

10. How can a Layer 3 MPLS VPN provider support customers with an overlapping IP address space?
    a. Each customer IP prefix is assigned a different RT value.
    b. Each customer IP prefix is appended with a unique RD value.
    c. Each customer route is injected into a separate GRE tunnel inside the MPSL core.
    d. Each customer route is injected into a separate VPWS tunnel inside the MPSL core.

Chapter 9

Enterprise-Managed WANs

Upon completing this chapter, you will be able to

- Describe enterprise-managed VPNs
- Describe GRE basics
- Describe multipoint GRE basics
- Describe IPsec basics
- Describe GRE over IPsec
- Describe IPsec with VTI
- Describe IPsec with dynamic VTI
- Describe DMVPN basics
- Understand and describe DMVPN Phase 1
- Understand and describe DMVPN Phase 2
- Understand and describe DMVPN Phase 3
- Describe MPLS/VPN over GRE/DMVPN
- Explain DMVPN redundancy
- Describe SSL VPN basics
- Describe FlexVPN basics
- Describe FlexVPN architecture
- Describe FlexVPN capabilities
- Describe FlexVPN configuration blocks
- Describe the GETVPN

In modern enterprises, the network is often dispersed over many locations requiring wide-area network (WAN) connectivity between one another. The WAN has empowered organizations to take advantage of improved efficiencies by consolidating and centralizing enterprise applications within private or public data center environments. There are many different ways to design and implement the WAN. The most common drivers influencing design and implementation decisions are usually associated with cost and reliability.

The WAN must deliver an uncompromised workforce experience while providing reliable connectivity for remote-site users to access critical business applications. The WAN will continue to grow in its importance as trends such as bring your own device (BYOD), cloud, the Internet of Everything (IoE), and digital transformation continue to highlight opportunities associated with effectively connecting people, processes, data, and things.

When designing and implementing the WAN, you can build your own infrastructure, lease a virtual private network (VPN) solution from a service provider, or configure your own overlaid WAN using a VPN solution, leveraging the Internet as a transport. Many organizations combine these solutions. One example of combining solutions would be enterprises that augment their premium Multiprotocol Label Switching (MPLS) transport with additional capacity, thus leveraging Internet services to create an enterprise-managed VPN to use as a fallback path in an Active/Standby deployment model for critical site locations.

Enterprise-managed VPNs that take advantage of broadband Internet connectivity services are usually the cheapest option, resulting in dramatic bandwidth, price, and performance benefits. If properly implemented, these VPNs can offer a perfectly safe and scalable solution over an unsecured public network. This chapter focuses on the enterprise-managed WAN based on VPN solutions and the various technologies, features, and options that make them possible.

Enterprise-Managed VPN Overview

VPN connections enable users to send data between remote-site locations and to access centralized corporate resources in a secure and efficient manner. The two main categories of VPN solutions are

- Remote VPN solutions
- Site-to-site VPN solutions

The goal of remote VPN solutions is to connect specific users through device-specific capabilities to one another and to centralized resources. An example of a modern remote VPN solution is SSLVPN. Remote VPN solutions typically require users to have special software on their devices to establish connectivity back to the enterprise.

The goal of site-to-site VPN solutions, and the focus of this chapter, is to connect two LANs across two or more remote-site locations over a third-party transport to form an enterprise-managed VPN. Examples of these VPN solutions are Generic Routing

Encapsulation (GRE), Internet Protocol Security (IPsec), GRE over IPsec, Dynamic Multipoint Virtual Private Network (DMVPN), and many other enterprise-managed VPN solutions that are covered in this chapter. A common capability introduced by many of these solutions is to create virtual tunnels and overlays to forward traffic. Deploying enterprise-managed VPNs usually involves network equipment dependencies.

Enterprise-managed VPNs are the right option if you want to implement your own routing infrastructure without provider involvement. Many organizations prefer this approach because it results in a consistent routing operational model and provides future flexibility associated with provider migrations. Enterprise-managed VPN connections are established over a third-party infrastructure and can take advantage of Internet or provider-managed VPNs for underlying transport connectivity.

Enterprise-managed VPNs that take advantage of the Internet are relatively cheap in comparison to those that rely on provider-managed VPN services. The drawback of using the Internet as an underlying transport technology is that there is no quality of service (QoS) support. Internet service providers transport data with "best effort," and as a result, there is no service-level agreement (SLA) to guarantee minimum service levels. Furthermore, when you extend private networks over a public network such as the Internet, the VPN connections are established over an insecure infrastructure. Incorporating encryption in such cases is highly recommended, and often mandatory, because sending data in clear text can expose sensitive information to attackers and result in compliance issues.

To overcome these drawbacks, enterprises can use provider-managed VPN services to lay the foundation for the underlying network and implement enterprise-managed VPN solutions over the provider infrastructure. The motivation for implementing an enterprise-managed VPN over a provider-managed VPN is that these services typically do come with SLAs in place for connections. To promote operational consistency and to minimize risk with a focus on security, you can establish traffic encryption even when you use provider-managed VPN services; this is a good practice. The drawback of using provider-managed VPNs is that this solution is often more expensive than VPN solutions over the Internet.

The following sections explore the various technologies available, which are typically incorporated into designing enterprise-managed VPN solutions.

GRE Overview

Establishing an enterprise-managed VPN requires a solution that can tunnel packets, and perhaps even multicast, over the underlying transport infrastructure.

Generic Routing Encapsulation (GRE), which uses protocol number 47, was developed by Cisco and is now standardized by the Internet Engineering Task Force (IETF). This protocol provides the capability to tunnel any unicast or multicast packets.

In addition to supporting multicast, this solution supports the use of routing protocols over the tunneling mechanism. This technology, in its most basic form, creates a virtual point-to-point connection between two routers, leveraging a tunnel source interface and destination IP address on each side. The router encapsulates traffic with a GRE header and a new IP header. This new packet is then forwarded to the router on the other end of the tunnel using the external IP header for forwarding decisions. The router on the other side of the tunnel strips the outer IP header and GRE header and forwards packets based on the routing table.

Two endpoints of the GRE tunnel act as if they are connected directly. The appearance that endpoints are directly connected means that you implement routing in the same way as you would for normal routed interfaces. You have flexibility to use common Interior Gateway Protocols (IGP), such as the Routing Information Protocol (RIP), Enhanced Interior Gateway Routing Protocol (EIGRP), and Open Shortest Path First (OSPF); and Exterior Gateway Protocols (EGPs), such as the Border Gateway Protocol (BGP). When you implement routing, you must be careful to avoid recursive loops. A recursive loop would happen if you misconfigure a router in such a way that it attempts to route to the tunnel destination address through the tunnel using the tunnel interface. Recursive loops can cause temporary instability as a result of route flapping elsewhere in the network. You can avoid such situations with proper filtering or by using a different routing protocol instance for the GRE tunnels than what is used by the transport network.

GRE is usually implemented as part of a hub-and-spoke topology design, as shown in Figure 9-1.

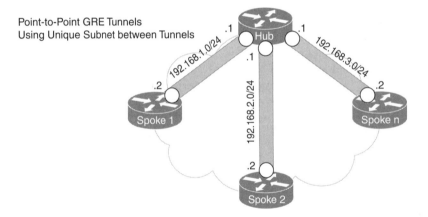

Figure 9-1 *Point-to-point GRE Tunneling over Hub-and-Spoke Topology*

In this type of design, the hub router must establish a separate point-to-point tunnel with each spoke router. This design requires the use of a unique subnet on each of the point-to-point connections between the sites. Those wanting to add high availability to this type of GRE design usually implement two routers at the central site and one router at the branch office. Each hub router at the central site has independent connectivity to the WAN. The branch router is then connected to the WAN via two upstream connections and leverages two separate GRE tunnels over each of these connections for high availability. Each tunnel would terminate to one hub router at the central site, and the routing protocol would be tuned to select a primary GRE tunnel to the central site.

The main advantage of the GRE tunnel is that it can transport protocols that would not normally pass the network. One example is tunneling multicast traffic over the Internet using a GRE tunnel between two sites. Traditionally, the only concern around using GRE in this way across an insecure transport is that GRE does not natively provide any cryptographic traffic protection. In these situations, GRE is usually combined with IPsec to ensure the necessary traffic protection properties are in place. A disadvantage is that the GRE standard does not define any keepalive mechanism. Cisco offers a proprietary GRE keepalive solution to address this concern. When you implement GRE tunnels, you can have MTU and IP fragmentation-related issues. GRE adds an extra 24 bytes (a 4-byte GRE header and a 20-byte new IP header) to the packet. You must configure the appropriate MTU value to support extra headers. Although well documented, this consideration is often overlooked or misunderstood.

Multipoint GRE Overview

Because classic GRE is a point-to-point technology and several limitations and scalability issues associated with provisioning point-to-point can exist, in many cases, you need something more capable. The multipoint GRE (mGRE) extends the GRE solution by adding multipoint support, which means that the single GRE interface supports multiple GRE tunnel connections simultaneously. Figure 9-2 shows an mGRE.

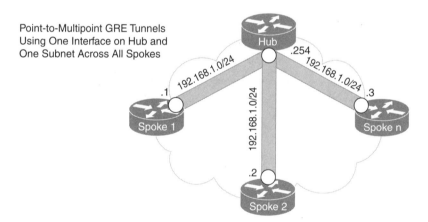

Figure 9-2 *Multipoint GRE Tunneling over Hub-and-Spoke Topology*

Because only one tunnel is needed for all other multipoint GRE peers, mGRE greatly simplifies the overall configuration. All GRE tunnels use the same subnet, which results in the hubs no longer requiring a unique subnet for each spoke-to-spoke connection. Just like classic GRE tunnels, mGRE tunnels support unicast, multicast, and broadcast traffic.

When you use point-to-point GRE tunnels, you manually specify the tunnel source and destination. With multipoint GRE, you still need to specify the tunnel source, but the learning of the peers happens dynamically. To dynamically learn about peers, you need a special protocol that maps the tunnel IP address to the physical nonbroadcast multi-access (NBMA) IP address. Cisco leverages a protocol called Next-Hop Resolution Protocol (NHRP) to achieve this (NHRP is described in IETF RFC 2332). NHRP is used similarly as the Address Resolution Protocol (ARP) on Ethernet. The NHRP dynamically registers mapping of the tunnel interface address and physical (NBMA) address to the other peers. This dynamic registration also allows the use of dynamically assigned addresses.

Point-to-Point and Multipoint GRE Comparison

Because you can choose from two types of GRE with several differences, it might be beneficial to examine characteristics of each type side by side in a table. Table 9-1 presents much of the information already shared in a simplified format.

Table 9-1 *Point-to-Point versus Multipoint GRE: Summary of Characteristics*

Point-to-Point GRE	Multipoint GRE
Typically used for simple point-to-point tunnels that emulate a point-to-point WAN link or on spoke routers in hub-and-spoke VPNs.	Typically used on hub routers in hub-and-spoke topologies or on all routers in mesh or partial-mesh topologies.
On each device, a separate GRE tunnel interface is configured for each GRE peer.	A single GRE interface is configured for multiple GRE tunnels.
A unique subnet is needed for each GRE tunnel.	The same subnet is configured for all GRE tunnels.
This does not require NHRP because other peers have a statically configured destination address.	This requires NHRP to build dynamic GRE tunnels and to learn about the IP addresses of the other peers.
This supports unicast, multicast, and broadcast traffic.	This supports unicast, multicast, and broadcast traffic.

You can mix point-to-point and point-to-multipoint GRE tunnels in your environment. Figure 9-3 shows three options for implementing GRE networks using GRE or mGRE functionality.

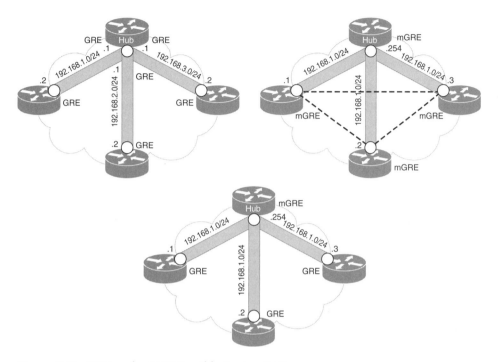

Figure 9-3 *GRE and mGRE Possible Design Options*

1. In the leftmost diagram, a hub-and-spoke network uses a set of point-to-point tunnels using only GRE interfaces. On the hub, you would need to create as many GRE interfaces as there are spokes, and on a spoke, you would require one GRE interface. All traffic between spokes flows strictly over the hub.

2. The middle diagram shows the hub that is optimized with an mGRE interface. In this setup, only a single interface is required on the hub. However, you must deploy NHRP for the hub to learn spoke addresses and correctly provision the spoke-to-hub GRE tunnels.

3. In the rightmost diagram, all devices in a hub-and-spoke network use an mGRE interface. Using NHRP, these devices can establish a partial mesh or full mesh of GRE tunnels by configuring only a single mGRE interface on each device. This option greatly simplifies the configuration and improves manageability.

GRE is a powerful solution for designing and implementing enterprise-managed VPNs; however, GRE alone may not always be adequate in addressing all requirements. As already mentioned, when you are creating GRE overlays over insecure transport connectivity, GRE is usually combined with IPsec to ensure the necessary traffic protection properties are in place. The next section explores IPsec independently before you dive deeper into a combined IPsec and GRE solution.

IPsec Overview

IPsec is designed to provide interoperable, high-quality, and cryptographically based transmission security to IP traffic. IPsec is defined in RFC 4301. It offers data confidentiality, data integrity, data origin authentication, and anti-replay security services.

IPsec provides security services at the IP layer, offering protection for IP and upper-layer protocols. It enables a system to select security protocols, determines the algorithms to use, and negotiates any cryptographic keys that are required to provide the requested services. IPsec can protect one or more paths between a pair of network devices. The IPsec protocol provides IP network layer encryption and defines a new set of headers to be added to IP datagrams. The new headers furnish information for securing the payload of the IP packet.

IPsec combines the following security protocols:

- **Internet Key Exchange** (IKE) provides key management to IPsec.
- **Authentication Header** (AH) defines a user traffic encapsulation that provides data integrity, data origin authentication, and protection against replay to user traffic.
- **Encapsulating Security Payload** (ESP) defines a user traffic encapsulation that provides data integrity, data origin authentication, protection against replays, and confidentiality to user traffic.

The concept of a Security Association (SA) is fundamental to IPsec. Both AH and ESP use SAs, and a major function of IKE is to establish and maintain SAs. An SA is a simple description of the current traffic protection parameters (algorithms, keys, traffic specification, and so on) that would be applied to specific user traffic flows. Security services are provided to an SA by using either AH or ESP. If AH or ESP protection is applied to a traffic stream, two (or more) SAs are created to provide protection to the traffic stream. To secure typical, bidirectional communication between two hosts or between two security gateways, you need two SAs (one in each direction).

IKE operates in two distinct phases:

- **Phase 1:** The first phase establishes the initial negotiation between two peers. Phase 1 begins with authentication in which crypto peers verify their identity with each other. When authenticated, the crypto peers agree upon the encryption algorithm, hash method, and other parameters. The peers establish bidirectional SAs. The goal of Phase 1 is for IKE to negotiate IPsec SA parameters and establish a secure channel for Phase 2.
- **Phase 2:** The goal of Phase 2 is to establish a secure channel for data exchange. The peers establish two (or more) unidirectional SAs. Phase 2 exchange is called the IKE quick mode.

It is not uncommon to hear that, in Phase 1, IKE can operate in either main mode or aggressive mode. The major characteristics of these modes are as follows:

- **Main mode:** This mode has three two-way exchanges between peers. It allows for more flexible IKE protection policy negotiation and always protects peer identity. A downside of main mode is that it does not support dynamically addressed peers when doing preshared key authentication. Dynamically addressed peers are supported only with PKI-facilitated authentication. The exception is when wildcard preshared keys are used. But the use of wildcard keys is strongly discouraged.

- **Aggressive mode:** In this mode, fewer exchanges are made, and with fewer packets. Therefore, it is faster than main mode. The downside of leveraging aggressive mode is that it does not protect peer identities because the names of communicating peers are sent over the untrusted network in the clear. The major benefit of aggressive mode is that it supports preshared key authentication for dynamically addressed peers.

IPsec, similar to IKE, also operates in one of two modes:

- **Tunnel mode:** This mode introduces a new IPsec header to the packet, and the complete user IP packet is encapsulated as the payload.

- **Transport mode:** This mode preserves the original IP header, and forwarding decisions are based on this original header.

Figure 9-4 compares how the transport and tunnel modes are affected by the use of AH versus ESP.

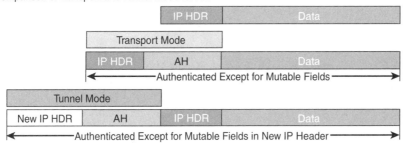

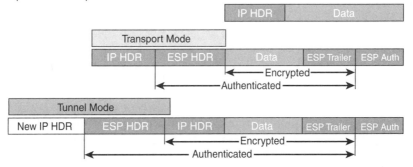

Figure 9-4 *IPsec Transport Mode versus Tunnel Mode when Using AH and ESP*

Referring to Figure 9-4, when IPsec operates with AH, the transport mode protects the external IP header along with the data payload. AH services protect all the fields in the header that do not change in transport. The AH header goes after the IP header and before the other higher-layer protocols. In tunnel mode, the entire original header is authenticated, and a new IP header is built. The new IP header is protected in the same way as the IP header in transport mode.

When IPsec operates with ESP, the IP payload is encrypted and original headers are left intact in transport mode. The ESP header is inserted after the IP header and before the upper-layer protocol header. The upper-layer protocols are encrypted and authenticated along with the ESP header. ESP does not authenticate the IP header. When ESP is used in tunnel mode, the original IP header is well protected because the entire original IP datagram is encrypted. With an ESP authentication mechanism, the original IP datagram and the ESP header are included; however, the new IP header is not included in the authentication.

Now that you have a better understanding of IPsec, you can shift your focus to an IPsec and GRE solution.

IPsec and GRE

When you consider IPsec and GRE independently, each has its limitations. Although IPsec provides a secure method for tunneling data across an IP network, it falls short in many design scenarios because of its inability to support IP broadcast, IP multicast, or multiprotocol traffic capabilities. These limitations prevent the use of protocols that rely on these features, such as routing protocols. Routing protocol support is critical to ensuring you can deliver a dynamic and scalable solution.

GRE, however, can be used to carry protocols such as IP broadcast or IP multicast, as well as non-IP protocols. The drawback of GRE, as already noted a few times, is that it does not provide any encryption mechanisms.

The ideal marriage is a solution that combines both technologies. You can use GRE tunnels to transfer wanted traffic and IPsec to encrypt the GRE tunnels. GRE over IPsec offers point-to-point tunneling capability. It is usually used during situations in which an enterprise must use routing protocols over the WAN and when traffic must be protected over the transport. The underlying transport can be Internet-based or even a provider-managed VPN. Point-to-point solutions such as this are appropriate for a small number of tunnels and can become an operational burden in larger deployments requiring considerable scale.

IPsec can be used in either tunnel mode or transport mode with a GRE over IPsec solution. Tunnel mode adds an extra 20 bytes to the total packet size, so this must be taken into consideration when configuring MTU and tcp-adjust MSS settings. Although both modes work with GRE over IPsec, certain scenarios require that you leverage a specific IPsec mode of operation. One example is when GRE over IPsec transits either a NAT or PAT device. When presented with this type of scenario, tunnel mode is required. The tunnel mode is also required if GRE tunnel endpoints and crypto tunnel endpoints are different.

The two options when implementing a GRE over IPsec solution are

- Using crypto maps:
  - The packet is routed to the tunnel interface.
  - The packet is encapsulated with GRE.
  - The encapsulated packet is forwarded in accordance with the routing table to the appropriate interface.
  - The encapsulated packet is encrypted using crypto map configuration.
- Using tunnel protection:
  - The packet is routed to the tunnel interface.
  - The GRE encapsulates the packet, whereas IPsec adds encryption to the GRE tunnel.
  - The encrypted and encapsulated packet is forwarded to the destination in accordance with the routing table.

The solution to leveraging crypto maps is more complex, and therefore, it is recommended that you use the tunnel protection method when possible. Sometimes when you perform encryption and encapsulation on different devices, you need to use crypto maps.

The following sections explore some alternatives to leveraging GRE over IPsec, such as virtual tunnel interfaces (VTI) and dynamic virtual tunnel interfaces (DVTI).

IPsec and Virtual Tunnel Interface

An IPsec virtual tunnel interface is an alternative to the GRE tunnels over IPsec and provides another mechanism to support VPNs. A VTI supports native IPsec tunneling and allows common interface commands and capabilities to be applied directly to the IPsec tunnels, leveraging a routable interface type. VTIs support interoperability with standards-based IPsec installations of other vendors.

The use of IPsec VTIs is popular because they greatly simplify the configuration process and offer an easy way to define protection between sites to form an overlay network, as shown in Figure 9-5.

Figure 9-5 *Site-to-Site IPsec Tunnel*

VTIs have the following characteristics:

- They behave as a regular tunnel, one for each remote site of the VPN.
- Their encapsulation must be either IPsec ESP or AH.
- Their line protocol depends on the state of the VPN tunnel (IPsec security associations).

A major benefit of IPsec VTIs is that the configuration does not require a static mapping of IPsec sessions to a physical interface. When you use the VTI approach, you configure a virtual tunnel interface and apply an IPsec profile on it using tunnel protection. This approach results in fewer configuration lines because crypto maps are automatically generated for each tunnel when tunnel protection is applied. Features for plaintext packets are configured on the VTI, whereas features for encrypted packets are applied on the physical interface.

The most common use cases for leveraging VTI configuration are for small-scale and hub-and-spoke topology deployments. Following is a review of VTI benefits followed by its limitations:

- **Simplified configuration:** Customers can use the virtual tunnel constructs to configure an IPsec peering to simplify the VPN configuration as compared to crypto maps or GRE IPsec tunnels.

- **Flexible interface feature support:** An IPsec VTI is an encapsulation that uses its Cisco IOS software interface. This characteristic offers the flexibility of defining features to run on either the physical interface that operates on encrypted traffic or the IPsec VTI that operates on clear-text traffic.

- **Multicast support:** Customers can use the IPsec VTIs to securely transfer multicast traffic, such as voice and video applications, from one site to another.

- **Improved scalability:** IPsec VTIs need fewer established SAs to cover different types of traffic such as unicast and multicast, thus enabling improved scaling.

- **Routable interface:** Like GRE IPsec, IPsec VTIs can natively support all types of IP routing protocols, offering improved scalability and redundancy.

VTI limitations include the following issues:

- **Lack of multiprotocol support:** The IPsec VTI is limited to only IP unicast and multicast traffic, as opposed to GRE tunnels, which have wider multiprotocol support.

- **No IPsec stateful failover:** Cisco IOS software IPsec stateful failover is not supported with IPsec VTIs. You can use alternative failover methods such as dynamic routing protocol capabilities to achieve similar functionality, but stateful failover is not inherent within the solution.

IPsec and Dynamic VTI

Dynamic VTI (DVTI) expands VTI functionality to provide highly scalable hub configuration capabilities as part of VPN deployments designed to support site-to-site and remote-access connectivity. Dynamic VTI functionality requires minimal configuration on the hub router when used for hub-and-spoke VPN deployments. For configuration, dynamic VTIs on the hub do not appear as tunnel interfaces but rather show up as virtual-access interfaces, which are automatically cloned from virtual template interfaces. The virtual template interface includes a set of common settings that are inherited by dynamic VTIs. The virtual template configuration includes the IPsec settings and any Cisco IOS software feature settings that would otherwise be configured on a regular interface such as QoS, NetFlow, ACLs, and so on. The hub fills in all other dynamic parameters, such as the tunnel address information of the spoke, as the remote spoke peer connects.

The spoke peer uses static VTI to initiate the VPN connection and to create the tunnel that triggers the creation of the hub DVTI. More specifically, dynamic VTIs are created when spoke peers create an IKE session to the hub device and negotiate IPsec policies. These dynamic tunnels provide on-demand separate virtual access interfaces for each VPN session. Figure 9-6 shows a DVTI hub-and-spoke VPN.

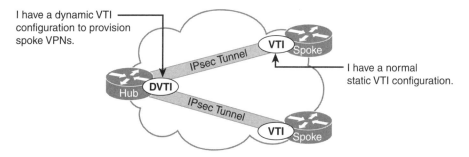

Figure 9-6 *Dynamic VTI over Hub-and-Spoke Network*

The most common use case for dynamic VTI is for large hub-and-spoke deployments, where simplified VPN provisioning on the hub router is wanted. You can also use a dynamic VTI implementation in environments in which spokes take advantage of dynamic WAN IP addressing.

Other Cisco proprietary VPN technologies expand on many of the capabilities that have already been discussed and that have gained in popularity over the last several years. The next section explores one of the most widely deployed Cisco VPN solutions.

DMVPN Overview

Cisco Dynamic Multipoint VPN (DMVPN) is a feature that simplifies the deployment of large hub-and-spoke, partially meshed, and fully meshed virtual private networks. DMVPN combines mGRE tunnels, IPsec encryption, and NHRP to provide simplified provisioning to better scale large and small IPsec VPNs. Although these capabilities have already been reviewed, the following is a consolidated summary of these three DMVPN pillars:

- **mGRE:** Multipoint GRE enables a single GRE interface to support multiple GRE tunnels and simplifies the complexity of the configuration. GRE tunnels provide support for IP multicast, which in turn enables you, as the network designer, to use routing protocols to distribute routing information and detect changes in the VPN. All DMVPN members use GRE or mGRE interfaces to build tunnels between devices.

- **NHRP:** In this client and server protocol (described in RFC 2332), the hub acts as an NHRP server and the spokes act as NHRP clients. The hub maintains an NHRP database of mappings between the outer (public, physical, NBMA interface) and tunnel (inside the tunnel interface) IP addresses of each spoke. Each spoke registers its public and internal tunnel addresses when it boots with the hub, which is also considered to be the Next-Hop Server (NHS). In partial-mesh and full-mesh deployments, the spokes query the NHRP database for the addresses of other spokes for the purpose of building direct spoke-to-spoke tunnels. NHRP reduces the configuration complexity of full-mesh and partial-mesh VPNs. NHRP spokes require only static configuration to communicate with the hub, and the hub shares database information in turn to facilitate spoke-to-spoke connectivity.

- **IPsec:** Internet Protocol Security provides transmission protection for GRE tunnels. DMVPNs form a permanent hub-and-spoke IPsec VPN that can dynamically reconfigures into partial-mesh or full-mesh VPNs as needed.

Major features of the DMVPN solution include the following:

- Configuration reduction
- Zero-touch deployment (ZTD)
- Dynamic routing protocol support
- QoS and per tunnel QoS support
- Hub-and-spoke multicast support
- Support for dynamically addressed peers
- Support for devices behind NAT
- Partial-mesh and full-mesh VPN capabilities
- Capability to be used with or without IPsec encryption

As a result of leveraging mGRE, which takes advantage of a single interface configuration on the hub router to support all spoke connectivity, with DMVPN you can greatly reduce configuration on the hub router. NHRP coupled with dynamic routing makes zero-touch deployments possible. The NHRP provides dynamic registration of the spoke routers, whereas dynamic routing protocols running over DMVPN provide automatic spoke route distribution, allowing for scalable end-to-end IP connectivity. It is possible not only to configure Hierarchical QoS for tunneled traffic but also to implement per tunnel QoS policies that result in shaping traffic down to the committed information rate for each remote-site location before nesting QoS under the class-default per site shaper. DMVPN supports spoke routers that take advantage of dynamic IP addressing and uses NHRP to register the dynamic IP addresses of the spoke routers within the hub router. In addition to supporting dynamic IP addressing on the spokes, the DMVPN solution supports spoke routers behind dynamic NAT. Hub routers are also supported behind NAT but must use static NAT configuration given that all spokes will leverage static NHRP mappings to communicate with the hub.

DMVPN with or without IPsec encryption is a powerful solution when partial-mesh or full-mesh capability is required. It is always important to design with a long-term vision in mind. This typically translates to selecting solutions such as DMVPN that offer the necessary flexibility and adaptability to introduce new capabilities without having to rip, replace, and redesign the infrastructure while going through the plan, build, and manage life cycle.

DMVPN supports two deployment models:

- **Hub and spoke:** A strict hub-and-spoke DMVPN deployment model requires each branch to be configured with a point-to-point GRE interface to the hub. All traffic between spoke networks must flow through the hub router. DMVPN provides scalable configuration to the hub router but does not facilitate direct spoke-to-spoke communication.

- **Spoke-to-spoke:** A spoke-to-spoke DMVPN deployment model requires each branch to be configured with an mGRE interface in which dynamic spoke-to-spoke tunnels are used for the spoke-to-spoke traffic. In this model, DMVPN provides a scalable configuration model for all involved devices and also allows spoke devices to dynamically peer and establish optimal routing paths. DMVPN will not immediately produce a partially meshed or fully meshed topology. DMVPN initially establishes a permanent hub-and-spoke topology, from which a partial mesh or full mesh is dynamically generated based on traffic patterns and DMVPN Phase 2 or Phase 3 configuration, which is discussed later in this chapter (DMVPN Phase 2 subsection).

Figure 9-7 shows both the hub-and-spoke and spoke-to-spoke deployment models.

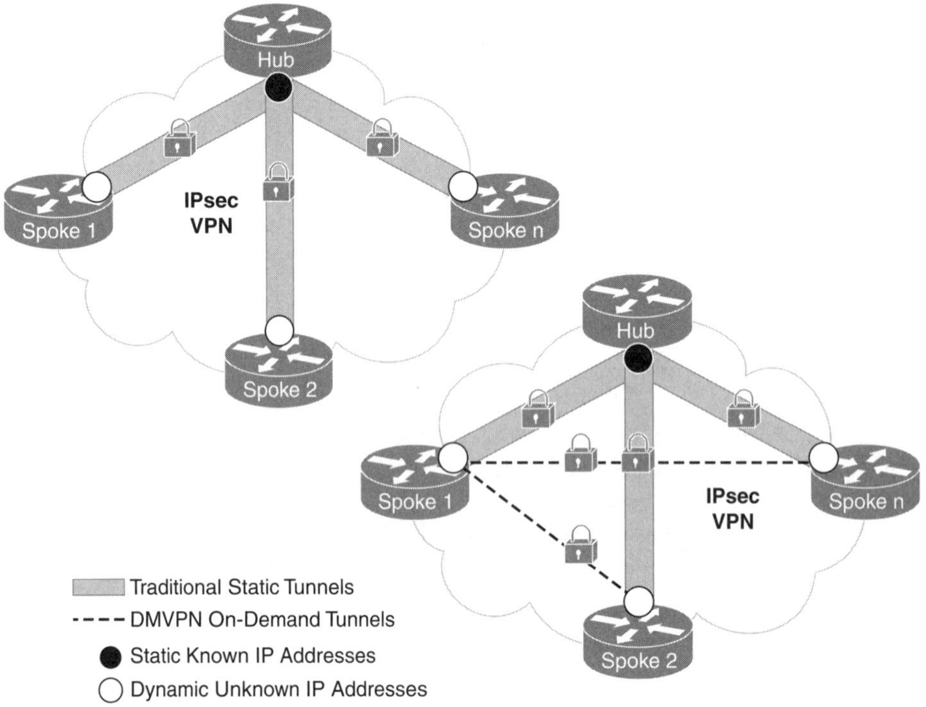

Figure 9-7 *Hub-and-Spoke and Spoke-to-Spoke Communication Models*

DMVPN offers several benefits but has a few limitations in the areas of encryption management and troubleshooting.

Following are the DMVPN major benefits:

- The creation of a scalable fully meshed VPN topology with many peers, where tunnels are dynamically set up as needed.

- Relatively little ongoing configuration effort given that the configuration of hub routers does not change as new peers are added to the network.

- Advanced feature capabilities such as dynamic routing protocol configuration, quality of service methods, security features, multicast, and so on.

- Support over both private and public networks that do not support customer routing information, such as the Internet.

Following are the DMVPN limitations:

- Public Key Infrastructure (PKI) authentication of peers is required to provide scalable spoke-to-spoke IKE authentication.

- Troubleshooting DMVPN is more complex compared to troubleshooting classic IPsec tunnels due to reliance on NHRP and mGRE technologies.

You might wonder what some of the most common deployment examples are when DMVPN is selected as the preferred technology.

The most common DMVPN deployment examples are as follows:

- **Large number of low-bandwidth spokes:** A practical example includes a bank ATM network. These networks are usually large with many low-bandwidth spokes that require connectivity to the hub site for back-end processing. The DMVPN enables these sites to connect over the Internet, providing privacy and data integrity while meeting the performance requirements of business-critical applications.

- SOHO **access to the corporate environment:** The DMVPN can provide work access from small or home offices. The solution supports a large number of spokes that need access to the corporate data center resources, including centralized dial tone services for extended VoIP deployments. DMVPN spoke-to-spoke connectivity is ideal for supporting peer-to-peer traffic patterns such as voice and video communications.

- **Enterprise extranet:** Large enterprises frequently require connectivity to many business partners. You can use the DMVPN to secure traffic between the enterprise and various partner sites. The solution can provide network segregation by helping to ensure that no spoke-to-spoke traffic is allowed by controlling this through the hub.

- **Enterprise WAN connectivity backup:** Perhaps one of the most common use cases has been to leverage the DMVPN over the Internet as a backup solution for private WANs.

- **Service provider VPN services:** The DMVPN enables service providers to offer managed VPN services. Traffic from multiple customers can be aggregated in a single provider edge router and kept isolated using features such as virtual routing and forwarding (VRF).

Depending on your design requirements and use case, the DMVPN supports three versions of implementation referred to as phases. Each phase provides unique benefits and has caveats that must be understood to ensure successful execution of hub-and-spoke, partial-mesh, and full-mesh deployment models.

DMVPN Phase 1

DMVPN Phase 1 is the basic DMVPN deployment model. In Phase 1, as shown in Figure 9-8, the hub router uses mGRE to connect to the spoke routers. The spoke routers use regular point-to-point GRE tunnels.

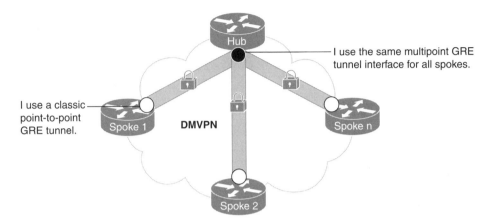

Figure 9-8 *DMVPN Phase 1*

Although all routers in DMVPN Phase 1 must use the same subnet, the spoke routers can only directly reach the hub and must go through the hub to get to any other spokes. The main benefits of DMVPN Phase 1 are the simplified configuration on the hub routers and controlled spoke-to-spoke communications for circumstances in which this functionality would prove useful. In DMVPN Phase 1, the hub acts as an NHRP server. The spokes register with the hub, which means that they announce mapping between the tunnel IP address and the address on the physical interface. In this way, the hub knows how to reach each spoke and records this information in a database. Because the registration process is triggered by the spoke and happens automatically at the hub, the DMVPN enables dynamically assigned IP addresses on the spoke routers.

The disadvantage of DMVPN Phase 1 in many enterprise uses cases is the inability to establish spoke-to-spoke tunnels. Spoke-to-spoke connectivity is often required to accommodate improved traffic handling and application performance.

You can use almost any routing protocol as part of a DMVPN Phase 1 deployment. Because DMVPN Phase 1 does not allow spoke-to-spoke tunnel establishment, all traffic must go through the hub router; therefore, the next hop must always be the hub router. A common approach to routing with DMVPN Phase 1 deployments is to have only a default route pointing back to the hub configured on the spoke routers. This default route can be configured statically or advertised from the hub through a routing protocol.

When you use EIGRP as a routing protocol in the DMVPN, you must understand the rule of split horizon. Split horizon prevents routing loops in the network. The rule states that the router should never advertise a route out of the interface through which it learns that route. When using DMVPN Phase 1, the hub uses only one interface to connect to all spokes. When the hub receives the routing update from one spoke, it must deliver the same update out of the same interface. Split horizon is enabled by default and prevents this behavior on the hub router. You can do one of the three things to ensure that spokes reach other spokes through the hub:

- Disable split horizon.

- Leverage summarization at the hub if spoke routes can be aggregated as part of a shorter matching prefix.

- Leverage a catchall default route pointing back to the hub if conflicting with the direct Internet attach and split-tunnel configuration is not in place.

If you're using OSPF as the routing protocol in the DMVPN, you must use the point-to-multipoint network type on hub-and-spoke routers. The default OSPF network type on the tunnel interface is point-to-point. If you leave the default network type, the OSPF adjacency will flap continuously between spoke routers. When configuring the point-to-multipoint network type, OSPF treats this network type as a collection of point-to-point links.

If you decide to use BGP as the routing protocol in your DMVPN, you should consider using eBGP to accommodate a simplified design and simplified overall provisioning. iBGP does not announce prefixes that are received through iBGP to other iBGP peers and will require configuring the DMVPN hub router as a route reflector. When using eBGP, you need to configure the next-hop-self option because eBGP does not change next-hop attributes when peers are in the same subnet. If you examine this closely in the context of DMVPN, when you configure eBGP peering relationships between IP addresses on the tunnel interfaces, the spoke announces prefixes with the next-hop IP address of the tunnel interface. When prefixes come to the hub router, this router announces prefixes to the other spokes and does not change the next-hop attribute. The result of this situation is that spokes will not have reachability to the networks behind other spokes because the next-hop IPs of these spokes are not available.

DMVPN Phase 2

To overcome the limitations of DMVPN Phase 1 and to enable direct spoke-to-spoke tunnel capability, you need to prepare the infrastructure by configuring multipoint GRE on all hub-and-spoke router tunnel interfaces, as shown in Figure 9-9.

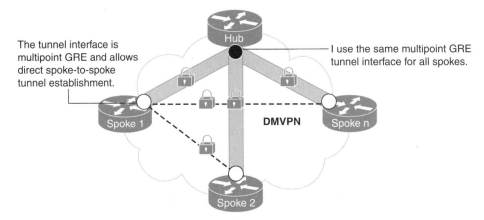

Figure 9-9 *DMVPN Phase 2*

This model will ensure that when the router establishes a direct spoke-to-spoke tunnel, it can send data directly to the spoke without the need to send data through hub router. This feature applies only for unicast traffic. When you're leveraging the DMVPN, multicast traffic can be sent only between hub-and-spoke routers. This limitation results in routing adjacencies being established only between the hub-and-spoke routers. If you want routing adjacencies directly between spoke routers to support certain design scenarios, you must statically configure neighbors on the spoke routers.

NHRP serves two functions in DMVPN Phase 2. The first function is similar to DMVPN Phase 1 in which NHRP is used for dynamic spoke registration and can accommodate spokes with dynamic IP addresses. The second function of NHRP with DMVPN Phase 2 is for on-demand tunnel destination resolution. When a spoke wants to communicate to some other spoke based on unmodified next-hop information, it uses NHRP to ask the hub about the other spoke's tunnel IP address to real IP address mapping. For DMVPN Phase 2 to work successfully, the spoke routers must have full reachability information, including the full routing table and the unmodified tunnel next-hop IP address of the other spoke. The requirement for full reachability information means that leveraging summarization on the hub router is not supported with DMVPN Phase 2. This is an important limitation to keep in mind when designing for scalability in large networks. Next, look at the role that different routing protocols play in DMVPN Phase 2 deployments.

When using EIGRP with DMVPN Phase 2, you should not only disable split horizon on the hub router but should also disable the next-hop-self option to ensure that the next-hop information is unchanged. This configuration tells the hub router to set the next-hop IP addressing information to the IP address of the spoke that originated the route. When the receiving spoke receives the route, it sees the IP address of the tunnel interface on the other spoke router as the next-hop IP address. When the spoke wants to send data to this network, it tries to establish a direct spoke-to-spoke tunnel based on multipoint GRE tunnel interface configuration and next-hop routing information.

When using OSPF as part of a DMVPN Phase 2 deployment, remember that the DMVPN behaves like a LAN segment. Because of this LAN-like behavior, when leveraging OSPF as the routing protocol, you should configure the OSPF network type as broadcast on all router tunnel interfaces. You can also use the OSPF network type of nonbroadcast, but this would require statically configuring neighbor statements on the hub router pointing to each of the spoke router tunnel IP addresses. Configuring the OSPF network type as point-to-multipoint would result in all traffic continuing to flow through the hub router and would prevent you from achieving a Phase 2 deployment model. Because OSPF DR/BDR election is performed in the broadcast segment when tunnel interfaces are configured with the network type broadcast, it is critical to configure your hub router to win the election process. Not only should you set the OSPF DR priority to the highest value on the hub, but you should also set the DR priority on all spoke routers to zero. Setting a priority of zero prevents spoke routers from participating in the DR/BDR election process. Figure 9-10 shows EIGRP and OSPF considerations discussed as part of this section.

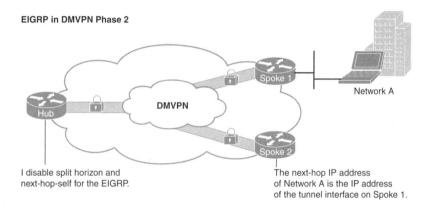

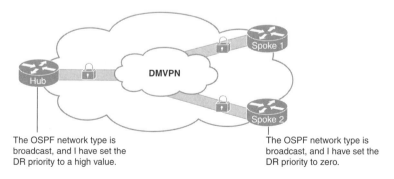

Figure 9-10 *EIGRP and OSPF over DMVPN Phase 2*

Now take a closer look at DMVPN Phase 2 operations. When a spoke wants to send traffic destined to the network on the other spoke, it checks the routing table. The next-hop IP address in the routing table is pointing directly to the other spoke router. If the direct tunnel was not already established, the following procedure is used:

Step 1. **NHRP Query:** The spoke sends an NHRP query to the NHRP server (NHS/DMVPN hub) to resolve the next-hop IP address to the tunnel endpoint address.

Step 2. **NHS Response:** The NHRP server sends an NHRP reply to the spoke routers with the correct mapping information that was stored during the initial spoke-to-hub registration process.

Step 3. **IPsec Trigger:** The spoke router receives the NHRP response from the hub, and this triggers the IPsec process for direct spoke-to-spoke tunnel establishment.

Step 4. **Unidirectional Tunnel Establishment:** After the IPsec tunnel is created, all packets bypass the hub. At this point, the spoke-to-spoke tunnel can pass traffic in one direction only.

Step 5. **Reverse Direction NHRP Query:** To provide bidirectional connectivity, the other spoke also needs to leverage unmodified next-hop information. The other spoke sends an NHRP query when the first packet needs to be forwarded. When the NHRP mapping is in place and the GRE association is built, the response packet will be sent directly to the spoke.

DMVPN Phase 2 is a common and widely leveraged VPN deployment model. As a result of limitations with scalability, however, many enterprise organizations choose DMVPN Phase 3 for initial deployments or are in the process of migrating existing deployments from Phase 2 to Phase 3.

DMVPN Phase 3

DMVPN Phase 3 is similar to DMVPN Phase 2 because it enables direct spoke-to-spoke tunnel creation to support optimized traffic handling. Now examine similarities and differences by exploring DMVPN Phase 3 operations:

Step 1. **Registration:** The initial step in DMVPN Phase 3 is similar to the one in DMVPN Phase 2. The spoke router registers tunnel and outer IP address mapping to the hub router. This registration enables the hub to dynamically discover all spokes.

Step 2. **Routing:** After the initial connectivity has been established, the hub and spoke can establish a routing adjacency to exchange routes. In DMVPN Phase 2, the hub routers must preserve the next-hop IP address when sending the route to the other spokes. In DMVPN Phase 3, the hub router does not need to preserve the IP next-hop information. Unlike Phase 2, DMVPN Phase 3 also supports sending summary information or even simply only sending default routing information as part of the routing advertisement. The ability to leverage route summarization enables you to greatly reduce the size of the routing table on the spoke routers taking part in large DMVPN deployments.

Step 3. First Packet: When the spoke router wants to send IP packets to the other spoke routers, it sends the first packet to the hub router.

Step 4. NHRP Redirect: The hub router forwards packets to the correct spoke, but it also replies to the originator of the traffic with NHRP redirects. This redirect message tells the originator that the forwarding is suboptimal and that it should send traffic directly to the other spoke. The message contains the destination IP address of the original IP packet.

Step 5. NHRP Request: The spoke then sends an NHRP request for the original IP address using the routing table.

Step 6. Request Forward: The request will traverse the hub router, which will forward this request to the correct spoke.

Step 7. Direct Response: When the other spoke receives the NHRP request, it responds directly to the originator.

Step 8. NHRP Table Rewrite: When the response reaches the originator, it knows the outer IP address of the destination and can rewrite the NHRP table with the correct entry.

If you are interested in migrating from DMVPN Phase 2 to Phase 3, you need to add the IP NHRP Redirect command to the hub tunnel interface and the IP NHRP Shortcut command to all spoke router tunnel interfaces. The next set of changes depend on the routing protocol used and relate to no longer needing to preserve IP next-hop information.

If you are leveraging EIGRP as the routing protocol, it is no longer necessary to disable next-hop-self on the hub router, and therefore, it is recommended that you remove this configuration. Split horizon can stay disabled, and you can now use summarization commands to reduce the number of routes on the DMVPN spokes.

If you want to migrate from DMVPN Phase 2 to Phase 3 and if you are using OSPF, change the network type to point-to-multipoint on all hubs and spokes. After making this change, you can also remove DR/BDR-related ip ospf priority settings because this is no longer needed when configuring OSPF point-to-multipoint network types.

Figure 9-11 shows EIGRP and OSPF considerations when leveraging DMVPN Phase 3.

294 Chapter 9: Enterprise-Managed WANs

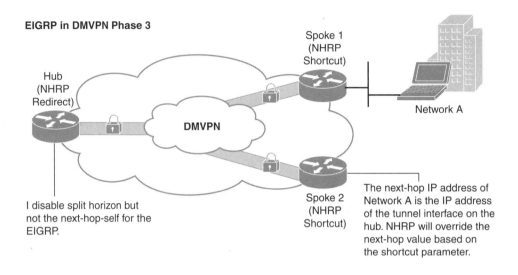

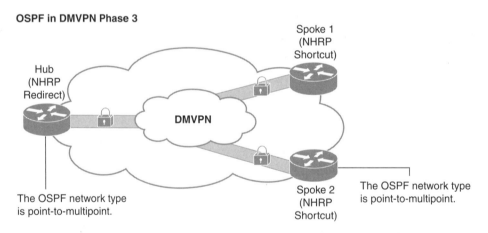

Figure 9-11 *EIGRP and OSPF over DMVPN Phase 2*

DMVPN Phase 3 scalability enhancements such as routing protocol summarization make it an ideal choice for most modern DMVPN deployments. In addition to route summarization capabilities, DMVPN Phase 3 also introduces support for hierarchical hub designs, such as the one shown in Figure 9-12.

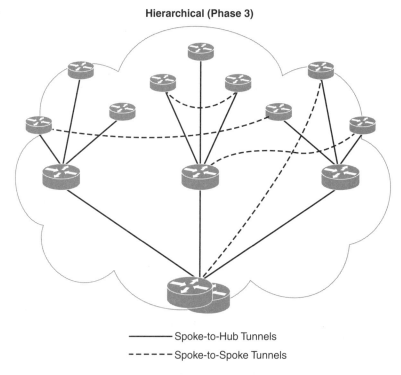

Figure 9-12 *Hierarchical DMVPN Hub Design*

Case Study: EIGRP DMVPN

This section leverages a case study with additional detail to gain a better understanding of the three DMVPN phases using the most commonly selected routing protocol, EIGRP. No matter which DMVPN phase is used or how complex the topology is, EIGRP routers will always establish adjacencies in a hub-and-spoke manner. This, in turn, reduces the number of total adjacencies and spoke hardware requirements and allows for greater scalability.

EIGRP over DMVPN Phase 1

When leveraging a DMVPN Phase 1 hub-and-spoke-only deployment model, DMVPN relays multicast between hub and spokes, allowing EIGRP adjacencies to form. As shown in Figure 9-13, all spoke routers establish adjacencies only with the hub router because there is no direct path between the spokes.

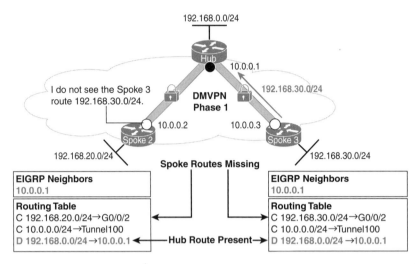

Figure 9-13 *DMVPN Phase 1: Initial Connectivity*

The Spoke 3 router in this diagram advertises its connected network 192.168.30.0/24 to the hub router, which, after receiving the route, places it in its routing table. Although the hub has established an adjacency with the Spoke 2 router, the 192.168.30.0/24 network is not present in the Spoke 2 router's routing table. Perhaps you recall what would cause this behavior. Is it that the hub router is not advertising the 192.168.30.0/24 network to Spoke 2, or is it that the Spoke 2 router is not installing the received route in its routing table? Previous sections introduced you to the rule of split horizon, which prevents a route from being advertised out of the same interface from which it was learned. Figure 9-14 shows that when you disable the split horizon, the route gets advertised and installed.

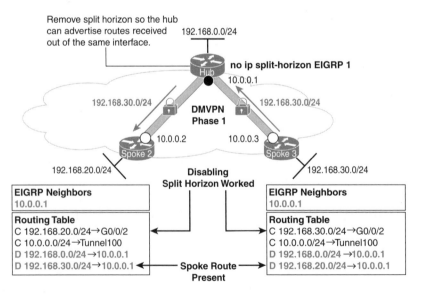

Figure 9-14 *EIGRP Split Horizon over DMVPN*

When using EIGRP to route through the DMVPN cloud, always disable split horizon on the hub router to ensure that routes get propagated from one spoke router to the other.

EIGRP over DMVPN Phase 2

DMVPN Phase 2 allows dynamic establishment of mGRE tunnels between the spoke routers when needed; however, spoke-to-spoke tunnels do not relay multicast, and thus, spoke-to-spoke EIGRP adjacencies are not established. This tremendously reduces the number of established adjacencies in DMVPN mesh networks with a high number of spokes and enables you to use low-end routers in your branches. Figure 9-15 shows that as all spoke networks are advertised through the hub, the hub serves as the next hop for all spoke-to-spoke communication, rendering any established spoke-to-spoke tunnels useless.

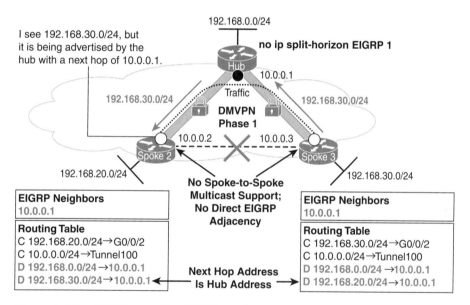

Figure 9-15 *EIGRP over DMVPN Phase 2: Initial Connectivity*

Do you recall how to keep the hub-and-spoke EIGRP topology yet use the full mesh of DMVPN to forward traffic as part of a DMVPN Phase 2 deployment model? Perhaps you remember the technique, as shown in Figure 9-16.

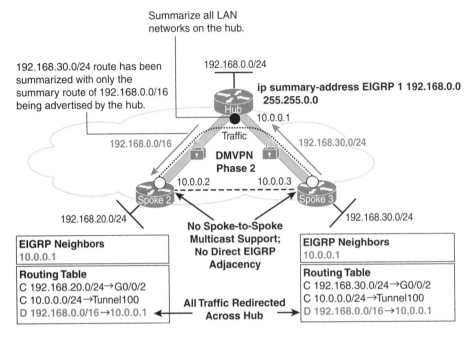

Figure 9-16 *Summarizing Spoke Routes at the DMVPN Hub*

The hub router can still relay the advertisements that it receives from the spoke routers; however, it must not state itself as a next hop for those routes. You must configure the hub to advertise the network that it receives from the spokes by disabling split horizon; however, you must also ensure that you keep the spoke IP address as the next hop. By disabling the ip next-hop-self behavior, you can see from the Spoke 2 routing table that it received the 192.168.30.0/24 route from the hub router, with the unmodified next-hop address of the Spoke 3 router. With this configuration in place, spoke-to-spoke traffic is now forwarded directly between the spokes. When using a DMVPN Phase 2 deployment model, you must configure the hub router with the **no next-hop-self** command.

As the number of DMVPN spokes rises, so does the number of advertised routes. You determine that you want to counter the rising number of routes by using summarization. Because all the routes are advertised through the hub, you decide to implement summarization on the hub to control the situation. The hub now advertises only a summary network to the spokes. Summarization reduces the number of advertised routes, but now all spoke-to-spoke traffic flows through the hub again because the next hop of the summary route is the hub. Figure 9-17 displays the impact of introducing the summary.

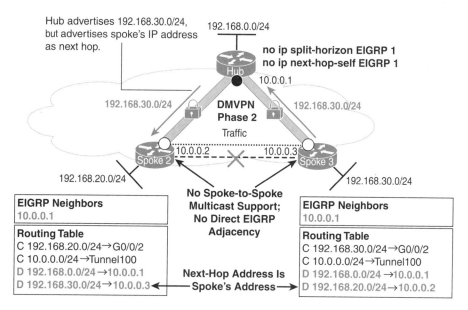

Figure 9-17 *EIGRP over DMVPN Phase 2: Enable Direct Spoke-to-Spoke Communication*

EIGRP over DMVPN Phase 3

Let's take this design a step forward by optimizing routing advertisement. First, you need to know if you can summarize all networks that are advertised by spokes, while optimally routing through the DMVPN cloud. Is it possible to do this using a Phase 2 deployment model, or do you need to consider migrating to DMVPN Phase 3? Figure 9-18 shows that leveraging summarization while supporting spoke-to-spoke connectivity requires migration to a DMVPN Phase 3 deployment model.

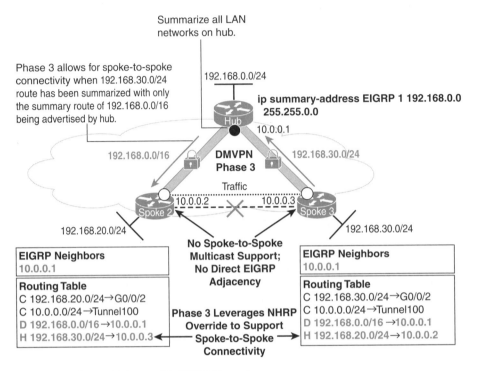

Figure 9-18 *EIGRP over DMVPN Phase 3*

Both DMVPN Phase 2 and DMVPN Phase 3 enable you to build partial- or full-mesh networks, but only DMVPN Phase 3 enables you to perform optimal full-mesh routing with simple, summarized EIGRP advertising. This is made possible by NHRP Phase 3 improvements that enable the hub to issue redirects to spokes. Figure 9-19 shows how this works.

EIGRP configuration remains simple. The hub router peers with spokes, and the split horizon rule is removed on the hub. The hub advertises all the networks that it receives from the spokes, stating itself as the next hop. You can easily do a summarization on the hub to reduce the number of advertised networks to each of the spoke routers.

A packet is sent from the Spoke 2 LAN, destined to the Spoke 3 LAN address. Spoke 2 looks into its routing table and sees that there is a summary network entry with the hub router as its next hop. A packet is forwarded toward the hub router, which then forwards it to Spoke 3. Up until this point, this routing behavior sounds a lot like a DMVPN Phase 2 EIGRP deployment leveraging a next-hop-self configuration. So how is it possible that DMVPN Phase 3 is better than DMVPN Phase 2?

Case Study: EIGRP DMVPN   301

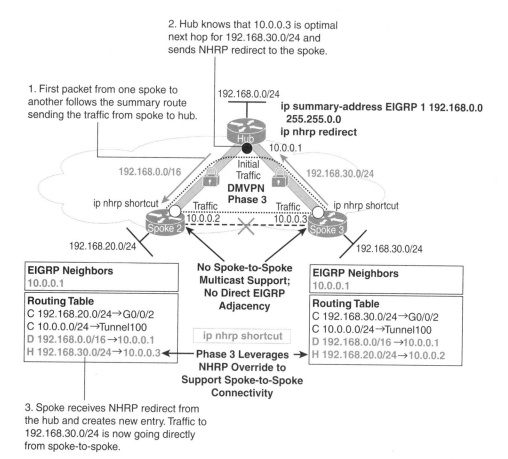

Figure 9-19 *EIGRP over DMVPN—NHRP Redirect*

The hub router has Spoke 3 listed as the optimal next hop for the Spoke 3 LAN address. When the hub router is configured for **ip nhrp redirect** under the tunnel interface configuration, it sends an NHRP redirect message to Spoke 2. This redirect message notifies Spoke 2 that the packets for the Spoke 3 LAN are better forwarded directly to the Spoke 3 router.

The Spoke 3 router receives the NHRP redirect from the hub and, when configured with **ip nhrp shortcut** under the tunnel interface configuration, it creates a new NHRP entry in its routing table. The new NHRP entry overrides the initial routing pointer to the hub as the next hop. The Spoke 3 router shows up as the NHRP next hop override for the traffic that is destined to the Spoke 3 LAN subnet, and the traffic now forwards directly across the spoke-to-spoke tunnel to the Spoke 3 router.

DMVPN Phase 1–3 Summary

Before moving to DMVPN redundancy, scalability, and other advanced DMVPN use cases, let's close out these last several sections by comparing each of the DMVPN phases to one another. Table 9-2 provides a summary comparison.

Table 9-2 *DMVPN Phase 1–3 Comparison*

Phase 1	Phase 2	Phase 3
■ Hub-and-spoke functionality only	■ Spoke-to-spoke functionality	■ Spoke-to-spoke functionality
■ Point-to-point GRE interface configuration on spokes	■ mGRE interface configuration on hubs and spokes	■ mGRE interface configuration on hubs and spokes
■ mGRE configuration on hubs	■ Direct spoke-to-spoke data traffic reduces load on hubs and provides optimal traffic handling for peer-to-peer applications	■ Direct spoke-to-spoke data traffic reduces load on hubs and provides optimal traffic handling for peer-to-peer applications
■ Simplified and smaller configuration on hubs		
■ Support for dynamically addressed CPEs (NAT)	■ Spokes must have full routing table and therefore summarization not supported	■ Spokes don't need full routing table and therefore can summarize to support improved scale
■ Support for routing protocols and multicast	■ Spoke-spoke tunnel triggered by spoke itself	■ Spoke-spoke tunnel triggered by hubs (requires the spoke to have the **ip nhrp shortcut** command configured)
■ Spokes don't need full routing table and therefore can summarize on hubs	■ Routing protocol limitations	
	■ Multihub deployments must interconnect hubs in a daisy-chain fashion	■ Removes routing protocol limitations such as requirement for **no ip next-hop-self**

In simple words:

- Phase 1 allows for simple hub-and-spoke topologies.
- DMVPN Phase 2 and DMVPN Phase 3 allow complex hub-and-spoke, full-mesh, or hybrid topologies.
- DMVPN Phase 3 adds greater scalability and support for hierarchical designs.

DMVPN and Redundancy

A common approach to providing high availability in the DMVPNs is to implement multiple hub routers at the central site.

Figure 9-20 presents the two typical deployment options that are most commonly present within enterprise environments:

- Dual hub dual DMVPN cloud
- Dual hub single DMVPN cloud

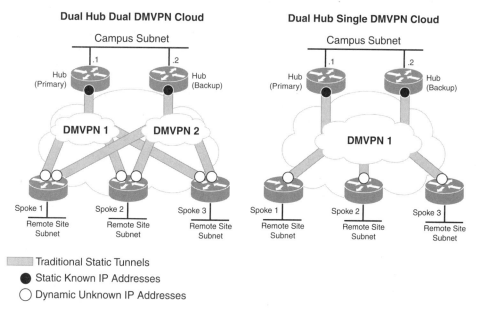

Figure 9-20 *Common DMVPN Dual Hub Deployment Models*

> **Note** Although dual hub is mentioned, you can use more than two routers at the central site for high availability. Dual hub is just a typical deployment.

In both topologies, at least two hub routers are deployed for redundancy, and the second hub router provides high availability. The hub may be on the same DMVPN subnet as the primary hub router as with a single DMVPN cloud topology or dual hub single DMVPN design. The second hub router can also service its own DMVPN subnet, which is known as a dual DMVPN cloud topology or dual hub dual DMVPN design. Both dual hub single DMVPN and dual hub dual DMVPN cloud topologies rely on routing protocols running inside the tunnels to determine tunnel path selection.

The difference between the two topologies is apparent on the branch router. With a single DMVPN subnet, the branch router has a single mGRE tunnel, and both hub routers are mapped to this tunnel through this mGRE interface. In a dual DMVPN topology, the branch router has a unique tunnel pointing to each of the unique hub routers. Standard routing protocols such as EIGRP, BGP, or OSPF determine the active hub over either topology. In the single DMVPN topology, the hubs appear as two different next hops via the one mGRE tunnel interface. In the dual DMVPN topology, the hubs appear as two different next hops via the two GRE or mGRE interfaces.

In general, the single DMVPN cloud topology is best when dynamic spoke-spoke tunnels are required because spoke-spoke tunnels can only be built within a DMVPN cloud, not between DMVPN clouds. The dual DMVPN cloud topology is often easier for hub-and-spoke-only networks. It can be easier to configure the routing protocol to prefer one DMVPN cloud (hub) over the other. The reason for this is that the router receives routing information from the hubs on different tunnel interfaces. These are simply recommendations and not requirements because either DMVPN cloud topology can be configured for either hub-and-spoke only or spoke-spoke networks. DMVPN cloud topologies can also be used in combination to meet the requirements for more complex networks.

The next section includes a detailed case study to explore a slightly more advanced DMVPN deployment use case that involves taking advantage of GRE/DMVPN to deliver MPLS/VPN-style services capabilities.

Case Study: MPLS/VPN over GRE/DMVPN

In this case, you are working at a company that has several hundred remote branch offices. Each branch has a single router that connects back in a hub-and-spoke fashion to a central site that leverages two hub routers for aggregation and high availability. The ISP provides the connectivity between branch offices and the central site, and the hub routers provide connectivity back to other parts of the infrastructure. You have implemented point-to-point GRE tunnels with IPsec protection on top of the service provider transport network. You are leveraging a dual hub dual DMVPN cloud topology design, which means that there are two GRE tunnels from each branch office to the central site. You have tweaked the EIGRP routing protocol to select one tunnel as the primary path and the other as a backup. Figure 9-21 depicts the current WAN setup.

Multiple departments are using the common branch infrastructure. You want to maintain isolation between the traffic from the different departments, and the current solution does not provide enough scalability to address such a requirement. You are currently using access lists to limit the connectivity between each segment. Although segments must be separated, some traffic must still pass from one segment to the other. You are manually allowing access to accommodate such use cases.

Case Study: MPLS/VPN over GRE/DMVPN

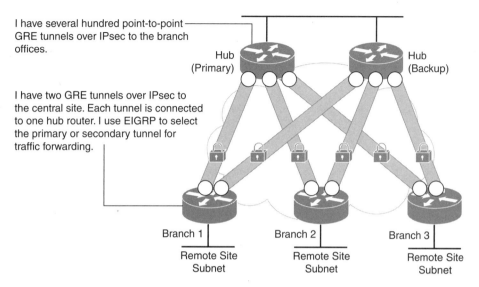

Figure 9-21 *Current EIGRP over GRE Design*

You want to upgrade your current network with a solution that meets the following requirements:

- The solution must be scalable.
- The solution must reduce the workload for configuration of the new branch office.
- The traffic between departments must be isolated.
- The security policy between departments must be centrally managed.

The current method of using point-to-point GRE tunnels over IPsec adds a considerable amount of management overhead. When you add a new branch office, you must configure a new tunnel interface on both the hub router and on the spoke router. With so many branch offices, the configuration on the hub routers has become huge and is relatively hard to maintain. You are thinking about an optimal solution for VPN tunnel provisioning while keeping in mind that most of the traffic today and for the foreseeable future is between each branch office and the central site, with occasional branch-to-branch communications. Naturally, you are leaning toward a VPN technology that is designed to ideally address hub-and-spoke topology requirements. As shown in Figure 9-22, you decide to upgrade the transport network to leverage DMVPN. To maintain a highly available solution, you provision a dual hub single DMVPN cloud design, which means that both routers at the central site are configured as hub routers for the same DMVPN cloud.

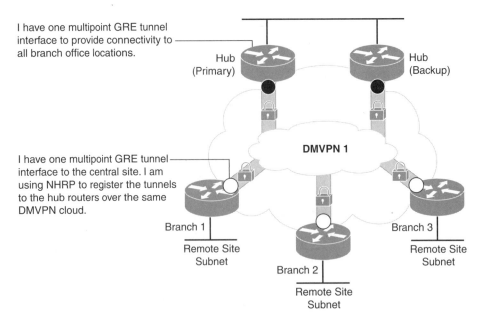

Figure 9-22 *Proposed Design: DMVPN Based*

With this design, each of the hub routers is configured with a single multipoint GRE tunnel interface and supports a zero-touch dynamic registration of the spoke routers through NHRP. IP connectivity is established between the sites, leveraging routing protocol configuration. The optimized solution results in an immediate reduction in the configuration from several hundred tunnel interfaces to a single interface, which provides connectivity for all branch routers.

To successfully migrate branches to the new DMVPN cloud, you have configured multipoint GRE tunnel interfaces on each of the branch routers. The multipoint GRE mode of configuration is needed because you are transitioning from a design that uses independent tunnel interfaces connecting to each hub to a single interface configuration that must communicate with two hub routers over the same transport.

You maintain GRE protection by using the IPsec-integrated capability with preshared key authentication. You are planning to migrate to internal PKI for IPsec peer authentication at a later time to enhance overall security and manageability of the solution.

After you upgrade the transport network, you move forward with a design to address traffic isolation requirements at the branch office. The router at each site is currently deployed as a router on a stick. A router on a stick configuration means that the router is trunking down to the switch leveraging dot1q encapsulation and is configured with routable subinterfaces, providing default gateway functionality for hosts on each of the VLAN segments broken out by department. One of the best ways to isolate traffic for these routable interfaces is to use the virtual routing and forwarding (VRF) technology available on the routers. A VRF consists of an IP routing table, a derived forwarding table, a set of interfaces that use the forwarding table, and a set of rules and routing protocols that determine what goes into the forwarding table. Simply put, a VRF is a mechanism to create several independent virtual routing tables on the same routing device. Using VRF in this way is often referred to as VRF-Lite. Through the use of VRF-Lite, you can completely isolate traffic forwarding between departments. Implementing this solution is as simple as configuring a VRF for each department and then putting each subinterface acting as gateway for the hosts contained within a departmental VLAN into a separate VRF, as shown in Figure 9-23.

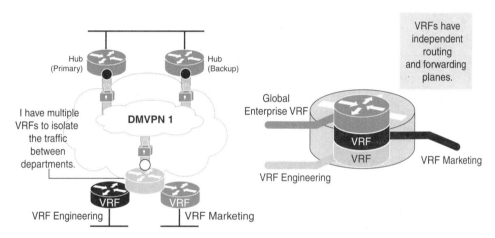

Figure 9-23 *Traffic Isolation Using VRF-Lite*

After you have successfully isolated traffic from different departments within the branch, you still need a solution to forward traffic between these VRFs and the central site. Furthermore, one of the requirements was that you need to be able to centrally manage which traffic can pass between VRFs. You can achieve this requirement by forwarding traffic to the central site, where you can perform the security check and forward the traffic back to the branch office. These requirements could be addressed by configuring a separate multipoint GRE tunnel interface for each department on the branch routers and hub routers and allocating these interfaces to the same VRFs that were leveraged for subinterface configuration. This results in end-to-end VRF-Lite–based segmentation. An example of leveraging VRF-Lite to create multiple DVMPN clouds is shown in Figure 9-24.

308   Chapter 9: Enterprise-Managed WANs

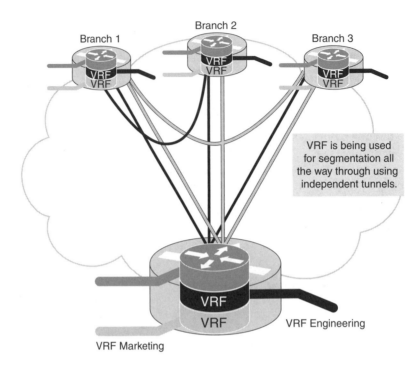

Figure 9-24 *DMVPN per VRF*

The problem with this approach is that it doesn't scale and adds additional configuration overhead. Each VRF creates the need for an additional multipoint GRE tunnel interface to be configured, which results in the need for separate IPsec connectivity and increased resource utilization. The most scalable solution that can send isolated traffic over a common infrastructure without the need for redundant configuration is an L3 Multiprotocol Label Switching (MPLS) VPN. Figure 9-25 shows an example of RFC 25470DMVPN, which is essentially MPLS running over a DMVPN.

Service providers typically leverage MPLS to isolate traffic between different customers. In your case, you can consider IT as the service provider and each department as your customer. Implementing an L3 MPLS VPN solution would allow you to transfer traffic from multiple departments across the common DMVPN transport while isolating the traffic from each other. With an L3 MPLS VPN solution, you would also have a separate routing table for each department on the devices terminating each end of the VPN. Figure 9-26 provides a view of the design.

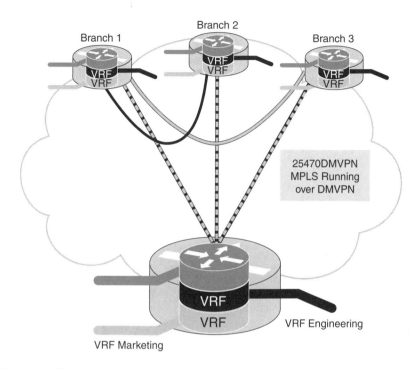

- ▬▬ VRF Engineering Tunnels
- ═══ VRF Marketing Tunnels
- ▀▀▀ VRF Marketing/Engineering Tunnels

Figure 9-25 *MPLS over DMVPN*

Solution implementation requires VRF configuration for each department as well as a route distinguisher and route targets for each VRF on the hub routers. To transfer routes from the branch office to the central site, you need to use Multiprotocol BGP (MP-BGP), which enables you to transfer VPNv4 routes. You decided to use external BGP as the routing protocol to facilitate IP connectivity between the central site and branch offices, where each branch office uses its own autonomous system (AS) number. Given that this is a private BGP deployment, you are using private AS space. To ensure that all traffic goes through the central site, you decide to send only a default route to the branch routers from the central site hub routers. You will use MP-BGP policy to select which hub router will act as the primary versus secondary path. You are announcing all routes to the central site from the branch office to allow dynamically learned routes at the central site.

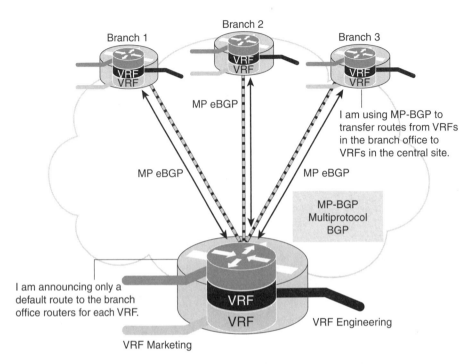

Figure 9-26 *Route Separation with VRFs and MP-BGP*

You have connected the hub routers to the switch at the central site. You have configured trunking from the switch to the routers. You have determined VLAN to VRF mappings. Similar to the branch deployment, you have implemented a router-on-a-stick solution on the hub routers. The difference is that these interfaces are routing to independent subinterfaces broken out for isolated transport on a central firewall. This solution enables you to continue to isolate traffic between VRFs at the central site and to leverage a single point dedicated for policy enforcement. The solution is shown in Figure 9-27.

The point where you will perform security checks on the traffic will be the firewall. The firewall again uses multiple subinterfaces, providing segmented connectivity from the hub routers. All security policy is implemented on the firewall subinterfaces, and this, in turn, enables you to control which traffic will pass between VRFs and which traffic will be denied.

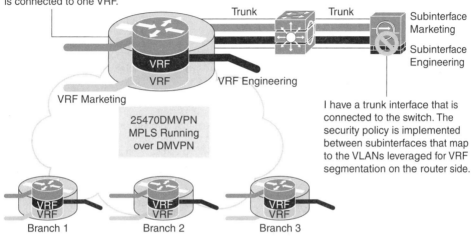

Figure 9-27 *Centralized Firewall for Inter-VLAN/VPN Routing*

With this solution, you have achieved traffic isolation at the branch office and centrally managed a security check for such traffic. When you send traffic from one department and it is destined to the other department at the branch office, the traffic must go through the central firewall, as shown in Figure 9-28.

The traffic is first forwarded to the router at the branch office. The branch router performs a VRF routing table check to find the destination for the packet. Because you are sending only the default route to the branch office, the traffic is forwarded through the WAN using MPLS over the DMVPN. The traffic arrives at the hub router, which performs a routing table check for the specific VRF. The packet is forwarded through the hub router VRF interface over the VLAN that is mapped to the dedicated firewall subinterface. The firewall performs a security check on the packet. If the packet is allowed, the firewall forwards the packet back to the hub router. When the packet arrives at the destination VRF, the hub router performs a routing table check and forwards the packet to the correct branch router according to the routing table. The packet is forwarded through the WAN using MPLS. When the packet arrives at the correct router, this router delivers the packet to the end host.

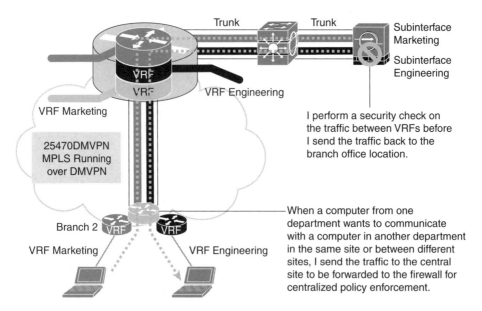

Figure 9-28 *Inter-VLAN/VPN Routing: Traffic Flow*

After the testing phase, you verify that the solution works as expected.

With this solution, you gain the following benefits:

- Traffic isolation between departments at the branch routers
- Configuration reduction on the central site routers
- Zero-touch deployments for the new branch offices
- Centrally managed security policy between departments

Although the solution meets the requirements, as part of your long-term design planning, you must consider some drawbacks in using this solution. As you can see, the local traffic must be transferred through the WAN twice before it is forwarded to the host in the same branch office. If the need for internal branch cross-department communication increases significantly, this could result in suboptimal routing. You must consider staffing knowledge and familiarity with advanced protocols such as MPLS that may be perceived as being more complex than the previous solution that was in place leveraging point-to-point GRE tunnels.

Now it's time to shift the focus to a few other VPN solutions before closing out the chapter.

SSL VPN Overview

The Secure Sockets Layer (SSL) VPN enables your company to extend access to its secure enterprise network to any authorized user by providing remote-access connectivity through an SSL-enabled VPN gateway. Secure remote-access connectivity is possible from almost any Internet-enabled location using only a web browser that natively supports SSL encryption. In addition to supporting corporate-managed devices and locations, one of the benefits of SSL VPN is the capability to support access from noncorporate machines and locations, including home computers, Internet kiosks, and wireless hotspots. These locations are difficult places to deploy and manage the VPN client software and remote configuration required to support IPsec VPN connectivity.

SSL VPN delivers the three modes of access shown in Figure 9-29.

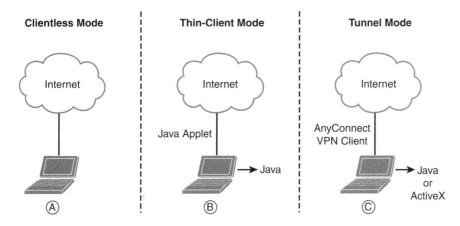

Figure 9-29 *SSL VPN Access Modes*

- **Clientless:** Clientless mode provides secure access to private web resources and web content. This mode is useful for accessing most content that you would expect to access in a web browser. Examples include intranet access, Internet access, databases, and online tools that employ a web interface.

- **Thin client:** Thin-client mode extends the capability of the cryptographic functions of the web browser. This option enables remote access to TCP-based applications such as POP3, SMTP, IMAP, Telnet, and SSH. The remote user downloads a Java applet by clicking the link that is provided on the portal page or by downloading the applet automatically. The Java applet acts as a TCP proxy on the client machine for the services that are configured on the gateway.

- **Tunnel mode:** Full tunnel client mode offers extensive application support through its dynamically downloadable Cisco AnyConnect VPN Client for SSL VPN. Full tunnel client mode delivers a lightweight, centrally configured, and easy-to-support SSL VPN tunneling client that provides network layer access to virtually any application.

FlexVPN Overview

Deploying IPsec VPN over IP networks can be complex and often results in high costs associated with deploying multiple types of VPN solutions to meet different types of connectivity requirements.

FlexVPN was created to simplify the deployment of VPNs and designed to address the complexity associated with deploying multiple solutions. FlexVPN covers all types of VPN connectivity: remote access, teleworker, site to site, mobility, managed security services, and others.

FlexVPN is a robust, standards-based encryption technology that helps enable organizations to securely connect branch offices and remote users. The solution can provide significant cost savings in comparison to supporting multiple separate types of VPN solutions such as GRE, Crypto, and VTI-based solutions. FlexVPN relies on open-standards–based IKEv2 as a security technology and also provides many specific enhancements to provide high levels of security, added value, and competitive differentiation.

FlexVPN provides the following benefits:

- **Transport network:** The solution can be deployed over a public Internet or private MPLS VPN.

- **Deployment style:** The solution was designed for the concentration of both site-to-site and remote-access VPNs. A single FlexVPN deployment can accept both types of connection requests at the same time.

- **Failover redundancy:** Three different kinds of redundancy models can be implemented with FlexVPN: dynamic routing protocols, IKEv2-based dynamic route distribution with server clustering, and IPsec/IKEv2 active/standby stateful failover between two chassis.

- **Third-party compatibility:** The FlexVPN solution provides compatibility with any IKEv2-based third-party VPN vendors, including native VPN clients from Apple iOS and Android devices.

- **IP multicast support:** FlexVPN natively supports IP multicast.

- **Superior QoS:** The architecture of FlexVPN easily allows hierarchical QoS to be integrated at the per tunnel or per SA basis.

- **Centralized policy control:** Dynamic VPN policies can be fully integrated with the use of an AAA/RADIUS server and applied on a per peer basis. These dynamic policies include split-tunnel policy, encryption network policy, VRF selection, DNS server resolution (for remote access), and so on.

- **VRF awareness:** The FlexVPN supports both Inside VRF and front-door VRF for an end-to-end VRF path isolation deployment. You can also manage the inside VRF assignment policy with the centralized AAA server.

FlexVPN Architecture

FlexVPN offers a simple but modular framework that extensively uses the tunnel interface paradigm while remaining compatible with legacy VPN implementations using crypto maps. FlexVPN is the Cisco implementation of the IKEv2 standard; it supports a single configuration approach for all VPN types. IKEv2 is a next-generation key management protocol that is based on RFC 4306 and is an enhancement of the IKE protocol. IKEv2 is used for performing mutual authentication and establishing and maintaining SAs.

FlexVPN supports per peer configurations of service parameters, such as QoS, firewall mechanisms, policies, and VRF-related settings. It is ideal for service aggregation that encompasses both remote-access and site-to-site VPNs. It provides improved service management through integration with external AAA databases and works well in multitenancy scenarios.

FlexVPN Capabilities

FlexVPN supports a wide range of capabilities for both site-to-site and remote-access VPN deployments. Perhaps the easiest way to understand FlexVPN capabilities is to conduct a VPN capability comparison. Table 9-3 provides a summary of VPN capabilities across a number of VPN solutions.

Table 9-3 *VPN Capability Comparison*

	EasyVPN	DMVPN	Crypto MAP	Flex VPN
Dynamic Routing	No	Yes	No	Yes
Spoke-to-Spoke Direct	No	Yes	No	Yes
Remote Access	Yes	No	Yes	Yes
Configuration Push	Yes	No	No	Yes
Per-Peer Configuration	Yes	No	No	Yes
Per-Peer QoS	Yes	Yes—Group	No	Yes
Full AAA Management	Yes	No	No	Yes

FlexVPN Configuration Blocks

To implement FlexVPN on the router, you need to configure several building blocks with custom and default values. Figure 9-30 provides a FlexVPN configuration block overview.

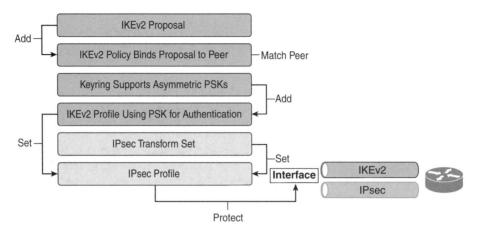

Figure 9-30 *FlexVPN Configuration Block*

As shown in the diagram, the configuration blocks for FlexVPN are

- **IKEv2 proposal:** Defines the protection attributes to be used in the negotiation of the IKEv2 SA. After you create an IKEv2 proposal, attach it to an IKEv2 policy so that the proposal is picked for negotiation.

- **IKEv2 policy:** Binds the proposal to a VPN peer. The IKEv2 policy references the IKEv2 proposal.

- **IKEv2 keyring:** Enables you to define preshared keys, which can be asymmetric.

- **IKEv2 profile:** Provides a repository of nonnegotiable parameters of the IKE SA, such as the VPN peer address and authentication methods to be used. There is no default IKEv2 profile, so you must configure one and attach it to an IPsec profile on the initiator. If preshared key authentication is used, the IKEv2 profile references the IKEv2 keyring.

- **IPsec transform set:** Specifies an acceptable combination of security protocols and algorithms for the IPsec SA.

- **IPsec profile:** Summarizes FlexVPN settings into a single profile that can be applied to an interface. The IPsec profile references the IPsec transform set and the IKEv2 profile.

To minimize FlexVPN configuration, you can use an IKEv2 feature called Smart Defaults. This feature includes default settings for all configuration blocks except the IKEv2 profile and keyring. IKEv2 Smart Defaults can also be customized for specific use cases; however, this practice is not typically recommended.

GETVPN

The final VPN technology discussed is the Cisco Group Encrypted Transport VPN (GETVPN). Fully meshed VPNs present both a scalability and manageability challenge. Historically, many customers have usually avoided using full-mesh VPNs. The GETVPN technology provides a tunnelless VPN solution to address these challenges and enables organizations to easily deploy complex, redundant, fully meshed, and secure networks.

GETVPN offers a new standards-based IPsec security model that is based on the concept of "trusted" group members. Trusted member routers use a common security methodology that is independent of any point-to-point IPsec tunnel relationship.

Group controllers, otherwise known as key servers, and group members are the two key components in the GETVPN architecture. The key server authenticates all group members, performs admission control to the GETVPN domain, and creates and supplies group authentication keys and SAs to group members. Group members provide the transmission protection service to sensitive site-to-site (member-to-member) traffic. Figure 9-31 shows the general GETVPN protocol flow.

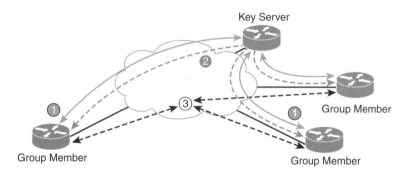

① Group members register with the key server.
② The key server pushes IPsec policy and keys to the group members.
③ The group members can securely communicate with each other.

Figure 9-31 *GETVPN Protocol Flow*

A key server distributes keys and policies to all registered and authenticated group members. By distributing keys and policies from a centralized point and by sharing the same group SA with authenticated group members, you greatly simplify key distribution and management.

Communication among a key server and group members is encrypted and secured using the IKE Group Domain of Interpretation (GDOI) protocol. IKE GDOI is a standards-based ISAKMP group key management protocol that is designed to provide secure group communications and is standardized in RFC 3547. GETVPN uses IKE GDOI operating over UDP port 848 as the group keying mechanism. IKE GDOI supports the use of two keys. The Traffic Encryption Key (TEK) is used to protect the traffic between group members, whereas the Key Encryption Key (KEK) is used to protect rekeys (key refresh) between key servers and group members. The key server distributes the TEK to all group members. The group members use the downloaded TEK to communicate securely among the group and to create and verify IPsec packets. The key server also distributes the KEK, which group members use to decrypt the incoming rekey messages from the key server.

One major difference of GDOI IKE is that GDOI IKE SAs do not need to linger between members after initial establishment. The GDOI IKE SA can be left to quickly expire after a group member has authenticated to the key server and obtained the group policy. The second major difference is that GDOI IKE sessions do not get established between all peers in a VPN. The sessions are established only between each group member and the key server (or multiple key servers for redundancy). Another notable difference of a GDOI-based VPN is that all group members use the same set of session keys to protect network traffic. This is different from classic IPsec VPN deployments, where each pair of peers has a private set of IPsec SAs that is only shared between the two peers.

The group members need to register to the key server to receive policies from the key server. Upon receiving registration messages from a group member, the key server generates the information that contains the rekey policy (one KEK) and the new IPsec SAs (multiple TEK attributes, traffic encryption policy, lifetime, source, and destination information about the traffic that must be protected, and the Security Parameter Index [SPI] ID that is associated with each TEK). The new IPsec SA is then sent to the group member.

In the GETVPN data plane, group members that have appropriate group IPsec SAs can protect traffic and send the traffic to other group members. These group members can decrypt the packets because they have the same group IPsec SAs.

GETVPN uses rekey messages to refresh IPsec SAs (session keys) outside of IKE sessions. When the group IPsec SAs are about to expire, one single rekey message for a particular group is generated on the key server. No new IKE sessions are created for the rekey message distribution.

Following are two rekeying options:

- **Unicast rekeying:** When you use unicast rekeying with many group members, the key server generates rekey messages for only a few group members at a time. The key server also ensures that all group members receive the rekey messages for the new SA before the old SA expires. This process helps reduce latency issues. In addition, when a unicast group receives the rekey message from the key server, a group member sends an encrypted ACK message to the key server. It uses the keys that are received as part of the rekey message.

- **Multicast rekeying:** With multicast rekeying, the key server sends out multicast rekeys to the group members. It sends out a single multicast rekey packet to the core, and the core does the replication for all group members. Because the group member does not send any acknowledgment, rekeys will be retransmitted two or three times during every rekey period. Using multicast transport is efficient and highly recommended for a larger network. In turn, multicast rekeying reduces the load on the key server to process the rekey messages for each group member and the acknowledgments received from every group member. Moreover, the group member does not send any acknowledgments, as required in the unicast transport mechanism.

If the enterprise network is multicast-capable, it is recommended that you use multicast rekeying, which is a more scalable mechanism.

The following are some general guidelines for rekeying:

- If most group members are only capable of unicast, use unicast rekeying.
- If most group members are capable of multicast (and the entire transport network is capable of multicast), use multicast rekeying.

GETVPN has the following benefits:

- Configuration is scalable because the configuration does not grow significantly when adding group members in a fully meshed scenario.
- It provides scalable support for multicast traffic.

There are, however, a few limitations:

- VPN addresses must be routable in the transport network. This limitation is a direct consequence of original IP header preservation, and in most cases prevents GETVPN from being used over the Internet.
- The compromise of a peer can have a detrimental effect on the security of other peers because group keys are shared and an attacker could decrypt any traffic in the GETVPN.
- Key servers must be available during rekeys and registration for the entire network to work.

You can use GETVPN-based networks in various WAN environments, including IP and MPLS. MPLS VPNs that use this transmission protection technology are highly scalable, manageable, and cost effective; in addition, they meet regulatory-mandated transmission protection requirements. The flexible nature of GETVPN enables security-conscious enterprises to manage their own network security over a service provider WAN service or to offload encryption services to their providers. GETVPN simplifies securing large Layer 2 or MPLS networks that require partial- or full-mesh connectivity.

When you are designing a GETVPN, you have several deployment choices. You need to decide if you will be using preshared key or PKI-based authentication. Using preshared key is simpler, but security is generally stronger when using a PKI infrastructure. When you are using preshared key, you cannot use dynamically addressed group members. You must use PKI-based authentication for this task. To provide high availability, you can have multiple key servers. Each key server is an active key server that handles requests from the group members. One of the key servers is a primary key server and is used to update policies to the other key servers.

You should consider three main guidelines when implementing a VPN using GETVPN technology:

- It is recommended that you consider GETVPN as your primary technology to implement scalable fully meshed connectivity with several private sites.

- When you are implementing GETVPN over the Internet, it is mandatory that you use routable IP addresses on all networks that are included in the VPN. Usually, this option is not possible because enterprises use RFC 1918–based private addresses inside their internal networks.

- In a GETVPN, there is no scalability issue with the PSK approach because you need to configure only a limited number of IKE sessions. Other criteria must be used to decide between PSK and PKI, especially weighing the complexity of PKI against possible security issues (weak PSKs) with PSKs.

Summary

In this chapter, you learned how both site-to-site and remote-access VPN connections enable users to send data between remote-site locations and to access centralized corporate resources in a secure and efficient manner.

- How to use point-to-point and multipoint GRE tunnels to establish private routing over public transport

- How to leverage IPsec to protect GRE tunnel connectivity

- Simplified and scalable VPN infrastructure provisioning with DMVPN

- The three modes of implementation for DMVPN based on use case (Phases 1, 2, and 3)

- Consolidation of site-to-site and remote-access VPN functionality with FlexVPN

Review Questions

After answering the following questions, please refer to Appendix A, "Answers to Review Questions," for the answers.

1. Which answers are true about multipoint GRE? (Select two.)
   a. It needs a unique subnet for each tunnel.
   b. It supports only unicast.
   c. It uses a single interface for all GRE peers.
   d. It uses the same subnet for all tunnels.
   e. It is used to encrypt traffic between multiple sites.

2. Match the DMVPN phases with the best description.

   DMVPN Phase 2   It does not allow spoke-to-spoke tunnels.

   DMVPN Phase 1   It allows spoke-to-spoke tunnels, but you need full reachability.

   DMVPN Phase 3   It allows spoke-to-spoke tunnels, and you can send only the default route to the spokes.

3. Which two rekeying mechanisms can be used in GETVPN? (Select two.)
   a. Broadcast rekeying
   b. Multicast rekeying
   c. Encrypted rekeying
   d. Local rekeying
   e. Unicast rekeying

4. When you are implementing GRE tunnels, why might you experience MTU and IP fragmentation-related issues?
   a. GRE adds an extra 22 bytes.
   b. GRE adds a 2-byte GRE header and a new 22-byte IP header.
   c. GRE adds an extra 4-byte GRE header and a new 18-byte IP header.
   d. GRE adds an extra 4-byte GRE header and a new 20-byte IP header.

5. When implementing multipoint GRE tunnels, which of the following do you need to specify?
   a. Source interface
   b. Destination IP
   c. Both a and b
   d. NHBP protocol mapping

6. Which entry is incorrect and needs to be reversed?

	Point-to-point GRE	**Multipoint GRE**
a.	■ Typically used for simple point-to-point tunnels that emulate a point-to-point WAN link, or on spoke routers in hub-and-spoke VPNs.	■ Typically used on hub routers in hub-and-spoke topologies, or on all routers in mesh or partial-mesh topologies.
b.	■ On each device, there is a separate GRE tunnel interface that is configured for each GRE peer.	■ A single GRE interface is configured for multiple GRE tunnels.
c.	■ The same subnet is configured for all GRE tunnels.	■ A unique subnet is needed for each GRE tunnel.
d.	■ Does not require NHRP because other peers have a statically configured destination address.	■ Requires NHRP to build dynamic GRE tunnels and to learn about the IP addresses of the other peer.
e.	■ Supports unicast, multicast, and broadcast traffic.	■ Supports unicast, multicast, and broadcast traffic.

7. Match the security protocol with the best description.

Internet Key Exchange (IKE)   Defines a user traffic encapsulation that provides data integrity, data origin authentication, and protection against replay to user traffic.

Authentication Header (AH)   Provides key management to IPsec

Encapsulating Security Payload (ESP)   Defines a user traffic encapsulation that provides data integrity, data origin authentication, protection against replays, and confidentiality to user traffic.

8. What are some limitations of VTI? (Select two.)
  a. It doesn't support multicast.
  b. It requires more established SAs to cover different types of traffic such as unicast and multicast.
  c. It is limited to only IP unicast and multicast traffic, as opposed to GRE tunnels, which have a wider multiprotocol support.
  d. IPsec stateful failover is not supported with IPsec VTIs.

Chapter 10

Enterprise WAN Resiliency Design

Upon completing this chapter, you will be able to

- Describe WAN remote sites
- Identify common MPLS WAN design models
- Identify common Layer 2 WAN design models
- Identify common VPN WAN design models
- Identify 3G/4G VPN design models
- Connect remote sites using the local Internet
- Describe the remote-site LAN
- Explain some redundancy and connectivity use cases
- Describe basic traffic engineering techniques
- Describe IWAN basics
- Describe intelligent WAN design basics
- Describe the IWAN hybrid design model
- Describe Cisco PfR basics
- Describe Cisco PfR versions
- Describe Cisco PfR operations
- Identify Cisco PfR topologies
- Identify Cisco PfR design and deployment considerations

- Describe the basic differences between Cisco APIC-EM and Cisco One-PK
- Describe the benefits of using Cisco APIC-EM to manage WAN and access network services
- Identify capabilities of Cisco APIC-EM for the management of enterprise WAN and access

Organizations have spent the last several years consolidating and centralizing the majority of their applications and services across both private and public cloud data center environments. Many of these same organizations have spent a significant amount of money to incorporate data center resiliency as part of the overall DC design to ensure business continuity in the event of central-site outages. Given this shift toward application centralization, the enterprise WAN architecture that interconnects remote-site LANs to centralized resources plays a critical role in business survival. Businesses depend on the availability and performance of the network and often pay a premium for WAN services that come with service-level agreements (SLA) to meet enterprise application requirements.

Organizations are vulnerable to the impact that network conditions and outages have on workforce productivity and business operations and often invest in redundant circuits and, in some cases, even redundant hardware to ensure the appropriate level of resiliency.

Multiple WAN transport offerings can be used simultaneously to create a robust, secure, and cost-effective WAN, including MPLS VPNs, Internet, Cellular (3G/LTE), and Carrier Ethernet. Internet-based IP VPNs, as discussed in Chapter 8, "Service Provider–Managed VPNs," offer attractive bandwidth pricing and can augment premium MPLS offerings or replace MPLS in some scenarios. A flexible network architecture should include many of the common WAN transport offerings as options without significantly increasing the complexity of the overall design.

This chapter focuses on different WAN design models and technologies and describes how you can use them to optimize your WAN connections.

WAN Remote-Site Overview

Most remote sites are designed with a single-router WAN edge. However, certain remote-site types require a dual-router WAN edge. Dual-router candidate sites include regional office or remote campus locations with large user populations, or sites with business-critical needs that justify additional redundancy to remove single points of failure such as contact center facilities or distribution warehouses. The size of the remote-site LAN depends on factors such as the number of connected users and the physical layout of the remote site.

The remote-site WAN routing platform selection is driven by logical design requirements, and the determined specification is tied closely to factors such as bandwidth, aggregated services, component redundancy, and other factors affecting performance, scale, and resiliency. Cisco Integrated Services Routers (ISR) support modular additions and, in more recent releases, bandwidth performance upgrades. Your ability to implement a solution design with various potential router choices is one of the benefits of a modular design approach focused on accommodating long-term needs.

You must consider many factors in the selection of WAN remote-site routers. One of these factors is the capability to process the expected amount and type of traffic. Other areas of consideration are to ensure that there are enough interfaces and module slots, and the necessary licensing capability to enable the set of features required to support the agreed-upon design.

After the WAN design has been determined, the general topology that is used for various remote sites should essentially be the same, regardless of site type. The differences associated with various WAN transport options are apparent after you begin the deployment and configuration of the WAN routers.

Table 10-1 summarizes common WAN transport design models and includes a breakdown of single-router, dual-router, and combined primary and secondary transport services deployment options.

Table 10-1 *WAN Aggregation and WAN Remote-Site Transport Options*

WAN Aggregation Design Model (Primary)	WAN Aggregation Design Model (Secondary)	WAN Remote-Site Routers	WAN Transports	Primary Transport	Secondary Transport
MPLS Static	—	Single	Single	MPLS VPN	—
MPLS Dynamic					
Dual MPLS					
Layer 2 Simple	—	Single	Single	MetroE/ VPLS	—
Layer 2 Trunked					
DMVPN Only	—	Single	Single	Internet	—
Dual DMVPN					
DMVPN Only	—	Single	Single	Internet 3G/4G	—
Dual DMVPN					
Dual MPLS	Dual MPLS	Single	Dual	MPLS VPN A	MPLS VPN B
MPLS Static	DMVPN Backup Shared	Single	Dual	MPLS VPN	Internet
MPLS Dynamic					
Dual MPLS	DMVPN Backup Dedicated				

WAN Aggregation Design Model (Primary)	WAN Aggregation Design Model (Secondary)	WAN Remote-Site Routers	WAN Transports	Primary Transport	Secondary Transport
MPLS Static MPLS Dynamic Dual MPLS	DMVPN Backup Shared DMVPN Backup Dedicated	Single	Dual	MPLS VPN	Internet 3G/4G
Layer 2 Simple Layer 2 Trunked	DMVPN Backup Dedicated	Single	Dual	MetroE/VPLS	Internet
Dual DMVPN	Dual DMVPN	Single	Dual	Internet	Internet
Dual MPLS	Dual MPLS	Dual	Dual	MPLS VPN A	MPLS VPN B
MPLS Dynamic Dual MPLS	DMVPN Backup Dedicated	Dual	Dual	MPLS VPN	Internet
MPLS Dynamic Dual MPLS	DMVPN Backup Dedicated	Dual	Dual	MPLS VPN	Internet 3G/4G
Layer 2 Simple Layer 2 Trunked	DMVPN Backup Dedicated	Dual	Dual	MetroE/VPLS	Internet
Dual DMVPN	Dual DMVPN	Dual	Dual	Internet	Internet

MPLS Layer 3 WAN Design Models

MPLS Layer 3 VPNs use a peer-to-peer VPN model that leverages Multiprotocol BGP (mBGP) within the provider network to distribute private prefix and VPN-related information. This peer-to-peer model enables subscribers to outsource to service providers the enterprise's site-to-site routing responsibility. This design model typically results in islands of enterprise campus and remote-site Interior Gateway Protocol (IGP) routing deployments interconnected with service provider edge to customer edge eBGP relationships.

The MPLS WAN aggregation (hub) designs include one or two WAN edge routers. When WAN edge routers are referred to in the context of the connection to a carrier or service provider, they are typically known as customer edge (CE) routers. All WAN edge CE routers at the hub site typically connect into a LAN distribution layer.

The WAN transport options include MPLS VPNs used as a primary or secondary transport. Each transport connects to a dedicated CE router at the hub site. A similar method of connection and configuration is leveraged for both hubs.

Three common MPLS WAN aggregation design models take advantage of either static or dynamic routing with the MPLS service provider. The primary difference between the various designs is the use of the routing protocols. Several router platform options with differing levels of performance and resiliency capabilities are suitable for each model.

Each of the design models uses LAN connections into either a collapsed core/distribution layer or a dedicated WAN distribution layer. No functional differences exist between these two methods from the WAN aggregation perspective.

In all WAN aggregation designs, tasks such as IP route summarization are performed at the distribution layer. Other various devices support WAN edge services, such as application optimization and encryption, and these devices should also connect into the distribution layer.

Each MPLS carrier terminates to a dedicated WAN router with a primary goal of eliminating any single points of failure.

The three typical MPLS WAN aggregation design models are depicted in Figure 10-1.

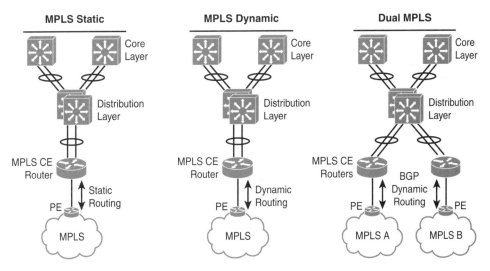

Figure 10-1 *WAN Aggregation Design Models*

Following are design recommendations for WAN connectivity options in Table 10-1:

- MPLS Static:
    - Appropriate for smaller deployments
    - Uses static routing between the CE and PE routers

- Uses a single MPLS service provider
- Requires the MPLS service provider to inject static routes and to advertise existing and future site prefixes on behalf of the customer

■ MPLS Dynamic:

- Appropriate for medium-sized WANs
- Uses dynamic routing between the CE and PE routers
- Uses a single MPLS service provider
- Typically leverages eBGP for PE-CE peering

■ Dual MPLS:

- Appropriate for larger WANs
- Uses dynamic routing between the CE and PE routers
- Typically leverages eBGP for PE-CE peering
- Usually uses multiple CE routers for high availability

The three typical WAN remote-site design models are shown in Figure 10-2:

- MPLS WAN nonredundant
- MPLS WAN with redundant link
- MPLS WAN with redundant link and router

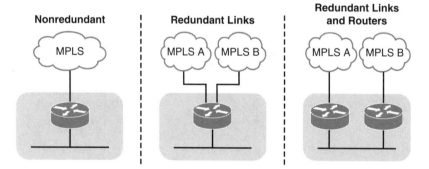

Figure 10-2 *WAN Remote-site Design Models*

The nonredundant variant is the only one that is compatible with the single-carrier design models (MPLS Static or MPLS Dynamic). The redundant variants are compatible with the Dual MPLS design model. If you have implemented the Dual MPLS design model, you may also connect a nonredundant remote site to either carrier.

The typical remote site uses only a single WAN router due to the impact of constraints such as affordability. Certain remote sites that are critical in nature may use a dual-router design model. These remote sites are usually regional offices, locations with many users, or sites that are business critical and need additional redundancy to remove single points of failure.

Common Layer 2 WAN Design Models

Layer 2 WAN transports are now widely available from service providers. The most common implementations of Layer 2 WAN are used to provide Ethernet over the WAN using either a point-to-point service (EoMPLS) or point-to-multipoint service (VPLS). Many service providers also offer Carrier Ethernet or Metro Ethernet services that are typically limited to a relatively small geographic area.

The two main WAN aggregation design models are shown in Figure 10-3.

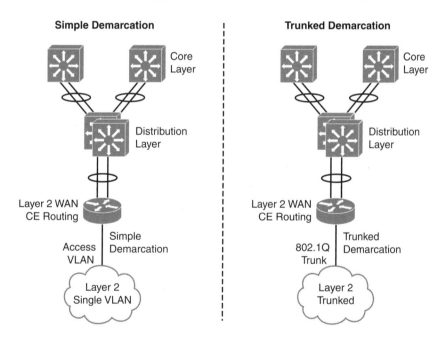

Figure 10-3 *Layer 2 WAN Aggregation Design Models*

The design can use either *simple demarcation* (a link with one VLAN) or *trunked demarcation* (multiple VLANs). The primary difference between the simple demarcation and trunked demarcation design model is the number of broadcast domains or VLANs that are used to communicate with a subset of remote-site routers.

When you use the simple demarcation design model, the service provider connects your equipment using a single VLAN. This VLAN provides Layer 2 connectivity between the central site and the remote site. When you use the trunked demarcation design model, you connect your central and remote sites using 802.1Q VLAN tagging. Service providers often refer to a trunked service as Q-in-Q tunneling (QinQ).

Each of the design models uses LAN connections into either a collapsed core/distribution layer or a dedicated WAN distribution layer. There are no functional differences between these two methods from the WAN-aggregation perspective.

In the WAN aggregation design, tasks such as IP route summarization are performed at the distribution layer. Other various devices support WAN edge services, such as application optimization and encryption, and these devices should also connect into the distribution layer.

As you can see in Figure 10-4, the remote site typically includes a single WAN edge router.

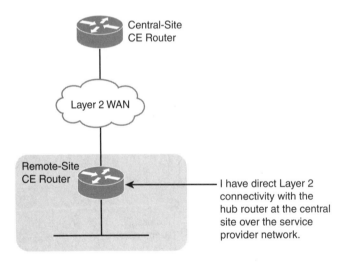

Figure 10-4 *Single WAN Edge Router*

This CE router is connected to the service provider network and has direct Layer 2 connectivity with the hub router at the central site.

Based on the design model, it can be implemented in the simple or trunked demarcation design model depending on enterprise customer requirements and provider-offered services. With a Layer 2 WAN design model, the enterprise customer is responsible for all end-to-end routing over the WAN. Unlike with MPLS services, no routing peering relationships exist between CE and PE devices. Although this chapter does not cover the dual-layer 2 WAN design option, it is nevertheless a valid design option for those companies leaning in this direction.

Common VPN WAN Design Models

As discussed in Chapter 8, the VPN WAN typically uses the Internet as WAN transport technology. The Internet is essentially a large-scale public WAN composed of multiple interconnected service providers. The Internet can provide reliable high-performance connectivity between various locations, although it lacks any explicit guarantees for these connections. Despite the "best effort" nature, the Internet is a sensible choice for a primary transport when it is not feasible to connect with another transport option. Additional resiliency can be introduced into an existing design using MPLS or Layer 2 WAN services by using the Internet as an alternate transport option.

Given its extensive capabilities, Dynamic Multipoint Virtual Private Network (DMVPN), as covered in Chapter 8, has been the most widely deployed option to provide VPN WAN services. DMVPN is a highly scalable solution supporting on-demand full-mesh connectivity with a simple hub-and-spoke configuration and a zero-touch hub deployment model for adding remote sites. The capability to support dynamic routing, multicast, and spoke routers that have dynamically assigned IP addresses are other factors that make it an ideal choice.

Multiple WAN aggregation design models are widely used. The DMVPN Only design model uses only an Internet VPN as the transport. The Dual DMVPN design model uses Internet VPN as both the primary and secondary transport while taking advantage of redundant Internet service providers.

In both the DMVPN Only and Dual DMVPN design models, the VPN hub routers are connected into the firewall DMZ interface rather than being connected directly with Internet service provider routers. The DMZ interface is contained within the Internet edge, providing an additional layer of security. Both design models can use one or two hub routers. Figure 10-5 provides a visual representation of both the DMVPN Only and Dual DMVPN design models.

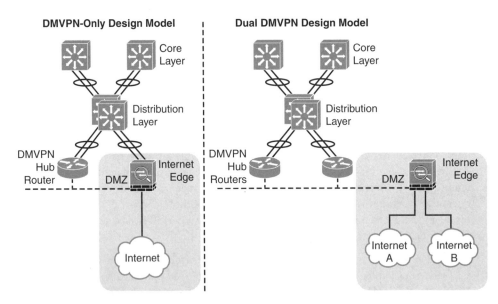

Figure 10-5 *DMVPN Only Design Model*

As you can see in Figure 10-5, when using the DMVPN Only design model, you have only one Internet service provider at the central site. In contrast, the Dual DMVPN design model uses two Internet service providers to provide high availability. Similar to the MPLS and Layer 2 WAN design models, each of the VPN WAN design models has LAN connections into either a collapsed core/distribution layer or a dedicated WAN distribution layer. Also, as with the other design options, from a WAN aggregation perspective, there are no functional differences between these two methods. IP route summarization and similar tasks are consistently performed at the distribution layer as common best practice.

The DMVPN Backup design models use the Internet VPN as a backup to an existing primary MPLS WAN or Layer 2 WAN transport. The primary difference between the DMVPN Backup designs is whether the VPN hub is implemented on an existing MPLS CE router, which is referred to as DMVPN Backup Shared, or the VPN hub is implemented on a dedicated VPN hub router, which is referred to as DMVPN Backup Dedicated. Figure 10-6 provides a visual comparison of DMVPN Backup Shared versus DMVPN Backup Dedicated.

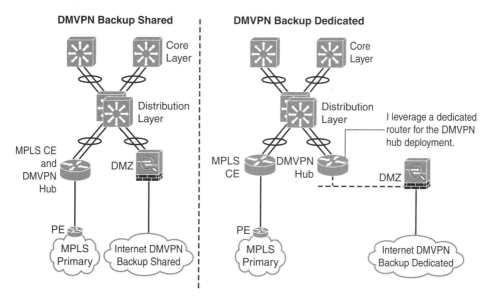

Figure 10-6 *DMVPN Backup Shared Versus DMVPN Backup Dedicated*

In the DMVPN Backup Shared design model, the DMVPN hub router is also the MPLS CE router. If you do not want to dedicate a separate physical interface for DMVPN WAN connectivity, it is possible to leverage a subinterface on the router using the connection that is already in place between the router and the distribution or core layer. The connection to the Internet is established through this newly defined subinterface and a firewall interface that is contained within the Internet edge. This option for connectivity removes the requirement to leverage a dedicated interface and DMZ for this design model.

In the DMVPN Backup Dedicated design models, the DMVPN hub routers connect to the Internet indirectly through a firewall DMZ interface contained within the Internet edge. The VPN hub routers are connected into the firewall DMZ interface, rather than being connected directly with Internet service provider routers.

The DMVPN Backup Dedicated design has multiple variants. The difference between them is the type of primary transport. Some of the DMVPN Backup Dedicated designs are

- DMVPN Backup Dedicated design model with MPLS Dynamic as primary transport
- DMVPN Backup Dedicated design model with Dual MPLS as primary transport
- DMVPN Backup Dedicated design model with Layer 2 WAN as primary transport

There are multiple options for WAN remote-site designs. These options are based on various combinations of WAN transports mapped to the site-specific requirements for service levels and redundancy. The remote-site designs include single or dual WAN edge routers. These routers can be either CE routers (for MPLS or Layer 2 WAN) or VPN spoke routers. In some cases, a single WAN edge router can perform the role of both the CE router and VPN spoke router. Figure 10-7 highlights various remote-site single-router and dual-router WAN design options.

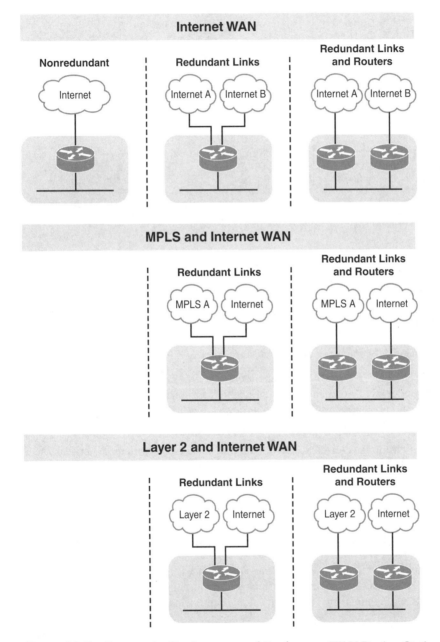

Figure 10-7 *Remote-site Single-router and Dual-router WAN Design Options*

As you can see from Figure 10-7, the possible combinations based on WAN transport include

- Internet WAN:
    - Nonredundant
    - Redundant links
    - Redundant links and routers
- MPLS and Internet WAN:
    - Redundant links
    - Redundant links and routers
- Layer 2 WAN and Internet WAN:
    - Redundant links
    - Redundant links and routers

3G/4G VPN Design Models

Copper and fiber connectivity are not always an option when connecting a remote branch. Cellular connectivity provides an alternative solution for such cases and is becoming more common. Figure 10-8 shows that the same VPN design models used for the Internet are also supported with 3G/4G connectivity.

An Internet VPN running over a 3G or 4G wireless WAN is typically used as a backup solution for MPLS or Layer 2 WAN primary transport. It is important to note, however, that this type of connectivity can also be used as the primary connectivity for smaller remote branches. The 3G/4G WAN interfaces usually use dynamic IP addresses. DMVPN is especially useful for this deployment option considering it supports dynamically addressed spoke routers.

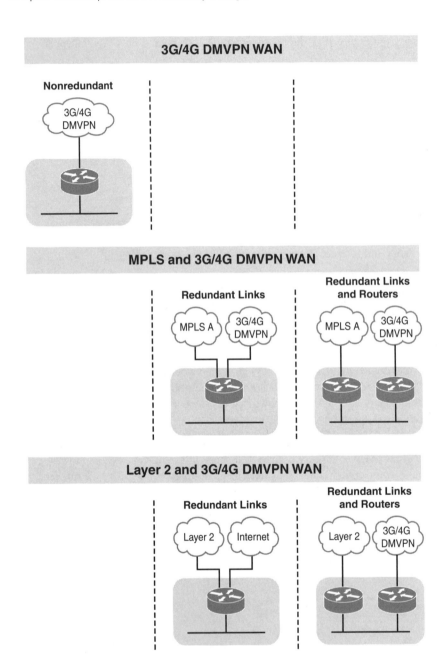

Figure 10-8 *VPN Design Model over 3G/4G Connectivity*

Remote Site Using Local Internet

Traditionally, many of the applications and services that the remote-site workers use have been centrally located and consolidated within the enterprise data center or data centers. With trends such as public cloud and Internet-hosted public software as a service application, there are benefits in providing local Internet access at each remote-site location.

The remote-site design provides the remote office with local Internet access solutions for web browsing and cloud services. This solution is referred to as the local Internet model, and a comparison between the Central Internet and Local Internet models is shown in Figure 10-9.

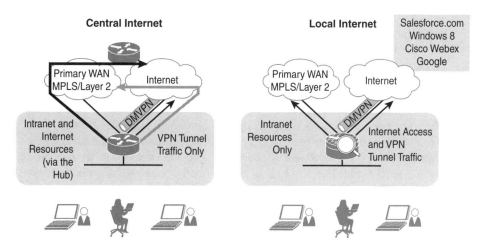

Figure 10-9 *Central Internet Versus Local Internet Models*

With the Local Internet model, user web traffic and hosted cloud services traffic are permitted to use the local Internet link in a split-tunneling manner. In this model, a default route is generated locally, connecting each remote site directly to the Internet provider. Private WAN connections using DMVPN over an Internet, MPLS, or Layer 2 WAN provide internal routes to the data center and campus. In some configurations, backup Internet routing is provided over the private WAN connections.

Local Internet traffic is forwarded directly to the Internet by using the default route. This default route is directed at the next-hop router in the ISP network. Because RFC 1918 addresses are used for internal networks, all Internet-bound traffic is translated to a public address by using PAT on the ISP-connected interface. In addition to PAT, it is also important to provide stateful inspection to enforce a policy that allows return traffic only for sessions that are initiated by internal users.

When you are leveraging a local Internet model, if a front door virtual routing and forwarding (fVRF) instance is not used along with the DMVPN design to segment the routing table, a default route over Internet-based VPN tunnels cannot be allowed because route flapping can occur. In the case where the fVRF is missing, backup Internet routing is not possible over these VPN tunnels, and therefore the recommended best practice is to filter the central-site default route from being learned over the tunnel interface. Ensuring the default route to the local ISP is preferred over the central-site default route by leveraging a lower administrative distance also helps to avoid issues if the default route is not filtered due to misconfigurations. Central Internet fallback is possible with MPLS-based WAN services. Central Internet fallback is also possible with VPN-based WAN services when a combination of fVRF, DMVPN, and route leaking are leveraged as part of the solution design. Please reference the following Cisco validated design guides for more information on this advanced topic:

- VPN WAN Technology Design Guide
- VPN Remote Site over 3G/4G Technology Design Guide

Table 10-2 summarizes the WAN transport options for remote sites using the local Internet. It is important to note that the remote-site routing configuration changes when local Internet access is deployed. For instance, you need to ensure that no default route is received over the tunnel interface to send Internet traffic using the local Internet link, while traffic destined to the hub or remote sites must go over the tunnel interface (see Figure 10-9).

Table 10-2 *WAN Transport Options for Remote Sites Using Local Internet*

WAN-Aggregation Design Model (Primary)	WAN-Aggregation Design Model (Secondary)	WAN Remote-Site Routers	WAN Transports	Primary Transport	Secondary Transport
DMVPN Only Dual DMVPN	—	Single	Single	Internet	—
DMVPN Only Dual DMVPN	—	Single	Single	Internet 3G/4G	
MPLS Static MPLS Dynamic Dual MPLS	DMVPN Backup Shared DMVPN Backup Dedicated	Single	Dual	MPLS VPN	Internet

WAN-Aggregation Design Model (Primary)	WAN-Aggregation Design Model (Secondary)	WAN Remote-Site Routers	WAN Transports	Primary Transport	Secondary Transport
MPLS Static MPLS Dynamic Dual MPLS	DMVPN Backup Shared DMVPN Backup Dedicated	Single	Dual	MPLS VPN	Internet 3G/4G
Layer 2 Simple Layer 2 Trunked	DMVPN Backup Dedicated	Single	Dual	MetroE/VPLS	Internet
Dual DMVPN	Dual DMVPN	Single	Dual	Internet	Internet
MPLS Dynamic Dual MPLS	DMVPN Backup Dedicated	Dual	Dual	MPLS VPN	Internet
MPLS Dynamic Dual MPLS	DMVPN Backup Dedicated	Dual	Dual	MPLS VPN	Internet 3G/4G
Layer 2 Simple Layer 2 Trunked	DMVPN Backup Dedicated	Dual	Dual	MetroE/VPLS	Internet
Dual DMVPN	Dual DMVPN	Dual	Dual	Internet	Internet

Remote-Site LAN

The primary role of the WAN is to interconnect primary-site and remote-site LANs. At remote sites, the LAN topology depends on the number of connected users and physical geography of the site.

You have different options when you are designing a remote-site network. Large sites may require the use of a distribution layer to support multiple access layer switches. Other sites might require only an access layer switch that is directly connected to the WAN remote-site routers. The main design options included in Figure 10-10 are

- Single or dual WAN remote-site routers
- Single or dual WAN transport
- A LAN topology that can be access only or distribution/access layer

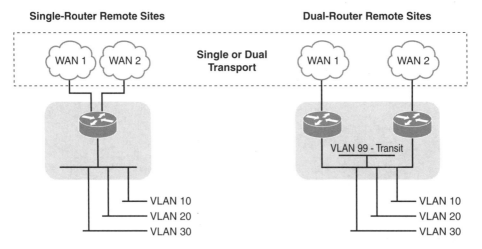

Figure 10-10 *Remote-site LAN Design Options*

For consistency and modularity, you should configure all WAN remote sites with the same VLAN assignment scheme, as depicted in Figure 10-11.

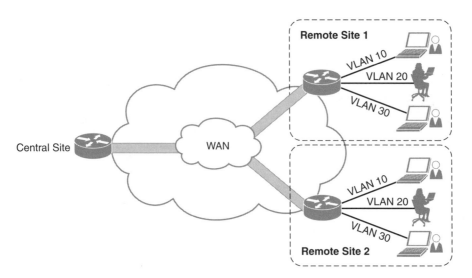

Figure 10-11 *Remote-site LAN: VLAN Assignment Scheme*

This model can be easily scaled to additional access closets by adding a distribution layer. Figure 10-12 shows the impact of adding a distribution layer in the design.

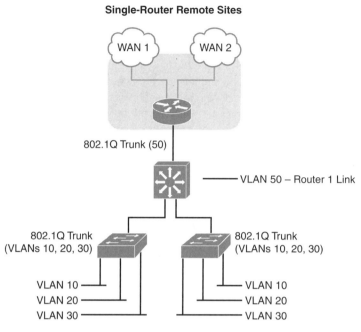

Figure 10-12 *Two-tier Remote-site LAN Design*

WAN remote sites that do not require additional LAN distribution layer routing devices are considered flat or, from a LAN perspective, they are considered unrouted Layer 2 sites. The attached WAN routers provide all Layer 3 services. The access switches can support services such as data and voice by using multiple VLANs. The benefit of this design is that you can configure all access switches identically regardless of the number of sites in this configuration.

IP subnets are assigned on a per-VLAN basis. Usually, you can use the /24 mask for the access layer even if fewer than 254 IP addresses are required. You must configure the connection between the router and the access switch for 802.1Q VLAN trunking with subinterfaces on the router that map to the respective VLANs on the switch. The various router subinterfaces act as the IP default gateways for each of the IP subnet and VLAN combinations.

Flat Layer 2 design can be extended to a dual-router edge. This design change introduces some additional complexity. You will usually run a routing protocol internally within the remote site with a dual-router design. The routing protocol is configured between the routers. The dual-router designs also warrant an additional transit network component that is required for proper routing in certain scenarios. In these cases, traffic flow from a remote-site host might be sent to a destination that is reachable via the alternate WAN transport (for example, a dual MPLS remote-site communicating with an MPLS-B-only remote site). The primary WAN transport router then forwards the traffic back out the same data interface where it was received from the LAN to send it to the alternate WAN transport router. This router then forwards the traffic to the proper destination. This problem is referred to as *hairpinning*.

The appropriate method to avoid sending the traffic out the same interface is to introduce an additional link between the routers and designate the link as a transit network. No hosts are connected to the transit network, and it is used only for router-router communication. The routing protocol runs between router subinterfaces assigned to the transit network. No additional router interfaces are required with this design modification because the 802.1Q VLAN trunk configuration can easily accommodate an additional subinterface.

Because there are two routers per subnet and the router subinterfaces are still providing default gateway functionality, you must implement a First-Hop Redundancy Protocol (FHRP). You can use Hot Standby Router Protocol (HSRP), Virtual Router Redundancy Protocol (VRRP), or Gateway Load Balancing Protocol (GLBP). FHRP offers high availability by providing first-hop routing redundancy for IP hosts configured with a default gateway IP address. Figure 10-13 builds on Figure 10-10 by layering on FHRP and, more specifically, HSRP services.

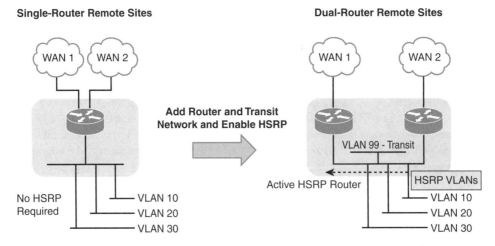

Figure 10-13 *Remote-site LAN Design with FHRP and Transit VLAN*

In a dual-router design with routers leveraging an FHRP such as HSRP, something is needed to trigger HSRP failover from Active to Standby when the connected WAN path becomes unavailable. Enhanced Object Tracking (EOT) provides a consistent methodology for various router and switching features to conditionally modify their operation based on information objects available in other processes. A few examples of objects that can be tracked include the Interface Line Protocol, IP route reachability, and IP SLA reachability. To improve convergence times after a primary WAN failure, the router can monitor the reachability of a next-hop IP neighbor (MPLS PE, Layer 2 WAN CE, or DMVPN hub) by using EOT and IP SLA. This combination allows for a router to give up its active HSRP role if its upstream neighbor becomes unresponsive. Integrated services capabilities such as these, when leveraged as part of a holistic design approach, provide additional network resiliency.

Large remote sites may require a LAN environment similar to that of a small campus LAN that includes a distribution layer and access layer, as depicted in Figure 10-14.

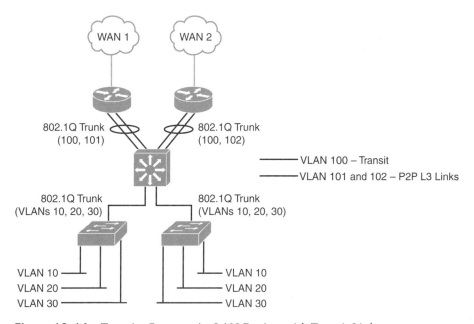

Figure 10-14 *Two-tier Remote-site LAN Design with Transit Link*

This topology works well with either a single- or dual-router WAN edge. To implement this design, the routers should connect via EtherChannel links to the distribution switch. These EtherChannel links are configured as 802.1Q VLAN trunks. This EtherChannel should support both a routed point-to-point link for routing with the distribution switch (VLAN 101 and VLAN 102), and in the dual-router design, to provide a transit network for direct communication between the WAN routers (VLAN 100).

The LAN distribution switch handles access layer routing, with VLANs trunked to access switches. No FHRP is required at the WAN edge when the design includes a distribution layer.

Case Study: Redundancy and Connectivity

As you know from the previous sections, today it is more feasible for some organizations to use a VPN technology over the public Internet as a WAN transport to provide a flexible and cost-effective connectivity model. This case study takes you through a sample design scenario that will leverage the Internet connectivity as a WAN transport. Also, this case study discusses how to optimize the availability of such WAN design.

344 Chapter 10: Enterprise WAN Resiliency Design

In this case, you are working as a network architect in the Bank of POLONA and have been tasked with developing a new WAN design to better accommodate the company's business needs. The WAN interconnects a large number of ATMs, many branch offices, and several regional offices.

ATM WAN Design

Your first step is to design an ATM WAN. An ATM deployment represents a small remote-site type. Based on the business needs, you should consider the following details and requirements as part of the overall design:

- Business users can tolerate ATM unavailability for a couple of hours.
- Only one or two ATMs will be connected at each site.
- Physical WAN connectivity is not available for all sites.
- ATMs have low-speed connectivity requirements.

As depicted in Figure 10-15, based on the requirements, you have decided to leverage the Internet as the primary option for transport network connectivity. The Internet is a cheap alternative to provider-managed VPNs. Most of the sites will be connected with a physical connection; however, the sites where physical connectivity is not available will be connected with 3G/4G cellular network services.

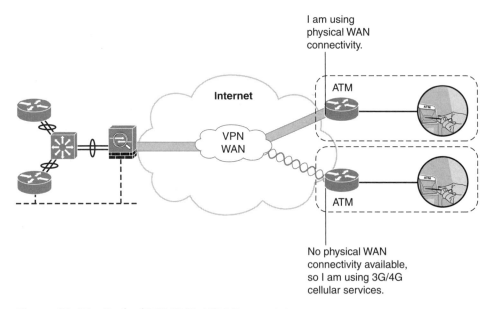

Figure 10-15 *Bank of POLONA ATM Connectivity*

You will use a single-router deployment model with no link and router redundancy at this time. If business continuity needs justify the need for additional spending, different levels of redundancy can easily be incorporated later based on your modular design approach.

As shown in Figure 10-16, you will use two routers at the central site. Both routers will be connected to the distribution layer of the central-site network. The connection to the Internet will be established through a firewall within the Internet edge. The Internet edge is already implemented with connectivity to two Internet service providers and uses BGP to announce the public IP address space.

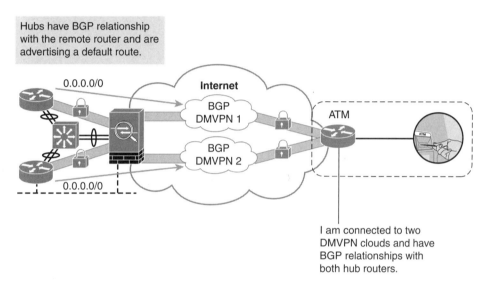

Figure 10-16 *Central-Site Internet, DMVPN, and LAN Connectivity*

As you can see in Figure 10-16, to provide ATM connectivity to the central site, you have decided that you will implement the DMVPN solution. The DMVPN will be built on top of the Internet transport network connectivity.

Each of the hub routers will map to a unique DMVPN cloud. One hub will be set up to leverage the Backup Dedicated design model while the other hub will leverage the Backup Shared design model. You are planning to support the aggregation of multiple WAN services on the hub using the Backup Shared design model and have decided to conserve physical interfaces by using a subinterface mapping to a firewall interface that is contained within the Internet edge. The remote routers will have two tunnels. One tunnel will be used for the first DMVPN cloud, and the second tunnel will be used for the second DMVPN cloud. The ATMs do not need connectivity between each other; therefore, you decide to use a DMVPN Phase 1 deployment model.

To implement a scalable routing solution for your ATM WAN, you will use BGP as the routing protocol in the DMVPN overlay. Because ATMs do not need Internet access, you decide to configure static routes pointing to the next-hop gateway for the public

IP addresses of the hub routers. Connectivity to private central site networks will be addressed by sending a default route to the remote routers through the DMVPN overlays via BGP. The remote routers will announce a connected LAN to the central hub routers. With BGP, you have many options available to implement some sort of traffic engineering based on best path selection. You can define a BGP policy leveraging attributes such as Weight or Local Preference at the remote-site edge to route half of the remote sites through the first hub router and the other half through the second hub router. With this solution, you can achieve load-sharing capabilities across both available paths, while still having a backup route in the event of a hub failure. For more information on leveraging BGP best path selection capabilities, see Chapter 5, "Border Gateway Protocol Design."

Remote-Site (Branch Office) WAN Design

After you have successfully designed your ATM WAN, your next step is to design a WAN for the branch offices. Based on business needs, you have identified the following requirements:

- The branch office will have up to 20 users.
- All business applications will be hosted in the data center at the central site.
- The users will take advantage of data, voice, and video services.
- Users will connect to the Internet through the central site.
- The branch office can tolerate 2 hours of unavailability.

Because branch users cannot tolerate long outages and are leveraging numerous types of applications and services, you must implement a highly available and high-performing solution. You decided to use an MPLS network as the primary connectivity for all your branch offices and implement an SLA with the service provider to provide acceptable service levels to support your application requirements. The service provider has agreed to fix connectivity issues within 4 hours. This agreement translates to a reasonable balance of cost and SLA for the MPLS service offering. Because this repair time is more than your users at the branch office can tolerate, you need to design a backup solution. You have decided that the optimal solution to address business continuity requirements is to leverage Internet VPN for backup connectivity. Each router at the branch office will connect to the MPLS network as the primary path and the Internet VPN as the backup path.

To save on costs, you decide to use the same hub routers that you used for ATM WAN design. You will connect one of the existing hub routers to the MPLS network using the DMVPN Backup Shared design model. Figure 10-17 provides a high-level design overview.

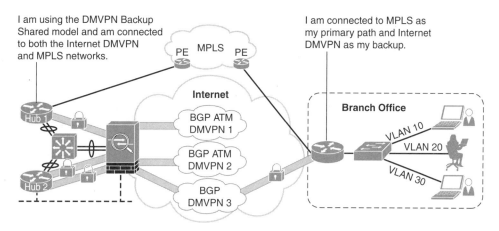

Figure 10-17 *Remote-site High-level WAN Design*

As you can see in Figure 10-17, you will use a flat routing model at the remote site. The WAN router will provide all Layer 3 services and will be configured as a router on a stick. The access switches will simply provide access layer connectivity for users and devices at the remote site. You will use VLAN segmentation at the remote sites and will take advantage of the same VLAN assignment scheme across all locations based on best practice recommendations. Leveraging the same VLAN assignment scheme will enable you to configure all of the access switches across all sites in an identical fashion.

Figure 10-18 continues to dive deeper into additional design details.

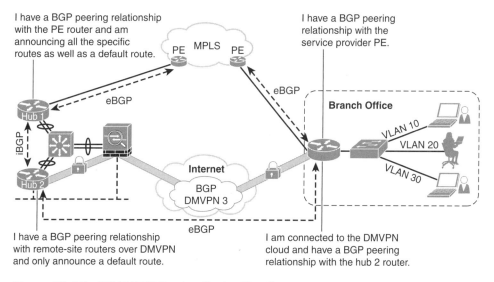

Figure 10-18 *WAN BGP Peering Design Details*

As you can see in Figure 10-18, you will establish a BGP peering relationship with the MPLS service provider PE routers. You will announce all specific routes and the default route to the PE router from the central site. You will also have a BGP session with a PE router at each remote branch office router. You will announce connected LANs through BGP to the PE routers at the remote site.

To implement a backup solution, you will establish a new DMVPN cloud. The hub router for the DMVPN cloud will be the second router at the central site. You will also establish a BGP session from the remote office router to the central hub router and will announce only the default route from the hub router to the remote site. You will announce the LAN-connected routes to the hub routers from the remote-site router.

You will need to use the BGP routing policy at the central site to steer your traffic to the remote site primarily through the MPLS network. Considering that both hubs have an iBGP peering relationship, you decide to use local preference to influence route preference.

With BGP in place, you can continue to implement various traffic engineering capabilities. An example of this would be to send business-critical data through the MPLS network and Internet traffic through the DMVPN.

Regional Offices WAN Design

The final area of focus is to provide connectivity for the regional offices. These offices have special requirements:

- There can be up to 100 users in the regional office.
- All business applications will be hosted in the data center at the central site.
- The users need data, voice, and video traffic.
- Users will connect to the Internet through the central site.
- The regional office can tolerate half an hour of unavailability.
- High-speed connectivity to the central site is needed.

Because regional offices have the highest availability demands, you have decided to implement a dual MPLS solution, as displayed in Figure 10-19.

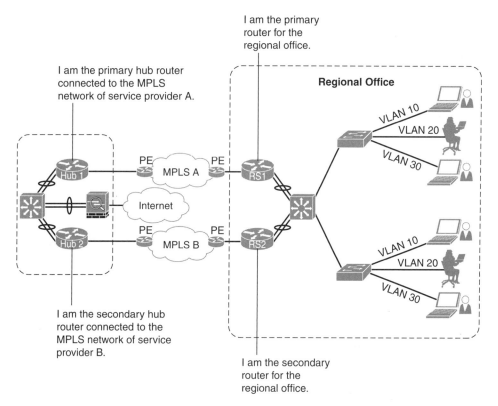

Figure 10-19 *Regional Office WAN Design (Dual MPLS)*

Each of the hub routers will be connected to a unique MPLS provider. You have decided to reuse the same MPLS network selected for branch office connectivity and will select a second MPLS network for redundancy on the second hub router.

Because there is a high demand for availability, you will implement two routers at the regional office. The two routers will provide redundancy in case of failure of one of the routers. You will also implement distribution layer switches, which will provide Layer 3 services to the LAN users.

The design with dual links to the central site and dual routers at the regional office enables you to meet the demands for availability.

Figure 10-20 provides a closer look at the regional office routing design considerations.

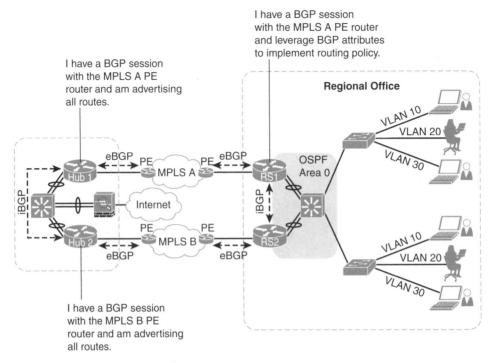

Figure 10-20 *Regional Office Routing Design*

As you can see in this diagram, you will establish BGP routing from your hub routers to the PE routers at the central site. You will also establish BGP routing with PE routers at the regional offices. OSPF routing will be used at the regional office between the WAN routers and distribution switches. The use of a routing protocol such as OSPF will accommodate dynamic rerouting from the distribution switches to the edge routers in the event of WAN failures. You can redistribute specific routes or inject only the default route to the distribution switches from the WAN edge routers. One method for influencing path preference is to leverage the longest match by redistributing specifics on one router and inject a default route from the other router. Another option is to redistribute with OSPF Metric Type 1 on one router and OSPF Metric Type 2 on the other. Routes learned with OSPF Metric Type 1 are always preferred over those learned with Metric Type 2. See Chapter 3, "OSPF Design," for more information regarding OSPF design considerations.

The other options for traffic engineering include using BGP as the routing protocol within the WAN. You can create a routing policy to load balance between both MPLS networks. Some regional offices can use the MPLS A network as the primary path, whereas other regional offices use the MPLS B network as the primary path. Local Preference could be one option for configuring a BGP policy to implement such a solution.

This concludes the redundancy and connectivity use case. Table 10-3 summarizes the overall next-generation WAN design you came up with.

Table 10-3 *WAN Transport Options for Remote Sites Using Local Internet*

	WAN Aggregation Design Model (Primary)	WAN Aggregation Design Model (Secondary)	WAN Remote Routers Single/Dual	WAN Transports (Single/Dual)	Primary Transport	Secondary Transport
ATM WAN	Dual DMVPN		Single	Single	Internet VPN	
Branch Office WAN	MPLS Dynamic	DMVPN Backup Shared	Single	Dual	MPLS	Internet VPN
Regional Office WAN	Dual MPLS	Dual MPLS	Dual	Dual	MPLS VPN A	MPLS VPN B

As with any design project, it is important to look at requirements associated with multiple potentially related initiatives while considering interdependencies and opportunities to maximize leverage of assets.

Basic Traffic Engineering Techniques

In the Bank of POLONA design case study in the preceding section, you developed a WAN design taking advantage of multiple WAN links to the remote sites for the branch office and regional office deployments. There are two modes of operation when configuring WAN forwarding in environments with multiple links toward the central site:

- Active/failover
- Load balancing

When using the active/failover mode, only one WAN link is active and considered as the primary path. The other link is provisioned to provide backup connectivity. When the primary WAN link fails, the backup link is designed to automatically take over. This mode provides symmetric routing, with traffic flowing along the same path in both directions. Symmetric routing simplifies troubleshooting because bidirectional traffic flows always traverse the same links. The active/failover mode is typically used in the majority of WAN designs. The IGP routing protocols can be easily implemented to accommodate active/failover scenarios.

When you use the load-balancing mode, both links are active. If one of the WAN links fails, the other link automatically takes over and begins forwarding all traffic. This mode makes troubleshooting more difficult, because the traffic could traverse one link in one direction and the other link in the other direction, resulting in nondeterministic behavior.

Sometimes it makes sense to welcome additional complexity to use all the WAN links and bandwidth available. Although some traffic engineering techniques and ideas were shared as part of the Bank of POLONA design scenario, this section explicitly reviews some of the basic traffic engineering techniques available with BGP to effectively load-balance traffic over multiple transport networks.

As discussed in Chapter 5, BGP is the most common and often most appropriate protocol for performing traffic engineering. BGP already includes tools that allow forwarding traffic based on routing policy.

Implementing inbound or outbound load distribution with BGP from a remote-site perspective is made possible as a result of the following options:

- **Using the weight attribute:** This option is available only when you have a single-router design. This attribute is a Cisco proprietary BGP attribute. If you want to influence routing with the weight attribute, you can set a higher value for the routes that are received from a specific BGP neighbor (DMVPN hub or SP PE router). The routes with a higher weight attribute value will be selected as the primary routes.

- **Using the local preference attribute:** This attribute is similar to the weight attribute, but unlike weight, local preference can also be leveraged as part of a dual-router or multirouter design. When you want to send some traffic over a specific link, you simply need to set the local preference for routes received through that link or a specific BGP neighbor to some higher value. The outbound traffic will then be forwarded out of that WAN link.

- **Using the MED attribute:** With the MED attribute you can influence how the traffic will flow into your network. An example of this would be to set the MED to a lower value for specific routes as the router advertises them. A lower MED informs remote routers as to whether a specific link has a lower cost and should be used for traffic to specific destinations.

- **AS prepending:** It is possible to prepend extra AS numbers to specific routes. With AS prepending, you will make routes less desirable and can influence traffic forwarding into your network.

The example depicted in Figure 10-21 addresses a basic traffic engineering scenario focused on achieving the following conditions:

Case Study: Redundancy and Connectivity   353

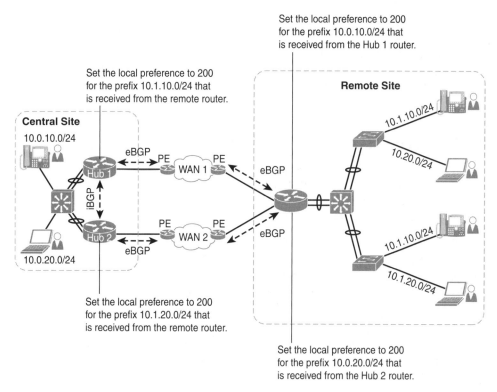

Figure 10-21 *Traffic Engineering Using BGP Attributes*

- Data traffic between networks 10.0.10.0/24 and 10.1.10.0/24 must be forwarded over WAN link 1.

- Voice traffic between networks 10.0.20.0/24 and 10.1.20.0/24 must be forwarded over WAN link 2.

You can achieve the desired data forwarding by using local preference on all routers. The following provides a breakdown of the routing policy displayed in Figure 10-21:

- On the Hub1 router, set the local preference to 200 for the prefix 10.1.10.0/24 that is received from the remote router.

- On the Hub2 router, set the local preference to 200 for the prefix 10.1.20.0/24 that is received from the remote router.

- On the remote router, set the local preference to 200 for the prefix 10.0.10.0/24 that is received from the Hub1 router.

- On the remote router, set the local preference to 200 for the prefix 10.0.20.0/24 that is received from the Hub2 router.

There are many options for classifying traffic and optimizing routing policy with BGP. Nevertheless, traditional approaches such as these may or may not be sufficient in addressing next-generation enterprise customer demands and the desire to route traffic based on greater levels of intelligence. In the next section, we explore Cisco's next-generation WAN (NGWAN) based on software-defined WAN (SDWAN) solutions known as Intelligent WAN (or IWAN).

NGWAN, SDWAN, and IWAN Solution Overview

Media-rich applications, an increased number of devices connecting to the network, guest access, Internet of Things (IoT), cloud offerings, and other factors cause not only a higher demand for bandwidth at the branch but also result in the need for organizations to reconsider the impact associated with a change in traffic patterns.

Until recently, the only way to get reliable connectivity with predictable performance was to take advantage of a private WAN using MPLS or leased-line services. Carrier-based MPLS and leased-line services can be expensive and are not always a cost-effective option to support growing bandwidth requirements for remote-site connectivity. Organizations are looking for ways to their lower operating budget while adequately providing the network transport for a remote site.

Cheaper Internet connections have become more reliable and are more economical compared to dedicated links; however, businesses are primarily deploying Internet VPN in their smaller sites or as a backup path given perceived risks and performance inadequacies. Price-to-performance gains have become too attractive to ignore, and organizations would like to take advantage of cheaper bandwidth at branch locations, without compromising application performance, availability, or security.

Cisco IWAN enables organizations to take advantage of performance-enhancing innovative capabilities to deliver an uncompromised experience over any connection. Cisco IWAN empowers IT organizations to provide more bandwidth to their branch office locations by using less-expensive WAN transport options without affecting performance, security, or reliability. With the IWAN solution, traffic is dynamically routed based on application visibility, SLAs, endpoint type, and network conditions to deliver the best-quality experience. The realized savings from IWAN not only potentially pay for the infrastructure upgrades but also free resources for business innovation.

Figure 10-22 depicts the most commonly sought-after capability requirements addressed by IWAN and considered when evaluating SD WAN (software-defined WAN) solution offerings.

NGWAN, SDWAN, and IWAN Solution Overview 355

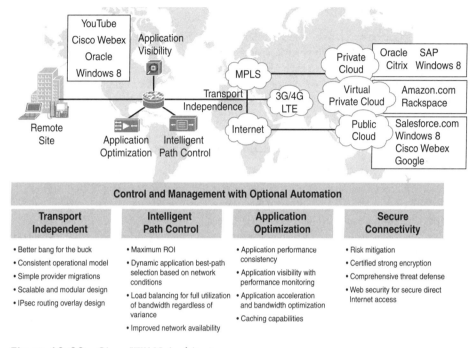

Figure 10-22 *Cisco IWAN Architecture*

When organizations consider the current state of their WAN and the journey to the next-generation WAN, it is important to look at the big picture and all the capability requirements necessary to address the long-term needs of the business. It is obvious that the primary initial drivers from a business perspective are cost reduction, improved application performance, accelerated delivery of new services, and flexibility to innovate by addressing the technical constraints that limit the introduction of new technologies necessary to impact overall business capabilities.

The technical capability requirements shown in Figure 10-22 that typically come up and that are used for next-generation solution evaluation are

- Transport-independent design (TID)
- Intelligent path control (IPC)
- Application optimization (AO)
- Secure connectivity (SC)

In addition to the four pillars of TID, IPC, AO, and SC, the overall manageability of the solution cannot be overlooked. Solution manageability can affect uptime and either simplify or complicate the troubleshooting process. We examine the details of each of these capability requirements before moving on to the IWAN design overview.

Transport-Independent Design

Organizations are asking for a transport-independent design. Given aggressive pricing associated with different carrier options and the desire to get the best bang for the buck, organizations are looking at ways to realize carrier and WAN transport flexibility. They envision a consistent operational model over all access networks to eliminate routing complexity while addressing scalability, modularity, and security. Leveraging a transport-independent design model simplifies provider migrations and does not involve a complete redesign or fancy workarounds to address a change in business needs. Internet with an IPsec routing overlay is typically the solution that many organizations consider and deploy.

IWAN leverages a combination of front door virtual routing forwarding (fVRF) and DMVPN-based overlays across all available connectivity. Hiding away the underlying transport with a unique fVRF and making it accessible only by the DMVPN overlay enables organizations to use any available connectivity and provides the flexibility to add or replace network connections without having to modify the network architecture.

Intelligent Path Control

Organizations realize that to optimize application performance and to implement SLAs, they need the intelligent path control capability. Intelligent path control is more than the path redirection available with the classical routing technology. Application best path selection involves defining a path preference tied to SLAs that protect critical traffic. SLAs are based on the measurement of metrics such as delay, loss, and jitter and are in the context of per application thresholds required for optimal performance. Nonclassified best effort class traffic needs to be efficiently load-balanced across the WAN links regardless of bandwidth discrepancies.

IWAN takes advantage of Cisco Performance Routing (PfR) to improve application delivery and WAN efficiency. Cisco PfR dynamically controls data packet forwarding decisions by looking at application type, performance, policies, and path status.

Application Optimization

Many applications are hidden by HTTP. Organizations need to be able to see those applications to optimize them so that they can get better performance. Organizations want to know what's on their networks and be able to control it. Imagine having the capability to monitor and report on hundreds of applications and then having the capability to apply the necessary QoS policy. The goal is to easily and appropriately allocate bandwidth as well as priority to critical applications while limiting resource utilization for those applications that are not as critical.

In several situations, organizations want to realize even greater performance benefits through the use of application acceleration and caching solutions. They envision immediate page loads, file downloads, pre positioning of content files, and the benefits of further bandwidth savings that result from enabling additional optimization and HTTP/HTTPS caching capabilities.

IWAN leverages Cisco Application Visibility and Control (AVC), Cisco Wide Area Application Services (WAAS), and the Akamai Connect feature capability to provide visibility into and help organizations optimize application performance over WAN links.

Secure Connectivity

The capability of providing certified strong encryption with AES-256-GCM support is becoming increasingly more important to protect information from intrusion. With direct Internet services out at the branch site to provide secure transport between locations and to critical data center resources, organizations realize that they now also have the flexibility to route Internet-bound traffic directly out of these circuits if they choose to do so. Traffic patterns are changing as Public SaaS productivity applications become more prevalent. When the traffic is destined for the Internet, routing traffic back through centralized Data Center Internet connectivity often results in suboptimal traffic patterns.

Security is typically the reason that organizations might delay the decision to use direct Internet Access at a branch location. At a bare minimum, with multiple distributed Internet touchpoints, organizations are concerned with how they will secure them. Features such as NAT, firewalling, and web security are becoming more important at the remote-site WAN edge to accommodate a shift to decentralized Internet services.

IWAN takes advantage of integrated services capabilities within routing platforms such as NAT, zone-based policy firewall (ZFW), and Cisco Web Security (CWS) Cloud Connector to ensure that the solution provides the level of security required to meet next-generation WAN requirements.

Management

Organizations are requesting simplified models for provisioning WAN services, and IT tends to gravitate toward wizard-based and automated deployment offerings. Organizations with a large number of sites typically would like to ship hardware directly from the manufacturer to the end-site destination without having to configure the hardware in a staging facility prior to sending it out. Plug-and-play deployment is a "nice to have" for many organizations, but a necessity for others that seek to accelerate site turn-up.

Cisco provides comprehensive management options to help organizations achieve the full benefits of the Cisco IWAN experience and covers all Day 0 (design and prepare), Day 1 (install and make operational), and Day 2 (monitor, optimize throughout, troubleshoot) activities. One of the more common management solution options includes Cisco Prime Infrastructure for on-premises management, either standalone or integrated with LiveAction for advanced visualization of application performance metrics. Another common management solution option leverages Glue Networks for cloud-based and multitenant software-defined WANs. The management solution growing in increasing popularity since its release is the Cisco Application Policy Infrastructure Controller (APIC) with the Enterprise Module (EM) leveraging the integrated IWAN Application module. APIC-EM simplifies and streamlines the management of network services that are provided by access routers and switches. The separately licensed IWAN application for APIC-EM greatly simplifies WAN deployments by providing a highly intuitive, policy-based interface that helps IT abstract network complexity and design for business intent.

Organizations must consider TID, IPC, AO, SC, and management capabilities holistically as they embark on the journey to design and deploy the next-generation WAN. Focusing on long-term design considerations will ensure sustainable outcomes and the most consistent application experience for branch users. IWAN offers the flexibility to focus on only a few pillars based on immediate priorities such as transport-independent design and intelligent path control based on the design requirements and priorities, and later you can build it up by adding other capabilities such as WAN optimization and caching to help applications run faster. The following sections explore IWAN design and PfR-specific details.

IWAN Design Overview

The *Cisco Intelligent WAN (IWAN)* provides a transport-independent solution that enables highly available, secure, and optimized connectivity for multiple remote-site LANs.

The transport-independent design simplifies the WAN deployment by using an IPsec VPN overlay over all WAN transport options including MPLS, Internet, and Cellular (3G/4G). Leveraging VPN overlays on top of all transport connectivity and not just to accommodate Internet VPN deployments reduces routing and security complexity and provides flexibility in choosing providers and transport options. As highlighted in the previous section, Cisco Dynamic Multipoint VPN (DMVPN) is the technology used to establish the IWAN IPsec overlay.

The IWAN architecture leverages two or more providers for resiliency and application availability. Provider path diversity provides the foundation for Cisco Performance Routing (PfR) to route around fluctuations in the providers' performance to protect against not only blackout, but also brownout situations.

Internet connections are typically included in discussions that are relevant to the Internet edge module and data center design conversations. Remote-site routers also commonly have Internet connections used to provide augmented transport connectivity, but these routers do not necessarily provide the same breadth of services as appliances leveraged within the Internet edge module. For security and other reasons, Internet access at remote sites is often routed through the primary site.

Two common IWAN design models use Internet as a transport technology:

- Hybrid WAN design
- Dual Internet WAN design

The IWAN Hybrid WAN design model uses MPLS paired with Internet VPN for WAN transport connectivity. In this design model, the MPLS WAN can provide more bandwidth for the critical classes of services that are needed for key applications and can provide SLA guarantees for these applications. The IWAN Dual Internet design model uses a pair of Internet service providers to further reduce cost while maintaining a high level of resiliency for the WAN.

The IWAN WAN aggregation (hub) designs include two WAN edge routers. WAN aggregation routers that terminate VPN traffic are also referred to as VPN hub routers. In the context of IWAN, an MPLS A CE router is also used as a VPN hub router. Just like with traditional design models, when taking advantage of IWAN design models, the WAN aggregation routers always connect into a pair of distribution layer switches.

IWAN Hybrid Design Model

The IWAN Hybrid design model uses a single MPLS VPN provider and a single Internet provider, as shown in Figure 10-23.

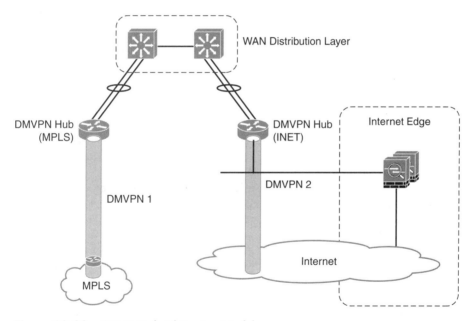

Figure 10-23 *IWAN Hybrid Design Model*

The hub router connects to the Internet indirectly through a firewall DMZ interface.

The IWAN hybrid design requires dual WAN aggregation routers to support the pair of DMVPN clouds. Those two clouds are required to provide resilient connections to all remote sites.

The IWAN Hybrid design uses fVRF on both transport links. The fVRF provides control plane separation from the providers and an additional security layer between inside and outside networks. Figure 10-24 provides a visual overview of fVRF functionality.

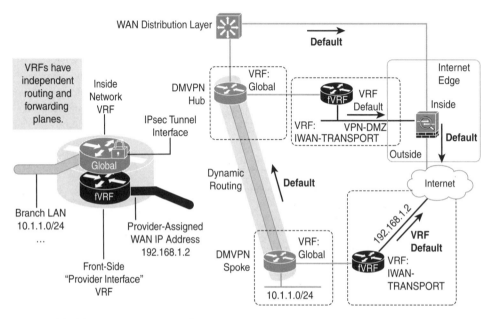

Figure 10-24 *IWAN: Front-end VRF*

VRF allows multiple instances of a routing table to coexist within the same router at the same time. The WAN physical interface is in its own VRF routing traffic over the transport network (Internet or MPLS) to allow DMVPN tunnels to be established. The global VRF routes the traffic through the established DMVPN tunnels providing end-to-end site-to-site connectivity. Given that the routing instances are independent, it is possible to use the same overlapping IP addresses within the public and private addressing space without conflicting with each other.

IWAN uses VRF to provide the following:

- Default route separation between user traffic and the DMVPN tunnel establishment
- Control and data plane separation between inside and outside networks for security purposes

Traditionally, organizations do not allow direct Internet access for remote users, and as a result, any remote-site hosts that access the Internet must do so via the Internet edge at the primary site or data center. Remote-site routers require a default route for all external and Internet destinations. If organizations continue to forbid direct Internet access, the default route at the remote-site edge must force traffic across the primary or secondary WAN transport DMVPN tunnels. DMVPN also has a default route requirement to establish tunnels between sites as part of a DMVPN Phase 3 deployment. The default route for the user traffic over DMVPN conflicts with the default route needed for DMVPN to establish tunnels between sites. Also, you could only send a summary from the hub that summarizes the branch subnets toward the branch routers over the DMVPN tunnel if the design requires using local Internet link for access the Internet.

Using VRFs on the router solves the problem associated with needing multiple default routes at the remote-site edge. A router can have multiple routing tables that are kept logically separate on the device. This separation is similar to a virtual router from a forwarding plane perspective. The global VRF corresponds to the traditional routing table, and additional VRFs are given names and, in some design use cases, route distinguisher (RD) values.

Certain features on the router are VRF-aware, including static routing, routing protocols, interface forwarding, and IPsec tunneling. This set of features is used with DMVPN to permit the use of multiple default routes for both the DMVPN hub routers and DMVPN spoke routers. One of the options is to use a global VRF for user traffic routing and a VRF for each WAN physical interface specifically used for DMVPN tunnel establishment. This combination of features is referred to as fVRF because the VRF faces the WAN, and the router internal LAN and DMVPN tunnel interfaces all remain in the global VRF.

The use of fVRF with DMVPN for all transport connectivity provides the necessary foundation for layering on innovative feature capabilities such as PfR.

Cisco PfR Overview

Performance routing (PfR) has been available for more than 10 years and started originally as Optimized Edge Routing (OER). PfRv2 introduced application routing based on real-time performance metrics, and PfRv3 was designed from the ground up with configuration simplification and enhanced scalability in mind.

Figure 10-25 provides a comparison of OER, PfRv2, and PfRv3.

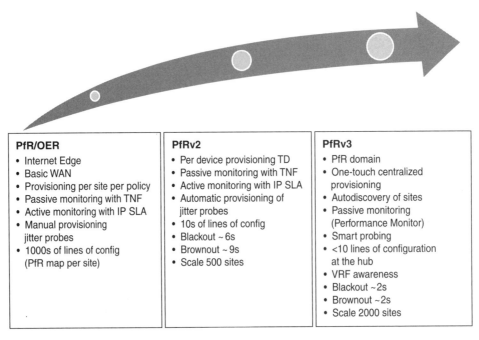

Figure 10-25 *Comparison of OER, PfRv2, and PfRv3*

Cisco PfR Operations

Cisco PfRv2 leverages a five-stage operational lifecycle based on different performance metrics to enhance WAN performance. Figure 10-26 provides a visual overview.

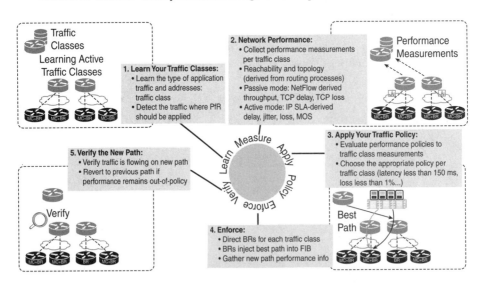

Figure 10-26 *PfRv2 Operational Lifecycle*

As you can see in Figure 10-26, the five stages of PfRv2 are

- **Learn:** The master controller tells the border router to learn "interesting" applications, called traffic classes (TC). These traffic classes could be a destination prefix with or without the port, DSCP, source prefix, or even application using Network-Based Application Recognition (NBAR). This profiling process can be entirely automatic based on the top talkers (using NetFlow) or configured manually.

- **Measure:** The Cisco PfR collects traffic class statistics for learned applications:

  - **Monitor Modes:** Passive, Active, Both, Fast, Special (Cat6K)
  - NetFlow for UDP (bandwidth) and TCP flows (availability, delay, bandwidth, loss)
  - IP SLA for TCP and UDP flows (availability, delay, loss, jitter, MOS)

- **Apply policy:** Use measured application data to determine whether the managed traffic class is out of policy (OOP) and if an alternate path can meet the policy requirements.

- **Enforce:**

  - **Prefix Control:** Direct border routers (BRs) for each traffic class and inject BGP or Static routes.
  - **Application Control:** Dynamic route-map/PBR for traffic classes that are defined by ACLs, NBAR. Unsupported routing protocols are OSPF, IS-IS, or border routers running a mix of routing protocols.

- **Verify:** Verify that traffic flowing on the new path matches the policy and reverts to a healthier path if performance remains out of policy and such a path is available.

Cisco IWAN and PfRv3

The version of Cisco Performance Routing (PfR) used as part of the IWAN 2.0 solution is Performance Routing Version 3 (PfRv3). PfRv3 is a one-touch provisioning and multi-site coordination solution that simplifies network provisioning. It enables intelligence of Cisco devices to improve application performance and availability. PfRv3 is an application-based policy-driven framework that provides multisite-aware bandwidth and path control optimization for WAN and cloud-based applications.

PfRv3 monitors network performance and selects the best path for each application based on criteria such as reachability, delay, jitter, and loss. PfRv3 evenly distributes traffic and maintains equivalent link utilization levels while load-balancing traffic.

PfRv3 is tightly integrated with existing AVC components such as performance monitoring, quality of service (QoS), and NBAR2. PfRv3 is useful for enterprise and managed service providers looking for ways to increase their WAN reliability and availability while saving costs.

PfRv3 includes the following key improvements:

- **Enterprise domain:** All sites belong to an enterprise domain and are connected with peering. The peering mechanism is used for service exchange, network automatic discovery, and single-touch provisioning. This peering mechanism was introduced with Cisco Performance Routing version 2 (PfRv2) as a feature called Target Discovery (TD), but this peering feature has been greatly enhanced to become the core of Cisco PfRv3.

- **Application centric:** The Cisco PfRv3 solution is more focused on applications. It provides a simple way to provision policies based on application visibility and classification. Application classification is based on Cisco's deep packet inspection engine, Network-Based Application Recognition version 2 (NBAR2). The solution provides visibility into applications and traffic flows by integrating with Unified Monitoring (Performance Monitor). Application visibility includes bandwidth, performance, correlation to QoS queues, and so on.

- **Simple provisioning:** Cisco PfRv3 has simplified policies with pre existing templates. The policy configuration is in a central location and is distributed to all sites via peering. This solution simplifies provisioning and ensures consistency across the entire network.

- **Automatic discovery:** Enterprise sites are discovered using peering. Each site peers with the hub site. Prefixes specific to sites are advertised along with a site ID. The site prefix to site ID mapping is used for monitoring and optimization. This mapping is also used for creating reports for specific sites. WAN interfaces at each site are discovered using a special probing mechanism. This probing mechanism further reduces provisioning on the branch sites to simply the overall PfRv3 deployment.

- **Scalable passive monitoring:** Cisco PfRv3 uses Unified Monitoring (also called Performance Monitor) to monitor traffic going into WAN links and traffic coming from the WAN links. It monitors performance metrics per the Differentiated Services Code Point (DSCP) rather than monitoring on a per flow or per prefix basis.

- **Smart probing:** Cisco PfRv3 uses a lightweight probing mechanism that will generate traffic when there is no traffic as well as with data traffic. The router generates RTP traffic, which enables you to measure jitter and packet loss via regular Performance Monitors. It reduces the need for control messages to carry statistics back to the sender.

- **Scaling:** Cisco PfRv3 uses the platform hardware wherever possible to generate the probes on the border routers. Apart from artificial probes, Cisco PfRv3 also uses the existing traffic for probing. When there is no traffic, however, Cisco PfRv3 uses its own probes to measure important metrics such as delay and jitter. As part of the IWAN 2.0 release, Cisco PfRv3, as part of the IWAN solution offering, is able to scale to a 2000-branch deployment. As compared to previous versions, Scalable Passive Monitoring and Smart Probe capability are what allow Cisco PfRv3 to achieve this level of scale.

- **VRF support:** Cisco PfRv3 is VRF aware. Whenever you require segmenting your network into different logical networks using separate DMVPN tunnels, Cisco PfRv3 instances can be created for each VRF.

A device can play different roles in PfRv3 configuration, as displayed within Figure 10-27 and described in the following list.

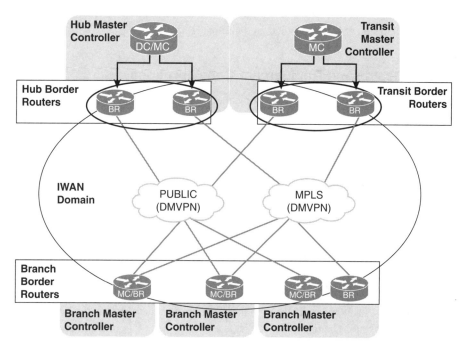

Figure 10-27 *Device Roles with PfRv3*

- **Hub master controller (MC):** The master controller at the hub site, which can be either a data center or headquarters. All policies are configured on the hub MC. It acts as master controller for the site and makes optimization decisions.

- **Hub border router:** The border controller at the hub site. The WAN interface terminates in the hub border routers. PfRv3 is enabled on these interfaces. A hub BR can support only one transport. You can have multiple hub border devices. A hub BR will generate discovery probes to help branch sites discover their external interfaces.

- **Transit master controller:** The master controller at a transit site, which can be either a data center or headquarters. It acts as a master controller for the site.

- **Transit border router:** The border controller at a transit site. The WAN interface terminates in the transit border routers. PfRv3 is enabled on these interfaces. A transit BR can support only one transport. You can have multiple transit border devices. A transit BR will generate discovery probes to help branch sites discover their external interfaces.

- **Branch master controller:** The branch master controller is the master controller at the branch site. There is no policy configuration on this device. It receives policy from the hub MC. This device acts as master controller for that site for making optimization decisions.

- **Branch border router:** The border device at the branch site. There is no configuration other than enabling the PfRv3 border MC on the device. The WAN interface that terminates on the device is detected automatically.

Cisco PfRv3 Design and Deployment Considerations

Cisco PfRv3 deployment must be carefully planned. The following are some aspects to consider when integrating Cisco PfRv3 as part of an IWAN design and deployment:

- You should evaluate the routing protocols and policies that are used in the WAN and decide how the Cisco PfR will both integrate and influence the routing decisions. Depending on the routing protocol that is in use on the network, there could be potential caveats. Although EIGRP and BGP are the preferred protocols because PfRv3 has the capability to reference secondary paths included within the topology database of these routing protocols, both EIGRP and BGP offer the most stable and scalable routing design over hub-and-spoke topology and a more flexible design optimization over DMVPN.

- You will need to decide which routers will be border routers and master controllers. The routers that are connected to the exits of each site should be configured as border routers. Each site needs its own master controller that controls the border routers for that site. The master controller is a control plane function and can be combined on a border router or run on a separate router. The main consideration is scale. On the branch site, the master controller function can easily be implemented on one of the border routers. At the main WAN hub or data center sites, it is better to implement a separate router as the master controller to scale to support the projected number of traffic classes. On the primary site, you will provision the hub master controller. Secondary or tertiary data centers will need to be configured with a transit master controller.

- You will need to determine what type of traffic you want to control and define a domain policy on the hub master controller to be sent over the peering infrastructure to all the branch master controllers. Policies can be defined per application or per Differentiated Service Code Point (DSCP). You cannot mix and match DSCP and application-based policies in the same class group. Traffic that does not match any of the classification and match statements falls into a default group, which will be routed by default or load-balanced if load balancing is enabled (in both cases, no performance measurement is done).

- You should decide which performance metrics you want to measure as part of the domain policy. Examples include delay, loss, and jitter. Predefined policy templates are available for selection with PfRv3 and include the most common applications and associated best practice threshold values. Figure 10-28 shows these predefined policy templates. It is also possible to define custom policies based on unique application requirements.

Predefined Template	Threshold Definition
Voice	priority 1 one-way-delay threshold 150 threshold 150 (msec) priority 2 packet-loss-rate threshold 1 (%) priority 2 byte-loss-rate threshold 1 (%) priority 3 jitter 30 (msec)
Real-time Video	priority 1 packet-loss-rate threshold 1 (%) priority 1 byte-loss-rate threshold 1 (%) priority 2 one-way-delay threshold 150 (msec) priority 3 jitter 20 (msec)
Low-latency Data	priority 1 one-way-delay threshold 100 (msec) priority 2 byte-loss-rate threshold 5 (%) priority 2 packet-loss-rate threshold 5 (%)

Predefined Template	Threshold Definition
Bulk Data	priority 1 one-way-delay threshold 300 (msec) priority 2 byte-loss-rate threshold 5 (%) priority 2 packet-loss-rate threshold 5 (%)
Best Effort	priority 1 one-way-delay threshold 500 (msec) priority 2 byte-loss-rate threshold 10 (%) priority 2 packet-loss-rate threshold 10 (%)
Scavenger	priority 1 one-way-delay threshold 500 (msec) priority 2 byte-loss-rate threshold 50 (%) priority 2 packet-loss-rate threshold 50 (%)

Figure 10-28 *PfRv3: Predefined Policy Templates*

Enterprise WAN and Access Management

IT organizations are looking at trends such as Software-Defined Networking (SDN) to provide the necessary level of programmability and automated network control to help them rapidly respond to new business opportunities.

Figure 10-29 illustrates two design options enabling the use of network programmability.

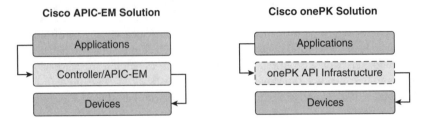

Figure 10-29 *Network Programmability: Options*

The Cisco Application Policy Infrastructure Controller Enterprise Module (APIC-EM) provides an opportunity to leverage open programmability APIs to manage network services through a single controller. This capability provides you with abstraction of the network, thus further simplifying the management of network services.

onePK is an easy-to-use toolkit for development, automation, and rapid service creation; it enables direct access to individual devices, thus enabling you to extend the functionality that is provided by these devices.

For scalability, ease of use, and faster development of new applications, you should choose the solution with the Cisco APIC-EM. For maximum flexibility and customizability of individual devices, you should choose the solution in which APIs on the devices are used leveraging onePK. It is important to note that there is an increased development burden when applications need to control individual devices and the network as a whole, such as when using onePK independent of controller capabilities.

APIC-EM

The end goal for many organizations is automated provisioning and a controller that can manage the entire enterprise infrastructure. This is a definitely a journey, but the Cisco APIC-EM is several steps along the path. Use the Cisco APIC-EM to simplify and streamline the management of network services that are provided by WAN and access routers and switches. The Cisco APIC-EM provides an open and programmable approach to networking through open APIs for policy-based management and security. The approach automates what has typically been a tedious manual configuration.

The controller provisions network services consistently and provides rich network information and analytics across all network resources: LAN and WAN, wired and wireless, and physical and virtual infrastructures. This visibility enables you to optimize services and support new applications and business models. The controller bridges the gap between open, programmable network elements and the applications that communicate with them, automating the provisioning of the entire end-to-end infrastructure.

In the past, it was not uncommon to suffer from stovepipe development and a lack of flexibility, making it slow to add functionality. These challenges are a result of siloes of components and features with no solution context and no predefined workflows.

APIC-EM is an evolution to a layered approach, where abstraction is key. This abstraction will enable you to leverage common functions such as the PKI service, plug-and-play services, and network discovery. The Cisco APIC-EM abstracts the device layer, making it possible to leverage the configuration rendering for network devices over many different applications. This, in turn, allows for a quicker development of modular applications that leverage the services infrastructure provided by APIC-EM through RESTful APIs.

The applications interface to the APIC-EM controller abstracts and masks the complexity of managing individual network devices. Many partners are evolving their own solutions and infrastructure components to ride on top of the APIC-EM controller, which will result in the creation of additional applications that customers can continue to use to realize additional value.

Cisco and partner network management applications such as Cisco Prime, GluWare, and LiveAction have started leveraging the APIC-EM controller for provisioning and analytics as well as for reporting and analysis.

Figure 10-30 illustrates the evolution to next-generation management capabilities made possible with APIC-EM.

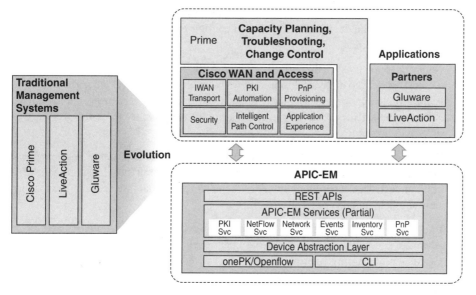

Figure 10-30 *Next-generation Management Powered by APIC-EM*

The Cisco APIC-EM simplifies and streamlines network operations while also reducing cost. It frees the IT department to focus on business innovation by deploying new network devices and applications rapidly. Some of the benefits of APIC-EM are

- Consistency across the enterprise network, which keeps downtime to a minimum and lowers operational complexity and associated cost.

- Automated end-to-end provisioning and configuration to enable rapid deployment of applications and services. Provisioning times drop from months to hours.

- Open and programmable network devices, policy, data, and analytics to drive business innovation by providing easy access to network intelligence.

- Support for both greenfield and brownfield deployments, which empowers IT to implement programmability and automation within the existing infrastructure that is already in place.

Design of APIC-EM

Following are some of the features of APIC-EM that are developed or in development and that could potentially be leveraged as part of the solution design:

- **Network information database:** The Cisco APIC-EM periodically scans the network to create a "single source of truth" for IT. This inventory includes all network devices, along with an abstraction for the entire enterprise network. This database allows applications to be device-independent, so configuration differences between devices are not a problem.

- **Network topology visualization:** The Cisco APIC-EM autodiscovers and maps network devices to a physical topology with detailed device-level data. The autovisualization feature provides a highly interactive mechanism for viewing and troubleshooting the network. One very useful feature is the capability to easily customize its GUI.

- **Zero-touch deployment:** When the controller scanner discovers a new network device, it creates a network information database entry for it and then automatically configures it. This capability eliminates the need for manual intervention, thus saving time and helping prevent errors.

- **Plug-and-Play:** Cisco Network Plug-and-Play provides a highly secure, scalable, seamless, and unified zero-touch-deployment experience for customers across Cisco's entire enterprise network portfolio of wired and wireless devices. It reduces the burden on enterprises by greatly simplifying the deployment process for new devices, which also can significantly lower operating expenditures (OpEx).

- **Cisco Intelligent WAN (IWAN) application:** The separately licensed IWAN application for APIC-EM greatly simplifies the provisioning of IWAN profiles with simple business policies.

- **Public Key Infrastructure:** The PKI service provides an integrated authentication server for automated key management. It automates the lifecycle management of issuing, renewing, and revoking the PKI X.509 certificate for apps such as IWAN.

This service greatly simplifies the process of establishing and maintaining trust in the network.

- **Path Trace application:** Inspection, interrogation, and remediation of network problems rely on manual techniques today, which may be slow and inaccurate and also quite expensive. Given a five-tuple description, the Path Trace application solves this problem by automating inspection and visualization of the path taken by a flow between two endpoints in the network.

- **Identity Manager:** It is possible to track user identities and endpoints by exchanging information with the Cisco Identity Services Engine (ISE). The result is highly sophisticated per-user policy enforcement, which can improve mobile security policies (including BYOD policies) across the enterprise network.

- **Policy Manager:** To enhance security, the controller translates business policy into network device-level policy. It can enforce abstracted policy for certain users at various times of the day, across wired and wireless networks. It gathers network analytics that help IT initiate policy enforcement across the enterprise network.

- **ACL analysis:** The controller accelerates ACL management. It queries and analyzes ACLs on each network device. This feature helps IT simplify and accelerate troubleshooting by quickly identifying ACL misconfigurations.

- **QoS deployment and change management:** This feature enables you to quickly set and enforce QoS priority policies, while remaining confident that network devices automatically stay in compliance. This feature helps keep application traffic behaving consistently and in accordance with QoS SLAs.

Summary

- Typical MPLS WAN design models:
    - MPLS Static or Dynamic
    - Dual MPLS
- Typical Layer 2 WAN design models:
    - Layer 2 Simple Demarcation
    - Layer 2 Trunked Demarcation
- Typical overlay (VPN):
    - DMVPN Only
    - Dual DMPVN
    - DMVPN Backup Shared or Dedicated

- IWAN:
  - Transport-independent design with fVRF and DMVPN
  - Intelligent path control with PfR
- Management:
  - Cisco APIC-EM
  - Cisco onePK

Review Questions

After answering the following questions, please refer to Appendix A, "Answers to Review Questions," for the answers.

1. Match the typical VPN WAN design model with the best description of it.

DMVPN Backup Dedicated	Design model that uses only Internet VPN as transport
DMVPN Only	Design model that uses two Internet connections
DMVPN Backup Shared	Design model that uses the Internet as a secondary link and implements the VPN hub on an existing MPLS router
Dual DMVPN	Design model that uses the Internet as a secondary link and implements the VPN hub on dedicated router

2. Which of the following best describes IWAN?
   a. The IWAN allows transport-independent connectivity.
   b. The IWAN allows only static routing.
   c. Because only encrypted traffic is transported, application visibility is not possible with the IWAN.
   d. The IWAN needs special encrypting devices to provide an acceptable security level.

3. Which of the following best describes PfR?
   a. PfR enables adaptive routing adjustments.
   b. PfR uses a static set of connection parameters to perform adaptive routing adjustments.
   c. There are two versions of PfR.
   d. The designated router makes decisions about which outbound path to use.

4. Which capabilities are required to leverage a local Internet model where user web traffic and hosted cloud services traffic are permitted to use the local Internet link in a split-tunneling manner as part of a VPN overlay design?
   a. NAT/PAT
   b. Front door VRF
   c. Default route out of interface and pointing to INET PE next hop
   d. All of the above

5. What should be taken into consideration when leveraging a dual-router edge design? (Select three.)
   a. Types of routers deployed
   b. Additional transit network component that is required for proper routing in certain scenarios
   c. Run a routing protocol internally within the remote site
   d. Leverage a FHRP between the routers
   e. IPSLA between the routers

6. What are the four common capability pillars typically leveraged to evaluate next-generation WAN solutions such as IWAN?
   a. Transport-dependent design, intelligent path control, application optimization, secure connectivity
   b. Transport-independent design, intelligent path control, application optimization, secure connectivity
   c. Private connectivity, intelligent path control, application optimization, secure connectivity
   d. Hybrid connectivity, intelligent path control, application optimization, secure connectivity

7. Match the NGWAN capability pillar to the IWAN technology solution.

   TID   PfR

   IPC   WAAS and Akamai Connect

   AO   ZFW, NAT, CWS

   SC   fVRF and DMVPN

8. What was the name of the PfR version 1 capability?
   a. Optimized Edge Routing
   b. Optimized Efficient Routing
   c. Optimized Effective Routing
   d. Optimized Endpoint Routing

Chapter 11

Multitier Enterprise Data Center Designs

Upon completing this chapter, you will be able to

- Explain how to connect the server room to the enterprise LAN (Case Study)
- Explain the benefits of a two-tier data center network architecture (Case Study)
- Explain the benefits of a three-tier data center network architecture (Case Study)
- Describe the specifics of data center inter-VLAN routing
- Compare the top of rack and end of row designs
- Describe how fabric extenders affect the data center network architecture
- Explain some data center high-availability mechanisms
- Describe NIC teaming

The design of any network and, specifically, a data center network (DCN) must always be driven by the requirement of applications. As a result, the design of today's data center networks faces constant challenges, such as rapid application growth, unpredictable traffic characteristics, workload mobility, resource optimization, and critical data security, all within the limited costs of deploying new resources. Therefore, as a network architect or designer, you should hedge these challenges with a modular and scalable data center network design that meets today's design requirements and offers the flexibility to grow in the future with any major redesign.

This chapter uses design case studies to cover some sample design scenarios of the possible and common data center network designs for small, medium, and large DCNs. Chapter 12, "New Trends and Techniques to a Design Modern Data Center," and Chapter 13, "Cisco Application-Centric Infrastructure (ACI)," cover the technologies and designs of modern data centers.

Case Study 1: Small Data Centers (Connecting Servers to an Enterprise LAN)

ABC Corp. is a small enterprise with approximately 70 internal users located in one building. Also, 15 remote (home-based) users are connected over the Internet. Currently, the network that ABC Corp. uses is based on the collapsed core/distribution architecture, as shown in Figure 11-1. To satisfy the needs of internal users, ABC Corp. has to deploy a small group of rack-mountable servers. Servers will house e-mail, file-sharing, and database applications. The server room has already been outfitted. However, ABC Corp. network engineers must decide how the servers will be connected into the enterprise LAN.

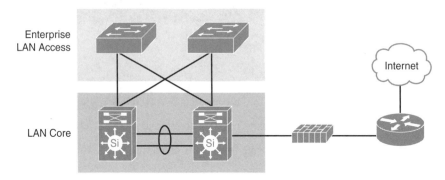

Figure 11-1 *ABC Corp. DC LAN-1*

Based on the current LAN architecture and the scale of the network, to provide network connectivity for the servers and cleanly integrate them with network security capabilities—that is, an existing enterprise LAN firewall—you should connect the servers to the existing enterprise LAN collapsed core switches. This design will offer a simple and cost-effective design that meets the requirements of ABC Corp., providing that enough ports are available. In addition, ideally you should bundle the collapsed core switches with VSS, vPC, or a similar technology to achieve a simple and highly fault-tolerant solution facilitated by redundant uplink connections using the concept of Multichassis EtherChannel (MEC) usage, as shown in Figure 11-2.

> **Note** The MEC enables you to establish PortChannel over physical links connected not to one but to two physical switches in the VSS or vPC bundle. If you are using a nonclustered switch (VSS, vPC, or Stackwise), it will be difficult to avoid a single point of failure; you will need to rely mainly on the server's NIC teaming being set up in active/passive and you will need to detect failure scenarios.

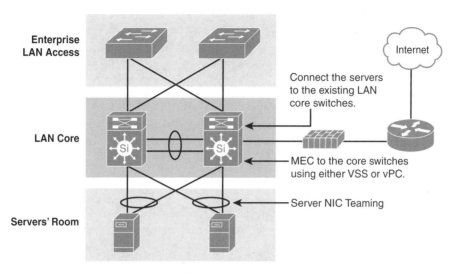

Figure 11-2 *ABC Corp. DC LAN-2*

As a network designer, you should always consider any future growth in your design. For instance when the number of ABC Corp. servers increases, the current enterprise LAN collapsed core switches might not provide enough switch ports. In this case, you need to place additional server room access switches between the servers and enterprise LAN collapsed core switches to solve that problem, as shown in Figure 11-3. Therefore, you must always ask about the current and future plans before providing any design.

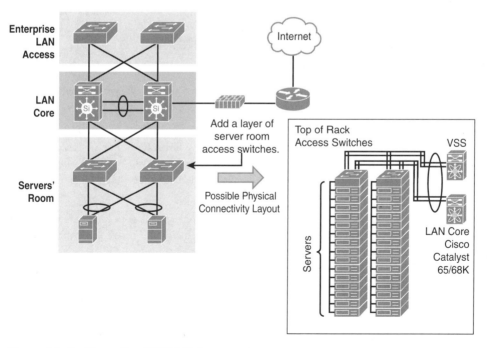

Figure 11-3 *Extending DC LAN Access*

> **Note** In Figure 11-3, Cisco fabric extender (FEX) switches (FEX is covered later in the "End of Row Versus Top of Rack Design" section) provide additional server room access ports/switches, and these switches act like remote line cards and cannot be considered as an additional network layer in this design.

Any switch with sufficient port capacities can be used as a server room switch. However, to achieve fault tolerance between the servers and server room switches, you should use switches with switch-clustering capabilities (VSS, vPC, Stackwise) to allow the use of the MEC connectivity model.

> **Note** Both the server room switch and the client LAN access switch connect devices to the network. The difference between the two methods that changes the switch model is the requirement in the LAN access for Power over Ethernet (PoE). Although PoE-capable devices are not typical in the server room, using PoE-capable switches offers a benefit worth considering: The minor initial cost savings of a non-PoE switch may not be worth the benefits of using the same switch across multiple modules of your local LAN. The ability to use a single switch type between multiple modules can lower operational costs by allowing for simpler sparing and management, and also provide a better chance of reuse as the organization grows. That said, some purpose-built data center switches such as the Cisco Nexus family switch offer capabilities designed for data center networks. For a small data center network (server room), you can consider low-end models if any feature of these switches is required.

Case Study 2: Two-Tier Data Center Network Architecture

ABC Corp. decided to expand its business in which a higher level of data center performance, scalability, and applications services availability is required by the business.

Multiple hardware platforms and technologies must be integrated to deliver the expected levels of performance and availability to application end users. A scalable, high-performance data center demands switching platforms that are designed for the data center, such as the Cisco Nexus family.

As you know from the preceding case study, smaller enterprises with mediocre data center requirements often deploy data center switches as their enterprise LAN collapsed core switches. A single pair of switches provides the wanted data center and LAN core capabilities while using firewall, IPS/IDS, and other appliances for both the enterprise LAN and data center.

This design has its drawbacks, however, when the number of servers increases. LAN collapsed core switches might not provide enough switch ports, and the LAN firewall, IPS/IDS, and other appliances might not suffice for data center requirements. Therefore, adding a layer of data center access/aggregation switches between the LAN core and servers solves that problem. With this design model (see Figure 11-4), the aggregation provides ports and bandwidth aggregation. Also, if the added access switches are Cisco Nexus switches, you can increase access port capacity to a significantly higher number by considering Cisco FEX.

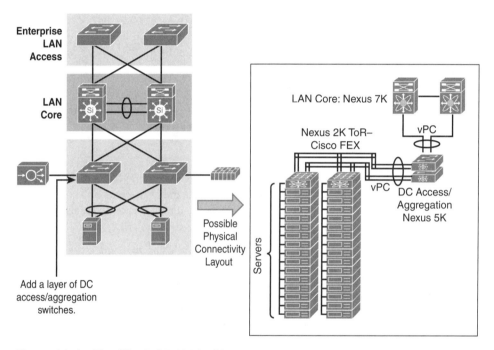

Figure 11-4 *Two-Tier DC LAN Architecture*

The added data center switches will be connected northbound to the LAN core and southbound to servers and other appliances.

Note Northbound connections lead to a higher-level layer (that is, in the direction of the core). Southbound connections lead to a lower layer (that is, in the direction of the end nodes). Terms describe a typical layered network topology mimicking the orientation of a typical map, where north is represented on top of the map.

> **Note** You must be careful when you increase the number of access ports because doing so will reduce access to the uplink oversubscription ratio, which you need to keep as small as possible in the data center design. *Oversubscription* occurs when the ingress capacity exceeds the egress capacity. For example, for 48x 10G attached servers, the access switch needs at least 480 Gbps of port capacity toward the upstream or distribution layer to provide 1:1 oversubscription (1:1 here means zero or no subscription). However, if the access switch has only 2x 10G uplinks, in this case the oversubscription is 24:1. Although not every network is required to provide 1:1 performance, oversubscription needs to be minimized in modern large-scale DCNs (for example, ideally 4:1 or 3:1). Keep in mind that when an oversubscription occurs, quality of service (QoS) is almost always needed to protect important applications during congestion periods (see Chapter 17, "Campus, WAN, and Data Center QoS Design," for more details about QoS design in the data center).

Case Study 3: Three-Tier Data Center Network Architecture

As the data center grows, so does the number of servers and required connections. Data center aggregation switches do not provide a sufficient number of ports, and connecting every server to a limited number of access switch and pair aggregation switches becomes a nuisance.

To solve the problem, the network needs to be redesigned using an architecture that supports a larger scale of access and aggregation switches. In a three-tier architecture, the following occurs:

- The access layer increases the number of available ports, but more important, it reduces the number of required cables. Servers are now connected to the nearest access switch.

- The access switches are connected northbound to aggregation switches with a pair of copper or optical cables.

- The aggregation switches are also connected in the same manner to core switches, but with this architecture, the data center can have multiple pairs of aggregation switches connected to a pair of core switches to support large-scale data center networks.

- With this architecture, the services and appliances are connected to the aggregation switches.

Figure 11-5 shows a typical three-tier data center network architecture.

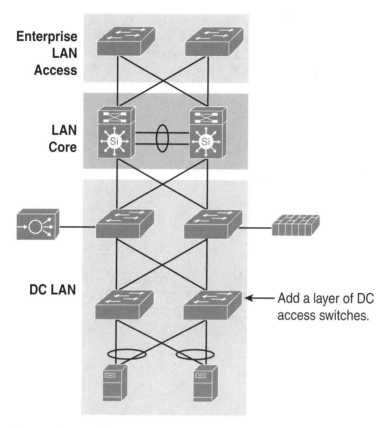

Figure 11-5 *Three-Tier Data Center Network Architecture*

In addition, as a network designer, you need to be aware of some design approaches that can be used with this architecture, including the following:

- Inter-VLAN routing to decide which layer to apply the demarcation between Layer 3 and Layer 2 domains in such an architecture
- Top of rack (ToR) versus end of row (EoR) access switch connectivity models
- Cisco fabric extender (FEX) at the access layer
- Availability and performance optimization

The following subsections cover these points in more detail.

Data Center Inter-VLAN Routing

With the multitier data center network architecture, you need to decide which layer will perform the inter-VLAN routing. This decision dictates the choice of switches (Layer 2 or Layer 3) in the aggregation layer. Also, the topology is dictated by the type of data center workload and predominant traffic flows.

Consider that the demarcation point between a Layer 3 and Layer 2 domain at the data center aggregation layer (Inter-VLAN routing) is preferred in data centers with servers that perform identical tasks and are typically placed behind load balancers, such as web services. As shown in Figure 11-6, traffic flows run mostly between the servers and the network core, whereas communication between the servers is sparse. Such traffic flows enable you to reduce the size of the Layer 2 domain and avoid the problems that occur in large Layer 2 domains. Inter-VLAN routing in the aggregation layer requires Layer 3 switches.

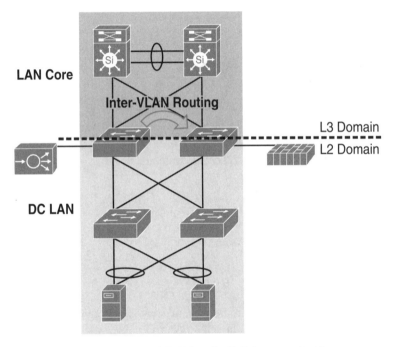

Figure 11-6 *Inter-VLAN VLAN at the DC Aggregation Layer*

A typical enterprise data center, which hosts servers running virtual machines, however, has different requirements. (In general, you may face some challenges with this architecture; this issue will be discussed in the following chapter.) For instance, active VM migration and other traffic flows between the physical servers prefer larger Layer 2 domains. One possible design model is that the Inter-VLAN routing can be done in the core, and the aggregation layer requires only Layer 2 switches, as shown in Figure 11-7. However, this design introduces some challenges in large-scale networks, such as reduced performance because of the increased Layer 2 flooding domain. (Any broadcast or unknown unicast flooding can cause a big issue here.)

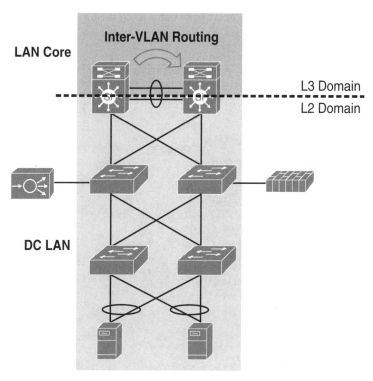

Figure 11-7 *Inter-VLAN at the DC Core Layer*

End of Row Versus Top of Rack Design

Bigger data centers typically have multiple rows of racks. EoR design describes a topology in which all servers in a row connect to the access switch residing in the last rack in a row. EoR access switches are typically modular switches with a sufficient number of ports to provide connectivity for hundreds of servers.

ToR design describes a topology with an access switch on top of every rack, with all servers in a rack connected to it. ToR access switches are typically switches with 24 or 48 ports and an optical fiber connection to aggregation switches.

Figure 11-8 shows a combination of both EoR and ToR connectivity models.

Combination of EoR and ToR Cabling

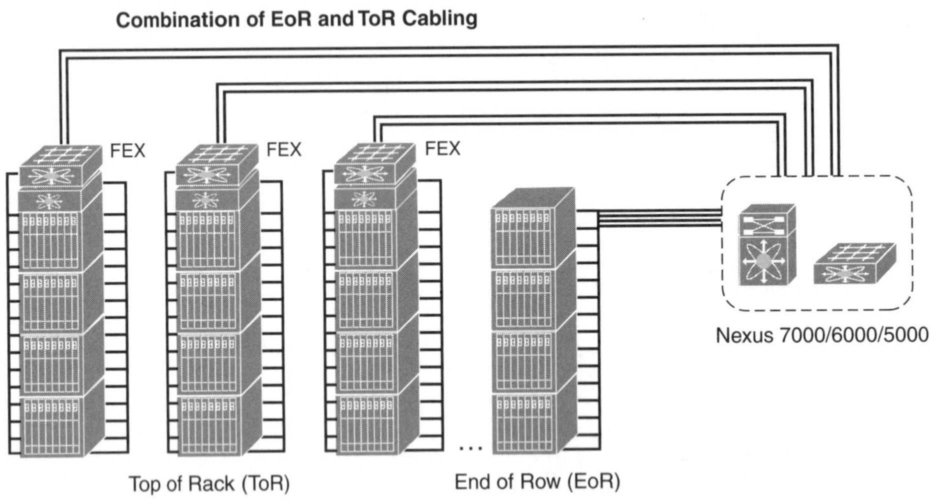

Figure 11-8 *EoR and ToR Connectivity Models*

Note EoR describes a design with access switches positioned at the end, start, or middle of the row. For a redundant design, one row switch may be positioned at the start and the other at the end of the row. However, ToR topology can have the access switch on the top, on the bottom, or in the middle of the rack. Redundant topology typically consists of two switches per rack.

EoR requires a smaller number of capable switches. EoR reduces the management overhead, simplifies STP topology, and requires fewer ports in the aggregation layer. However, in large-scale networks, EoR may require extensive copper cabling from hundreds of servers to the end of the row and more infrastructure for patching and cabling. This translates to more operational complexity.

In contrast, ToR contains the servers' copper cabling in the rack, reducing the cable and patching infrastructure and using fiber connections with higher capacity. In addition, ToR physical topology is more modular because each rack presents a module that can be upgraded and changed with no effect on the other racks. ToR, however, requires a larger number of switches, thus increasing the management overhead. More ports are required in the aggregation layer, and the STP topology gains complexity.

Fabric Extenders

Fabric extenders, also known as port extenders, follow the ToR concept but solve some of its shortcomings. As with ToR access switches, FEXes are typically mounted on the top of each rack. However, FEXes do not behave like normal switches but rather like line cards of the aggregation switch. FEXes extend the aggregation switch data plane to the top of each rack, while obeying a single control plane in its master switch, as shown in Figure 11-9.

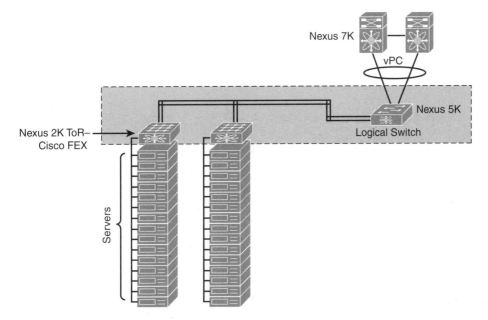

Figure 11-9 *Fabric Extenders (FEX)*

Because multiple FEXes and parent switches behave as a single aggregation switch, FEX usage reduces the number of managed switches and removes a layer in STP topology. Current-generation FEXes cannot switch traffic between the local ports. All traffic is forwarded to the parent switch. So, FEX usage is ideal when most of the traffic flows between the servers and network core, and not between the servers that are connected to the same FEX.

Nevertheless, an FEX-based design provides the benefits of a physical ToR design and a logical EoR design at the same time. As shown in Figure 11-10, this design reduces both the number of required connections to the aggregation and core layer and to the number of managed switches; it also reduces the STP domain.

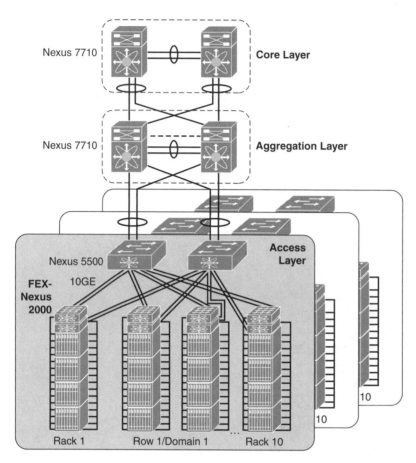

Figure 11-10 *DC LAN Connectivity Optimization with Cisco FEX*

Figure 11-11 shows the various possible connectivity models of the Cisco FEX (Cisco Nexus 2000 series and 5500 series switches).

Case Study 3: Three-Tier Data Center Network Architecture   387

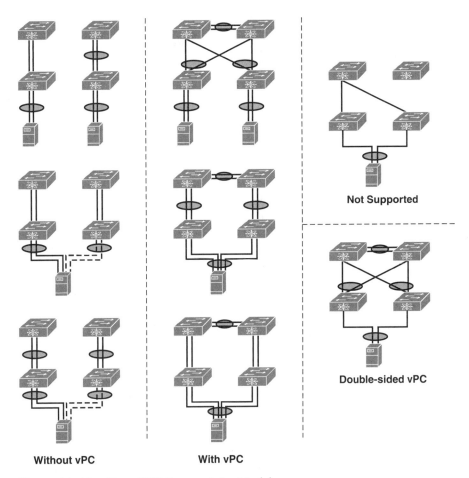

Figure 11-11 *Cisco FEX Connectivity Models*

Note You must refer to the data sheet of the Cisco Nexus 2000 series switch model before considering any of the previously mentioned connectivity models to ensure the selected switch model supports the intended connectivity model.

Furthermore, some of the Cisco FEX models (such as FEX-2232TM-E) enable you to extend the reach of 10G Ethernet/FCoE to a distributed line card (ToR). When FCoE is required at the host's access level, the connectivity models of the FEX to the upstream parent switch (for example, Nexus 5500 series) will be limited. Nexus 2232 needs to be single-homed to upstream Nexus 5000 (straight through N2K) to ensure SAN A and SAN B isolation, as shown in Figure 11-12.

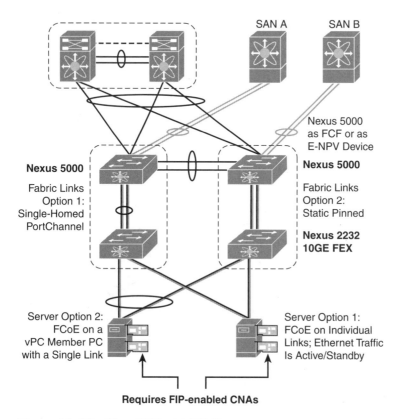

Figure 11-12 *Cisco FEX with FCoE*

> **Note** The FCoE Initialization Protocol (FIP) uses the native VLAN. Therefore, all FCoE links should be trunked to carry the FCoE VLAN and the native VLAN. Also, Generation 2 (FIP-enabled) CNAs are required for host connections to the Cisco Nexus 2232 Fabric Extender host interfaces.

Data Center High Availability

Relying solely on STP with this hierarchical DC LAN architecture will typically block some of the Layer 2 connections to prevent Layer 2 loops, rendering one-half of the data center connections useless.

As a network designer, you first should ask, "How can the blocked connections be put in use?" Hypothetically, careful planning of multiple STP instances can be considered as one of the possible solutions. However, practically, it is hard to maintain perfect load balancing in a data center. There is a better solution, which is based on bundling redundant connections between physical devices with PortChannel to reduce or completely remove the number of loops in Layer 2 topology. However, to bundle ports on a different chassis into a PortChannel with Multichassis EtherChannel (MEC), the two switches on the same layer must be bundled together into one logical unit. In an enterprise LAN, you can achieve this bundling by stacking (VSS, StackWise) physical switches in a single logical unit. However, neither of these two technologies is available on Cisco Nexus data center switches. Instead, Cisco Nexus data center switches introduce the virtual PortChannel vPC technology.

Contrary to VSS, vPC does not bundle two switches into one logical switch. vPC allows links that are physically connected to two different Cisco Nexus switches to appear as a single PortChannel to a third device. Unlike spanning tree, vPC provides Layer 2 multipathing and load balancing over both uplinks to two different switches. This offers true active/active uplinks, thus doubling the available network bandwidth, as shown in Figure 11-13.

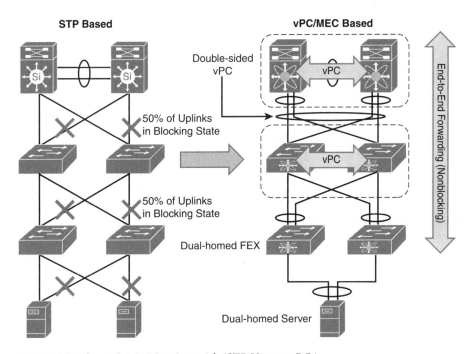

Figure 11-13 *DC LAN Design with (STP Versus vPC)*

vPC requires a peer keepalive link, which sends heartbeat messages between the two vPC peer devices and also the interswitch link between the vPC peers to be deployed as vPC peer-link, as shown in Figure 11-14.

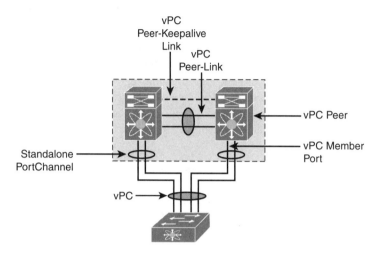

Figure 11-14 *vPC Components*

When fabric extenders are connected to data center switches bound with vPC, there can be different possible topologies to achieve access network redundancy. As shown in Figure 11-11, fabric extenders can be dual-homed when wired to data center switches bound with Enhanced vPC, supported by the Cisco Nexus 5500 series. This enables a dual-homed FEX topology, where any dual-homed FEX keeps forwarding traffic even if one of the data center switches fails.

In single-homed FEX topology, fabric extenders are connected to a single master (parent) switch, which does not require vPC between the master switches. However, to use MEC between the fabric extenders and the servers, data center switches must use vPC. However, with this topology, data center switch failure also results in fabric extender failure. There will be no service downtime because the servers are kept connected to the second data center switch's fabric extender (assuming the right NIC teaming is deployed at the server level).

Furthermore, Cisco vPC and VSS MEC technologies offer the flexibility to integrate pairs of nodes configured as VSS and vPC, providing an end-to-end forwarding (nonblocking) path, as shown in Figure 11-15. (For example, you may have existing Cisco catalyst switches deployed with VSS where vPC and VSS interoperability will offer investment protection, in this case, for the existing network equipment.)

Case Study 3: Three-Tier Data Center Network Architecture 391

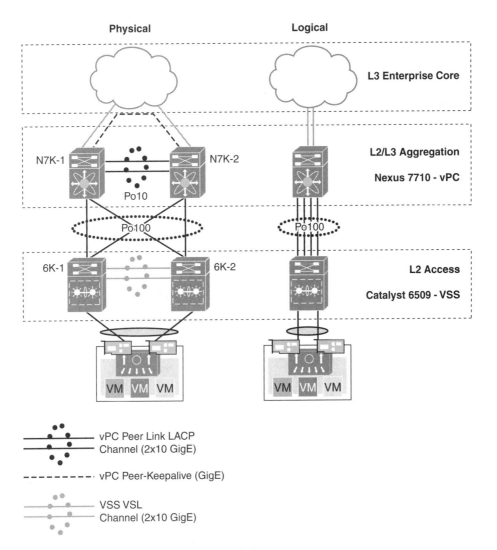

Figure 11-15 *vPC and VSS Interoperability*

> **Note** Although vPC eliminates the limitations of STP blocking, STP must be enabled as a protective mechanism if any misconfiguration or miscabling in the network occurs to avoid any Layer 2 loops that can lead to a blackout or degraded performance. Figure 11-16 shows the recommended STP configurations in a vPC environment. Nevertheless, it is strongly recommended that you enable STP as a protective mechanism in case of misconfiguration or miscabling.

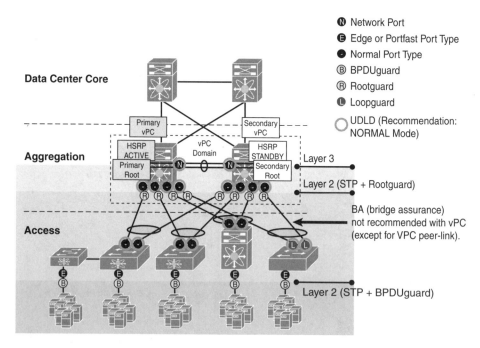

Figure 11-16 *STP Configurations in a vPC Environment*

Network Interface Controller Teaming

To provide redundancy, servers are typically connected to one or two switches with two redundant connections. As end nodes, servers do not forward frames and do not run STP. To utilize dual connections, servers use NIC teaming. The following are the two primary NIC teaming models (see Figure 11-17):

- **Active/passive NIC teaming:** Enables multiple network adapters to be placed into a team to prevent a connectivity loss if an active connection outage occurs. Active/passive-teamed NICs can be connected to a single switch or multiple switches without any additional requirements on the switch. However, because the passive NIC is not in use, it offers no bandwidth aggregation.

- **Active/active NIC teaming:** Enables multiple network adapters to be placed into a team. This way, you can improve the bandwidth by using bandwidth aggregation and prevent connectivity loss if an outage of one of the connections occurs. Active/active NIC teaming requires PortChannel configuration on the upstream switch and vPC or VSS MEC configuration on upstream switches if the server is connected to two different switches.

Case Study 3: Three-Tier Data Center Network Architecture   393

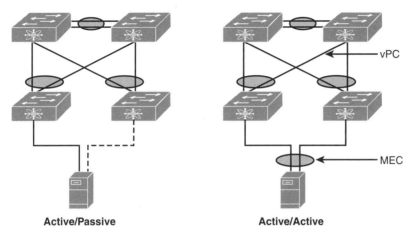

Figure 11-17 *Server NIC Teaming*

This concept is also applicable to virtualized environments in which each physical server hosts multiple virtual machines (VM), as shown in Figure 11-18.

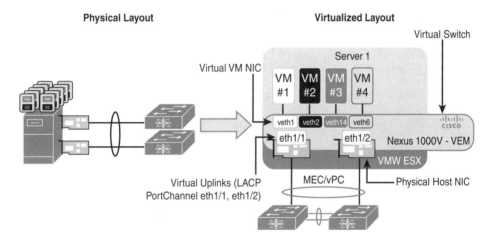

Figure 11-18 *NIC Teaming with Virtual Machines*

Note With active/active NIC teaming, PortChannel can be established with either manual configuration on the server and switch side or through the use of the Link Aggregation Control Protocol (LACP).

Summary

- The data center can be integrated with the enterprise core using the following architectures:
    - Two-tier architecture (LAN core and DC aggregation/access)
    - Three-tier architecture (LAN core, DC aggregation, and DC access)
- With tiered architecture, it is almost always recommended to place the demarcation point between Layer 2 and Layer 3 at the aggregation layer, along with DC services such as firewalls and load balancers.
- Different DC access architectures are available, including ToR, EoR, and Cisco FEX. Each has its advantages and limitations.
- Cisco FEX offers a flexible DC access design that supports various access architectures and connectivity models.
- High-availability mechanisms achieve highly available DC communication and avoid STP blocking limitations; they include vPC, MEC, dual-homed FEX, and dual-homed servers with NIC teaming.

Review Questions

After answering the following questions, refer to Appendix A, "Answers to Review Questions," for the answers.

1. Match the access layer designs/technologies with their properties.

Access Layer Designs/Technologies	Properties
Top of Rack	Simplifies STP topology, requires extensive cabling
End of Row	Reduces cabling, expands STP topology
Fabric Extenders	Reduces STP topology, does not allow local switching

2. Match the data center design model with its attributes.

DC Design Model	Attributes
Two-tier	Scalable and offers nonblocking solution
Three-tier	Limited scalability
Three tiers with vPC	Scalable; however, STP reduces the overall solution efficiency

3. Which NIC teaming statement is correct?
   a. Active/passive NIC teaming requires PortChannel configuration on the upstream switch.
   b. Active/active NIC teaming improves bandwidth using bandwidth aggregation.
   c. Active/active NIC teaming is possible only on links terminated on the same upstream switch.
   d. Active/passive NIC teaming is established using LACP.

4. Which statement is correct? (Select two.)
   a. Inter-VLAN routing at the core layer offers a more scalable and stable DC design.
   b. Inter-VLAN routing at the aggregation layer offers a better fault isolation design.
   c. vPC and VSS cannot be integrated.
   d. vPC and VSS provide the capability to be integrated.
   e. By using the Cisco Nexus series switch, you can either use vPC or VSS to configure MEC between access and distribution switches.

5. A small retail company wants to enhance its current DC performance. Which of the following would you suggest to this retailer? (Select two.)
   a. Use MSTP with VLAN load distribution across the aggregation switches.
   b. Consider MEC between the access and aggregation layers.
   c. Always consider links bundling between the different DC layers.
   d. Consider EoR architecture.
   e. Perform inter-VLAN routing at the core layer.

Chapter 12

New Trends and Techniques to Design Modern Data Centers

Upon completing this chapter, you will be able to

- Identify and explain the limitations of traditional data center network architectures
- Explain modern design techniques of data center networks
- Describe the different protocols and overlay protocols used in today's networks
- Define software-defined networking (SDN)
- Explain the benefits of SDN and the associated challenges
- Design a multitenant data center network

Preceding chapters discussed classical data center network design models, which are based on the multitiered design model. Today, applications and business demands are driving technology requirements and designs. This chapter discusses the changes in business and application needs and how they drive technological design requirements. Then it analyzes the various design approaches and protocols commonly used in response to these changes.

The Need for a New Network Architecture

As discussed in the preceding chapter, classical data centers are structured with a three-tier architecture that has core, aggregation, and access layers, or a two-tier collapsed core that has the aggregation and core layer functions combined into one layer. Smaller data centers may even take advantage of a single pair of switches. This architecture accommodates a north-south traffic pattern in which client data comes in from the WAN or Internet to be processed by a server in the data center and is then pushed back out of the data center. This is common for applications like web services, where most communication is between an external client and an internal server. The north-south traffic pattern permits hardware oversubscription because most traffic is funneled in and out through the lower-bandwidth WAN or Internet bottleneck.

Based on data center applications and service requirements, the traditional way of building hierarchical-tree–structured, or tiered, networks is not suited to the dynamic nature of modern computing and storage needs. The following computing trends shape the need for a new network architecture:

- **Changing traffic patterns:** The data center is shifting away from traditional client/server application architectures to models in which significantly more data is transferred from machine to machine. The result is a shift from north-south traffic patterns to more east-west traffic in the data center. Content from the enterprise also needs to be accessible at anytime from anywhere. In addition, many corporate IT departments are showing great interest in moving to public, private, or hybrid cloud environments.

- **The consumerization of IT:** Users are demanding more bring-your-own-device (BYOD) flexibility so that personal laptops, tablets, and smartphones can be used to access corporate information. A result of this trend is a greater emphasis on the protection of corporate data with security policies and enforcement.

- **The rise of cloud services:** Public cloud services available from companies such as Amazon.com, Microsoft, and Google have given corporate IT departments a glimpse of self-service IT and demonstrate how agile applications and services can be. Organizations are now demanding the same service levels from their own IT departments. However, unlike public cloud environments, private cloud environments need to meet strict security and compliance requirements, which cannot be sacrificed for increased agility.

- **Big data means more bandwidth:** Enterprises are investing in big data applications to facilitate better business decision making. However, these applications require massive parallel processing across hundreds or thousands of servers. The demand to handle huge data sets is placing greater stress and load on the network and driving the need for greater capacity.

Limitations of Current Networking Technology

The *Open Networking Foundation (ONF)* is a user-led organization dedicated to the promotion and adoption of software-defined networking (SDN). The ONF published a white paper titled "Software-Defined Networking: The New Norm for Networks."[1] This ONF paper discusses significant limitations of current networking technologies that must be overcome to meet modern IT requirements. These challenges are presented in the context of a traditional requirement—that is, providing stable, resilient, yet static connectivity. However, the computing trends mentioned earlier require networks to support rapid deployment of applications. They also require the network to scale to accommodate increased workloads with greater agility, while also keeping costs at a minimum. Thus, the traditional approach has substantial limitations, such as the following:[2]

- **Complexity that leads to stasis:** The abundance of networking protocols and features defined in isolation has greatly increased network complexity. The ONF paper states that each protocol is "solving a specific problem and without the benefit of any fundamental abstractions." In addition, old technologies were often recycled as quick fixes to address new business requirements. An example of this recycled approach is the loose use of VLANs in current networks. Initially, the purpose of VLANs was to create smaller broadcast domains. Today, VLANs are used as policy and security domains for isolation. This use has created complex dependencies that increase security risks and reduce agility because a change in security policy requires a change in the broadcast and forwarding domain, whereas a change in VLANs may also impact security policy.

- **Inconsistent policies:** Security and quality of service (QoS) policies in current networks need to be manually configured or scripted across hundreds or thousands of network devices. This requirement makes policy changes extremely complicated for organizations to implement without significant investment in scripting language skills or tools that can automate configuration changes. Manual configuration is prone to error and can lead to many hours of troubleshooting to discover which line of a security or QoS access control list (ACL) was entered incorrectly for a given device.

- **Limited scalability:** As application workloads change and demand for network bandwidth increases, the IT department either needs to be satisfied with an oversubscribed static network or needs to grow with the demands of the organization. Unfortunately, the majority of traditional networks are statically provisioned in such a way that increasing the number of endpoints, services, or bandwidth requires substantial planning and redesign of the network. Server virtualization and private cloud deployments are challenging IT networking professionals to reevaluate their architecture. Some may choose to massively overprovision the network to accommodate the dynamic nature of virtual machines, which can be deployed on demand and instantiated anywhere on the network, but most need to evaluate new ways to design the network.

- **Bandwidth aggregation:** With the classical three-tier architecture, east-west traffic between the workload within the data center residing in different subnets or point of delivery (POD) may end up traversing the data center access, aggregation, and core layers. This can typically lead to reduced bandwidth along the path; as the higher traffic goes into the hierarchy, the more path aggregation between all traffic flows will be. Also, this leads to increased latency.

The following section covers the architectures, protocols, and design techniques that aim to meet today's modern data center requirements and that aim to overcome the limitations.

Modern Data Center Design Techniques and Architectures

This section discusses the fundamental designs and protocols used today to overcome the concerns and limitations described in the preceding section for the traditional data center design model. You need to understand that each design or protocol discussed in this chapter may not individually overcome the design concerns and limitations of the traditional design model, and when this is the case, you should consider a combination of these elements to achieve the desired goal. For example, you might need to consider a spine-leaf architecture along with an overlay protocol such as VXLAN to achieve an agile and a flexible modern data center network in which you can achieve host mobility and maintain the same IP addressing no matter where the host is physically connected to the data center network and without hitting scalability limitations of the extended L2 VLANs design.

Chapter 13, "Cisco Application-Centric Infrastructure," explains how the Cisco Application-Centric Infrastructure (ACI) solution overcomes the limitations of traditional data center designs and how to meet the new trends and requirements of today's modern data centers using a policy-based approach that focuses on applications combined with automation, programmability, and centralized provisioning. This can help network operators to deploy the network based on application requirements in the form of policies and eliminate the need to translate to the complexity of current network constraints.

Note In this chapter you develop a foundational knowledge so that you understand ACI concepts and design. Therefore, you should read and understand the concepts and protocols covered in this chapter prior to reading Chapter 13.

Spine-Leaf Data Center Design

Spine-leaf topologies are based on the Clos network architecture. The term originates from Charles Clos at Bell Laboratories. In 1953, he published a paper describing a mathematical theory of a multipathing, nonblocking, multiple-stage network topology to switch telephone calls through.

Today, Clos's original thoughts on design are applied to the modern spine-leaf topology. Spine-leaf is typically deployed as two layers: *spines* (like an aggregation layer) and *leaves* (like an access layer), as shown in Figure 12-1. With the spine-leaf architecture (Clos), each leaf is one hop anyway from any other leaf switch; therefore, it promotes high-bandwidth, low-latency, nonblocking server-to-server connectivity.

Modern Data Center Design Techniques and Architectures 401

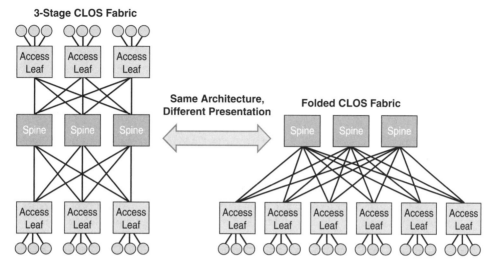

Figure 12-1 *Spine-leaf Architecture*

Leaf switches provide devices access to the fabric (the network of spine and leaf switches) and are typically deployed at the top of the rack. All devices connect to the leaf switches. Devices may include servers, Layer 4 to 7 services (firewalls and load balancers), and WAN or Internet routers. Leaf switches do not connect to other leaf switches. However, every leaf should connect to every spine in a full mesh. Some ports on the leaf will be used for end devices (typically at 1 Gb or 10 Gb), and some ports will be used for the spine connections (at 40 Gb or 100 Gb).

Spine switches connect to all leaf switches and are typically deployed at the end or middle of the row. Spine switches do not connect to other spine switches. Spines serve as backbone interconnects for leaf switches. Spines connect only to leaves.

All devices connected to the fabric are an equal number of hops away from one another. This delivers predictable latency and high bandwidth between servers. Figure 12-1 shows a typical spine-leaf design.

In this architecture, Cisco Nexus 9000 series switches enable data center operators of small to midsize networks to start with a few switches and implement a pay-as-you-grow model. When more access ports are needed, more leaves can be added. When more bandwidth is needed, more spines can be added. In both cases, there will be no need to do any change to the design, cabling, or addressing of the underlay infrastructure.

Furthermore, if you want to take this design model to the next step in the data center evolution, you should consider a virtual network overlay technology (also known as virtual overlay fabric). With this approach, you can still maintain Layer 2 reachability between servers without relying on STP and its inefficiencies. The next section covers network overlays in more detail.

Network Overlays

In a modern data center network, one of the common approaches to overcome some of the limitations mentioned previously is to use *networking overlay protocols*. This is primarily derived by the needs of today's data centers, where multitier applications need to communicate with other application tiers or services, no matter where the application is located physically within the data center network.

In general, the concept of an overlay refers to the capability to encapsulate packets sent by an application or service along with the targeted destination's location before sending it across the network. Then, when the packet arrives at the targeted destination, it will be decapsulated and delivered in its original format, such as with an 802.1Q tag. The encapsulation and decapsulation are facilitated by an overlay protocol that transforms the application's communication to be more location-independent, separating the location from the identity and facilitating the creation of multiple separate logical networks, as shown in Figure 12-2. Most common overlay protocols today use either MAC-in-MAC encapsulation, such as IETF Transparent Interconnection of Lots of Links (TRILL), and Cisco FabricPath. MAC-in-IP can be achieved using NVGRE or Virtual Extensible LAN (VXLAN). The following sections discuss Cisco FabricPath (FP) and VXLAN in more detail.

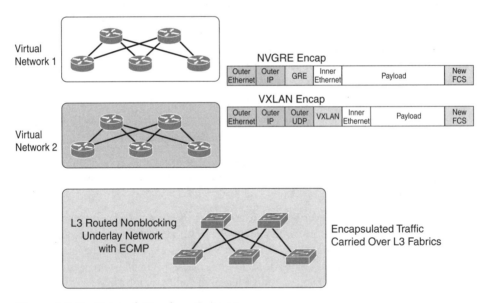

Figure 12-2 *Network Overlays Concept*

Cisco Fabric Path

Commonly, Layer 2 connectivity is required between data center switches. As you know from the previous chapter, using Spanning-Tree Protocol (STP) blocks all the redundant connections, as shown in Figure 12-3. As a result, switches forward frames based on

MAC table entries only through nonblocked links, resulting in suboptimal traffic flow and stressing nonblocked connections and other switches more than necessary, which will lead to inefficient links and bandwidth utilization.

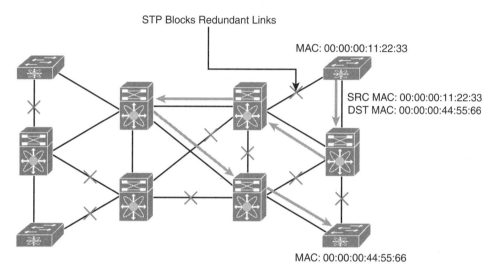

Figure 12-3 *STP Limitation in the DC Network*

In addition, even if you consider a multichassis link aggregation (mLAG) concept here, such as VSS or vPC, in most of the implementations, this concept limits your upstream switches/spine nodes to only two, as shown in Figure 12-4, and limits the data center network to scale out in large DC environments.

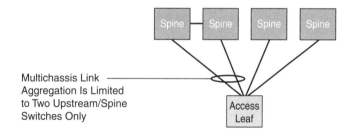

Figure 12-4 *mLAG Scale-out Limitation*

One of the network overlay technologies to overcome STP issues in such designs is Cisco FabricPath (FP). *Cisco FabricPath* technology, supported on Cisco Nexus data center switches, is the Cisco implementation of TRILL. Cisco FabricPath brings routing techniques from Layer 3 to solve Layer 2 loop problems.

Cisco FabricPath switching allows multipath networking at Layer 2 and encapsulates the entire Layer 2 frame with a new Cisco FabricPath header. Cisco FabricPath links are point to point. Devices encapsulate frames at the ingress edge port of the Cisco FabricPath network and de-encapsulate frames on the egress edge port of the Cisco FabricPath network. This new encapsulation allows the core of the Cisco FabricPath network to be hidden (through overlay technology) from the host state information, reducing the scaling requirements of Cisco FabricPath core devices.

Because Cisco FabricPath encompasses the entire Ethernet frame in a new encapsulation, all nodes on the Cisco FabricPath network need to support Cisco FabricPath to look up and forward the frame throughout the rest of the network. Cisco FabricPath uses extensions to the Intermediate System-to-Intermediate System (IS-IS) protocol to exchange unicast and multicast location and reachability information and to forward traffic in the network using Cisco FabricPath headers. (IS-IS forms the underlay network for the FabricPath and enables the underlay fabric to be a nonblocking Layer 3-routed network with ECMP forwarding.) Because IS-IS is a dynamic link-state routing protocol, it can detect changes in the network topology and calculate loop-free routes to all other nodes in the network, with each node having a complete link-state database that describes the state of the entire network.

To better understand the forwarding logic of the Cisco FabricPath, now consider the sample scenario shown in Figure 12-5 and outlined in the following steps.

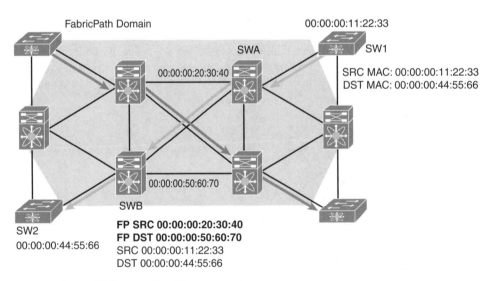

Figure 12-5 *FP Forwarding Figure*

Step 1. SW1 sends a frame with the source MAC address 00:00:00:11:22:33 and destination MAC address 00:00:00:22:33:44 to the SWA switch in the FabricPath domain.

Step 2. SWA looks into its Layer 2 routing table that is populated by a control protocol, which is built on top of an IS-IS routing protocol. It finds out that the best route to a destination MAC address leads through SWB. SWA adds a FabricPath header to the existing frame with a FabricPath source MAC set to its own MAC address and FabricPath destination MAC set to SWB MAC. SWA then sends the frame to SWB.

Step 3. SWB receives the frame and removes the FabricPath header. It then sends the frame to destination SW2.

In addition, FabricPath forwarding is performed only inside a FabricPath domain. FabricPath switches that connect to hosts or classical switches are called edge switches. Edge switches forward frames to other FabricPath switches using FabricPath routing, while performing classic switching with classic switches outside the FabricPath domain. To avoid the need for STP between the FabricPath domain and classic switch, you can use vPC with MEC. You can achieve this by using a configuration construct called an emulated switch. The emulated switch implementations in FabricPath, where two FabricPath edge switches provide a vPC to a third-party device, is called vPC+, as shown in Figure 12-6.

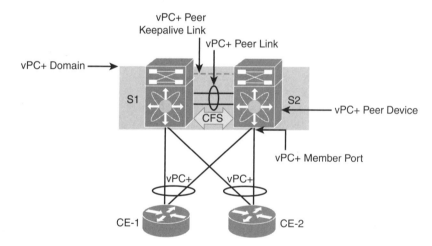

- S1 and S2 are vPC+ peer devices. vPC+ domain supports two vPC+ peer devices.
- The vPC+ peer link is the interswitch link between the two vPC+ peer devices.
  The vPC+ peer link is used for both data traffic and control-plane information synchronization.
- CFS runs over the vPC peer link to synchronize information between vPC+ peer devices (MAC address, vPC+ state, IGMP snooping). Only MAC addresses learned through vPC+ member ports are synchronized across the two vPC+ peer devices.
- The vPC+ peer keepalive link is used to monitor the presence of the neighbor vPC+ peer device.
- vPC+ is a combination of two vPC+ member ports: one vPC+ member port on S1 and one vPC+ member port on S2.

Figure 12-6 *vPC+ Domain Components*

Figure 12-7 shows vPC+ possible topologies.

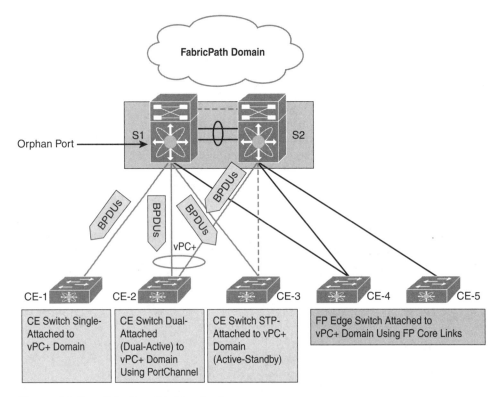

Figure 12-7 *vPC+ Possible Topologies*

> **Note** Although CiscoFabric Path is based on the same concept as the industry standard TRILL, Cisco FabricPath offers more capabilities. For example, it can optimize DCN efficiency and manageability by considering the FabricPath multitopology design. FabricPath also enhances FHRP gateway services by providing the four active HSRP peers in active-active mode (also known as Anycast HSRP), whereas TRILL forwards traffic based on the traditional active-standby mode, as shown in Figure 12-8.

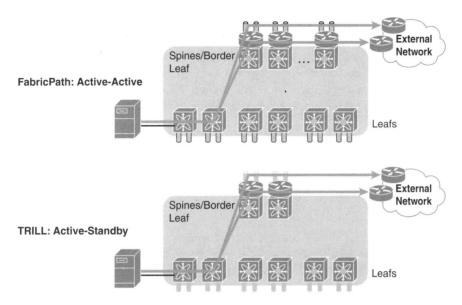

Figure 12-8 *FHRP: TRILL Versus FP*

Virtual Extensible LAN (VXLAN)

VXLAN is an encapsulation method that extends Layer 2 traffic over a Layer 3 or an IP-based network. VXLAN relies on multicast in the network core. Cisco, in partnership with other leading vendors, proposed the VXLAN standard to the IETF as a solution to the data center network challenges posed by traditional VLAN technology. The VXLAN standard provides for elastic workload placement and higher scalability of Layer 2 segmentation that is required by today's application demands.

As its name indicates, VXLAN is designed to provide the same Ethernet Layer 2 network services as VLAN does today, but with greater extensibility and flexibility. Compared to VLAN, VXLAN offers the following benefits:

- **Flexible placement of multitenant segments throughout the data center:** It provides a solution to extend Layer 2 segments over the underlying shared network infrastructure so that tenant workload can be placed across physical pods in the data center.

- **Higher scalability to address more Layer 2 segments:** VLANs use a 12-bit VLAN ID to address Layer 2 segments, which results in limiting scalability of only 4094 VLANs. VXLAN uses a 24-bit segment ID known as the VXLAN network identifier (VNID), which enables up to 16 million VXLAN segments to coexist in the same administrative domain.

- **Better utilization of available network paths in the underlying infrastructure:** VLAN uses the Spanning-Tree Protocol for loop prevention, which doesn't use one-half of the network links in a network by blocking redundant paths. In contrast, VXLAN packets are transferred through the underlying network based on its Layer 3 header and can take complete advantage of Layer 3 routing, equal-cost multipath (ECMP) routing, and link aggregation protocols to use all available paths.

VXLAN is a Layer 2 overlay scheme over a Layer 3 network and is categorized as a MAC-in-IP overlay protocol; specifically, it uses MAC-in-UDP encapsulation to provide a means to extend Layer 2 segments across the data center network. VXLAN is a solution to support a flexible, large-scale multitenant environment over a shared common physical infrastructure. The transport protocol over the physical data center network is IP plus UDP.

VXLAN defines a MAC-in-UDP encapsulation scheme in which the original Layer 2 frame has a VXLAN header added and is then placed in a UDP-IP packet. With this MAC-in-UDP encapsulation, VXLAN tunnels a Layer 2 network over a Layer 3 network.

VXLAN introduces an 8-byte VXLAN header that consists of a 24-bit VNID and a few reserved bits. The VXLAN header, together with the original Ethernet frame, goes in the UDP payload. The 24-bit VNID is used to identify Layer 2 segments and to maintain Layer 2 isolation between the segments. With all 24 bits in VNID, VXLAN can support 16 million LAN segments.

Note Because of the MAC-to-UDP encapsulation, VXLAN introduces a 50-byte overhead to the original frames. Therefore, the maximum transmission unit (MTU) in the transport network needs to be increased by 50 bytes. If the overlays use a 1500-byte MTU, the transport network needs to be configured to accommodate 1550-byte packets at a minimum. In the transport network, jumbo-frame support is required if the overlay applications tend to use frame sizes larger than 1500 bytes.

VXLAN Tunnel Endpoint

VXLAN uses *VXLAN tunnel endpoint (VTEP)* devices to map tenants' end devices to VXLAN segments and to perform VXLAN encapsulation and de-encapsulation. Each VTEP function has two interfaces: one is a switch interface on the local LAN segment to support local endpoint communication through bridging, and the other is an IP interface to the transport IP network, as shown in Figure 12-9.

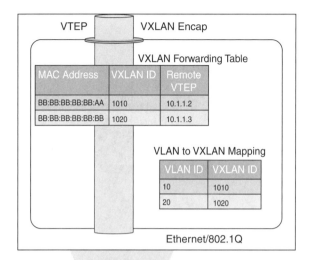
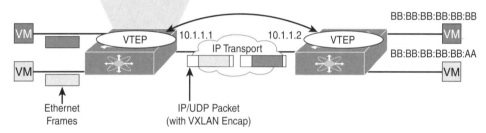

Figure 12-9 *VXLAN Tunnel Endpoint*

The IP interface has a unique IP address that identifies the VTEP device on the transport IP network known as the infrastructure VLAN. The VTEP device uses this IP address to encapsulate Ethernet frames and transmits the encapsulated packets to the transport network through the IP interface. A VTEP device also discovers the remote VTEPs for its VXLAN segments and learns remote MAC Address-to-VTEP mappings through its IP interface. The functional components of VTEPs and the logical topology that is created for Layer 2 connectivity across the transport IP network are shown in Figure 12-10.

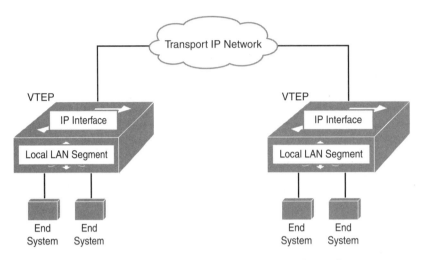

Figure 12-10 *VTEP Functional Components (Logical Interfaces)*

Figure 12-10 shows that each VTEP has two interfaces:

- Local LAN interface
- Interface to the transport IP network

The IP interface has a unique IP address that identifies the VTEP on the transport IP network. The VXLAN segments are independent of the underlying network topology; conversely, the underlying IP network between VTEPs is independent of the VXLAN overlay. It routes the encapsulated packets based on the outer IP address header, which has the initiating VTEP as the source IP address and the terminating VTEP as the destination IP address.

In Figure 12-9, you can see that each VTEP has two tables that it relies on when frames need to be encapsulated. When a frame enters VTEP on the LAN side, VTEP looks into the VLAN to VXLAN map to determine into which VXLAN the frame will be encapsulated. VTEP then looks into the MAC to VTEP map and compares the frame's destination MAC address and its VXLAN to determine the IP address of the remote VTEP. The frame is then encapsulated in a stateless VXLAN tunnel and sent over an IP transport network to the remote VTEP IP address using UDP.

If VTEP receives a broadcast frame or a frame with a destination MAC address that is not present in MAC to a VTEP map, VTEP floods the frame to an IP multicast group. Every VXLAN has an assigned IP multicast group, and all VTEPs with nodes in that VXLAN are joined to that multicast group. This behavior is analogue to the traditional Ethernet model, but it limits flooding only to VTEPs that listen to assigned multicast IP. The following section covers the VXLAN forwarding in more details.

> **Note** VTEP devices must use an identical destination UDP port. However, some switches introduce a level of entropy in the source UDP port. When the transport network uses an ECMP or LACP hashing algorithm that takes the UDP source port as an input for hashing, this achieves the best load-sharing results for VXLAN encapsulated traffic.

Remote VTEP Discovery and Tenant Address Learning

The typical VXLAN deployment (such as on Cisco Nexus 9000 series switches in non-ACI mode) uses existing Layer 2 mechanisms (flooding and dynamic MAC address learning) to do the following:[3]

- Transport broadcast, unknown unicast, and multicast traffic (BUM traffic).
- Discover remote VTEPs.
- Learn remote host MAC addresses and MAC-to-VTEP mappings for each VXLAN segment.

For these traffic types, IP multicast reduces the flooding scope of the set of hosts that are participating in the VXLAN segment. Each *VXLAN segment*, or VNID, is mapped to an IP multicast group in the transport IP network. Each VTEP device is independently configured and joins this multicast group as an IP host through the Internet Group Management Protocol (IGMP). The IGMP joins trigger Protocol Independent Multicast (PIM) joins and signaling through the transport network for the particular multicast group. The multicast distribution tree for this group is built through the transport network based on the locations of participating VTEPs.[4]

Based on the previous VXLAN deployment model, it uses the classic Layer 2 data plane flooding and learning mechanisms for remote VTEP discovery and tenant address learning. For example, in the scenario shown Figure 12-11, the tenant VXLAN segment has VNID 10 and uses the multicast group 239.1.1.1 over the transport network. It has three participating VTEPs in the data center. Assume that no address learning has been performed between locations. End System A (with IP-A, MAC-A) starts IP communication with End System B (with IP-B, MAC-B).

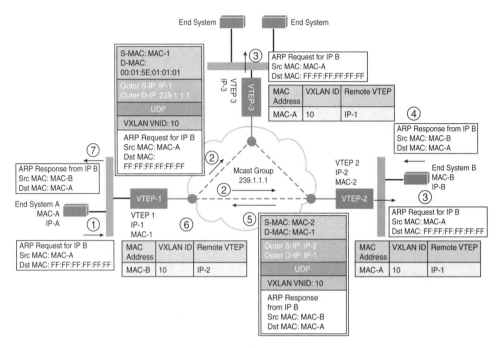

Figure 12-11 *Remote VETP Discovery*

The sequence of steps is as follows (refer to Figure 12-11):[5]

Step 1. End System A sends out an Address Resolution Protocol (ARP) request for IP-B on its Layer 2 VXLAN.

Step 2. VTEP-1 receives the ARP request. It does not yet have a mapping for IP-B. VTEP-1 encapsulates the ARP request in an IP multicast packet and forwards it to the VXLAN multicast group. The encapsulated multicast packet has the IP address of VTEP-1 as the source IP address and the VXLAN multicast group address as the destination IP address.

Step 3. The IP multicast packet is distributed to all members in the tree. VTEP-2 and VTEP-3 receive the encapsulated multicast packet because they've joined the VXLAN multicast group. They de-encapsulate the packet and check its VNID in the VXLAN header. If it matches their configured VXLAN segment VNID, they forward the ARP request to their local VXLAN. They also learn the IP address of VTEP-1 from the outer IP address header and inspect the packet to learn the MAC address of End System A, placing this mapping in the local table.

Step 4. End System B receives the ARP request forwarded by VTEP-2. It responds with its own MAC address (MAC-B) and learns the IP-A-to-MAC-A mapping.

Step 5. VTEP-2 receives the ARP reply of End System B that has MAC-A as the destination MAC address. It now knows about MAC-A-to-IP-1 mapping. It can use the unicast tunnel to forward the ARP reply back to VTEP-1. In the encapsulated unicast packet, the source IP address is IP-2, and the destination IP address is IP-1. The ARP reply is encapsulated in the UDP payload.

Step 6. VTEP-1 receives the encapsulated ARP reply from VTEP-2. It de-encapsulates and forwards the ARP reply to End System A. It also learns the IP address of VTEP-2 from the outer IP address header and inspects the original packet to learn MAC-B-to-IP-2 mapping.

Step 7. Subsequent IP packets between End Systems A and B are unicast forwarded, based on the mapping information on VTEP-1 and VTEP-2, using the VXLAN tunnel between them.

VTEP-1 can optionally perform proxy ARPs for subsequent ARP requests for IP-B to reduce the flooding over the transport network.

VXLAN Control-Plane Optimization

The initial IETF VXLAN standards (RFC 7348) defined a multicast-based flood-and-learn VXLAN without a control plane. It relied on data-driven flood-and-learn behavior for remote VXLAN tunnel endpoint (VTEP) peer discovery and remote end-host learning. The overlay broadcast, unknown unicast, and multicast traffic are encapsulated into multicast VXLAN packets and transported to remote VTEP switches through the underlay multicast forwarding. Flooding in such a deployment can present a challenge for the scalability of the solution. The requirement to enable multicast capabilities in the underlay network also presents a challenge because some organizations do not want to enable multicast in their data centers or WANs.

To overcome the limitations of the flood-and-learn VXLAN as defined in RFC 7348, organizations can use *Multiprotocol Border Gateway Protocol Ethernet Virtual Private Network (MP-BGP EVPN)* as the control plane for VXLAN. The IETF has defined MP-BGP EVPN as the standards-based control plane for VXLAN overlays. The MP-BGP EVPN control plane provides protocol-based VTEP peer discovery and end-host reachability information distribution that allows more scalable VXLAN overlay network designs suitable for private and public clouds. The MP-BGP EVPN control plane introduces a set of features that reduce or eliminate traffic flooding in the overlay network and enable optimal forwarding for both west-east and south-north traffic.[6]

The MP-BGP EVPN control plane offers the following main benefits:[7]

- The MP-BGP EVPN protocol is based on industry standards, allowing multivendor interoperability.

- It enables control-plane learning of end-host Layer 2 and Layer 3 reachability information, enabling organizations to build more robust and scalable VXLAN overlay networks.

- It uses the proven, mature MP-BGP VPN technology to support scalable multitenant VXLAN overlay networks.

- The EVPN address family carries both Layer 2 and Layer 3 reachability information, thus providing integrated bridging and routing in VXLAN overlay networks.

- It minimizes network flooding through protocol-based host MAC/IP route distribution and Address Resolution Protocol (ARP) suppression on the local VTEPs.

- It provides optimal forwarding for east-west and north-south traffic and supports workload mobility with the distributed anycast function.

- It provides VTEP peer discovery and authentication, mitigating the risk of rogue VTEPs in the VXLAN overlay network.

- It provides mechanisms for building active-active multihoming at Layer 2.

Note Although many of the MP-BGP EVPN functions and design are platform-independent, the Cisco Nexus 9000 series is the first switch platform that supports this protocol as a VXLAN control plane when operating in standalone mode (non-ACI).

Software-Defined Networking

Traditional networks consist of several devices (for example, routers, switches, and more), each equipped with its software and networking functionality:

- The *data plane* is responsible for the forwarding of frames or packets.

- The *control plane* is responsible for controlling the forwarding tables that are used by the data plane. The control plane of routers and switches has seen enormous development in the past few decades, which gives the network good capabilities but also increases complexity. This complexity has been further increased by the introduction of modern solutions and requirements such as mobility, cloud, bring your own device (BYOD), enhanced security requirements, and so on.

The control plane consumes more hardware resources because it runs on CPU, whereas the data plane runs on dedicated hardware. Based on that, the control plane is the intelligence of the network element, whereas the data plane (also referred to as the forwarding plane) is responsible for receiving and forwarding packets. Table 12-1 compares the network control plane and data plane.

Table 12-1 *Control Plane Versus Data Plane*

Processing Plane	Where It Runs	How Fast These Processes Run	Type of Processes Performed
Control Plane	Switch CPU (in the software)	Thousands of packets per second	Routing protocols, Spanning-Tree Protocol, SYSLOG, authentication authorization accounting, netflow data export, CLI, SNMP
Data Plane	Dedicated Hardware ASICs	Millions or billions of packets per second	Layers 2 and 3 switching, MPLS forwarding, VRF forwarding, QOS marking, classification, policing, netflow collection, security access control lists

Figure 12-12 shows how the SDN architecture changes the networking paradigm by removing "intelligence" from individual devices and transferring it to a central controller. In other words, network control is decoupled from forwarding and is directly programmable through a central controller.

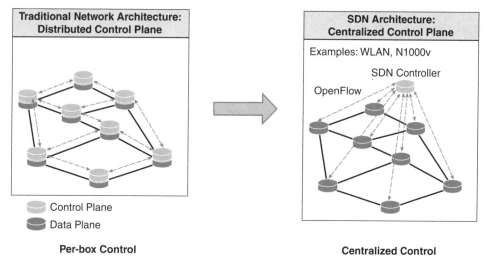

Figure 12-12 *Traditional Network Architecture Versus SDN Architecture*

The typical controller that is based on ONF standards uses OpenFlow to control individual devices (southbound API) and provide an abstracted network view to upstream applications using a northbound API, as shown in Figure 12-13. This SDN approach enables network operators to deploy services and policies centrally to meet the rapidly changing needs of today's businesses, without having to visit every switch or router in the network.

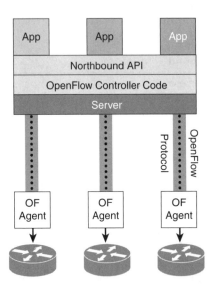

Figure 12-13 *ONF OpenFlow*

How SDN Can Help

As you know from previous discussions, the new trends and evolution of applications' needs are directly affecting the architecture and design models and directions of today's data center and enterprise networks. Therefore, SDN must factor for the new technology requirements (highlighted earlier in this chapter), where network architectures need to support a higher level of scalability and more sophisticated policies to cope with these changes. The capability to automate and push these policies in a simplified and centralized manner is key to providing a manageable solution at a scale.

Various surveys by networking publications, plus informational RFCs, such as RFC 3535, list the requirements that end users have associated with SDN:

- Capability to automate provisioning and management.
- Flexibility of resource utilization that enables easy provisioning, modification, or releasing of resources.
- Improved security that offers more flexible security service insertion that goes beyond a simple perimeter security concept at the edge of the network.
- Application awareness in network management to enable applications to easily interact with the network or network management to acquire the required resources from the network.

- Increased scalability. The scalability of physical resources should enable seamless modifications in the underlying infrastructure without the need for complex infrastructure management.

- Need for networks to be configured as a whole with the capability to implement network-wide policies.

- Support for creation and dynamic movement of virtual machines. Mobility of resources enables provisioned resources to be mobile internally or even be able to move to external (for example, cloud) locations.

- Support for creation of a private or hybrid cloud.

- Need for networks to be configured as a whole.

- Need for text-based configuration for simplified revision control

- Network-wide management that is required to enable an application to manage services end-to-end. This means a need for network management tools more advanced than Simple Network Management Protocol (SNMP) and a command-line interface (CLI).

- Abstraction of devices and network technologies that enable software developers to create solutions that integrate with network management without needing in-depth knowledge of the underlying network topology and the technologies that are used in it.

According to ONF, the most important aspects of SDN are "network operators and administrators" who can "programmatically configure this simplified network abstraction rather than having to hand-code tens of thousands of lines of configuration scattered among thousands of devices. In addition, leveraging the SDN controller's centralized intelligence, IT can alter network behavior in real-time and deploy new applications and network services in a matter of hours or days."[8]

Note OpenFlow is the ONF standard; however, it is not necessary for an SDN solution.

Selection Criteria of SDN Solutions

The preceding sections covered the primary drivers for the need for data center architectures and design, along with SDN and the benefits for modern data center requirements. This section highlights the primary factors that you, as a network designer, need to consider when selecting or evaluating an SDN solution. Many factors should be taken into account when selecting any technology solution; however, for SDN, you should consider the following minimum points:

> **Note** The following factors are only technology related and are not intended to decide whether SDN is the right solution for you or whether your organization is ready to consider SDN.

- **Policy-based centralized control:** One of the primary promises and benefits of an SDN concept is centralized provisioning and network programmability, where a network administrator can define and push configurations, policies, and more from the SDN controller without the need to configure every single device in the data forwarding path. That said, it is critical to understand that this does not mean you must have separation between them. Actually, some protocols and technology solutions achieve the SDN vision without taking off the intelligence from the network component. In the following chapter, you will see how the Cisco ACI with its declarative SDN controller model takes the SDN to the next level.

- **SDN controller characteristics:** As you know from the preceding sections, the SDN controller is a vital key element of the SDN architecture and there could be a variety of SDN controllers to consider when selecting your SDN solution. As a simple rule, if you consider a proprietary controller or controller that supports only a limited SDN policy model and vendors (not multivendor-capable), you will be limited with the flexibility and capabilities of this SDN solution. In other words, you need an SDN controller that can interoperate and integrate with different vendors as well as provide the capability to create and push sophisticated policies centrally that align with application needs and business polices. For example, the Cisco ACI enables network operators to produce complex polices using a simplified graphical user interface (GUI), and it can be pushed later to the data center fabric switches. (In a few minutes, you can create and rule out end-to-end data center communication and policies.) In addition, from a multivendor interoperability point of view, currently a number of ecosystem partners have become ACI-compliant, including F5, Citrix, Check Point, and others.

- **Capability to integrate with automation tools:** In today's cloud-based and multitenant virtualized data centers, automation is one of the key elements an SDN solution must support. Integration between the SDN controller and cloud automation tools means that data center operators will be able to instruct individual infrastructure components (switches, servers, firewalls, and so on) to align with other applications and service needs in an automated manner. For example, Cisco has developed an open source plug-in for OpenStack Neutron that enables OpenStack tenants to transparently configure and manage a network based on the Cisco ACI. This plug-in, Cisco Application Policy Infrastructure Controller (APIC), automatically translates OpenStack Neutron API commands for networks, subnets, routers, and so on into an ACI application network profile.

- **Flexibility to integrate with security services:** One of the main concerns associated with adoption of an SDN solution is security. Considering an SDN solution and controller that offer the flexibility to integrate with various types of network security services such as firewalls and IPS (both physical and virtual nodes) from different vendors will, to a large extent, help maintain current levels of the security model with more optimized and automated provisioning and manageability approaches.

SDN Requirements

SDN defines a set of requirements that must be met to provide the required benefits:

- Application awareness in network management enables applications to easily interact with the network or network management to acquire the required resources from the network.

- Network-wide management is required to enable an application to manage services end to end.

- Abstraction of devices and network technologies enables software developers to create solutions that integrate with network management without having in-depth knowledge of the underlying network topology and the technologies that are used in it.

- Flexibility of resource utilization enables easy provisioning, modification, or releasing of resources.

- Mobility of resources enables provisioned resources to be mobile either internally or even be able to move to external (for example, cloud) locations.

- Scalability of physical resources should enable seamless modifications in the underlying infrastructure without the need for complex infrastructure management.

SDN Challenges

In general, one of the main problems with SDN today is that it is not mature enough compared to the existing technologies used in enterprise environments. Today's routers and switches are packed with features enabling efficient and secure communication. The SDN environment cannot guarantee similar levels of network services by using available SDN controllers and applications. Another important aspect in the SDN approach requires the use of "dumb" switches that support OpenFlow and expect to be told by the controller what to do. These switches, also called white box switches, are generic hardware with reduced control and management features when compared to standard switches.[9]

Although SDN, software-based virtual overlays, and OpenFlow present some interesting solutions for both traditional and emerging computing workloads. Today, only a small number of data centers have adopted software overlays and OpenFlow in their production environments (at press time). This lack of adoption can be attributed to a new set of challenges, including the following:[10]

- **New operational complexities:** Software-based virtual overlays are difficult to manage and troubleshoot. The software-based virtual overlay approach cannot address the complexity of managing the underlying physical infrastructure. The fundamental problem is that they have little or no relationship with the underlying physical infrastructure. For instance, if there is any drop in the underlay network, this cannot easily be traced back to the service or application that was affected. Furthermore, the software-based virtual overlay may be managed by a different team, with a different skillset, that isn't equipped to troubleshoot end-to-end network connectivity issues, leading to finger-pointing across IT operations departments and possibly vendors. This drawback is potentially more severe in traditional networks, in which flexibility is limited, but at least such networks have predictability and deterministic points of failure for which a single IT operations group takes ownership.

- **OpenFlow protocols that are too primitive and concrete for the data center:** OpenFlow in a network switch applies a match function on the incoming packet (typically based on an existing network field attribute such as a source MAC address or destination IP address) and then takes some form of action, which may depend on the switch implementation but typically involves forwarding the packet out through a given physical or logical port.

- For most data center use cases, such detailed control is not required, because bandwidth (and hence paths) in the data center is typically abundant. Therefore, detailed path decisions based on network header parameters may not be needed and may incur unnecessary overhead for data center network administrators to manage.

- In addition, the OpenFlow protocol assumes a particular hardware architecture using a series of generic table lookups that generate actions to apply to the packet. This specific view of the underlying hardware architecture limits scalability and portability. A higher level of abstraction allows different specific hardware architectures to provide specific benefits while still meeting the requirements of the APIs.

- **Merchant silicon that is not optimized for OpenFlow today:** Most merchant silicon available in the market today has been optimized for general data center workloads. Typically, such deployments mandate allocation of a large amount of memory to forwarding tables to perform longest-prefix match and adjacency, Address Resolution Protocol (ARP), and MAC and IP address binding lookups; and a finite amount of memory to ACLs, typically using ternary content-addressable memory (TCAM) that is optimized for masking, packet matching, and action sets. OpenFlow tables use the latter form of memory in switches. Unfortunately, forwarding memory is not easily changeable with ACL memory, so the total amount of memory available to install flow entries in today's modern merchant silicon is somewhat limited. As mentioned earlier, if any misses occur, packets may be unexpectedly dropped or forwarded to the SDN controller for further processing.

- **Security challenges:** Anyone with access to the servers that host the control software can potentially control the entire network (for more details, refer to Chapter 22, "Designing Enterprise Infrastructure Security"). Several security features that are typically deployed in enterprise networks will not fit into a controller-based environment. Administrative access control that is traditionally performed by each individual device will no longer scale because you perform bulk transactions through a controller, which in turn may execute many commands on several devices.

Furthermore, the traditional AAA model is replaced by RBAC in central controllers, allowing granular access control by mapping user groups to roles, which in turn defines privileges on the central system (not on individual devices). In addition, enterprises also internally organize their IT departments into so-called silos, such as the network, server, storage, and security departments. These departments have traditionally exhibited a level of independence that allowed them to build their own systems to manage their part of the IT environment. With SDN, you want to be able to have simple end-to-end management of services, which touches all aspects of the environment—servers, storage, network, and so on.

Consequently, although a typical OpenFlow-based SDN architecture can bring several benefits to data center operators, it may introduce a new set of limitations because it lacks scalability, visibility, and security and is associated with complexity and disjoint overlays when used in large-scale data center networks. Therefore, Cisco introduced a new approach and architecture that is driven from the SDN concept with more emphasis on the most important part in the data center: it is an application called the Application-Centric Infrastructure (ACI). Chapter 13 covers the Cisco ACI in more detail and how it can help network architects and operators overcome the limitations and complexities of the traditional as well as the typical OpenFlow-based SDN data center solutions.

Direction of Nontraditional SDN

When you design an enterprise or data center network environment using SDN principles, you should consider the following design directions:

- Reuse existing infrastructure (investment protection).

- Reuse existing technologies (mature) instead of increasing risks using OpenFlow.

- Use overlay networking to enable application-driven end-to-end connectivity (for example, VLANs, VXLAN, Cisco Intelligent WAN [IWAN]).

- Use an orchestrator to enable open programmability (for example, representational state transfer [REST]) and provide abstraction of network devices and topologies (simplification of service provisioning by using open APIs).

- Choose the suitable Cisco products and software-defined networking (SDN) controller to optimize the management of the targeted environment:

  - Cisco Application Policy Infrastructure Controller (Cisco APIC) for the Data Center

  - Cisco Application Policy Infrastructure Controller Enterprise Module (Cisco APIC-EM) for WAN and Access

> **Note** *REST* is an architecture style for designing networked applications. The idea is that, rather than using complex mechanisms such as The Common Object Request Broker Architecture (CORBA), Remote Procedure Call (RPC), or Simple Object Access Protocol (SOAP) to connect between machines, simple HTTP is used to make calls between machines.

Multitenant Data Center

Virtualization of compute and storage resources adds a layer of abstraction, unifying data center resources into a single resource cloud and enabling resource sharing across and outside the organization. Sharing of physical resources among different entities, however, results in security and resource overutilization risks. Logical isolation of shared virtual resources is called multitenancy. In such an environment, data center resources and traffic paths should be logically separated in multiple tenants to achieve scalable workload distribution and fulfill security demands.

A *tenant* is a user community with some level of shared affinity. A tenant might be a customer in an IaaS cloud. Within an enterprise, a tenant may be a business unit, department, or workgroup. Or when a data center hosts a multitiered application, a tenant could be a single application layer (for instance, a web, application, or database layer). Deploying multiple tenants in a shared, common infrastructure optimizes resource utilization at lower cost but requires designs that address secure tenant separation to ensure end-to-end path isolation and meet tenant requirements.

Secure Tenant Separation

A *multitenant data center* separates multiple resources: network, compute, storage, and application. Network separation is achieved with the use of different path isolation techniques to logically divide a shared infrastructure into multiple (per tenant) virtual networks.

Path isolation is implemented in end-to-end fashion across the multiple hierarchical layers of the infrastructure and includes the following (see Figure 12-14):

- **Network Layer 3 separation (core/aggregation layers):** VRF-Lite implemented at core and aggregation layers provides per tenant isolation at Layer 3, with separate dedicated per tenant routing and forwarding tables ensuring that no intertenant traffic within the data center will be allowed, unless explicitly configured.

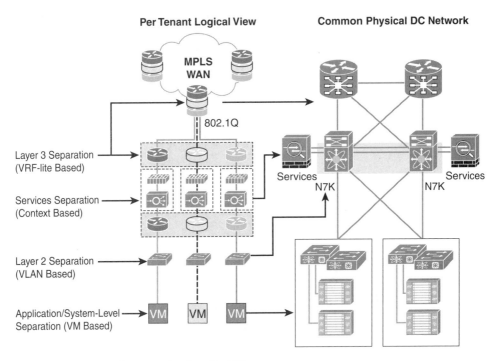

Figure 12-14 *Multitenant End-to-End Figure*

- **Network Layer 2 separation (access, virtual access):** VLANs provide isolation and identification of tenant traffic across the Layer 2 domain, and more generally, across shared links throughout the infrastructure.

- **Network services separation (services core, compute):** On a physical appliance or service module form factors, dedicated contexts or zones provide the means for virtualized security, load balancing, NAT, and SSL offload services and the application of unique per tenant policies at the VLAN level of granularity. Similarly, dedicated virtual appliances provide for unique per tenant services within the compute layer of the infrastructure at the virtual machine level of granularity.

Layer 3 Separation with VRF-Lite

Tenant separation on Layer 2 is done using VLANs. Virtual routing and forwarding (VRF) achieves a similar separation on Layer 3. As you know from Chapter 8, "Service Provider–Managed VPNs," *VRF* is a technology that allows a router to hold multiple independent routing tables. Interfaces are assigned to a certain VRF to form an isolated network path.

A side benefit of separated routing and forwarding instances is the support for overlapping IP addresses. Overlapping IP address space is common in a public cloud, in a merger, or in other situations involving IP addressing transitions in private enterprises.

In Figure 12-15, traffic that enter a core switch in the ingress direction through the interface that is assigned to VRF A is destined to the 192.168.0.100. The core switch performs a lookup in the VRF A routing table and forwards traffic to the aggregation switch through the Layer 3 interface that is assigned to VRF A. The Layer 3 interface can be either a physical port or a VLAN SVI. When the DC aggregation switch receives traffic through the Layer 3 interface that is assigned to VRF A, it performs a lookup in the VRF A routing table and forwards traffic to the VLAN 1 switch virtual interface (SVI). Traffic is then sent through VLAN 1 to the destination server.

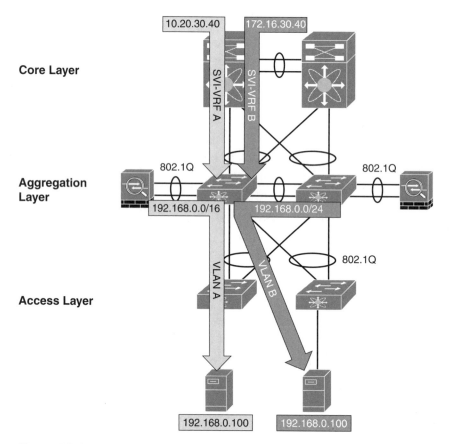

Figure 12-15 *Two-tier DC LAN Architecture*

VRFs are commonly used in service provider networks in combination with multiprotocol label switching (MPLS), where VRFs provide routing and forwarding isolation, and MPLS provides traffic isolation on the connections. VRFs may, however, be used without MPLS, with traffic isolation provided by either per-VRF assigned connections or IP VPNs. VRF implementation without the MPLS is called VRF-Lite.

Device-Level Virtualization and Separation

Cisco Nexus switches introduce support for virtual device contexts (VDCs). A VDC enables the switches to be virtualized at the device level. Each configured VDC presents itself as a unique device, further expanding tenant separation not only on data and control planes, but also on the management plane. A VDC runs as a separate logical entity within the switch, maintaining its own unique set of running software processes, having its own configuration, and being managed by a separate administrator.

As shown in Figure 12-16, each VDC contains its own unique and independent set of VLANs and VRFs. Physical ports can be assigned to a specific VDC, thus allowing the hardware data plane to be virtualized also. Within each VDC, a separate management domain can manage the VDC itself, thus allowing the management plane itself to also be virtualized.

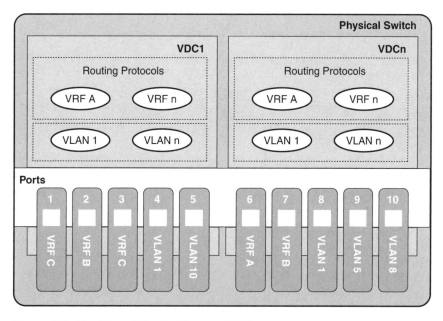

Figure 12-16 *Virtual Device Context VDC*

Case Study: Multitenant Data Center

In this case study, you need to design a hybrid multitenant data center that suits the requirements of enterprise internally and externally accessible e-commerce applications. In this design, you need to meet the following data center requirements:

- Host your enterprise's internal services, such as e-mail, collaboration, and others. Most services run on dedicated physical servers.

- Host an enterprise e-commerce application, accessible from the public Internet. Some internal services require e-commerce application database access.

- The e-commerce application should consist of multiple virtual servers. A physical load balancer should be utilized to distribute the load.

- The highest practical tenant separation is wanted.

- Only one management authority manages all data center devices.

426 Chapter 12: New Trends and Techniques to Design Modern Data Centers

To isolate traffic that comes from the Internet or from private traffic, you use two VRFs in the Layer 3 network. All traffic passes through a single physical firewall, where it is separated with the use of public and private contexts (device-level virtualization). You could use VDC on data center switches, but because the whole infrastructure is managed by a single entity, there is no need for management plane separation.

You can use VLANs to separate traffic in a Layer 2 network. Private servers require little communication between each other, so a network-centric topology is used. E-commerce application servers are virtualized and connected to the aggregation layer via a virtual switch. VLAN segmentation on the virtual switch exposes only web VLAN northbound toward the aggregation layer; all other communication between the application tier is kept inside the virtualized network (see Figure 12-17).

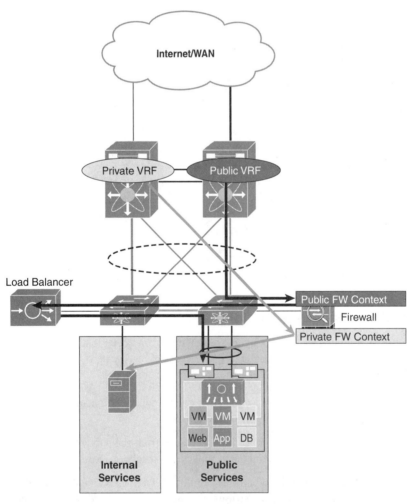

Figure 12-17 *Path Separation in a Multitenant Data Center Environment*

Microsegmentation with Overlay Networks

Classic security models are hard to adapt to multitier application requirements. Public and private services are not sealed from one another. Internal business applications may need access to e-commerce applications and databases. Some application flows may need to extend outside the private cloud tenant. Application tiers may be distributed across the Layer 2 boundaries of the data center.

In modern data centers, you can solve these problems with overlay networking. Services that need direct communication are placed in a common VXLAN, providing Layer 2 connectivity independent of physical location or the underlying Layer 3 network. The OVERLAY network allows services to freely communicate across Layer 2 boundaries, while their communication is isolated from other services.

In this case study, public traffic is encapsulated in a VXLAN as soon as it enters the data center and is sent to the load balancer through the VXLAN 1000. The load balancer forwards traffic through the VXLAN 1010 to the public server. Simultaneously, public servers are part of VXLAN 3000, used by internal business applications to access some of the e-commerce application APIs and databases, while being isolated from public traffic (see Figure 12-18).

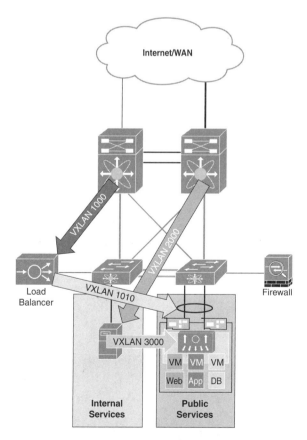

Figure 12-18 *Microsegmentation with the Overlay Network (VXLAN)*

> **Note** The Cisco ACI takes this overlay microsegmentation a step further, by introducing the endpoint groups and contract concepts (these concepts are covered in the following chapter). With these ACI concepts, data center architects, designers, and administrators can focus on application communicating requirements and leave the ACI fabric to offload the complexity of the configurations by automatically (through GUI or API integration) deploying and enforcing the desired microsegmentation policies between applications (no matter if the applications are using physical [bare metal] or virtualized systems).

Summary

- Multitiered data center network architecture introduces several limitations to large-scale modern data center environments driven by the requirements of system virtualizations, VM mobility, and cloud solutions.
- Spine-leaf (Clos) architecture offers more scalable and efficient architecture for today's data center design needs.
- Cisco FabricPath brings Layer 3 routing mechanisms to solve Layer 2 problems.
- Overlay Networking (VXLAN) extends the number of V(X)LANs and stretches the Layer 2 domain.
- Consider SDN principles in existing enterprise and data center environments.
- With Cisco APIC solutions, you can standardize and automate the management of your network, whether it's a data center or WAN.
- Redesign security for devices and data to fit the new SDN-based architecture.
- Carefully select an SDN solution that uses a controller that is intelligent and flexible enough to integrate with multivendor network services and offer a true policy-based design model.
- Virtualization of compute and storage resources enables resource sharing, security, and resource overutilization risks.
- Multitenancy is the logical isolation of shared virtual resources. It can serve different purposes and is achieved in different ways:
- Device management
    - VDC, contexts
- Layer 3 network
    - VRF-Lite (Lite = VRF without MPLS)
- Layer 2 network
    - VLANs
- Overlay networks
    - VXLAN

Review Questions

After answering the following questions, refer to Appendix A, "Answers to Review Questions," for the answers.

1. Which statement about Cisco FabricPath is correct?
    a. Cisco FabricPath significantly improves STP convergence time.
    b. Cisco FabricPath uses OSPF as a control protocol.
    c. Cisco FabricPath switches cannot share a Layer 2 domain with non-FabricPath switches.
    d. Cisco FabricPath adds FabricPath headers to existing frames with a destination MAC address set to the next switch in path.

2. Which of the statements about VXLAN are correct? (Select two.)
    a. VXLAN encapsulates Ethernet frames within TCP packets.
    b. VXLAN supports 16 million logical networks.
    c. Frame encapsulation is performed by VTEP.
    d. Frames are only encapsulated on end hosts.
    e. If VTEP receives a broadcast frame, it broadcasts it to all other VTEPs in the network.

3. Match tenant separation technologies with their descriptions.

Technology	Description
VRF-Lite	Provides Layer 3 separation in conjunction with MPLS. (Source: Multitenant Data Center)
VDC	Provides Layer 3 separation without the need for MPLS
VLAN	Provides Layer 2 separation
VRF	Provides data, control, and management plane separation

4. Which one of the following is a recommended architecture for a modern data center with virtualization and cloud services?
    a. Three-tier architecture
    b. Collapsed core/aggregation architecture
    c. Clos architecture
    d. Flat architecture

5. Which statement about TRILL is correct?
    a. Supports anycast HSRP
    b. Supports active-standby HSRP
    c. Supports vPC+

6. Which statement about VXLAN is correct?
   a. A Layer 2 path between the VTEPs is a must.
   b. Any routed transport can be used between the VTEPs.
   c. VXLAN is a MAC-in-MAC tunneling mechanism.
   d. VXLAN cannot be considered as a network overlay technology.

7. Which statement about SDN is correct? (Select two.)
   a. SDN may introduce new challenges to today's networks such as security concerns.
   b. Any SDN solution must use OpenFlow protocol.
   c. SDN offers the capability to automate network provisioning and simplify its manageability.
   d. The SDN controller is an optional component in any SDN solution.

8. What are the drivers to consider multitenant data centers? (Select two.)
   a. They enable you to use the same physical infrastructure by different virtual networks or groups.
   b. They offer the capability to support cloud-based data center networks.
   c. They reduce the load from the network.
   d. They provide less bandwidth utilization.

References

1. "Is Cisco Application Centric Infrastructure an SDN Technology?," http://www.cisco.com/c/en/us/solutions/collateral/data-center-virtualization/application-centric-infrastructure/white-paper-c11-733456.html

2. See note 1 above.

3. "VXLAN Overview: Cisco Nexus 9000 Series Switches," http://www.cisco.com

4. See note 3 above.

5. See note 3 above.

6. "VXLAN Network with MP-BGP EVPN Control Plane Design Guide," http://www.cisco.com

7. See note 6 above.

8. "Cisco Application Centric Infrastructure (ACI) - Endpoint Groups (EPG) Usage and Design," http://www.cisco.com

9. "Is Cisco Application Centric Infrastructure an SDN Technology?," http://www.cisco.com/c/en/us/solutions/collateral/data-center-virtualization/application-centric-infrastructure/white-paper-c11-733456.html

10. See note 9 above.

Chapter 13

Cisco Application-Centric Infrastructure

Upon completing this chapter, you will be able to

- Understand the Cisco ACI architecture for a data center
- Describe the characteristics of the Cisco ACI fabric
- Explain the role of network virtualization overlay technologies in the SDN solution that is based on the Cisco ACI
- Describe the design building blocks for the Cisco ACI for the data center
- Explain how endpoint groups are used to describe applications for policy-based management of the underlying infrastructure
- Describe the requirements and challenges of designing application profiles using the Cisco ACI
- Describe the requirements for designing a Cisco APIC network application profile for a known existing application and an unknown existing application
- Explain how to connect the Cisco ACI to external Layer 2 and Layer 3 networks

The Cisco Application-Centric Infrastructure (ACI) delivers software flexibility with the scalability of hardware performance that provides a robust transport network for today's dynamic workloads. The ACI is built on a network fabric that combines time-tested protocols with new innovations to create a highly flexible, scalable, and resilient architecture of low-latency, high-bandwidth links. These benefits are achieved through the integration of physical and virtual environments under one policy model for networks, servers, storage, services, and security.

In this chapter, you learn how to use the Cisco ACI to operate and maintain an enterprise-grade data center and the applications that are hosted in the data center.

ACI Characteristics

The ACI in the data center is a holistic policy-based Software-Defined Network (SDN) architecture. Key characteristics of the ACI include

- Simplified automation by an application-driven policy model
- Application velocity. Any workload. Anywhere
- Centralized visibility with real-time application health monitoring
- Open software flexibility for DevOps teams and ecosystem partner integration
- Investment protection through integration with the existing fabric infrastructure (for example, Nexus 7000)
- Scalable performance and multitenancy in hardware

Through the Cisco ACI, customers are reducing application deployment times from weeks to minutes. It also dramatically improves IT alignment with business objectives and policy requirements. What drives ACI speed and efficiencies is the common policy-based operating model the ACI introduces across the ACI-ready network and security elements. This model is facilitated through leveraging a policy-based solution. Therefore, the ACI is able to enhance modern data center networking models, overcome the limitations of siloed data center structures, and considerably reduce data center operational complexity and costs (capital expenditures, operating expenditures, provisioning time, and so on).

How the Cisco ACI Addresses Current Networking Limitations

Chapter 12, "New Trends and Techniques to Design Modern Data Centers," highlights the primary limitations of traditional data center network design in today's modern businesses. The Cisco ACI addresses traditional networking limitations. It is built using a balanced approach that weighs the best software against the best hardware, custom silicon against merchant silicon, centralized models against distributed models, and the need to address old problems against the need to meet new challenges. It tackles business challenges rather than championing only one particular technology approach.

The Cisco ACI addresses current network limitations as follows:[1]

- **Removes complexity that leads to stasis:** The Cisco ACI removes complexity from the network. It sets out to decouple policy from forwarding by allowing network routing and switching to be completely distributed across the entire fabric. Cisco ACI packet forwarding across the fabric uses a combination of merchant and custom silicon to deliver standards-based Virtual Extensible LAN (VXLAN) bridging and routing with no performance penalty or negative impact on the user or application.

- In addition, the Cisco ACI can apply policy without the need to derive this information from network information (such as IP addresses). It does this by populating each VXLAN frame with a 16-bit ID to uniquely identify the originating (source) group of the packet as specified in the group-based policy VXLAN Internet Engineering Task Force (IETF) draft. This approach provides outstanding flexibility for end users, allowing users to modify network policies with little network knowledge and no negative impact on network forwarding.

- The Cisco ACI further simplifies policies by introducing an abstraction model—a group-based policy—so that end users can define connectivity using higher-level abstracted constructs instead of concrete networking semantics. This model enables Cisco ACI end users to define policy rules without knowledge of networking, opening the way for application administrators and developers to directly interact with Cisco ACI policies to express their intent without the need to involve IT network administrators.

- **Ensures consistent policies:** One of the biggest challenges in managing network policies across a large network is the requirement to touch a large number of devices and make sure that the policy configuration remains consistent. The Cisco ACI addresses this challenge by offloading this task to the Cisco Application Policy Infrastructure Controller (APIC), which is the central policy authority and the central point of management for the Cisco ACI and associated physical and virtual services. The end user simply needs to specify on the Cisco APIC the desired intent of group-based policy, and the Cisco APIC distributes the policy to all the nodes in the Cisco ACI fabric.

- The Cisco APIC uses a variant of promise theory, with full formal separation between the abstract logical model and the concrete model, and with no configuration performed on concrete entities. Concrete entities are configured implicitly as a side effect of the logical model implementation. This implementation of promise theory provides policy consistency throughout the network at scale.

- **Provides the ability to scale:** The Cisco ACI is designed to scale transparently throughout its deployment, supporting changes in connectivity, bandwidth, tenants, and policies. The spine-and-leaf topology of the Cisco ACI fabric supports a scale-out design approach. If additional physical connectivity is required, you can add leaf nodes by connecting them to the spines. Similarly, if additional bandwidth or redundancy is required, you can introduce additional spine nodes. This scale-out deployment model also enables end users to start small and later scale to extremely large environments, thereby reducing the initial capital expenditure required to implement a scalable fabric. However, the addition of new devices does not mean an increased number of management points. After registering the new devices on the Cisco ACI fabric through the Cisco APIC, the end user can administer the entire fabric, including the new devices, from the central Cisco APIC. Introduction of the new devices requires no intervention by the administrator.

- Tenants and policies also use a scale-out approach. Policies are centrally stored on the fabric and are rendered to fabric nodes as required. The Cisco APIC policy repository itself is a scale-out clustered database. It can increase from 3 to more than 31 nodes in a single cluster, depending on the scale of tenants and policies required. Even with additional cluster nodes, all nodes are considered active, and policies can be managed on any cluster member.

- **Is vendor-independent:** A complete Cisco ACI deployment will likely include Layer 4 through 7 services, virtual networking, computing, storage resources, WAN routers, and northbound orchestration services. A main strength of Cisco ACI is its openness, with its published APIs, Layer 4 through 7 device packages, and use of the open OpFlex protocol. With these open APIs, plug-ins, and protocols, end users can incrementally add functions to their solutions without the need to wait for a single vendor to introduce new capabilities.

Cisco ACI Architecture Components

The Cisco ACI architecture is a combination of high-performance hardware and software innovation and intelligence integrated with two important concepts from SDN solutions: overlays and centralized control. However, the ACI utilizes different approaches and offers capabilities that go beyond the typical SDN offering, or what is known as OpenFlow-based SDN. The Cisco ACI Solution architecture consists of

- Centralized policy management called the Cisco Application Policy Infrastructure Controller (APIC)
- The new Cisco ACI high-performance fabric hardware with software and hardware innovations
- A Cisco application virtual switch (AVS) for the virtual network edge
- Integrated physical and virtual infrastructure
- An open ecosystem of network, storage, management, and orchestration vendors

Cisco Application Policy Infrastructure Controller (APIC)

In general, modern data center operators and IT staff need policies that are consistent across the entire network. However, one of the main challenges in managing policies in existing networks is the number of devices to which policies need to be applied, coupled with the need to ensure consistency. The Cisco Application Policy Infrastructure Controller (APIC) addresses this issue.

Figure 13-1 illustrates the Cisco *Open Network Environment (ONE) architecture*. The ONE architecture uses the Cisco APIC for the data center, which is a key architectural component of ACI to simplify and streamline the management of hosted applications in the data center. The Cisco APIC provides an open and programmable approach to networking through open APIs for policy-based management and security. Data center operators can use representational state transfer (REST)-based calls (through XML or JavaScript Object Notation [JSON]) to provision, manage, monitor, or troubleshoot the system.

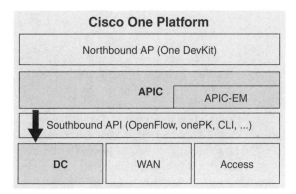

Figure 13-1 *Cisco ONE*

This approach automates and unifies applications, networking, cloud, and security teams in defining application requirements that avoid the complexity of what has typically been a tedious manual and siloed approach among different IT teams.

For architecture, the Cisco APIC is a distributed system implemented as a cluster of controllers. It provides a single point of control, a central API, a central repository for global data, and a repository for group-based policy data for Cisco ACI.

The Cisco APIC communicates with the Cisco ACI fabric to distribute policies to the points of attachment and to provide several critical administrative functions to the fabric. However, the Cisco APIC is not directly involved in data-plane forwarding, so a complete failure or disconnection of all Cisco APIC elements in a cluster will not result in any loss of forwarding capabilities, increasing overall system reliability.

Furthermore, the Cisco APIC also provides full native support for multitenancy, so multiple interested groups (internal or external to the organization) can share the Cisco

ACI fabric securely yet still be allowed access to shared resources if required. The Cisco APIC also has full, detailed support for role-based access control (RBAC) down to each managed object in the system, so privileges (read, write, or both) can be granted per role across the entire fabric.

Main features of the Cisco APIC include

- Application-centric network policies
- Data model-based declarative provisioning
- Application, topology monitoring, and troubleshooting
- Third-party integration (Layer 4 through 7 services, storage, computing, WAN)
- Image management (spine and leaf)
- Cisco ACI inventory and configuration
- Implementation on a distributed framework across a cluster of appliances

The APIC manages and automates the underlying forwarding components and Layer 4–Layer 7 service devices. Utilizing the APIC visibility into both the virtual and physical infrastructure as well as end-to-end knowledge of the application based on the application profile, the APIC is able to calculate an application health score. This health score represents the application's network health across virtual and physical resources including Layer 4–Layer 7 devices. It includes jitter, latency, congestion, failures, packet drops, and so on.

The health score provides enhanced visibility on both application and tenant levels. The health score can create further value when it is used to trigger automated events at specific thresholds. This enables the network to respond automatically to application health, making changes before users are impacted.

APIC Approach Within the ACI Architecture

The Cisco APIC policy uses an object-oriented approach based on promise theory. Promise theory is based on declarative, scalable control of intelligent objects, in comparison to legacy imperative models, which can be thought of as heavyweight, top-down management.

As depicted in Figure 13-2, the policy controller tells the network devices what it needs to be enabled/configured in order to satisfy the requirement for an application; however, it does not tell the device how to do it, and the device can do it using its own features and capabilities to achieve the same end result.

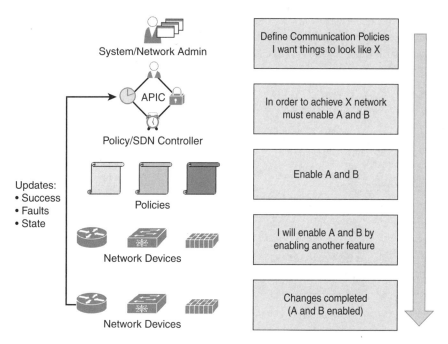

Figure 13-2 *Cisco ACI Declarative Approach*

The APIC centrally pushes policies to the underlying infrastructure using an extensible policy protocol designed to exchange the abstract policy between a network controller and a set of smart devices capable of rendering policy called OpFlex. Unlike OpenFlow, which is an agent-driven technology and allows only network operators to manage specific elements with the OpenFlow controller, OpFlex is designed to work as part of a declarative control system. Therefore, it offers the flexibility to data center operators to push policies to various network infrastructure elements, whether they are virtual, physical, or Layer 4–7 devices, and the abstract policies can be shared on demand.

Cisco ACI Fabric

As discussed previously, workloads continue to evolve, and traffic is becoming more east-west based. Networks need to respond faster to dynamic virtualized and cloud-based workloads and accommodate traffic growth as data sets become larger.

The Cisco ACI fabric architecture is designed based on one of the most efficient and scalable network design models: a spine-and-leaf bipartite graph or Clos architecture, in which every leaf is connected to every spine over 40/100 Gigabit links, and the converse. Also, with this architecture, each leaf node is one hop away from any other leaf node across the fabric. As discussed in the preceding chapter, the beauty of this architecture is that full-mesh connectivity is not required, yet it can offer an optimal forwarding path between any two endpoints with a minimal number of hops/latency combined with ECMP load distribution. In other words, the spine nodes don't connect to each other, and leaf nodes don't connect to each other, as shown in Figure 13-3.

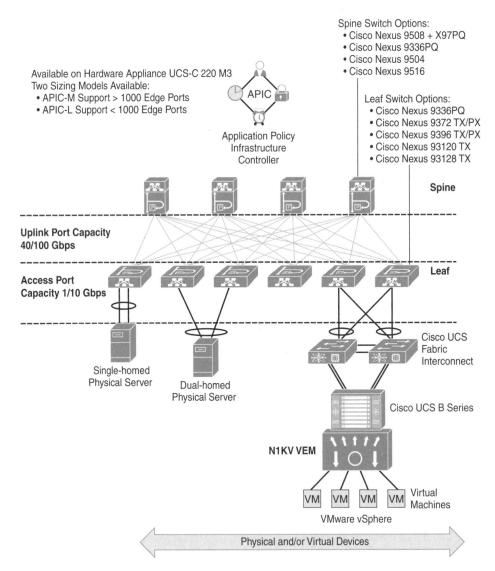

Figure 13-3 *ACI Spines and Leaves Fabric Architecture*

To reduce the likelihood of hotspots of activity forming in the fabric, all devices (regardless of their functions) connect at the leaf nodes of the fabric. This way, the fabric can simply scale the number of devices connected, by adding more leaf nodes. If the amount of cross-sectional bandwidth that is servicing the fabric needs to be increased, the administrator simply has to add spine nodes. This flexibility allows the fabric to start as a small environment but gradually grow to a much larger environment if the need arises. The fabric is also built using standards-based IP routed interfaces, offering greater stability in larger scale-out deployments. At the time of this writing, the typical spine-and-leaf fabric consists of two layers of Cisco Nexus 9000 series devices (see Figure 13-3):

- **Spine switches:** The top-level high-performance switches interconnect all leaf devices; therefore, spine devices constitute the backbone of the fabric and provide the mapping database function. The hardware used for the spine is designed specifically to provide this function at a high scale. The mapping database is stored in a redundant fashion within each spine, and it is replicated among spine switches so that if a spine disappears, traffic forwarding continues. Modular spine switches have a greater mapping database storage capacity; in fact, the mapping database is shared across fabric cards, so the more fabric cards, the more endpoints can be stored. The use of more fabric cards also depends on the forwarding capacity that you want to give to line cards. As mentioned earlier, no direct link is allowed or required between the spine switches.

- **Leaf switches:** The bottom-level switches connect all servers or other parts of the network to the fabric. In fact, the leaf devices can connect to any device, and they are the place at which policies are enforced. Leaf devices also provide the capability to route and to bridge to external network infrastructures (campus, WAN, connectivity to a Multiprotocol Label Switching Virtual Private Network [MPLS VPN] cloud, and so on). In this case, they are sometimes referred to as border leaf devices. Also, leaf switches can be the attachment point simultaneously for workloads and for the border leaf to provide connectivity to the WAN or to an MPLS VPN cloud.

The Nexus switches must run the ACI fabric mode to enable the ACI fabric. Alternatively, they may run in a standard NX-OS mode. In this case, they are regarded as any other type of individual device. (As mentioned in the preceding chapter, you can run BGP-EVPN as the control plane for the VXLAN in this mode; however, you won't get the capabilities and applications' visibility you have with the ACI mode.)

The Cisco APIC is a physical appliance that is connected to the leaf layer and is responsible for initial bootstrapping of the fabric (hence, the requirement to be a physical device because the virtual environment depends on the availability of the fabric). The Cisco APIC is a physically distributed but logically centralized controller that provides DHCP, bootstrap configuration, and image management to the fabric for automated startup and upgrades, as illustrated in Figure 13-4.

- Applications fully use clustered and replicated controller (N+1, N+2, etc.)
- Any node can service any user for any operation
- Seamless APIC node adds and deletes
- Fully automated APIC software cluster upgrade with redundancy during upgrade
- Cluster size driven by transaction rate requirements
- APIC is not in the data path

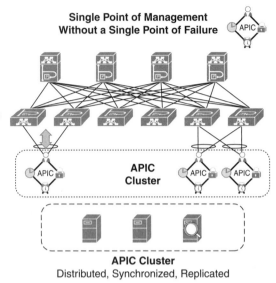

Figure 13-4 *ACI APIC Cluster*

The Cisco Nexus ACI fabric software is bundled as an ISO image, which can be installed on the Cisco APIC appliance server through the serial console. The Cisco Nexus ACI Software ISO contains the Cisco APIC image, the firmware image for the leaf node, the firmware image for the spine node, the default fabric infrastructure policies, and the protocols that are required for operation.

The recommended minimum sizing has the following requirements:

- Three or more Cisco APIC controllers that are dual-connected to different leaf switches for maximum resilience. Note that the fabric is manageable even with just one controller and operational without a controller.

- At least two spine devices for resilience and also load balancing. The spine can easily scale out simply by adding additional switches.

- At least two leaf devices for resilience and also load balancing. The leaves can easily scale out by adding additional leaf switches. Every leaf should be connected to all spine devices.

The Cisco ACI fabric is a highly scalable, multipath, high-performance leaf-and-spine architecture that provides a VXLAN overlay for the tenant space—the network that business applications, departments, and customers use. The Cisco ACI fabric also implements the concept of infrastructure space, which is securely isolated in the fabric. This is also the place where all topology discovery, fabric management, and infrastructure addressing are performed.

ACI Network Virtualization Overlays

The Cisco ACI fabric is an IP-based fabric that implements an integrated overlay, allowing any subnet to be placed anywhere in the fabric and support a fabric-wide mobility domain for virtualized workloads. Spanning-Tree Protocol (STP) is not required in the Cisco ACI fabric and leaf switches. To achieve this, the Cisco ACI network solution uses an overlay that is based on VXLAN (discussed in Chapter 12) to virtualize the physical infrastructure. This overlay, like most overlays, requires the data path at the edge of the network to map from the tenant endpoint address in the packet, its identifier, to the location of the endpoint, its locator. This mapping occurs in the tunnel endpoint (TEP).

Because overlay networks are "virtual" by nature, they are agile, dynamic, and suitable for automation and software control. In a Cisco ACI environment, VXLAN is used to encapsulate traffic inside the fabric. In other words, each leaf switch acts as a hardware VXLAN tunnel endpoint (VTEP). In addition, as discussed in the previous chapter, VXLAN is a MAC-in-IP type of encapsulation that requires a Layer 3 underlay-routed transport network to establish the connectivity between the VTEPs. The Cisco ACI fabric is designed to provide a zero-touch operation experience topology with autodiscovery, automated configuration, and infrastructure addressing using industry-standard protocols including Intermediate System-to-Intermediate System (IS-IS) to facilitate establishing the overlay connectivity between the VTEPs over the dynamically discovered and built Layer 3 routed network between the spine and leaf switches using IS-IS as the underlay routing protocol (inside the fabric only), as illustrated in Figure 13-5.

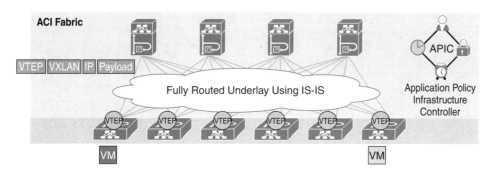

Figure 13-5 *ACI Fabric Underlay and Overlay*

The Cisco ACI fabric decouples the tenant endpoint address, its identifier, from the location of that endpoint, which is defined by its locator, or the VXLAN termination endpoint address.

Forwarding within the fabric is between VTEPs and an extender VXLAN header format referred to as the VXLAN policy header. The VTEP maps the internal tenant MAC or IP address to a location using a distributed mapping database. The Cisco ACI supports full Layer 2 and Layer 3 forwarding semantics; no changes are required to applications or endpoint IP stacks. VLAN IDs will have local significance at the leaf switch level only, as the ingress leaf switch swaps the external VLAN, VXLAN, and Network Virtualization using Generic Routing Encapsulation (NVGRE) tags with an internal VXLAN tag; and this tag will be swapped with the respective tag at the egress leaf switch. Figure 13-6 illustrates an example of ACI fabric encapsulation normalization.

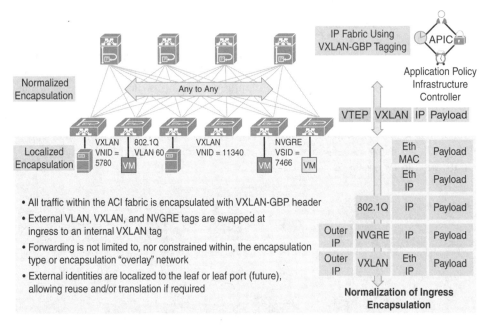

Figure 13-6 *ACI Fabric Encapsulation Normalization*

To better understand the packet forwarding and encapsulation normalization concept inside the ACI fabric, Figure 13-7 summarizes the packet forwarding process between two endpoints across the ACI fabric using seven steps.

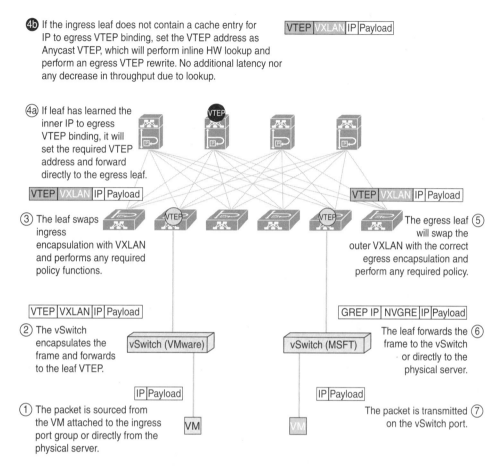

Figure 13-7 *Unicast Packet Forwarding Across the ACI Fabric*

In the Cisco ACI fabric, some extensions have been added to the VXLAN header to allow the segmentation of endpoint groups (EPG) and the management of filtering rules. These extensions also support the enhanced load-balancing techniques used in the fabric. (The next section discusses the EPG concept in more detail.)

The ACI enhanced VXLAN (eVXLAN) header provides a tagging mechanism to identify properties associated with frames forwarded through an ACI-capable fabric. It is an extension of the Layer 2 Locator/ID Separation Protocol (LISP) (draft-smith-lisp-layer2-01) with the additional policy group, load and path metric, counter and ingress port, and encapsulation information. The eVXLAN header is not associated with a specific Layer 2 segment or Layer 3 domain but provides a multifunction tagging mechanism used in ACI Application Defined Networking-enabled fabric, as shown in Figure 13-8.

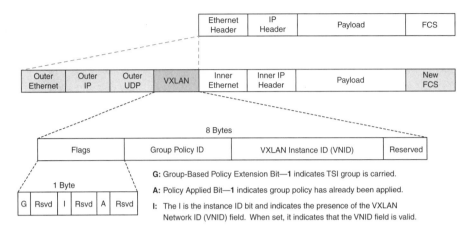

Figure 13-8 *ACI Enhanced VXLAN (eVXLAN) Header*

Note As shown in Figure 13-8, the Cisco ACI uses the reserved fields of the regular VXLAN header for other purposes. The source group indicates the source Tenant System Interface (TSI) group membership. In other words, this field is used to represent the endpoint group to which the endpoint that is the source of the packet belongs. This information allows the filtering policy to be consistently applied regardless of the location of an endpoint.

With this forwarding approach, ACI provides "multi-hypervisor" encapsulation normalization, which facilitates a seamless and unified transport for different hypervisor vendors and overlay technologies, whether they are based on VLAN, VXLAN, or NVGRE networks for both virtual and physical nodes. As shown in Figure 13-9, ACI simplifies the network provisioning deployment to support the multi-hypervisor and allows data center operators to choose a hypervisor vendor without restriction.

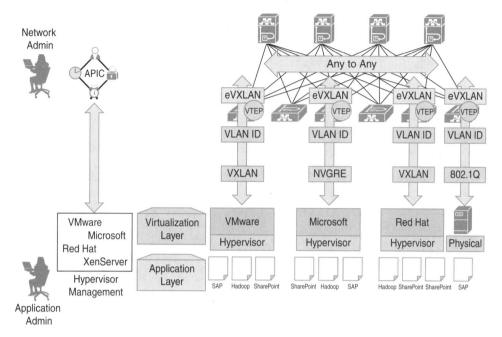

Figure 13-9 *Multi-Hypervisor–Ready Fabric*

As illustrated earlier in Figure 13-6, when applications are hosted by different hypervisor types, different host-level encapsulation might need to be used (such as VXLAN and NVGRE). ACI simplifies this communication and makes it transparent to the network administrator through the concept of encapsulation normalization.

Note If any VLAN allocation is required at the leaf port switch level, the network administer normally does not need to configure it manually. The administrator needs to define only an access policy (specifying basic access attributes such as port type and VLAN pool range). The rest will be part of the provisioning process of the application network profile (ANP), which is covered in the following section.

Unlike the deployment of Nexus 9000 series switches in non-ACI mode (covered in the preceding chapter), which use BGP-EVPN as the control plane for the VXLAN, in ACI mode, the control plane and forwarding are based on a concept called a mapping database. A mapping database offers increased visibility of host locations and addresses across the fabric with more efficient communication. The mapping database in ACI is maintained by the fabric that contains the mapping for each endpoint attached to the network (identifier) and the address of the tunnel endpoint that it sits behind (locator). The endpoint address is both the MAC address and the IP address of the endpoint plus the logical network that it resides in (the VRF instance). The mapping database in the spine is replicated for redundancy and is synchronized across all spines. Normally, when an ingress leaf switch forwards a packet, it checks its local cache of the mapping database first. If it does not find the endpoint address it is looking for, it will encapsulate the packet to the proxy function residing in the spine switch and forward it as unicast for further lookup for the required address that can be connected to another leaf switch. Or, it can be an external address and reachable through a border leaf. With this approach, the tables on each leaf need to contain the following information:

- The Local Station Table (LST) needs to contain only the IP and MAC addresses of locally attached hosts.

- The Global Station Table (GST) needs to contain only the information about the IP and MAC addresses of remote hosts with which the local hosts have an active conversation.

For new flow and conversations and for entries that have aged out, the spine proxy is used as an inline-mapping database to provide location services for the remote leaf. With this approach, even if entries in the GST age out, the fabric never needs to be flooded (see Figure 13-10).

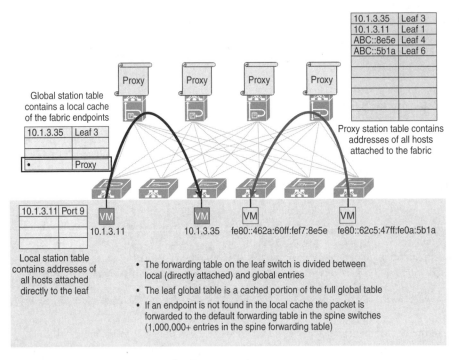

Figure 13-10 *ACI Proxy and Inline Mapping*

Note For Layer 2 forwarding in the presence of silent hosts (such as hosts that do not send traffic out periodically), you may want to change the unknown unicast flooding configuration option or the ARP flooding option. However, the system default configuration is such that there is seldom a need to change these configurations. The concept of a bridge domain is described later in this chapter.

Application Design Principles with the Cisco ACI Policy Model

Applications influence business. They include web portals that generate revenue, human resources (HR) systems that help to onboard new employees, imaging systems that support patient care, and so on. While the group of applications used differs between industry and between businesses within an industry, one thing remains constant: an application is not an isolated process running on a virtual machine (VM). Applications are ecosystems of interconnected components: some physical, some virtual, some legacy, and some new.

These application ecosystems are complex interconnections of components and tiers, the end result of which promotes business value. For instance, when a user tries to access a certain application over a thin client (using the virtual desktop infrastructure, or VDI), the process of entering the login credentials to receive the desired application interface could be complete in a few seconds. On the back end, a VDI and virtualized application instances will pass the user's credentials to an authorization system. Once the user is authorized as a valid user, the information is passed to the virtualized application system along with the access request to initiate the application session. It then retrieves the relevant data from the data store, such as a network file system (NFS) storage device. Finally, this information is formatted and compiled through a presentation layer and presented back to the user through thin client devices.

This interaction to provide a single login experience to the user requires several tiers and components spread across both front-end and back-end data center networks. These application components may exist in virtual or physical layers, and the transactions are most likely subject to various network services, including security and compliance checks, as shown in Figure 13-11.

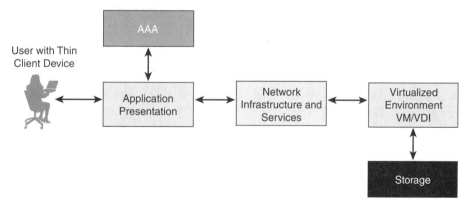

Figure 13-11 *Sample Application View*

In fact, applications are not as simple as software running on a VM. The complexities within application connectivity go well beyond the scope of what is shown in Figure 13-11 when TCP/UDP ports, service chaining, and more are added. This complete ecosystem is what provides the desired end result to the user or system using the application.[2]

That being said, today's networks mostly do not treat applications in the way they are structured (as described previously). Instead, today's networks almost always group applications by virtual LAN (VLAN) and subnet and apply connectivity and policy based on those constructs. This leads to restrictions on how applications can be grouped and how policy can be applied to those applications, as illustrated in Figure 13-12. With this traditional approach, it is like you have a disconnect or inefficient translation between an application's language and network language.

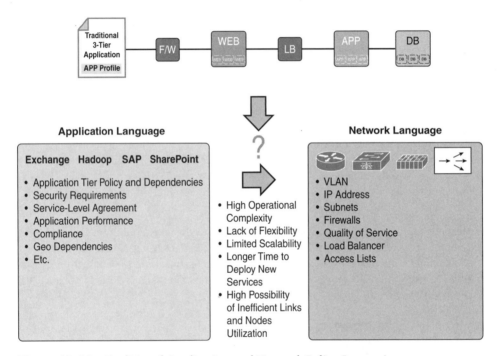

Figure 13-12 *Traditional Application and Network Policy Interaction*

Typically, one or more applications are grouped into VLANs, and then IP subnets are mapped to those VLANs. From there, connectivity through routing is configured, and network services are applied to the subnet addressing. Therefore, the manual configurations, process, and coupled constructs of this design model lead to slower deployment, higher configuration error rates, and reduced auditability. Consequently, this creates significant business impact with the current methodology.

On the other hand, Figure 13-13 illustrates how Cisco ACI mined the gap between the application and network languages with the policy-based model that is primarily enabled by the Cisco APIC. In this approach, the traditional tiered application can now be effortlessly deployed in the ACI fabric simply by defining the objects and the communication requirements between them.

Application Design Principles with the Cisco ACI Policy Model   449

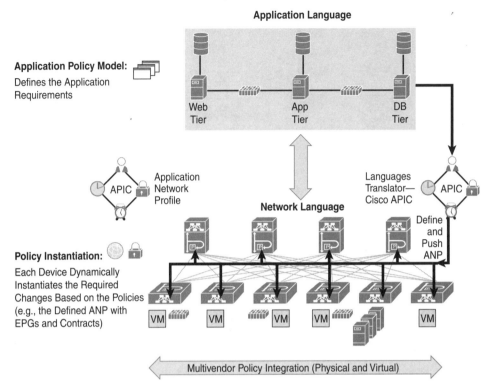

Figure 13-13 *Cisco ACI Policy-based Approach*

The following are the primary principles to build application polices and communications with the ACI policy-based data center design model:

- **Application network profile (ANP):** This profile contains the entire application policy. In fact, ANPs are designed to be modeled in a logical manner that matches the way applications are designed and deployed (overcoming the disconnect between the application language and the networking language).

- **Endpoint groups (EPG):** A policy consists of a number of endpoint groups, which are typically one or more servers in the same segment.

- **Contracts:** Policy contracts define the communication requirements between EPGs.

This approach will overcome the siloed approach and manual configurations and provide the capability to abstract the complexity of the network infrastructure and polices so that it is not visible to the network operator, as illustrated in Figure 13-14. (This approach is divided into three stages in sequence.) These principles are discussed in more detail in the following sections.

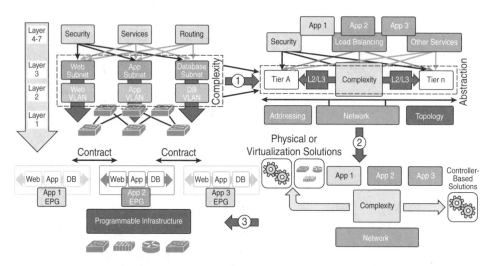

Figure 13-14 *The Abstraction of the Applications and Policies Complexities*

What Is an Endpoint Group in Cisco ACI?

Endpoint groups (EPG) are collections of similar endpoints representing an application tier or set of services. They provide a logical grouping for objects that require similar policy. For example, an EPG could be a group of components that make up an application's web tier. Endpoints themselves are defined using NIC, vNIC, MAC addresses, IP addresses, DNS names, and VM tags with extensibility for future methods of identifying application components. For instance, Figure 13-15 shows an EPG that contains web services (both HTTP and HTTPS) defined regardless of their IP subnet (different IP subnets under a single EPG). In this example, regardless of the separate subnets, policy is applied to both HTTPS and HTTP services within this EPG. This helps data center operators separate the addressing of the applications from its mapping and policy enforcement across the ACI fabric.[3]

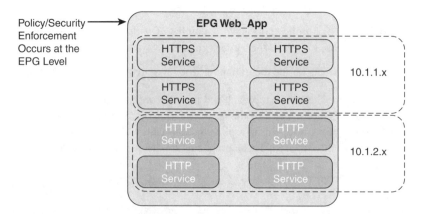

Figure 13-15 *ACI EPG Application Mapping*

EPGs are designed for flexibility, enabling them to be customized to one or more deployment models a given customer might choose. The EPGs themselves are then used to define where policy is applied. Within the Cisco ACI fabric, policy is applied between EPGs, therefore defining how EPGs communicate with one another. Also, EPGs and the associated policies are designed to be extensible in the future to policy application within an EPG itself.

The implementation of EPGs within the fabric provides several valuable benefits. EPGs act as a single policy enforcement point for a group of contained objects. This simplifies configuration of these policies and ensures that it is consistent. Additional policy is applied based not on subnet, but rather on the EPG itself. This means that IP addressing changes to the endpoint itself do not necessarily change its policy, as is commonly the case in traditional networks (the exception here is an endpoint defined by its IP). Alternatively, moving an endpoint to another EPG would apply the new policy to the leaf switch to which the endpoint is connected and define new behavior for that endpoint based on the new EPG.[4]

Design EPGs

ACI EPGs provide a new model for mapping applications to a network. Rather than using forwarding constructs such as addressing or VLANs to apply connectivity and policy, EPGs use a grouping of application endpoints. EPGs act as a container for collections of applications, or for application components and tiers that can be used to apply forwarding and policy logic. They allow the separation of network policy, security, and forwarding from addressing and instead apply it to logical application boundaries.

In any typical ACI deployment (but not always), the endpoint groups require the following components:

- Collection of servers
- Contracts (provided and consumed): a contract defines which Layer 4 protocol and port is allowed (everything else is denied)
- Bridge domain
- Network

Contracts define inbound and outbound permit, deny, and QoS rules and policies, such as redirect. Contracts allow both simple and complex definitions of the way that an EPG communicates with other EPGs, depending on the requirements of the environment. Although contracts are enforced between EPGs, they are connected to EPGs using provider-consumer relationships. Essentially, one EPG provides a contract, and other EPGs consume that contract. Also, this policy model allows for both unidirectional and bidirectional policy enforcement (see Figure 13-16).

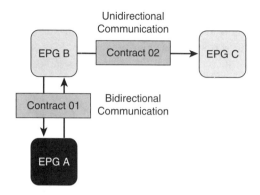

Figure 13-16 *Contracts' Policy Enforcement Models*

In other words, to build a design with the Cisco ACI policy-based approach, you must do the following:

- Identify and group together endpoints. In the Cisco ACI model, you achieve this by using EPGs.

- Determine how these grouped endpoints communicate with each other. In the Cisco ACI, you achieve this by creating policies and associating them with contracts as connection points between EPGs.

Figure 13-17 shows the basic three-tier web application used previously with some common additional connectivity that would be required in the real world. This diagram shows shared network services, NFS, and management, which would be used by all three tiers as well as other EPGs within the fabric. In these cases, the contract provides a reusable policy defining how the NFS and MGMT EPGs produce functions or services that can be consumed by other EPGs.

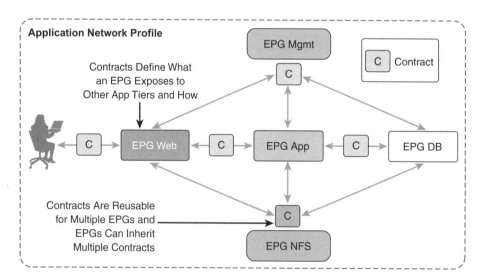

Figure 13-17 *Multitier Application Design Logic in Cisco ACI*

After defining objects such as EPGs and contracts, the data center operator can define the application network profile to be pushed by the ACI APIC and provisioned by the ACI fabric switches, as illustrated in Figure 13-18. With this approach, network operators do not need to worry about defining and applying manual complex configurations such as VLANs and ACLs.

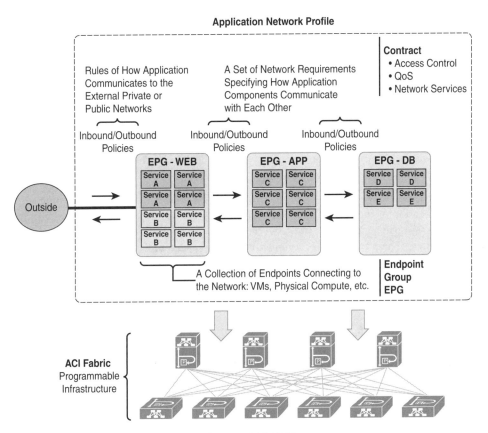

Figure 13-18 *Logical Construct of Cisco ACI ANP*

Note As discussed earlier in this chapter, the eVXLAN source group is used as a tag/label to identify the specific endpoint for each application function (EPG), in which it enables the ACI to map policy configuration to the packet level and facilities. By doing so, it achieves the following:

- Policy enforcement between an ingress or source application tier (EPG) and an egress or destination application tier (EPG)
- Policy that can be enforced at the source or destination

ACI Fabric Access Polices

The preceding sections described how the Cisco ACI with application network profiles (ANP) can provide a layer of abstraction that remove the complexities data center network operators normally deal with, such as mapping ports and applications to VLANs and then mapping each VLAN to a VRF, defining ACLs, and so on.

However, the data center network operator still needs to provision basic setup for the leaf switches to specify access-related parameters such as VLAN pools, which leaf switches and ports need to be used, and how they need to be configured (such as providing external connectivity, trunk, or vPC). (As we know in ACI, a VLAN has local significance at the leaf node level only.) Also, some other access parameters, including port speed, LLDP, CDP, and storm control, can be configured.

On the other hand, the underlying philosophy of the Cisco ACI is that the infrastructure administrator can categorize servers based on their requirements. For example, virtualized servers with hypervisors can be connected at a 10 Gigabit Ethernet, nonvirtualized servers can be connected at 1 Gigabit Ethernet, and so on.

Cisco ACI provides a way to keep the promised level of abstraction when defining the connection of the servers or any external entity to the fabric. At the same time, it demystifies the configurations of the physical ports for both small- and large-scale data centers. The infrastructure administrator prepares a template of configurations for servers connected with active-standby teaming, PortChannels, and vPCs and bundles all the settings for the ports into a policy group. The administrator then creates objects that select interfaces of the fabric in ranges that share the same policy-group configuration.

With this approach, the DC network operator or administrator can define the required policies and templates once to provision the desired VLANs and interface policies on the leaf nodes and ports. Then the administrator can rely on the EPGs and ANP to group hosts and services and to control the communication across the fabric using the application policy-based model discussed earlier in this chapter. Figure 13-19 shows how to create the logical structure of ACI fabric access policies.

Furthermore, you can create policies that apply not to just one switch at a time but to multiple switches. This capability is very useful for the configuration of vPCs.

Application Design Principles with the Cisco ACI Policy Model   455

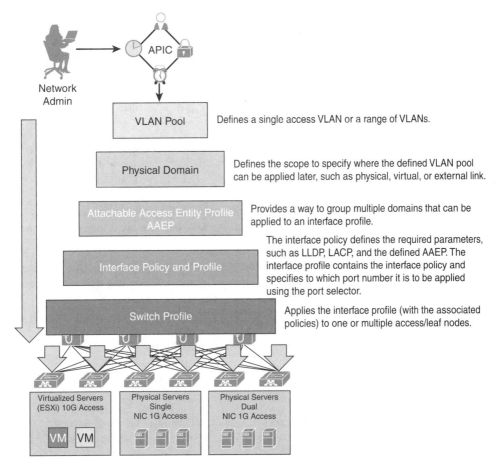

Figure 13-19 *Logical Structure of ACI Fabric Access Polices*

From a network operation point of view, the main advantage of this approach is that you can effectively apply configurations in a more logical manner. For instance, if you want to add one port to the set of physical servers, you just need to add an interface to the interface profile. If you want to change the physical port settings, you just make that change in the interface policy group. If you want to add a VLAN to the range, you could just modify the physical domain.

Note This configuration can be achieved with a single REST call, which offers the capability to manage very large-scale data center networks with complex configuration requirements in a simple and automated manner.

Building Blocks of a Tenant in the Cisco ACI

Although the exact use and definition of a tenant in today's modern data center networks can vary from solution to solution, its general concept is still the same. A tenant is a logical or physical entity that resides on a data center network to serve a certain user group (such as a marketing team tenant, guest tenant, research & development tenant). In a modern multitenant data center network, multiple tenants normally utilize the same underlying infrastructure with logical separations at higher layers (Layers 2 to 7).

In the Cisco ACI, a *tenant* is a logical container or a folder for application policies. It can represent an actual tenant, an organization, or a domain, or it can just be used for the convenience of organizing information.[5] In the Cisco ACI, typically all application configurations are part of a tenant because it represents a unit of isolation from a policy perspective and does not represent a private network. Within a tenant, you can define one or more Layer 3 networks (VRF instances/contexts), one or more bridge domains per network, and EPGs to divide the bridge domains.

The bridge domains identify properties influencing forwarding behavior. In fact, a bridge domain is a container for subnets that can act as a broadcast or flooding domain if broadcast or flooding is enabled (this is rarely needed). The bridge domain is not a VLAN, although it can act similar to a VLAN. You instead should think of it as a distributed switch, which, on a leaf, can be translated locally as a VLAN with local significance. Whenever you create an EPG, you need to reference a bridge domain.

The relationships among the various objects are as follows:

- The EPG points to a bridge domain BD.
- The bridge domain points to a Layer 3 network (BD can be defined as Layer 2 where no routing is enabled, or as a routed BD where Layer 3 is enabled along with a pervasive gateway capability).
- EPGs are grouped into application network profiles, and the application profiles can span multiple bridge domains. By grouping EPGs into application profiles, the administrator makes the network aware of the relationship among application components.

Figure 13-20 illustrates the relationship among these building blocks of a tenant.

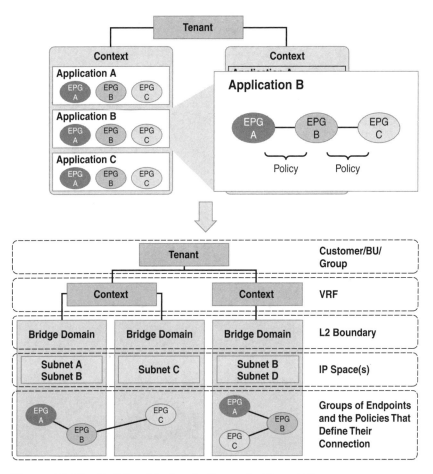

Figure 13-20 *Building Blocks of a Tenant in Cisco ACI*

The bridging domains and routing instances to move IP packets across the fabric provide the transport infrastructure for the workloads defined in the EPGs. The relationship between EPGs through contracts can span application profiles and even tenants.

Figure 13-21 summarizes the relationships of the ACI objects (networks, bridge domains, EPGs, and ANPs). Any disconnect among these objects can lead to broken communication. Therefore, it is crucial that network designers understand the relationship between these objects.

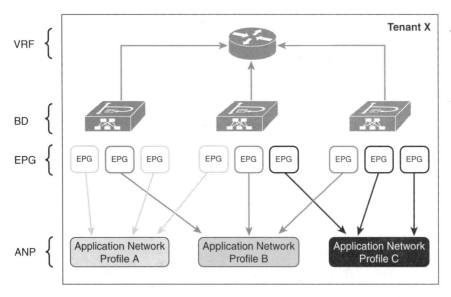

Figure 13-21 *Relationship between the ACI Objects*

Based on Figure 13-21, in Cisco ACI, all application configuration is part of a tenant. Within a tenant, you define one or more Layer 3 networks (VRF instances/contexts), one or more bridge domains per network, and EPGs to divide the bridge domains. Figure 13-22 depicts the structure of these objects in an ACI construct.

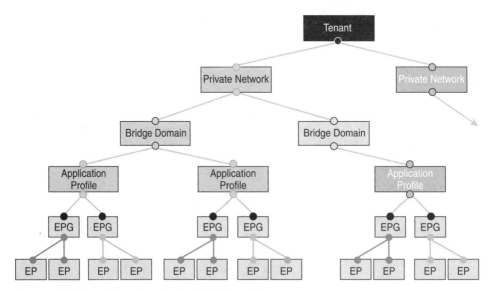

Figure 13-22 *Hierarchy of the ACI Fabric Objects*

Note Cisco ACI offers the capability to insert Layer 4 through Layer 7 functions using an approach called a *service graph*. The industry normally refers to the capability to add Layer 4 through Layer 7 devices in the path between endpoints as *service insertion*. The Cisco ACI service graph technology can be considered a superset of service insertion. One of several innovations in the area of service insertion is that the Cisco ACI enables you to concatenate functions offered by individual Layer 4 through Layer 7 devices instead of simply connecting discrete boxes in sequence. A service graph is a variation of the concept of a contract. As we know from the preceding section, in the Cisco ACI policy model, a contract connects two endpoint groups (EPGs). A contract can also offer functions such as traffic filtering, traffic load balancing, and SSL offloading. The Cisco ACI locates the devices that provide such functions and inserts them into the path as defined by the service graph policy.

Crafting Applications Design with the Cisco ACI

One of the primary philosophies of the Cisco ACI is to transform the data center network design so that it is policy driven. The goal is to focus on application needs and business polices that are irrelevant to the device or application location within the ACI fabric (no matter where it is connected, what IP or VLAN is used). This capability is primarily enabled by the application's profiling concept (ANP) and its subcomponents (EPGs, BDs, contracts, service insertion), as illustrated in Figure 13-23. The simplicity of the application profile modeling requires only a relatively small set of data describing either existing or new applications. An optimized design can then be modeled and implemented using the Cisco Application Policy Infrastructure Controller application network profiles.

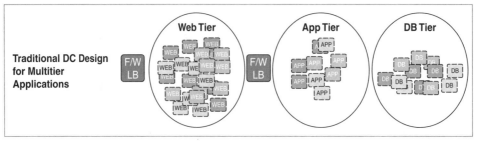
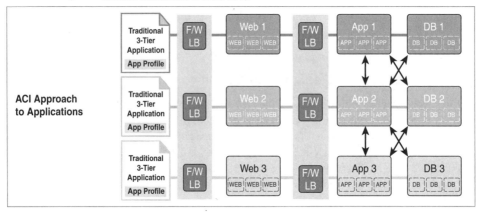

Figure 13-23 *Application Network Profile Discovery*

However, often there is lack of documentation regarding an existing (potentially large) set of applications that are in production. Lack of such information may prevent the proper design of an equivalent application using the Cisco APIC.

Therefore, as a network designer, you need the following information to design an application profile in the Cisco APIC:

- Application architecture
- Addressing and routing
- Security functionality (for example, protocols and ports used)

This means a thorough analysis of the existing environment must precede other application design steps in order to provide a reliable set of information describing the migrated applications. You can complete this analysis using any of a number of ways, such as inspecting running configurations of devices to determine applications, devices, relations, connectivity rules, and so on.

ACI Interaction with External Layer 2 Connections and Networks

The section discusses how the ACI interacts with external Layer 2 links and domains.

To create a basic Layer 2 network in the ACI, without any Layer 3 routing, you simply need to start with the basics. First, consider creating one or more bridge domains and EPGs. You can then decide whether to configure the bridge domains for hardware-proxy mode or for flood-and-learn mode based on communication.

Note When you are creating any configuration or design in the Cisco ACI, for objects to be instantiated and, as a result, programmed into the hardware, they must meet the requirements of the object model. In other words, if a reference is missing, the object will not be instantiated.

In the Cisco ACI object model, the bridge domain is a child of the VRF instance. So, even if you need a purely Layer 2 network, you still need to create a VRF instance and associate the bridge domain with that VRF instance.

That being said, this approach doesn't mean that the configuration consumes VRF hardware resources. In fact, if you don't enable routing, no VRF resources will be allocated in hardware.

The following steps are required to create a simple Layer 2 network in the Cisco ACI:

Step 1. Create a VRF instance.

Step 2. Create a bridge domain (without enabling unicast routing) and associate the bridge domain with the VRF instance. Also, the bridge domain must not be provided with a subnet IP address (SVI IP address).

Step 3. Configure the bridge domain for either optimized switching (also called hardware-proxy mode; that is, using the mapping database) or the traditional flood-and-learn behavior (if there are silent hosts, as discussed earlier in this chapter).

Step 4. Create EPGs and make sure that they have a relationship with a bridge domain. (EPGs and the bridge domain do not have a one-to-one relationship; you can have multiple EPGs in the same bridge domain.)

Step 5. Create contracts between EPGs as necessary. If you want all EPGs to be able to talk to each other without any filtering, you can set the VRF instance as unenforced.

Step 6. Create switch and port access polices (profiles) to assign the desired parameters and VLANs to the access leaf switches and ports.

> **Note** When extending a Layer 2 bridged domain to an external Layer 2 domain in migration scenarios where the Layer 3 default gateway may still reside in the external network, you need to consider the following parameters when creating the bridge domain BD in ACI:
>
> - Enable flooding of the Layer 2 unknown unicast.
> - Enable ARP flooding.
> - Disable unicast routing (it can be enabled later when the migration is completed and the endpoints will use the ACI for the Layer 3 default gateway).

The following sections cover how to extend a Layer 2 domain created using the preceding steps outside the ACI fabric that might be required to achieve any or all of the following connectivity requirements:

Step 1. Connect the physical workload to ACI.

Step 2. Connect Hypervisor platforms that operate without integration with APIC.

Step 3. Connect the legacy network to ACI (it could be an STP- or vPC-based network).

Step 4. Extend a BD/EPG to support Layer 2 Data Center Interconnect (DCI).

Connecting ACI to the Outside Layer 2 Domain

This section covers the two primary methods to extend the Layer 2 flooding domain from the ACI fabric to an external network such as an existing legacy network during the migration phase or to support a Layer 2 data center interconnect DCI using VLAN peering.

Extending the Existing EPG

To extend an existing EPG, you need to manually assign a port to a VLAN. In turn, it is mapped to an EPG, to extend an existing EPG beyond the ACI fabric under the same bridge domain and single policy group (EPG), as illustrated in Figure 13-24.

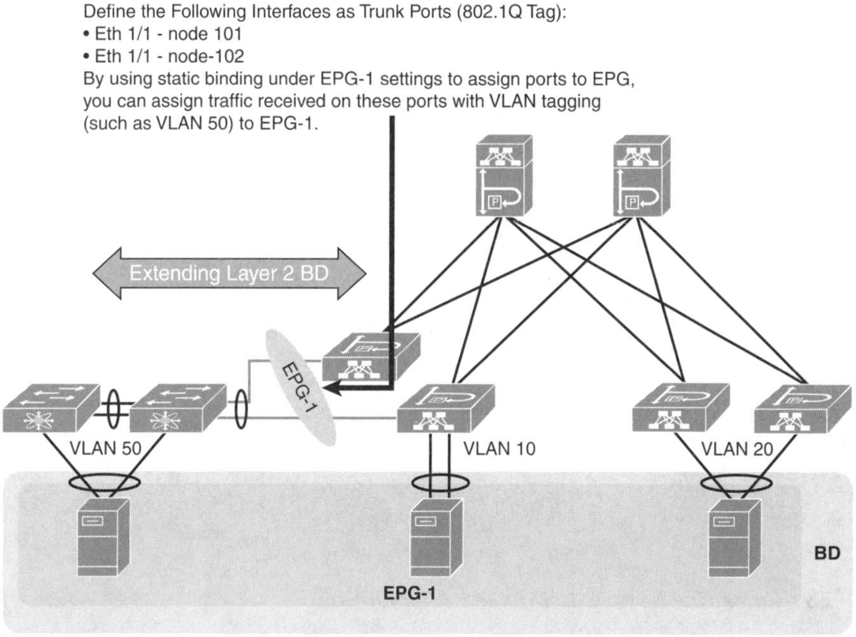
Define the Following Interfaces as Trunk Ports (802.1Q Tag):
• Eth 1/1 - node 101
• Eth 1/1 - node-102
By using static binding under EPG-1 settings to assign ports to EPG, you can assign traffic received on these ports with VLAN tagging (such as VLAN 50) to EPG-1.
Extending Layer 2 BD
EPG-1
VLAN 50
VLAN 10
VLAN 20
BD
EPG-1

Figure 13-24 *Extending Layer 2 Using the Port to EPG Option*

As shown in Figure 13-24, although hosts connected to the ACI fabric and the legacy network belong to the same subnet/bridge domain, the VLAN ID used at the leaf node level can be different because it has leaf switch-wide significance only within the ACI fabric. Communication between endpoints is based on the application network profile's ANP model discussed earlier in this chapter (controlled by the defend tenants, contest BD, EPG and contracts). Because the endpoints in Figure 13-24 are all part of the same BD and EPG, no additional configuration is required to allow the communication between these endpoints.

Layer 2 Outside Connection (L2Out)

The L2Out option also provides Layer 2 extension from the ACI fabric to an external (outside) bridged network. Unlike the previous option, this option is designed specifically to provide connectivity to outside bridged networks. The network operator needs to define a separate external endpoint group under the "external bridged network." Then a contract can be defined to enable the communication between the internal EPG (any EPG defined under the application profile that needs to use the external Layer 2 outside connection) and the external EPG, as depicted in Figure 13-25.

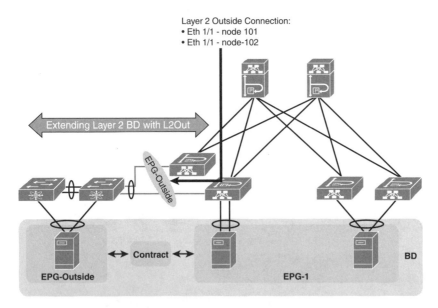

Figure 13-25 *Extending Layer 2 Using the L2Out Option*

> **Note** Although both options described here use the same bridge domain to connect external Layer 2 entities as directly attached endpoints, the L2Out option places external endpoints under external EPGs, which offer more granular policy control because policies will be applied between the internal and the external EPG. In addition, flooding between the two domains will be contained because Layer 2 flooding is not allowed, by default, between different EPGs in the Cisco ACI.

ACI Integration with STP-Based Layer LAN

Although the Cisco ACI fabric does not run Spanning-Tree Protocol natively, it does forward spanning-tree bridge protocol data units (BPDU) between ports within an EPG. For example, in the scenarios depicted in Figure 13-26, switches A and B are connected to a different port on a different Cisco ACI leaf switch; however, these ports reside in the same EPG of the external Layer 2 outside EPG. In this scenario, the Cisco ACI fabric floods BPDU frames within the same EPG. With this behavior, switches A and B will act as if they are connected directly to each other (the ACI will appear as a Layer 2 transport). As a result, the segment between switch B and the Cisco ACI fabric is blocked. This means external devices can leverage STP/BPDU to prevent any potential Layer 2 loops. Also, the Cisco ACI offers other protection mechanisms against external loops, such as the following:

- Link Layer Discovery Protocol (LLDP) detects direct loopback cables between any two switches in the same fabric.

- Mis-Cabling Protocol (MCP) is a new link-level loopback packet that detects an external Layer 2 forwarding loop.

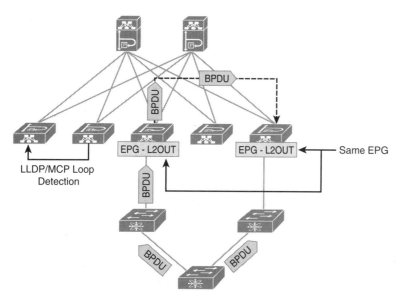

Figure 13-26 *ACI Interaction with External Layer 2 STP-based Network*

In Figure 13-26, both L2Out options belong to the same EPG; otherwise, Layer 2 flooding and BPDU won't be forwarded between different EPGs even if they reside within the same BD.

In addition, with this behavior, there will be hardware forwarding only and no interaction with CPU on leaf or spine switches for standard BPDU frames. This protects CPU against any Layer 2 flood that is occurring externally.

ACI Routing

As you know from the previous sections, ACI fabric decouples the tenant endpoint address, its "identifier," from the location of that endpoint that is defined by its "locator," or VTEP address. Thus, the forwarding within the fabric is between VTEPs, and the VTEPs perform internal tenant MAC or IP address mapping to location using the distributed mapping database concept.

This capability enables the ACI fabric to support full Layer 2 and Layer 3 forwarding semantics, where no changes are required to applications or endpoint IP stacks. The following sections discuss the main component of the ACI fabric architecture to perform Layer 3 routing and forwarding within the ACI fabric as well as between the ACI fabric and external networks.

First-Hop Layer 3 Default Gateway in ACI

With the Cisco ACI, network operators and designers do not need to worry about considering additional protocols to provide Layer 3 gateway services such as HSRP because the Cisco ACI offers what is known as "Pervasive SVI," which provides a distributed default gateway. This Anycast gateway is global across the fabric and configured on top of rack (ToR) leaf switches wherever the bridge domain of a tenant is present. In addition, the subnet default gateway addresses are programmed in all leaves with endpoints present for the specific tenant IP subnet. This not only helps to reduce design and operation complexity but also helps to a large extent to optimize traffic forwarding across the ACI fabric. When a packet needs to be routed to another leaf or external network, it does not need to span the network to reach its default gateway that could reside on another leaf, as illustrated in Figure 13-27.

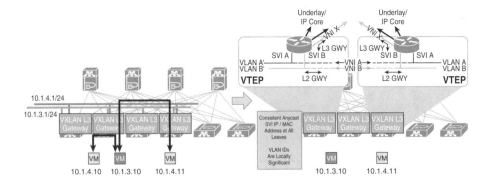

- The same Anycast SVI IP/MAC is used at all VTEPs/ToRs.
- A host will always find its SVI anywhere it moves.

Figure 13-27 *ACI Distributed Default Gateway (Pervasive SVI)*

That said, the Cisco ACI still supports the external gateway, which is commonly used when the fabric is deployed to provide Layer 2 transport only for a specific tenant, or if the organization security standards require that the default gateway must be a firewall, as shown in Figure 13-28. Also, using the external default gateway as a temporary approach helps during migration scenarios (refer to this chapter case study for more details).

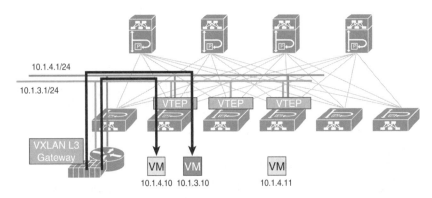

Figure 13-28 *ACI External Default Gateway*

Border Leaves

The border leaves are ACI leaf nodes that provide Layer 3 connections to the outside (an external network can be either a Layer 3 routed network such as WAN/Internet or Layer 2 such as Data Center Interconnect). Any ACI leaf node can be used as a border leaf node. There is no limitation to the number of leaf switches that you can use as border leaves. The number depends on the network scale, number of external and redundant connections, and so on. The border leaf can also be used to connect to compute, IP storage, and service appliances. In large-scale design scenarios, it may be preferred to have border leaf switches separated from the leaves that connect to compute and service appliances for scalability reasons. In this case, these border leaves are referred to as service leaves to distinguish them from the border leaves that connect the ACI to external network. Both service leaf nodes and border leaf nodes perform the same function, which is providing connectivity to external nodes or networks, as illustrated in Figure 13-29.

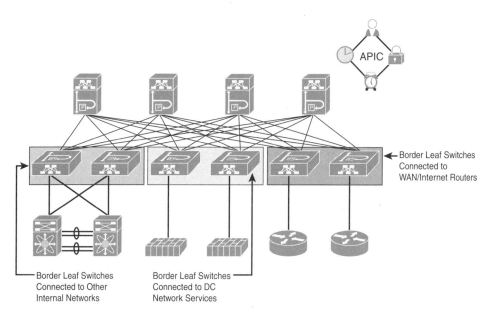

Figure 13-29 *Showing ACI with Connectivity to the External Network, Services, and So On*

> **Note** Like any typical network node, the border leaf switches support the following interface types to connect to external networks (see Figure 13-30):
>
> - **Layer 3 interface (routed):** Used when connecting to dedicated external devices per tenant/VRF.
> - **Subinterface with 802.1Q tagging:** Used when connecting to shared external devices across tenants/VRFs (VRF-Lite).
> - **Switched virtual interface (SVI):** Used when connecting to devices that require Layer 2 connectivity between devices. Used when both Layer 3 and Layer 2 connections are required on the same interface.

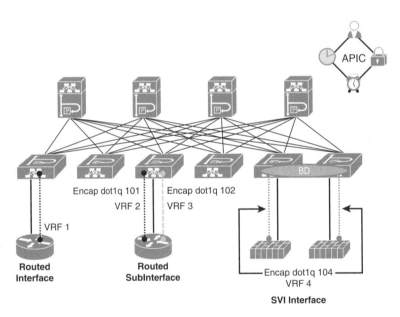

Figure 13-30 *Cisco ACI-supported Interface Types to Connect to External Networks*

Route Propagation inside the ACI Fabric

At the time of this writing, within the ACI fabric, Multiprotocol BGP (MP-BGP) is used between leaf and spine switches to propagate external routes within the ACI fabric. In addition, the BGP route reflector technology is enabled on the spine switches to support a large number of leaf switches within a single fabric. With this architecture, all of the leaf and spine switches are in one single BGP autonomous system (AS). The use of MP-BGP facilitates routes' propagation of different tenant networks without adding any control plane complexity (different routing instances are not required across the ACI fabric). Consequently, when the border leaf node learns the external routes, it can then redistribute the external routes of a given VRF to an MP-BGP address family VPN version 4 (or VPN version 6). With address family VPN version 4, MP-BGP maintains a separate BGP routing table for each VRF. Within MP-BGP, the border leaf advertises routes to a spine switch, which is a BGP route reflector. The routes are then propagated to all the leaves where the VRFs (or private network in the APIC GUI's terminology) are instantiated. Figure 13-31 illustrates the routing protocol across the ACI fabric as well as between the border leaf and external router with VRF-lite.

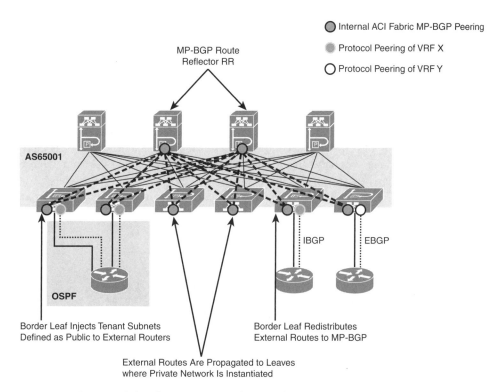

Figure 13-31 *High-level Architecture of ACI Fabric Route Propagation*

> **Note** The recent versions of the Cisco ACI support the ACI fabric to act as a transit network between different L3Out connections, but you may need to configure an "export route control policy" for the transit prefix to allow the ACI fabric to advertise it out through another L3Out connection.

As shown in Figure 13-31, the spine nodes only have MP-BGP sessions with the leaf nodes. They don't have BGP sessions with any external router; therefore, they can't be used as BGP RR for that purpose. Also, the same AS number is used for internal MP-BGP as well as for the iBGP session between the border leaf switches and external routers. In addition, Cisco ACI border leaf switches offer the flexibility to set BGP community or extended community values for tenant routes using an outbound BGP policy.

> **Note** MP-BGP is not enabled, by default, in the ACI fabric. For a deployment scenario in which the ACI fabric is used as Layer 2 fabric or there is no need for a Layer 3 outside connection, MP-BGP is not required. To enable MP-BGP, configure BGP policy on the APIC to specify the BGP ASN and specify spine nodes as BGP route reflectors. After these two are configured, the APIC will take care of the rest, such as configuring IBGP peering between the leaf and the spine, and specifying leaves as route reflector clients. It will also automatically generate the required configuration for route redistribution on the border leaf.

Connecting the ACI Fabric to External Layer 3 Domains

As you know from the previous section, the ACI enables you to define an L2Out connection to provide connectivity with an external network using a Layer 2 interconnection. In this case, you need to define a separate external EGP for the L2Out and then define a contract between any internal EPG and this external EPG that requires the communication over this connection. Similarly, the Layer 3 external connection (also known as Layer 3 out or L3Out) uses the same logic. However, it is used to provide Layer 3 connectivity (routed), where typically you will need to have more configurations such as an interface (physical or SVI) IP address and define the routing protocol used with the external peer and its attributes.

> **Note** Before configuring any Layer 3 external routed connection, ensure that routing and MP-BGP are enabled. Also, make sure that the required access polices (covered earlier in this chapter) are configured and applied to the targeted leaf node/interface, in which you can specify the VLAN ID(s) if you want to define Layer 3 SVI(s). Enabling MP-BGP in Cisco ACI is as simple as selecting the spines that will operate as BGP route reflectors and configuring the autonomous system number (ASN).

In fact, creating L3Out is a simple task as long you understand the required objects and the policy construct logic. To create an external L3Out, you need to consider the following logic:

Step 1. Create external routed networks.

Step 2. Add/select a Layer 3 border leaf node for the Layer 3 outside connection.

Step 3. Add/select a Layer 3 interface profile for the Layer 3 outside connection.

Step 4. Repeat Steps 2 and 3 if you need to add additional leaf nodes/interfaces.

Step 5. Configure an external EPG. The ACI fabric maps external Layer 3 endpoints/ routes to the external EPG by using the IP prefix and mask. One or more external EPGs can be supported for each Layer 3 outside connection, depending on whether the user wants to apply a different policy for different groups of external endpoints. You may treat all outside endpoints equally and create only one external EPG.

Step 6. Configure a contract between the external and the internal EPG. The ACI policy model requires a contract between the external and internal EPGs. Without this, all connectivity to the outside will be blocked, even if external routes are learned properly. This is part of the security model of ACI.

Note For a subnet in a bridge domain to be announced to the outside, ensure that the following configuration is in place: the subnet must be configured under the bridge domain and the EPG, and marked as advertised externally (or public). Also, you should mark the subnet as shared if you need to leak it to other VRFs.

Integration and Migration to ACI Connectivity Options

ACI provides the flexibility for existing data center environments to be integrated or migrated to the new fabric using any of the following options (see Figure 13-32):

- Migration of hosts to the new fabric
- Migration of fabric extenders (FEX) to the ACI fabric
- Migration of the aggregating Cisco Nexus 5x00 series switches and dependent FEXs to the ACI fabric
- Interconnection of the entire existing data center to the ACI fabric (using L3Out, L2Out, or both depends on the application requirements and migration approach)

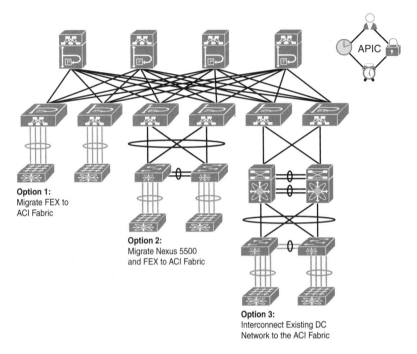

Figure 13-32 *Integration and Migration Options to ACI*

In addition, one of the valid approaches to grow your existing data center toward ACI is to start adding data center access switches as Nexus 9300 series using vPC (to act as the leaf switches), as shown in Figure 13-33.

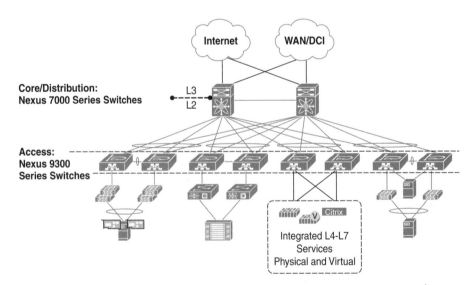

Figure 13-33 *Growing the Existing DC toward ACI: Stage 1*

In the next step, you can migrate the existing Nexus 9300 access switches gradually so that they are connected to the ACI fabric spine switches, such as Nexus 9500 series switches, to act as leaf switches, as shown in Figure 13-34.

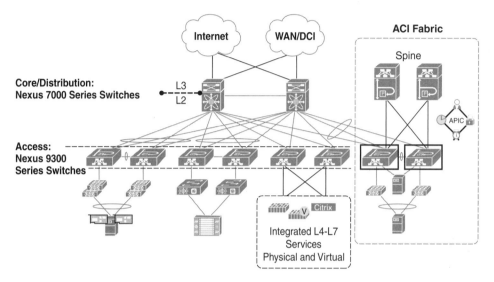

Figure 13-34 *Growing the Existing DC toward ACI: Stage 2*

Whichever solution you choose, you should ensure Layer 2 connectivity between the host segment and the leaf in order to benefit from the Cisco APIC's capability to manage services end to end.

Summary

Today's data center architects and operators have many choices to make in designing and implementing the data center LAN. After decisions to meet business requirements for application agility and network performance, the most critical decisions the data center architect makes pertain to the operation of the data center LAN. Operating costs often far outweigh the actual cost of the equipment that is purchased. A solution with implicit automation and self-provisioning can offer operation advantages over traditional switching infrastructure. It is also conceptually easier to manage the data center network as a whole entity rather than to manage multiple separate switches.

As you learned from this chapter, the Cisco Application-Centric Infrastructure (ACI) combines traditional high-performance switching technologies (Cisco 9000 series switches) with advanced management and automation capabilities. This ultimately will enable data center operators to accelerate application deployment, simplify operations, and treat the network as a resource pool similar to the way that servers and storage resources are treated today. This approach is known as a zero-touch fabric.

Several elements of the Cisco ACI fabric are designed to enable this zero-touch operation experience:

- A logically central but physically distributed controller for policy
- Easy startup with topology autodiscovery, automated configuration, and infrastructure addressing
- A simple and automated policy-based upgrade process and automated image management

In addition, the Cisco ACI policy-model eliminates the disconnect between application language and network language; this is primarily facilitated by the application network profile. However, as a network designer, you need to have a good understanding of application communication requirements. Without this information, it will be a challenge to design an application-driven communication model. Table 13-1 summarizes the different design requirements and the possible solutions using Cisco ACI capabilities and features.

Table 13-1 *Summary of Cisco ACI Solution to Common Design Needs*

Design Requirement	Solution
Network-wide management	APIC Controller
Open programming interfaces	REST with XML or JSON
	Partner ecosystem
	DevNet community (https://developer.cisco.com)
Abstraction of devices and network topologies	EPGs and contracts
	Automation of physical infrastructure configuration
Flexibility of resource utilization	Orchestration
Mobility of resources	ACI fabric mode
	CDP or LLDP
Microsegmentation	EPGs and contracts
Flexible and easy-to-manage data center services	ACI Service insertion
VM level network visibility and control	Hypervisor integration with the Cisco ACI APIC Controller

Review Questions

After answering the following questions, please refer to Appendix A, "Answers to Review Questions," for the answers.

1. Which statement about the Cisco ACI is correct? (Select two.)
   a. Cisco ACI is a policy-based data center solution.
   b. Cisco ACI is a FabricPath-based data center solution.
   c. Cisco ACI focuses on application communication requirements.
   d. Cisco ACI focuses on routing protocol communication requirements to meet application needs.
   e. Cisco ACI relies on a three-tier data center design model.

2. Which statement about the Cisco ACI is correct?
   a. Cisco ACI provides an any-to-any Fabric communication-based FabricPath overlay
   b. Cisco ACI provides an any-to-any Fabric communication-based VXLAN overlay.
   c. Cisco ACI focuses on application communication requirements.
   d. Cisco ACI does not support Clos architecture.
   e. Cisco ACI relies on a three-tier data center design model.

3. Match each Cisco ACI object with its descriptions:

ACI Object	Description
EPG	Represents a private network and is equivalent to VRF
Contract	Provides a mean of grouping endpoints based on a certain common communication requirement or application attribute
NAP	Allows or denies communication between EPGs
Context	Contains EPGs and contracts for a given application or service that can be applied to the ACI fabric

4. Which statement about ACI border leaf is correct?
   a. A switch that connects the ACI links only
   b. Any leaf switch that connects the ACI fabric to any external link or service
   c. A switch that provides VXLAN gateway service to communicate with legacy Layer VLANs

5. Which statement about the ACI bridge domain is correct?
   a. It's an ACI object that provides function similar to Layer 3 VRF.
   b. It's an ACI object that provides function similar to Layer 2 VLAN.
   c. It provides a transport underlay for VXLAN VTEPs.

6. What are the drivers to consider ACI in large multitenant data centers? (Select two.)
   a. Enables you to manage complex application communications requirements from a single management and controller interface
   b. Does not use overlays such as VXLAN
   c. Provides a next-generation data center model that combines both SDN automation and provisioning capability with high-performance underlay hardware
   d. Provides less bandwidth utilization

7. Which statement about Cisco ACI APIC correct?
   a. Is a switch that connects the ACI ACI links only
   b. Is the Cisco ACI SDN controller that provides centralized management and monitoring to the entire ACI fabric
   c. Provides monitoring and reporting functions only

8. Which statement about VXLAN in Cisco ACI is correct?
   a. VXLAN encapsulates Ethernet frames within TCP packets.
   b. Each leaf switch will have a VTEP per tenant or VRF.
   c. Each leaf switch will have a single VTEP for all the defined tenants or VRF.
   d. Frames are encapsulated only on end hosts.

References

1. "Is Cisco Application Centric Infrastructure an SDN Technology?," http://www.cisco.com/c/en/us/solutions/collateral/data-center-virtualization/application-centric-infrastructure/white-paper-c11-733456.html

2. "Cisco Application Centric Infrastructure (ACI) - Endpoint Groups (EPG) Usage and Design," http://www.cisco.com

3. See note 2 above.

4. See note 2 above.

5. L. Avramov & M. Portol, *The Policy Driven Data Center with ACI*, (Cisco Press, 2014).

Chapter 14

Data Center Connections

Upon completing this chapter, you will be able to

- Name the data center traffic flow directions
- Describe data center traffic flow types
- Describe the need for data center interconnection
- Identify the IP address mobility problem
- Explain dark fiber DCI topologies
- Describe EoMPLS DCI
- Describe VPLS DCI
- Describe AToMoGRE
- Identify Layer 2 DCI caveats
- Identify and describe the differences between Layer 2 and Layer 3 DCI
- Describe OTV DCI
- Identify overlay networking DCI caveats

Server-to-server communication, high-availability clusters, networking, and security may require Layer 2 connectivity maintained across different access layer switches. In many instances, Layer 2 functionality must extend beyond a single data center, particularly when a campus framework extends beyond its original geography, spanning multiple long-distance data centers. Cisco recommends isolating and reducing Layer 2 networks to their smallest diameter, limited to the access layer.

Traffic flows between the data center and external devices, and communication between services and applications within a data center dictate the data center network design, specifically the Data Center Interconnect (DCI). This chapter focuses on how to identify predominant traffic flows in your data center and how to design a network that will fulfill capacity and resiliency requirements. Then it discusses what requirements and solutions you need to consider when designing a DCI.

Data Center Traffic Flows

This section covers the different directions and types of traffic flows in a data center.

Traffic Flow Directions

Data center traffic flows in three directions (see Figure 14-1):

- **North-south traffic:** This traffic enters or exits the data center and typically flows between the clients that are located outside the data center and servers in the data center.
- **East-west traffic:** This traffic flows between the servers or devices in the data center and does not leave the data center.
- **Inter-DC traffic:** This traffic flows between multiple data centers across the DCI.

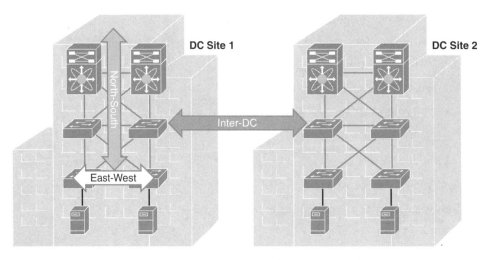

Figure 14-1 *Data Center Traffic Flow Directions*

> **Note** North-south and east-west terms describe traffic flow directions based on a network topology scheme in which the core is positioned on top (north) and servers at the bottom (south). Also, east-west traffic can span the DCI between two data centers.

Unlike in a campus network, in a typical data center the dominant volume traverses in an east-west direction. The Cisco Global Cloud Index estimates that 76 percent of global data center traffic traverses east-west, 17 percent traverses north-south, and 7 percent traverses between the data centers.

Traffic volume and direction dictate not only the oversubscription of a data center topology, but also the position of a Layer 2 or Layer 3 border. Strong north-south traffic prefers a small Layer 2 domain with Inter-VLAN routing in the aggregation layer. However, predominant east-west traffic advocates a large Layer 2 domain with Inter-VLAN routing in the core layer.

Note As you know from the preceding chapter, with the Cisco ACI, you will have more optimized inter-VLAN routing for inter- and intra-DC traffic flows using the concept of a distributed (Anycast) default gateway.

Traffic Flow Types

Client-server traffic is typically north-south traffic that enters or exits the data center and flows between the clients that are located outside the data center and servers in the data center. Nevertheless, the use of firewalls and load balancers adds a component of east-west traffic between the appliances and servers, as shown in Figure 14-2. You must carefully plan oversubscription of links between the core and aggregation layers to provide sufficient bandwidth for a number of servers.

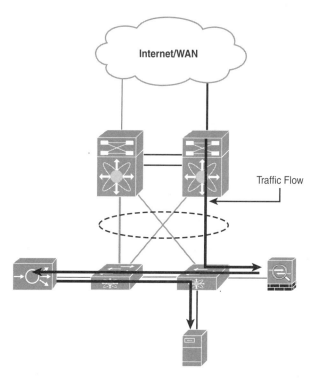

Figure 14-2 *Typical North-South Traffic Passing through Data Center Services*

Server-server traffic is typically east-west traffic, which never exits the data center or sometimes is limited to a single Layer 2 domain. It can flow directly from server to server, or if there are security and scalability demands, appliances such as firewalls and load balancers can be put in between. Typical server-server traffic follows (see Figure 14-3):

- Virtual machine (VM) migration
- Communication between the application server and the database (tier applications)
- State and transaction replications between servers in the same cluster, and so on

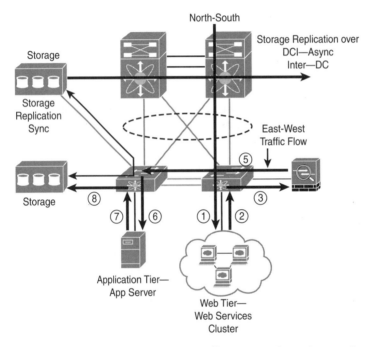

Figure 14-3 *Typical East-West Traffic Passing through Data Center Services*

When server-server traffic flows between servers in different data centers, it traverses the DCI. You must carefully tailor Inter-DCI traffic because the DCI link capacity is typically magnitudes lower than the capacity available inside the data center.

The third traffic type in modern data centers is storage traffic. NFS, iSCSI, FCoE, and other storage protocols utilize the existing data center network for their traffic. There are three types of storage traffic: server-storage traffic, synchronous replication between storage arrays, and asynchronous replication between storage arrays. Server-storage traffic and synchronous replication require low latency and may demand extra mechanisms such as lossless Ethernet or Jumbo frame. Therefore, they are typically kept inside a Layer 2 domain, do not transit any other appliances, and are considered east-west traffic, as shown in Figure 14-4.

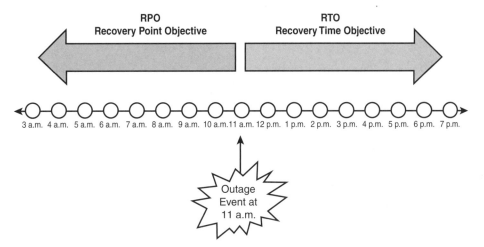

Figure 14-4 *RPO and RTO*

Note Standard Ethernet is a best-effort medium, which means that it lacks any form of flow control. If congestion or collisions occur, Ethernet drops packets. A set of network technologies, including IEEE Data Center Bridging, enables Ethernet fabrics to support lossless transmission, making them suitable for carrying all types of SAN traffic.

When storage replication between dislocated data centers is required, storage traffic has to traverse the DCI. Unless the data centers are suitably close together (100–200 km), DCI's capacity, latency, and reliability are not suitable for synchronous replication; consequently, the asynchronous replication is more commonly used over DCI.

With synchronous replication, all data committed on the first storage array is synchronized to the second storage array, before the server gets an acknowledgment that data is committed. With asynchronous replication, commits on the first storage array are queued and sent to the second storage array when possible, resulting in potential data loss if the first storage array fails.

> **Note** During the planning of storage replication over a DCI, network architects need to consider two important factors (see Figure 14-4):
>
> - **Recovery Point Objective (RPO):** This is the amount of data loss that's deemed acceptable, defined by the application, if an outage occurs. RPO can range from zero data loss to minutes or hours of data loss, depending on the criticality of the application or data. For example, synchronous data replication is capable of offering low to zero data loss RPO; however, it can be an expensive choice with distance limitations because of its high-bandwidth and low-latency requirements.
>
> - **Recovery Time Objective (RTO):** This is the amount of time to recover critical business processes to users from initial outage, ranging from zero time to many minutes or hours.
>
> Ideally, the level of criticality of a business application should define the acceptable RPO and RTO target if a planned or unplanned outage occurs.

The Need for DCI

Today's businesses rely to a large extent on technology to facilitate achieving their business goals. Therefore, availability of business-critical applications and technology solutions is key for any business to continue its operation and succeed. Consequently, business continuity is a fundamental requirement for today's businesses. Business continuity (BC), also referred to as business continuity planning (BCP), aims to build a standard plan to keep business operations intact during and after any failure scenario. BCP is a fundamental requirement for some organizations that cannot tolerate any service outage, such as health care, financial services, and online retailers. Typically, this is driven by either a huge cost caused by any simple outage or by the critical provided services, such as health-care services, which cannot accept any downtime. Disaster recovery is one of the mechanisms that helps to achieve BC by having a redundant component that can be used in failure scenarios, such as recovering a failed server using a redundant server that can be located in the same physical location or a different location.

The deployment of geographically dispersed data centers enables the data center designer to put in place effective disaster-avoidance and disaster-recovery mechanisms that increase the availability of the applications. Geographic dispersion also enables optimization of the application response through improved facility placement and allows flexible mobility of workloads across data centers to avoid demand hotspots and fully utilizes available capacity.

To enable all benefits of geographically dispersed data centers, different types of communication may be required between the data centers (see Figure 14-5):

- The typical VM and IP address mobility requires Layer 2 DCI. However, this goal is also achievable over Layer 3 DCI using advanced technologies such as LISP.

- Transaction replication of a database cluster or application synchronization of an application cluster requires Layer 3 communication over a DCI (some legacy applications may need Layer 2).

- Storage replication requirements differ, depending on the storage protocol used. FC requires Layer 1 DCI (fiber optics), FCoE Layer 2 DCI, iSCSI Layer 3 DCI, and so on.

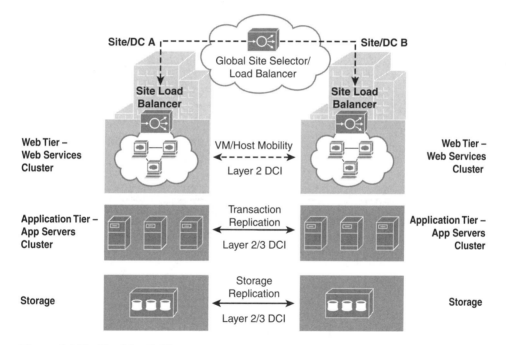

Figure 14-5 *Need for DCI*

IP Address Mobility

As mentioned earlier, Layer 2 DCI enables simple VM and IP address mobility. However, some implications with this design need to be considered. For instance, in Figure 14-6, see the virtual server at the Site A data center with the 203.0.113.100 public IP. Traffic leaves the local VLAN through the 203.0.113.1 gateway and is forwarded through the core layer and out to the Internet.

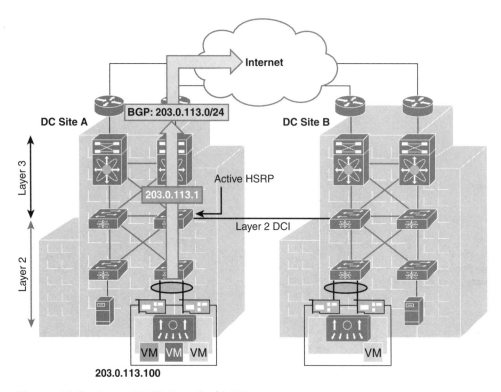

Figure 14-6 *Layer 2 DCI: Stretched LAN*

When the VM is migrated into the Site B data center, it keeps its IP address and still belongs to the same VLAN. Its gateway, however, remains on Site A, and the IP network it belongs to is still advertised into the Internet from Site A. VLAN traffic is thus forwarded from Site B across the Layer 2 DCI to Site A and then rerouted to the Internet, as shown in Figure 14-7.

IP Address Mobility 485

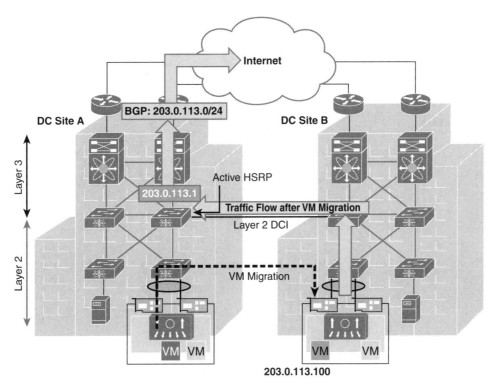

Figure 14-7 *Layer 2 DCI: Egress Traffic Flow*

As a network designer proposing a design like this, you should ask the question, "What happens when the DCI fails?" VM's default gateway is now unreachable.

Although this problem could be addressed by using FHRP with default gateways on both sites, there is still a question of return traffic because the BGP still advertises the subnet from Site A. Some of the servers from the same subnet could still be running on Site A, as shown in Figure 14-8, so BGP advertising of the same network from Site B is not a solution and may cause the *split brain* issue. This occurs when servers from different data centers serve the content to different parts of the Internet without synchronization with each other while the DCI is down. Split brain may lead to state inconsistency and data corruption.

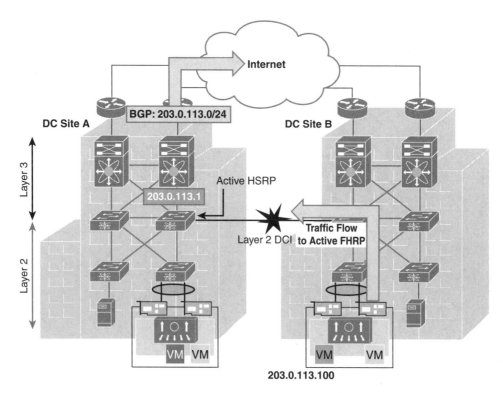

Figure 14-8 *Layer 2 DCI Failure Scenario*

Another issue occurs with VM migration. Figure 14-9 shows two VMs that have their default gateways in another data center. When a VM at Site B is communicating with a VM at Site A, its traffic goes from Site B through the DCI to Site A, to its default gateway. The default gateway forwards the traffic back through the DCI to Site B based on the routing table entry. The VLAN 20 default gateway at Site B accepts the traffic and, based on its content addressable memory (CAM) table, sends it through VLAN 20 back to the server located on Site A.

IP Address Mobility 487

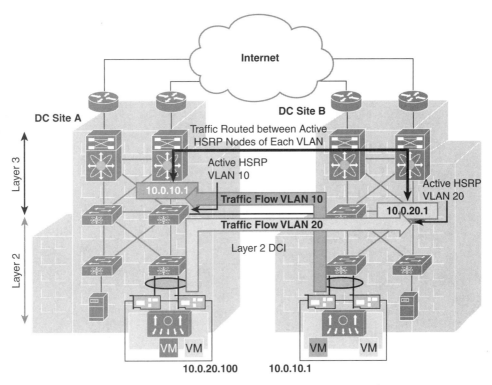

Figure 14-9 *Layer 2 DCI Traffic Trombone*

In this worst-case scenario, traffic must traverse the DCI three times before reaching its destination host; this effect is called a *traffic trombone*, which occurs when a single traffic flow keeps traversing the DCI. If you have a large volume of traffic traversing the DCI that interconnects two data centers located in different geographical locations, this can reduce application performance and ultimately will impact the user's experience.

The issue of IP mobility is not easily solvable because the IP address expresses two pieces of information in a single address: device identity and device position in the network. Several initiatives exist that separate those two pieces of information in two separate addressing spaces—for instance, LISP IP/host-level mobility awareness, as illustrated in Figure 14-10.

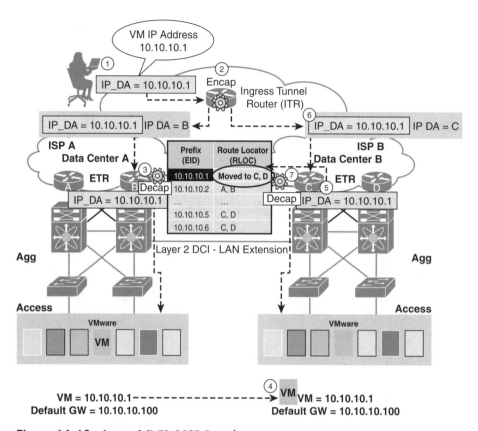

Figure 14-10 *Layer 2 DCI: LISP Based*

The steps shown in Figure 14-10 are summarized here:

Step 1. The Ingress Tunnel Router (ITR) consults the directory to get the Route Locator (RLOC) for the destination endpoint ID (EID).

Step 2. The ITR IP-in-IP encapsulates traffic to send it to the RLOC address.

Step 3. The Egress Tunnel Routers (ETR) receive and decapsulate traffic.

Up to Step 3, the traffic is directed to the local (home) DC where the VM/host is located; the subsequent steps describe the traffic handling when a VM moves to the secondary (remote) DC.

Step 4. The VM with IP 10.10.10.1 moves to the second DC (DC B).

Step 5. The ETR updates the mapping DB or the RLOC to map the VM host IP /23 10.10.10.1/32 to point to nodes/xTR C and D in DC B.

Step 6. New sessions destined to the host with IP 10.10.10.1 will be routed to DC B.

Step 7. The ETRs receive and decapsulate traffic.

You must focus not only on the ingress traffic flow optimization, but for egress traffic direction, you also need to achieve FHRP localization. (For example, you need to filter HSRP messages over the Layer 2 DCI to ensure symmetrical routing for both inbound and outbound traffic flows after VM or host migration.) Therefore, in this scenario, the default gateway Virtual MAC (vMAC) and IP addresses (vIP) in both data centers should remain consistent, because the mobile workload would most likely continue to send packets to the same GW IP address after the live mobility event is completed. Virtual MAC consistency is usually achieved in extended subnet mode by configuring the same HSRP group associated with the same subnet in separate data center sites. Also, usually HSRP filtering is configured, leveraging ACLs to drop Hellos and prevent the exchange across the LAN extension connection.

Note With LISP, the remote sites or the edge gateway interfacing non-LISP sites (also known as the Proxy tunnel router) need to be LISP-capable for LISP to operate as expected.

Stretching your high-availability server cluster with VM mobility across multiple data centers might not be a good idea due to the increased Layer 2 flooding domains. You should utilize a second data center as a DRC instead. That, however, is not always a network engineer's choice. For instance:

- Applications that require Layer 2 connectivity will still need a LAN extension (Layer 2 clustering, and so on).
- Traffic for legacy applications may not be routable, so it will still need to use LAN to be extended across DCs.

Furthermore, you must understand that considering IP or host mobility with a stretched LAN over DCI (Layer 2 DCI) introduces the following challenges for ingress traffic:

- Subnets are spread across locations.
- Subnet information in the routing tables is not specific enough.
- Routing doesn't know if a server has moved between locations.
- Traffic may be sent to the location in which the application is not available.

To mitigate or overcome the challenges, consider one of the following options for the DCI when possible:

- Layer 3 DCI with DNS redirection (this option works for applications that can be reached by name)
- Layer 2 or Layer 3 DCI with LISP (host-based routing)
- Layer 3 DCI with Anycast routes' advertisement (this concept is covered later in the "Layer 3 DCI" section)

Case Study: Dark Fiber DCI

Dark fiber can be considered a Layer 1 type of service. It is popular among many customers today because it allows the transport of various types of traffic, native Ethernet, IP, and MPLS, including SAN traffic. It tends to be expensive, especially as the number of sites increases. Dark fiber is commonly used to build Wavelength Division Multiplexer networks (most commonly Dense Wavelength Division Multiplexer Device, or DWDM), spanning Layer 2 Ethernet over MAN distances up to 100 km, providing Layer 2 DCI.

Note The term *dark fiber* refers to the fiber capacity that is installed but not in use (that is, not lit up); therefore, it is available for lease.

Note WDM is a technology that multiplexes a number of optical carrier signals onto a single optical fiber by using different wavelengths of laser light. WDM provides the media layer to initiate the various point-to-point physical layers (built from each available wavelength of the optical link). There are two common types of WDM:

- **CWDM:** Coarse Wavelength Division Multiplexing can be used with WDM systems that need fewer than eight active wavelengths per fiber.
- **DWDM:** Dense Wavelength Division Multiplexing can be used with WDM systems with more than eight active wavelengths per fiber. At press time, it can provide up to 96 DWDM wavelengths over a single pair of fibers.

In this case study, your company has two data centers. You need to establish a point-to-point DCI. A dark fiber DWDM link is available between the two sites, enabling you to initiate multiple Layer 2 connections. As a network designer, you need to think first about the following question: "Which data center layer(s) should the DC interconnect be placed at and how?" (see Figure 14-11).

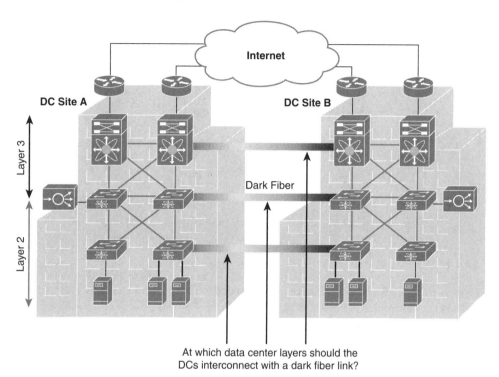

Figure 14-11 *Where to Place DCI Dark Fiber*

Although you could use either access or aggregation layer switches to extend your LAN between two sites, it is recommended that you interconnect the data centers over a dark fiber using the aggregation layers of each DC.

To achieve this, you need to connect one aggregation switch at Site A with the aggregation switch at Site B and the other aggregation switch at Site A with another aggregation switch at Site B. To exclude any Layer 2 loops, bundle the two links in a Multichassis EtherChannel (MEC) and join the aggregation switches on both sites with vPC/VSS. This approach supports an end-to-end, fully redundant Layer 2 network without the need for STP, as illustrated in Figure 14-12. However, you should keep STP enabled as the last resort in case of software or fiber or cable misconfigurations.

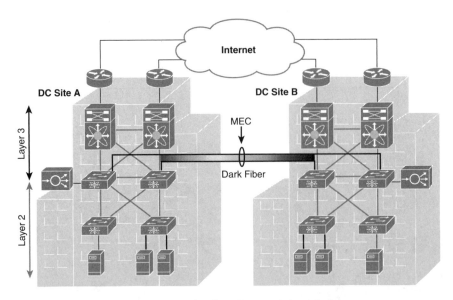

Figure 14-12 *Layer 2 DCI Dark Fiber Connectivity Model*

Now assume the number of data centers you need to interconnect increases. Four remote data centers are interconnected using a DWDM ring. DWDM provides the media layer to initiate the various point-to-point physical layers (see Figure 14-13). How will you connect the four data centers with a loop-free Layer 2 topology?

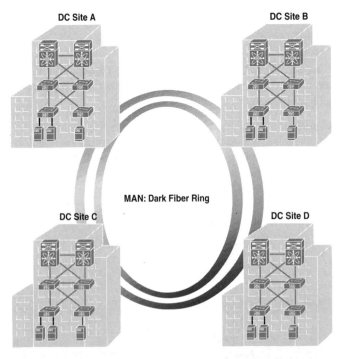

Figure 14-13 *Multisite Layer 2 DCI over DWDM Ring*

A logical star topology offers a scalable, loop-free interconnection for all data centers. In this design model, you need to establish a Layer 2 core with redundant switches clustered using vPC/VSS to allow MEC between the aggregation layer of each DC and the newly added Layer 2 core, as shown in Figure 14-14. The Layer 2 core, however, needs to be placed on one of the existing sites. Where will you place the redundant Layer 2 core switches to achieve the best scalability, redundancy, and lowest latency?

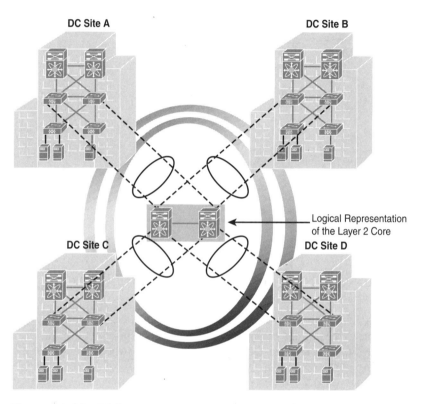

Figure 14-14 *Multisite Layer 2 DCI Using Logical Start Connectivity Model*

Note If you are using Clos architecture in your DC, you should use the border leaf nodes to connect the DCI link(s).

A crucial architecture point is that you spread physical switches that comprise the Layer 2 core onto different remote sites, thus offering high availability. Consequently, you need to establish a logical point-to-point connection between the Layer 2 core switches using DWDM and bundle them with vPC/VSS, as shown in Figure 14-15.

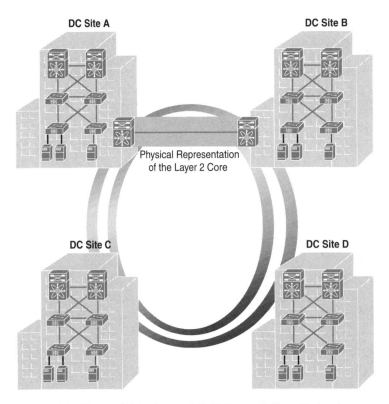

Figure 14-15 *Multisite Layer 2 DCI: Layer 2 Core Redundancy*

The logical point-to-point connections are laid out to produce a virtual star topology with the Layer 2 core as the hub and the aggregation pairs as the spokes. One of the aggregation switches at Site A is connected to the Layer 2 core A switch using the local link. The other aggregation switch at Site A is connected to the Layer 2 core B switch at Site B, using one of the available DWDM point-to-point links created between Sites A and B. Sites B, C, and D are configured in a similar manner.

Applying this same interconnection methodology to all sites yields a highly flexible design. The only limitation is the maximum number of uplinks available from the Layer 2 core and the maximum number of wavelengths available from the DWDM ring. In addition, the more you extend a Layer 2 domain, the larger the flooding domain will be across different DC locations, which can lead to a higher degree of instability (Layer 2 storms) and suboptimal routing.

Pseudowire DCI

As you know from the preceding section, dark fiber is an expensive connectivity model, might not be available on-site (geographical distribution limitation), and has its range limits (scalability). Today's service providers (such as Carrier Ethernet) typically offer a less expensive service: pseudowires. Pseudowire is an emulation of a point-to-point connection over a packet-switched network. Ethernet over MPLS (EoMPLS) is a typical service provider pseudowire service that offers a point-to-point Ethernet connection. Any ingress Layer 2 traffic on one location will be transported and delivered to the remote location as is, whether it is data or a control packet. (Refer to Chapter 8, "Service Provider Managed VPNs," for more details.)

When you are interconnecting two data centers, best practice is to bundle two Ethernet pseudowires and then disable STP between the locations to contain STP topology changes inside the location (see Figure 14-16).

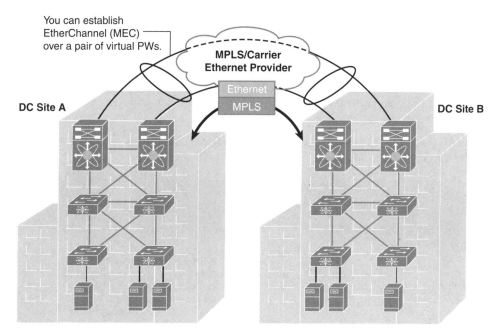

Figure 14-16 *Layer 2 DCI: Pseudowire Based*

Virtual Private LAN Service DCI

As you know from Chapter 8, the Virtual Private LAN Service (VPLS) is a class of VPN that supports the connection of multiple sites in a single bridged domain over a managed IP or MPLS network. VPLS presents an Ethernet interface to customers, while the service provider network acts as a switched LAN.

Because the VSS/vPC pair of switches now connects to the VPLS network that emulates an IEEE Ethernet bridge, the use of EtherChannel is no longer possible. Layer 2 loops in the network need to be solved with the use of STP. The introduction of STP in DCI not only blocks some of the redundant links but also extends the STP domain across the DCI. This action is undesirable because it floods BPDUs across DCIs, resulting in bridge forwarding table flushes at Site B when topology changes happen on Site A, and so on.

Advanced VPLS (A-VPLS) is the Cisco enhancement of the existing Layer 2 VPN VPLS solution. It extends the MEC concept into the VPLS network, allowing the use of MEC on redundant links across the VPLS network as long as the switches on the customer's site are in VSS/vPC. Figure 14-17 shows the classical VPLS and A-VPLS connectivity models from a DCI perspective. The Cisco Layer 2 VPN A-VPLS feature introduces the following enhancements to VPLS:

- Capability to load-balance traffic across multiple core interfaces using equal-cost multipathing (ECMP), while the typical VPLS cannot support active/active attachment circuits/paths

- Command-line interface (CLI) enhancements to facilitate configuration of the L2VPN A-VPLS feature

- Support for redundant Cisco Data Center Interconnect (DCI) and provider-edge switches

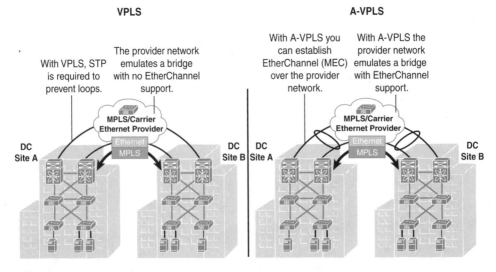

Figure 14-17 *VPLS versus A-VPLS*

Customer-Managed Layer 2 DCI Deployment Models

The preceding sections covered the different possible L2VPN-based DCI options, including pseudowire and VPLS. The model covered in these sections is based on the fact that the service provider (for example, Carrier Ethernet) is responsible for provisioning the required Layer 2 connectivity model to the customer for DCI purposes, whether it is point-to-point or multipoint-to-multipoint. However, in some scenarios, the enterprise customers have their own managed WAN/MAN routed network, and they need to overlay a Layer 2 DCI technology using any of the discussed technologies in this chapter. Figure 14-18 depicts these two different provisioning models.

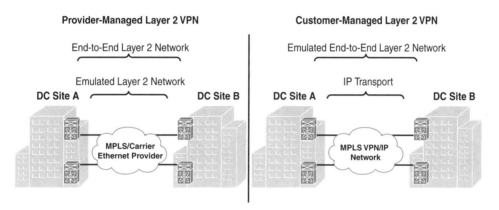

Figure 14-18 *Layer 2 VPN Provisioning Models*

Any Transport over MPLS over GRE

When service providers do not provide Layer 2 VPN services or when DCI needs to be established over an existing enterprise IP core, EoMPLS and VPLS cannot be used natively. You need to create an overlay to logically interconnect the enterprise devices in the different data centers and enable MPLS inside the overlay/tunnel. You typically achieve this result by using GRE tunnels. EoMPLS or VPLS traffic is encapsulated on a GRE tunnel, allowing Layer 2 traffic to flow over an existing IP core. The solution is called "any transport over MPLS over GRE" (AToMoGRE).

The resulting design is identical to deployment over the service provider's MPLS network. This approach enables the enterprise to build EoMPLS point-to-point across connections between two sites, while these connections are being transported over the existing IP core, as illustrated in Figure 14-19. MPLS does not need to be deployed in the core network.

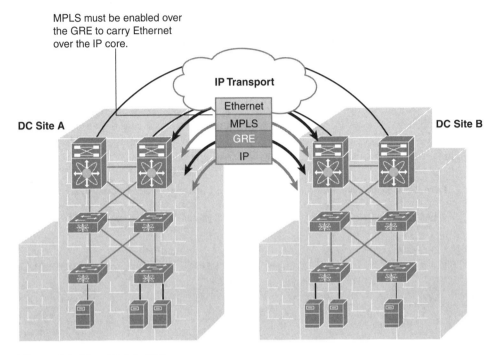

Figure 14-19 *AToMoGRE*

If the enterprise requirement wants to interconnect multiple sites in a multipoint fashion, VPLS is the recommended technology. Like EoMPLS, it can be transported over IP using a GRE tunnel.

When you are interconnecting two data centers, the best practice is to bundle two Ethernet pseudowires and then disable STP between the locations to contain STP topology changes inside the location.

Note You can also create point-to-point Layer 2 tunnels over native IP networks using L2TPv3.

Customer-Managed Layer 2 DCI Deployment

Unlike with AToMoGRE, in some scenarios, the enterprise customer owns the WAN/MAN core; therefore, it is possible to make it MPLS enabled (if it's not already enabled) so that you can overlay a Layer 2 VPN technology on top of it, such as point-to-point pseudowire, multipoint VPLS, or A-VPLS. As you learned earlier in the "Case Study:

Dark Fiber DCI" section, you should almost always deploy dark fiber DCI at the DC aggregation layer. In contrast, from a design point view, the aforementioned DCI technologies, such as AToMoGRE, pseudowire, and A-VPLS, can have different possible deployment models where you can apply the actual DCI relevant configuration. (Each model uses a different DC layer, and each has its own use case. In other words, there is no single best practice that must always be used.) The following are the most common deployment models:

- **Core layer deployment model:** The pseudowire, VPLS, or A-VPLS instances can be initiated from the core layer. An additional link needs to be connected from the aggregation to the core layer, and this link needs to be configured as a trunk link. Only VLANs that need to be transported across the Layer 3 domain should be allowed; all other VLANs should be disallowed, as shown in Figure 14-20.

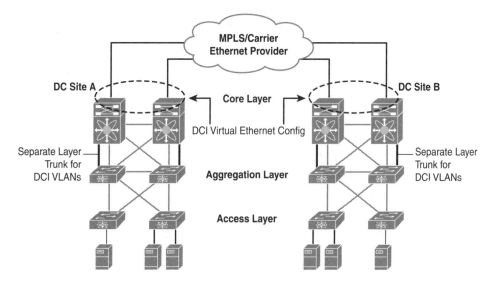

Figure 14-20 *DCI at the Core Layer Deployment Model*

- **Aggregation layer deployment model:** Most networks initiate their Layer 3 and Layer 2 boundaries from the aggregation layer. With this model, you almost never need to consider adding any additional link for the VLANs that need to be extended over the DCI, as shown in Figure 14-21. However, you need to ensure that your aggregation layer hardware and software support the DCI technology used, such as A-VPLS.

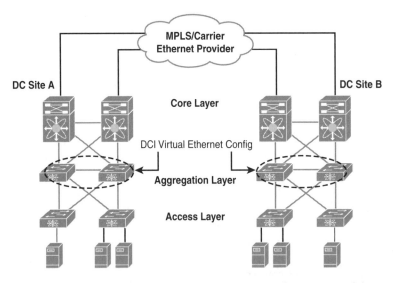

Figure 14-21 *DCI at the Aggregation Layer Deployment Model*

> **Note** If no specific requirement or design constraint mandates the use of any other deployment model, you should consider the aggregation layer deployment model due to its simplicity compared to the other models.

- **Separate DCI layer deployment model:** A separate layer can be created to extend the Layer 2 domain. This type of setup is useful in mixed-platform networks or large networks with multiple aggregation-layer switches, as shown in Figure 14-22.

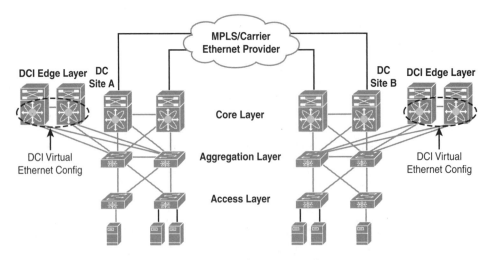

Figure 14-22 *DCI at Separate Layer Deployment Mode*

Layer 2 DCI Caveats

Existing mechanisms for the extension of Layer 2 connectivity are less than optimal in addressing connectivity and independence requirements and present many challenges and limitations.

Following are some of the challenges:

- **Data-plane learning and flooding:** The extension of Layer 2 domains across multiple data centers can cause the data centers to share failures that would normally have been isolated when interconnecting data centers over an IP network. These failures propagate freely over the open Layer 2 flood domain.

- **Layer 2 addressing is flat and nonhierarchical:** MAC addresses identify hosts; they do not point to their locations. It makes troubleshooting large Layer 2 topologies challenging. Layer 2 addressing is nonsummarizable, resulting in uncontrolled address-table growth for all devices in the Layer 2 domain.

- **Spanning tree across the DCI:** If a customer site is multihomed, STP needs to be running across the DCI core to prevent Layer 2 loops. Redundant links are blocked and their bandwidth wasted.

- **Multicast:** There is no native multicast replication support. When DCI consists of multiple pseudowires, multicast frames are flooded out through all pseudowires.

- **Complex operations:** Layer 2 VPNs can provide extended Layer 2 connectivity between data centers, but that will usually involve a mix of complex protocols, distributed provisioning, and an operationally intensive hierarchical scaling model. A simple overlay protocol with built-in capabilities and point-to-cloud provisioning is crucial to reducing the cost of providing this connectivity.

Therefore, in general, as a network architect, you should avoid considering a LAN extension unless it is a must for certain critical business applications. In this case, you may also look into advanced technologies that optimize Layer 2 DCI behavior, such as Overlay Transport Virtualization (OTV). Otherwise, you should always aim to use Layer 3 DCI.

Overlay Transport Virtualization DCI

AToMoGRE solutions require establishment of intermediate layers: MPLS. OTV is an IP-based functionality that has been designed from the ground up to provide Layer 2 extension capabilities over any transport infrastructure: Layer 2, Layer 3, MPLS, and so on.

As shown in Figure 14-23, the only requirement from the transport infrastructure is providing IP connectivity between remote data center sites. In addition, OTV provides an overlay that enables Layer 2 connectivity between separate Layer 2 domains while keeping these domains independent and preserving the fault-isolation, resiliency, and load-balancing benefits of an IP-based interconnection.

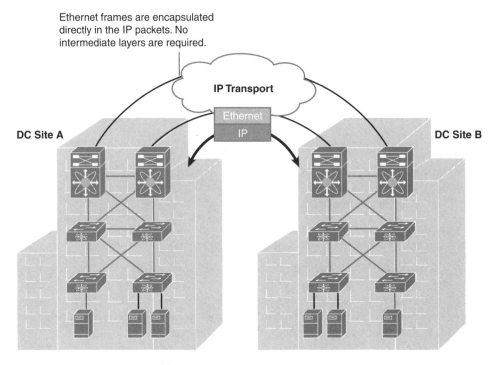

Figure 14-23 *OTV-Based DCI*

OTV introduces the concept of dynamic encapsulation for Layer 2 flows that need to be sent to remote locations. Each Ethernet frame is individually encapsulated into an IP packet and delivered across the transport network. Dynamic encapsulation eliminates the need to establish pseudowires between data centers.

In addition, OTV introduces the concept of "MAC routing." A control plane protocol is used to exchange MAC reachability information between network devices providing LAN extension functionality. This is a significant shift from Layer 2 switching that leverages data-plane learning, and it is justified by the need to limit flooding of Layer 2 traffic across the transport infrastructure. If the destination MAC address information is unknown, traffic is dropped (not flooded), preventing waste of precious bandwidth across the WAN.

The following are the main elements that construct OTV-based DCI (see Figure 14-24):

- The *edge device* is responsible for performing all the OTV functionality.
- The *internal interfaces* are those interfaces of the edge devices that face the site and carry at least one of the VLANs extended through OTV.
- The *join interface* is one of the uplink interfaces of the edge device. It is a point-to-point routed interface and can be a single physical interface as well as a port channel (which has higher resiliency).
- The *overlay interface* is a new virtual interface where all the OTV configuration is placed; it encapsulates the site's Layer 2 frames in IP unicast or multicast packets that are then sent to the other sites.

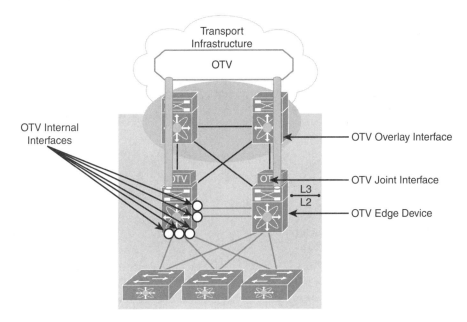

Figure 14-24 *OTV Solution Elements*

OTV encapsulation is performed in OTV edge devices, which are positioned at the edge of the Layer 2 domain. When the OTV edge device on Site A learns a new MAC address on its internal interface, via traditional Ethernet MAC learning, the OTV edge device then creates an OTV update message, containing the information about the MAC address.
It then sends that message across the IP network to all other OTV edge devices. MAC reachability information is imported in the OTV edge device's CAM. The only difference with a traditional CAM entry is that instead of being associated with a physical interface, OTV entries refer to the IP address of the originating OTV edge device.

When a Layer 2 frame is received at the OTV edge device, a Layer 2 lookup is performed. If MAC information in CAM points to an IP address of the remote OTV edge device, rather than a physical interface, the Ethernet frame is encapsulated in an IP packet and sent over the IP network to the remote OTV edge device.

The following steps summarize the traffic flow between two servers located in the same LAN segment across two data centers using OTV as the DCI solution. The frame goes from Server 1 (MAC 1) on Site A to Server 3 (MAC 3) on Site B (see Figure 14-25).

Step 1. Server 1 sends a frame to Server 3.

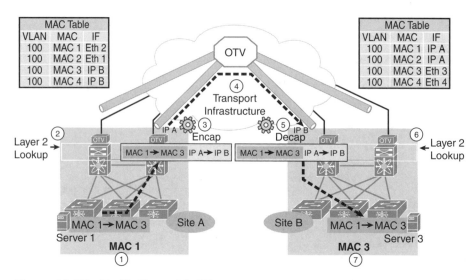

Figure 14-25 *Traffic Flow with OTV*

Step 2. The Layer 2 frame arrives at the Site A OTV edge device. A classic Layer 2 lookup on the destination MAC address takes place. The destination MAC address, MAC 3, is reachable through an IP address, which indicates that MAC 3 is not a local MAC. MAC 3 is, in fact, reachable through IP B, which is the IP address of the join-interface of the OTV Edge Device in site B.

Step 3. MAC 3 is reachable through IP B. The edge device then encapsulates the original frame into an IP packet where the *IP_SA* is IP A and the *IP_DA* is IP B.

Step 4. The encapsulated packet is now passed to the core, which will deliver it to its destination: the OTV edge device on Site B associated with IP address IP B.

Step 5. The OTV Edge Device on Site B with IP address B receives and decapsulates the packet. You now have the original Layer 2 frame.

Step 6. Another classic Layer 2 lookup is then performed on the frame. MAC 3 is now reachable through a physical interface. It's actually a local MAC.

Step 7. The Layer 2 frame is delivered to its destination server.

Note The routing protocol used to implement the OTV control plane is IS-IS. It was selected because it is a standard-based protocol, originally designed with the capability of carrying MAC address information.

OTV provides a native built-in multihoming capability with automatic detection, critical to increasing high availability of the overall solution. Two or more devices can be leveraged in each data center to provide LAN extension functionality without running the risk of creating an end-to-end loop. OTV does not require STP extended across the DCI.

OTV also provides other optimizations. OTV edge devices snoop ARP replies and signal IP to MAC bindings to remote nodes, thus reducing ARP broadcasts. OTV uses native IP multicast to help ensure optimal replication of multicast, broadcast, and signaling traffic.

Note OTV is currently supported on Cisco Nexus 7000 and Cisco ASR 1000 series routers.

Note As shown in Figure 14-26, considering LISP along with OTV will help you achieve ingress and egress localization with IP/VM mobility and avoid the standard limitations of extended LAN over a layer DCI.

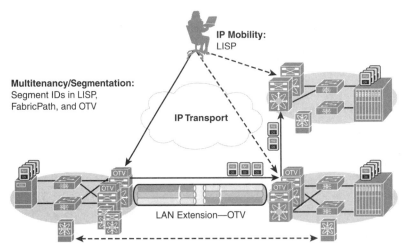

Figure 14-26 *IP Mobility with LISP and OTV*

Figure 14-27 summarizes the roles and places in the network and where to deploy LISP and OTV in typical interconnected DC networks.

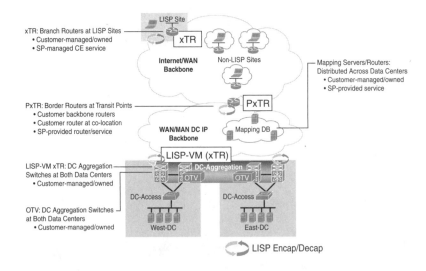

Figure 14-27 *Where to Deploy LISP and OTV*

Overlay Networking DCI

Overlay network protocols, such as VXLAN, are designed to span Layer 2 networks across the underlying IP network. Can they be used to provide Layer 2 DCI?

VXLAN was designed to address a different problem. It was designed to run within a single data center. VXLAN lacks the control plane and relies on standard Layer 2 data-plane addresses learning with unicast flooding, extending the Layer 2 fault domain across multiple data centers. Due to the MAC-in-IP encapsulation, VXLAN requires a 1600-byte MTU to accommodate the additional 24-bit header. While jumbo frames are readily supported inside a data center, it is not always the case on IP connections between the data centers.

Note VXLAN is not a DCI technology in its current state. You should use other technologies, such as OTV.

Layer 3 DCI

A Layer 3-based data center interconnection offers a simpler and more predictable design compared to the Layer 2 DCI. However, as covered earlier in this chapter, the design choice must always be derived from the upper-layer requirements, such as applications to achieve desired BC goals. Therefore, if the Layer 2 extension between data centers is not a must from a technical point of view, you should consider the routed or Layer 3-based DCI in this case because the routed DCI will help to avoid several design and operational complexities associated with the Layer 2 DCI (as discussed earlier in this chapter). For example, with the Layer 3 DCI model, fault domains will be contained within each site (following the fault-isolation principle). In turn, the model will provide a more stable and reliable DCI solution. The following are the common possible options to advertise data center networks when Layer 3 DCI is used (see Figure 14-28):

- **Option 1:** Each site has its own IP range (either a full or divided range). At the same time, each site advertises the other site's IP range (such as a summary of both sites' IP ranges, if this information is summarizable) for failover purposes.

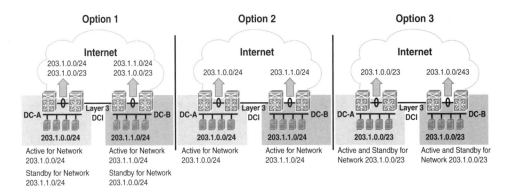

Figure 14-28 *Layer 3-based DCI with Different IP Advertisement Models*

- **Option 2:** Each site has its own IP range, and each DC/site is only required to provide connectivity to its local resources. (If one DC fails, it will not be reachable via the DCI, and the DCI here is used mainly for internal services' and systems' communications, such as replication, migration, and so on.)

- **Option 3:** Each site has the same IP range or a different IP range (with NAT at the edge); however, the advertised IP range is the same from each site. This model is also known as the "Anycast" model. With this approach, the DC sites will work in active-active mode, and load distribution across the data centers will be based on the geographical location of the traffic sources because the Internet route traffic moves from the source to the closest (in hops) DC site (for example, the path with lowest number of hops). With this model, users trying to access DC services will be routed to the closest DC site and automatically routed to the next closest site in case of a DC failure.

Nevertheless, the approach you should choose must be based on the business, applications, and functional requirements of the interconnected DCs.

For example, Figure 14-29 shows an organization using the Layer 3 DCI (using the Option 2 design model, described earlier). In this scenario, the site/DC selection is first performed by the global site selector (GSS). This is accomplished commonly based on DNS in which the main service or application is accessed via the GSS using a single name /URL such as www.example.com, and each site has its own local load balancer with its own virtual IP address (VIP) that points to the site/DC local resources. With this approach, this organization can achieve active-active interconnected data centers. As previously described, with this design model (option 2), the DCI is used only for data center services communications, such as data replication. In case of any DC site failure, the GSS will direct all traffic to the remaining DC site only.

Note GSS functionality can be provided either by the ISP or by the customer.

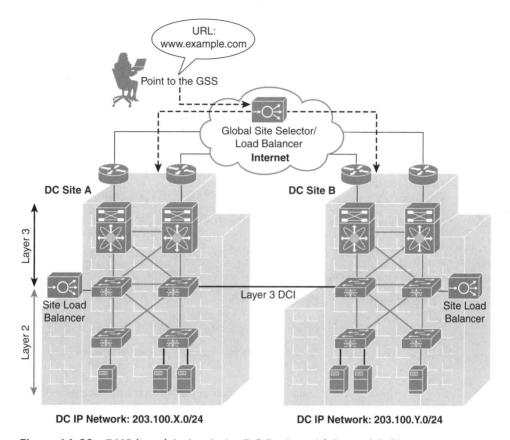

Figure 14-29 *DNS-based Active-Active DC Design with Layer 3 DCI*

Summary

- DCI is needed for
    - VM mobility (Layer 2, or Layer 3 with IP/host mobility routing such as LISP)
    - Transaction replication (Layer 3)
    - Storage replication (Layers 1, 2, 3)
- IP address mobility with Layer 2 DCI has caveats, including split brain and traffic trombone.
- Dark fiber is good for establishing any kind of DCI over Layer 1, but it might not be available and its range is less than 100 km.
- Service provider VPNs are EoMPLS (point-to-point) and VPLS (multisite).
- Enterprise-managed VPNs are

- EoMPLSoGRE
- L2VPN over enterprise-managed MPLS WAN/MAN
- OTV (Ethernet over IP, preferred)

Review Questions

After answering the following questions, please refer to Appendix A, "Answers to Review Questions," for the answers.

1. Which of the following DCI statements is true?
   a. Data centers require a Layer 2 DCI.
   b. A Layer 2 DCI should be avoided, unless absolutely required by the applications.
   c. Asynchronous storage replication requires a Layer 2 DCI.
   d. IP address mobility problems are easily solvable with a Layer 2 DCI.

2. Match the DCI technology with its description.

DCI Technology	Description
Dark Fiber	Limited range, used to build DWDM networks
VPLS	Uses pseudowires, enterprise-managed VPN over Layer 3 network
OTV	Supports connection of multiple sites. SP managed VPN.
EoMPLSoGRE	Transports Layer 2 over Layer 3 network. Has control plane protocol and does not use data-plane flooding for address learning.

3. Which statement about OTV is true?
   a. OTV requires configuration of GRE tunnels.
   b. OTV edge devices do not use traditional Ethernet MAC learning.
   c. OTV edge devices do not import MAC reachability information in their CAM, but in their routing table.
   d. OTV edge devices snoop ARP replies and signal IP to MAC bindings to remote nodes, reducing ARP broadcasts.

4. Match the data center flow with the correct description.

Data Center Flows	Description
Inter-DC	Enters or exits the data center and typically flows between the clients that are located outside the data center and servers in the data center
North-south	Flows between the servers or devices in the data center and does not leave the data center
East-west	Flows across the DCI

5. Which statements about data center traffic flows are true? (Select two.)
   a. VM migration is a typical east-west traffic.
   b. FC requires lossless Ethernet extension.
   c. Load balancers add a north-south component to existing east-west traffic.
   d. Only synchronous storage replication is possible over a long-distance DCI.
   e. Multitier applications increase the amount of east-west traffic.

6. Match the DCI technology with the correct design requirements.

DCI Technology	Design Requirements
DWDM Dark Fiber	Provides active-active DC design, provides VM mobility; each DC has its IP range; DCI must be used for data replication and VM migration traffic only
P2P AToMoGRE	Provides LAN extension between multiple data center sites
OTV	Interconnects two data centers only over IP transport
Layer 3 DCI + LISP	Interconnects two data centers only with the capability to provide separate 10 Gbps for transport for storage replication (FC) and separate 10 Gbps for Layer 2 DCI traffic over single physical link.

7. Which statements about avoiding a traffic trombone between data centers are true? (Select two.)
   a. You need to align the ingress and egress traffic flows within the same DC.
   b. Layer 3 DCI will always lead to a traffic trombone issue.
   c. Localizing FHRP per DC and using an IP/host mobility routing protocol such as LISP will help to avoid a traffic trombone issue.
   d. By using A-VPLS, you can overcome a traffic trombone issue.

8. Which statements about L2VPN-based DCI are true? (Select two.)
   a. VPLS provides the capability to use flow-based load balancing over different edge DCI devices.
   b. A-VPLS provides the capability to use load balancing over different edge DCI devices.
   c. L2VPN technologies such as VPLS can be established over any IP transport to emulate a Layer 2 bridged network.
   d. OTV provides a built-in capability to localize the active FHRP per DC site.

Chapter 15

QoS Overview

Upon completing this chapter, you will be able to

- Describe and compare the IntServ and DiffServ QoS models
- Provide an overview of classification and marking tools
- Understand Layer 2 marking with CoS
- Understand Layer 3 marking with ToS
- Understand Layer 3 marking with DSCP and PHB
- Understand Layer 2.5 marking with MPLS experimental bits
- Understand Layer 7 classification with NBAR
- Explain and contrast the role and usage of policers and shapers
- Describe token bucket algorithms
- Describe single-rate three-color markers
- Understand the two-rate three-color marker and compare it to a single-rate three-color marker
- Explain the concept of queuing
- Describe buffer control with Tx-Ring
- Describe fair queuing
- Describe CBWFQ queuing tools
- Describe LLQ queuing tools
- Describe DSCP-based WRED
- Describe IP ECN

Quality of service (QoS) is a foundational network technology that has been around for a while and that is still necessary regardless of the substantial increase in network link speeds over the years. This chapter focuses on the fundamental building blocks of QoS. Subsequent chapters leverage this foundational knowledge and dive deeper into general QoS design principles as well as QoS design for individual parts of the network.

QoS Overview

QoS is a crucial element of any administrative policy that mandates how to handle application traffic on a network. The fundamental purpose of QoS is to manage contention for network resources and maximize the end-user experience of a session. Given that not all packets are equal, they should not be treated equally.

In any network in which networked applications require differentiated levels of service, traffic must be sorted into different classes upon which QoS is applied. Classification and marking are two critical functions of any successful QoS implementation. Traffic policing and traffic shaping are two QoS techniques that can limit the amount of bandwidth that a specific application, user, or class of traffic can use on a link. You can use congestion avoidance mechanisms to reduce the negative effects of congestion by penalizing the most aggressive traffic streams when software queues begin to fill. However, congestion management techniques can provide you with an effective means to manage software queues and to allocate the required bandwidth to specific applications when congestion exists.

IntServ versus DiffServ

Two different models exist for addressing QoS on a network. The Integrated Services (IntServ) model was introduced to supplement the best-effort delivery by setting aside some bandwidth for applications that require bandwidth and delay guarantees. IntServ expects applications to signal their requirements to the network. The Differentiated Services (DiffServ) model was added to provide greater scalability for addressing QoS requirements for IP packets.

Some applications, such as high-definition videoconferencing, require consistent, dedicated bandwidth to provide a sufficient experience for users. IntServ was introduced to guarantee predictable network behavior for these types of applications. Because IntServ reserves bandwidth throughout a network, no other traffic can use the reserved bandwidth.

IntServ provides hard QoS guarantees such as bandwidth, delay, and packet-loss rates end to end. These guarantees ensure both predictable and guaranteed service levels for applications. There will be no effect on traffic when guarantees are made because QoS requirements are negotiated on establishment of the connection, and Connection Admission Control (CAC) ensures that no new traffic will violate existing guarantees. These guarantees require an end-to-end QoS approach, which introduces both complexity and scalability limitations. Because each node needs to build and maintain state per flow, in large-scale networks with thousands or millions of flows, this introduces control plane complexity and adds extra overhead on the network devices along the flow path.

Using IntServ is like having a private courier airplane or truck that is dedicated to the delivery of your traffic. This model ensures quality and delivery, but it is expensive and has scalability issues.

DiffServ was designed to overcome the limitations of the IntServ models. DiffServ provides a cost-effective and scalable "almost guaranteed" QoS model. With the DiffServ model, QoS mechanisms are used without prior signaling, and QoS characteristics (for example, bandwidth and delay) are managed on a hop-by-hop basis with policies that are established independently at each device in the network. This approach is not considered an end-to-end QoS strategy because end-to-end guarantees cannot be enforced. It is important to note, however, that DiffServ is a more scalable approach to implementing QoS because hundreds or potentially thousands of applications can be mapped into a smaller set of classes upon which similar sets of QoS behaviors can be implemented. Although QoS mechanisms in this approach are enforced and applied on a hop-by-hop basis, uniformly applying a global policy to each consistent traffic class provides both flexibility and scalability.

With DiffServ, network traffic is divided into classes that are based on business requirements. Each of the classes can then be assigned a different level of service. As the packets traverse a network, each of the network devices identifies the packet class and services the packets according to this class. You can choose many levels of service with DiffServ. Examples of implementing different levels of service include voice traffic from IP phones being given preferential treatment over all other application traffic and e-mail being given best-effort service. Nonbusiness, or scavenger, traffic can either be given poor service or blocked entirely.

DiffServ works like a package delivery service. You request (and pay for) a level of service when you send your package. Throughout the package delivery process, the level of service is recognized, and your package is given either preferential or normal treatment, depending on what you requested.

DiffServ, as noted, is highly scalable and provides many different levels of quality service configuration; however, it does have the following drawbacks:

- No absolute guarantee of service quality can be made.
- It requires a set of complex mechanisms to work in concert throughout the network.

Table 15-1 provides a summary comparison of the IntServ versus DiffServ characteristics covered in this section.

Table 15-1 *IntServ versus DiffServ Characteristics*

Integrated Services (IntServ)	Differentiated Services (DiffServ)
IntServ is similar to a private courier service.	DiffServ is similar to a package delivery service.
An application signals requirement to the network.	Classification identifies network traffic.
It guarantees predictable network behavior.	Network QoS policy enforces differentiated treatment of traffic classes.
No other traffic can use reserved bandwidth.	The user defines level of service for each traffic class.

Classification and Marking

This section defines and explains the need and design of QoS classification and marketing. It also discusses different classifications and marking mechanisms and design considerations of each.

Classifications and Marking Tools

Packet classification uses a traffic descriptor to categorize a packet within a specific group to define this packet. Marking is related to classification and allows network devices to leverage a specific traffic descriptor to classify a packet or frame.

Commonly used traffic descriptors include

- Class of service (CoS)
- Incoming interface
- IP precedence
- Differentiated Services Code Point (DSCP)
- Source address
- Destination address
- Application
- MPLS EXP bits

After the packet has been defined or classified, the packet is then accessible for QoS handling on the network. Packet classification creates an opportunity for you to partition network traffic into multiple priority levels or classes of service. When traffic descriptors are used to classify traffic, the source agrees to adhere to the contracted terms, and the network promises a specific level of QoS. Different QoS mechanisms, such as traffic policing, traffic shaping, and queuing techniques, use the traffic descriptor of the packet (that is, the classification of the packet) to ensure adherence to the defined agreement.

Classification and marking should always take place at the network edge, typically in the wiring closet, in IP phones or at network endpoints. It is recommended that classification occur as close to the source of the traffic as possible to ensure traffic flows receive the desired treatment from its entry point to the network all the way to the destination or exit point (hop by hop).

The concept of trust is key for deploying QoS. When an end device such as a workstation or an IP phone marks a packet with a CoS or DSCP value, a switch or router has the option of accepting or not accepting values from the end device. If the switch or router chooses to accept the values, the switch or router trusts the end device. If the switch or router trusts the end device, it does not need to do any reclassification of packets coming from the device as they enter the interface. If the switch or router does not trust the device, it must perform a reclassification to determine the appropriate QoS value for the packets coming from the device in through the interface. Switches and routers are generally set to not trust end devices and must specifically be configured to trust packets coming from an interface.

Figure 15-1 shows the typically used traffic descriptors including CoS, DSCP, IP precedence, and MPLS EXP bits. Marking can be used to set information in the Layer 2 or Layer 3 packet headers.

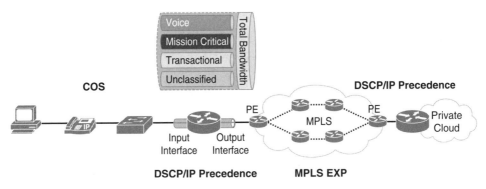

Figure 15-1 *QoS Traffic Descriptors*

Marking a packet or frame with its classification allows network devices to easily distinguish the marked packet or frame as belonging to a specific class. After the packets or frames are identified as belonging to a specific class, other QoS mechanisms can use these markings to uniformly apply QoS policies. The following sections explore classification and marking in greater detail.

Layer 2 Marking: IEEE 802.1Q/p Class of Service

The packet classification and marking options that are available at the data link layer depend on the Layer 2 technology. Each Layer 2 technology has its own mechanism for classification and marking. For the marking to persist beyond the Layer 2 network, translation of the relevant field must take place.

The 802.1Q standard is an IEEE specification for implementing VLANs in Layer 2 switched networks. As shown in Figure 15-2, the 802.1Q specification defines two 2-byte fields, Tag Protocol Identifier (TPID) and Tag Control Information (TCI), which are inserted within an Ethernet frame following the Source Address (SA) field.

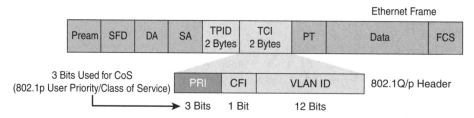

Figure 15-2 *802.1Q Layer 2 QoS Tagging*

The TPID field is currently fixed and assigned the value 0x8100. The TCI field is composed of three fields:

- **User priority bits (3 bits):** The IEEE 802.1p standard defines the specifications of this 3-bit field. These bits can mark packets as belonging to a specific CoS. The CoS markings use the three 802.1p user priority bits and allow a Layer 2 Ethernet frame to be marked with eight levels of priority (values 0–7). The 3 bits allow a direct correspondence with IPv4 (IP precedence) type of service (ToS) values. The 802.1p specification defines these standard definitions for each CoS:

    - CoS 7 (111): network
    - CoS 6 (110): Internet
    - CoS 5 (101): critical
    - CoS 4 (100): flash-override
    - CoS 3 (011): flash
    - CoS 2 (010): immediate
    - CoS 1 (001): priority
    - CoS 0 (000): routine

    One disadvantage of using CoS marking is that frames lose their CoS markings when transiting a non-802.1Q or non-802.1p link. Non-802.1Q/802.1p links include any type of non-Ethernet WAN link. When designing end-to-end QoS, you should consider a more permanent marking mechanism for network transit, such as Layer 3 IP DSCP marking. This goal is typically accomplished by translating a CoS marking into another marker or simply using a different marking mechanism to begin with.

- **CFI (1 bit):** This bit indicates whether the bit order is canonical or noncanonical. The Canonical Format Indicator (CFI) bit is used for compatibility between Ethernet and Token Ring networks.

- **VLAN identifier, or VLAN ID (12 bits):** The VLAN ID field is a 12-bit field that defines the VLAN that is used by 802.1Q. Because the field is 12 bits restricts the number of VLANs that are supported by 802.1Q to 4096.

> **Note** Legacy Layer 2 WAN transports such as ATM and frame-relay carry QoS markings in their headers.

Layer 3 Marking: IP Type of Service

Link layer media often changes as a packet travels from its source to its destination. As noted in the previous section, the CoS field does not exist in a standard Ethernet frame, and therefore, CoS markings at the link layer are not preserved as packets traverse nontrunked or non-Ethernet networks. Using marking at Layer 3 provides a more permanent marker that is preserved from source to destination. At Layer 3, IP packets are commonly classified based on source or destination IP address, packet length, or the contents of the ToS byte.

Figure 15-3 provides a closer look at the header of an IPv4 packet and, in particular, the ToS byte.

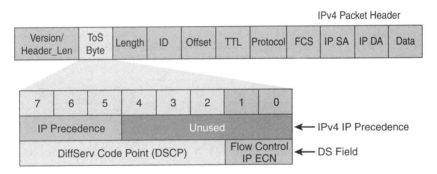

Figure 15-3 *IPv4 Header—ToS*

IP precedence uses three precedence bits in the ToS field of the IPv4 header to specify the service class for each packet. IP precedence values range from 0 to 7 and enable you to partition traffic in up to six usable classes of service. It is important to note that values 6 and 7 are reserved for internal network use.

The newer DiffServ model supersedes and is backward compatible with IP precedence. This has resulted in making IP precedence practically obsolete. DiffServ redefines the ToS byte as the DiffServ field and uses six prioritization bits that permit classification of up to 64 values (0 to 63), of which 32 are commonly used. A DiffServ value is called a DSCP value.

With DiffServ, packet classification categorizes network traffic into multiple priority levels or classes of service. Packet classification uses the DSCP traffic descriptor to categorize a packet within a specific group to define this packet. After the packet has been defined (classified), the packet is then accessible for QoS handling on the network.

The first 6 bits of the ToS byte are used for marking while the last 2 bits are reserved for flow control and explicit congestion notification (ECN).

ECN allows end-to-end notification of network congestion without dropping packets. ECN is an optional feature that may be used between two ECN-enabled endpoints when the underlying network infrastructure also supports this capability. When ECN is successfully negotiated, an ECN-aware router may set a mark in the IP header instead of dropping a packet to signal impending congestion. The receiver of the packet echoes the congestion indication to the sender, which reduces its transmission rate as though it detected a dropped packet. Because ECN marking in routers depends on some form of active queue management, routers must be configured with a suitable queue discipline to perform ECN marking. Cisco IOS routers perform ECN marking if configured with the weighted random early detection (WRED) queuing discipline.

Layer 3 Marking: DSCP Per-Hop Behaviors

Commonly, different per-hop behavior (PHB) values are used in today's networks, and they are based on the DSCP values of IP packets. Table 15-2 provides a breakdown of PHB and includes the associated use as well as DSCP bit settings.

Table 15-2 *IETF PHB Definitions*

PHB	Use	DSCP Bit Setting
Default	Used for best-effort service	Bits 5 to 7 of DSCP = 000
EF	Used for low-delay service	Bits 5 to 7 of DSCP = 101
AF	Used for guaranteed bandwidth service	Bits 5 to 7 of DSCP = 001, 010, 011, or 100
Class selector	Used for backward compatibility with non-DiffServ-compliant devices (RFC 1812 devices)	Bits 2 to 4 of DSCP = 000

Figure 15-4 provides a visual depiction of the mapping between PHB and DSCP bit settings.

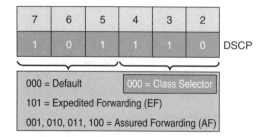

Figure 15-4 *PHB–DSCP Bit Mapping*

The EF PHB is intended to provide a guaranteed bandwidth rate with the lowest possible delay. This is achieved by providing prioritized forwarding for the EF PHB. Prioritized forwarding results in this PHB policing excess bandwidth so that other classes that are not using this PHB are not starved for bandwidth.

Packets requiring EF PHB should be marked with a DSCP binary value of 101110, or 46, as depicted in Figure 15-5; non-DiffServ–compliant devices will regard the EF DSCP value as IP precedence 5. This precedence is the highest user-definable IP precedence and is typically used for delay-sensitive traffic such as VoIP.

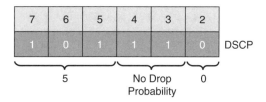

Figure 15-5 *EF and AF Marking*

The *AF PHB* defines a method by which different forwarding assurances can be given to the packets. Four standard defined AF classes are represented by the aaa values 001, 010, 011, and 100, as shown in Figure 15-6. Each class should be treated independently and should have allocated bandwidth that is based on the QoS policy.

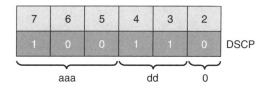

Figure 15-6 *AF Marking Standard Classes*

AF drop probability indicates the drop priorities of traffic within the AF classes. Each AF class is assigned an IP precedence and has three drop probabilities: low, medium, and high. Figure 15-7 provides a look into the relationship between drop probability and AF values.

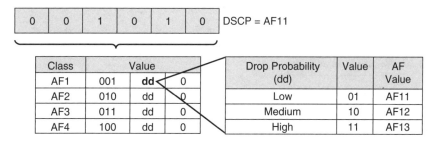

Figure 15-7 *AF/IPPrec Dropping Probabilities*

AFxy defined in RFC 2597 is an AF in which the value x corresponds to the IP precedence values 1 through 4, and value y corresponds to the drop preference value 1, 2, or 3. It is possible to calculate the DSCP value for an AF PHB by multiplying the IP precedence value by 8, multiplying the drop preference by 2, and then adding these values together. For example, the DSCP value for AF23 would be equal to $((2 * 8) + (3 * 2)) = 22$.

Table 15-3 illustrates the DSCP coding for specifying the AF class with the drop probability.

Table 15-3 *DSCP Dropping Probability*

Drop	AF1x	AF2x	AF3x	AF4x
Low	AF11 = DSCP 10 or 001010	AF21 = DSCP 18 or 010010	AF31 = DSCP 26 or 011010	AF41 = DSCP 34 or 100010
Medium	AF12 = DSCP 12 or 001100	AF22 = DSCP 20 or 010100	AF32 = DSCP 28 or 011100	AF42 = DSCP 36 or 100100
High	AF13 = DSCP 14 or 001110	AF23 = DSCP 22 or 010110	AF33 = DSCP 30 or 011110	AF43 = DSCP 38 or 100110

Table 15-4 applies the calculation that was just shared to come up with the same values referred to in Table 15-3.

Table 15-4 *DSCP Dropping Probability Calculation*

Drop	AF1x	AF2x	AF3x	AF4x
Low	AF11 = $((1 * 8) + (1 * 2)) = 10$	AF21 = $((2 * 8) + (1 * 2)) = 18$	AF31 = $((3 * 8) + (1 * 2)) = 26$	AF41 = $((4 * 8) + (1 * 2)) = 34$
Medium	AF12 = $((1 * 8) + (2 * 2)) = 12$	AF22 = $((2 * 8) + (2 * 2)) = 20$	AF32 = $((3 * 8) + (2 * 2)) = 28$	AF42 = $((4 * 8) + (2 * 2)) = 36$
High	AF13 = $((1 * 8) + (3 * 2)) = 14$	AF23 = $((2 * 8) + (3 * 2)) = 22$	AF33 = $((3 * 8) + (3 * 2)) = 30$	AF43 = $((4 * 8) + (3 * 2)) = 38$

The meaning of the 8 bits in the DiffServ DS field of the IP packet shown in Figure 15-8 have changed over time to meet the expanding requirements of IP networks.

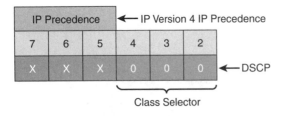

Figure 15-8 *IP Packet DiffServ DS Field*

As previously noted, originally the DS field was referred to as the ToS field, and the first 3 bits of the field (bits 5 to 7) defined a packet IP precedence value. A packet could be assigned one of six priorities based on the IP precedence value. As noted in RFC 791, IP precedence 5 (101) was the highest priority that could be assigned.

RFC 2474 replaced the ToS field with the DS field. The class-selector PHB and range of eight values were defined to provide backward compatibility for DSCP with ToS-based IP precedence. RFC 1812 simply prioritizes packets according to the precedence value, essentially mapping IP precedence to DSCP. The *PHB* is defined as the probability of timely forwarding. Packets with higher IP precedence should be on average forwarded in less time than packets with lower IP precedence during an interface congestion period.

The last 3 bits of the DSCP, bits 2–4, set to 0, identify a class-selector PHB. You can calculate the DSCP value for a CS PHB by multiplying the class number by 8. For example, the DSCP value for CS3 would be equal to (3 * 8) = 24.

Table 15-5 provides a detailed view of DSCP to IP precedence mappings and includes both binary and decimal DS field values for your reference.

Table 15-5 *DSP to IP Precedence Mapping*

DSCP Value	DS Field Value		IP Precedence
	Binary	Decimal	
CS0	000 000	0	0
CS1	001 000	8	1
AF11	001 010	10	1
AF12	001 100	12	1
AF13	001 110	14	1
CS2	010 000	16	2
AF21	010 010	18	2
AF22	010 100	20	2
AF23	010 110	22	2
CS3	011 000	24	3
AF31	011 010	26	3
AF32	011 100	28	3
AF33	011 110	30	3
CS4	100 000	32	4
AF41	100 010	34	4
AF42	100 100	36	4
AF43	100 110	38	4
CS5	101 000	40	5
EF	101 110	46	5
CS6	110 000	48	6
CS7	111 000	56	7

Layer 2.5 Marking: MPLS Experimental Bits

Marking within an MPLS environment falls somewhere between Layer 2 and Layer 3 and requires a different type of descriptor. The MPLS EXP field is a 3-bit field in the MPLS header that you can use to define the QoS treatment and per-hop behavior that a node should give to a packet.

As previously noted, when a customer transmits IP packets from one site to another, the IP precedence field specifies the class of service. The packet is given the wanted treatment, such as guaranteed bandwidth or latency based on the IP precedence marking. If the service provider network is an MPLS network, the IP precedence bits are copied into the MPLS EXP field at the edge of the network. In many cases and depending on the service offering, the service provider might want to set QoS for a MPLS packet to a different value.

The MPLS EXP field enables the service provider to provide QoS without overwriting the value in the customer IP precedence field. The IP header remains available for customer use, and the IP packet marking is not required to change as the packet travels through the MPLS network. Figure 15-9 provides a visual breakdown of the MPLS header and specifically the MPLS EXP field.

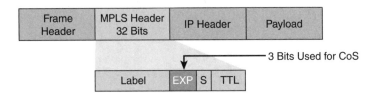

Figure 15-9 *MPLS Header*

Following are some important basic facts about MPLS QoS markings:

- MPLS uses a 32-bit label field referred to as a shim header that is inserted between Layer 2 and Layer 3 headers in frame mode.

- The 3-bit MPLS EXP field is used for QoS marking and supports up to eight classes of service.

- The IP precedence or DSCP field is not directly visible to MPLS label switch routers.

- By default, Cisco IOS software copies the three most significant bits of the DSCP or the IP precedence of the IP packet to the EXP field.

- The 3-bit MPLS EXP field is preserved throughout the MPLS network.

Mapping QoS Markings between OSI Layers

Unlike data link layer headers, IP headers are preserved end to end when IP packets are transported across a network. You might assume that this means that the IP layer is the most logical place to mark packets for end-to-end QoS. Marking traffic strictly at the IP layer is not always practical given that some edge devices can mark frames only at the data link layer, and many other network devices operate only at the Layer 2. With different marking mechanisms supported from Layer 2 to Layer 3, the capability to map QoS marking between the layers is essential to ensure interoperability and to provide true end-to-end QoS.

Enterprise networks frequently are composed of sites with a switched LAN. Providing end-to-end QoS through this type of an environment requires that CoS markings that are set at the LAN edge be mapped into QoS markings such as IP precedence or DSCP for transit through campus or WAN routers. Campus and WAN routers can also map the QoS markings to new data link headers for transit across the switched LAN. In this way, QoS can be preserved and uniformly applied across the enterprise.

Service providers offering IP services typically have a requirement to provide robust QoS solutions to their customers. The capability to map Layer 3 QoS to Layer 2 CoS enables these providers to offer a complete end-to-end QoS solution that does not depend on any specific link layer technology.

Compatibility between an MPLS transport layer and Layer 3 QoS is also achieved by mapping between MPLS EXP bits and the IP precedence or DSCP bits. A service provider can map the customer Layer 3 QoS marking as is or change it to fit an agreed-upon SLA. The information in the MPLS EXP bits can be carried end to end in the MPLS network, independent of the transport media. In addition, the Layer 3 marking can remain unchanged so that when the packet leaves the service provider MPLS network, the original QoS markings remain intact (unless MPLS QoS uniform tunneling mode is used in which the remarking of EXP will be reflected on the IP marking). In this way, a service provider offering MPLS services can ensure there is no break in a true end-to-end enterprise QoS solution. Figure 15-10 shows a mapping between the layers.

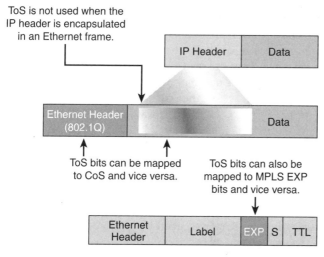

Figure 15-10 *ToS to EXP Mapping*

Layer 7 Classification: NBAR/NBAR2

Cisco *Network-Based Application Recognition (NBAR)*, a feature in Cisco IOS software shown in Figure 15-11, performs stateful bidirectional deep packet inspection of traffic as it flows through the network and identifies applications based on information in the packet payload.

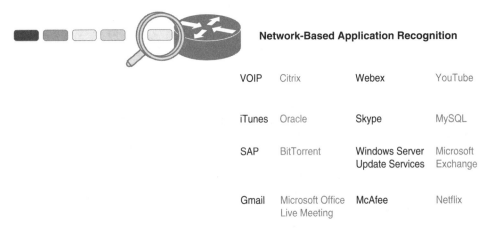

Figure 15-11 *Cisco NBAR*

Cisco NBAR can recognize a wide variety of protocols and applications, including web-based applications as well as client and server applications that dynamically assign TCP or UDP port numbers. After protocols and application have been intelligently classified leveraging NBAR, the network can invoke specific services for these protocols or applications.

When used in active mode, Cisco NBAR is enabled within the Modular QoS CLI MQC structure to classify traffic. Of course, the criterion for classifying packets into class maps using NBAR depends on whether the packet matches a specific protocol or application known to NBAR. Custom applications can be defined as part of the NBAR classification engine. Using MQC, network traffic matching a specific network protocol such as Citrix can be placed into one traffic class, while traffic that matches a different network protocol such as Skype can be placed into another traffic class. After traffic has been classified in this way, you can then set different Layer 3 marking values to different classes of traffic.

When used in passive mode, NBAR protocol discovery is enabled on a per-interface basis to discover and provide real-time statistics on applications traversing the network.

Next-generation NBAR, or *NBAR2*, is a fully backward-compatible re-architecture of Cisco NBAR with advanced classification techniques, improved accuracy, and support for more signatures. NBAR2 is supported on multiple devices including ISR-G2, ASR1000, ISR-4000, CSR1000, ASA-CX, and Cisco Wireless LAN Controllers (WLC).

Cisco NBAR protocol and signature support can be updated by installing newer Packet Description Language Modules (PDLM) for NBAR systems or Protocol Packs for NBAR2 systems. Support for modular upgrades allows for nondisruptive updates to the NBAR capabilities as updating of the base IOS image is not required.

Policers and Shapers

Traffic policing and *traffic shaping* are traffic-conditioning mechanisms that are used in a network to control the traffic rate. Both mechanisms differentiate traffic through the use of classification, and both measure the rate of traffic and compare that rate to the configured traffic-shaping or traffic-policing policy. Figure 15-12 highlights the difference between traffic shaping and traffic policing.

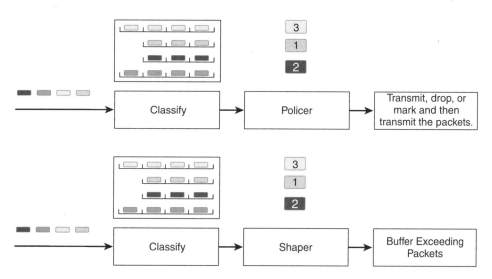

Figure 15-12 *Traffic Handling (Policing versus Shaping)*

The difference between traffic shaping and traffic policing can be described in terms of buffering versus dropping excess traffic:

- Traffic shaping buffers excessive traffic so that the traffic stays within the wanted rate. With traffic shaping, traffic bursts are smoothed out by queuing the excess traffic to produce a steadier flow of data. Reducing traffic bursts helps to reduce network congestion.

- Traffic policing drops excess traffic to control traffic flow within specified rate limits. Traffic policing does not introduce any delay to traffic that conforms to traffic policies. Traffic policing can cause more TCP retransmissions because traffic in excess of specified limits is dropped.

Traffic shaping is commonly used to shape outbound traffic flows when the outbound line rate is higher than the target subscription rate. Customers subscribing to service provider services supporting an Ethernet handoff will typically want to shape traffic outbound on the customer edge (CE) equipment to match the subscribed to committed information rate, or CIR (the maximum allowed contractual rate).

The service provider typically polices incoming traffic on the provider edge (PE) equipment to match the CIR, and therefore, shaping on the customer end will avoid unnecessary policing and drops on the PE, which are put in place to address excess traffic flows. An example of this scenario is highlighted in Figure 15-13 and shows a Fast Ethernet interface connecting to a service provider offering with a committed information rate of 20 Mbps.

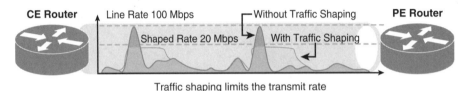

Figure 15-13 *Traffic Shaping with Fractional Interface Bandwidth*

Shaping in this example is used to smooth the traffic. It does so by storing excess traffic in a shaping queue, which in turn increases the buffer utilization on the router and causes variable packet delay.

Traffic shaping can also interact with a Frame Relay network, adapting to indications of Layer 2 congestion in the WAN. For example, if the backward explicit congestion notification (BECN) bit is received, the router can lower the rate limit to help reduce congestion in the Frame Relay network.

Traffic-policing mechanisms such as class-based policing have marking capabilities in addition to rate-limiting capabilities. Instead of dropping the excess traffic, traffic policing can alternatively re-mark excess traffic with a lower priority before it is sent out. Traffic shaping, however, does not support this capability. Traffic shaping is only able to delay excess traffic bursts to conform to a specified rate.

You can apply policing to either the inbound or outbound direction, while shaping can be applied only in the outbound direction. Policing drops nonconforming traffic instead of queuing the traffic-like shaping. Traffic policing is more efficient for memory utilization than traffic shaping because no additional queuing of packets is needed.

Both traffic policing and traffic shaping mechanisms ensure that traffic does not exceed a bandwidth limit, but each mechanism has a different impact on the traffic:

- Shaping increases packet delay and causes jitter, which makes it not ideal for delay-sensitive applications such as VoIP.
- Policing drops packets more often, generally causing more retransmissions of connection-oriented protocols such as TCP.

Traffic shaping is typically used for the following:

- Preventing and managing congestion in networks where asymmetric bandwidths are used along the traffic path. If shaping is not used, buffering can occur at the slow (usually the remote) end, which can lead to queuing (causing delays) and overflow (causing drops).

- Preventing the dropping of noncompliant traffic by the service provider by not allowing the traffic to burst above the subscribed (committed) rate. The customer can keep local control of traffic regulation.

Traffic policing is typically used to satisfy one of these requirements:

- Limiting the access rate on an interface when high-speed physical infrastructure is used in transport. Service providers typically use rate limiting to offer customers subrate access, as referred to in Figure 15-13.

- Engineering bandwidth so that traffic rates of certain applications or classes of traffic follow a specified traffic rate policy. For example, rate-limiting traffic from file-sharing applications to a maximum of 500 kbps.

- Re-marking excess traffic with a lower priority at Layer 2 or Layer 3 or both, before sending the excess traffic out. Cisco class-based traffic policing can be configured to mark packets at both Layer 2 and Layer 3. For example, excess traffic can be re-marked to a lower DSCP value and also have the Frame Relay DE bit set before the packet is sent out.

Table 15-6 compares traffic shaping versus traffic policing characteristics.

Table 15-6 *Traffic Shaping versus Traffic Policing Characteristics*

Traffic-Shaping Characteristics	Traffic-Policing Characteristics
Outgoing direction only	Incoming and outgoing directions
Queues out of profile packets until a buffer gets full	Drops out of profile packets
Buffering minimizes TCP retransmits	Dropping causes TCP retransmits
Does not support marking or remarking	Supports packet marking or remarking
Supports interaction with Frame Relay congestion indication	Less buffer usage (shaping requires an additional shaping queuing system)

Token Bucket Algorithms

Although they do not credit tokens in the same way, Cisco IOS policers and shapers are modeled after token bucket algorithms. A general and simplified explanation follows and does not necessarily strictly represent how each algorithm on each Cisco platform operates. There are many variations in the implementation details and across products and software releases.

Token bucket algorithms are metering engines that keep track of how much traffic can be sent to conform to a specified traffic rate. A token permits a single unit (usually a bit, but can be a byte) of traffic to be sent. Tokens are granted at the beginning of a specific time increment, usually every second, according to the specified rate called the committed information rate (CIR). The CIR is the access bit rate that is contracted in the SLA with a service provider.

If the CIR is set to 8000 bps, 8000 tokens are placed in a bucket at the beginning of the time period. Each time a bit of traffic is offered to the policer, the bucket is checked for tokens. If there are tokens in the bucket, the traffic is viewed as conforming to the rate, and the typical action is to send the traffic. One token is removed from the bucket for each bit of traffic passed. When the bucket runs out of tokens, any additional offered traffic is considered to exceed the rate, and the exceed action is taken, which is typically either to re-mark or drop the traffic.

Note At the end of the second, there might be unused tokens. The handling of unused tokens is a key differentiator among different types of policers.

Because the interface clock rate cannot change to enforce CIR policy, the only way to impose a rate limit on an interface is to use *time-division multiplexing (*TDM*)*, which is a technique in which information from multiple channels can be allocated bandwidth on a single wire based on preassigned time slots. With TDM, when a rate limit (or CIR) is imposed on an interface, the traffic is allocated a subsecond time slice during which it can be sent. This subsecond time slice is referred to as the time interval (or Tc). For example, if an 8-Kbps CIR is imposed on a 64-Kbps link, traffic can be sent for an interval of 125 ms (64,000 bps / 8000 bits).

The entire amount that is allowed by the CIR (8000 bits) could theoretically be sent at once, but then the algorithm would have to wait 875 ms before it could send any more data to comply with the rate limit, causing excessive interpacket delays. Therefore, to smooth out the allowed flow over each second, the CIR is divided into smaller units, referred to as the committed burst (Bc), which is the sustained number of bits that can be sent per Tc interval. These smaller units are sent over multiple instances during a single second. Continuing with the previous example, if the Bc is set to 1000, each committed burst can take only 15.6 ms (1000 bits / 64,000 bps) to send traffic out the interface at the clock rate. The algorithm waits 109.4 ms (125 ms – 15.6 ms) and sends another 15.6 ms of data (1000 bits). This process is repeated a total of eight times during each second. The data transmission "bursts" comprising a Bc of 1000, and therefore, a Tc of 125 ms is illustrated in the bottom portion of Figure 15-14.

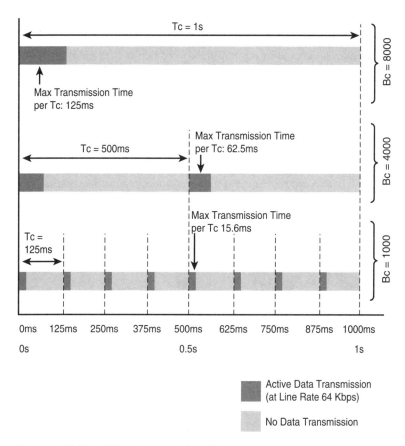

Figure 15-14 *Token Bucket Algorithm*

A packet or frame of 1500 bytes constitutes (1500 * 8) 12,000 bits. At 1000 bits (the Bc value) for each time slice (the value of Tc, in this case 125 ms), it takes 12 time slices to send the entire packet. Each time slice is 125 ms, and therefore, the entire packet takes 1.5 seconds to be sent in its entirety, resulting in small bursts of 100 bits each at line rate transmission speed.

The token bucket algorithm is as follows: Bc = CIR * Tc (Bits = Rate * Time)

Cisco IOS software does not allow the explicit definition of the interval (Tc). Instead, IOS takes the CIR and Bc values as arguments and derives the interval and the number of bursts per second. For example, if the CIR is 8000 and the Bc is set to 4000, 2 bursts occur per second, meaning that the Tc = 500 ms. The resulting transmission of a Bc value of 4000 is illustrated in the middle part of Figure 15-14. If the Bc is set to 2000, 4 bursts occur per second (Tc = 250 ms). If the Bc is set to 1000, 8 bursts occur per second (Tc = 125 ms). The resulting transmission of a Bc value of 8000 is illustrated in the top part of Figure 15-14.

Policing Tools: Single-Rate Three-Color Marker

Dual-bucket policing allows tokens to be accumulated based on the CIR, up to the Bc, with excess tokens accumulated in a second bucket up to the excess burst (Be). Technically, you can configure class-based traffic policing to support excess bursting capability. With excess bursting, after the first token bucket is filled to Bc, extra (excess) tokens can be accumulated in a second token bucket. Be is the maximum amount of excess traffic over and above Bc that can be sent during the time interval *after* a period of inactivity. With a single rate-metering mechanism, the second token bucket with a maximum size of Be fills at the same rate (CIR) as the first token bucket. If the second token bucket fills up to capacity, no more tokens can be accumulated and the excess tokens are discarded. This mechanism is illustrated in Figure 15-15.

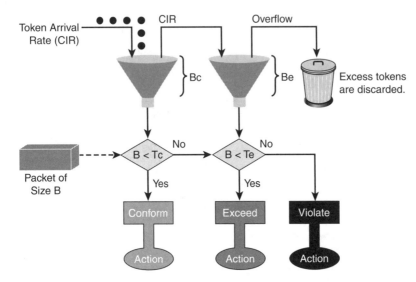

Figure 15-15 *Dual-token Bucket*

When you are using a dual-token bucket model, the measured traffic rate can be identified in three states or three colors:

- **Conforming:** There are enough tokens in the first token bucket with a maximum size of Bc.
- **Exceeding:** There are not enough tokens in the first token bucket, but there are enough tokens in the second token bucket with a maximum size of Be.
- **Violating:** There are not enough tokens in the first or second token bucket.

With dual-token bucket traffic policing, the typical actions that are performed are sending all conforming traffic, re-marking to a lower priority, sending all exceeding traffic, and dropping all violating traffic. The main benefit of using a dual-token bucket method is the ability to distinguish between traffic that exceeds the Bc but not the Be. A different policy can be applied to packets in the Be category, providing a greater level of design flexibility. Using a coin bank example, think of the CIR as the savings rate of one dollar per day. Bc is how much you can save into the bank, such as one dollar per day. Tc is the interval at which you put money into the coin bank, which equals one day. A Be of five dollars enables you to burst over the average spending rate of one dollar per day if you are not spending one dollar per day.

The single-rate three-color policer's tolerance of temporary bursts results in fewer TCP retransmissions and is therefore more efficient in terms of bandwidth utilization. This is a highly suitable tool for marking according to RFC 2597 AF classes (AFx1, AFx2, and AFx3), which have three "colors" or drop preferences defined per class, which was covered earlier in this chapter. Using a three-color policer generally makes sense only if the actions taken for each color differ. If the actions for two or more colors are the same, a simpler policer resulting in a less complex QoS policy definition is more suitable.

> **Note** If "Conform and Exceed" conditions are defined as part of the QoS class-policy configuration, you are only defining two colors. If the "violate" condition is added also, you will have three-color policer that offers more specific traffic conditioning/treatment.

Policing Tools: Two-Rate Three-Color Marker

With *dual-rate metering*, the traffic rate can be enforced according to two separate rates: CIR and peak information rate (PIR). The single-rate three-color marker/policer is a significant improvement for policing traffic. It makes allowance for temporary traffic bursts as long as the overall average transmitted rate is equal to or below the CIR. In some situations with a single-rate three-color policer, the variation in the number of accumulated excess burst credits could cause a degree of unpredictability in traffic flows. To improve on this and address this issue, a two-rate three-color marker/policer is defined in RFC 2698. This policer addresses the PIR, which is unpredictable in the RFC 2697 model. Furthermore, the two-rate three-color marker/policer allows for a sustainable excess burst, which negates the need to accumulate credits to accommodate temporary bursts and allows for different actions for the traffic exceeding the different burst values.

The two-rate three-color policer also uses an algorithm with two token buckets, but the logic varies slightly. Instead of transferring unused tokens from one bucket to another, this policer has two separate buckets that are filled each second with two separate token rates. The first bucket is filled with the PIR tokens, and the second bucket is filled with the CIR tokens. The two-rate three-color policer is illustrated in Figure 15-16.

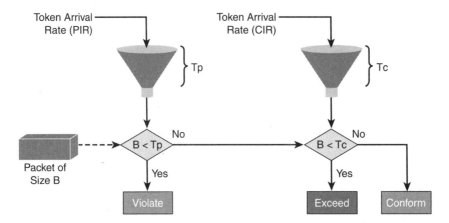

Figure 15-16 *Two-rate Three-color Policer*

Dual-rate metering supports a higher level of bandwidth management and supports a sustained excess rate, which is based on the PIR. With dual-rate metering, the PIR token bucket is replenished when a packet arrives. The number of bytes that is replenished is based on both the configured PIR and the packet arrival rate:

(Current Packet Arrival Time − Previous Packet Arrival Time) ∗ PIR

The CIR token bucket is also replenished when a packet arrives, but the number of bytes that are replenished is based on both the configured CIR and the packet arrival rate:

(Current Packet Arrival Time − Previous Packet Arrival Time) ∗ CIR

When a packet arrives, the PIR token bucket is first checked to see if there are enough tokens in the PIR token bucket to send the packet. The violating condition occurs if there are not enough tokens in the PIR token bucket to transmit the packet. If there are enough tokens in the PIR token bucket to send the packet, the CIR token bucket is checked. The exceeding condition occurs if there are enough tokens in the PIR token bucket to transmit the packet but not enough tokens in the CIR token bucket to transmit the packet. The conforming condition occurs if there are enough tokens in the CIR bucket to transmit the packet.

The two-rate policer marks packets as either conforming, exceeding, or violating a specified rate:

- If $B > Tp$, the packet is marked as violating the specified rate.

- If $B > Tc$, the packet is marked as exceeding the specified rate, and the Tp token bucket is updated as $Tp = Tp - B$.

- If the packet is marked as conforming to the specified rate, both token buckets (Tc and Tp) are updated as $Tp = Tp - B$ and $Tc = Tc - B$.

In addition to rate limiting, traffic policing using dual-rate metering allows marking of traffic according to whether the packet conforms, exceeds, or violates a specified rate. Within these three categories, users can decide the packet treatment. An example of manipulating the packet treatment could be configuring a policing policy in such a way that conforming packets are transmitted, exceeding packets are transmitted with a decreased priority, and violating packets are dropped.

Queuing Tools

Congestion management tools, including queuing tools, apply to interfaces that may experience congestion. Whenever packets enter a device faster than they can exit, the potential for congestion exists and queuing mechanisms apply. It is important to note that although queuing tools are in place, they are activated only when congestion exists. In the absence of congestion, packets are sent as soon as they arrive. When congestion occurs, packets must be buffered or queued in temporary storage for subsequent scheduling of these backed-up packets to mitigate dropping. Congestion management encompasses both queuing and scheduling, as depicted in Figure 15-17.

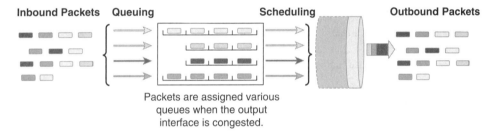

Figure 15-17 *Queuing and Scheduling*

Queuing, which is also referred to as buffering, is the logic of ordering packets in linked output buffers. Queuing processes are engaged when an interface is experiencing congestion and are deactivated when congestion clears. As queues fill, packets can be reordered so that higher priority packets exit the device sooner than lower priority ones.

Scheduling is the process of deciding which packet to send next. Scheduling, unlike queuing, occurs regardless of whether the interface is experiencing congestion.

There is a long history of queuing algorithms in Cisco IOS software. The older methods are insufficient for modern rich-media networks because they predate these traffic types. The key legacy queuing methods, all of which predate the MQC architecture, include

- **First-in, first-out queuing:** *FIFO* is a single queue with packets sent in the exact order they arrived.
- **Priority queuing:** PQ is a set of four queues that are served in strict-priority order. This method's major drawback is the potential for starvation of lower-priority traffic.

- **Custom queuing:** CQ is a set of 16 queues with a round-robin scheduler. It provides bandwidth guarantees and prevents starvation but does not provide the strict priority that is required by delay-sensitive, real-time flows.
- **Weighted fair queuing:** The WFQ algorithm divides the interface's bandwidth by the number of flows weighted by IP precedence (or IPP) and ensures an equitable distribution of bandwidth for all applications. This method provides better service for high-priority real-time flows but lacks a bandwidth guarantee for any particular flow.
- **IP RTP priority queuing:** *PQ-WFQ* is a transient method providing a single strict-priority queue for real-time traffic in addition to a WFQ complex for other traffic. LLQ soon superseded PQ-WFQ.

The current, and much newer, queuing mechanisms that are recommended and suitable for rich-media networks and present in MQC sought to combine the best features of the legacy algorithms while at the same time attempting to minimize their drawbacks. Real-time, delay-sensitive traffic requires two attributes of a queuing algorithm: an absolute bandwidth guarantee and a delay guarantee. In the presence of real-time traffic, it is critical not to starve other traffic types. The current recommended queuing algorithms include

- **Class-based weighted fair queuing:** A hybrid CBWFQ queuing algorithm combining a bandwidth guarantee from CQ with dynamic fairness to other flows within a class of traffic from WFQ. It does not provide a latency guarantee and as such is suitable only for data traffic management.
- **Low-latency queuing:** The *LLQ* method adds a strict-priority capability to CBWFQ and is therefore suitable for mixes of real-time and non-real–time traffic. It provides both latency and bandwidth guarantees.

Tx-Ring

Queuing and scheduling happen at various layers for any particular traffic flow. The most sophisticated queuing algorithms exist at Layer 3 and are independent of the interface type. Layer 3 queuing methods typically consider only the IP packet overhead in its bandwidth provisioning. On the Cisco IOS router platforms, Layer 3 queuing can also be configured in a hierarchical manner so that a cascade of Layer 3 queues feed traffic to lower-layer queues.

Queuing also occurs at Layer 2, for certain interface types, to accommodate media-specific requirements and idiosyncrasies, such as the older technologies for ATM and Frame Relay circuits. When the Layer 2 queues fill up, they in turn push back packets into the Layer 3 queues.

A final queue, usually referred to as a *transmit ring (Tx-Ring)*, is located within the Layer 1 device driver. Tx-Rings are media- and hardware-dependent and can operate quite differently on different routers, cards, and modules. When the Tx-Ring queue fills up, the higher-level queues are pressed into service, and this is essentially when QoS becomes active on the device.

Device driver level queuing at Layer 1 is done as the last egress point before transmission. The Tx-Ring Layer 1 queuing mechanism is a relatively small FIFO queue and is the final output buffer for a WAN interface. Its purpose is to maximize the physical link bandwidth utilization by matching the outbound transmission rate with the physical interface rate. Figure 15-18 illustrates the Tx-Ring operation.

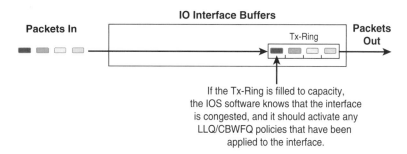

Figure 15-18 *Tx-Ring*

If the Tx-Ring fills to capacity, the interface is considered congested and the software activates any LLQ/CBWFQ policies that have been applied to the interface. The size of the Tx-Ring depends on the hardware, software, Layer 2 media, and queuing algorithm that are configured on the interface.

Fair Queuing

WFQ was developed to resolve some of the problems of basic queuing methods, such as queue starvation, delay, and jitter. WFQ dynamically divides available bandwidth by a calculation that is based on the total number of flows and the weight of each given flow. Bandwidth cannot be guaranteed because the number of flows is constantly changing and therefore so is the allocated bandwidth to each flow.

When FIFO queuing is used, traffic is sent in the order it is received without regard for bandwidth consumption or associated delays. File transfers and other high-volume applications can generate a series of packets that can consume all the available bandwidth and effectively deprive other traffic flows of bandwidth.

The idea of WFQ is to

- Have a dedicated queue for each flow that results in no starvation, delay, or jitter within the queue
- Allocate bandwidth fairly and accurately among all flows to ensure minimum scheduling delay and guaranteed service
- Use IP precedence as a weight value when allocating bandwidth

The WFQ scheduler, illustrated in Figure 15-19, is a simulation of a TDM system.

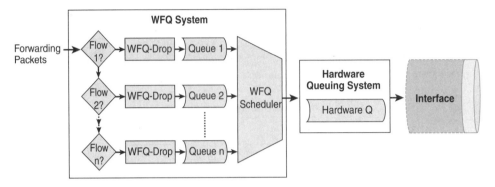

Figure 15-19 *WFQ Scheduler*

WFQ adapts to the number of active flows or queues in an attempt to allocate equal amounts of bandwidth to each flow. Flows with small packets, such as interactive flows, get much better service because they do not need a great deal of bandwidth. Flows with small packets do, however, have a need for low delay, which WFQ naturally accommodates as a result of the underlying algorithm.

The classification of flows in WFQ is automatic and does not support manually defined classification. The dropping mechanism is not a simple tail drop and instead drops packets of the most aggressive flows.

A flow is identified that is based on information that is taken from the IP header and the TCP or UDP headers, such as

- Source IP address
- Destination IP address
- Protocol number (identifying TCP or UDP)
- ToS field
- Source TCP or UDP port number
- Destination TCP or UDP port number

WFQ provides a simple mechanism of providing guaranteed throughput for all flows and is widely supported across Cisco platforms and software versions. The most obvious limitations are that it does not support the configuration of explicit classification of traffic or fixed bandwidth guarantees.

CBWFQ

Class-based weighted fair queuing (CBWFQ) is an extension of WFQ that enables network administrators to create a queuing policy that is specific to network requirements.

CBWFQ provides the capability to define traffic classes that are based on match criteria such as protocols, ACLs, and input interfaces. Packets satisfying the match criteria for a class constitute the traffic for that class. A queue is reserved for each class, and traffic belonging to a class is directed to that class queue.

After a class has been defined according to its match criteria, you can assign characteristics to it. Characterizing a class involves assigning it the minimum bandwidth that it will have access to during periods of congestion. You can also specify the queue limit for the class, which is the maximum number of packets that are allowed to accumulate in the class queue. Packets belonging to a class are subject to the bandwidth and queue limits that characterize the class. After a queue has reached its configured queue limit, what happens next depends on how the class policy is configured and whether enqueuing of extra packets to the class causes tail drops or random packet drops.

CBWFQ enables the creation of up to 256 queues, serving up to 256 classes of traffic. Each queue is serviced based on the bandwidth that is assigned to the class. CBWFQ is configured using the **bandwidth** keyword in a policy map. With CBWFQ, a minimum bandwidth is explicitly defined and enforced. The bandwidth can be specified in absolute or percentage terms.

If congestion occurs, the Layer 1 Tx-Ring for the interface fills up and pushes packets back into the Layer 3 CBWFQ queues if configured. Each CBWFQ class is assigned its own queue. CBWFQ queues may also have a fair-queuing presorter applied using the **fair-queue** keyword within a policy map to manage multiple flows contending for a single queue fairly. In addition, each CBWFQ queue is serviced in a weighted round-robin (WRR) fashion based on the bandwidth assigned to each class. The CBWFQ scheduler then forwards packets to the Tx-Ring. Figure 15-20 illustrates CBWFQ.

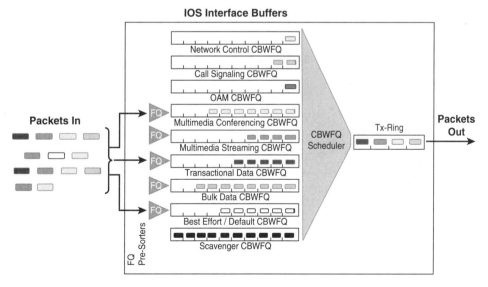

Figure 15-20 *CBWFQ Scheduler Queuing Tools—LLQ*

The LLQ feature brings strict-priority queuing to CBWFQ. Strict-priority queuing gives delay-sensitive data such as voice and video preferential treatment over other traffic by allowing this traffic to be dequeued and sent first before packets in other queues are dequeued.

Although weighted fair queue provides a fair share of bandwidth to every flow, and provides fair scheduling of its queues, it cannot provide guaranteed bandwidth and low delay to select applications. Without LLQ capability, voice traffic may still compete with other aggressive flows in the WFQ queuing system because the WFQ system lacks priority scheduling for time-critical traffic classes.

For CBWFQ, the weight for a packet belonging to a specific class is derived from the bandwidth that was assigned to the class when it was configured. Therefore, the bandwidth assigned to the packets of a class determines the order in which packets are sent. If all packets are serviced fairly based on weight, no class of packets may be granted strict priority. Not having strict priority poses problems for voice traffic because it is largely intolerant of delay and especially intolerant of jitter.

LLQ enables the use of a single strict-priority queue within CBWFQ at the class level. This introduces the capability to direct traffic belonging to a class to the CBWFQ strict-priority queue. Enqueueing class traffic to the strict-priority queue involves configuring the **priority** command for the class after specifying the named class within a policy map. Classes to which the **priority** command is applied are considered priority classes. Within a policy map, you can give one or more classes priority status. When multiple classes within a single policy map are configured as priority classes, all traffic from these classes is enqueued to a single strict-priority queue.

All real-time traffic should use the priority queue. Figure 15-21 illustrates three real-time classes of traffic all funneling into the priority queue of LLQ while other classes of traffic use the CBWFQ algorithm.

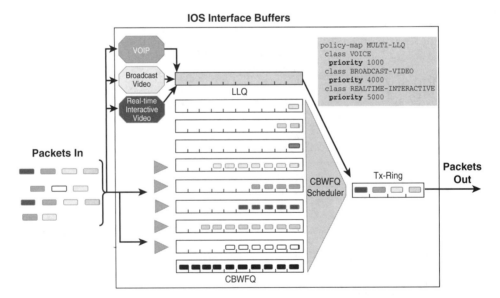

Figure 15-21 *QoS—Queuing*

Multiple classes of real-time traffic can be defined, and separate bandwidth guarantees given to each, but a single priority queue schedules all that combined traffic. As with CBWFQ, you can configure LLQ with absolute or percentage-based bandwidth allocations.

LLQ includes an implicit policer that limits the bandwidth that can be consumed by traffic in the real-time queue and thus prevents bandwidth starvation of the non-real-time flows serviced by the CBWFQ scheduler. The policing rate for this implicit policer is the bandwidth allocated to the class, and traffic exceeding this rate is tail dropped.

When CBWFQ is configured as the queuing system, it creates a number of queues, into which it classifies traffic classes. These queues are then scheduled with a WFQ-like scheduler, which can guarantee bandwidth to each class.

If LLQ is used within the CBWFQ system, it creates an additional priority queue in the WFQ system, which is serviced by a strict-priority scheduler. Any class of traffic can therefore be attached to a service policy, which uses priority scheduling, and hence can be prioritized over other classes.

Dropping Tools

This section discusses the DSCP-based WRED and IP ECN dropping tools.

DSCP-Based WRED

Buffering memory is a limited resource on any interface. When queuing, buffers fill up, and packets might be dropped either as they arrive, which is referred to as a *tail drop*, or selectively dropped before all buffers are filled. Selective dropping of packets when queues are filling up is referred to as *congestion avoidance*. Queuing algorithms manage the front of a queue, and congestion avoidance mechanisms manage the tail of a queue.

A router can handle multiple concurrent TCP sessions. It is likely that when traffic exceeds the queue limit, it exceeds this limit due to the bursty nature of packet networks. However, there is also a high probability that excessive traffic depth caused by packet bursts is temporary and that traffic does not stay excessively deep except either at points where traffic flows merge or at edge routers.

If the receiving router drops all traffic that exceeds the queue limit, as is done with tail drop by default, many TCP sessions simultaneously go into slow-start. So, traffic temporarily slows down to the extreme and then all flows slow-start again, creating a condition called *global synchronization*.

Global synchronization occurs as waves of congestion crest only to be followed by troughs, during which the transmission link is not fully used. Global synchronization of TCP hosts can occur because packets are dropped all at once. Global synchronization occurs when multiple TCP hosts reduce their transmission rates in response to packet dropping. When congestion is reduced, their transmission rates are increased. The most important point is that the waves of transmission known as global synchronization result in significant link underutilization. Figure 15-22 shows the suboptimal bandwidth utilization that tail drop has on TCP traffic.

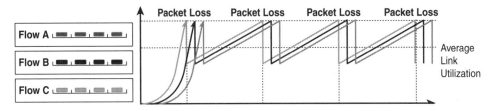

Figure 15-22 *Suboptimal Bandwidth Utilization and Tail Drop*

For this reason, random dropping congestion avoidance mechanisms are much more effective in managing TCP traffic. Although this figure may be somewhat theoretical, it does illustrate visually the effects of managing TCP traffic queuing; in practice, these "waves" may happen to a larger or smaller extent depending on the actual traffic characteristics and flow patterns present.

Random early detection (RED) counters the effects of TCP global synchronization by randomly dropping packets before the queues fill to capacity. Randomly dropping packets instead of dropping them all at once, as is done in a tail drop, avoids global synchronization of TCP streams. RED monitors the buffer depth and performs early discards or drops on random packets when the minimum defined queue threshold is exceeded. The dropping strategy is based primarily on the average queue length, which means that RED will be more likely to drop an incoming packet than when the average queue length is shorter.

> **Note** Cisco IOS Software does not support pure RED; it supports weighted RED. However, if all the packets assigned to an interface or class have the same DSCP markings, the effective resulting policy is simply RED.

Because RED drops packets randomly, it has no per-flow intelligence. The rationale is that an aggressive flow will represent most of the arriving traffic, so it is likely that RED will drop a packet of an aggressive session. RED punishes more aggressive sessions with a higher statistical probability and somewhat selectively slows down the most significant cause of congestion. Directing one TCP session at a time to slow down allows for full utilization of the bandwidth, rather than utilization that manifests itself as crests and troughs of traffic.

As a result of implementing RED, the problem of TCP global synchronization is less likely to occur, and TCP can utilize link bandwidth more efficiently. In RED implementations, the average queue size also decreases significantly, as the possibility of the queue filling up is reduced. This smaller queue size is due to very aggressive dropping in the event of traffic bursts, when the queue is already quite full.

RED distributes losses over time and normally maintains a low queue depth while absorbing traffic spikes. The probability of a packet being dropped is based on three configurable parameters that are contained within the RED profile:

- **Minimum threshold:** When the average queue length is equal to or above the minimum threshold, RED starts dropping packets. The rate of packet drops increases linearly as the average queue size increases, until the average queue size reaches the maximum threshold.

- **Maximum threshold:** When the average queue size is above the maximum threshold, all packets are dropped.

- **Mark probability denominator:** This value is the fraction of packets that are dropped when the average queue depth is at the maximum threshold. For example, if the denominator is 512, one out of every 512 packets is dropped when the average queue is at the maximum threshold. The linear increase of packet drops from the minimum threshold (0 drops) to the maximum threshold is based on this parameter and the queue size between the minimum and maximum thresholds.

Drop probability is illustrated in Figure 15-23.

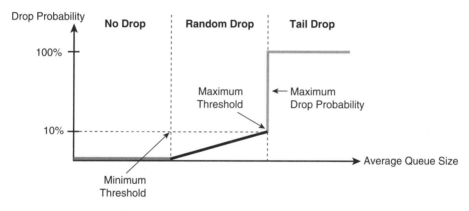

Figure 15-23 *Drop Probability*

The minimum threshold value should be set high enough to maximize the link utilization. If the minimum threshold is too low, packets may be dropped unnecessarily, and the transmission link will not be fully used.

The difference between the maximum threshold and the minimum threshold should be large enough to avoid global synchronization. If the difference is too small, many packets may be dropped at once, resulting in global synchronization.

The mark probability has the effect of controlling the number of packets that are dropped when the average queue length reaches the maximum threshold. If the value is set too low, it will result in too many dropped packets. If the value is set too large, RED dropping can be rendered ineffective.

Based on the average queue size, RED has three dropping modes:

- **No drop:** When the average queue size is between 0 and the configured minimum threshold, no drops occur and all packets are queued.

- **Random drop:** When the average queue size is between the configured minimum threshold and the configured maximum threshold, random drops occur, which is linearly proportional to the mark probability denominator and the average queue length.

- **Full drop (tail drop):** When the average queue size is at or higher than the maximum threshold, RED performs a full (tail) drop in the queue. This tail drop is unlikely because RED should slow down TCP traffic ahead of congestion. If a lot of non-TCP traffic is present, RED cannot effectively drop traffic to reduce congestion, and tail drops are likely to occur.

The idea behind using WRED is both to maintain the queue length at a level somewhere between the minimum and maximum thresholds and to implement different drop policies for different classes of traffic. WRED can selectively discard lower-priority traffic when the interface becomes congested, and it can provide differentiated performance characteristics for different classes of service. You can also configure WRED to achieve nonweighted RED behavior.

WRED can use multiple different RED profiles, where each profile is identified by the minimum threshold, maximum threshold, and maximum drop probability. The WRED profile selection could, for example, be selected based on DSCP values, as shown in Figure 15-24.

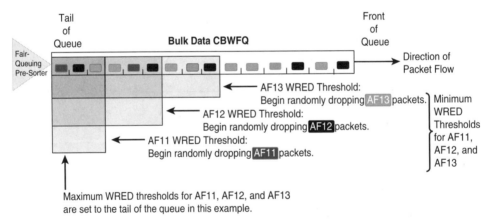

Figure 15-24 *DSCP-Based WRED*

WRED reduces the chances of tail drop by selectively dropping packets when the output interface begins to show signs of congestion. By dropping some packets early rather than waiting until the queue is full, WRED avoids dropping large numbers of packets all at once and minimizes the chances of global synchronization. As a result, WRED maximizes the utilization of transmission lines.

WRED is useful only when the bulk of the traffic is TCP traffic. When TCP is transmitted, dropped packets indicate congestion, so the packet source reduces its transmission rate. With other protocols, packet sources might not respond or might continue to resend dropped packets at the same rate, and so dropping packets might not decrease congestion.

The router constantly updates the WRED algorithm with the calculated average queue length, which is based on the recent history of queue lengths.

In addition, in the traffic profile there are parameters to define the drop characteristics that WRED uses, such as the minimum threshold, maximum threshold, and mark probability denominator. These parameters define the WRED probability slopes. Figure 15-25 illustrates WRED in action.

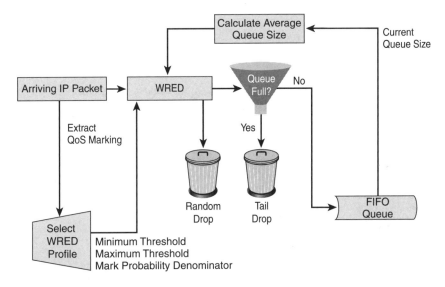

Figure 15-25 *WRED Process Flow*

When a packet arrives at the output queue, the QoS marking value is used to select the correct WRED profile for the packet. The packet is then passed to WRED for processing. Based on the selected traffic profile and the average queue length, WRED calculates the probability for dropping the current packet. If the average queue length is greater than the minimum threshold but less than the maximum threshold, WRED will either queue the packet or perform a random drop. If the average queue length is less than the minimum threshold, the packet is passed to the output queue.

If the queue is already full, the packet is tail dropped. Otherwise, the packet will eventually be transmitted out onto the interface.

WRED profiles can be manually set. To avoid the need for setting all WRED parameters in a router, 64 values are defined for DSCP-based WRED. Therefore, the default settings should suffice in most deployments. As illustrated in Figure 15-26, Cisco IOS DSCP-based WRED configures itself by default so that the minimum threshold for EF DiffServ is high, increasing the probability of no drops being applied to that traffic class.

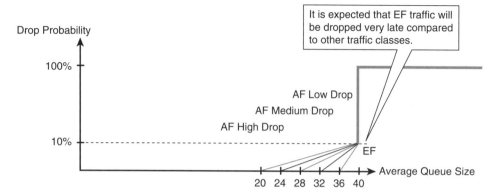

Figure 15-26 *Cisco IOS DSCP-based WRED Dropping Probability*

EF traffic is expected to be dropped late, compared to other traffic classes, and the EF traffic is then prioritized in the event of congestion.

There are four defined AF classes. Each class should be treated independently and have bandwidth allocated that is based on the QoS policy. For each AF DiffServ traffic class, Cisco IOS DSCP-based WRED configures itself by default for three different profiles, depending on the drop preference bits. All AF classes are initially marked with Drop Preference 1 (lowest drop preference), but in transit policers may mark down the classes to Drop Preference 2 or Drop Preference 3, if the classes are exceeding or violating administratively defined traffic rates. Table 15-7 lists the EF and AF profiles.

Table 15-7 *EF and AF Profiles*

Assured Forwarding Class	Drop Probability	(Class) DSCP	Default Minimum Threshold
EF Class	—	(EF) 101110	36
AF Class 1	Low	(AF11) 001010	32
	Medium	(AF12) 001100	28
	High	(AF13) 001110	24
AF Class 2	Low	(AF21) 010010	32
	Medium	(AF22) 010100	28
	High	(AF23) 010110	24
AF Class 3	Low	(AF31) 011010	32
	Medium	(AF32) 011100	28
	High	(AF33) 011110	24
AF Class 4	Low	(AF41) 100010	32
	Medium	(AF42) 100100	28
	High	(AF43) 100110	24

IP ECN

TCP determines how many unacknowledged packets it can send by gradually increasing the number of packets the session sends until it experiences a dropped packet; this adjustment is known as *TCP windowing*. As a result of this process, TCP tends to cause router queues to build up at network bottleneck points. When queues become full, tail drop begins dropping all incoming packets until there is room in the queue. Tail drop does not provide differential treatment, and therefore, some of the fragile flow packets, which are sensitive to latency, may be dropped. In addition, tail drop can lead to global synchronization of packet loss across multiple flows, as highlighted in the previous section.

Active queue management mechanisms such as WRED detect congestion before queues fill and overflow. As a result of selectively discarding packets, these mechanisms provide congestion indication to end nodes. Therefore, active queue management and congestion avoidance mechanisms can reduce queuing delays for all traffic that shares a specific queue. In addition, active queue management means that it is no longer necessary to rely on buffer overflow as the only means of indicating congestion.

Packet dropping in these mechanisms is based on the average queue length exceeding a predefined threshold, rather than only when queues overflow. However, because packets are dropped before queues actually overflow, the router dropping the packet is not always constrained by memory limitations and required to drop the packet.

Explicit congestion notification (ECN) enables network devices to mark an ECN bit to notify hosts that congestion has been experienced. On Cisco IOS routers, ECN is an extension to WRED functionality.

WRED is an active queue management mechanism that uses packet drops as a congestion indicator for endpoints. Packets are dropped by WRED based on the average queue length exceeding a specific set of predefined threshold values (minimum and maximum thresholds). ECN is an extension to WRED, in that ECN marks packets instead of dropping them when the average queue length exceeds a specific threshold value. With RFC 3168, the addition of ECN to IP active queue management allows routers to signal that the router has experienced congestion instead of relying on the use of packet drops. When congestion signaling is used, aggressive flows can be slowed, thus reducing the impact of congestion and packet loss on latency-sensitive flows.

RFC 3168 redefines the DiffServ field to contain an ECN-specific field, as illustrated in Figure 15-27.

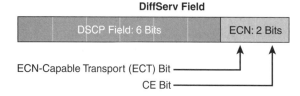

ECT Bit	CE Bit	Result
0	0	Not ECN-capable Transport
0	1	ECN-capable Transport (1)
1	0	ECN-capable Transport (0)
1	1	Congestion Experienced

Figure 15-27 *ECN Field*

The ECN field consists of the last two low-order bits of the DiffServ field. These last two bits are the ECT bit and the CE bit. The different ECT and CE bit combinations in the ECN field have the following meanings:

- **00:** This ECN field combination indicates that a packet is not using ECN.
- **01 and 10:** These ECN field combinations, called ECT(1) and ECT(0), respectively, are set by the data sender to indicate that the endpoints of the transport protocol are ECN-capable. Routers will treat these two field combinations identically. Data senders can use either one or both of these two combinations.
- **11:** This ECN field combination indicates to the endpoints that congestion has been experienced and that packets arriving at a full queue of a router will be dropped.

When ECN is configured with WRED, routers and end hosts use this marking as a signal that the network is congested, and they will slow down the rate at which packets are sent. Also, ECN must be interoperable with non-ECN–compliant devices. Because ECN is configured as an extension to WRED, packets are treated differently by WRED when ECN has been enabled.

If the average queue length is below the defined WRED minimum threshold, all packets are queued and transmitted normally. This behavior is identical to devices that are configured to use non-ECN–enabled WRED. If the average queue length is greater than the maximum threshold, packets are tail dropped. This behavior is identical to devices that are configured to use non-ECN–enabled WRED. If the number of packets in the queue is between the minimum threshold and the maximum threshold, one of these scenarios will occur:

- If the ECN field on the packet indicates that the endpoints are ECN-capable, meaning that the ECT bit is set to 1 and the CE bit is set to 0 or the ECT bit is set to 0 and the CE bit is set to 1, and the WRED algorithm determines that the packet should have been dropped based on the drop probability, the ECN process is used instead of the packet being dropped.

- If the ECN field on the packet indicates that neither endpoint is ECN-capable, meaning that the ECT bit is set to 0 and the CE bit is set to 0, the packet may be dropped based on the WRED drop probability. This action is the identical treatment that a packet receives when WRED is enabled without ECN configured on the router.

The ECN operation relies on interaction between ECN-capable hosts and ECN-capable network devices, as illustrated in Figure 15-28.

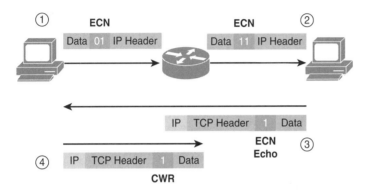

Figure 15-28 *ECN Operation*

The following steps (illustrated in Figure 15-28) explain how ECN signaling can prevent packet drops by causing a host that is transmitting TCP packets to reduce its transmission rate:

Step 1. The sender (host A) sets the ECN bits in the IP headers of all data packets to 01 or 10 to indicate to the network that it is capable of participating in ECN.

Step 2. If the following conditions exist, the router sets the ECN bits to 11 (Congestion Experienced) and sends the packet on to the receiver (host B):

- The ECN field in the packet indicates that the endpoints are ECN-capable.
- The network is congested, or congestion is imminent.
- The WRED algorithm determines that the packet should be dropped based on the drop probability.

Step 3. When host B sees the 11 (Congestion Experienced) marking, it sets an ECN Echo Bit ECE flag in the TCP header of the next packet it sends back to host A. The purpose of this flag is to tell host A to slow down its transmissions.

Step 4. When host A receives the packet with the ECE flag, it reduces its congestion window to slow down its transmission rate. Host A then sets a Congestion Window Reduced (CWR) bit flag in the TCP header of the first new packet that it sends to host B. This flag informs host B that host A has reduced its window and slowed transmission.

ECN has the following characteristics:

- TCP congestion controls are not suited to applications that are sensitive to delay or packet loss.
- It removes the need to rely on packet loss as a congestion indicator.
- It marks packets instead of dropping them when the average queue length exceeds a specific threshold value.
- It enables routers and end hosts to use ECN marking as a signal that the network is congested and will send packets at a slower rate.

Summary

- Classification involves identifying and splitting traffic into different classes.
- Marking involves marking each packet as a member of a network class so that the packet class can be quickly recognized throughout the network.
- Marking can be on the data link and network layers.
- NBAR is a classification engine that can recognize a wide variety of protocols and applications.
- Traffic policing and traffic shaping are traffic-conditioning mechanisms that are used in a network to control the traffic rate.
- CBWFQ is a mechanism that is used to guarantee bandwidth to classes, while LLQ guarantees the low-latency propagation of packets.
- RED is a mechanism that randomly drops packets before a queue is full.
- ECN allows a network device to indicate to hosts that congestion has been experienced.

Review Questions

After answering the following questions, please refer to Appendix A, "Answers to Review Questions," for the answers.

1. Which MQC feature allows traffic to be classified by a packet support value?
    a. LDPM
    b. NBAR
    c. Service maps
    d. Service classes

2. What does LLQ bring to CBWFQ?
   a. Strict-priority scheduling
   b. Alternate priority scheduling
   c. Non-policed queues for low-latency traffic
   d. Special voice traffic classification and dispatch

3. What are the traffic drop modes in RED? (Choose three.)
   a. No drop
   b. Full drop
   c. Random drop
   d. Deferred drop
   e. Tail drop

4. Which option describes a major difference between traffic policing and traffic shaping?
   a. Traffic policing drops excess traffic, whereas traffic shaping delays excess traffic by queuing it.
   b. Traffic policing is applied in only the outbound direction, whereas traffic shaping can be applied in both the inbound and outbound directions.
   c. Traffic policing is not available on Cisco Catalyst switches, whereas traffic shaping is available on Cisco Catalyst switches.
   d. Traffic policing requires policing queues to buffer excess traffic, whereas traffic shaping does not require any queues to buffer excess traffic.

5. Which of the following are characteristics of DiffServ? (Choose two.)
   a. QoS mechanisms are used without prior signaling.
   b. QoS characteristics (for example, bandwidth and delay) are managed on a hop-by-hop basis with policies that are established independently at each device in the network.
   c. DiffServ provides hard QoS guarantees such as bandwidth, delay, and packet loss rates end to end.
   d. QoS requirements are negotiated upon establishment of the connection, and Connection Admission Control (CAC) ensures that no new traffic will violate existing guarantees.
   e. DiffServ is compared to having a private courier airplane or truck that is dedicated to the delivery of your traffic.

6. What are the three fields that make up the TCI field?
   a. User Priority Bits, CDI, VLAN Identifier
   b. CFI, CDI, VLAN Identifier
   c. User Priority Bits, CFI, VLAN Identifier
   d. Device Priority Bits, CFI, VLAN Identifier

7. Which of the following are incorrect?

PHB	Use	DSCP Bit Settings
a. Default	Used for best-effort service	Bits 5 to 7 of DSCP = 000
b. EF	Used for low-delay service	Bits 5 to 7 of DSCP = 111
c. AF	Used for guaranteed bandwidth service	Bits 5 to 7 of DSCP = 001, 010, 011, or 100
d. Class selector	Used for backward compatibility with non-DiffServ-compliant devices (RFC 1812 devices)	Bits 2 to 4 of DSCP = 000

8. Which of the following has the highest drop probability?
   a. AF11
   b. AF12
   c. AF13
   d. AF21

Chapter 16

QoS Design Principles and Best Practices

Upon completing this chapter, you will be able to

- Describe basic classification and marking design principles
- Describe basic policing and remarking design principles
- Explain queuing design principles
- Explain basic dropping design principles
- Explain what are per-hop behavior queue design principles
- Explain the role of RFC 4594 recommendation
- List and describe QoS strategy models
- Describe the 4-class QoS strategy model
- Describe the 8-class QoS strategy model
- Describe the 12-class QoS strategy model

Now that we have covered the various tools for enabling quality of service (QoS) in the network, it is possible to create a QoS strategy that best meets an organization's requirements. This chapter presents some best practice QoS design principles and QoS strategy models that are used to implement the numerous QoS tools we have at our disposal. Remember that usually more than one solution fits the given QoS requirements, so simplifying the models leveraged can significantly accelerate and ensure proper QoS deployment.

QoS Overview

Quality of service is critical to ensuring application performance consistency and optimized end-user experiences. As discussed in Chapter 15, "QoS Overview," the fundamental purpose of QoS is to manage contention for network resources while addressing applications that require differentiated levels of service. Prior to developing a QoS strategy, you must perform the proper discovery to identify current and future applications and application characteristics within the environment. This information, coupled with an understanding of the end-to-end network design and traffic patterns, will drive the QoS design strategy model that is most appropriate for the business. Following are some common questions that you need to answer:

- What traffic needs to be classified and marked?

- Is it possible to leverage a 4-class, 8-class, or 12-class QoS strategy model from end to end?

- Will traffic-marking characteristics stay in place as data traverses the infrastructure?

- What traffic needs to be prioritized?

- What traffic requires bandwidth reservations?

- What traffic needs to be policed?

- Is shaping required at the WAN edge or at other places within the infrastructure such as the Data Center Interconnect (DCI)?

- How can congestion management and congestion avoidance techniques be leveraged to optimize TCP traffic?

Classification and Marking Design Principles

The first fundamental design principle is that QoS policies should always be enabled in hardware whenever possible. Some Cisco routers perform QoS in software, and such behavior can increase the load on the CPU. Cisco Catalyst switches have dedicated hardware called application-specific integrated circuits (ASIC), which are used to perform QoS operations. Switches can perform complex QoS policies under maximum traffic load without any marginal CPU spike. Some platforms, such as the Cisco ASR, can perform QoS operations (such as queuing) in dedicated hardware ASICs, but other functions (such as deep packet inspection) are still processed in software via the CPU.

Based on design recommendations, classification and marking should be done closest to the source of traffic as administratively and technically possible. This design principle promotes DiffServ and per-hop behaviors (PHB) as the recommended end-to-end design.

Note "As administratively close as possible" refers to an administrative domain, in scenarios in which you are not controlling the end-to-end traffic flow path of a packet; you need to classify/mark as close to the source as possible within your administrative domain.

As a rule, it is not recommended to trust markings set by end users leveraging PCs or other endpoint devices. End users can intentionally or unintentionally abuse QoS policies that trust markings of end devices. If users and unclassified applications take advantage of the configured QoS policy as a result of trusting end devices, this can result in easily starving priority queues with nonpriority traffic, ruining quality of service for real-time applications. However, if QoS markings for end devices and associated applications are administered centrally across the enterprise, this can be an acceptable design option. An additional area of exception might also include wireless devices that can leverage Wireless Multimedia (WMM) QoS provisioning in the upstream direction.

The next important recommendation is to use Differentiated Services Code Point (DSCP) marking whenever technically possible. DSCP markings are the recommended method for marking IP traffic for the following reasons:

- It has support for end-to-end Layer 3 marking.

- It is a more granular method of marking that supports 64 levels as compared to class of service (CoS) and MPLS Experimental EXP, which have 8 levels.

- It is more extensible than Layer 2 markings as these markings are lost when media changes.

To provide interoperability on the border between enterprise and service provider networks, you should use standard-based DSCP PHB markings because the use of such markings can streamline interoperability and compliance with service provider classes of service. Classification and marking design principles covered in this section are illustrated in Figure 16-1.

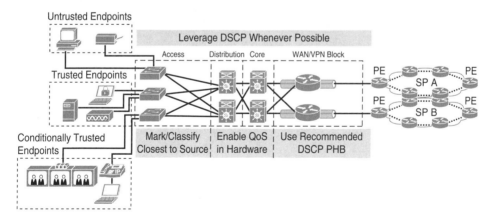

Figure 16-1 *QoS Classification and Marking Architecture*

Policing and Remarking Design Principles

Traffic that is unwanted should be discarded as soon as possible to preserve network resources from unnecessary consumption. Undesirable traffic can be the result of denial of service (DoS) or worm attacks. Furthermore, excessive unwanted traffic could cause a network outage as a result of high impact on the CPU and memory resources of network devices. Malicious traffic can mask under legitimate TCP/UDP ports that are used by well-known applications, and this traffic can create large amounts of unwanted traffic. Traffic behavior must be monitored and marked down as close as possible to the source under such circumstances.

Traffic should be marked down using RFC recommendations. Those recommendations ensure interoperability and end-to-end QoS network design. Examples of these recommendations are RFC 2597 and RFC 2698, where excess traffic with marking of AFx1 should be marked down to AFx2 or AFx3. Note that 2 or 3 in AFx2 and AFx3 represent drop probability. This markdown principle should be combined properly with other QoS tools. For example, with DSCP-based WRED, AFx2 should be dropped more aggressively than AFx1 but less aggressively than AFx3. Figure 16-2 illustrates the policing and remarking design principles covered in this section.

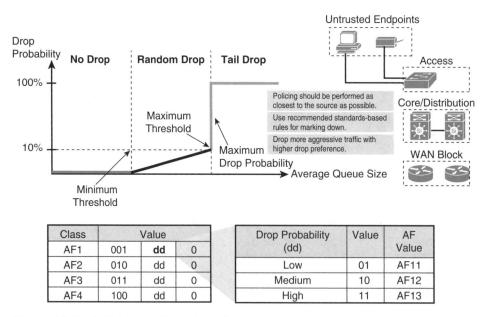

Figure 16-2 *Policing and Remarking Concepts*

Queuing Design Principles

The only way to provide QoS service guarantees to business-critical applications is to enable queuing to every node that has the potential for congestion. Queuing should be enabled regardless of whether congestion is occurring rarely or frequently. Although frequently deployed at the WAN edge, this principle must be applied not only to congested WAN links but also within the campus network. Speed mismatch, link aggregation, and link subscription ratios can create congestion in the network devices by filling up queuing buffers.

Because each distinctive application class requires unique QoS service requirements, it is recommended you provide a distinctive queue for each traffic class. One of the main justifications for leveraging distinctive queues is that each QoS service class can accept certain QoS-enabled behaviors such as bandwidth allocation and dropping ratios.

It is recommended you use a minimum of four standards-based queuing behaviors on all platforms and service provider links when deploying end-to-end QoS across the network infrastructure:

- RFC 3246 Expedited Forwarding PHB (used for real-time traffic)
- RFC 2597 Assured Forwarding PHB (used for guaranteed bandwidth queue)
- RFC 2474 Default Forwarding PHB (default nonprioritized queue, best effort)
- RFC 3662 Lower Effort Per-Domain Behavior (less than best-effort queue, bandwidth constrained)

Dropping Design Principles

As covered in Chapter 15, congestion avoidance mechanisms are used to selectively drop packets when a predefined limit is reached. As a review, by dropping packets early, congestion avoidance helps prevent bottlenecks downstream the network. Congestion avoidance mechanisms include RED and WRED. If WRED is designed per recommendations where every traffic class has its own queue, WRED should be used for only some types of queues (not necessarily all of them).

It is recommended that WRED not be used for the strict-priority queue, scavenger traffic queue, and control traffic queue. Traffic for the strict-priority queue and control traffic queue are highly sensitive to dropping. Scavenger traffic is often provisioned with a small amount of bandwidth, typically below 1 percent, and for this type of queue, WRED is not needed. Considering that the WRED feature is performed in software, enabling WRED for scavenger traffic class will consume additional CPU resources with no significant gain.

For AF-marked queues with DSCP-based WRED, typically traffic marked with AFx3 is more aggressively dropped than AFx2, which is in turn more aggressively dropped than AFx1.

All traffic types that are not explicitly defined in other queues fall into default (DF) traffic class. For this traffic class, it is recommended to enable WRED. WRED should be enabled in the default queue because, as explained in Chapter 15, it increases throughput by reducing the TCP synchronization effect. In the case of the default queue where all different traffic types are equally marked with a DSCP value of zero, there is no mechanism to fairly weight less aggressive applications when WRED is not enabled.

Per-Hop Behavior Queue Design Principles

The goal of convergence in the network is to enable voice, video, and data applications to seamlessly coexist in the network by providing each with appropriate QoS service expectations and guarantees.

When real-time applications are the only ones that consume link bandwidth, non-real–time applications' performance can be significantly degraded. Extensive testing results show that there is significant performance impact on non-real–time applications when more than one-third of the links is used by real-time applications as part of a strict-priority queue. Thus, it is recommended that no more than a third of link bandwidth be used for strict-priority queuing. This principle prevents non-real–time applications from being dropped out of their required QoS recommendations. In other words, it is recommended that no more than 33 percent of the bandwidth be used for the expedite forwarding (EF) queue. It is also important to note that this 33 percent design principle is simply a best practices design recommendation and not necessarily a mandatory rule.

It is recommended that a minimum of one queue be provisioned for assured forwarding per-hop behavior (AF PHB), but up to four subclasses can be defined within the AF class: AF1x, AF2x, AF3x, and AF4x. Each queue belonging to the specified AF subclass must have a bandwidth guarantee that corresponds to the application requirements of that traffic subclass.

The default forwarding (DF) class consists of all traffic that is not explicitly defined in other queues. If an enterprise is using many applications, it is important to have adequate space for those traffic types. It is recommended that typically 25 percent of link bandwidth be used for this service class. Figure 16-3 illustrates an example of bandwidth allocation leveraging these recommended best practices.

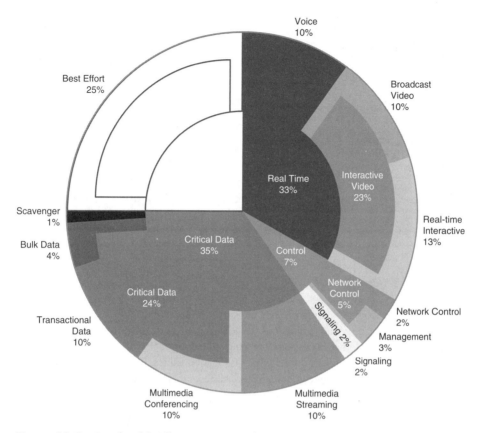

Figure 16-3 *Bandwidth Allocation Example*

RFC 4594 QoS Recommendation

RFC 4594 QoS provides guidelines for marking, queuing, and dropping principles for different types of traffic. Cisco has made a minor modification to its adoption of RFC 4594, namely the switching of Call-Signaling and Broadcast Video markings (to CS3 and CS5, respectively). A summary of Cisco's implementation of RFC 4594 is presented in Figure 16-4.

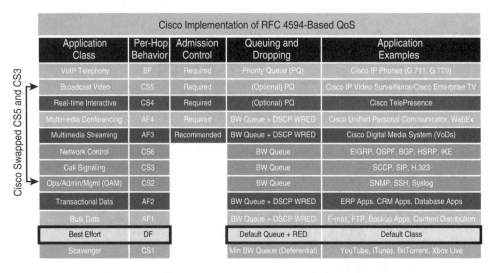

Figure 16-4 *QoS Marking—RFC 4594*

RFC 4594 is the recommendation but not the standard; it resides in the category of draft proposal RFCs. It recommends guidelines on how to configure 14 traffic classes that are associated with 28 different code-point marking values. Note that some of the PHBs shown in Figure 16-4 include multiple DSCP-associated values. For example, the AF class for multimedia streaming can have AF31, AF32, and AF33 DSCP values. RFC 4594 includes information on which PHBs should be used for certain traffic types and also what queuing and dropping mechanism should be used for that same traffic class.

Some sample recommendations highlighted in Figure 16-4 include

- Voice traffic should be marked to EF/DSCP 46.
- Voice should be queued using strict-priority queuing.
- Broadcast video traffic should be marked to CS5/DSCP 40.
- Multimedia conferencing should be treated with an AF PHB, provisioned with a guaranteed-bandwidth queue.

RFC 4594 is not a final RFC standard and will more than likely continue to be developed considering that needs and trends for QoS application requirements change over the time.

QoS Strategy Models

Before applying any QoS tools, organizations need to define the strategy and goals for different applications running in their network. This will result in defining a certain number of traffic classes to meet the end-to-end QoS objectives of an organization.

Three basic QoS strategy models can be deployed, depending on the granularity of applications running within an organization's network:

- 4-Class QoS Strategy Model
- 8-Class QoS Strategy Model
- 12-Class QoS Strategy Model

Although the more classes you define, the more specific and granular traffic treatment will be per application, the selection of a certain strategy model must be based on application requirements coupled with the WAN provider QoS model (if there is any WANs with QoS). The following sections provide a detailed view into each of these QoS strategy models.

4-Class QoS Strategy

The 4-class QoS strategy model is the simplest of the three models (in terms of QoS polices) and typically accounts for telephony, signaling, transactional/mission-critical, and best-effort data. When businesses deploy telephony applications in their network, three classes of traffic are typically required (telephony, signaling, and default/best effort).

Typically, the fourth class is the Assured Forwarding (AF) class. The AF class is used for transactional and mission-critical data applications such as SQL databases. The AF class can also be used for multimedia conferencing, multimedia streaming, and bulk data applications.

The 4-class QoS strategy model, as shown in Figure 16-5, is an example of where an organization has deployed IP telephony. In addition to separating telephony, signaling, and default/best-effort traffic, the organization has defined one mission-critical transactional data class.

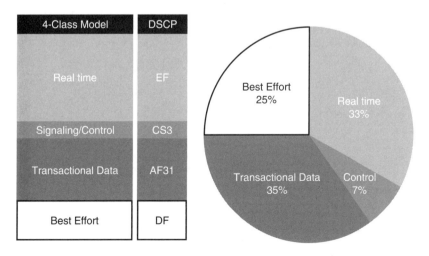

Figure 16-5 *The 4-Class QoS Strategy Model*

The four traffic classes of QoS markings and guarantees are as follows:

- **Voice (Real time):** Marked with EF and provisioned to leverage up to one-third of link bandwidth
- **Signaling:** Marked with CS3 and provisioned to leverage a minimum of 7 percent of link bandwidth
- **Mission-critical data (Transactional Data):** Marked with AF31 and provisioned to leverage 35 percent of link bandwidth
- **Default (best-effort data):** Marked with DF and provisioned to take advantage of 25 percent of link bandwidth

Voice and signaling guarantees must be selected based on the volume of voice calls and the VoIP codec that is used through the given link. Mission-critical data is selected based on the decision of the director of each company department who has given info about critical business application needs to the networking team.

8-Class QoS Strategy

The 8-class QoS strategy model builds upon the 4-class model and includes the following additional classes:

- Multimedia conferencing
- Multimedia streaming
- Network control
- Scavenger

The two additional multimedia traffic types in this model are multimedia conferencing and multimedia streaming. The explicitly defined network control traffic class is used for applications such as network routing protocol updates or network infrastructure control traffic such as OAM. The 8-class QoS strategy model is illustrated in Figure 16-6.

QoS Strategy Models   563

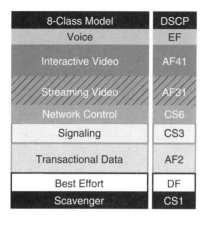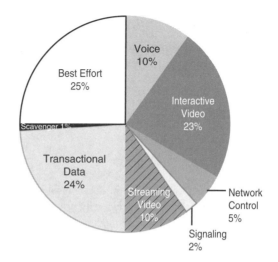

Figure 16-6 *The 8-Class QoS Strategy Model*

As can be seen from Figure 16-6, the recommendations for each traffic class in this model are as follows:

- **Voice:** Marked with EF and limited to 10 percent of link bandwidth in a strict-priority queue

- **Multimedia conferencing (Interactive video):** Marked with AF41 or sometimes as EF and limited to 23 percent of link bandwidth in a strict-priority queue

- **Multimedia streaming:** Marked with AF31 and guaranteed 10 percent of link bandwidth with WRED enabled

- **Network control:** Marked with CS6 and guaranteed 5 percent of link bandwidth

- **Signaling:** Marked with CS3 and provisioned with minimum of 2 percent of link bandwidth

- **Transactional data:** Marked with AF21 and provisioned with 24 percent of link bandwidth with WRED enabled

- **Default (best-effort data):** Marked with DF and provisioned with 25 percent of link bandwidth

- **Scavenger:** Marked with CS1 and provisioned with a maximum of 1 percent of link bandwidth

Note It is important to note the difference as some traffic types, such as voice traffic, are limited by bandwidth defined in a strict-priority queue, and other traffic types, such as multimedia streaming, have guaranteed provisioned bandwidth.

12-Class QoS Strategy

The 12-class QoS strategy model builds upon the 8-class model and includes the following additional classes:

- Real-time Interactive
- Broadcast Video
- Management/OAM
- Bulk Data

The 12-class QoS strategy model represents Cisco's interpretation of the RFC 4594 recommendation and, as previously noted, incorporates a slight modification by swapping the markings used for signaling and broadcast video. The 12-class QoS strategy model is illustrated in Figure 16-7.

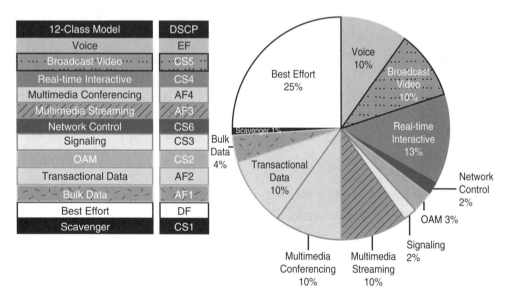

Figure 16-7 *The 12-Class QoS Strategy Model*

As can be seen from Figure 16-7, the recommendations for each traffic class in this model are as follows:

- **Voice:** Marked with EF and limited to 10 percent of link bandwidth in a strict-priority queue

- **Broadcast video:** Marked with CS5 or sometimes as EF and limited to 10 percent of link bandwidth in a strict-priority queue

- **Real-time interactive:** Marked with CS4 or sometimes as EF and limited to 13 percent of link bandwidth in a strict-priority queue

- **Multimedia conferencing:** Marked with AF41 or sometimes as EF and limited to 10 percent of link bandwidth in a strict-priority queue
- **Multimedia streaming:** Marked with AF31 and guaranteed 10 percent of link bandwidth with WRED enabled
- **Network control:** Marked with CS6 and provisioned as guaranteed bandwidth 2 percent of link bandwidth
- **Signaling:** Marked with CS3 and provisioned with a minimum of 2 percent of link bandwidth
- **Management/OAM:** Marked with CS2 and provisioned with a minimum of 3 percent of link bandwidth
- **Transactional data:** Marked with AF21 and provisioned with 10 percent of link bandwidth with WRED enabled
- **Bulk data:** Marked with AF11 and provisioned with 4 percent of link bandwidth with WRED enabled
- **Default (best-effort data):** Marked with DF and provisioned with 25 percent of link bandwidth
- **Scavenger:** Marked with CS1 and provisioned with a maximum of 1 percent of link bandwidth

Summary

- Use QoS policies in hardware rather than in software whenever possible.
- Classify, mark, and police applications as close to the source as possible.
- Use DSCP marking whenever possible.
- Define a queue for the traffic class and enable queuing on each node that has potential congestion.
- Limit the strict-priority queue to one-third of the link bandwidth.
- Do not use WRED for priority or scavenger traffic classes.
- Use one of the three QoS strategy models to govern end-to-end QoS design.

Review Questions

After answering the following questions, please refer to Appendix A, "Answers to Review Questions," for the answers.

1. Which of the following is recommended for a QoS queuing design?
    a. You should implement queuing policy very selectively.
    b. Classes should share queues in order to save resources.

c. You should use at minimum 4 classes of queuing behavior.
d. You should use at minimum 11 classes of queuing behavior.

2. Match the application classes with their PHBs as per RFC 4594.

    VoIP Telephony   EF

    Transactional Data   CS1

    Network Control   CS6

    Call Signaling   CS4

    Real-time Interactive AF21

3. Select the four classes of the 4-class QoS model.
    a. Voice, signaling, mission-critical data, and best effort
    b. Video, signaling, mission-critical data, and best effort
    c. Voice, signaling, mission-critical data, and scavenger
    d. Real-time interactive, signaling, mission-critical data, and best effort

4. Why is it recommended to leverage DSCP markings wherever possible?
    a. Support for end-to-end Layer 3 marking.
    b. It is a more granular method of marking that supports 64 levels as compared to CoS and MPLS EXP, which have 8 levels.
    c. It is more extensible than Layer 2 markings because these markings are lost when media change.
    d. All the above.
    e. None of the above.

5. Traffic should be marked down using which RFC recommendations? (Select two.)
    a. RFC 2957
    b. RFC 2597
    c. RFC 2698
    d. RFC 2968

Chapter 17

Campus, WAN, and Data Center QoS Design

Upon completing this chapter, you will be able to

- Describe the need for QoS in campus networks
- Explain the difference between VoIP and video QoS provisioning
- Describe bursts and explain the need for appropriate buffer size
- Provide general recommendations for trust boundaries
- Explain trust boundaries on examples
- Explain the dynamic trust state when a predefined condition has been met
- Describe recommended classification, marking, and policing models at the ingress
- Describe recommended queuing and dropping models at the egress
- Provide general recommendations for EtherChannel QoS design
- Provide an example of campus QoS design
- Explain the need for WAN and branch QoS
- Describe platform performance considerations
- Describe latency and jitter considerations
- Describe queuing considerations
- Explain use of QoS on the WAN/branch edge devices on the example
- Describe the need for QoS in data center networks
- Explain the main principles of high-performance trading architectures
- Describe the design principles for big data center architecture QoS design
- Describe QoS design in virtualized multiservice architectures
- Explain data center bridging tools
- Explain the case study illustrating QoS design in a data center

The case for quality of service (QoS) for WAN and VPN connectivity is fairly straightforward because of the relatively low-speed bandwidth links at the WAN/VPN edge. When you are considering other Places-in-the-Network (PIN), such as Gigabit/10 Gigabit campus networks and 10/40/100 Gigabit data center networks, the need for QoS is sometimes overlooked or even challenged. The reason for this lack of consideration could be that network administrators equate QoS with queuing policies only. The QoS toolset extends considerably beyond just queuing tools that you need to consider for a sustainable end-to-end QoS design. Classification, marking, and policing all are important QoS functions that need to be performed optimally within all PINs.

Campus QoS Overview

The primary goal of a campus QoS is not to manage latency or jitter but to cope with packet loss when buffers of network devices are filled up. Contemporary endpoints mostly have 1 Gbps connections to the access layer. With a large number of endpoints operating simultaneously, it is easy to fill up buffers and cause packet drops. Even with powerful line cards on core switches, buffers can be filled up in a few milliseconds. Real-time applications such as high-definition video could suffer even from low-rate packet drops. Surprisingly, HD video users can discern the impact to the video experience when even 1 out of 10,000 packets is dropped.

- The secondary goal of campus QoS is to manage and differentiate application data traffic at the access layer. The strategic QoS design principles covered in Chapter 16, "QoS Design Principles and Best Practices," are relevant when you are designing and deploying QoS in the campus network: always perform QoS in hardware rather than software when a choice exists.

- Classify and mark applications as close to their sources as technically and administratively feasible.

- Police unwanted traffic flows as close to their sources as possible.

- Enable queuing policies at every node where the potential for congestion exists, regardless of how rarely this may occur.

- Protect the control plane and data plane by enabling control plane policing (on platforms supporting this feature) as well as data plane policing (scavenger-class QoS) on campus network switches to mitigate and constrain network attacks.

VoIP and Video

The first step in implementing QoS is identifying the traffic on the network and determining QoS requirements for the traffic. Voice and video are typically regarded as highly critical and important traffic types.

Voice traffic has extremely stringent QoS requirements. Voice traffic usually generates a smooth demand on bandwidth and has a minimal impact on other traffic classes as long as the voice traffic is managed properly.

Although voice packets are typically small (60 to 120 bytes), they cannot tolerate delay or drops. The result of delays and drops is poor and often unacceptable voice quality. A typical voice call requires 17 to 106 kbps of guaranteed priority bandwidth in addition to an extra 150 bps per call to address voice-control traffic requirements.

Videoconferencing applications have QoS requirements that are similar to voice. However, videoconferencing traffic is often greedy in nature and, as a result, can affect other traffic classes. Therefore, you need to understand the videoconferencing requirements for a network and also provision carefully for it. The minimum bandwidth for a videoconferencing stream requires the actual bandwidth of the stream in addition to traffic overhead. Figure 17-1 shows the similarities and differences of voice and video traffic.

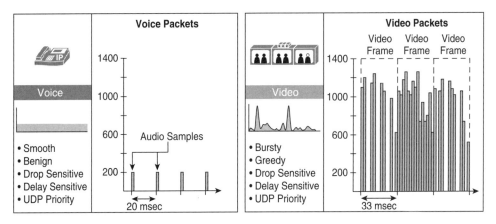

Figure 17-1 *Voice and Video Traffic Flow Characteristics*

Buffers and Bursts

The protocols that have been developed have adapted to the bursty nature of data networks, and brief outages are survivable for certain types of traffic, such as e-mail or web browsing. However, for sensitive real-time applications, as indicated with the example of HD video, even small packet loss can be noticeable. If you want to avoid packet drops on fragile applications, it is critical to increase buffer space and bandwidth to accommodate bursts. Different platforms and line cards have different capabilities, leading to this question: How long can queue buffers accommodate line-rate bursts? Figure 17-2 illustrates why you must consider the point at which to begin dropping regardless of whether you have 1 Gbps or 10 Gbps deployed within the infrastructure.

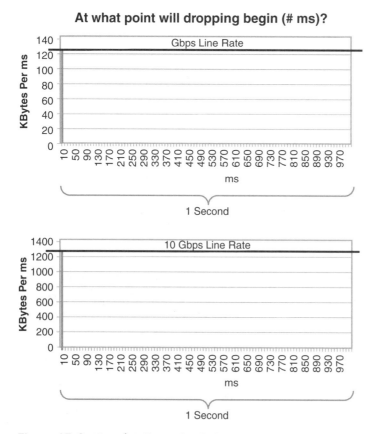

Figure 17-2 *Interface Dropping Point*

Increasing the bandwidth for a particular queue does not necessarily mean increasing buffer space for that queue. For example, you can allocate buffers for the strict-priority and scavenger queues to be tuned and indirectly proportional to their bandwidth allocations, whereas all other traffic types are directly proportional to their bandwidth allocations.

Not all platforms support buffer allocations. On platforms that support this feature, per-queue buffer allocations can be configured. For example, bandwidth allocation for the priority queue can be one-third of the bandwidth allocation among all queues on a given port. Buffer allocations have less impact than tuning bandwidth for the queue and serve to complement the scheduling policy on ports.

Trust States and Boundaries

If the switch or router trusts the end device, it does not need to do any reclassification of packets coming to that interface. Switches and routers are generally set to not trust end devices and must specifically be configured to trust packets coming from an interface.

Ideally, as covered in Chapter 16, classification should be performed as close to the source as possible.

To understand the operation of various trust states, let's look at how three static states can be leveraged at the switch port level:

- **Untrusted:** The port discards any Layer 2 or Layer 3 markings and generates an internal DSCP value of 0 for the packet.
- **Trust CoS:** The port accepts CoS marking and calculates the internal DSCP value according to the default or predefined CoS-DSCP mapping.
- **Trust DSCP:** The port trusts the DSCP marking and sets the internal DSCP value to the value that matches the received DSCP value.

In addition to the static configuration of trust, Cisco Catalyst switches also can define the dynamic trust state, in which trusting on the port dynamically depends on endpoint identification according to the trust policy. Such endpoint identification depends on the Cisco Discovery Protocol (CDP) and is supported only for Cisco end devices. Figure 17-3 shows typical trust states and boundaries.

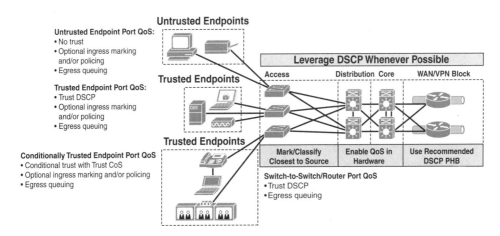

Figure 17-3 *Trust States and Boundaries*

Trust States and Boundaries Example

Figure 17-4 explains key points in placing trust boundaries at different ports in the network.

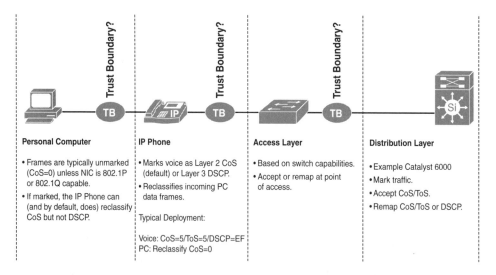

Figure 17-4 *Placement of Trust Boundary Considerations*

Consider the campus network containing IP telephony and host endpoints. Frames can be marked as important by using Layer 2 CoS settings or by leveraging the IP precedence or DSCP bits in the ToS and DiffServ field of the IPv4 header. Cisco IP Phones can mark voice packets as high priority using CoS and ToS. By default, the IP Phone sends 802.1P-tagged packets with the CoS and ToS set to a value of 5 for voice packets. Because most PCs do not have an 802.1Q-capable NIC, they send untagged packets that do not have an 802.1P field. Unless the applications running on the PC send packets with a specific CoS value, this field is 0.

To protect against unwanted and unauthorized prioritization of applications, even if the PC sends tagged frames with a specific CoS value, the Cisco IP Phones can zero out this value before sending the frame to the switch. This is the default behavior. Voice frames coming from the IP Phone have a CoS value of 5, and data frames coming from the PC have a CoS value of 0. If the DSCP is set, the IP Phone cannot re-mark the DSCP, and this must be performed at the switching layer.

If the end device is not a trusted device, the access layer switch can perform the reclassification function, if that switch can do so. If the device cannot, the reclassification task falls to the distribution layer device. If reclassification cannot be performed at one of these two layers, a Cisco IOS software upgrade, hardware upgrade, or both may be necessary to address the QoS needs of the organization.

Dynamic Trust State

The trust state can be dynamically set when a predefined condition has been met. On a Cisco switchport, you can set the condition that end device must belong to for the condition to be successfully fulfilled. This condition is checked using CDP in such a way that the end device provides its own information, such as platform and capabilities, to the switch. Figure 17-5 shows an example of a dynamic conditional trust state.

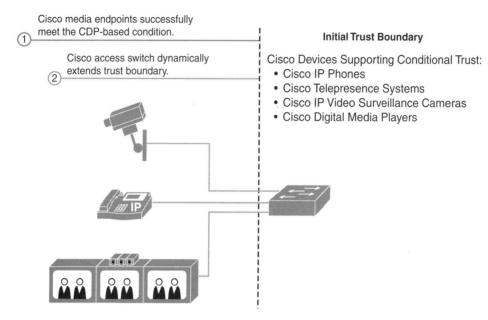

Figure 17-5 *Dynamic Conditional Trust State*

In this example, the Cisco Telepresence System and Cisco IP Phone can provide platform information to access a switch, and the switch can start trusting markings if the end device type matches with predefined type of conditions. Other end devices that can be conditionally trusted are also Cisco IP surveillance cameras and Cisco digital media players.

Classification/Marking/Policing QoS Model

When you are designing QoS, the second layer to look at after selecting the desired trust boundary model is marking and classification. For classification, marking, and policing, QoS policies should be applied in the ingress direction at the switch port. At the access layer, the QoS model that is applied assumes a port trust state or an explicit classification and a marking policy that is applied to the switch port. When designing end-to-end QoS, you need to take into account strategic QoS models such as the 4-, 8-, and 12-class models that will be leveraged to accommodate QoS requirements throughout the organization. Care should be taken to understand the application classes that are present at the access layer of the network and whether the application traffic is sourced from a trusted or untrusted endpoint.

Not every type of application should be classified at the access layer edge because some types of traffic, such as routing updates, should never be received from an endpoint. Similarly, OAM traffic is commonly generated from networking devices, but not from endpoints. Traffic sourcing from Cisco IP Phones should be trusted and classified at the edge, but voice traffic can also be sourced from PCs using voice applications such as Cisco Jabber. In some cases, it is simpler to classify voice traffic according to a range of UDP ports that are used for RTP traffic.

Policing can be applied to monitor transactional data, bulk data, and best effort flows while performing dropping or marking-down actions if such traffic violates predefined limits. As a last step in ingress QoS processing, you can optionally leverage ingress queuing. Ingress queuing is supported on some platforms, and its operation depends greatly on the platform on which ingress queuing is performed.

Figure 17-6 illustrates an example of applying a QoS model at ingress that maps to an eight-class QoS strategy model. Marking, classification, policing, and dropping/re-marking policies are applied for each of the eight traffic classes.

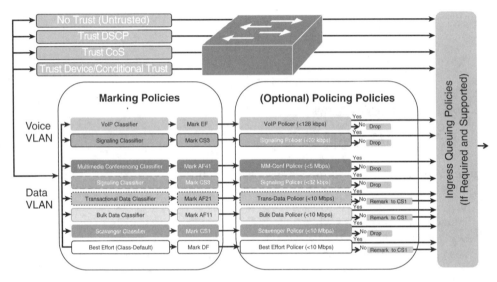

Figure 17-6 *QoS Policy to Map to an Eight-class QoS*

Queuing/Dropping Recommendations

Queuing and dropping of packets on Cisco Catalyst switches are commonly performed at the egress. Cisco Catalyst switches use hardware-based queues; therefore, the number of queues depends on the actual platform. You need to use queuing policies on egress ports with a 1P3QyT queuing structure, where 1P represent one strict-priority queue, 3 represents the number of nonpriority queues, and y represents the number of drop thresholds for nonpriority queues. In this case, 1P3Q8T would translate to the following:

- 1 strict-**Priority** Queue
- 3 nonpriority **Queues**, each with
- 8 drop **Thresholds** per Queue

As shown in Figure 17-7, minimum standard-based queuing behaviors are supported per a four-class QoS model, where real-time traffic should be provisioned to leverage no more than 33 percent of bandwidth, best effort should be provisioned with 25 percent of bandwidth, and scavenger (less than best effort) traffic should be minimally provisioned.

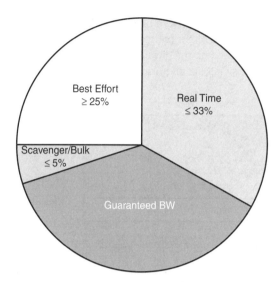

Figure 17-7 *Typical Queuing Behaviors of a Four-class QoS Model*

Congestion-avoidance mechanisms should be enabled only on nonpriority queues because priority queues will be policed by default as part of the low-latency queuing (LLQ) mechanism.

Link Aggregation "EtherChannel" QoS Design

Multiple-Gigabit Ethernet or 10-Gigabit Ethernet interfaces can be bundled into a single logical interface referred to as link aggregation of an EtherChannel interface. When deploying EtherChannel QoS, you need to know platform-specific requirements to decide whether to apply policy on the physical or logical interface. Following are two major considerations when implementing QoS on EtherChannel interfaces:

- **Load balancing:** Typically, EtherChannel load balancing is performed by source and/or destination MAC address or source and/or destination IP address; destination port number also can be used as part of the load-balancing hashing algorithm. However, EtherChannel load balancing does not take into account bandwidth of each flow but instead relies on statistical probability that a large number of flows results in less or more equally distributed load across the links. When loads are balanced using the source and destination IP mechanism, packets belonging to a single flow retain the packet order for that flow.

- **Configuration of physical links:** EtherChannel technology has no awareness of a configuration of individual physical links consisting of an EtherChannel port group. If one link in an EtherChannel port group fails, the remaining physical links would be used for traffic crossing the EtherChannel link. In that situation, an EtherChannel failover mechanism can allocate more real-time traffic across links that cannot accommodate the load, which can in turn lead to degraded QoS of real-time applications.

To decide whether to apply the EtherChannel QoS policy on a physical or logical interface in an ingress direction, you must be aware of the platform used. For egress direction, EtherChannel QoS can always be applied on the physical interface. Figure 17-8 provides a sample breakdown for a few of the switching platforms leveraged within the campus network.

Platform	QoS Policies Applied to the (Logical) PortChannel Interface	QoS Policies Applied to the (Physical) Port-Member Interfaces
Catalyst 2960-X		Ingress and Egress
Catalyst 3650/3850	Ingress	Egress
Catalyst 4500	Ingress	Egress
Catalyst 6500	Ingress	Egress

Figure 17-8 *Sample Ingress QoS Policy Application Breakdown of Different Cisco Switching Platforms*

Practical Example of Campus QoS Design

Figure 17-9 shows an example of campus QoS design, which this section covers thoroughly.

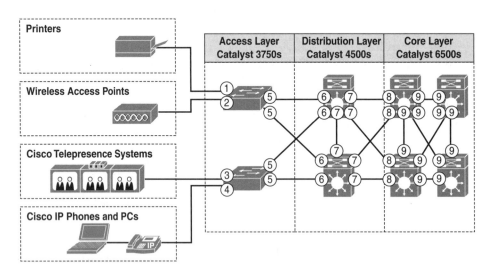

Figure 17-9 *Campus QoS Design: Sample Topology*

Company A has a campus network consisting of different types of endpoints such as PCs, printers, Cisco IP Phones, Cisco Telepresence endpoints, and Cisco wireless access points. The network administrator wants to ensure that endpoints have the correct classification, marking, and policing applied to them. The administrator also wants to limit the guest VLAN to 2 Mbps per each flow.

These campus QoS policies are designed as follows:

- Policy 1 for untrusted endpoints (applied on Catalyst 3750-X for printer devices):
    - Disable trust
    - Enable ingress and egress 1P1Q3T queuing per eight-class QoS model

    ```
    C3750(config)# interface GigabitEthernet 1/0/1
    C3750(config-if)# switchport access vlan 10
    C3750(config-if)# no mls qos trust
    ```

- Policy 2 for trusted endpoints (applied on Catalyst 3750-X for Cisco wireless access points):
    - Enable DSCP trust
    - Enable ingress and egress 1P1Q3T queuing per eight-class QoS model

    ```
    C3750(config)# interface GigabitEthernet 1/0/2
    C3750(config-if)# switchport access vlan 10
    C3750(config-if)# mls qos trust dscp
    ```

- Policy 3 for conditionally trusted endpoints (applied on Catalyst 3750-X for Cisco Telepresence devices):
    - Enable DSCP trust conditionally (if connected device is Cisco Telepresence System [CTS])
    - Enable ingress and egress 1P1Q3T queuing per eight-class QoS model

    ```
    C3750(config)# interface GigabitEthernet 1/0/3
    C3750(config-if)# switchport access vlan 10
    C3750(config-if)# switchport voice vlan 110
    C3750(config-if)# spanning-tree portfast
    C3750(config-if)# mls qos trust device cts
    ! Port is configured to conditionally trust the CTS endpoint
    C3750(config-if)# mls qos trust dscp
    ! Port is configured to statically trust DSCP
    ```

- Policy 4 for conditionally trusted endpoints (applied on Catalyst 3750-X for daisy-chained Cisco IP Phone and PC):
    - Enable CoS trust if the connected device is a Cisco IP Phone
    - Enable ingress and egress 1P1Q3T queuing per eight-class QoS model

```
C3750(config)# ip access-list extended SIGNALING
C3750(config-ext-nacl)# remark SCCP
C3750(config-ext-nacl)# permit tcp any any eq 2000
C3750(config-ext-nacl)# remark SIP
C3750(config-ext-nacl)# permit tcp any any range 5060 5061
C3750(config)# ip access-list extended MULTIMEDIA-CONFERENCING
C3750(config-ext-nacl)# remark CISCO-JABBER-RTP
C3750(config-ext-nacl)# permit udp any any range 16384 32767
C3750(config-ext-nacl)# remark MICROSOFT-LYNC
C3750(config-ext-nacl)# permit tcp any any range 50000 59999
C3750(config)# ip access-list extended TRANSACTIONAL-DATA
C3750(config-ext-nacl)# remark HTTPS
C3750(config-ext-nacl)# permit tcp any any eq 443
C3750(config-ext-nacl)# remark CITRIX
C3750(config-ext-nacl)# permit tcp any any eq 3389
C3750(config-ext-nacl)# permit tcp any any eq 5985
C3750(config-ext-nacl)# permit tcp any any eq 8080
C3750(config)# ip access-list extended BULK-DATA
C3750(config-ext-nacl)# remark FTP
C3750(config-ext-nacl)# permit tcp any any eq ftp
C3750(config-ext-nacl)# permit tcp any any eq ftp-data
C3750(config-ext-nacl)# remark SSH/SFTP
C3750(config-ext-nacl)# permit tcp any any eq 22
C3750(config-ext-nacl)# remark SMTP/SECURE SMTP
C3750(config-ext-nacl)# permit tcp any any eq smtp
C3750(config-ext-nacl)# permit tcp any any eq 465
C3750(config)# ip access-list extended SCAVENGER
C3750(config-ext-nacl)# remark BITTORRENT
C3750(config-ext-nacl)# permit tcp any any range 6881 6999
C3750(config-ext-nacl)# remark APPLE ITUNES MUSIC SHARING
C3750(config-ext-nacl)# permit tcp any any eq 3689
C3750(config-ext-nacl)# permit udp any any eq 3689
C3750(config)# ip access-list extended DEFAULT
C3750(config-ext-nacl)# remark EXPLICIT CLASS-DEFAULT
C3750(config-ext-nacl)# permit ip any any
C3750(config-cmap)# class-map match-all VOICE
C3750(config-cmap)# match dscp ef
! VoIP is trusted (from the VVLAN)
C3750(config-cmap)# class-map match-any SIGNALING
```

```
C3750(config-cmap)# match dscp cs3
! Signaling is trusted (from the VVLAN)
C3750(config-cmap)# match access-group name SIGNALING
C3750(config-cmap)# class-map match-all MULTIMEDIA-CONFERENCING
C3750(config-cmap)# match access-group name MULTIMEDIA-CONFERENCING
C3750(config-cmap)# class-map match-all TRANSACTIONAL-DATA
C3750(config-cmap)# match access-group name TRANSACTIONAL-DATA
C3750(config-cmap)# class-map match-all BULK-DATA
C3750(config-cmap)# match access-group name BULK-DATA
C3750(config-cmap)# class-map match-all SCAVENGER
C3750(config-cmap)# match access-group name SCAVENGER
C3750(config-cmap)# class-map match-all DEFAULT
C3750(config-cmap)# match access-group name DEFAULT
C3750(config-cmap)# policy-map PC-MARKING
C3750(config-pmap-c)# class VOICE
C3750(config-pmap-c)# set dscp ef
C3750(config-pmap-c)# class SIGNALING
C3750(config-pmap-c)# set dscp cs3
C3750(config-pmap-c)# class MULTIMEDIA-CONFERENCING
C3750(config-pmap-c)# set dscp af41
C3750(config-pmap-c)# class TRANSACTIONAL-DATA
C3750(config-pmap-c)# set dscp af21
C3750(config-pmap-c)# class BULK-DATA
C3750(config-pmap-c)# set dscp af11
C3750(config-pmap-c)# class SCAVENGER
C3750(config-pmap-c)# set dscp cs1
C3750(config-pmap-c)# class DEFAULT
C3750(config-pmap-c)# set dscp default
C3750(config)# interface range GigabitEthernet 1/0/4-45
C3750(config-if-range)# switchport access vlan 10
C3750(config-if-range)# switchport voice vlan 110
C3750(config-if-range)# mls qos trust device cisco-phone
! The interface is set to conditionally trust Cisco IP Phones
C3750(config-if-range)# mls qos trust cos
! CoS trust will be dynamically extended to Cisco IP Phones
C3750(config-if-range)# service-policy input PC-MARKING
! Attaches the PC-MARKING policy to the interface(s)
```

Figure 17-10 illustrates the eight-class 1P1Q3T ingress queuing design.

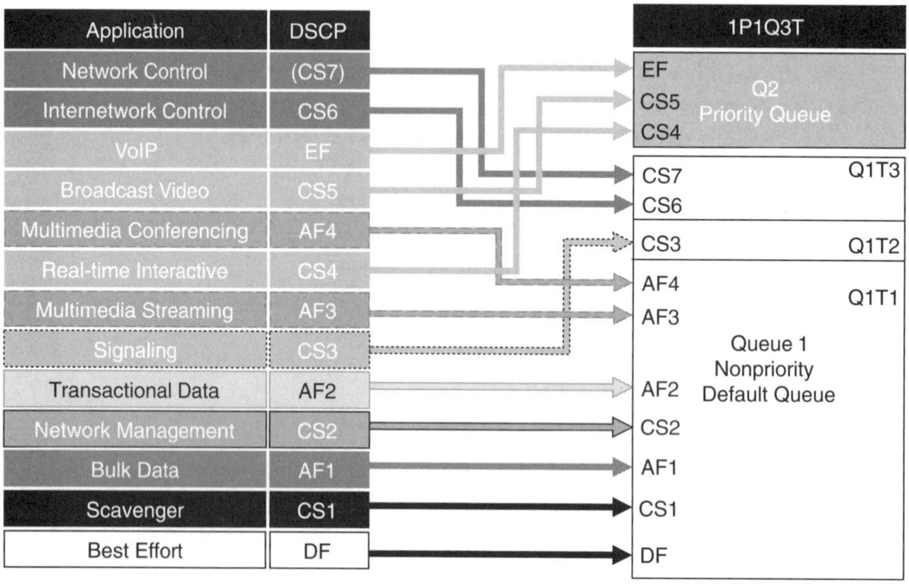

Figure 17-10 *Eight-class 1P1Q3T Ingress Queuing*

Following is the corresponding configuration of the eight-class 1P1Q3T ingress queuing design.

```
! This section provides Eight-Class 1P1Q3T Ingress Queuing Design:
C3750(config)# mls qos srr-queue input priority-queue 2 bandwidth 30
 ! Q2 is enabled as a strict-priority ingress queue with 30% BW
C3750(config)# mls qos srr-queue input bandwidth 70 30
 ! Q1 is assigned 70% BW via SRR shared weights
 ! Q2 SRR shared weight is ignored (as it has been configured as a PQ)
C3750(config)# mls qos srr-queue input buffers 90 10
 ! Q1 is assigned 90% of queuing buffers and Q2 (PQ) is assigned 10%
C3750(config)# mls qos srr-queue input threshold 1 80 90
 ! Q1 thresholds are configured at 80% (Q1T1) and 90% (Q1T2)
 ! Q1T3 is implicitly set at 100% (the tail of the queue)
 ! Q2 thresholds are all set (by default) to 100% (the tail of Q2)
 ! This section configures ingress CoS-to-Queue mappings
C3750(config)# mls qos srr-queue input cos-map queue 1 threshold 1 0 1 2
 ! CoS values 0, 1 and 2 are mapped to Q1T1
C3750(config)# mls qos srr-queue input cos-map queue 1 threshold 2 3
 ! CoS value 3 is mapped to ingress Q1T2
C3750(config)# mls qos srr-queue input cos-map queue 1 threshold 3 6 7
 ! CoS values 6 and 7 are mapped to ingress Q1T3
C3750(config)# mls qos srr-queue input cos-map queue 2 threshold 1 4 5
 ! CoS values 4 and 5 are mapped to ingress Q2 (the PQ)
```

```
! This section configures ingress DSCP-to-Queue Mappings
C3750(config)# mls qos srr-queue input dscp-map queue 1 threshold 1 0 8 10 12 14
! DSCP DF, CS1 and AF1 are mapped to ingress Q1T1
C3750(config)# mls qos srr-queue input dscp-map queue 1 threshold 1 16 18 20 22
! DSCP CS2 and AF2 are mapped to ingress Q1T1
C3750(config)# mls qos srr-queue input dscp-map queue 1 threshold 1 26 28 30 34 36 38
! DSCP AF3 and AF4 are mapped to ingress Q1T1
C3750(config)# mls qos srr-queue input dscp-map queue 1 threshold 2 24
! DSCP CS3 is mapped to ingress Q1T2
C3750(config)# mls qos srr-queue input dscp-map queue 1 threshold 3 48 56
! DSCP CS6 and CS7 are mapped to ingress Q1T3 (the tail of Q1)
C3750(config)# mls qos srr-queue input dscp-map queue 2 threshold 3 32 40 46
! DSCP CS4, CS5 and EF are mapped to ingress Q2T3 (the tail of the PQ)
```

Figure 17-11 illustrates the eight-class 1P1Q3T egress queuing design followed by the corresponding configuration.

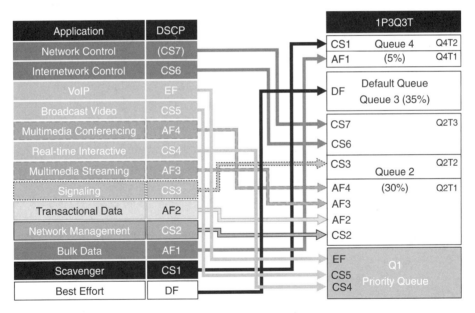

Figure 17-11 *Eight-class 1P1Q3T Egress Queuing*

Following is the corresponding configuration of the eight-class 1P1Q3T egress queuing design.

```
! This section provides Eight-Class 1P3Q3T Egress Queuing Design:
! This section configures buffers and thresholds on Q1 through Q4
C3750(config)# mls qos queue-set output 1 buffers 15 30 35 20
! Queue buffers are allocated
C3750(config)# mls qos queue-set output 1 threshold 1 100 100 100 100
```

```
! All Q1 (PQ) Thresholds are set to 100%
C3750(config)# mls qos queue-set output 1 threshold 2 80 90 100 400
! Q2T1 is set to 80%; Q2T2 is set to 90%;
! Q2 Reserve Threshold is set to 100%;
! Q2 Maximum (Overflow) Threshold is set to 400%
C3750(config)# mls qos queue-set output 1 threshold 3 100 100 100 400
! Q3T1 is set to 100%, as all packets are marked the same weight in Q3
! Q3 Reserve Threshold is set to 100%;
! Q3 Maximum (Overflow) Threshold is set to 400%
C3750(config)# mls qos queue-set output 1 threshold 4 60 100 100 400
! Q4T1 is set to 60%; Q4T2 is set to 100%
! Q4 Reserve Threshold is set to 100%;
! Q4 Maximum (Overflow) Threshold is set to 400%
! This section configures egress CoS-to-Queue mappings
C3750(config)# mls qos srr-queue output cos-map queue 1 threshold 3 4 5
! CoS 4 and 5 are mapped to egress Q1T3 (the tail of the PQ)
C3750(config)# mls qos srr-queue output cos-map queue 2 threshold 1 2
! CoS 2 is mapped to egress Q2T1
C3750(config)# mls qos srr-queue output cos-map queue 2 threshold 2 3
! CoS 3 is mapped to egress Q2T2
C3750(config)# mls qos srr-queue output cos-map queue 2 threshold 3 6 7
! CoS 6 and 7 are mapped to Q2T3
C3750(config)# mls qos srr-queue output cos-map queue 3 threshold 3 0
! CoS 0 is mapped to Q3T3 (the tail of the default queue)
C3750(config)# mls qos srr-queue output cos-map queue 4 threshold 3 1
! CoS 1 is mapped to Q4T3 (tail of the less-than-best-effort queue)
! This section configures egress DSCP-to-Queue mappings
C3750(config)# mls qos srr-queue output dscp-map queue 1 threshold 3 32 40 46
! DSCP CS4, CS5 and EF are mapped to egress Q1T3 (tail of the PQ)
C3750(config)# mls qos srr-queue output dscp-map queue 2 threshold 1 16 18 20 22
! DSCP CS2 and AF2 are mapped to egress Q2T1
C3750(config)# mls qos srr-queue output dscp-map queue 2 threshold 1 26 28 30 34
 36 38
! DSCP AF3 and AF4 are mapped to egress Q2T1
C3750(config)# mls qos srr-queue output dscp-map queue 2 threshold 2 24
! DSCP CS3 is mapped to egress Q2T2
C3750(config)# mls qos srr-queue output dscp-map queue 2 threshold 3 48 56
! DSCP CS6 and CS7 are mapped to egress Q2T3
C3750(config)# mls qos srr-queue output dscp-map queue 3 threshold 3 0
! DSCP DF is mapped to egress Q3T3 (tail of the best effort queue)
C3750(config)# mls qos srr-queue output dscp-map queue 4 threshold 1 8
! DSCP CS1 is mapped to egress Q4T1
C3750(config)# mls qos srr-queue output dscp-map queue 4 threshold 2 10 12 14
! This section configures interface egress queuing parameters
C3750(config)# interface range GigabitEthernet1/0/1-48
```

```
C3750(config-if-range)# queue-set 1
! The interface(s) is assigned to queue-set 1
C3750(config-if-range)# srr-queue bandwidth share 1 30 35 5
! The SRR sharing weights are set to allocate 30% BW to Q2
! 35% BW to Q3 and 5% BW to Q4
! Q1 SRR sharing weight is ignored, as it will be configured as a PQ
C3750(config-if-range)# priority-queue out
! Q1 is enabled as a strict-priority queue
```

- Policy 5 for uplink ports on the access layer (applied on Catalyst 3750-X in the outbound direction toward the distribution layer):
  - Enable DSCP trust
  - Enable ingress and egress 1P1Q3T queuing per eight-class QoS model

```
! Physical EtherChannel member-ports
C3750(config)# interface range TenGigabitEthernet1/0/1-2
C3750(config-if-range)# description PORT-CHANNEL1-PHYSICAL-PORT-MEMBER
C3750(config-if-range)# switchport mode trunk
C3750(config-if-range)# switchport trunk encapsulation dot1q
C3750(config-if-range)# switchport trunk allowed vlan 10,99,110
C3750(config-if-range)# channel-group 1 mode auto
! Associates the physical ports with the logical EtherChannel bundle
C3750(config-if-range)# mls qos trust dscp
! The physical port-member interfaces are set to statically trust DSCP
C3750(config-if-range)# queue-set 1
! The interfaces are assigned to queue-set 1
C3750(config-if-range)# srr-queue bandwidth share 1 30 35 5
! The SRR sharing weights are set to allocate 30% BW to Q2
! 35% BW to Q3 and 5% BW to Q4
! Q1 SRR sharing weight is ignored, as it will be configured as a PQ
C3750(config-if-range)# priority-queue out
! Q1 is enabled as a strict-priority queue
```

- Policy 6 for downstream ports on the distribution layer (applied on Catalyst 4500 in the inbound direction toward the access layer):
  - Enable DSCP trust by default
  - Enable 1P7Q1T+DBL egress queuing per eight-class QoS model

```
C4500(config)# ip access-list extended GUEST-VLAN-SUBNET
C4500(config-ext-nacl)# permit ip 192.168.10.0 0.0.0.255 any
C4500(config)# flow record FLOW-RECORD-1
C4500(config-flow-record)# match ipv4 source address
C4500(config)# class-map match-all GUEST-VLAN-SUBNET
C4500(config-cmap)# match access-group name GUEST-VLAN-SUBNET
```

```
C4500(config-cmap)# match flow record FLOW-RECORD-1
C4500(config)# policy-map GUEST-VLAN-2MBS-MICROFLOW-POLICER
C4500(config-pmap)# class GUEST-VLAN-SUBNET
C4500(config-pmap-c)# police cir 2m
C4500(config-pmap-c-police)# conform-action transmit
C4500(config-pmap-c-police)# exceed-action drop
! Specifies each discrete microflow is to be limited to 2 Mbps
! This section configures the logical port channel interface
C4500(config)# interface Port-channel1
C4500(config-if)# description ETHERCHANNEL-LOGICAL-INTERFACE
C4500(config-if)# switchport mode trunk
C4500(config-if)# switchport trunk encapsulation dot1q
C4500(config-if)# switchport trunk allowed vlan 10,99,110
C4500(config-if)# service-policy input GUEST-VLAN-2MBS-MICROFLOW-POLICER
! This section configures 1P3Q1T+DBL queuing on physical port-member interfaces
C4500(config)# interface range TenGigabitEthernet1/1-2
C4500(config-if-range)# description PORT-CHANNEL1-PORT-MEMBER
C4500(config-if-range)# switchport mode trunk
C4500(config-if-range)# switchport trunk encapsulation dot1q
C4500(config-if-range)# switchport trunk allowed vlan 10,99,110
C4500(config-if-range)# channel-group 1 mode auto
C4500(config-if-range)# service-policy output 1P7Q1T-QUEUING
```

- Policy 7 for upstream ports on the distribution layer (applied on Catalyst 4500 in the outbound direction toward the core layer):

    - DSCP trust by default
    - Enable 1P7Q1T+DBL egress queuing per eight-class QoS model

```
! This section configures the class maps for the egress queuing policy
C4500(config)# class-map match-any PRIORITY-QUEUE
C4500(config-cmap)# match dscp ef
C4500(config-cmap)# match dscp cs4
C4500(config)# class-map match-all MULTIMEDIA-CONFERENCING-QUEUE
C4500(config-cmap)# match dscp af41 af42 af43
C4500(config)# class-map match-all SIGNALING-QUEUE
C4500(config-cmap)# match dscp cs3
C4500(config)# class-map match-all TRANSACTIONAL-DATA-QUEUE
C4500(config-cmap)# match dscp af21 af22 af23
C4500(config)# class-map match-all BULK-DATA-QUEUE
C4500(config-cmap)# match dscp af11 af12 af13
C4500(config)# class-map match-all SCAVENGER-QUEUE
C4500(config-cmap)# match dscp cs1
! This section configures the 1P7Q1T+DBL egress queuing policy map
C4500(config)# policy-map 1P7Q1T+DBL
```

```
C4500(config-pmap-c)# class PRIORITY-QUEUE
C4500(config-pmap-c)# priority
C4500(config-pmap-c)# class MULTIMEDIA-CONFERENCING-QUEUE
C4500(config-pmap-c)# bandwidth remaining percent 10
C4500(config-pmap-c)# dbl
C4500(config-pmap-c)# class SIGNALING-QUEUE
C4500(config-pmap-c)# bandwidth remaining percent 2
C4500(config-pmap-c)# class TRANSACTIONAL-DATA-QUEUE
C4500(config-pmap-c)# bandwidth remaining percent 25
C4500(config-pmap-c)# dbl
C4500(config-pmap-c)# class BULK-DATA-QUEUE
C4500(config-pmap-c)# bandwidth remaining percent 4
C4500(config-pmap-c)# dbl
C4500(config-pmap-c)# class SCAVENGER-QUEUE
C4500(config-pmap-c)# bandwidth remaining percent 1
C4500(config-pmap-c)# class class-default
C4500(config-pmap-c)# bandwidth remaining percent 25
C4500(config-pmap-c)# dbl
! This section attaches the egress queuing policy to the interface(s)
C4500(config)# interface range TenGigabitEthernet 1/1-8
C4500(config-if-range)# service-policy output 1P7Q1T+DBL
```

- Policy 8 for downstream ports on the core layer (applied on Catalyst 6500 in the inbound direction from the distribution layer):

    - DSCP trust by default

    - Enable 1P7Q4T egress queuing and 8Q4T egress queuing per eight-class QoS model

```
! This section configures the class maps for the queuing policy maps
C6500(config-cmap)# class-map type lan-queuing REALTIME-QUEUE
C6500(config-cmap)# match dscp ef cs4
C6500(config-cmap)# class-map type lan-queuing SIGNALING-QUEUE
C6500(config-cmap)# match dscp cs3
C6500(config-cmap)# class-map type lan-queuing MULTIMEDIA-CONF-QUEUE
C6500(config-cmap)# match dscp af41 af42 af43
C6500(config-cmap)# class-map type lan-queuing TRANSACTIONAL-DATA-QUEUE
C6500(config-cmap)# match dscp af21 af22 af23
C6500(config-cmap)# class-map type lan-queuing BULK-DATA-QUEUE
C6500(config-cmap)# match dscp af11 af12 af13
C6500(config-cmap)# class-map type lan-queuing SCAVENGER-QUEUE
C6500(config-cmap)# match dscp cs1
! This section configures the eight-class ingress (8Q4T) policy map
C6500(config-pmap)# policy-map type lan-queuing INGRESS-8Q4T
C6500(config-pmap)# class REALTIME-QUEUE
```

```
C6500(config-pmap-c)# bandwidth percent 33
C6500(config-pmap-c)# class SIGNALING-QUEUE
C6500(config-pmap-c)# bandwidth percent 2
C6500(config-pmap-c)# class MULTIMEDIA-CONF-QUEUE
C6500(config-pmap-c)# bandwidth percent 10
C6500(config-pmap-c)# random-detect dscp-based
C6500(config-pmap-c)# random-detect dscp af41 percent 80 100
C6500(config-pmap-c)# random-detect dscp af42 percent 70 100
C6500(config-pmap-c)# random-detect dscp af43 percent 60 100
C6500(config-pmap-c)# class TRANSACTIONAL-DATA-QUEUE
C6500(config-pmap-c)# bandwidth percent 25
C6500(config-pmap-c)# random-detect dscp-based
C6500(config-pmap-c)# random-detect dscp af21 percent 80 100
C6500(config-pmap-c)# random-detect dscp af22 percent 70 100
C6500(config-pmap-c)# random-detect dscp af23 percent 60 100
C6500(config-pmap-c)# class BULK-DATA-QUEUE
C6500(config-pmap-c)# bandwidth percent 4
C6500(config-pmap-c)# random-detect dscp-based
C6500(config-pmap-c)# random-detect dscp af11 percent 80 100
C6500(config-pmap-c)# random-detect dscp af12 percent 70 100
C6500(config-pmap-c)# random-detect dscp af13 percent 60 100
C6500(config-pmap-c)# class SCAVENGER-QUEUE
C6500(config-pmap-c)# bandwidth percent 1
C6500(config-pmap-c)# class class-default
C6500(config-pmap-c)# random-detect dscp-based
C6500(config-pmap-c)# random-detect dscp default percent 80 100
! This section configures the eight-class egress (1P7Q4T) policy map
C6500(config-pmap)# policy-map type lan-queuing EGRESS-1P7Q4T
C6500(config-pmap)# class REALTIME-QUEUE
C6500(config-pmap-c)# priority
! Enables strict-priority queuing on the REALTIME-QUEUE
C6500(config-pmap-c)# class SIGNALING-QUEUE
C6500(config-pmap-c)# bandwidth remaining percent 2
C6500(config-pmap-c)# class MULTIMEDIA-CONF-QUEUE
C6500(config-pmap-c)# bandwidth remaining percent 10
C6500(config-pmap-c)# random-detect dscp-based
C6500(config-pmap-c)# random-detect dscp af41 percent 80 100
C6500(config-pmap-c)# random-detect dscp af42 percent 70 100
C6500(config-pmap-c)# random-detect dscp af43 percent 60 100
! DSCP-based WRED is enabled and tuned for AF4 PHB
C6500(config-pmap-c)# class TRANSACTIONAL-DATA-QUEUE
C6500(config-pmap-c)# bandwidth remaining percent 25
C6500(config-pmap-c)# random-detect dscp-based
C6500(config-pmap-c)# random-detect dscp af21 percent 80 100
C6500(config-pmap-c)# random-detect dscp af22 percent 70 100
```

```
C6500(config-pmap-c)# random-detect dscp af23 percent 60 100
C6500(config-pmap-c)# class BULK-DATA-QUEUE
C6500(config-pmap-c)# bandwidth remaining percent 4
C6500(config-pmap-c)# random-detect dscp-based
C6500(config-pmap-c)# random-detect dscp af11 percent 80 100
C6500(config-pmap-c)# random-detect dscp af12 percent 70 100
C6500(config-pmap-c)# random-detect dscp af13 percent 60 100
C6500(config-pmap-c)# class SCAVENGER-QUEUE
C6500(config-pmap-c)# bandwidth remaining percent 1
C6500(config-pmap-c)# class class-default
C6500(config-pmap-c)# random-detect dscp-based
C6500(config-pmap-c)# random-detect dscp default percent 80 100
! This section applies ingress and egress policies
C6500(config)# interface range TenGigabitEthernet 3/1-8
C6500(config-if-range)# service-policy type lan-queuing input INGRESS-8Q4T
C6500(config-if-range)# service-policy type lan-queuing output EGRESS-1P7Q4T
```

- Policy 9 for upstream ports on the core layer (applied on Catalyst 6500 in the core layer):
  - DSCP trust by default
  - Enable 2P6Q4T egress queuing and 2P6Q4T egress queuing per eight-class QoS model

```
C6500(config-cmap)# class-map type lan-queuing REALTIME-VOICE-QUEUE
C6500(config-cmap)# match dscp ef
C6500(config-cmap)# class-map type lan-queuing REALTIME-VIDEO-QUEUE
C6500(config-cmap)# match dscp ef cs4
C6500(config-cmap)# class-map type lan-queuing SIGNALING-QUEUE
C6500(config-cmap)# match dscp cs3
C6500(config-cmap)# class-map type lan-queuing MULTIMEDIA-CONF-QUEUE
C6500(config-cmap)# match dscp af41 af42 af43
C6500(config-cmap)# class-map type lan-queuing TRANSACTIONAL-DATA-QUEUE
C6500(config-cmap)# match dscp af21 af22 af23
C6500(config-cmap)# class-map type lan-queuing BULK-DATA-QUEUE
C6500(config-cmap)# match dscp af11 af12 af13
C6500(config-cmap)# class-map type lan-queuing SCAVENGER-QUEUE
C6500(config-cmap)# match dscp cs1
C6500(config-pmap)# policy-map type lan-queuing 2P6Q4T
C6500(config-pmap)# class REALTIME-VOICE-QUEUE
C6500(config-pmap-c)# priority level 1
C6500(config-pmap)# class REALTIME-VIDEO-QUEUE
C6500(config-pmap-c)# priority level 2
C6500(config-pmap-c)# class SIGNALING-QUEUE
C6500(config-pmap-c)# bandwidth remaining percent 2
```

```
C6500(config-pmap-c)# class MULTIMEDIA-CONF-QUEUE
C6500(config-pmap-c)# bandwidth remaining percent 10
C6500(config-pmap-c)# random-detect dscp-based
C6500(config-pmap-c)# random-detect dscp af41 percent 80 100
C6500(config-pmap-c)# random-detect dscp af42 percent 70 100
C6500(config-pmap-c)# random-detect dscp af43 percent 60 100
C6500(config-pmap-c)# class TRANSACTIONAL-DATA-QUEUE
C6500(config-pmap-c)# bandwidth remaining percent 25
C6500(config-pmap-c)# random-detect dscp-based
C6500(config-pmap-c)# random-detect dscp af21 percent 80 100
C6500(config-pmap-c)# random-detect dscp af22 percent 70 100
C6500(config-pmap-c)# random-detect dscp af23 percent 60 100
C6500(config-pmap-c)# class BULK-DATA-QUEUE
C6500(config-pmap-c)# bandwidth remaining percent 4
C6500(config-pmap-c)# random-detect dscp-based
C6500(config-pmap-c)# random-detect dscp af11 percent 80 100
C6500(config-pmap-c)# random-detect dscp af12 percent 70 100
C6500(config-pmap-c)# random-detect dscp af13 percent 60 100
C6500(config-pmap-c)# class SCAVENGER-QUEUE
C6500(config-pmap-c)# bandwidth remaining percent 1
C6500(config-pmap-c)# class class-default
C6500(config-pmap-c)# random-detect dscp-based
C6500(config-pmap-c)# random-detect dscp default percent 80 100
! This section attaches the ingress and egress queuing policies to the interface
C6500(config)# interface FortyGigabitEthernet 1/1
C6500(config-if)# service-policy type lan-queuing input 2P6Q4T
C6500(config-if)# service-policy type lan-queuing output 2P6Q4T
```

All traffic markings to signaling, real-time interactive, voice, best effort, and so on should be enforced according to an eight-class QoS design model.

WAN QoS Overview

The same design principles applicable to campus networks are applied to the WAN/branch QoS design. There are, however, some distinct recommendations associated with applying QoS to WAN/branch edge devices.

Packet loss and jitter are most apparent on WAN and branch devices. As a result, QoS in those places must be carefully considered because it can have a major impact on the quality of real-time applications and the overall user experience.

A major problem with the WAN/branch edge is associated with low-speed links when compared to the speeds of the LAN/campus network. The difference in those speeds can lead to filled buffers and packet loss. On the lower-speed links at the WAN edge, a packet can be significantly delayed. A delayed packet is just as bad as a dropped packet, because sometimes a packet is delayed too much, and this delay results in it being dropped at the receiver due to exceeding the de-jitter buffer space. To properly cope with packet loss and jitter, you must implement appropriate queuing policies.

The WAN/branch edge devices enable the use of QoS tools such as Medianet or Application Visibility and Control (AVC) to enhance classification granularity. Whether focusing on campus networks, data centers, WANs, or VPNs, you need to follow the same strategic QoS and best practice design principles across the entire infrastructure to ensure a sustainable and effective end-to-end QoS design. Recommendations previously covered include

- Performing QoS in hardware whenever possible
- Classifying and marking applications as close as possible to the source
- Policing unwanted traffic flows as close to their sources as possible
- Enabling queuing at every node that has potential for congestion
- Enabling control plane policing to protect the data and control planes

Platform Performance Considerations

When choosing a WAN/branch router, you must be aware of several platform-performance considerations for QoS configuration. Although many of the Cisco routers perform QoS operations in software, which may result in increased CPU cycles when deploying QoS, it is dependent on the selected platform—for example, Cisco ASRs that perform QoS operations in both software and hardware. Therefore, hardware acceleration features, link speeds, policy complexity, packet rates, and packet sizes influence platform selection. It is important to ensure that the selected platform fulfills current and near future performance requirements.

Enabling QoS in the Cisco IOS has several advantages:

- It provides cross-platform consistency of QoS features like LLQ and CBWFQ.
- Syntax of the QoS configuration is consistent as a result of the modular QoS CLI MQC configuration approach being shared in all platforms.
- Rich set of QoS features, such as NBAR/NBAR2 or hierarchical QoS, is not available on Catalyst switch platforms.

Figure 17-12 shows product platforms and related performance capacity examples that you can use as a reference for planning.

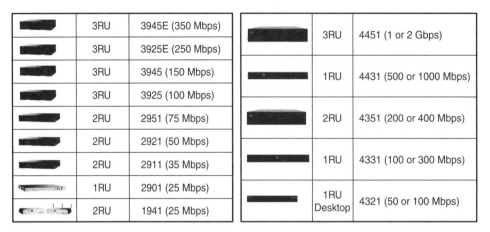

Figure 17-12 *Cisco Platform Performance Capacity Examples*

Note Numbers shown in Figure 17-12 are illustrative; refer to www.cisco.com for updated lists.

Note ISR G2 and ISR 4K routers are typically leveraged as branch routers. ASRs are usually used as WAN aggregation routers.

Latency and Jitter Considerations

Latency and jitter are important factors when you are deploying real-time applications over WANs. Control of latency and jitter is performed by using reliable WAN links supported by QoS tools.

The ITU G.114 recommendation states that one-way latency for real-time applications such as voice and video should not exceed 150 ms. To stay within this limit, you must understand factors that influence overall delay in the network, such as

- Serialization delay
- Propagation delay
- Queuing delay

Some types of delay, such as serialization and propagation delay, are fixed. The network administrator cannot control them. Serialization delay mainly depends on the line rate (circuit speed), and propagation delay depends on the physical distance between the sender and the receiver. However, queuing delay is a variable type of delay and depends on the congestion in the device that processes the packet. For delay-sensitive packets, you can apply a queuing policy that will shorten the time that a packet stays in the queue of the device that is congested. You must send real-time traffic packets onto the wire first because they must be received within the de-jitter buffer time limits. Any received packet that is delayed beyond the de-jitter buffer limit is as good as lost. Such cases affect overall real-time application quality and end-user experience.

Queuing Considerations

Because it is important to control various types of delays, such as queuing delays, you must consider queuing when planning and implementing end-to-end QoS across the network.

You need to be aware of a few facts when designing queuing policies in the network. The final output when sending frames onto the wire is the Tx-Ring. The Tx-Ring is a FIFO queue that maximizes bandwidth by matching the output packet rate to the rate of the physical interface. On certain Cisco platforms, the Tx-Ring can be configured to allow a deeper or shallower queue. Lowering the value of the Tx-Ring enforces the IOS software queuing engine to queue packets sooner and more often, resulting in overall lower jitter and delay values for priority traffic. On the other side, setting a Tx-Ring too low can cause higher CPU utilization. Remember this when making trade-offs between delay or jitter and CPU utilization.

For queuing in software, you can use three basic queuing management strategies on WAN/branch edge devices:

- **CBWFQ:** Use this queuing algorithm to guarantee minimum bandwidth to certain traffic classes.

- **LLQ:** Use this queuing algorithm to transport real-time traffic applications within the priority queue and to guarantee a minimum bandwidth to other traffic types. This approach enables protection of real-time traffic (such as voice and video conferencing) and prevents other traffic types from interfering with the real-time traffic. However, be aware that the priority queue is always limited by the rate that is configured within a given class because an implicit policer is applied for the priority traffic class.

- **WRED:** Use this congestion-avoidance algorithm for TCP-based applications to avoid congestion by dropping lower-priority packets before congestion occurs.

LLQ recommendations for the WAN/branch edge should be familiar; they are as follows:

- Provision no more than 33 percent of link bandwidth capacity for LLQ.
- Do not enable the WRED mechanism for LLQ.

CBWFQ recommendations for the WAN/branch edge are as follows:

- On CBWFQ, separate classes are assigned bandwidth allocations according to application requirements.

- Depending on the class of the traffic, you may use DSCP-based WRED to minimize TCP global synchronization.

- For the control CBWFQ traffic class, it is not recommended that you enable fair-queuing pre-sorters or DSCP-based WRED because those packets should never be dropped or reordered.

- For multimedia and data CBWFQ, fair-queuing pre-sorters and DSCP-based WRED can be enabled.

- For scavenger CBWFQ, it is not recommended that you enable pre-sorters or DSCP-based WRED.

- For the default CBWFQ class, you can enable pre-sorters or DSCP-based WRED if needed. It is recommended that you allocate a minimum of 25 percent of bandwidth to this traffic type. However, this is just a generic best practice recommendation that may not always be the right percentage for your requirements; therefore, gathering and understanding application requirements in terms of amount of bandwidth is key to achieve a successful QoS design.

Note CBWFQ queues may also have a fair-queuing pre-sorter applied to them so that multiple flows contending for a single queue are managed fairly.

Shaping Considerations

With WAN interfaces using Ethernet as an access technology, the demarcation point between the enterprise and the service provider might no longer have a physical-interface bandwidth constraint. Instead, a specified amount of access bandwidth is contracted with the service provider. To ensure the offered load to the service provider does not exceed the contracted rate that results in the carrier discarding traffic, you need to configure shaping in the outbound direction on the physical interface. This shaping is accomplished with a QoS service policy.

A QoS service policy is configured on the outside Ethernet interface, and this parent policy includes a shaper that then references a second or subordinate (child) policy that enables queuing within the shaped rate. This deployment model is referred to as a Hierarchical Class-Based Weighted Fair Queuing (HCBWFQ) configuration. When configuring the shape average command, you must ensure that the value matches the contracted bandwidth rate from the service provider to avoid traffic being policed and dropped inbound at the service provider PE. Figure 17-13 illustrates HCBWFQ.

WAN QoS Overview   593

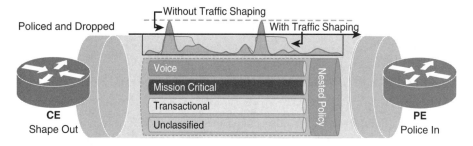

Figure 17-13 *Hierarchical Class-based Weighted Fair Queuing*

Practical Example of WAN and Branch QoS

Figure 17-14 shows a WAN/VPN QoS design.

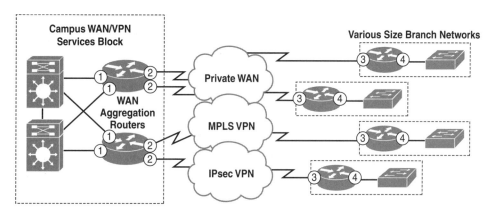

Figure 17-14 *WAN/VPN QoS Design*

As you can see in Figure 17-14, Company A has the following networks:

- Hub-and-spoke network topology with WAN links over a private WAN
- MPLS VPN
- IPsec over the Internet

The company wants to deploy QoS over all WAN links to provide a quality experience for real-time applications. Policies 1–4 are applied at different points on network WAN/branch edge devices as follows:

- Policy 1 is for the WAN aggregator LAN edge and enables ingress DSCP trust as well as optional ingress NBAR2 classification and marking. Egress LLQ/CBWFQ/WRED may also be enabled if required.

- Policy 2 is for the WAN aggregator WAN edge and enables ingress DSCP trust as well as egress LLQ/CBWFQ/WRED. RSVP policies or VPN-specific policies may also be enabled.

- Policy 3 is for the branch WAN edge and enables ingress DSCP trust as well as egress LLQ/CBWFQ/WRED. RSVP policies or VPN-specific policies may also be enabled.

- Policy 4 is for the branch LAN edge and enables ingress DSCP trust as well as NBAR2 classification and marking. Egress LLQ/CBWFQ/WRED policies may be applied if required.

Data Center QoS Overview

Although the principles applied to the DC QoS design are similar to QoS design in a campus network, QoS design must be carefully considered in the DC also. The primary goal of QoS in a data center is to manage packet loss. In 10/40/100 Gigabit Ethernet data centers, only a few milliseconds of congestion can cause severe packet loss. Hardware buffering and queuing may not cope with the specific data center protocols that require lossless service.

You need to consider the following important roles of QoS design in data center networks:

- Perform QoS in hardware whenever possible. The Cisco Nexus switching platform can perform QoS actions in ASICs, offloading CPU resources for other operations. This capability gives you the opportunity to enable QoS policies on the Nexus platform at the line rate.

- Classify and mark applications as close as possible to the traffic source. This approach, covered as part of campus QoS design, is a general QoS design principle and should also be followed in data center networks.

- Police traffic closest to the source as administratively possible. The goal is to offload the CPU of the network devices and preserve the throughput and bandwidth of links.

- Enable queuing on every node that could be potentially congested. This principle is important in data centers where oversubscription ratios of multigigabit Ethernet links create the potential for congestion.

- Enable control plane policing. This step is recommended to improve the security of the data center infrastructure.

High-Performance Trading Architecture

High-performance trading (HPT) data centers have minimal QoS requirements because the goal of those data centers is to eliminate oversubscription, and this renders QoS in such environments unnecessary. Financial institutions use the HPT architecture to increase execution speeds and gain competitive advantage.

Figure 17-15 shows low-latency platforms such as the Nexus 3000, which are used because they minimize oversubscription and provide high-speed processing at a line rate.

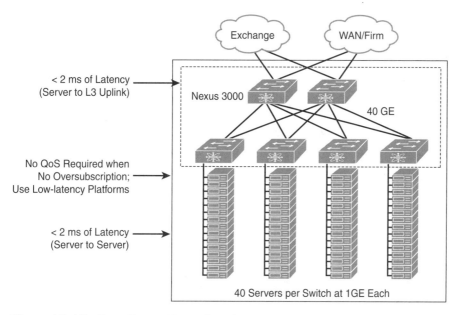

Figure 17-15 *Data Center Network with Low Latency*

In data centers that have an access, distribution, and core layer hierarchy, the traffic from the access layer going to the core must traverse the distribution layer providing aggregation services. To avoid congestion in the distribution layer, you need to provide enough bandwidth and buffer space on distribution layer platforms to accommodate the downstream access layer devices. When you leverage adequate platforms with enough high-bandwidth ports provisioned from core to access, you avoid oversubscription.

Big Data Architecture

Big data architectures were designed to process complex and large sets of data that are not easy to handle with traditional architectures. In cluster-based architectures of big data centers, computing and storage reside within individual servers that form clusters, as shown in Figure 17-16.

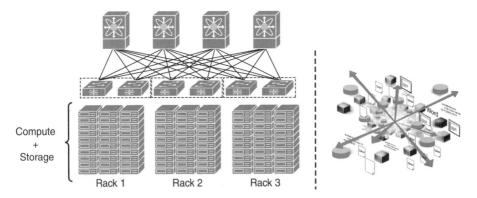

Figure 17-16 *Big Data System Architecture*

QoS tools and design are required to support those architectures. The applied tools are similar to the tools that are applied in campus networks, such as classification, marking, and ingress and egress queuing. The reason for this is that the primary focus is mainly on extending the trust boundary and the queuing that is applied in every node.

Case Study: Virtualized Multiservice Architectures

Data center architectures have shifted in recent years because of virtualization and cloud technologies delivering infrastructure offerings in the form of platform as a service (PaaS). Those changes have resulted in the following factors:

- Applications are not bound to a physical server anymore.
- Storage is no longer bound to a physical disk (different instances).
- The network is no longer bound to hardware network devices.

From a QoS perspective, lossless data center and virtualization protocols must be implemented to support services such as Live Migration or vMotion. In multitenant data center architectures, the same QoS tools and designs are applied with a new consideration, and in this case the marking models also identify the class of customer service and are not strictly related to application traffic classes.

Cisco Virtualized Multiservice Data Centers (VMDC) leverage virtualization and cloud technologies to create a single compute, storage, network, and management platform. This platform is designed to increase efficiency, scalability, and operations simplicity of a data center network. An example highlighting the building blocks of Virtualized Multiservice Architectures is the Cisco Virtualized Multiservice Validated Design illustrated in Figure 17-17.

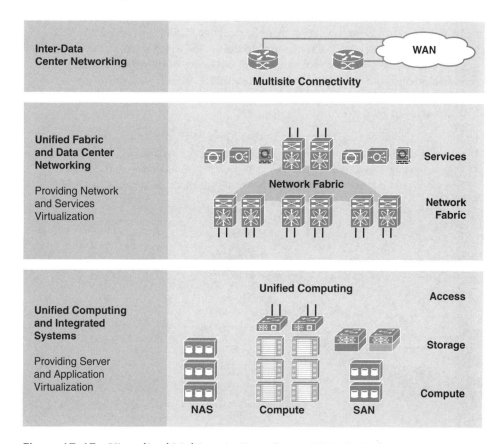

Figure 17-17 *Virtualized Multiservice Data Center (VMDC) Architecture*

This validated design is a result of testing and documenting solutions that bring together networking, computing, storage resources, and services. The Cisco VMDC Validated Design is also used to provide QoS recommendations for implementing QoS tools such as policing, classification, and marking, while at the same time implementing trust boundaries on a platform basis.

Data Center Bridging Toolset

In addition to classification, marking, queuing, and dropping, QoS operations in data centers also require lossless transport for some SAN protocols like Fibre Channel over Ethernet (FCoE). Traditional Ethernet cannot guarantee the lossless transport requirements of Fibre Channel. The IEEE has developed several extensions to Ethernet that are designed to meet those challenges. Those enhancements fall into a toolset that is called the Data Center Bridging (DCB) toolset.

Legacy flow control uses Ethernet Flow Control (EFC) that is defined in IEEE 802.3x, which defines the PAUSE frame. If the sending station, which can be a server or a network device, is transmitting faster than the receiving station can process traffic, the receiving station sends a PAUSE frame back to the sender, which instructs the sending station to temporarily stop transmission. The disadvantage of this method is that the transmission of traffic to other servers that are available for receiving traffic is also stopped. The resulting delay to other traffic is called Head of Line (HOL) blocking and is a disadvantage of EFC.

Introduced in 2008 by the Data Center Bridging Task Force, the Priority-based Flow Control (PFC) mechanism improves the EFC HOL behavior. When PFC is used, the PAUSE frame contains a specific CoS value. When PFC is implemented, the sending station stops only the transmission of traffic with a specific CoS value. Figure 17-18 provides an example of PFC in action.

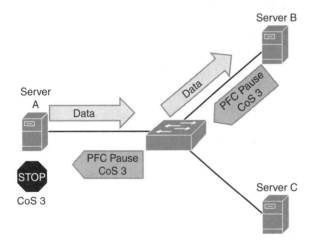

Figure 17-18 *Priority-based Flow Control*

In this example, server B experiences congestion in buffers and sends a PAUSE frame to the data center switch. If the data center switch has no buffering capacity, it sends its own PFC PAUSE frame to server A. Upon receiving the PFC PAUSE frame with a CoS 3 value, server A temporarily stops transmission of CoS 3 traffic. It also continues to send all other CoS priority traffic. The only flow that suffers from HOL blocking in this case is the CoS 3 flow that is intended for server C. In this way, PFC significantly reduces HOL blocking and increases the network throughput.

Data Center QoS Overview

Case Study: DC QoS Application

Figure 17-19 illustrates an example of a DC QoS design.

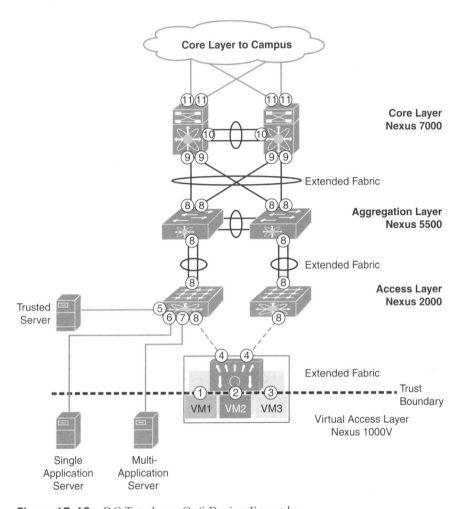

Figure 17-19 *DC Topology: QoS Design Example*

Company A has a data center and wants to deploy QoS to ensure the appropriate application experience. The design must accommodate the following capabilities:

- Virtual machine control protocols
- vMotion
- FCoE

The data center network of company A consists of the following components:

- Cisco Nexus 1000V switches
- Cisco Nexus 5500s with Nexus with 2000 Fabric Extenders
- Cisco Nexus 7000s

It decided to follow several strategic goals:

- It dedicated a CoS 3 virtual lane to FCoE, which is the default CoS value for FCoE.
- It plans to connect another data center via OTV and wants its policy to support this overlay.
- It decided not to implement a policed server model because it polices only on an aggregate basis, rather than on a microflow basis.

The resulting policies referred to in Figure 17-19 that are applied on different points on the network devices are divided into three categories:

- Data Center Virtual Access-Edge Policies (Policies 1 to 4)
- Data Center Access/Aggregation Layer QoS policy (Policies 5 to 8)
- Data Center Core-Layer QoS Policies (Policies 9 to 11)

These policies are summarized as follows:

- Policy 1 is for trusted virtual machines and trusts CoS and DSCP markings.
- Policy 2 is for single-application virtual machines and explicitly defines QoS markings.
- Policy 3 is for multi-application virtual machines and matches traffic with an ACL to then define explicit QoS markings for this traffic class.
- Policy 4 is for network-edge queuing and enables CoS-based CBWFQ per an eight-class strategic model.
- Policy 5 is for trusted servers and trusts CoS and DSCP markings, while at the same time enabling ingress and egress queuing per an eight-class model. (No-drop service for FCoE is enabled by default.)
- Policy 6 is for single application servers and explicitly defines QoS markings, while enabling ingress and egress queuing per an eight-class model. (No-drop service for FCoE is enabled by default.)
- Policy 7 is for multi-application servers and matches traffic with an ACL and defines explicit QoS markings for this traffic class, while enabling ingress and egress queuing per an eight-class model. (No-drop service for FCoE is enabled by default.)

- Policy 8 is for network-edge queuing on Nexus 5500/2000 and trusts CoS and DSCP markings, while enabling ingress and egress queuing per an eight-class model. (No-drop service for FCoE is enabled by default.)
- Policy 9 is for network-edge queuing on Nexus 7000 and trusts CoS and DSCP markings, while enabling ingress and egress queuing per an eight-class model and enabling no-drop service for FCoE.
- Policy 10 is for network-edge queuing (including OTV edges) on Nexus 7000 and trusts CoS and DSCP markings, while enabling ingress and egress queuing per an eight-class model.
- Policy 11 is for DSCP mutation between the data center and campus and enables mapping of DSCP CS3 markings from the campus to DSCP 33 in the data center, while enabling ingress and egress queuing per an eight-class model.

Summary

QoS design considerations for campus networks include

- The primary goal of campus QoS is to manage packet loss.
- Voice and video traffic have similar QoS requirements, but the video profile is bursty and consumes more bandwidth.
- Appropriate bandwidth and buffer size must be configured to accommodate bursts.
- Static and dynamic trust boundaries have to be set as close to the source as possible.
- It is recommended that classification, marking, and policing be performed on the switch port at egress.
- A minimum of 1P3QyT egress queuing on all switch ports is recommended.
- Depending on the platform and load-balancing method used, QoS for EtherChannel can be applied on physical or logical ports.

The QoS design considerations for the WAN/branch edge devices include

- The primary goal of WAN and branch QoS is to manage packet loss and jitter.
- Choose the appropriate platform that meets application performance requirements.
- Comply to ITU G.114 delay and jitter recommendations by selecting a reliable ISP and choosing the appropriate queuing algorithm.
- Tune Tx-Ring only if necessary.
- Use software queuing mechanisms such as LLQ and CBWFQ.
- Leverage HCBWFQ configuration when the contracted provider rate is less than the physical interface rate.
- You can follow some best practice rules when applying policies on WAN/branch edge devices.

The QoS design considerations for the data center network include

- The primary goal of DC QoS is to manage packet loss.
- In HPT architectures, the primary goal is to avoid oversubscription.
- QoS tools in big data architectures are similar to the tools that are applied in campus networks.
- Virtualized cloud-based data centers must implement some protocols that require lossless service.
- The PFC mechanism enhances transport in the data center by inserting PAUSE frames for specific CoS values.
- Different policies are applied per type of device and for different positions in the data center network.
- You must always identify and understand the key drivers to consider QoS based on the place in the network (refer to Table 17-1).

Table 17-1 *Comparison of QoS Design Drivers and Considerations Based on the PIN*

	WAN	**Campus**	**Data Center**
Drivers	Avoid congestion and packet loss due to lower bandwidth to provide traffic prioritization across the WAN Traffic flows prioritization and policing over expensive WAN links Security	More for traffic prioritization to avoid unexpected congestions Security	Avoid packet loss for sensitive applications (requires low or ultra-low latency) Security
Trust boundary	External WAN edge interface (QoS marking and mapping)	Access switch port or IP phone (extended boundary)	Data center access switches (ToR)
QoS processing	Performed in hardware or software; depends on the platform	Almost always performed in hardware (switches)	Almost always performed in hardware (switches)
Number of Queues	Limited; deepens on the supported number of queues (Classes) by WAN provider) commonly four or six classes/queues	Flexible; deepens on application requirements	Flexible; deepens on application requirements

Review Questions

After answering the following questions, please refer to Appendix A, "Answers to Review Questions," for the answers.

1. What is the primary reason to enable QoS in a campus network?
   a. To manage packet loss
   b. To manage jitter
   c. To manage latency
   d. To manage application data traffic

2. Which properties apply to video traffic in a campus network?
   a. Smooth, benign, UDP priority
   b. Smooth, greedy, UDP priority
   c. Bursty, greedy, drop sensitive
   d. Bursty, drop sensitive, benign

3. What is the primary goal of enabling QoS in a data center network?
   a. To manage jitter
   b. To classify and mark traffic at virtual access edge
   c. To classify and mark traffic at physical access edge
   d. To manage packet loss

4. Match the data center architectures with their properties.

Virtualized multiservice architectures	Minimal QoS requirements
Big data architecture	Requirements similar to campus network requirements
High-performance trading architecture	Not only application traffic classes, but also class of customer service needs to be identified

5. Which statements about recommended QoS design in the data center are true? (Select two.)
   a. Avoid enabling control plane policing.
   b. Perform QoS in software whenever possible.
   c. Enable queuing on every node that could be potentially congested.
   d. Police traffic as close to the source as possible.
   e. Classify traffic as far away from the traffic source as possible.

6. Which statement about latency and jitter is true?
   a. Latency and jitter on different provider networks will always be the same.
   b. You can only influence variable delay such as a queuing delay.
   c. Latency should not exceed 30 ms.
   d. Jitter should not exceed 150 ms.

7. Which statement about LLQ recommendations on a WAN is true?
   a. Limit to 50 percent of bandwidth; enable WRED.
   b. Limit to 33 percent of bandwidth; enable WRED.
   c. Limit to 66 percent of bandwidth; do not enable WRED.
   d. Limit to 33 percent of bandwidth; do not enable WRED.

8. Which strategic QoS principle applies to WAN?
   a. Perform QoS in software whenever possible.
   b. Classify and mark an application as close as possible to the source.
   c. Disable queuing at every node that has potential for congestion.
   d. Disable control plane policing to protect the data and control planes.

Chapter 18

MPLS VPN QoS Design

Upon completing this chapter, you will be able to

- Identify the need for QoS as part of an MPLS VPN deployment
- Describe Layer 2 WAN QoS administration
- Describe MPLS VPN QoS administration
- List and describe the MPLS DiffServ tunneling modes
- Provide an example that illustrates the MPLS VPN QoS roles

Quality of service (QoS) has become an integral part of a multiservice, converged network, and service implementation. Multiprotocol Label Switching Virtual Private Networks (MPLS VPNs) have rapidly gained popularity over private WAN alternatives because they offer a single source of information for the design, deployment, and implementation of QoS-enabled services. The migration to an MPLS VPN from a private WAN requires a significant paradigm shift when addressing QoS design. This chapter covers the basics of designing QoS for MPLS VPNs.

The Need for QoS in MPLS VPN

MPLS VPNs provide fully meshed Layer 3 virtual WAN services to all interconnected customer edge (CE) routers, as shown in Figure 18-1.

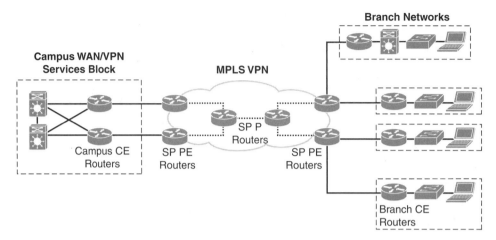

Figure 18-1 *MPLS VPN Connectivity Model*

One of the main reasons for using MPLS VPN is its any-to-any connectivity capability. The full-mesh nature of MPLS VPN poses significant QoS implications to enterprise customers and service providers alike. Enterprise customer subscribers must closely cooperate with their service providers to ensure end-to-end service levels because you cannot achieve these service levels independent of service provider policies.

You can view the MPLS VPN QoS design from two distinct perspectives:

- The enterprise customer subscribing to the MPLS VPN service
- The service provider provisioning edge and core QoS within the MPLS VPN service

Regardless of the perspective, enterprise and service provider QoS designs must be consistent and complementary. The service provider IP core provides high-speed packet transport.

In the provider network, all the markings, policing, and shaping should be performed only at the provider edge (PE) router on the PE-to-CE link, and not in the core. Only the edge requires a complex QoS policy. In the core, only queuing and dropping are required. The queuing and dropping operation will be based on the markings that are done at the PE. The reason for these procedures is the any-to-any and full-mesh nature of MPLS VPNs, where enterprise subscribers depend on their service providers to provision PE-to-CE QoS policies that are consistent with their CE-to-PE policies. In addition to these PE-to-CE policies, service providers will likely implement ingress policers on their PEs to identify whether the traffic flows from the customer are in or out of contract. Optionally, service providers may also provision QoS policies within their core networks using DiffServ or MPLS traffic engineering (TE) to maximize the use of underutilized links and to optimize the transport of traffic impacted by latency, loss, and jitter.

The dual role of QoS in the private WAN and branch networks consists of managing packet loss and jitter by queuing policies and enhancing classification granularity by leveraging deep-packet inspection engines. Additionally, the role of QoS over the MPLS VPN may be expanded to include the following:

- Shaping traffic to contracted service rates
- Performing hierarchical queuing and dropping within these shaped rates
- Mapping enterprise-to-service provider class of service markings
- Policing traffic classes according to contracted rates
- Restoring packet markings

Layer 2 Private WAN QoS Administration

Due to cost, scalability, and manageability constraints, traditional private WAN designs rarely use full-mesh models. Instead, most Layer 2 WAN designs revolve around a hub-and-spoke model, implementing either a centralized hub design or the more efficient regional hub design. Considering that private WANs are usually deployed in either a point-to-point or a hub-and-spoke topology, a Layer 2 private WAN QoS design is more straightforward than an MPLS VPN QoS design.

Under such hub-and-spoke designs, QoS is primarily administered at the hub router, which takes on the role of WAN aggregator within the enterprise. As long as the service provider meets the contracted service levels, the packets that are received at remote branches will reflect the scheduling policies of the hub router. The WAN aggregator controls not only campus-to-branch traffic but also branch-to-branch traffic, which is homed through the hub. Figure 18-2 illustrates the hub-and-spoke QoS design model.

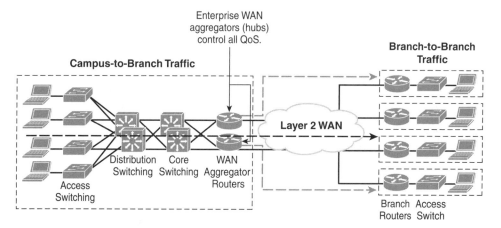

Figure 18-2 *Layer 2 Hub-and-Spoke WAN QoS Design Model*

Fully Meshed MPLS VPN QoS Administration

Under a full-mesh design, the hub router still administers QoS for all campus-to-branch traffic, but it no longer fully controls the QoS for branch-to-branch traffic. Although it might appear that the only required workaround for this new scenario is to ensure that QoS is provisioned on all branch routers, this workaround is insufficient because it addresses only part of the issue.

For example, consider the case of provisioning any-to-any multimedia conferencing. As with a traditional Layer 2 WAN design, a scheduling policy to prioritize multimedia conferencing on the WAN aggregator is required. The enterprise must also properly provision similar priority scheduling for multimedia conferencing on the branch routers. In this manner, any multimedia-conferencing calls from the campus to the branch and from branch to branch are protected against traffic of lesser importance flowing between the same sites and causing congestion. The complexity of the fully meshed model arises when considering that contending traffic might not always come from the same sites but could come from any site. Furthermore, the enterprise no longer fully controls QoS for branch-to-branch traffic because this traffic is no longer homed through a hub. Continuing the example, if a multimedia-conferencing call is set up between two branches and a user from one of the branches also initiates a large FTP download from the central site, the potential for oversubscription of the PE-to-CE link from the fully meshed MPLS VPN cloud into one of the branches becomes real and will likely cause drops impacting the multimedia-conferencing call.

The only way to guarantee service levels in such a scenario is for the service provider to provision QoS scheduling that is compatible with the enterprise's policies on all PE links to remote branches. This is what creates the paradigm shift in QoS administration for fully meshed topologies. Enterprises and service providers must cooperate to jointly administer QoS over MPLS VPNs, as shown in Figure 18-3.

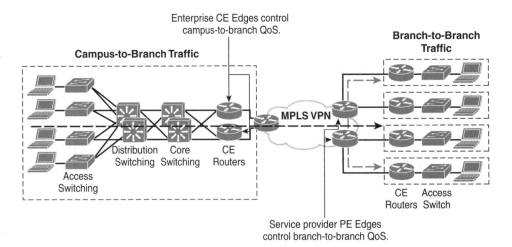

Figure 18-3 *QoS over MPLS VPN*

Therefore, queuing policies are mandatory on CE and PE router egress edges because of the full-mesh implications associated with MPLS VPNs. In addition, PE routers will have ingress policing policies to enforce SLAs.

QoS policies on provider core routers are optional. Such policies are optional because some service providers overprovision their MPLS core networks and, as such, do not require any additional QoS policies within their backbones; however, other providers might implement simplified DiffServ policies within their cores or might even deploy MPLS TE to handle congestion scenarios within backbone infrastructure that has not been overprovisioned.

MPLS DiffServ Tunneling Modes

The previous section focused on the QoS at the MPLS VPN edge; this section discusses the considerations and design options of QoS design within and across the MPLS VPN.

DiffServ tunneling modes introduce a new per-hop behavior (PHB), which allows differentiated QoS in a service provider's network. The tunneling mode is defined at the edge of the network, normally in the PE LSRs at both ingress and egress.

MPLS can tunnel the QoS markings of a packet and create QoS transparency for the customer. It is possible to mark the MPLS EXP field in the service provider network independently of the PHB marked by the customer in the IP Precedence or DSCP fields. A service provider may choose from an existing array of classification criteria, including or excluding the IP PHB marking, to classify those packets into a different PHB. The PHB behavior is then marked only in the MPLS EXP field during label imposition. This marking is useful to a service provider that requires SLA enforcement of the customer packets by promoting or demoting the PHB of a packet, without regard to the QoS marking scheme and without overwriting the IP PHB markings of the customer.

Considering that MPLS labels include 3 bits that are commonly used for QoS marking, you can tunnel DiffServ to preserve the Layer 3 DiffServ markings through a service provider MPLS VPN cloud, while still performing remarking via MPLS EXP bits within the cloud to indicate in-contract or out-of-contract traffic.

It is up to service providers to define the class of service (CoS) models they will offer to their subscribers. There is no one-size-fits-all model because these CoS models are often a key component of a service provider's competitive differentiation strategy. Most service providers have four and six class QoS model offerings, whereas a few offer eight or more classes of service.

Whenever multiple service provider models are presented as options, the subscriber should select the model that most closely aligns with the strategic end-to-end QoS model.

RFC 3270 defines three distinct modes of MPLS DiffServ tunneling:

- **Uniform mode:** DiffServ tunneling uniform mode has only one layer of QoS, which reaches end to end. The ingress PE router copies the DSCP from the incoming IP packet into the MPLS EXP bits of the imposed labels. As the EXP bits travel through the core, they may or may not be modified by intermediate P routers. At the egress P router, the EXP bits are copied to the EXP bits of the newly exposed label. Finally, at the egress PE router, the EXP bits are copied to the DSCP bits of the newly exposed IP packet.

- **Short-pipe mode:** DiffServ tunneling short-pipe mode uses the same rules and techniques across the core. The difference is at the egress PE router where the newly exposed IP packets for outbound queuing are classified based on the IP PHB from the DSCP value of the IP packet.

- **Pipe mode:** DiffServ tunneling pipe mode uses two layers of QoS: (1) an underlying QoS for the data, which remains unchanged when traversing the core; and (2) a per-core QoS, which is separate from that of the underlying IP packets. This per-core QoS PHB remains transparent to end users. When a packet reaches the edge of the MPLS core, the egress PE router classifies the newly exposed IP packets for outbound queuing based on the MPLS PHB from the EXP bits of the recently removed label.

Figure 18-4 illustrates the three MPLS DiffServ tunneling modes.

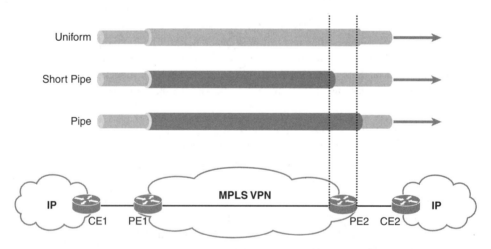

Figure 18-4 *MPLS DiffServ Tunneling Modes*

The type of DiffServ tunneling mode depends on the following factors:

- Whether customer and service provider are in the same QoS domain
- Whether the service provider maintains QoS transparency for the customer
- Whether the customer or service provider QoS policy is implied on the PE egress router

You need to understand the default behavior of the DSCP MPLS EXP bits, as shown in Figure 18-5, as a packet travels from one CE router to another CE router across an MPLS core.

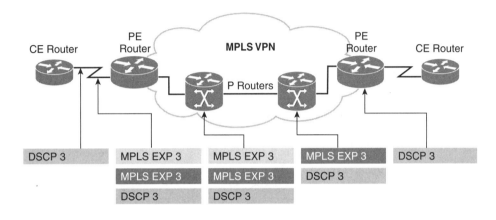

Figure 18-5 *Default Behavior of the DSCP MPLS EXP Bits*

Figure 18-5 shows the behavior is as follows:

- Imposition of the label (IP to label):
  - The IP precedence of the incoming IP packet is copied to the MPLS EXP bits of all pushed labels.
  - The first 3 bits of the DSCP bit are copied to the MPLS EXP bits of all pushed labels.
  - This technique is also known as ToS reflection.
- MPLS forwarding (label to label):
  - The EXP is copied to the new labels that are swapped and pushed during forwarding or imposition.
  - At label imposition, the underlying labels are not modified with the value of the new label that is being added to the current label stack.
  - At label disposition, the EXP bits are not copied to the newly exposed label EXP bits.
- Disposition of the label (label to IP):
  - At label disposition, the EXP bits are not copied to the IP precedence or DSCP field of the newly exposed IP packet.

Uniform Tunneling Mode

Uniform tunneling mode is generally used when the customer and the service provider share the same DiffServ domain, as in the case of an enterprise deploying its own MPLS VPN core. The outmost header is always used as the single meaningful information source about the QoS PHB. On the MPLS label imposition, the IP precedence classification is copied into the outermost experimental field of the label (the default behavior). As the EXP bits travel through the core, they may be modified by intermediate P routers. On the egress of the service provider network, when the label is popped, the router propagates the EXP bits down into the IP precedence or the DSCP field, which needs to be configured by the service provider on the egress PE router.

As shown in Figure 18-6, the enterprise customer's DSCP markings have been re-marked in transit by the SP in the MPLS Uniform DiffServ tunneling model.

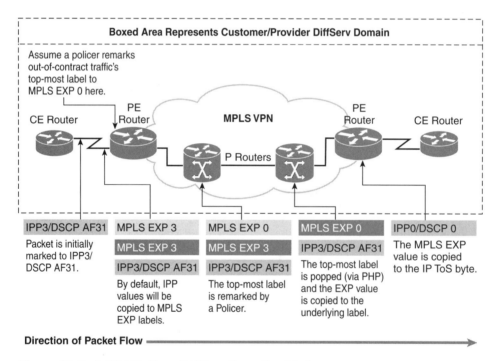

Figure 18-6 *MPLS Uniform DiffServ Tunneling Mode*

Short-Pipe Tunneling Mode

Short-pipe tunneling mode is used when the customer and the service provider are in different DiffServ domains. Short-pipe mode is useful when the service provider wants to enforce its own DiffServ policy, while maintaining DiffServ transparency. The outermost label is utilized as the single meaningful information source as it relates to the QoS PHB of the service provider. On the MPLS label imposition, the IP classification is not copied into the EXP of the outermost label. Rather, based on the QoS policy of the service provider, an appropriate value for the MPLS EXP is set on the ingress PE. The MPLS EXP value could be different from the original IP precedence or the DSCP. The MPLS EXP will accomplish the CoS marking on the topmost label but preserve the underlying IP DSCP. If the service provider reclassifies the traffic in the MPLS cloud for any reason, the EXP value of the topmost label is changed. On the egress of the service provider network, when the label is popped, the PE router will not affect the value of the underlying DSCP information. In this way, the MPLS EXP is not propagated to the DSCP field. Therefore, the DSCP transparency is maintained.

As shown in Figure 18-7, MPLS EXP values can be marked in any way that the SP wants to convey local significance and have no relation to the customer's packet-marking values. Therefore, the customer's markings are preserved in transit and are available to the customer as the packet exits the MPLS VPN.

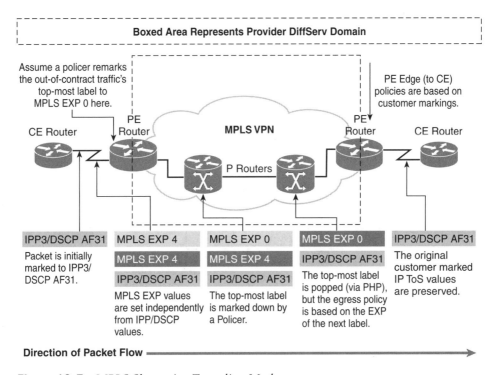

Figure 18-7 *MPLS Short-pipe Tunneling Mode*

> **Note** The egress PE in the short-pipe mode uses the original IP precedence or DSCP to classify the packet it sends to the enterprise network. The enterprise set the original IP precedence per its own QoS policy. The service provider may apply enterprise QoS policy at egress PE for traffic that is going toward the CE. In this example, the PE implements per-customer egress QoS policies for traffic toward the CE, granting customers maximum control of the packet's QoS treatment through the MPLS VPN.

In the case of any re-marking occurrence within the service provider's MPLS VPN cloud, changes are limited to the MPLS EXP re-marking only and are not propagated down to the underlying IP packet's ToS byte.

Pipe Tunneling Mode

The main difference between short-pipe mode and pipe mode MPLS DiffServ tunneling is that the PE egress policies toward the customer CEs are provisioned according to the service provider's explicit markings and re-markings, not the enterprise customer's IP DiffServ markings; however, these customer IP DiffServ markings are preserved. When a packet reaches the edge of the MPLS core, the egress PE router classifies the newly exposed IP packets for outbound queuing based on the MPLS PHB from the EXP bits of the recently removed label. As with short-pipe mode, any changes to label markings that occur within the service provider's cloud do not get propagated to the IP ToS byte when the packet leaves the MPLS network. Figure 18-8 illustrates the pipe mode MPLS DiffServ tunneling operation.

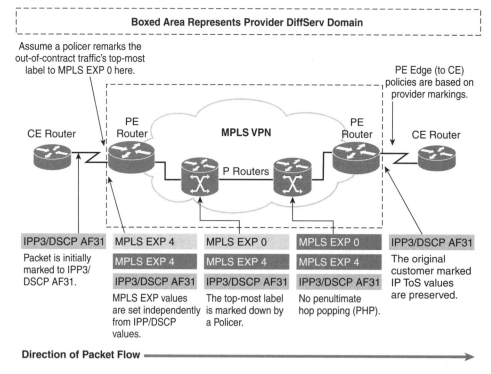

Figure 18-8 *MPLS Pipe Tunneling Mode*

This implementation avoids the additional operational overhead of per-customer configurations on each egress interface on the egress PE router. As referred to in the figure, pipe mode operation is identical to the short pipe, with the sole exception being that the final PE egress queuing policies are based on the service provider's markings (and not the customer's).

Sample MPLS VPN QoS Roles

Sometimes, the number of service provider CoS classes will match or exceed the number of application classes that an enterprise has defined in its strategic end-to-end QoS policy. However, this is typically not the case. When the number of enterprise application classes exceeds the number of service provider CoS classes, the enterprise administrator will need to map into the service provider's model, tactically and efficiently collapsing and combining application classes and performing any required re-marking in the process.

Here are some recommendations for enterprise-to-service provider mapping:

- Efficiently map enterprise application classes to service provider CoS classes.
- Balance service-level requirements for real-time voice and video applications with service provider premiums for real-time bandwidth.
- Avoid mixing control plane traffic with data plane traffic in a single service provider CoS.
- Separate TCP traffic from UDP traffic when mapping to service provider CoS classes.

Most service providers use the DSCP marking of packets that are offered to them to determine which service provider CoS the packet should be assigned to. Therefore, enterprises must mark or re-mark their traffic consistent with their service provider's admission criteria to gain the appropriate level of service.

A general DiffServ principle is to mark or trust traffic as close to the source as administratively and technically possible. However, certain traffic types might need to be re-marked before handoff to the service provider to gain admission to the correct class. If such a re-marking is required, it is recommended that the re-marking be performed at the CE's egress edge, not within the campus. The reason is that service provider service offerings will likely evolve or expand over time, and adjusting to such changes will be easier to manage if re-marking is performed at a single place—that place being the CE egress edge.

Figure 18-9 illustrates a typical QoS policy to role mapping.

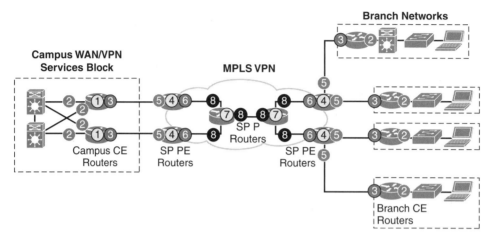

Figure 18-9 *MPLS VPN QoS Policy to Role Mapping*

The specific QoS policies for these roles referred to in Figure 18-9 follow:

1. Campus CE ingress/internal QoS: Ingress/internal QoS policies may be applied (if required).

2. CE LAN edge:
   - Ingress DSCP trust should be enabled (enabled by default).
   - Ingress NBAR2 classification and marking policies may be applied.
   - Egress LLQ/CBWFQ/WRED policies may be applied (if required).

3. CE VPN edge:
   - Ingress DSCP trust should be enabled (enabled by default).
   - Ingress NBAR2 classification and marking policies may be applied (to restore DSCP markings lost in transit).
   - Egress LLQ/CBWFQ/WRED policies may be applied (if required).
   - Egress LLQ/CBWFQ/WRED policies should be applied.
   - Egress hierarchical shaping with nested LLQ/CBWFQ/WRED policies may be applied.
   - Egress DSCP re-marking policies may be applied (to map application classes into specific service provider classes of service).

4. PE ingress/internal: Ingress/internal QoS policies may be applied (if required).

5. PE customer-facing edge:
   - Ingress DSCP trust should be enabled (enabled by default).
   - Ingress policing policies to meter customer traffic should be applied.
   - Ingress MPLS tunneling mode policies may be applied.
   - Egress MPLS tunneling mode policies may be applied.
   - Egress LLQ/CBWFQ/WRED policies should be applied.

6. PE core-facing edge:
   - Ingress DSCP trust should be enabled (enabled by default).
   - Ingress policing policies to meter customer traffic should be applied.
   - Egress MPLS EXP-based LLQ/CBWFQ policies should be applied.
   - Egress MPLS EXP-based WRED policies may be applied.

7. P (core router) ingress/internal QoS: Ingress/internal QoS policies may be applied (if required).

8. P edges:
   - Ingress DSCP trust should be enabled (enabled by default).
   - Egress MPLS EXP-based LLQ/CBWFQ policies may be applied (unless the core is overprovisioned or has MPLS TE enabled).
   - Egress MPLS EXP-based WRED policies may be applied.

Summary

- To achieve end-to-end service levels, both enterprise and service provider QoS designs must be consistent and complementary.
- Enterprise QoS policy needs to be translated to the service provider's QoS policy, which could include several QoS classes that are offered to the customer.
- Service providers can handle their QoS in different ways, defined in three different MPLS DiffServ modes.

Review Questions

After answering the following questions, please refer to Appendix A, "Answers to Review Questions," for the answers.

1. In which DiffServ tunneling modes does the service provider enforce its own DiffServ policy but maintain DiffServ transparency for the customer?
   a. Uniform mode only
   b. Short-pipe mode only

c. Pipe mode only
d. Uniform and pipe mode
e. Pipe and short-pipe mode
f. Uniform and short-pipe mode

2. Match the DiffServ tunneling modes with their properties.

Uniform mode   On PE egress, the customer QoS policy is implied.

Pipe mode   On PE egress, the service provider QoS policy is implied.

Short-pipe mode   The customer and service provider share the same DiffServ domain.

3. Which statements are correct regarding QoS administration in Layer 2 hub-and-spoke WAN design and in fully meshed MPLS VPN design? (Choose two.)
   a. In Layer 2 hub-and-spoke WAN design, the enterprise hub controls QoS for campus-to-branch and branch-to-branch traffic.
   b. In fully meshed MPLS VPN design, the enterprise hub controls QoS for campus-to-branch and branch-to-branch traffic.
   c. In Layer 2 hub-and-spoke WAN design, QoS is primarily administered at the spoke router.
   d. In Layer 2 hub-and-spoke WAN design, the service provider needs to provision QoS that is compatible with the enterprise's policies to guarantee end-to-end QoS service.
   e. In fully meshed MPLS VPN design, the service provider needs to provision QoS that is compatible with the enterprise's policies to guarantee end-to-end QoS service.

Chapter 19

IPsec VPN QoS Design

Upon completing this chapter, you will be able to

- Identify the need for QoS in IPsec VPN
- List VPN use cases and their QoS models
- Review IPsec options
- Describe IOS encryption and classification order of operations
- Identify MTU considerations
- Identify DMVPN QoS considerations
- Identify GET VPN QoS considerations
- Describe the impact that IPsec security association (SA) anti-replay has when QoS is enabled

The IPsec suite of technologies has become a ubiquitous element of enterprise networks. IPsec virtual private networks can be found in many places and are used to establish site-to-site data center interconnects as well as hub-and-spoke or partial-mesh networks connecting a large number of remote locations to the enterprise headquarters and to one another.

As with other forms of VPN, it is important to ensure a good user experience over the IPsec VPN transport. This chapter describes QoS-related considerations for IPsec VPNs.

The Need for QoS in IPsec VPN

Considering that IPsec is leveraged for a vast number of uses cases ranging from site-to-site interconnects to providing remote access services to home users, deploying IPsec VPNs introduces many new topics for consideration. This is especially true when using real-time applications that require QoS to ensure a quality user experience.

One of the most frequently implemented IPsec VPN use cases is the deployment of IPsec tunnels across a public network. Even though the increased bandwidth associated with Internet-based services typically offers higher speeds at a lower cost in most geographies, the Internet WAN still typically introduces a bottleneck as it offers lower bandwidth when compared to the LAN. The change from higher bandwidth in the LAN to lower bandwidth across the WAN, as illustrated in Figure 19-1, forces the network engineer to implement classification, marking, and queuing mechanisms to ensure that latency-sensitive applications receive preferred handling.

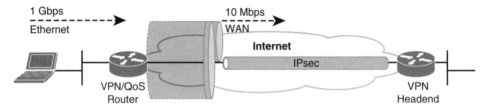

Figure 19-1 *Difference between LAN and WAN Bandwidth*

Scenarios such as this one depicted in Figure 19-1 require QoS configuration at the WAN edge to ensure that low-priority traffic is dropped or scheduled for delivery when resources are available.

Several challenges need to be taken into consideration when implementing well-known QoS mechanisms over IPsec architecture:

- **ToS byte preservation:** Although a normal IP packet includes the ToS byte inside the header, this information gets hidden from the queuing mechanism, as a new IP header is added while IPsec encrypts the original header.

- **Classification of encrypted data:** The categorization into traffic classes requires the identification of the traffic type, which can be obscured by the packet, which is being encrypted prior to the classification process.

- **Overhead:** Each tunneling mechanism adds additional header information to the original IP packet and, as a result, increases the size of the packet, thus reducing the amount of data being transported over the link.

- **Managing packet loss and jitter:** IPsec incorporates anti-replay capabilities to drop packets that may be fraudulently repeated or delayed. Packets that are dropped by the anti-replay feature can negatively affect latency-sensitive traffic.

VPN Use Cases and Their QoS Models

As already mentioned, IPsec can be implemented by leveraging manual site-to-site VPN tunnels between two dislocated sites or by connecting remote access users to the corporate network over the public network. Advanced IPsec implementations are also possible by leveraging the following technologies covered in Chapter 9, "Enterprise Managed WAN."

- **Dynamic Multipoint VPN (DMVPN):** Using a centralized architecture to build a scalable dynamic multipoint VPN. DMVPN offers the capability to build an on-demand full-mesh connectivity using a simple hub-and-spoke configuration.

- **GET VPN:** Using the underlying IP VPN routing infrastructure to implement a large-scale any-to-any IP connectivity through IPsec without the requirement for an overlay control plane. By eliminating point-to-point tunnels and associated overlay routing architecture, GET VPN allows for multicast replication and the greater level of scalability provided by the IP VPN topology.

Each VPN technology used to provide connectivity takes advantage of different QoS features and capabilities. DMVPN offers a unique per-tunnel QoS capability covered later in this chapter, and GET VPN preserves the original source and destination IP addressing, allowing it to also preserve the QoS policy configuration.

IPsec Refresher

IPsec VPNs can be configured in both point-to-point and point-to-multipoint topologies depending on the use case, headend device, and requested features. Furthermore, standard IPsec VPNs can be split into the following categories:

- **Tunnel Mode:** By using the default mode, the entire IP packet is protected by IPsec. The sending VPN router encrypts the original IP packet and adds a new IP header to the packet. A key advantage of the tunnel mode operation is that it supports multicast across the VPN tunnel and allows the implementation of routing protocols across the WAN.

- **Transport Mode:** Unlike tunnel mode, the transport mode does not encrypt the entire IP packet, but rather encrypts only the payload and preserves the original IP header. By preserving the original IP header, transport mode is not capable of supporting the implementation of services like multicast and routing protocols. Transport mode is often used with generic routing encapsulation (GRE), so the entire GRE tunnel is encrypted and supports multicast and routing protocols to be implemented within GRE.

Figure 19-2 shows a comparison of the two modes.

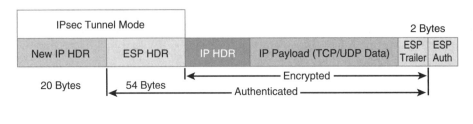

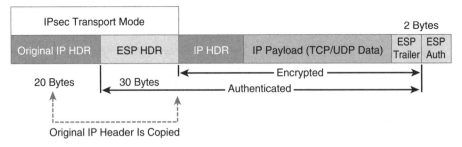

Figure 19-2 *IPsec VPN Modes*

GRE is a tunneling protocol that can encapsulate several network layer protocols inside a virtual point-to-point link over an IP network. By itself, GRE is a versatile and flexible protocol that is used to interconnect disparate networks and to support use cases such as

- Virtual Routing and Forwarding (VRF-Lite)
- DMVPN
- Transport of non-IP protocols
- Transport of multicast
- Transport of routing protocols

The challenge with GRE is that it does not provide any privacy and authentication mechanisms. Thus, using a combination with IPsec enables the network administrator to build secure connections between dislocated units using a public infrastructure.

The original IP packet is encapsulated by the GRE header, which in turn is encrypted by IPsec to provide privacy. Because IPsec introduces several additional headers to the original IP packet, the overhead is drastically increased. The IPsec with GRE packet is illustrated in Figure 19-3.

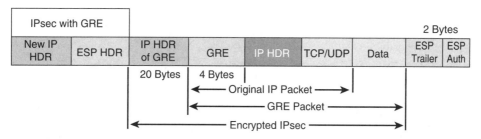

Figure 19-3 *IPsec with GRE Packet*

The VPN router is required to preserve the ToS value in the newly added IP header. If the ToS value is not preserved, the queuing mechanisms cannot prioritize latency-sensitive traffic as a result of the traffic being encrypted by IPsec.

Remote-access VPNs provide secure communications and access privileges depending on the remote user role. Remote-access VPNs extend the corporate network and applications to the remote users regardless of established site-to-site connectivity.

The Cisco primary remote-access VPN client is the AnyConnect Secure Mobility Client that supports both IPsec and Secure Sockets Layer (SSL) encryption. Although AnyConnect does not support any specific QoS classification, queuing, or policing tools, it does include Datagram Transport Layer Security (DTLS), which significantly improves the experience when using real-time applications.

When AnyConnect first connects to the headend device, a TCP-based SSL tunnel is set up. When the SSL session is fully established, the client negotiates a new UDP-based DTLS tunnel, which is reserved for the exclusive use of real-time applications. The UDP nature of DTLS allows the RTP voice and video packets to be transmitted unhindered. If any sudden packet loss or unexpected network events occur, the session does not pause and the lost packets are not re-sent. Rather, the consecutive packets continue to flow as normal, resulting in a more fluid experience associated with leveraging the voice or video software. For additional details regarding IPsec VPN and remote access, please refer Chapter 9.

IOS Encryption and Classification: Order of Operations

Previous sections provided an overview of the different VPN technologies and the packet header structure of each; this section takes it a step forward and discusses how QoS marking is treated when the original IP packet is encapsulated.

QoS classification is a process of matching one or more fields in the IP header of the packet and assigning the packet into a traffic class. However, when a packet is being encrypted, the original IP header is no longer visible, and the QoS mechanism becomes ineffective when applied to the original packet. To deal with this issue, Cisco IOS default operation is to copy the ToS field from the original IP header into the new IP header that encapsulates the original packet. This function is illustrated in Figure 19-4.

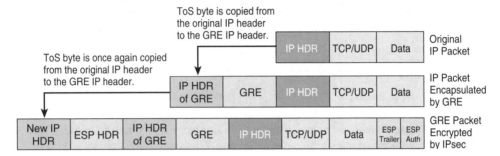

Figure 19-4 *Cisco IOS Default Operation with Regard to ToS Field with Encapsulation*

When this copying is performed, the classification process can still be accomplished, matching on the ToS value. The preservation behavior of Cisco IOS is available by default for IPsec, GRE, and IPsec-encrypted GRE-encapsulated traffic and requires no extra configuration by the network operator.

The limitation of the default behavior of Cisco IOS is that only the ToS byte is preserved. If classification based on other IP header fields is required, another mechanism is required. Examples of classification based on IP header fields other than ToS are

- Source IP address
- Destination IP address
- Source port
- Destination port
- Flags

The limitation of the Cisco IOS preservation mechanism is that only the ToS byte is copied from the original header into the new encapsulating header. Whenever you require the classification process to be implemented on the IP header field other than the ToS byte, this results in a reverse order of operation in IOS where classification takes place before encryption. When this is the case, it is necessary to use the IOS preclassify feature.

The preclassify feature clones the original IP header and keeps it in the router's memory with the intent to use it for the classification process after encryption. This mechanism has the effect of reversing the normal order of operation of Cisco IOS. The preclassify feature may be implemented on both IPsec and GRE tunnels. A key limitation with this approach is that the cloned IP header is applicable only on the encrypting router's outbound interface. Downstream routers would not be able to do QoS classification that is based on parameters other than the ToS.

If you are concerned that the QoS policy will later change to include matching criteria on other fields in the IP header, the best practice recommendation is to enable the preclassify feature on the VPN router.

MTU Considerations

Tunneling mechanisms will impact the size of the maximum transmission unit (MTU) due to added overhead. Whenever tunneling technologies are used in a network, there is always the risk of exceeding the MTU somewhere in the path. Unless jumbo frames are enabled end to end, it is critical to address MTU issues when using any kind of VPN technology because MTU issues can severely affect network connectivity. The impact of GRE and IPsec in terms of overhead is listed in Table 19-1.

Table 19-1 *Tunnel Types and Their Overhead*

Tunnel Type	Overhead
GRE	24 bytes
IPsec (Transport Mode)	36 bytes
IPsec (Tunnel Mode)	52 bytes
IPsec (Transport Mode) + GRE	60 bytes
IPsec (Tunnel Mode) + GRE	76 bytes

When you are using GRE and the packet enters the VPN router, it will encapsulate the original packet, increasing the overall size of the packet by 24 bytes, thus reducing the maximum unit size to 1476 if assuming a default MTU of 1500. Sending packets larger than 1476 will result in fragmentation and dropping.

In comparison to GRE, IPsec will not only add 24 bytes of overhead, but the overhead may vary based on the configured IPsec transform set. The maximum overhead could be up to 73 bytes, which is significantly more. IPsec will attempt a path MTU discovery to establish the maximum size and to help the router preemptively fragment packets that are larger than the supported network MTU size.

As a recommendation, it is always best to avoid fragmentation if possible and configure the MTU size based on the amount of overhead that is being introduced by the VPN technology. There is a maximum transmission unit (MTU) parameter for every link in an IP network, and typically, the MTU is 1500 bytes. IP packets larger than 1500 bytes must be fragmented when transmitted across these links. Fragmentation is not desirable and can impact network performance. To avoid fragmentation, the original packet size plus overhead must be 1500 bytes or less, which means that the sender must reduce the original packet size. To account for other potential overhead, Cisco recommends configuring tunnel interfaces with a 1400-byte MTU. There are dynamic methods for network clients to discover the path MTU, enabling the clients to reduce the size of packets they transmit. However, in many cases, these dynamic methods are unsuccessful, typically because security devices filter the necessary discovery traffic. This failure to discover the path MTU drives the need for a method that can reliably inform network clients of the appropriate packet size.

The solution is to implement the **ip tcp adjust mss [size]** command on the WAN routers, which influences the TCP maximum segment size (MSS) value reported by end hosts. The MSS defines the maximum amount of data that a host is willing to accept in a single TCP/IP datagram. The MSS value is sent as a TCP header option only in TCP SYN segments. Each side of a TCP connection reports its MSS value to the other side. The sending host is required to limit the size of data in a single TCP segment to a value less than or equal to the MSS reported by the receiving host. The IP and TCP headers combine for 40 bytes of overhead, so the typical MSS value reported by network clients will be 1460. Considering that encrypted tunnels will be set with a 1400-byte MTU, the MSS used by endpoints should be configured to be 1360 to minimize any impact of fragmentation. This means that it is necessary to implement the **ip tcp adjust mss 1360** command on all WAN-facing router interfaces.

Figure 19-5 illustrates the recommended practice of setting the MTU to 1400 to accommodate all of the most common GRE + IPsec implementations.

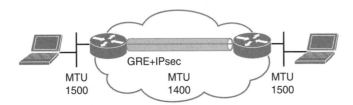

Tunnel Setting (AES256+SHA)	Recommended MTU
GRE/IPsec (Tunnel Mode)	1400 Bytes
GRE/IPsec (Transport Mode)	1400 Bytes

Figure 19-5 *Recommended MTU Setting with VPN*

DMVPN QoS Considerations

DMVPN, as illustrated in Figure 19-6, combines multipoint-GRE (mGRE), dynamic discovery of tunnel endpoints, and Next Hop Resolution Protocol (NHRP), which allows simple and fast deployment of hundreds of spokes seamlessly while allowing dynamic spoke-to-spoke tunnel establishment for optimized spoke-to-spoke communication.

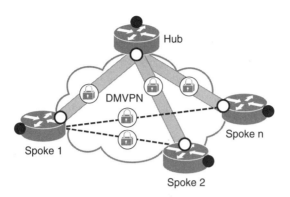

Figure 19-6 *DMVPN-based Network*

DMVPN is part of the IP transit network, and there is an implicit trust of the differentiated services code point (DSCP) markings of the packets that are received on the interface by both the hub-and-spoke VPN routers. Therefore, the primary QoS functions in a DMVPN topology are outbound hierarchical shaping and queuing of the specific traffic classes over the VPN tunnels.

A QoS challenge associated with DMVPN is that all the hub-and-spoke tunnels terminate on a single mGRE tunnel interface on the hub router. While applying a QoS policy for a site-to-site deployment would be the recommended method with DMVPN, there is only a single mGRE interface, which does not allow a per-site policy to be configured. The single policy would be able to control the QoS of the tunnel interface, but could not handle communication between spokes and could not avoid excessive communication between them.

Therefore, because DMVPN relies on mGRE tunnel interfaces, traditional QoS policies at the interface level do not work. To solve the problem, Cisco has implemented a feature that is called per-tunnel QoS for DMVPN. The per-tunnel QoS for DMVPN feature allows you to enable QoS on a per-tunnel or per-spoke basis when using DMVPN. The feature enables you to apply an outbound QoS service policy on the mGRE tunnel interface on the DMVPN hub, which is applied by the router to each spoke tunnel that the service policy is associated with. Figure 19-7 illustrates per-tunnel QoS shaping traffic from the DMVPN hub to the CIR of each spoke.

628 Chapter 19: IPsec VPN QoS Design

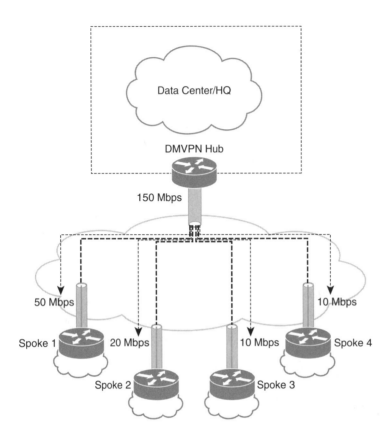

Figure 19-7 *DMVPN Per-tunnel QoS*

The effect of the new functionality is that it protects the spokes from excessive traffic between each other. A shaper is automatically applied by the system for each and every tunnel. This application in turn allows the router to implement differentiated services for data flows corresponding to each tunnel. This technique is called Hierarchical Queuing Framework (HQF). Using HQF, the QoS policy that is applied to the mGRE interface on the DMVPN hub enables you to shape the tunnel traffic to each spoke using a Parent Policy and then to apply differentiated services for various data flows going through each tunnel with class-based weighted faire queuing (CBWFQ) as part of a Child Policy.

Additionally, a key advantage of per-tunnel QoS for DMVPN feature is that it provides an automated generation of the QoS policy for each tunnel as the spoke registers at the hub, reducing manual configuration. DMVPN relies on NHRP for endpoint discovery, routing, and the per-tunnel QoS.

GET VPN QoS Considerations

As DMVPN provides hub-and-spoke architecture that is suitable for untrusted public networks such as the Internet, GET VPN is best suited for use in private networks such as MPLS that offer any-to-any services.

In the case of GET VPN, there is no concept of security association (SA) between specific routers in the network, meaning that there are no IPsec tunnels. GET VPN leverages the concept of a group SA, which is shared by all encrypting nodes in the network. Because all the routers in the GET VPN belong to one big group SA, there is no need to apply QoS on a per-site basis either; you simply need to configure QoS on the egress interface on each GET VPN router. The concept of per-tunnel QoS that was used for DMVPN is irrelevant in a GET VPN design.

Two types of routers are used in a GET VPN architecture:

- **Group Member (GM)** router is the device that does the actual encryption and decryption of packets as they traverse the router.
- **Key Server (KS)** is responsible for managing the encryption keys that are used by the group members.

Although there is always at least one GM router at each remote site in the network, there is only a single or a redundant pair of KS routers deployed for the entire GET VPN.

GET VPN uses both ToS preservation and preclassify mechanisms to allow classification of already-encrypted packets. Additionally, because GET VPN preserves the entire IP header, you can classify based on source and destination IP addresses without the use of the preclassify feature. Classification that is based on TCP and UDP port numbers, however, does require the preclassify feature to be enabled. Table 19-2 highlights the differences between DMVPN and GET VPN.

Table 19-2 *DMVPN Compared to GET VPN*

	DMVPN	GET VPN
Use Case	Public networks (Internet)	Private networks (MPLS)
Network Style	Hub-to-spoke/spoke-to-spoke	Any-to-any
Routing Architecture	Routing inside of GRE tunnels	Dynamic routing of native IPsec packets
Encryption Style	Point-to-point encryption	Group encryption
QoS Implementation	Per-tunnel QoS management through NHRP group membership. Uses a hierarchical shaper on the hub mGRE interface.	QoS is applied at each GET VPN Group Member because no tunnels are used. Typically uses a hierarchical shaper on the egress interface.
Multicast	Replication at the hub	Any-to-any (no need for the traffic to pass through the hub) IPsec SA Anti-Replay

IPsec SA anti-replay is a security service in which the decrypting router can reject duplicate packets and protect itself against replay attacks. Cisco QoS gives priority to high-priority packets, and as a result, this prioritization may cause some low-priority packets to be discarded. Cisco IOS provides anti-replay protection against an attacker duplicating encrypted packets. QoS queuing delays can cause anti-replay packet drops, so it is important to extend the window size to allow the router to keep track of more than the default of 64 packets to prevent the drops from occurring. Figure 19-8 shows the impact of anti-replay window sizing.

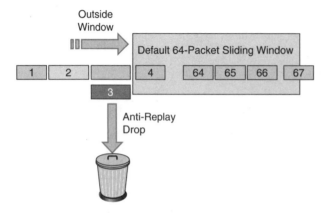

Figure 19-8 *Impact of Anti-replay Window Sizing*

Summary

- Tunneling mechanisms introduce the risk of exceeding the MTU, which can severely degrade network operation.

- When a QoS-classified packet is encrypted, the IP header and thus QoS classification are no longer visible.

- Cisco IOS, by default, copies the ToS field from the original IP header into the new IP header.

- DMVPN offers per-tunnel QoS configuration for spokes and zero-touch QoS deployment on hubs.

- With GET VPN, it is necessary to configure QoS on the egress interface of each GET VPN router.

- All routers in GET VPN belong to one group, so there is no need to apply per-site QoS.

Review Questions

After answering the following questions, please refer to Appendix A, "Answers to Review Questions," for the answers.

1. Which statements are true about Cisco IOS QoS classification? (Select two.)
   a. Cisco IOS, by default, copies the ToS field from the original IP header into a new IP header.
   b. Cisco IOS, by default, copies the CoS field from the original IP header into a new IP header.
   c. By default, encryption is performed prior to QoS classification.
   d. The preclassify feature may be implemented on IPsec, but not on IPsec GRE.
   e. Recommended practice is to enable the preclassify feature on Cisco ASA.

2. Which of the following is true about DMVPN QoS?
   a. You need to configure QoS on each group member.
   b. QoS configuration on all spokes is identical to the configuration on the hub.
   c. The primary function of QoS in DMVPN topology is reduction of network delay.
   d. Cisco IOS allows per-tunnel QoS design.

3. When a packet is being encrypted, the original IP header is no longer visible, and the QoS mechanism becomes ineffective when applied to the original packet. Which Cisco IOS operation addresses this issue?
   a. Cisco IOS, by default, copies the ToS field from the original IP header into a new IP header.
   b. Cisco IOS leverages a special command, **Copy ToS**, to copy the ToS field from the original IP header into new IP header.
   c. Cisco IOS leverages a special command, **ToS replicate**, to copy the ToS field from the original IP header into a new IP header.
   d. Cisco IOS is unable to address this issue.

Chapter 20

Enterprise IP Multicast Design

Upon completing this chapter, you will be able to

- Explain how IP multicast works
- Describe multicast groups
- Describe the IP multicast service model
- Describe the functions of a multicast network and multicast protocols
- Explain multicast forwarding and RPF checks
- Provide examples of RPF checks failing and succeeding
- Provide an overview of multicast protocol basics
- Identify multicast distribution trees
- Provide an overview of PIM-SM
- Describe the steps of a receiver joining the PIM-SM shared tree
- Describe how the source is registered to the RP
- Describe the multicast routing table
- Describe basic SSM concepts and an SSM scenario
- Describe bidirectional PIM and modifications for bidirectional operation
- Describe the DF election process and election messages

IP multicast is fundamentally changing the way that we live, work, play, and learn by providing innovative solutions that are simple, highly available, virtualized, open, and safe. This bandwidth conservation technology reduces traffic and server loads by simultaneously delivering a single stream of information to thousands of users.

Applications that take advantage of multicast technologies include videoconferencing; corporate communications; distance learning; and distribution of software, stock quotes, and news.

This chapter provides an introduction to IP multicast services. It presents the functional model of IP multicast and gives an overview of technologies that are present in IP multicasting. The chapter is composed of an introduction to IP multicast concepts followed by a discussion of distribution trees and protocols. This chapter also provides a detailed explanation of the most current scalable IP multicast routing protocol, Protocol-Independent Multicast—Sparse Mode (PIM-SM). You will become familiar with the determinism built into sparse mode multicast protocols and will develop the foundational knowledge required to prepare for learning more complex IP multicast designs and concepts.

How Does IP Multicast Work?

Because multicast is a different transmission mode from unicast, only protocols that are designed for multicast can be used with multicast. Multicast networks have source, network, and receiver segments. All these segments must perform specific functions to be able to deliver multicast traffic. The main idea of multicast is to replicate a single packet for multiple receivers. Figure 20-1 illustrates a multicast source host transmitting one copy of data and a network replicating the packet.

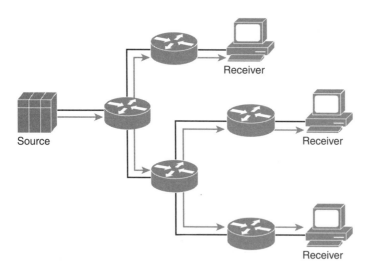

Figure 20-1 *Multicast in Action*

As you can see from Figure 20-1, the sender sends only one copy of a single data packet that is addressed to a group of receivers referred to as a multicast group. The downstream multicast routers replicate and forward the data packet to all the branches where receivers exist. Receivers express their interest in multicast traffic by registering at their first-hop router using Internet Group Management Protocol (IGMP) for IPv4 multicast or Multicast Listener Discovery (MLD) for IPv6 multicast.

Routers are responsible for replicating the packet and forwarding it to multiple recipients. Routers replicate the packet at any point where the network paths diverge. The reverse path forwarding (RPF) technique ensures that the packet is forwarded to the appropriate downstream paths without routing loops. The power of multicast is that each packet exists only in a single copy on any given network. The multicast source host may send to multiple receivers simultaneously by sending only one packet. Figure 20-2 illustrates what a similar transmission would look like with unicast.

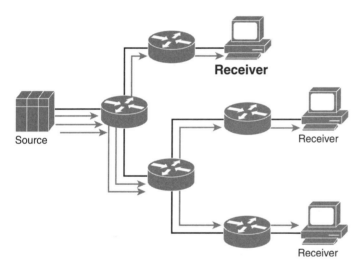

Figure 20-2 *Unicast in Action*

Multicast Group

A multicast address is associated with a group of interested receivers, as illustrated in Figure 20-3.

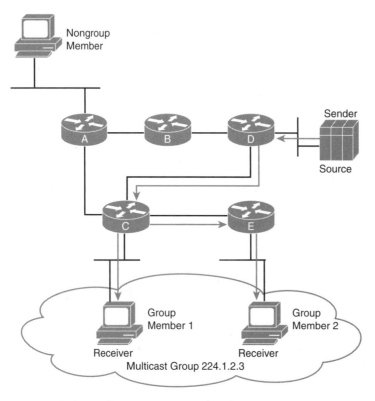

Figure 20-3 *Multicast Group Memberships*

According to RFC 3171, addresses 224.0.0.0 through 239.255.255.255, the former Class D addresses, are designated as multicast addresses in IPv4. Multicast addresses in IPv6 have the prefix FF00::/8. The sender sends a single datagram to the multicast address. The intermediary routers take care of making copies and sending a datagram to all receivers. The receivers have registered their interest in receiving the multicast data for that multicast address.

IP Multicast Service Model

IP multicast service models consist of three main components:

- Senders send to a multicast address.
- Receivers express an interest in a multicast address.
- Routers deliver traffic from the senders to the receivers.

How Does IP Multicast Work?   637

RFC 1112 specifies the host extensions for IP to support multicast:

- IP multicast allows hosts to join a group that receives multicast packets.
- IP multicast allows users to dynamically register (join or leave multicast groups) based on the applications they use.
- IP multicast uses IP datagrams to transmit data.

The multicast addresses are allocated dynamically and represent receiver groups, not the individual hosts. Receivers may dynamically join or leave an IP multicast group at any time by using IGMP or MLD messages. Messages are sent to the last-hop routers, which manage group membership. Routers use multicast routing protocols such as Protocol-Independent Multicast (PIM) to efficiently forward multicast data to multiple receivers. The routers listen to all multicast addresses and create multicast distribution trees, which are used for multicast packet forwarding.

Routers identify multicast traffic and forward the packets from senders toward the receivers. When the source becomes active, it starts sending the data without any indication. First-hop routers (FHR), to which the sources are directly connected, start forwarding the data to the network. Receivers that are interested in receiving IP multicast data register to the last-hop routers (LHR) using IGMP or MLD membership messages. Last-hop routers are those routers that have directly connected receivers. LHRs forward the group membership information of their receivers to the network so that the other routers are informed about which multicast flows are needed. Figure 20-4 shows a multicast source that is connected to an FHR, which forwards multicast packets into the network. Packets traverse shortest path trees (SPT) on their way to the receivers toward the last-hop router.

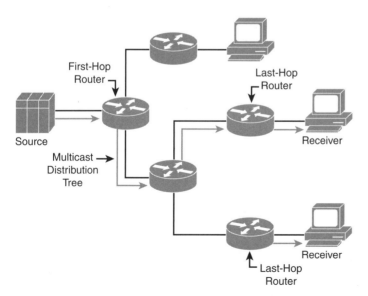

Figure 20-4 *First-hop Router, Last-hop Router, and Multicast Distribution Trees*

Functions of a Multicast Network

In a multicast network, routers build and maintain a multicast distribution tree as highlighted in the previous subsection and as illustrated in Figure 20-5.

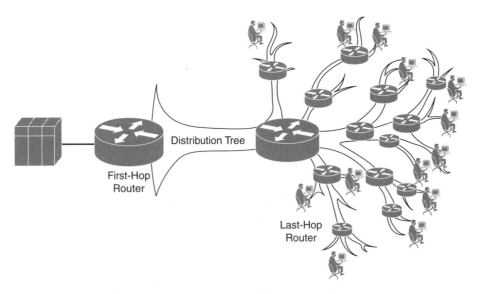

Figure 20-5 *Building and Maintaining a Multicast Distribution Tree*

The key steps for a properly functioning multicast network include the following:

Step 1. Learn about multicast group members and build an appropriate distribution tree.

Step 2. Identify multicast streams and forward them according to a distribution tree.

Step 3. Maintain group state at leaf segments and distribution trees in the whole network.

Step 4. Prevent loops and apply scoping and filtering.

As can be seen from these key steps, to build appropriate multicast distribution trees, the multicast network routers must learn about their multicast-enabled neighbors. As they build the multicast distribution trees, the routers start forwarding multicast traffic according to network needs. During normal operation, routers maintain the multicast distribution trees and multicast group state at leaf segments. The routers also prevent loops and apply scoping or filtering functions.

Multicast Protocols

Multicast protocols may differ depending on where in a multicast network they are implemented. No multicast protocol for source registering is used between the source and the first-hop router, such as IGMP, which is used between the last-hop router and the receiver. However, you do need multicast to be enabled on the interface facing the source/sender network. Multicast protocols are illustrated in Figure 20-6.

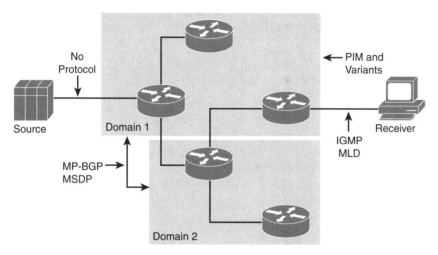

Figure 20-6 *Multicast Protocols*

Inside the multicast network, various multicast routing protocols are used. The multicast routing protocols may be separated into two groups based on intradomain versus interdomain functions:

- **Intradomain:** PIM and variants
- **Interdomain:** Multiprotocol Extensions for BGP (MP-BGP) in combination with Multicast Source Discovery Protocol (MSDP)

Between the last-hop router and the receivers, receivers use IGMP (for IPv4) or MLD (for IPv6) to report their multicast group membership to the router.

Multicast Forwarding and RPF Check

In unicast routing, when the router receives the packet, the decision whether to forward the packet is made depending on the destination address of the packet. In multicast routing, where to forward the multicast packet depends on where the packet came from. Multicast routers must know the origin of the packet in addition to its destination, which is the opposite of unicast routing.

The multicast packet is forwarded out of each interface that is in the outgoing interface list (OIL). OIL entries list the interfaces of the multicast neighbors that are downstream of the current router. Routers perform a reverse path forwarding (RPF) check to ensure that arriving multicast packets were received through the interface that is on the most direct path to the source that sent the packets.

> **Note** OILs also exist at the last-hop router (LHR) where there are no multicast neighbors downstream at all, only receivers. In other words, the OIL is a list of all outgoing interfaces where something has been communicated (via PIM JOIN or IGMP membership report) to this router that it is interested in that group.

An RPF check is always performed regarding the incoming interface, which is considered to be the RPF interface. The RPF check will succeed if the incoming interface is the shortest path to the source.

The router determines the RPF interface by the underlying unicast routing protocol or the dedicated multicast routing protocol in cases where one exists. An example of a dedicated multicast routing protocol is MP-BGP. It is important to note that the multicast routing protocol relies on the underlying unicast routing table. Any change in the unicast routing table immediately triggers an RPF recheck on most modern routers. Figure 20-7 illustrates the RPF process.

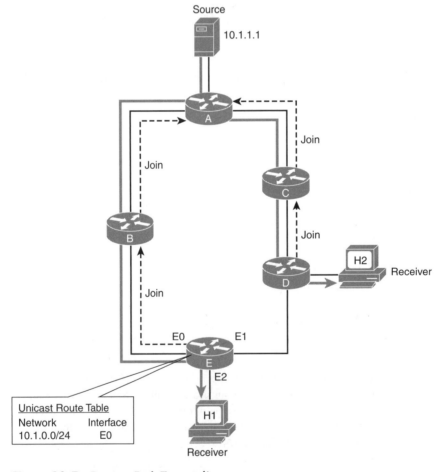

Figure 20-7 *Reverse Path Forwarding*

The RPF calculation is based on the source address. The best path to the source is found in the unicast routing table of the last-hop router and results in determining where to send the join. The join continues toward the source to build the multicast distribution tree creating the path, so multicast data can flow down the tree. This process is repeated for each receiver. In circumstances in which equal-cost multipath routing (ECMP) is used, the highest next hop IP address is used as the tiebreaker because there can be only a single path for the multicast stream.

Case Study 1: RPF Check Fails and Succeeds

The following case study, illustrated in Figure 20-8, shows two situations: when a multicast packet goes to the wrong interface, S0, and when it goes to the correct interface, S1.

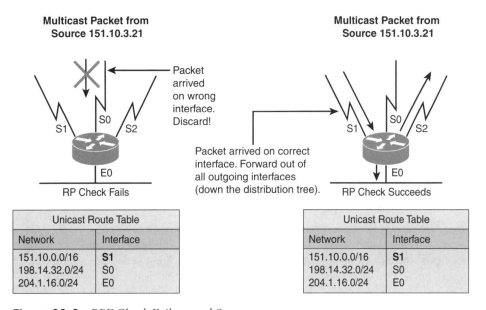

Figure 20-8 *RPF Check Failure and Success*

The diagram on the left in Figure 20-8 illustrates a failed RPF check, and the one on the right illustrates a successful RPF check:

- The router in the left diagram receives a multicast packet from source 151.10.3.21 on interface Serial 0. The router performs the RPF check by examining the unicast routing table. The unicast routing table indicates that interface Serial 1 is the shortest path to the network 151.10.0.0/16. Because interface Serial 0 is not the shortest path to the network from which the packet from the source 151.10.3.21 arrived, the RPF check fails, and the packet is discarded.

- The router in the right diagram receives a multicast packet from source 151.10.3.21 on interface Serial 1. The router performs the RPF check by looking into the unicast routing table. The unicast routing table indicates that interface Serial 1 is the shortest path to the network 151.10.0.0/16. Because interface Serial 1 is the shortest path to the network from which the packet from the source 151.10.3.21 arrived, the RPF check succeeds. With this success, the packet is forwarded on every interface in the outgoing interface list. In the right diagram, the OIL for the current multicast packet consists of interfaces Serial 2 and Ethernet 0, so the packet is forwarded on these interfaces.

Multicast Protocol Basics

Multicast distribution trees define the path that multicast traffic flows from the source to the receivers. The two types of multicast distribution trees are source-rooted trees (or SPTs) and shared trees.

With a source-rooted tree, a separate tree is built for each source to all members of a multicast group. Considering that the source-rooted tree takes a direct or shortest path from the source to its receivers, it is also referred to as an SPT.

Shared trees create multicast forwarding paths that rely on a central core router. This router serves as a Rendezvous Point (RP) between multicast sources and receivers. Sources initially send their multicast packets to the RP, which, in turn, forwards data through a shared tree to the members of the group. A shared tree can be less efficient than an SPT. In the shared-tree model, the paths between the source and the receivers are not necessarily the shortest, but it is important to note that a shared tree is less demanding on routers in terms of memory and CPU usage.

There are two types of multicast routing protocols: dense mode and sparse mode protocols. Dense mode protocols flood multicast traffic to all parts first and then prune the flows where there are no receivers by using a periodic flood-and-prune mechanism. Sparse mode protocols use an explicit join mechanism. With sparse mode protocols, distribution trees are built on demand by explicit tree join messages. The routers, which have directly connected receivers, will send join messages. Figure 20-9 shows an SPT between Source 1, Receiver 1, and Receiver 2.

Multicast Protocol Basics   643

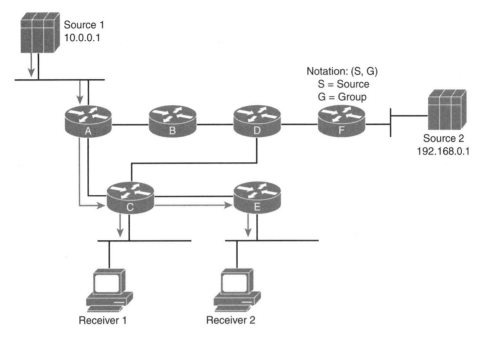

Figure 20-9 *Source Distribution Tree*

It is appropriately assumed that the path between the source and receivers over routers A, C, and E is the path with the lowest cost. Packets are forwarded down the SPT according to the pairs of source and group addresses. This is the reason the forwarding state that is associated with the SPT is referred to by the notation (S, G), which is pronounced *S comma G*. In this notation, S is the IP address of the source and G is the multicast group address. A separate SPT is built for every source S sending to a group G.

Figure 20-10 shows a shared distribution tree.

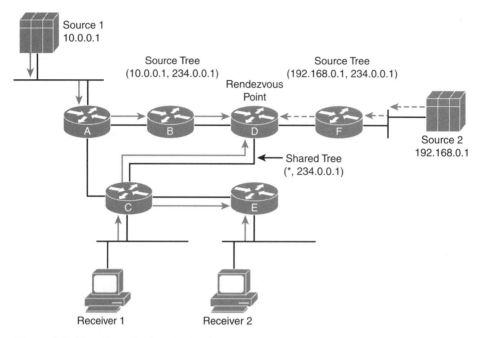

Figure 20-10 *Shared Distribution Tree*

Router D is the root of this shared tree. In PIM, the root of the shared tree is called an RP, as already mentioned. Packets are forwarded down the shared distribution tree to the receivers. The notation (*, G), pronounced *star comma G*, identifies the default forwarding state for the shared tree. The * symbol represents a wildcard entry, meaning that any source can be plugged into the notation, and G is the multicast group address.

Trees are always built backward. So the shared tree began when Receiver 1 sent an IGMP membership report and the LHR, router C, then created a (*,G) and added the interface Rx 1 as an OIL. Then it looks up who the RP is, where it is, and what the PIM RPF neighbor is. Next, it builds a PIM (*, G) join and sends it toward router D.

Figure 20-10 also shows traffic flow on two source-rooted trees in addition to the shared distribution tree. Source 1 and Source 2 send multicast packets toward an RP via the source-rooted trees. From the RP, the multicast packets flow through a shared distribution tree toward Receiver 1 and Receiver 2. Keep in mind that the sources are just sending. They will go wherever the trees are built. The RP sends PIM (S,G) joins back toward the root of the (S,G) tree, which is the first-hop router (FHR).

Multicast Distribution Trees Identification

It is important to be aware of the key differences between multicast distribution trees for better understanding of which multicast routing protocol is deployed in the network.

The multicast forwarding entries that appear in multicast forwarding tables may be read in the following way:

- **(S, G):** This notation indicates that a source S is sending to the group G.
- **(*, G):** This notation indicates that any source (*) is sending to the group G. These entries reflect the shared tree but are also created (in Cisco routers) for any existing (S, G) entry (refer to the following note).

> **Note** A source does not have to be sent for the (*,G) tree to be built. A receiver can send an IGMP membership report to its LHR. That creates a (*,G) and sends it to the RPF neighbor on the way to the RP. This will ultimately end up on the RP. It exists on the entire multicast distribution MDT path between the LHR and the RP while no source is sending yet at all. Also, for source-specific multicast (SSM), the (*,G) does not exist; that is, it is "not required for any (S,G) entry."

As already noted, SPT (S, G) state entries use more router memory. The reason for this is that there is an entry for each sender and group pair. However, because the traffic is sent over the optimal path to each receiver, the delay in packet delivery is minimized.

(*, G) state entries for shared distribution trees consume less router memory, but you may get suboptimal paths from a source to receivers, thus introducing an extra delay in packet delivery. It is important to choose the appropriate tree model to meet the demands of the application.

PIM-SM Overview

Protocol-Independent Multicast—Sparse Mode (PIM-SM) is a multicast routing protocol for IP networks. PIM-SM uses shared distribution trees that are rooted at the RP but that can also switch to the source-rooted distribution tree. PIM-SM uses the explicit join model. Receivers send either an IGMP membership report or an MLD (IPv6) to the LHR. The LHR creates a PIM (*,G) join once it knows who the RP is for that multicast group and then sends it to the designated RP. The RP is the root of a shared distribution tree that all multicast traffic flows down.

PIM-SM characteristics include

- Explicit join model via the RP.
- Receivers join to the RP via the last-hop router (LHR) (not directly).
- Senders register with the RP via the first-hop router (FHR) (not directly).
- Data flows down the shared tree and goes only to places that need the data from the sources.
- LHRs can join the source tree if the data rate exceeds the threshold.

To get multicast traffic to the RP for distribution down the shared tree, first-hop routers with directly connected senders send PIM register messages to the RP. Register messages cause the RP to send an (S, G) join toward the source. This activity enables multicast traffic to flow natively to the RP via an SPT and then down the shared tree.

LHRs may be configured with an SPT threshold, which, once exceeded, will cause the last-hop router to join the SPT. This action will cause the multicast traffic from the source to flow down the SPT directly to the last-hop router.

The following PIM-SM variants are available:

- **Bidirectional PIM (BIDIR-PIM):** Explicitly builds shared bidirectional trees. It never builds a shortest path tree, so it may have longer end-to-end delays than PIM-SM, but it scales well because it needs no source-specific state.

- **PIM Source-Specific Multicast (PIM-SSM):** Builds trees that are rooted in just one source, offering a more secure and scalable model for a limited number of applications.

PIMv6 is an implementation of the PIM-SM for IPv6. PIMv6 provides support for interdomain routing between domains and avoids the performance problems of earlier multicast routing protocols.

Receiver Joins PIM-SM Shared Tree

Figure 20-11 illustrates an active receiver joining multicast group G by multicasting an IGMP membership report.

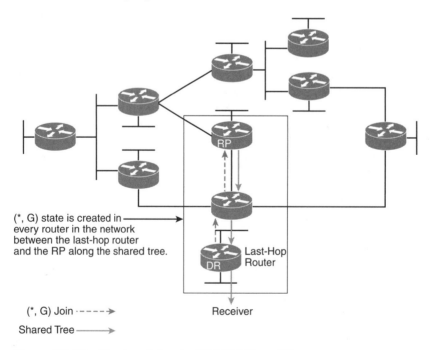

Figure 20-11 *Receiver Joins the PIM-SM Shared Tree*

In this example, a designated router (DR) on the LAN segment will receive IGMP membership reports. The DR knows the IP address of the RP router for group G and sends a (*, G) join for this group toward the RP. The join travels hop by hop toward the RP, building a branch of the shared tree that extends from the RP to the last-hop router directly connected to the receiver. At this point, group G traffic may flow down the shared tree to the receiver.

Registered to RP

As you can see in Figure 20-12, as soon as an active source for group G starts sending multicast packets, its first-hop DR registers the source with the RP.

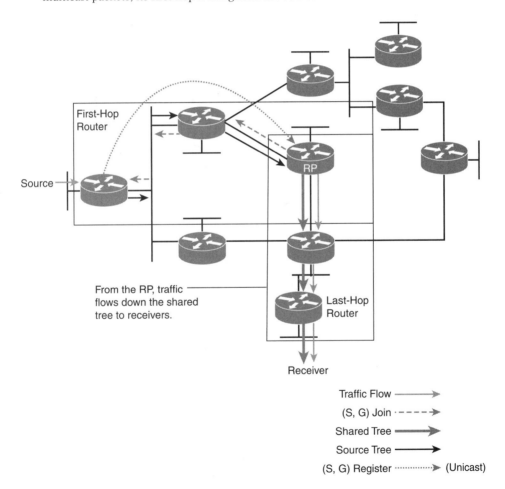

Figure 20-12 *RP Registration*

To register a source, the DR encapsulates the multicast packets in a PIM register message and sends the message to the RP using unicast. When the RP receives the unicast register message, it de-encapsulates the multicast packets inside the unicast register message.

The multicast packets are sent down the shared tree toward the receivers. At the same time, the RP initiates the building of an SPT from the source to the RP by sending (S, G) joins toward the source. The building of an SPT causes the creation of an (S, G) state in all routers along the SPT, including the RP. After the SPT is built from the first-hop router to the RP, the multicast traffic starts to flow from the source (S) to the RP.

When the RP begins receiving multicast data down the SPT from the source, it sends a unicast PIM register-stop message to the first-hop router, as illustrated in Figure 20-13.

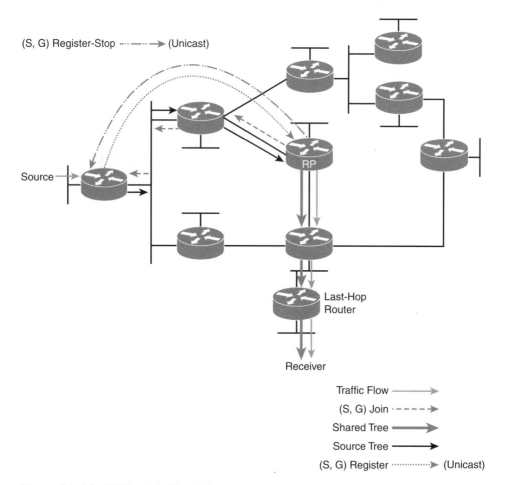

Figure 20-13 *RP Register-Stop Message*

The PIM register-stop message informs the first-hop router that it may stop sending the unicast register messages. At this point, the multicast traffic from the source is flowing down the SPT to the RP and, from there, down the shared tree to the receivers.

PIM-SM SPT Switchover

PIM-SM enables the last-hop router to switch to the SPT and bypass the RP if the multicast traffic rate is above a set threshold. This threshold is called the SPT threshold.

In Cisco routers, the default value of the SPT threshold is 0. Thus, as soon as the first packet arrives via the (*, G) shared tree, the default action for Cisco PIM-SM routers that are attached to active receivers is to immediately join the SPT to the source.

Figure 20-14 illustrates the last-hop router sending an (S, G) join message toward the source to join the SPT and bypass the RP.

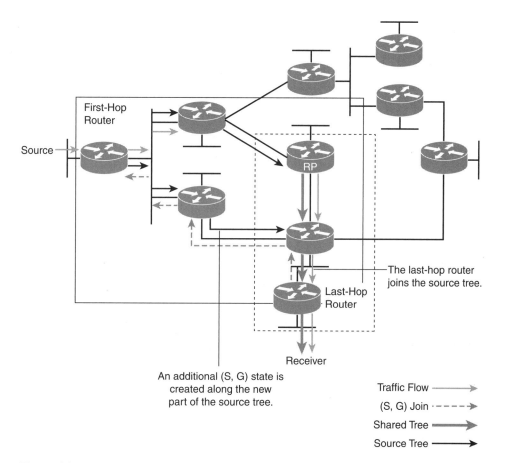

Figure 20-14 *PIM-SM SPT Switchover Last-hop Router Join*

The join message travels hop by hop to the first-hop router, creating another branch of the SPT. This action also creates an (S, G) state in all routers along this branch of the SPT.

As you can see in Figure 20-15, the (S, G) traffic is now flowing directly from the source to the receiver via the SPT.

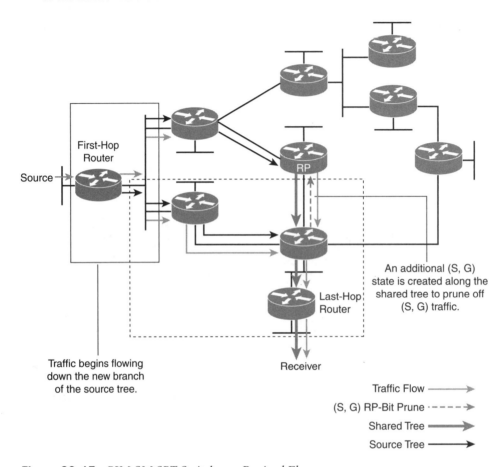

Figure 20-15 *PIM-SM SPT Switchover Revised Flow*

A special (S, G) RP-bit prune message is sent up the shared tree to prune the (S, G) traffic from the shared tree. After the (S, G) RP-bit prune message has reached the RP, the branch of the SPT from the source to the RP still exists. However, when the RP has received the (S, G) RP-bit prune message via all branches of the shared tree, the RP no longer needs (S, G) traffic. This result occurs because all receivers in the network are receiving the traffic via an SPT, bypassing the RP. The RP no longer needs the (S, G) traffic. Therefore, it will send (S, G) prune messages back toward the source to shut off the flow of now unnecessary (S, G) traffic, as illustrated in Figure 20-16.

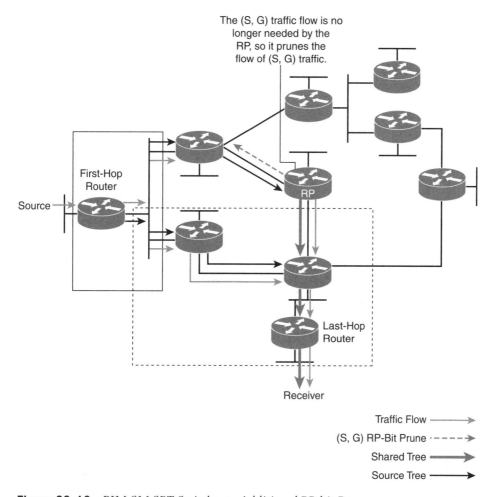

Figure 20-16 *PIM-SM SPT Switchover Additional RP-bit Prune*

When the (S, G) prune message reaches the first-hop router, it prunes the branch of the (S, G). This pruning will tear down the SPT that was built between the source and the RP. The traffic is now only flowing down the remaining branch of the (S, G)—the SPT built between the source and the last-hop router that initiated the switchover, as shown in Figure 20-17.

Chapter 20: Enterprise IP Multicast Design

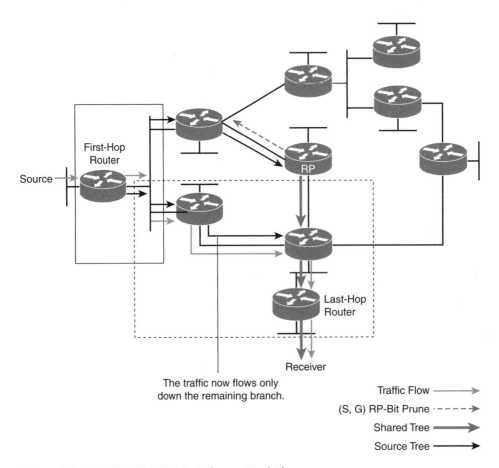

Figure 20-17 *PIM-SM SPT Switchover Final Flow*

Multicast Routing Table

Figure 20-18 shows a multicast routing table where two types of routes are present: (*, G) and (S, G).

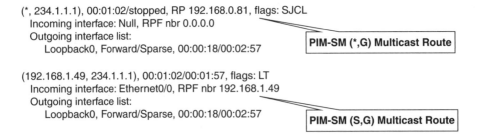

Figure 20-18 *Multicast Routing Table*

The incoming interface (IIF) is RPF checked for incoming multicast packets. The OIL is a list of interfaces where the multicast packet will be forwarded.

The PIM-SM (*, G) state rules are as follows:

- The (*, G) entry is created when a (*, G) join or an IGMP report is received. The latter condition may be simulated by manually configuring the router interface to join the group.
- (*, G) entries are also created automatically whenever an (S, G) entry for the group must be created. The (*, G) entry is created first; then the (S, G) entry is created.
- The IIF reflects the RPF interface and neighbor in the direction of the RP.
- The OIL of a PIM-SM (*, G) entry reflects interfaces with one of these attributes:
  - Have received a (*, G) join.
  - Are directly connected to a member that has joined the group.
  - Have been manually configured to join the group.
- (*, G) entries are deleted when the expire timer counts down to 0. This action occurs when only one of these conditions exists:
  - The OIL is null.
  - No child (S, G) entry exists.

The PIM-SM (S, G) state rules are as follows:

- (S, G) creation:
  - The receipt of an (S, G) join or prune message.
  - The receipt by the first-hop router of a packet from a directly connected source. This action will trigger the PIM-SM register process.
  - When a parent (*, G) is created, if it does not exist.
- (S, G) reflects forwarding of S to G:
  - IIF is the RPF interface toward the source. The exception to this rule occurs when the RP bit (R flag) is set in the (S, G) entry and the RPF interface is pointing up the shared tree. This action occurs after the SPT switchover and the router receives the RP-bit prune message to prune the (S, G) traffic from the shared tree. This mechanism allows duplicate (S, G) traffic to be blocked from flowing down the shared tree after a downstream router has switched to the SPT.
  - The OIL of the (S, G) entry is populated with a copy of the OIL from the parent (*, G) entry, without the IIF. The IIF must not appear in the OIL; otherwise, a multicast route loop may occur.
- (S, G) deletion:
  - In PIM-SM, the (S, G) entries are deleted when their expire timer counts down to 0. The expire timer is reset whenever an (S, G) packet is received and forwarded.

Basic SSM Concepts

Source-specific multicast (SSM) is a variant of a basic PIM-SM. SSM uses all the benefits of sparse mode protocols but eliminates the RPs and shared trees and only builds an SPT. SSM trees are built directly based on the receipt of group membership reports that request a given source. SSM is described in RFC 3569.

SSM is suitable for use when well-known sources exist either within the local PIM domain or within another PIM domain. The Multicast Source Discovery Protocol (MSDP), which is needed for interdomain multicast routing when regular PIM-SM is used within a domain, is no longer needed for SSM. MSDP is a multicast routing protocol that is used to interconnect multiple PIM-SM domains as well as to provide Anycast RP within a PIM-SM domain. MSDP is described in Chapter 21, "Rendezvous Point Distribution Solutions." A dedicated multicast group address range of 232.0.0.0/8 is used exclusively for SPTs for SSM. Routers are prevented from building a shared tree for any of the groups from this address range. The address range 232.0.0.0/8 is assigned for well-known global sources. SSM is a datagram delivery model that best supports one-to-many applications, also known as broadcast applications. Examples of applications in which SSM makes sense include video broadcasts, audio broadcasts, and stock market data.

The following are some well-known SSM characteristics:

- Allows the last-hop router to send an (S, G) join directly to the source without the creation of a shared tree

- Allows the first-hop router to respond to receiver-initiated join requests for specific sources within a group

- Uses IGMPv3 (IPv4) and MLDv2 (IPv6) to signal exactly which (S, G) SPT to join

- Supports elimination of share-tree state in the 232.0.0.0/8 range, simplifying address allocation

Figure 20-19 illustrates SSM in action.

Basic SSM Concepts 655

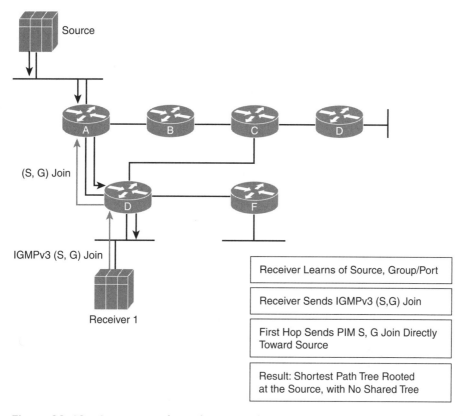

Figure 20-19 *Source-specific Multicast Mode*

As you can see in Figure 20-19, SSM allows the last-hop router to immediately send an (S, G) join toward the source. Thus, the PIM-SM (*, G) join toward the RP is eliminated, and the first-hop routers start forwarding the multicast traffic on the SPT from the very beginning. The SPT is built by receiving the first (S, G) join. The assigned address range of 232.0.0.0/8 also simplifies address allocation problems because it is a global range for sources that must be well known. Implementations in routers must not build any shared tree for those groups.

It is important to note that source-specific groups may coexist with other groups in PIM-SM domains.

SSM Scenario

The prerequisite for SSM deployment is a mechanism that allows hosts to report not only the group that they want to join but also the source for the group. This mechanism is built into the IGMPv3 standard. With IGMPv3, last-hop routers may receive IGMP membership reports requesting a specific multicast source and group traffic flow. The router responds by simply creating an (S, G) state and triggering an (S, G) join toward the source.

Exactly how a host learns about the existence of sources may occur via directory service, session announcements directly from sources, or some out-of-band mechanisms (for example, web pages). An out-of-band mechanism is illustrated in Figure 20-20.

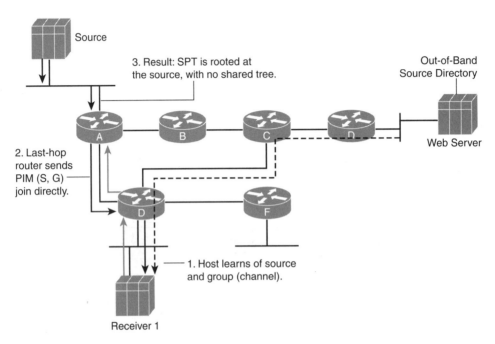

Figure 20-20 *SSM Out-of-band Source Directory*

The result of building an SPT from the beginning is that all of the PIM-SM mechanisms that are associated with an RP are eliminated. RPs for SSM groups are not needed because the discovery of sources is performed via some other method. In fact, routers must not build shared trees for groups in the SSM range (232.0.0.0/8).

There are several benefits of immediately building SPTs to a well-known source without the need for first building a shared tree. One of the main benefits concerns address management. Traditionally, it was necessary to acquire a unique IP multicast group address to ensure that a content source would not conflict with other possible sources sending on the shared tree.

In SSM, a unique IP multicast group address is no longer necessary. Traffic from each source is uniquely forwarded using only an SPT. Thus, different sources may use the same SSM multicast group addresses without concern about intermixing traffic flows.

Bidirectional PIM

PIM-SM is unidirectional in its native form. The traffic from sources to the RP initially flows encapsulated in register messages. This activity presents a significant burden because of the encapsulation and de-encapsulation mechanisms. Additionally, an SPT is built between the RP and the source, which results in (S, G) entries being created between the RP and the source.

Bidirectional PIM (BIDIR-PIM) is a variant of a basic PIM-SM model. Several multicast applications use a many-to-many multicast model in which each participant is a receiver as well as a sender. The (*, G) and (S, G) entries appear at points along the path from participants and the associated RP. Additional entries in the multicast routing table increase memory and CPU utilization. An increase of the overhead may become a significant issue in networks where the number of participants in the multicast group grows quite large.

A solid example of an application that takes advantage of BIDIR-PIM is a stock-trading application in which thousands of stock market traders perform trades via a multicast group. BIDIR-PIM eliminates the registration/encapsulation process and the (S, G) state. Packets are natively forwarded from a source to the RP using the (*, G) state only. This capability ensures that only (*, G) entries appear in multicast forwarding tables. BIDIR-PIM is illustrated in Figure 20-21.

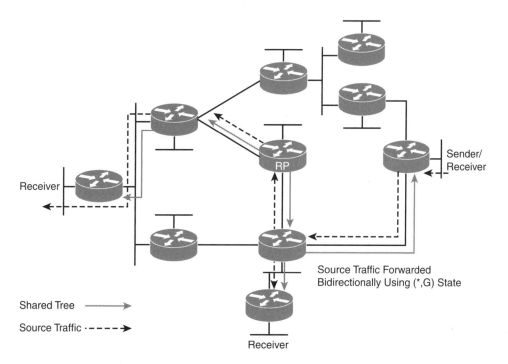

Figure 20-21 *Bidirectional PIM*

PIM Modifications for Bidirectional Operation

In BIDIR-PIM, the packet-forwarding rules have been improved over PIM-SM, allowing traffic to be passed up the shared tree toward the RP. To avoid a multicast packet that is looping, BIDIR-PIM introduces a new mechanism called the designated forwarder (DF), which establishes a loop-free SPT rooted at the RP.

The DF assumes the role of a designated router and has the following responsibilities:

- It is the only router that forwards packets traveling downstream (toward receiver segments) onto the link.
- It is the only router that picks up upstream-traveling packets (away from the source) off the link and forwards them toward the RP.

Use of this method ensures that only one copy of every packet will be sent to the RP, even if there are parallel equal-cost paths to the RP.

On every link in the network, the BIDIR-PIM routers participate in a procedure called DF election. The procedure selects one router as the DF for every RP of bidirectional groups. The router with the best unicast route to the RP is elected as a DF. An election tiebreaking process also occurs if there are parallel equal-cost paths to the RP. If the elected DF fails, it is detected via the normal PIM hello mechanism, and a new DF election process will be initiated.

A DF is selected for every RP of bidirectional groups. As a result, multiple routers may be elected as DF on any network segment, one for each RP. In addition, any particular router may be elected as DF on more than one interface.

DF Election

Multiaccess networks may have parallel paths, which can lead to group members receiving duplicate packets from multiple routers. To avoid this problem, PIM uses assert messages to elect a single PIM forwarder to forward the traffic. This process is illustrated in Figure 20-22.

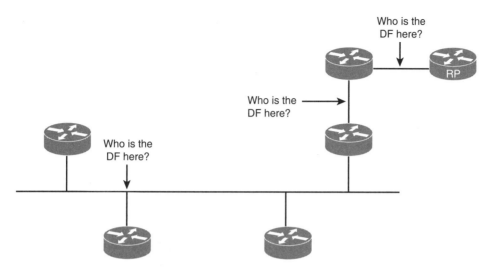

Figure 20-22 *BIDIR-PIM Designated Forwarder Election*

The BIDIR-PIM process of electing a DF on each link is similar to the PIM assert process. The BIDIR-PIM DF mechanism ensures that all the routers on the link have a consistent view of the same RP. To perform the election of the DF for a particular RP, routers on a link need to exchange their unicast routing metric information for reaching the RP. The election of a DF depends on the RP, not an individual group.

The DF election is based on unicast routing metrics and uses the same tiebreak rules that are employed by PIM assert processes. The router with the most preferred unicast routing metric to the RP becomes the DF.

The election process happens only once and occurs when information on a new RP becomes available. However, an update to the election is needed under the following conditions:

- A change occurs in the unicast metric to reach the RP for any of the routers on the link.
- The interface on which the RP is reachable changes to an interface for which the router was previously the DF.
- A new PIM neighbor is established on a link.
- The elected DF dies.

DF Election Messages

The DF election mechanism is based on four control messages that are exchanged between the routers on the link:

- **Offer message:** This message is used to advertise a router unicast metric to reach the RP. The other routers participating in the election of a DF compare the metric with their metric to reach the RP.

- **Winner message:** This message allows the winning router to announce to all routers on the link that it has won the DF election process. The DF also sends this message to reassert its status as the elected DF.

- **Backoff message:** This message is sent by the currently elected DF when it receives an offer message containing a better metric to the RP than its own. The DF records the received information and responds with a backoff message. The backoff message, therefore, is used to acknowledge that the sender (the active DF) has a worse metric back to the RP than the offering router. When the offering router receives the backoff message, it will assume the duties as the newly elected DF. The newly elected DF will send a winner message after a short time, while it allows unicast routing to stabilize.

- **Pass message:** This message is used by the acting DF to pass its function to another router that is offering a better metric. The old DF stops its tasks when the transmission is made.

Case Study 2: DF Election

This DF election case study shows how the DF is elected and what happens in situations in which the DF dies or the metric to the RP changes. In Figure 20-23, router B receives an offer with a better metric, assumes that it has lost the election, and backs off.

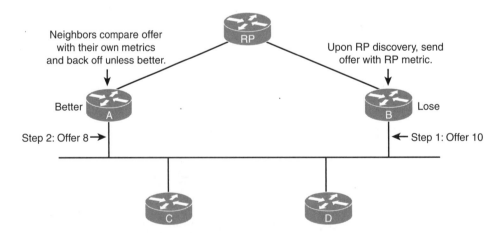

Figure 20-23 *Initial DF Election Process*

In Figure 20-24, router A has sent its offer three times and has not received another offer with a better metric. Winning the election as DF, router A assumes the role and announces its election by transmitting a winner message on the link. It also transmits its identity (IP address) and the metric it is using.

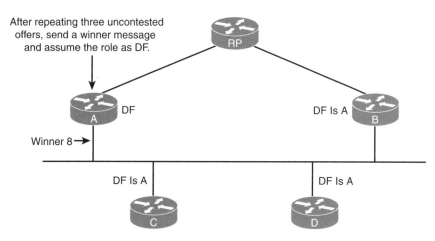

Figure 20-24 *Initial DF Election Result*

After the DF loses the path to the RP and its RPF interface becomes the same as the interface for which it is the DF, a standard DF election procedure starts. Routers that receive an infinite offer respond with their offers. The router with the best offer assumes the DF function and transmits a winner message. Loss of the path to the RP and change to the RPF interface are illustrated in Figure 20-25.

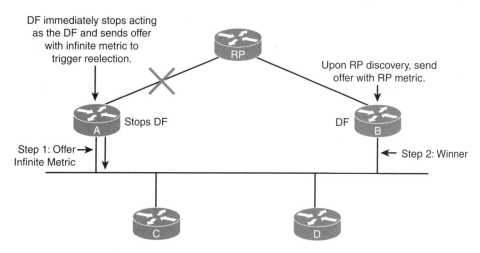

Figure 20-25 *DF Change during Unicast Routing Change*

In the situations in which the DF dies or the metric to the RP changes, the following will result:

- Downstream routers notice a change in the RPF information provided by unicast routing.
- Downstream routers trigger a reelection.
- If no downstream routers are available, the PIM neighbor timeout triggers a reelection.

When other metric changes occur, the following may happen:

- When the RP metric at a non-DF router changes to a value that is worse than that of the acting DF, no action is taken.
- When the metric at the DF improves, a winner message may be sent to update information in neighboring routers.
- When the metric at the DF becomes worse, three winner messages are sent to give a better candidate the opportunity to respond with an offer.

Summary

- Multicast sends a single packet to multiple receivers, thus reducing the network load closer to the source.
- Multicast uses the Class D IPv4 address space and FF00::/8 IPv6 prefix.
- Sources are the source of multicast streams, while receivers are the destination.
- A multicast network builds and maintains a distribution tree.
- The multicast network performs RPF checks to prevent multicast traffic loops.
- Multicast distribution trees are source-rooted and rooted at the meeting point.
- There are two notations in multicast for source-group pairings: (*, G) and (S, G).
- PIM-SM is the most widely used multicast routing protocol.
- DR joins the shared tree at the RP when a receiver joins a group.
- A shared tree is always built backward, from the last-hop router toward the RP.
- A source tree is created through PIM (S,G) joins hop by hop backward toward the source's IP address.
- The multicast tree can bypass the RP in certain situations.
- Different rules govern the creation, deletion, and maintenance of (*, G) and (S, G) states.
- SSM is a simplified solution for well-known sources.
- Bidirectional multicast uses the same tree for traffic from sources toward the RP and from the RP to receivers.

Review Questions

After answering the following questions, please refer to Appendix A, "Answers to Review Questions," for the answers.

1. Which protocol runs between the source and the first-hop router?
    a. IGMP
    b. MP-BGP
    c. MSDP
    d. PIM
    e. None of the above

2. How does an RPF check work?
    a. The routing table for unicast traffic is checked against the source address in the multicast datagram.
    b. The routing table for unicast traffic is checked against the source address in the unicast datagram.
    c. The routing table for multicast traffic is checked against the source address in the multicast datagram.
    d. The routing table for multicast traffic is checked against the source address in the unicast datagram.

3. Why does multicast routing use RPF information?
    a. To prevent forwarding loops
    b. To prevent switching loops
    c. All of the above
    d. None of the above

4. In the sparse mode multicast-enabled network, which router knows about all sources in the network?
    a. The first-hop router
    b. The rendezvous point
    c. The last-hop router
    d. All routers

5. Which two statements are true about (*, G) entries in the multicast routing table? (Choose two.)
    a. (*, G) is used for a particular source sending to a particular group.
    b. (*, G) is used for any source sending to a particular group.
    c. Traffic is forwarded via the shortest path from the source.
    d. Traffic is forwarded via a meeting point for a particular group.
    e. Traffic is always forwarded via the most optimal path.

6. For which two situations is SSM suitable? (Choose two.)
   a. For well-known sources
   b. For broadcast applications
   c. For random sources
   d. For many-to-many applications (video conference)
   e. For random sources and receivers

7. What is the default SSM range of IP multicast addresses?
   a. 223.0.0.0/8
   b. 232.1.0.0/24
   c. 232.0.0.0/8
   d. 232.1.0.0/16

8. Which two conditions are benefits of BIDIR-PIM? (Choose two.)
   a. All packets are encapsulated.
   b. The first packets from the source are not encapsulated.
   c. There are no (*, G) states.
   d. There are no (S, G) states.
   e. There are both (*, G) and (S, G) states.

9. Which router will become DF on the segment?
   a. The router with the best route to the receivers
   b. The router with the best route to the RP
   c. The router with the best route to the source
   d. The router with the best route to the BSR

10. Which condition would not trigger the process of re-electing a DF?
    a. A change in the unicast metric to reach the RP
    b. A change in the interface on which the RP is reachable
    c. Periodic triggering, every 3 minutes
    d. A new PIM neighbor on a link
    e. Death of an elected DF

Chapter 21

Rendezvous Point Distribution Solutions

Upon completing this chapter, you will be able to

- Describe rendezvous point discovery and point placement
- Describe Auto-RP, Auto-RP candidate RPs, and Auto-RP mapping agents
- Describe other routers that are not candidate RPs or mapping agents
- Provide an example of Auto-RP operations and Auto-RP scope issues
- Describe PIMv2 BSR, PIMv2 BSR candidate-RPs, and the PIMv2 BSR bootstrap router role
- Describe PIMv2 routers that are not BSRs or candidate RPs
- Describe the BSR flooding problem
- Describe IPv6 embedded RPs
- List and describe Anycast RP features
- Provide an overview of MSDP, MSDP neighbor relationship, and MSDP operation

This chapter provides an overview of Rendezvous Point (RP) distribution solutions. It explains the drawbacks of manual RP configuration and also describes the Auto-RP and BSR mechanisms. In addition to these common RP deployment options, the chapter also touches on the concept of Anycast RP, which works in combination with the Multicast Source Discovery Protocol (MSDP).

Rendezvous Point Discovery

Manual Rendezvous Point, sometimes referred to as static RP information configuration, although relatively easy to implement on a few devices within the infrastructure, does not scale to large environments. With a static RP deployment, the address of the RP must be configured on every router in the domain. If the network does not have many different RPs defined and/or they do not change very often, this could be the simplest method to define RPs.

There are, however, several problems associated with static RP configuration, including the following:

- The initial configuration of many routers is cumbersome (if a network provisioning and configuration tool is in place, configuring static RP across many devices should not be a major issue).

- Any change to the static configuration has a negative impact on the maintenance effort, which in the long term turns out to be even more troublesome than the initial provisioning. Although provisioning and configuration tools help simplify the configuration and provisioning part, any configuration change in a production environment typically requires a change window and may not be as quick and simple as required.

- Static RP information configuration does not support many scenarios leveraging redundant RPs, in which the network reachability changes (excluding the scenarios in which you have the RP defined with a redundancy protocol such as Anycast-MSDP).

Figure 21-1 illustrates challenges associated with an enterprise that has two uplinks to two service providers that offer multicasting services.

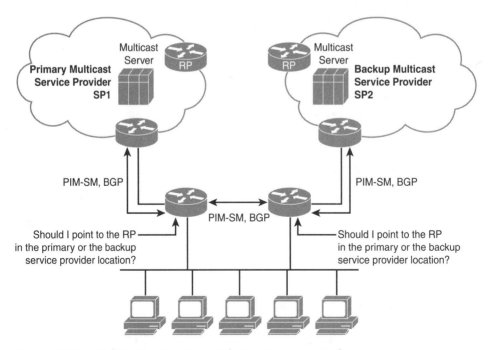

Figure 21-1 *Multicasting Services with Two Service Providers*

As can be seen from the diagram, the providers multicast to the same groups, but they have independent sources and RPs. The enterprise has Protocol-Independent Multicast—Sparse Mode (PIM-SM) and Border Gateway Protocol (BGP). These protocols peer with both service providers to exchange routing information and to build multicast distribution trees. SP1 is the primary provider, and SP2 is the backup, from which the multicast traffic should be received only if the connection to SP1 fails. Static RP information configuration does not support such requirements because the RP of SP1 has a different address than the RP of SP2. If the RP information of SP1 were configured on the enterprise routers, the RP selection would never fall back to the RP of SP2 in the event of a primary link failure.

In addition to the manual RP information configuration method, two mechanisms of dynamic RP discovery have been developed to improve scalability in large environments:

- **Auto-RP:** A method designed by Cisco
- **Bootstrap Router (BSR):** A standards-based mechanism

No matter which mechanism is used, as the designer, you must ensure that all routers have a consistent view. In other words, the same range of multicast groups has to be mapped to the same RP.

Table 21-1 compares the different kinds of RP deployments.

Table 21-1 *RP Deployment Comparison*

	Static RP	BSR	Auto-RP
Must be configured on every router	Yes	No (except on candidate BSRs and candidate RPs)	No (except on candidate RPs and mapping agents)
Supports IPv4 addresses	Yes	Yes	Yes
Supports IPv6 addresses	Yes	Yes	No
RP redundancy	No (unless used with Anycast RP)	Yes	Yes

Auto-RP and BSR are discussed in more detail in the following sections.

Rendezvous Placement

The decision as to which RP information distribution to use is not directly linked to the question of which routers should be declared as RPs or candidate RPs.

RPs can be almost anywhere. Theoretically, they do not even need to be on the path from the sources to the receiver. On the Cisco routers, the default Shortest Path Tree (SPT) threshold is set to 0. This default means that the distribution trees immediately switch to SPT, and the traffic itself does not flow via the RP. This concept was discussed in the previous chapter and is illustrated in Figure 21-2.

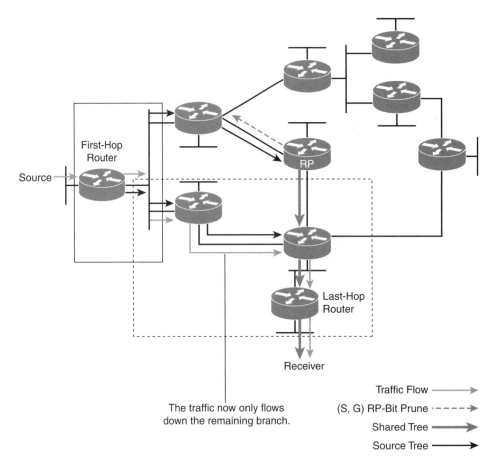

Figure 21-2 *PIM-SM SPT Switchover*

For other values of the SPT threshold, especially infinity, a placement closer to the source is recommended because the RP can become a congestion point.

Auto-RP

Auto-RP enables all routers in the network to automatically learn group-to-RP mappings. No special configuration steps must be taken, except on the routers that are to function as

- Candidate RPs
- Mapping agents

Multicast is used to distribute group-to-RP mapping information via two special multicast groups that are assigned with Internet Assigned Numbers Authority (IANA) addresses:

- Cisco announce group: 224.0.1.39
- Cisco discovery group: 224.0.1.40

Considering that multicast is used to distribute this information, a which-occurred-first situation can happen if the 224.0.1.39 and 224.0.1.40 groups operate in sparse mode. Routers would have to know the RP address before they can learn the address of the RPs via Auto-RP messages. Therefore, it is recommended that these groups run in PIM Dense Mode (PIM-DM) so that this information is flooded throughout the network. Figure 21-3 illustrates the role of the candidate RPs and mapping agents.

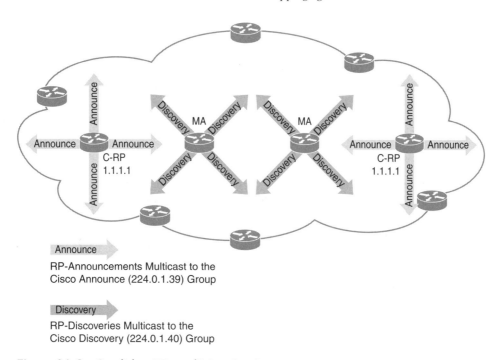

Figure 21-3 *Candidate RPs and Mapping Agents*

Multiple candidate RPs may be defined so that in the case of an RP failure, the other candidate RP can assume the responsibility of the RP.

Auto-RP can be configured to support administratively scoped zones, unlike the BSR mechanism, which is explained later in this chapter. Administratively scoped zones can be important when you are trying to prevent high-rate group traffic from leaving a campus and consuming too much bandwidth on the WAN links.

Auto-RP Candidate RPs

In Figure 21-3, an Auto-RP candidate RP is sending RP-announcement messages to the Cisco announce group (224.0.1.39). These messages announce the router as being a candidate RP. By default, the messages are sent every 60 seconds.

RP-announcement messages contain

- The group address range (the default is the all-multicast-groups address, or 224.0.0.0/4).
- The IP address of the candidate RP.
- A hold time, which is used to detect when the candidate RP has failed. This hold time is three times the announcement interval; therefore, the default value is 180 seconds.

Auto-RP Mapping Agents

An Auto-RP mapping agent joins the RP-announcement group (224.0.1.39) to receive RP announcements from a candidate RP. When a mapping agent receives an announcement, it does the following:

- Saves the announcement in the group-to-RP mapping cache
- Selects the candidate RP with the highest IP address as the RP for the group range

The hold times are used to expire an entry in the cache. This technique becomes useful if a candidate RP fails and is no longer sending periodic candidate-RP announcements. Via RP-discovery messages, the mapping agent periodically sends information on the elected RPs from its group-to-RP mapping cache to all routers in the network. RP-discovery messages are multicast to the Auto-RP–discovery group (224.0.1.40). They are sent every 60 seconds or when a change to the information in the group-to-mapping cache takes place.

Auto-RP and Other Routers

Cisco routers automatically join the Cisco discovery group (224.0.1.40) to receive the group-to-RP mapping information that is being multicast by the mapping agent in the network. No configuration is required to join this group. Group-to-RP mapping information that is contained in the RP-discovery messages is stored in the local group-to-RP mapping cache of the router. The router uses this information to map a group address to the IP address of the active RP for the group.

Case Study: Auto-RP Operation

Considering that other routers in the network will learn the group-to-RP mapping information from the mapping agents, it is important that this information is correct on the mapping agents. If the information is not correct, you must verify that the candidate

RPs are configured correctly. You must also verify that the mapping agent properly received the candidate-RP announcements.

If multiple mapping agents are in use, make sure that their group-to-RP mapping information is identical. If it is not, the routers in the network will oscillate between the different RPs selected by the agents. Again, it is important to make sure that all the mapping agents are properly receiving Auto-RP announcements from all candidate RPs in the network.

Group-to-RP mapping information should match the information of the mapping agents. If not, you must verify that the router is properly receiving Auto-RP–discovery messages from the agents.

Take care when configuring the time-to-live (TTL) scope on the RPs and mapping agents, especially with a redundant setup with multiple routers in those roles. If the TTL is too low, the messages may not reach all the destination routers. If the TTL is too high, an overlap will ensue, and you will need to ensure that the information offered by the multiple mapping agents is identical. Another challenge that you must consider is the need to constrain the message overflow into other administrative domains.

In this case study, we will examine the Auto-RP Operation process by highlighting the details that take place at each step. As shown in Figure 21-4, at time zero, the group-to-RP mapping caches in the mapping agents are empty because no RP announcements have been received.

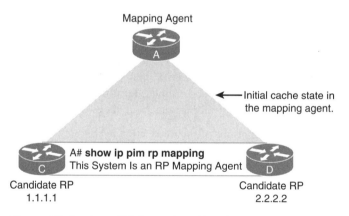

Figure 21-4 *Auto-RP Operation: Step 1*

The output of the Cisco IOS **show ip pim rp mapping** command shows that router A is a mapping agent and that the group-to-RP mapping cache is empty.

Routers C and D begin sending their RP-announcement messages to advertise themselves as RP candidates for all multicast groups. The mapping agent (router A) receives these

RP announcements and stores this information in its group-to-RP mapping cache, as illustrated in Figure 21-5.

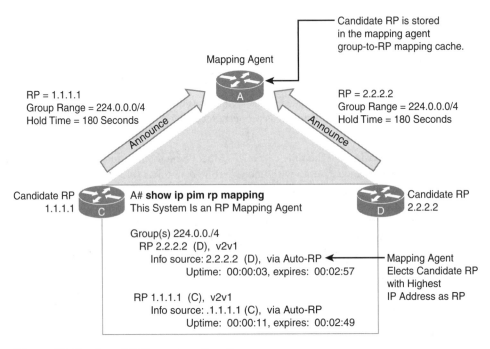

Figure 21-5 *Auto-RP Operation: Step 2*

The output on the mapping agent now shows both routers C and D as candidates for group range 224.0.0.0/4. The group range 224.0.0.0/4 means all multicast groups except for the Auto-RP groups, 224.0.1.39 and 224.0.1.40. The mapping agent then elects the candidate RP with the highest IP address as the active RP for the group range.

The mapping agent begins to advertise the results of the RP election to the rest of the network via Auto-RP–discovery messages, as depicted in Figure 21-6.

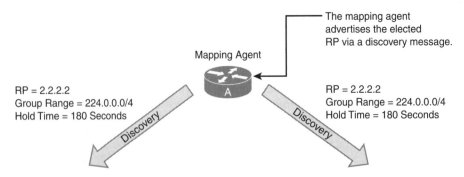

Figure 21-6 *Auto-RP Operation: Step 3*

It is critical that all mapping agents in the PIM-SM domain have identical information in their group-to-RP mapping caches to avoid having RP and receivers using different RPs that may not be fully synced up, as illustrated in Figure 21-7.

```
A# show ip pim rp mapping            B# show ip pim rp mapping
This System Is an RP Mapping Agent    This System Is an RP Mapping Agent

Group(s) 224.0.0./4                   Group(s) 224.0.0./4
  RP 2.2.2.2 (D), v2v1                  RP 2.2.2.2 (D), v2v1
    Info source: 2.2.2.2 (D), via Auto-RP   Info source: 2.2.2.2 (D), via Auto-RP
         Uptime: 00:00:03, expires: 00:02:57     Uptime: 00:00:03, expires: 00:02:57

  RP 1.1.1.1 (C), v2v1                  RP 1.1.1.1 (C), v2v1
    Info source: .1.1.1.1 (C), via Auto-RP   Info source: .1.1.1.1 (C), via Auto-RP
         Uptime: 00:00:11, expires: 00:02:49     Uptime: 00:00:11, expires: 00:02:49
```

Figure 21-7 *Auto-RP Operation: Step 4*

If the information in the mapping caches is not identical, it can cause the routers in the network to flip-flop between two different RPs. This is not the case with respect to this case study.

Figure 21-8 shows that router B is the first mapping agent to send its RP-discovery message containing the contents of its group-to-RP mapping cache.

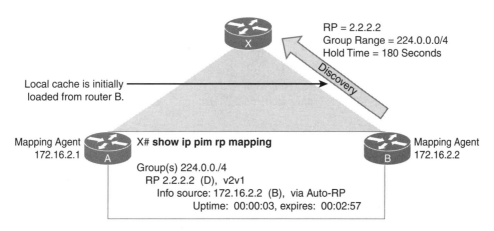

Figure 21-8 *Auto-RP Operation: Step 5*

The routers in the network all receive this RP-discovery message and install the information in their local group-to-RP mapping cache.

The output shows that the 2.2.2.2 router (router D, not shown in Figure 21-8) is currently selected as the RP for group range 224.0.0.0/4. It also shows that this information was most recently received from router B.

Router A sends an RP-discovery message containing the contents of its group-to-RP mapping cache, as depicted in Figure 21-9.

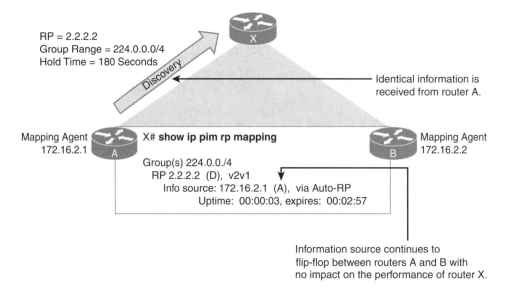

Figure 21-9 *Auto-RP Operation: Step 6*

The routers in the network receive this RP-discovery message and update the information in their local group-to-RP mapping cache. Because both mapping agents are sending identical information, the only thing that will change in the local group-to-RP mapping cache is the source of the information.

The output shows that the 2.2.2.2 router (router D, not shown in this diagram) is still selected as the RP for group range 224.0.0.0/4. However, the data reflects that this information was most recently received from router A. The flip-flop of the information source in the group-to-RP mapping cache of the local router has negligible impact on the router.

Auto-RP Scope Problem

Care must be taken in the selection of the TTL scope of RP-announcement messages. The RP-announcement messages should reach all the required mapping agents. Care must also be taken in the selection of the TTL scope of RP-discovery messages. The RP-discovery messages should reach all PIM-SM routers in the network.

Figure 21-10 highlights an Auto-RP scope candidate-RP problem where an arbitrary scope of 16 was used on the candidate-RP router. However, the maximum diameter of the network is greater than 16 hops, and in this case one mapping agent (router B) is farther away than 16 hops.

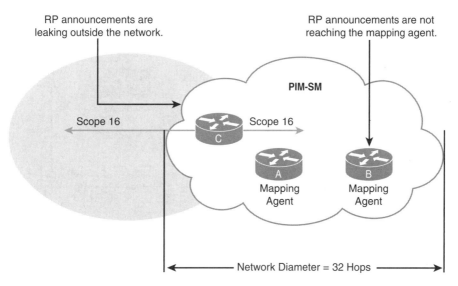

Figure 21-10 *Auto-RP Scope—Candidate-RP Problem*

As a result, this mapping agent does not receive the RP-announcement messages from the candidate RP. This lapse can cause the two mapping agents to have different information in their group-to-RP mapping caches. If this event occurs, each mapping agent will advertise a different router as the RP for a group, which will have disastrous results.

Also, the candidate RP is fewer than 16 hops away from the edge of the network. This arrangement can cause RP-announcement messages to leak into adjacent networks and produce Auto-RP problems in those networks.

Figure 21-11 highlights an Auto-RP scope mapping agent problem where an arbitrary scope of 16 was used on the mapping agent. However, the maximum diameter of the network is greater than 16 hops, and in this case, at least one router (router D) is farther away than 16 hops.

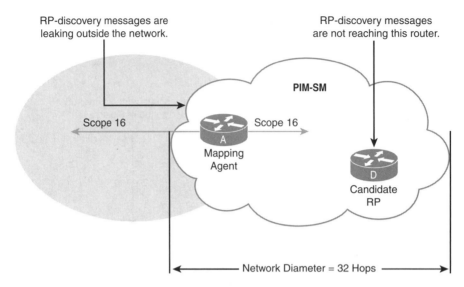

Figure 21-11 *Auto-RP Scope—Mapping Agent Problem*

As a result, this router does not receive the RP-discovery messages from the mapping agent. This lapse can result in the router having no group-to-RP mapping information. If this event occurs, the router will attempt to operate in dense mode for all multicast groups while other routers in the network work in sparse mode.

Also, the mapping agent is fewer than 16 hops away from the edge of the network. This arrangement can cause RP-discovery messages to leak into adjacent networks and produce Auto-RP problems in those networks.

PIMv2 BSR

The BSR is an IETF standards mechanism available in PIMv2; it is a standards-based alternative to Auto-RP. With BSR, a single router is elected as the BSR from a collection of candidate BSRs. If the current BSR fails, a new election is triggered. The election mechanism is preemptive based on the priority of the candidate BSR.

Candidate RPs send candidate-RP announcements directly to the BSR. Candidate RPs learn the IP address of the BSR via periodic BSR messages. The BSR does not elect the best RP for every group range it learns about, but rather for every group range known, the BSR builds a set of candidate RPs, including all the routers that advertised their willingness to serve as the RP for the group range. The BSR stores the collection of candidate-RP announcements in a database referred to as the RP set. The BSR periodically sends out BSR messages to the routers in the network to let them know that the BSR is still alive. BSR messages are flooded hop by hop throughout the network as multicasts to the all-PIM-routers group (224.0.0.13) with a TTL of 1. When a router receives a BSR message, it applies a reverse path forwarding (RPF) check, which is based on the source IP address in the packet. If the RPF check succeeds, the message is flooded out to all PIM-enabled interfaces.

BSR messages contain the following elements:

- The RP set, consisting of candidate-RP announcements
- The IP address of the BSR, so that candidate RPs know where to send their announcements

As a result of the packets being flooded throughout the network, the routers will receive the BSR messages. Each receiving router selects the active RP for each group range using a common hash algorithm that is run against the RP set. The routers in the network will select the same RP for a given group range. Contrary to the Auto-RP method, scoping cannot be used for BSR because scoping was not considered when BSR was designed. Candidate-RP announcements that are unicast to the BSR may cross multicast boundaries. Figure 21-12 illustrates the BSR election process.

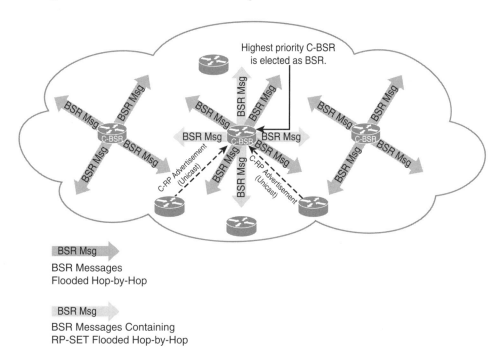

Figure 21-12 *BSR Election Process*

PIMv2 BSR: Candidate RPs

Candidate RPs periodically send candidate-RP messages directly to the BSR via unicast. They know the BSR address because the BSR messages have been periodically flooded to the all-PIM-routers group 224.0.0.13. The default interval for the candidate-RP messages is 60 seconds. The candidate-RP announcement messages contain the group range, candidate-RP address, and a hold time.

PIMv2 BSR: Bootstrap Router

The primary purpose of the BSR is to collect the candidate-RP announcements. These announcements are stored in a database that is called the RP set. The candidate-RP announcements are periodically flooded out to the other routers in the network using the BSR messages. When the BSR receives candidate-RP messages, these messages are accepted and stored. The BSR advertises BSR messages to all-PIM-routers (224.0.0.13) with a TTL of 1 every 60 seconds, or when changes are detected. Any new router with a higher BSR priority forces new election.

PIMv2 BSR: All PIMv2 Routers

The PIMv2 routers that are not BSRs or candidate RPs have an important role in the PIMv2 BSR process. PIMv2 routers perform as follows:

- Accept BSR messages that are based on the rules described earlier in this chapter. When a BSR message is accepted:

    - The RP set in the BSR message is stored in the local group-to-RP mapping cache.

    - The BSR message is forwarded to the other interfaces, except the one on which it was received.

- Select an RP using a hash algorithm:

    - The RP for a group is selected from the set of candidate RPs that advertised their candidacy for a matching group range.

    - The routers use the same hashing algorithm to select the RP from the set of candidate RPs in the RP set. Because the routers run the same algorithm on the same RP set, they will select the same RP for a given group.

    - The hashing algorithm permits multiple candidate RPs to load balance the duties of the RP across a range of groups. Only one candidate RP will be selected as the RP for any single group in the group range. However, the hash algorithm may select other candidate RPs as the RP for another group within the group range.

BSR Flooding Problem

BSR messages that are addressed to the multicast group 224.0.0.13 are propagated in a hop-by-hop fashion throughout the entire PIMv2 network, as illustrated in Figure 21-13.

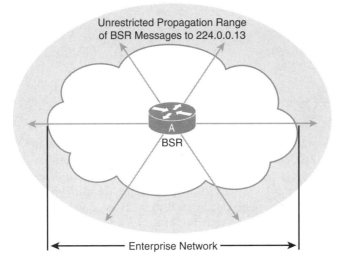

Figure 21-13 *BSR Flooding*

The leaf routers receive the packet, populate the local cache, and forward it across all other PIMv2 interfaces. The problem arises on domain borders that should not leak the information about enterprise RPs. Leaking this information can affect network performance because external domain RPs may be selected for the multicast distribution trees.

IPv6 Embedded Rendezvous Point

IPv6 embedded RP defined in RFC 3956 is an IPv6-only multicast feature, which simplifies the process of managing mapping between multicast groups and RPs. IPv6 embedded RP is a mechanism that eliminates the need for static configuration of IPv6 RPs on the multicast DRs. The IPv6 RP address for a given multicast group (address) is encoded inside the IPv6 multicast group, as illustrated in Figure 21-14.

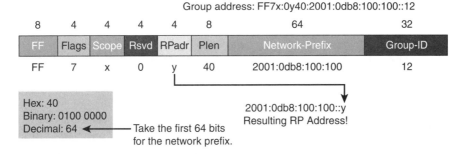

Figure 21-14 *IPv6 Embedded RPs*

The following is an example of the IPv6 embedded RP concept, which has the attributes listed:

- 16 RP addresses per network prefix
- 232 multicast groups per RP
- Guaranteed to be unique because of the enterprise-assigned /64 network that is used in the address

The example in Figure 21-14 shows the resulting IPv6 RP address that is taken from the IPv6 multicast group address. The 4 bits taken from the previously reserved range are used to specify one of 16 addresses, such as 1–15 (0 is reserved). Therefore, an address ending in ::16 or larger could not be an embedded RP. In the example, the mark bits are set to 0111, which means IPv6 RP is embedded in the IPv6 multicast group. Prefix length, or *Plen*, is set to 40, which means that 64 (all) bits of the network prefix are used to determine the IPv6 RP address. Group ID in the example is set to 12, and the IPv6 RP address (y) can range from 1 to 15. Using prefix embedding, any enterprise with a /64-bit prefix can generate a unique multicast address without consulting any organization or registering with IANA. IPv6 embedded RP adds the capability to also include 16 possible addresses for IPv6 RPs for the IPv6 multicast group.

IPv6 embedded RP is ideal as a replacement for static RP. No manual configuration of RP addresses is required because the address is embedded within a multicast group. However, if the RP address needs to change, the multicast address needs to change, which requires informing all interested applications. Routers that do not support IPv6 embedded RP can be statically configured or use other methods such as BSR.

The following key points summarize the use of IPv6 embedded RP:

- IPv6 embedded RP can be considered an automatic replacement to static IPv6 RP configuration.
- Routers that do not support IPv6 embedded RPs can be configured statically or via BSR.
- IPv6 embedded RP does not provide IPv6 RP redundancy as BSR or Anycast RP does.

Note The Cisco Auto-RP does not support IPv6. Anycast-RP PIM RFC 4610 with static RP is a common and reliable design option for IPv6 multicast.

Routers that serve as IPv6 embedded RPs must be configured for this specific multicast group. This process provides a safeguard mechanism that prohibits poor selection of RPs. When you specify exactly which multicast groups that an RP will stream traffic for, there is less likelihood that a high-rate group address will be sourced from a low-throughput RP. Without this safeguard, you could select RPs simply by specifying the IPv6 multicast address with an IPv6 embedded RP address, without consulting the network team. This may result in a possibility that an IPv6 embedded RP address could specify an IPv6 RP that could not process the multicast traffic.

> **Note** The IPv6 embedded RP solves the problem of helping multicast routers choose the right IPv6 RP, but it does not address the redundancy of RPs if the RP goes down.

Anycast RP Features

Anycast RP works with the Multicast Source Discovery Protocol (MSDP) to provide RP redundancy, rapid RP failover, and RP load balancing. Anycast RP is defined in RFC 3446. MSDP is a mechanism to connect multiple RPs.

The Anycast RP mechanism works as follows:

- Two or more routers are configured as the active RP for the same group range at the same time. This is normally a configuration error that would partition the PIM-SM domain. However, MSDP is used to prevent this from happening.
- Each RP is assigned the same RP address. This is usually accomplished using a loopback interface and private address space. Each router advertises its RP address as a host route in the unicast routing protocol.
- Sources and receivers use the closest RP, based on their unicast routing table.
- The Anycast RPs also establish MSDP peering relationships with one another. This allows each RP to learn which sources have been registered with the other Anycast RPs in the domain.
- The normal PIM-SM RP behavior causes the RP to join the source tree of active sources in the other parts of the network as necessary.

Anycast RP has the following benefits:

- RP backup without using Auto-RP or BSR
- RP failover at the speed of the unicast routing protocol

Anycast RP has the following feature requirements:

- It uses only one IP address for all RPs.
- RPs advertise the single IP address as a host route.
- MSDP is used between the RP routers.

Anycast RP Example

In Figure 21-15, two Anycast RPs, RP1 and RP2, are configured with the same IP address (10.1.1.1). They also establish MSDP peering between them. To establish MSDP peering, these RPs must use some other address than 10.1.1.1.

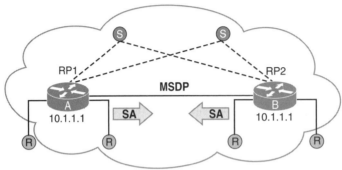

S Source

R Receiver

Figure 21-15 *Anycast RP Example*

Initially, the DRs (not shown in the diagram) for the sources and receivers register to the closest RP based on their unicast routing table entry for IP address 10.1.1.1. This action causes the DRs in the left part of the network to register or join to RP1 while the DRs in the right part register or join to RP2. When a new source registers with the nearest RP, that RP will send an MSDP SA message to its peer. This will cause the peer RP to join the SPT to the new source. Then the peer RP can pull the source traffic to itself and send it down the shared tree to its receivers.

Figure 21-16 illustrates what happens when RP1 goes down.

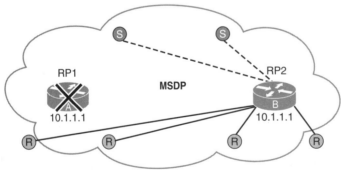

S Source

R Receiver

Figure 21-16 *Anycast RP Failure*

When the unicast routing protocol reconverges, all the DRs in the left part of the network can now see the route to 10.1.1.1 pointing toward RP2. The DRs in the left part of the network send new registers and joins to RP2, reestablishing the flow of traffic.

MSDP Protocol Overview

MSDP is a mechanism that connects multiple PIM-SM domains. MSDP allows multicast sources for a group to be known to all RPs in different domains. Each PIM-SM domain uses its own RPs and does not have to depend on RPs in other domains. An RP runs MSDP over TCP to discover multicast sources in other domains. Only SPTs are built between domains.

The following are some key MSDP protocol characteristics:

- Uses interdomain source trees
- Reduces the problem of locating active sources
- Allows RP or the last-hop receiver to join the interdomain source tree
- RPs know about all sources in a domain:
  - Sources cause a PIM register to the RP
  - They can tell RPs in other domains of their sources leveraging MSDP SA messages
- RPs know about receivers in a domain:
  - Via normal PIM (S, G) joins
  - Necessary only if there are receivers for the group

Anycast RP is a useful application of MSDP. With Anycast RP, a source may register with one RP, and receivers may join a different RP. This method is needed for RPs to exchange information about the active sources. All information exchange is done with MSDP.

MSDP Neighbor Relationship

Like BGP, MSDP establishes neighbor relationships with other MSDP peers using a TCP session to port 639. MSDP peers send keepalive messages every 60 seconds for a fixed period. The arrival of data performs the same function as the keepalive messages in terms of keeping the session from timing out. If no keepalive messages or data are received for 75 seconds, the TCP connection is reset and reopened. MSDP peers should exchange routing information using BGP. BGP is used to perform an RPF check of arriving SA messages and may use the Multicast Routing Information Base (MRIB), Unicast Routing Information Base (URIB), or both. Exceptions to this recommendation are when peering with only a single MSDP peer or when using an MSDP mesh group.

Case Study: MSDP Operation

The MSDP peers should also be the RPs in respective domains. These RPs are then connected via MSDP sessions, as depicted in Figure 21-17.

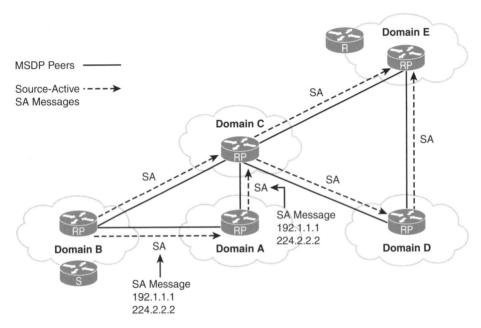

Figure 21-17 *MSDP Operation Case Study: Figure 1*

Figure 21-17 shows an example of PIM-SM domains A through E. Each domain has an RP, which is also an MSDP speaker. The solid lines between RPs represent the MSDP peer sessions via TCP, not actual physical connectivity between the domains. The physical connectivity between the domains is not shown in this figure.

Assume that a receiver in domain E joins multicast group 224.2.2.2. This join causes the DR that is labeled R to send a (*, G) join for this group to the RP.

This activity builds a branch of the shared tree from the RP in domain E to the DR as shown.

When a source goes active in domain B, the first-hop router S sends a PIM register message to the RP. This informs the RP in domain B that a source is active in the local domain. The RP responds by originating an (S, G) SA message for this source and sending it to its MSDP peers in domains A and C.

When the RPs in domains A and C receive the SA messages, the RPF information is checked. Then the SA messages are forwarded downstream to the MSDP peers of the domain E and D RPs.

MSDP Protocol Overview 685

The SA message traveling from domain A to domain C will fail the RPF check at the domain C RP (MSDP speaker). It will then be dropped because domain C has direct connectivity to domain B, where the source exists. However, the SA message arriving at domain C from domain B will pass the RPF check and be processed and forwarded to domains D and E and to A. The SA from domain C to domain A will fail the RPF check and will be dropped. Similarly, the SA from domain D to domain E will fail the RPF check and will be dropped.

Once the SA message arrives at the RP (MSDP speaker) in domain E, the RP sees that it has an active branch of the shared tree for group 224.2.2.2. The RP responds to the SA message by sending an (S, G) join toward the source in domain B. This is illustrated in Figure 21-18.

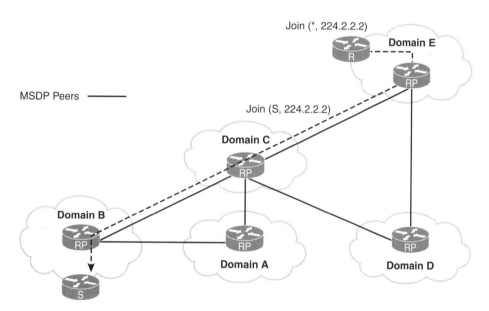

Figure 21-18 *MSDP Operation Case Study: Figure 2*

The (S, G) join will follow the multicast interdomain routing path from the RP in domain E to the source S in domain B. This multicast interdomain routing path is not necessarily the same path that the MSDP connections use. The BGP tables are used to determine the direction in which the (S, G) join is propagated toward the source.

When the (S, G) join message reaches the first-hop router in domain B, (S, G) traffic begins to flow to the RP in domain E via the SPT. This activity is shown in Figure 21-19.

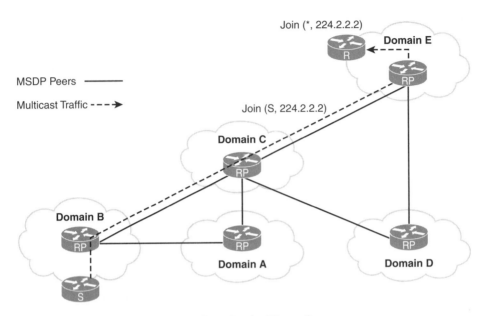

Figure 21-19 *MSDP Operation Case Study: Figure 3*

The (S, G) traffic will follow the path of the source tree that was built by the (S, G) join from the RP in domain E to source S.

When the (S, G) traffic reaches the last-hop router R in domain E, the last-hop router sends an (S, G) join toward the source in domain B.

The default SPT switchover threshold in PIM-SM for all groups is 0. This means that the switchover will happen immediately after the first multicast packet arrives. Depending on the physical topology of the domain, the shared tree path and the shortest tree path may overlap.

After the SPT switchover occurs in a last-hop router (router R), the (S, G) join from router R reaches source S. The (S, G) traffic from source S will now flow via the SPT to router R. The multicast traffic no longer needs to go through the RP in domain E.

Summary

- Static RP offers no fault tolerance.
- The two protocols for automatic RP discovery are Auto-RP and BSR.
- BSR periodically sends relevant RP information to all routers.
- BSR messages may be flooded outside the safe bounds, but a boundary can be configured to restrain BSR messages.
- The RP address can be embedded into a multicast group address.

- Anycast RP can be used to provide RP redundancy without the use of BSR or Auto-RP methods.
- MSDP SA messages are used to advertise active sources in the domain.

Review Questions

After answering the following questions, please refer to Appendix A, "Answers to Review Questions," for the answers.

1. Which statement describes the peer that initiates the MSDP connection and the duration of the keepalive timer?
   a. The peer with the lower IP address initiates the connection, and the keepalive timer is set at 75 seconds.
   b. The peer with the higher IP address initiates the connection, and the keepalive timer is set at 75 seconds.
   c. The peer with the lower IP address initiates the connection, and the keepalive timer is set at 60 seconds.
   d. The peer with the higher IP address initiates the connection, and the keepalive timer is set at 60 seconds.

2. Which addresses are involved in Auto-RP communications? (Select two.)
   a. 224.0.0.39
   b. 224.0.1.39
   c. 224.0.0.40
   d. 224.0.1.40
   e. 224.0.1.41

3. Which addresses are involved in BSR communications? (Select two.)
   a. 224.0.0.1
   b. 224.0.0.2
   c. 224.0.0.13
   d. Unicast to the BSR
   e. 224.0.0.40

4. Which method supports administrative scoping?
   a. Auto-RP
   b. BSR
   c. Auto-RP and BSR
   d. None of the above

5. How can MSDP be used inside a single domain?
   a. Use full-mesh MSDP sessions between all routers.
   b. Use MSDP instead of BGP.
   c. Use MSDP sessions between RPs.
   d. Use MSDP only between domains.

Chapter 22

Designing Security Services and Infrastructure Protection

Upon completing this chapter, you will be able to

- Describe network security zoning
- Describe Cisco modular network architecture
- Explain Cisco next-generation security products and features
- Describe Cisco network infrastructure protection
- Describe how to protect access to devices
- Describe how to protect routing infrastructure
- Describe how to protect network devices
- Explain how to enforce policy on network infrastructure devices using Layer 2 and Layer 3 data plane security controls
- Describe how to secure the switching infrastructure

Security is one of the most important aspects of modern network design. To protect the most critical resources, today's networks should be segmented, and proper control mechanisms should exist between those network segments. The design of secure networks should follow the common network architecture best practices and guidelines to provide the proper level of security. Cisco offers a wide range of next-generation products and technologies to meet modern security needs.

The network infrastructure is one of the foundation elements of enterprise IT infrastructure and is a critical business asset. Therefore, it is crucial to secure the network. You should take security into consideration in the designing phase of the network. To provide complete security of the network, begin by enforcing fundamental elements of network security. These elements can serve far more advanced security features and mechanisms.

Network Security Zoning

To restrict access between different parts of the network, use the concept of zoning. *Zoning* mitigates the risk of having one flat network without any access restrictions between different network segments. It does this by segmenting infrastructure services into logical groupings that have the same communication security policies and security requirements. It is a design approach that restricts communication to only those flows that are defined by security policy.

Zones are separated by *zone interface points*. A zone interface point provides a network interface between a zone and another zone. The zone interface point is implemented with network security devices. You can create each zone interface point by using a single component or a combination of components.

Many types of zones exist in the network. The most typical zones follow (see Figure 22-1):

- **Public zone:** An external zone that is not under control of the organization. Public services are located in this zone.
- **Public access zone:** A zone that hosts the public services of the organization and is often called the demilitarized zone (DMZ). These services can be accessed from the public zone. Typical services include e-mail proxy, web proxy, reverse proxy, and remote-access services.
- **Restricted zone:** An internal zone that hosts the most critical data services for the organization. Usually, this zone is the most secured zone, and access to this zone should be limited.

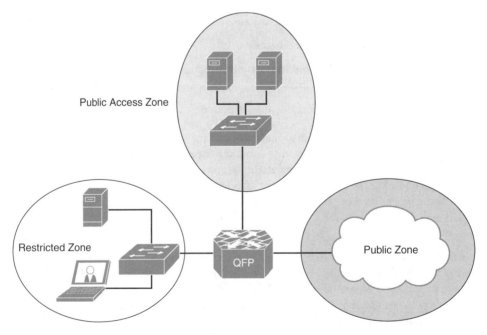

Figure 22-1 *Logical Security Zones*

> **Note** These examples describe the most typical zones. Many additional zones usually exist in modern networks and are based on design requirements, enterprise security policy, and needs.

To limit access between different zones, network security devices use the concept of *filtering*. The traffic that is not allowed to flow from one zone to another is filtered at the zone interface points. Security policy controls which traffic is allowed. In today's modern networks, this filtering can vary depending on various variables, such as the criticality of the applications, zones, and enterprise security policy standards. For instance, basic packet filtering may be based on the source, and destination IP/port or advanced filtering with deep packet inspection.

Cisco Modular Network Architecture

Cisco modular network architecture delivers defense-in-depth by positioning Cisco products and capabilities throughout the network and by using collaborative capabilities between the platforms. A wide range of security technologies is deployed in multiple layers. Products and capabilities are positioned where they deliver the most value, while facilitating collaboration and operation.

The Cisco modular network architecture follows these principles:

- **Defense-in-depth:** In Cisco modular network architecture, security is embedded throughout the network by following a defense-in-depth approach. For enhanced visibility and control, a rich set of security technologies and capabilities is deployed in multiple layers, under a common strategy and administrative control.

- **Modularity and flexibility:** In Cisco modular network architecture, all components are described by functional roles. The overall network infrastructure is divided into functional modules, such as the campus and the data center. Functional modules are then subdivided into more manageable and granular functional layers and blocks, such as the access layer and edge distribution layer. The modular designs result in added flexibility, which enables phased implementation for deployment plus selection of the best platforms and their eventual replacement as technology and the business need to evolve. Finally, modularity also accelerates the adoption of new services and roles.

- **Service availability and resiliency:** The Cisco modular network architecture incorporates several layers of redundancy to eliminate single points of failure and to maximize the availability of the network infrastructure.

- **Regulatory compliance:** The Cisco modular network architecture incorporates a rich set of security practices and functions that are commonly required by regulations and standards to facilitate the achievement of regulatory compliance.

- **Strive for operational efficiency:** The Cisco modular network architecture is designed to facilitate management and operations throughout the entire solution life cycle. Designs were conceived with simplicity to accelerate provisioning and to help troubleshoot and isolate problems quickly, effectively reducing operating expenditures.

- **Auditable implementations:** The Cisco modular network architecture designs accommodate a set of tools to measure and verify the operation and the enforcement of safeguards across the network.

- **Global information sharing and collaboration:** The Cisco modular network architecture uses information sharing and collaborative capabilities available on the Cisco products and platforms. Logging and event information that is generated from the devices in the network is centrally collected, trended, and correlated for maximum visibility.

As you know from Chapter 1, "Optimal Enterprise Campus Design," the Cisco modular network architecture consists of several functional modules. Each of these modules can be further subdivided into more manageable and granular functional layers and blocks, each serving a specific role in the network. Although these functional modules may vary from design to design based on various influencing factors such as targeted environment size and type of business, the most common modules follow (see Figure 22-2):

- **Enterprise core:** The core infrastructure is the main part of the network, which connects all other modules. The objective of this high-speed infrastructure is to provide a reliable and scalable Layer 2 or Layer 3 transport.

- **Intranet data center:** The objective of the intranet data center is to host many systems for serving applications and storing significant volumes of data. The data center also hosts network infrastructure that supports applications, including routers, switches, load balancers, and application acceleration. The intranet data center is designed to serve internal users and applications.

- **Enterprise campus:** The enterprise campus provides network access to users and devices. It may span over several floors or buildings in the same geographic location. Cisco modular network architecture includes a campus design that allows campus users to securely access any internal or external resource.

- **Enterprise Internet edge:** The Internet edge is the network architecture that provides connectivity to the Internet. It includes public services (DMZ), corporate Internet access, and remote-access VPN.

- **Enterprise WAN edge:** The WAN edge is the portion of the network infrastructure that aggregates the WAN links that connect geographically distant branch offices to a central site or regional hub site. The objective of the WAN is to provide users at the branches with the same network services as campus users at the central site. The Cisco modular network architecture includes a WAN edge design that allows branches and remote offices to securely communicate over a private WAN.

- **Enterprise branch:** Branches provide connectivity to users and devices at a remote location. They typically implement one or more LANs and connect to central sites via a private WAN or an Internet connection. The Cisco modular network architecture includes several branch designs that allow users and devices to securely access the network services.

- **Teleworker:** The term *teleworker* refers to any remote user such as a user with a home office connecting over the public Internet to the enterprise network.
- **E-commerce:** The term *e-commerce* refers to the enterprise block or module that hosts network and security devices to provide secure connectivity to e-commerce applications, mainly for external users or customers. This module should not necessarily be considered in every enterprise architecture (whether to do so depends on the business and services offered by the enterprise).
- **Partner and extranet:** These modules provide connectivity to external networks or users, such as business partners, over dedicated links or networks.
- **Management:** The architecture design includes a management network. The management network combines out-of-band (OOB) management and in-band (IB) management. The objective of the management network is to carry control and management plane traffic such as Network Time Protocol (NTP), Secure Shell (SSH), Simple Network Management Protocol (SNMP), and syslog.

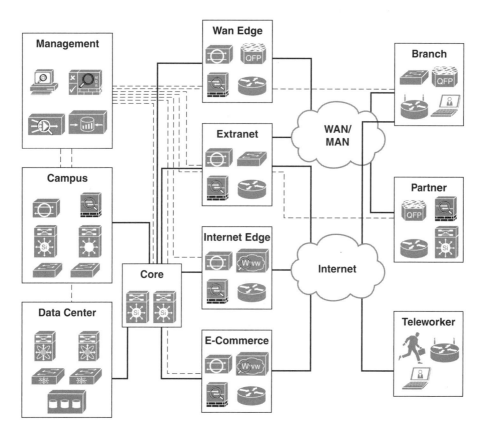

Figure 22-2 *Common Functional Modules of the Cisco Modular Enterprise Architecture*

By leveraging the Cisco enterprise modular architecture, Figure 22-3 shows the wide range of security technologies and products in an example of a network, which is built based on the modular network architecture design principles.

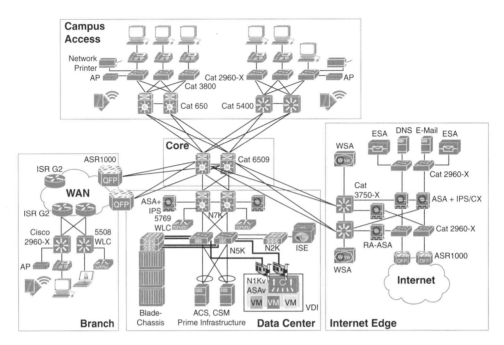

Figure 22-3 *Sample Application of Security Technologies and Product*

To provide more secure, manageable, and scalable security design, the Cisco modular network architecture must include several security zones. Some of the zones and the locations of these zones in the Cisco modular network architecture are as follows:

- **Public zone:** The public zone is outside the organization and is located in the enterprise Internet edge.

- **Public access zone:** The public access zone is used to host an organization's public services and secure access of the enterprise users to the public zone. It is located in the enterprise Internet edge.

- **Operations zone:** The operations zone hosts support services for internal users and services. This zone is usually located in the intranet data center functional module.

- **Restricted zone:** The restricted zone hosts most critical data services, and access should be limited to only necessary traffic. This zone is located in the intranet data center.

- **Management restricted zone:** This zone provides management for the network and other infrastructure. It should be secured to limit access to the management resources. This zone is hosted in the intranet data center.

When translating the security design from its high level (logical) form into a more detailed one where you need to start, decide which security or product you should select. You can use the following products and technologies to provide secure network design:

- **Secure network access:** Organizations today use a complex and diverse set of endpoints, both wired and wireless. The endpoints are located in the enterprise campus and enterprise branch in a Cisco modular network architecture. The main objective of those two functional modules is to provide secure network access and to protect endpoints from data loss, data theft, and privacy invasions. The security must focus on both wired and wireless endpoints.

- **VPN technologies:** To provide connectivity to the central site, organizations usually use network access such as the Internet or ISP WAN services, which are not secure from an organization's point of view. Therefore, organizations must use VPN technologies to provide secure access to the central site. VPN technologies are mainly used in the enterprise WAN edge and enterprise branch. To allow remote workers to connect to the organization's resources, remote-access VPN technologies are used at the enterprise Internet edge.

- **Firewalls/IPS:** Firewalls and IPS provide access control between different points of the network. These technologies are typically used in the enterprise Internet edge to control traffic between different security zones. Firewalls and IPS are also used in the intranet data center to control traffic between different network functional modules to applications and application stacks.

- **Infrastructure protection:** To provide high-level security to the organizational network, an infrastructure must be protected, and access to the devices must be limited to only authorized devices and employees. The infrastructure protection services should be taken into consideration in all functional modules of Cisco modular network architecture.

- **Content and application security:** Organizations can be vulnerable to attacks on data and content. Spam, phishing through e-mail, and web content attacks have all been used to provide an attacker access. To protect users against application layer attacks, the organization should deploy products like e-mail or web security appliances. These devices are usually deployed in the enterprise Internet edge.

- **Network and security management:** Network and security management tools are usually located in the management functional module. These tools provide central network and security management. They help organizations automate and simplify network management to reduce operational costs.

Cisco Next-Generation Security

To protect against modern threats (which are more sophisticated), Cisco offers next-generation products like the Cisco adaptive security appliance (ASA) 5500-X Next-Generation Firewall and Cisco FirePOWER Next-Generation intrusion prevention system (IPS).

The Cisco ASA 5500-X Series Next-Generation Firewall helps you balance security effectiveness with productivity. This solution offers the following highlighted features:

- Stateful firewall with advanced clustering
- Cisco Anyconnect remote access
- Granular application visibility and control (AVC) to support more than 3000 application-layer and risk-based controls
- Cisco FirePOWER Next-Generation IPS, which provides threat prevention and contextual awareness
- Filters on hundreds of millions of URLs in more than 80 categories
- Discovery and protection against advanced malware and threats
- Physical and virtual firewalling capabilities

Cisco ASA can be deployed in a wide range of form factors. The smallest appliance is Cisco ASA 5506-X for small business and small branch offices; it offers up to 250 Mbps of throughput. Cisco ASA 5512-X through Cisco ASA 5555-X are intended for small- to medium-sized enterprises, with throughput ranging from 300 Mbps to 1.75 Gbps. The high-end Cisco ASA product 5585-X with a different security services processor (SSP) can offer up to 15 Gbps of throughput per device and is intended for large Internet edge and data center networks.

The Cisco FirePOWER Next-Generation IPS solution integrates real-time contextual awareness, full-stack visibility, and intelligent security automation to deliver effective security, reliable performance, and lower cost of ownership. Threat protection can be expanded with optional subscription licenses to provide advanced malware protection (AMP) and application visibility and control.

The Cisco FirePOWER Next-Generation IPS can be deployed as a physical appliance. The 8000 Series appliances can provide from 15 Gbps to 60 Gbps of IPS throughput, whereas the 7000 series can provide from 50 Mbps to 1.25 Gbps of IPS throughput. The Cisco FirePower Next-Generation IPS can also be deployed as a virtual appliance or as an ASA with FirePOWER services.

Designing Infrastructure Protection

The first layer in securing a network infrastructure is enforcing the fundamental elements of network security. The fundamental elements of network security form a security baseline that creates a strong foundation on which more advanced methods and techniques can be built. If baseline security elements are not addressed, extra security technologies and features are typically useless. The following key areas are identified, and each will be covered in the subsequent sections in more detail:

- Securing infrastructure device access
- Securing routing infrastructure
- Device resiliency and survivability
- Network policy enforcement
- Securing switching infrastructure
- SDN security considerations

The functionality of a network device is typically segmented into three planes of operation:

- **Data plane:** The vast majority of packets handled by a router travel through it by way of the data plane (forwarding plane).
- **Control plane:** The spanning-tree protocol, routing control protocols, keepalives, ICMP with IP options, MPLS LDP, and packets destined to the local IP addresses of the router pass through the control plane.
- **Management plane:** Traffic from management protocols and other interactive access protocols, such as Telnet, Secure Shell (SSH), and SNMP, passes through the management plane.

To provide complete security of the network device, you must enforce security on all three planes. To protect the management plane, you must specially focus on securing infrastructure device access. Similarly, all control plane protocols should be secured. Therefore, you should secure your routing and switching infrastructure to protect the control plane of the network device. To protect your data plane, you should enforce network policy and secure switching infrastructure. Actually, secure networks must be built on a secure foundation; therefore, you should consider the following as a baseline or foundation to protect the preceding planes:

- **Control plane protection:** Protects the control plane traffic responsible for traffic forwarding by "locking down" services and routing protocols
- **Management plane protection:** Protects the management plane from unauthorized management access and polling and provides secure access for management and instrumentation
- **Data plane protection:** Protects the data plane from malicious traffic and protects data forwarded through the device

Infrastructure Device Access

Securing the network infrastructure requires securing management access to these infrastructure devices. It is critical to prevent unauthorized access.

Securing management access to the infrastructure devices is critical for network security. If the infrastructure device access is compromised, the security and management of the entire network can be compromised. Therefore, you should prevent unauthorized access.

Network infrastructure devices provide a range of different access mechanisms. Some of them are typically enabled by default, with minimal security associated with them. Therefore, you should review and properly configure each device before implementing it in production.

The key points to focus on when securing management access to an infrastructure device are as follows:

- **Restrict device accessibility:** Limit the permitted methods of access to only those methods that are needed for management. You should also limit the scope of IP addresses that can access the device via management protocols.
- **Present legal notification:** It is recommended that a legal notification banner be presented on all interactive sessions to ensure that users are notified of the security policy being enforced.
- **Authenticate access:** Ensure that device access is granted only to the authenticated users, groups, or services.
- **Authorize actions:** Restrict the actions and views that are permitted by any particular user, group, or service.
- **Ensure the confidentiality of data:** Protect locally stored sensitive data from viewing and copying by using encryption algorithms to store passwords and similar data. You should also avoid using unencrypted management protocols, such as Telnet or HTTP, and use SSH or HTTPS instead.
- **Log and account for all access:** Record who accessed the device, what the person was doing, and when this happened.

Many tools and mechanisms exist to protect network infrastructure devices. You should deploy them to reduce the risk of management access abuse. There are generally two independent mechanisms to secure management access to infrastructure devices:

- Use an out-of-band management philosophy that establishes a logically or physically separate network for management purposes. Such a network is isolated from network forwarding user traffic, so the chance of spoofing and intercepting management traffic is much lower. It may be acceptable to use unprotected (cleartext) management protocols, perhaps with weaker authentication. Usually, you can use console access via the terminal server or dedicated ports on the appliances.

- Use secure management protocols in an in-band management philosophy. These protocols include SSH, secure Hypertext Transfer Protocol (HTTPS), and Simple Network Management Protocol (SNMPv3). When an unsecure management protocol is used, you should use cryptographic protection, such as IPsec VPN.

    - It is also recommended that you deploy an IP address–based filter to allow access to the device management planes only from trusted hosts and networks. For devices using Cisco IOS Software, various mechanisms can be implemented to limit access to the device management plane: You can deploy IP address-based ACL filtering, which denies access to management IP addresses of the device on all device interfaces.

    - You can deploy service-specific ACLs that limit access to a specific management process (for example, a vty line).

    - You can deploy Cisco IOS Software Control Plane Protection, in which access control is provided at a virtual control plane interface.

    - You can deploy Cisco IOS Software Management Plane Protection, which enables you to designate a device's interface as the only interface over which management traffic is allowed to and from the device.

Routing Infrastructure

A routing protocol often needs to be protected to prevent access to unknown peers and to reject forged routing updates through the routing protocol. This action allows only trusted routers to participate in the routing.

Most routing protocols support both cleartext passwords (these passwords are included in updates) and hash-based algorithms to produce the message authentication code that is sent with updates. That means a shared secret is combined with information in a packet. A hash is then calculated from the combination. Therefore, knowing the packet contents and the resulting hash does not enable the reverse calculation of the original secret password. However, if the shared secret is not changed for a long time, the risk of disclosure is increased.

Different routing protocols support different authentication mechanisms, as shown in Table 22-1.

Table 22-1 *Routing Protocol Authentication Mechanisms*

Protocol	Authentication Mechanisms
Routing Information Protocol (RIPv2)	Cleartext Message Digest 5 (MD5)
Open Shortest Path First (OSPF)	MD5
Enhanced Interior Gateway Routing Protocol (EIGRP)	MD5
Border Gateway Protocol (BGP)	MD5

When implementing routing protocol authentication, follow these guidelines:

- Authenticate the routing protocol when a broadcast segment is shared by routers and untrusted end-stations.
- When possible, use HMAC-MD5 over cleartext authentication.
- Deploy strong shared secrets because keys are unlikely to be changed regularly.
- Try not to use the same secret on all routers in a domain.
- When changing keys, use key rollover, if supported.

When you are securing routing protocols, it is also recommended that you use the *passive interfaces* feature. This means that routing updates are sent only to networks that are needed. All other interfaces will not participate in routing. For example, it is recommended that you use this feature to disable routing updates in LANs.

The BGP also supports an extra check for the TTL. The feature is called TTL Security Check, which introduces EBGP protection against forged IP packets. When you enable this feature, the minimum TTL value for incoming packets is configured. BGP will establish and maintain the session only if the TTL value in the IP packet header is equal to or greater than the TTL value configured. If the value is less than the configured value, the packet is silently discarded and no ICMP message is generated.

To control the routing information that is accepted and transmitted to and from known peers, from a trusted or untrusted network, deploy routing information filtering. Two approaches are possible with route filtering. You can either accept or transmit only known good information and drop anything else, or you can drop known malicious routing information and accept or transmit everything else. Many different tools and mechanisms exist on network equipment to perform the route filtering functions, such as distribute lists, prefix lists, community lists, and redistribution with filtering.

Device Resiliency and Survivability

Routers and switches may be subject to attacks that indirectly affect the network availability. Possible attacks include DoS, Distributed DoS, flood attacks, reconnaissance, unauthorized access, and more. Several practices can be followed to preserve the resiliency and survivability of the network infrastructure devices.

You should follow these best practices to reduce the risk of attacks that may affect the network availability:

- **Disable unnecessary services:** Network devices come out-of-the-box with a list of services that are turned on. Some of the services are usually not required and therefore can be disabled. To help you determine which services should be disabled, you can identify open ports. You should also check that services like Bootstrap Protocol (BOOTP), IP source routing, Packet Assembler/Disassembler (PAD) services, IP directed broadcast, Proxy ARP, and others are disabled unless explicitly needed.

- **Protect the devices using infrastructure ACLs:** The infrastructure access control lists (iACLs) that filter traffic on the network edge are typically applied in the input direction on the interface that connects to the network users or external network. The iACL should be configured in such a way to drop and log all traffic that is destined to IP addresses of the network infrastructure devices and permit all other transit traffic.

- **Implement redundancy:** Networks are built from many hardware and software components that may fail or may be subject to attacks. Implement redundant components, which prevent single points of failure, improve availability of the network, and make it more resistant to attacks.

- **Protect the devices using CPPr/CoPP:** Control plane policing (CoPP) uses rate-limiting and drop traffic that is destined for the central processor of the network device. Policies are applied to a virtual aggregate CPU-bound queue, called the *control plane interface*. The queue receives all aggregated traffic that is destined for the control plane, management plane, and data plane that must be software-switched. Similarly, the control plane protection (CPP) rates limit and drop traffic that is destined for the CPU, but the traffic is automatically classified into three queues. They are the control plane host subinterface, which is traffic that is directly destined for one of the router interfaces (SSH, SNMP, IBGP, and so on); the control plane Cisco Express Forwarding-exception subinterface, which is traffic that is either redirected as a result of a configured input feature in the CEF packet forwarding path for process switching or directly enqueued in the control plane input queue by the interface driver (ARP, EBGP, LDP, and so on); and the control-plane transit subinterface, which is traffic that is software-switched by the CPU.

Network Policy Enforcement

Baseline network policy enforcement is primarily concerned with ensuring that traffic entering a network conforms to the network policy, including the IP address range and traffic types. Anomalous packets should be discarded as close to the edge of the network as possible to minimize the risk of exposure.

The two key steps to implement baseline network policy enforcement are

- Access edge filtering
- IP spoofing protection

All unnecessary traffic should be filtered as close to the edge as possible. You should protect access to the device itself using the infrastructure ACLs. With iACL, you control which traffic is allowed to the device. However, you should also filter traffic to the internal networks on the edge. You should use so-called transit ACLs. These ACLs are used to filter the traffic through the box. You should permit only authorized traffic to the internal networks.

IP spoofing protection involves discarding traffic that has an invalid source address. Spoofed traffic with an invalid source IP address may include traffic from either of the following:

- The RFC 1918 range, special-use IP address blocks, or the nonallocated IP address range
- The valid IP network address range, but not originated from the associated legitimate network

To limit the range of possible IP addresses for IP spoofing attacks to a valid IP network address range, implement filtering based on RFC 2827. This means that all IP addresses from the RFC 1918 range, special-use IP addresses, and the nonallocated IP address range should be filtered on the edge of the routers. You should also allow only traffic that is originated from your network block.

Several techniques exist to provide ingress traffic filtering:

- **Access control list (ACL):** ACLs are the traditional technique for filtering forged IP addresses. Because ACLs are not dynamic, you should use them in a limited manner. For example, you should filter an RFC 1918 address range, special-use IP addresses, and the nonallocated IP address range.
- **Unicast reverse pack forwarding (uRPF):** This dynamic technique discards packets with invalid source IP addresses based on a reverse-path lookup into the routing table. This technique offers minimal operational overhead and is scalable.
- **IP Source Guard:** This technique is used in switched environments to deny the use of forged MAC and source IP addresses. It is deployed on switching devices and is primarily designed for DHCP segments. Static addresses are also supported, but this technique introduces more operational complexity.
- **DHCP snooping and ARP inspection:** DHCP snooping is a security feature that validates DHCP messages; it also builds and maintains the DHCP snooping binding database. ARP inspection uses this database to validate ARP requests and responses and drop invalid ARP packets.

Switching Infrastructure

Baseline switching security is concerned with ensuring the availability of the Layer 2 switching networks. Several best practices can be followed to reduce security and other risks. The key steps to securing and preserving the switching infrastructure are

- Restricting broadcast domains
- Using spanning-tree (STP) security
- Using traffic filtering mechanisms
- Following VLAN best practices

The single LAN segment presents a single broadcast domain. This means that all unknown, multicast, and broadcast frames are forwarded through the LAN segment and may degrade performance in large networks. A single LAN segment also forms a single failure domain, which means that all clients on the LAN segment usually suffer during a failure. To avoid such problems, a good practice is to restrict the size of broadcast domain and to use hierarchical design principles to implement scalable and reliable LANs.

When implementing Layer 2 switch networks with STP, you should follow these guidelines to reduce security and operational risks:

- Disable VLAN dynamic trunk negotiation trunking on user ports.
- Use Per-VLAN Spanning Tree (PVST).
- Configure Bridge Protocol Data Units (BPDU) Guard.
- Configure STP Root Guard.
- Disable unused ports and put them into an unused VLAN.

You should implement traffic filtering mechanisms on the Layer 2 segment, such as port security or storm control. Port security can help mitigate MAC flooding and other Layer 2 CAM overflow attacks by restricting the MAC addresses that are allowed to send traffic on a particular port. Storm control can prevent broadcast, multicast, or unicast storms on the port. Storms can be caused by errors in protocol-stack implementation, mistakes in network configuration, or users issuing a DoS attack.

To prevent attacks, like VLAN hopping, you can follow common best practices:

- Restrict the VLAN IDs on trunk ports to only those VLAN IDs that are needed.
- Disable all unused ports and put them in an unused VLAN.
- Do not use VLAN 1 for anything.
- Configure all user-facing ports as nontrunking (Dynamic Trunking Protocol [DTP] off).
- Explicitly configure trunking on infrastructure ports.
- Use all tagged mode for the native VLAN on trunks.
- Set the default port status to disable.

SDN Security Considerations

Software-Defined Networks (SDN) have two properties that can be seen as attractive targets for malicious users and a source of headaches for less-prepared network operators. First is the capability to control the network with software, which is always subject to bugs and a score of other vulnerabilities. Second is the centralization of the intelligence in the controller. Anyone with access to the servers that host the control software can potentially control the entire network. The following are the most common groups of security threats associated with SDN solutions (also considered as challenges) that you must to take into consideration when designing any SDN infrastructure solution:

- **Forged or faked traffic flows:** These can be used to attack switches and controllers. This kind of attack can be malicious or nonmalicious (in the form of a faulty device). An attacker could target exhaustion of TCAMs in OpenFlow switches. Possible solutions are use of authentication systems and intrusion-detection systems.

- **Attacks on vulnerabilities in switches:** These attacks can cause quite a problem for your network. One single switch could be used to drop or slow down packets in the network, clone, or deviate network traffic (for example, for data theft purposes), or even inject traffic or forged requests to overload the controller or neighboring switches. Possible solutions are implementation of a trust management system and use of monitoring to detect abnormal behavior of network devices.

- **Attacks on control plane communications:** These attacks can generate denial of service attacks or data theft. Use of SSL/TSL does not guarantee secure communication, and this can compromise the controller-device link. The security of those communications is as strong as their weakest link, which could be a self-signed certificate, a compromised certificate authority, or vulnerable applications. Possible solutions are use of multiple trust certification authorities.

- **Attacks on and vulnerabilities in controllers:** These attacks are probably the most severe threats to SDNs. A faulty or malicious controller can compromise an entire network. A possible solution is employing diversity (of controllers, protocols, programming languages, and software), periodically refreshing the system to a clean and reliable state, and securing the controller.

- **Lack of standard mechanisms to ensure trust between the controller and management applications:** You can use mechanisms or protocols that are common in traditional networks to access the SDN network controller. These machines are already an exploitable target in current networks, the primary difference being that the threat surface as seen from a single compromised machine increases dramatically in SDNs. It becomes easy to reprogram the network from a single location. A possible solution is the use of protocols requiring double credential verification—for example, requiring credentials of two different users to access a server. It is also important that you have a plan in place such that you can recover the system and guarantee a reliable state after reboot.

- **Lack of trusted resources for forensics and remediation:** Having trusted resources in place would enable you to understand the cause of a detected problem and secure recovery. A possible solution is logging and tracing the common mechanisms in use. These logs should be stored in remote and secure environments.

Summary

- Segment network to network security zones.
- Filter traffic on zone interface points to limit flows to only allowed flows.
- Follow the architecture principles of Cisco modular network architecture when designing networks.
- Cisco offers next-generation products to meet modern security needs; they include
  - Cisco ASA 5500-X Next-Generation Firewall
  - Cisco FirePOWER Next-Generation IPS
- Enforce the fundamental elements of network security to create a strong foundation.
- Secure access to the infrastructure devices to prevent unauthorized access.
- Protect the routing infrastructure with authentication and route filtering.
- Preserve resiliency and survivability of the network devices by following best practices.
- Enforce network policy with edge filtering and IP spoofing protection.
- Protect the switching infrastructure by following best practices.

Review Questions

After answering the following questions, refer to Appendix A, "Answers to Review Questions," for the answers.

1. Which is the most appropriate description of the public zone?
   a. The zone connects external partners.
   b. The zone hosts critical data services.
   c. The zone is not under control of the organization.
   d. The zone hosts public services of the organization.

2. Match the functional modules with their proper description.

Enterprise Module	Description
Enterprise campus	High-speed infrastructure that connects all other modules
Enterprise Internet edge	Serves applications and stores data
Enterprise branch	Provides network access to users and devices
Enterprise WAN edge	Provides connectivity to the Internet
Intranet data center	Aggregates links from the branch offices
Enterprise core	Provides connectivity to users and devices at the remote locations

3. Which of the following are highlighted features of the Cisco ASA 5500-X Series Next-Generation Firewalls? (Select three.)
   a. Next-generation switching
   b. Next-generation mail gateway with advanced spam filtering
   c. Stateful firewall with advanced clustering
   d. Reverse-proxy with integrated web application firewall
   e. URL filtering
   f. Discovery and protection against advanced malware and threats

4. Match the key points that you need to focus on when securing management access with their proper descriptions.

Management access	Description
Log and account for all users	Limit the permitted methods and scope of IP addresses to connect to the device
Present legal notification	Notify users of the security policy enforcement
Authorize actions	Allow access only to the users who are allowed access
Restrict device accessibility	Restrict the actions and views that are permitted by the particular user
Ensure the confidentiality of data	Use encryption algorithms for storing and transferring sensitive data
Authenticate access	Record all accesses and actions that are performed by the connected user

5. Which of the following best describes the uRFP?
   a. It filters traffic that is based on source and destination IP addresses and ports.
   b. It discards packets with invalid source IP addresses based on reverse-path lookup in the routing table.
   c. It denies the packets with forged MAC and source IP addresses.
   d. It validates DHCP messages plus builds and maintains the DHCP snooping binding database.

6. Which are best practices to preserve resiliency and survivability of the network devices? (Select two.)
   a. Enable all possible services.
   b. Implement redundancy.
   c. Protect the devices using infrastructure ACLs.
   d. Implement IP Source Guard.
   e. Implement uRPF.

7. Which two are considered security challenges related to SDN? (Select two.)
   a. Attacks on control plane communications
   b. Attacks on data plane communications
   c. Attacks on and vulnerabilities in controllers
   d. Attacks on and vulnerabilities in LAN switches
   e. Attacks on and vulnerabilities in edge devices such as routers and firewalls

Chapter 23

Designing Firewall and IPS Solutions

Upon completing this chapter, you will be able to

- Provide an overview of firewall architectures
- Explain how to implement a firewall in a data center
- Identify the possible firewall modes and describe the corresponding network integration options
- Describe and compare virtualized and virtual firewalls
- Identify the high-availability options in firewalls
- Provide an overview of IPS architectures
- Describe FirePower IPS and data center high availability

When you are designing a network, it is important to implement proper security controls between untrusted and trusted networks. The firewalls can provide stateful packet filtering services, and they can also be extended with intrusion prevention system (IPS) devices to target modern security threats. This chapter describes common firewall and IPS architectures, high-availability modes, and firewall virtualization.

Firewall Architectures

Firewalls are used to protect resources and can be used in many locations in the enterprise reference architecture, such as the Internet edge, data center, or branch edge. When you start designing your firewall architecture, you should first collect business and security requirements and then design the architecture of the network accordingly. The design of network security components including firewalls can vary from network to network based on several variables, such as business type, applications requirements, criticality of the applications, and enterprise security policy standards; however, in general, the two common firewall architectures are as follows (see Figure 23-1):

- **Single-tier firewall architecture:** This is the most common firewall architecture, where a firewall has an inside and outside zone. The firewall can also host one or more demilitarized zones (DMZ) to provide public services to enterprises. This architecture is relatively simple and provides lower implementation and operational costs. But a single device is responsible for providing the security of the internal resources. If an attacker is able to compromise the firewall, the security of these resources is at risk.

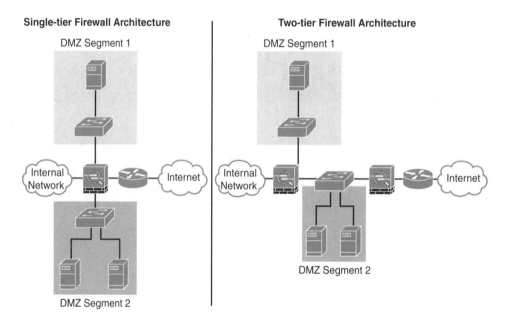

Figure 23-1 *Common Firewall Design Architectures*

- **Two-tier firewall architecture:** In this architecture, two firewalls are used to protect resources. One of the firewalls acts like an internal firewall, whereas the other acts as an external firewall. DMZs are located between both firewalls. An internal firewall is connected to the internal network, whereas an external firewall is connected to the external network. This architecture can increase the overall security level of the firewall system because an attacker must compromise the two firewalls to gain access to the protected resources. But this architecture increases complexity and cost from implementation and operational points of view.

The firewall system can also be extended with an IPS. The typical location of the IPS is directly after the internal interface of the firewall system. In this location, the IPS is able to see all traffic that is passing between internal networks and external segments. You can deploy the IPS in inline or promiscuous mode. When it is deployed in inline mode, traffic passes through the IPS, and the IPS is able to act according to the security policy. The IPS in promiscuous mode receives only a copy of the traffic and cannot block attacks in real time.

To provide extra security on the application layer, you can implement various proxy servers. A web proxy server can enforce the security policy for web browsing. An e-mail proxy server can control spam and other threats that are sent through an e-mail service. The web application firewall is responsible for protecting web applications that the organization publishes. The typical location of these services is in the DMZ segment. Figure 23-2 shows a typical DMZ design with different security services.

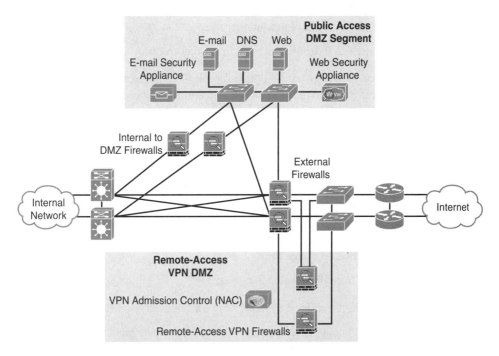

Figure 23-2 *Typical DMZ Design with Various Security Services*

A firewall can be deployed in different locations in the network. Typical network segments where you are able to find firewalls include the Internet edge, data center, and branch offices. When you are designing a firewall system, the location of the firewall is important due to different requirements.

The main purpose of the firewall in the Internet edge zone is to protect internal resources from external threats. Firewalls should offer stateful inspection in combination with deep packet inspection. Usually, firewalls host one or many DMZs to provide public services for outside hosts. The firewall must provide enough bandwidth to be able to serve the links that are provided by the ISP.

When you want to deploy a firewall service in the data center network, an excellent filtering point is located in the aggregation layer of the network. The firewall in the data center must provide high-throughput services. Cisco offers the Cisco Adaptive Security Appliance (ASA) 5585-X series firewall to meet high-throughput demands providing 10 Gbps of stateful packet filtering. It is usually a good practice to deploy the firewall in transparent mode. In this mode, the firewalls are configured in a Layer 2 mode and will bridge traffic between the interfaces. It is recommended that you deploy the firewalls in active-active design, which allows load sharing across the infrastructure.

Firewalls in branch offices enable the segmentation and enforcement of different security policy domains. These firewalls provide enhanced protection from unauthorized access that may be required if networks have different security level zones. Firewalls also offer more advanced inspection than access control lists (ACL). This inspection is especially needed when the branch office has local Internet access.

Cisco offers two options to integrate a firewall in the branch office network:

- **IOS Firewall:** A cost-effective firewall that is typically implemented in the branch edge router. It can be deployed as an interface-based firewall or as a zone-based firewall (ZBFW).
- **ASA:** A dedicated firewall enabling a highly scalable, high-performance, high-availability, and fully featured deployment.

Virtualized Firewalls

Firewall virtualization is mainly used in data center networks. The advantage of using firewall virtualization is scalability and flexibility. The use of automation tools can also reduce the operational workload and costs.

There are two types of firewall virtualization:

- **Multicontext mode:** Virtualized firewalls run on a single physical ASA appliance.
- **Virtual firewalls:** Virtual firewalls are software-only firewalls running in a hypervisor (virtual machine's manager).

The multicontext mode was originally designed for multitenant deployments. It is also commonly deployed in virtual routing and forwarding (VRF) environments, where VLANs map to VRFs, and each VRF has its own virtual firewall.

Virtual firewalls are mainly designed for cloud environments, where scalability and flexibility are the goals of designing a security infrastructure. Virtual firewalls are deployed directly on a hypervisor as a virtual machine.

Cisco offers three types of virtual firewalls:

- Virtual Security Gateway (VSG)
- ASA 1000V
- ASAv

You can partition a single ASA into multiple virtualized firewalls that are called security context. Each context is an independent firewall with its own security policy, interfaces, and administrators. Having multiple contexts is like having standalone firewalls.

When you deploy Cisco ASA in multicontext mode, the physical appliance host system configuration, which identifies basic settings for the security appliance, includes a list of contexts and the physical settings of its interfaces. By default, all contexts have unlimited access to the resources. To preserve the resources of an appliance, a good practice is to limit access to the resources using context resource management.

In multicontext mode, you can map one physical interface to one context when physical separation from another context is required. You can also map one physical interface to several contexts so that contexts share a single physical interface. A classifier algorithm is used to determine which context should process a particular inbound packet:

- **Unique interfaces:** If only one interface is associated with the ingress interface, the security appliance classifies the packet into that context.

- **Unique MAC addresses:** If multiple contexts share an interface, the classifier uses the packet's destination MAC address. The classifier compares it to the interface MAC address of each context sharing the interface. Because the shared interfaces do not have unique MAC addresses, you should configure unique MAC addresses, which can be configured manually or automatically.

- **NAT configuration:** If multiple firewall contexts share an interface (physical interface) and you do not configure unique MAC addresses, the classifier intercepts the packet. It performs destination IP address lookup and NAT configuration in each context.

You can implement all security context in routed mode or transparent mode, or you can implement some contexts in routed mode and some in transparent mode. The mixed mode is supported from version 8.5.(1).

Virtual Security Gateway (VSG) is a Layer 2 firewall that looks like a "bump in the wire" and runs as a virtual machine on a hypervisor. It is similar to a physical ASA that runs in transparent mode. The supported hypervisors are VMware or HyperV. VSG is managed via Virtual Network Management Center (VNMC). To implement VSG, you must first deploy Nexus 1000V, which is a requirement for implementation. VSG is typically implemented to protect east-west traffic, which is traffic between different servers in the access layer. Traffic can be in the same subnet or between VLANs.

Similar to VSG is the ASA 1000V, which is also a virtual firewall that runs on a hypervisor as a virtual machine. This software-only version runs ASA software, but with limited features. It is an edge firewall that complements the VSG. Traffic can, for example, first go through Cisco ASA 1000V, providing tenant edge security, and then go through VSG to provide security between virtual machines. To implement Cisco ASA 1000V, you also must implement Cisco Nexus 1000V.

Cisco Adaptive Security Virtual Appliance (ASAv) provides a complete ASA firewall running as a virtual machine. The ASAv does not require Nexus 1000V. Almost all ASA features are supported except ASA clustering, multicontext mode, EtherChannel interfaces, and active/active failover, which requires multicontext mode. ASAv is managed as a traditional ASA with CLI, Adaptive Security Device Manager (ASDM), or Cisco

Security Manager (CSM). ASAv supports the representational state transfer application programming interface (REST API) for programmatic management. It supports deployment in routed or transparent firewall mode and is usually deployed in multitenant environments, which requires scalability, stateful access control, or different types of VPN solutions. It can replace ASA 1000V and can also be used to complement VSG.

Table 23-1 compares the different Cisco Virtual Firewall models.

Table 23-1 *Comparison of Cisco Virtual Firewall Models*

ASAv	ASA 1000V	Virtual Security Gateway
Nexus 1000V not required	Nexus 1000V required	Nexus 1000V required
Routed and transparent mode	Routed mode only	Transparent mode only
Support for static and dynamic routing	Static routing only	Routing not supported
Support site-to-site IPsec and remote-access VPN	Supports site-to-site IPsec VPN	No VPN supported

Case Study 1: Separation of Application Tiers

Your e-commerce application follows a three-tiered functional model, consisting of web, application, and database tiers, as shown in Figure 23-3.

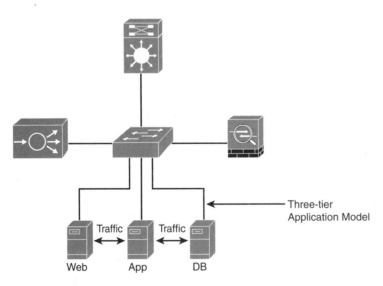

Figure 23-3 *Three-tiered e-Commerce Application Functional Model*

Servers in the web tier provide the public facing, front-end presentation services for the application. Servers in the application and database tiers function as the middleware and back-end processing components. Applications that are meant to be accessible over the public Internet represent the broadest scope and thus a major security concern.

The network-centric security model is the traditional approach. This method involves the use of VLANs within the Layer 2 domain to logically separate each tier of servers. Intertenant communication is established through routing at the aggregation layer. The network-centric method lends itself to designs in which some or all services are applied from outside the compute tier of the infrastructure. Flows between the VLANs are routed in the aggregation layer. Traffic typically flows through firewalls and load balancers before and in between the application tiers, as shown in Figure 23-4.

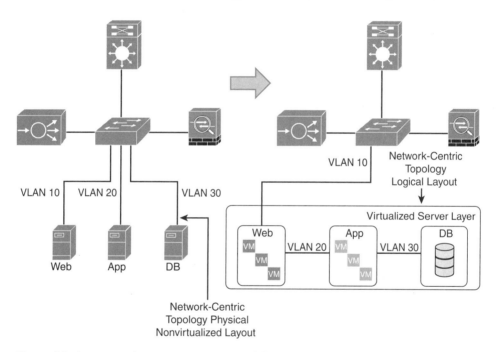

Figure 23-4 *Network-centric Security Model*

The server-centric method relies on the use of separate VM virtual network interface cards (vNICs) to daisychain server tiers together. This method relies on the virtualized server layer, leveraging the virtual switch (such as Cisco Nexus 1000v) strengths to classify and more optimally redirect traffic flows at the virtual access switching level of the infrastructure. Although this approach seems reasonable in theory, in practice, you will soon discover that it is too simplistic. One problem is that applications are complex; applications do not necessarily follow a strict hierarchical traffic flow pattern. Some applications may be written to function in a database-centric fashion, with communications flows to the middleware (application) and presentation (web) tiers from a database core. Another problem, particularly common for enterprise scenarios, is that some application flows may need to extend outside the private cloud tenant or workgroup container, across organizational boundaries, and perhaps from site to site.

Finally, application tiers may themselves be distributed, either logically or physically, across the data center or in a private case, across the enterprise campus. The result is unnecessary and suboptimal proliferation of policy enforcement points. Traffic may needlessly be required to traverse many firewalls on the path end to end from source to destination. As we learned in Chapter 13, "Cisco Application-Centric Infrastructure (ACI)," the policy model approach of the Cisco ACI along with service insertion automation on top of the spine-leaf network architecture offer more effective and efficient communication in such scenarios.

Securing East-West Traffic

While east-west in nature, server-server traffic still has to traverse up from access through the aggregation layer if you want to enforce security policies with the firewall appliance. It becomes even more obvious that the described traffic flow is suboptimal when the two servers reside as virtual machines (VM) on a single physical host. In that case, traffic has to flow from physical host through access layer to aggregation layer, just to be filtered by a firewall and forwarded back south to the same physical host, as shown in Figure 23-5.

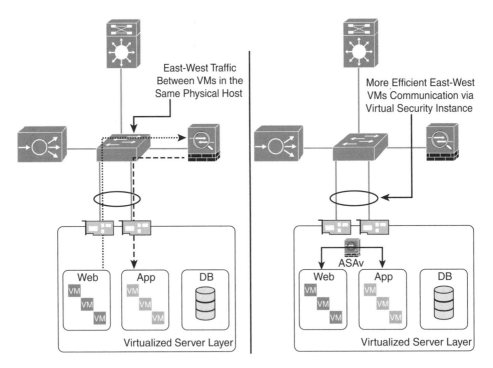

Figure 23-5 *East-West Traffic Between VMs*

It makes more sense to apply security policies on a physical host with a virtual firewall appliance, such as the Cisco Adaptive Security Virtual Appliance (ASAv) or Cisco Virtual Security Gateway (VSG). Virtual firewall appliances enforce policy to inter-VM traffic, without the need to hairpin traffic to physical firewalls. Cisco ASAv provides a comprehensive suite of virtualized security services that are designed specifically for DC environments: firewalling, NGFW, NGIPS, VPN, e-mail, and Web security services. Cisco VSG also supports dynamic provisioning of security policies and trust zones during VM instantiation and policy portability during VM movement. The goal is to apply the right security services as close as possible to the transaction, provide adequate and dynamic scalability, and deliver resiliency within the data center.

High performance of virtual firewalls is achieved by initializing multiple virtual firewalls as needed and leverage hybrid deployments with existing physical firewalls. To reduce management overhead, you can provision and manage virtual firewalls with SDN controllers, such as Cisco APIC, making them a perfect solution of an SDN-driven data center.

Case Study 2: Implementing Firewalls in a Data Center

To satisfy the latest security requirements for this case study, the enterprise has to deploy stateful packet filtering in the data center. The data center hosts a few hundred virtual machines on several servers. You must decide how to implement the firewall in the data center.

Note In this case study, the data center design is based on the multitier (three tier) architecture depicted in Figure 23-6.

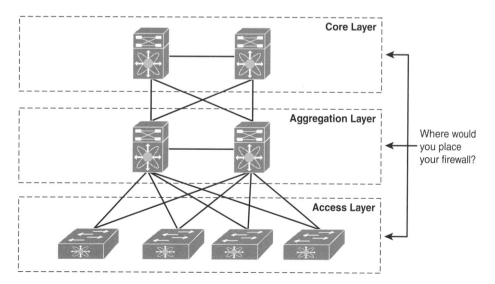

Figure 23-6 *Targeted Data Center Architecture*

The data center network is designed in a three-level architecture. The routing is already implemented between the network core and aggregation layer. The switch virtual interfaces (SVI) for VLANs in the access layer are located in the aggregation layer and represent the gateways for hosts. All IP addresses are already assigned. The first question you should think about is, "How do you integrate a firewall in such an environment?" Take into consideration the information provided earlier about the DC network architecture.

The best location to implement a firewall in the data center is in the aggregation layer (see Figure 23-7). It presents a convenient filtering point and the first layer of protection for the data center. The firewall must meet the high-performance requirements by providing 10 Gbps of stateful filtering.

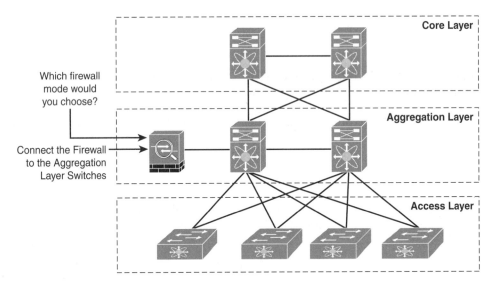

Figure 23-7 *Firewall Placement in the DC Network*

The second key question that you need to think about here is, "Which firewall mode would you choose for implementation?" A firewall is traditionally implemented as a routing hop and acts as a default gateway for hosts that are connected to one of the interfaces. Alternatively, a firewall can be implemented in such a way that Layer 3 devices do not see it.

A firewall can be implemented in the existing network in two different forwarding modes (see Figure 23-8):

- **Routed mode:** In routed mode, a firewall acts as a routing hop and presents itself as a router for hosts or routers that are connected to one of its networks. Traffic forwarding across the firewall is based on the destination IP address. To integrate a routed firewall into the existing network, you must change any addressing on the devices that are connected to the firewall. A firewall must participate in the routing protocol, or you must implement static routes. You also need to use NAT when you are connecting to the public networks.

- **Transparent mode:** In transparent mode, a firewall is a Layer 2 device that acts like a "bump in the wire." It is not seen as a routed hop to a connected device. When you use a transparent firewall, the same subnet is connected to the inside and outside interfaces. The firewall performs transparent bridging between the two interfaces. Traffic forwarding is based on the destination MAC address. Therefore, a firewall must support basic switching functionalities like MAC learning and similar. Because the transparent firewall is not a routing hop, readdressing is not needed when implementing the firewall in the existing network. This simplifies the implementation and network manageability.

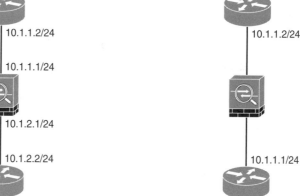

Figure 23-8 *Firewall Modes*

Transparent firewall architecture is popular in data center environments, where readdressing is often not possible and stateful filtering covers all basic security requirements, as illustrated in Figure 23-9.

Note When you are implementing a firewall in Internet edge or branch office segments, it is usually implemented in routed mode. The reason for this is that the firewall must participate in routing protocols, or static routes must be used. NAT is often needed in such deployments to translate internal IP addresses to the public addresses.

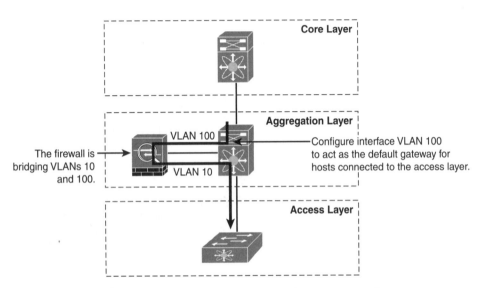

Figure 23-9 *Adding a Firewall in Transparent Mode a DC Network*

Case Study 3: Firewall High Availability

In this case study, the enterprise is hosting applications in the data center. The applications are protected with a firewall that provides stateful filtering. The goal of the enterprise is to upgrade the firewall system with high availability.

The firewall system is currently implemented with a single firewall providing stateful filtering. The firewall is connected to a pair of Nexus switches on the outside zone and to a pair of Nexus switches on the inside zone. The firewall is connected to the switches with EtherChannel technology, which provides interface-level high availability, as depicted in Figure 23-10.

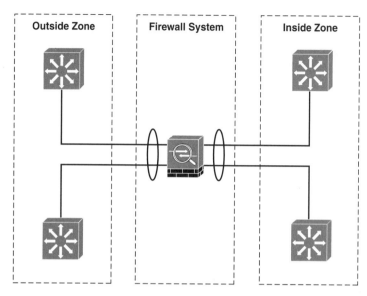

Figure 23-10 *Nonredundant Firewall Connectivity Design*

EtherChannel enables you to assign up to 16 interfaces to a bundle. (Only eight interfaces can be active; the remaining interfaces can act as standby links in case of interface failure.) The bundle acts as a single interface and traffic is load-balanced between ports. It is a best practice to use the Link Aggregation Control Protocol (LACP) for EtherChannel creation, which dynamically adds and removes interfaces to EtherChannel.

In this case, you have connected the firewall to multiple Nexus switches via EtherChannel. Virtual port-channel (vPC) technology is used on a pair of Nexus switches to provide Multichassis EtherChannel (MCE). Alternatively, you can use a virtual switching system (VSS) if you are using Catalyst switches. You do not need extra configuration on ASA to support VSS or vPC.

An alternative solution to provide interface-level high availability is to implement redundant interfaces. Redundant interfaces aggregate two physical interfaces into one logical interface. One of the redundant pair members becomes the active interface, and the other is the backup interface. Traffic is forwarded only on the active member. When the active member goes down, the passive member takes over. This mode does not support link aggregation and can be deployed only in interface pairs. You can configure up to eight pairs of redundant interfaces. It is a legacy technology that has been widely replaced with EtherChannel.

To provide unit-level high availability, you study the option to implement active/passive failover mode, where one firewall is actively forwarding traffic while the other is waiting for failover, as shown in Figure 23-11. In this mode, you connect two identical ASA devices in failover. ASA devices are connected with a dedicated failover link and optionally a state link. Data interfaces must be connected to the same broadcast domain. The ASA firewall is managed centrally on a primary device, and the configuration is automatically replicated to the secondary device. When you use stateful failover, the primary ASA device also replicates the connection table. Stateful failover is recommended to preserve all connections during failover. The state link that is used to replicate connections and other stateful data must be as fast as the fastest data link.

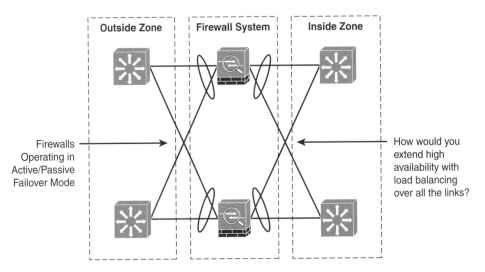

Figure 23-11 *ASA Firewall Active/Passive Failover Mode*

You can also implement active/active mode, which is supported only in multiple-context mode. You must manually add some context to the primary ASA device and some to the secondary. When failure occurs, all contexts are transferred to a single device.

How would you additionally upgrade high availability? Your goal is to meet the following requirements:

- High availability
- Scalability
- Utilization of all links
- High throughput
- Manageability

A better solution is to implement firewall clustering. In firewall clustering, multiple firewalls are joined in a cluster and act as one device. This solution offers the following:

- **High availability:** If one device in a cluster fails, the other devices take over.
- **Scalability:** You can always add an extra device in the future if there is a need for more throughput.

- **Utilization of all links:** All devices in a cluster are active devices; therefore, all links are utilized.

- **High throughput:** The throughput of a cluster is around 70 percent of combined throughput of all devices in a cluster.

- **Manageability:** A cluster acts as one device, and it is therefore also managed as one device.

Cisco ASA clustering, introduced in the 9.0 release, enables you to bundle multiple ASA devices into a single cluster. The data traffic is load-balanced between cluster members. The cluster acts as a single firewall, which means that configuration is managed on a single device and is synchronized to other devices in the cluster. When you combine multiple units into a cluster, you will get around 70 percent of the combined throughput. It means that you will get approximately 56 Gbps of throughput when you combine eight ASA 5585-X with SSP-40, which offers 10 Gbps. When you deploy a cluster, you must dedicate at least one hardware interface as the cluster control link, which is used for control traffic, monitoring, and state replication. You must properly size your cluster control link to match the expected throughput of each member. For example, if you use ASA 5585-X with SSP-60, which can pass 14 Gbps, your cluster control link should also pass 14 Gbps. Therefore, you could use two 10-gigabit Ethernet interfaces in EtherChannel for the cluster control link. It is recommended that you use local EtherChannel on each ASA for a control link to provide redundancy and aggregation, as illustrated in Figure 23-12.

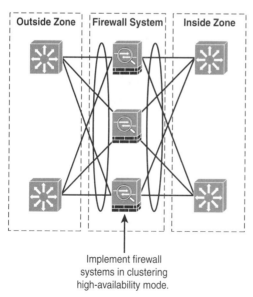

ASA Clustering Benefits:
- The capability to aggregate traffic to achieve higher throughput
- The capability to scale the number of ASA appliances into one logical firewall within the data center architecture
- True active/active model; in multicontext mode, every member for all contexts of the cluster are capable of forwarding every traffic flow
- Can force stateful flows to take a more symmetrical path, which improves predictability and session consistency
- Can operate in either Layer 2 or Layer 3 mode
- Supports single and multiple contexts (firewall virtualization)
- Clusterwide statistics are provided to track resource usage
- A single configuration is maintained across all units in the cluster using automatic configuration sync

Figure 23-12 *ASA Firewall Clustering*

You have decided to implement firewall clustering, where ASA devices in a cluster act as one device. Spanned EtherChannel is selected as the load-balancing method to forward traffic to the members of the cluster from the Nexus switches. You will still use the vPC technology on Nexus switches to provide Multichassis EtherChannel.

You can choose from three methods to load-balance traffic to the members of the cluster:

- **Spanned EtherChannel:** ASA uses a logical link aggregation construct called the Cluster Link Aggregation Control Protocol (cLACP). It is designed to extend standard LACP to multiple devices so that it can support span-cluster. EtherChannels need to span across the cluster. cLACP allows link aggregation between one switch, or a pair of switches, to multiple (more than two) ASAs in a cluster. It is the recommended method, which offers faster failure discovery, faster convergence time, and ease of configuration. In spanned EtherChannel, one or more interfaces are grouped into an EtherChannel that spans all units in the cluster. It can be configured in both routed and transparent firewall modes. It is recommended that you use the source and destination IP address hashing algorithm for load balancing. You can also use spanned EtherChannel with VSS or vPC. You can configure up to 32 active links in the spanned EtherChannel, but this feature requires that both switches in the vPC support EtherChannels with 16 active links. For switches that support 8 active links, you can configure up to 16 active links in the spanned EtherChannel when connecting to two switches in a VSS/vPC (see Figure 23-13).

- **Policy-Based Routing (PBR):** This method is supported in routed mode only, and it can be configured when you use individual interfaces on an ASA device. It means that interfaces are normal routed interfaces, where each interface has its own local IP address. The load balancing is configured on the upstream switch or router with PBR.

- **Equal-Cost Multipath Routing:** Similar to PBR, equal-cost multipath routing is supported in routed mode only, and it can also be configured on individual interfaces. To achieve load balancing, you must configure your routing on the upstream switch or router in such a way that traffic is forwarded based on the routing table in the network. It is recommended that you use dynamic routing instead of static.

Case Study 3: Firewall High Availability   725

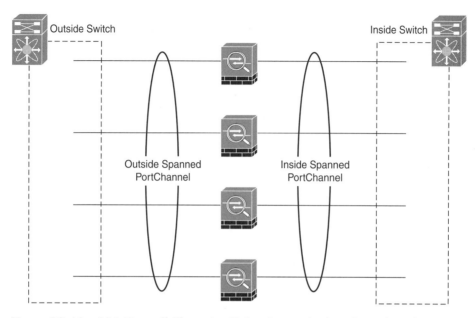

Figure 23-13 *ASA Firewall Clustering Using Spanned EtherChannel Mode*

> **Note** It is important to consider firewall connectivity when deployed in routed mode and the aggregation layer is using vPC. Unlike VSS, dynamic routing over vPC or vPC+ is not supported; therefore, you might need to consider using static routes or change the connectivity model of the firewalls, as shown in Figure 23-14.

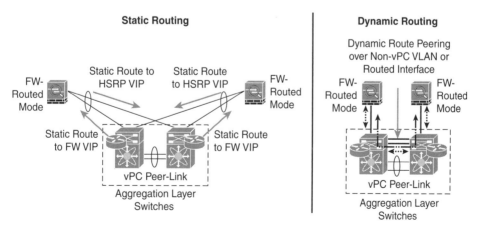

Figure 23-14 *Firewall Routing Design Options with vPC*

IPS Architectures

To provide protection against modern threats, you can integrate components such as IPS. Some firewalls already support IPS functionalities natively or using expansion modules. Alternatively, you can deploy IPS as a standalone appliance running on dedicated hardware or as virtual device.

You can deploy IPS on two locations relative to a firewall (see Figure 23-15):

- **Outside zone:** When you deploy the IPS on the outside of the firewall, the IPS may catch attacks and attempts before they even hit the firewall. This way, you can detect new attacks or trends and provide additional data for correlating with the other sensor. However, you will probably get many false positives. The reason is that you usually tune IPS in such deployments to be very sensitive to detect unwanted traffic. Because there will probably be many false positives, IPS is usually not used to prevent attacks.

- **Inside zone:** When you deploy the IPS on the inside of the firewall, the IPS will detect attacks that pass the firewall from outside to inside. This implementation also prevents suspicious traffic from leaving your network. The inside of the firewall is the typical location of the IPS. Because only the traffic that the firewall permits is inspected, you will probably receive fewer false positives.

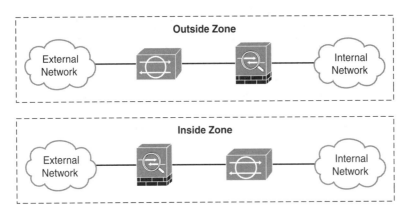

Figure 23-15 *IPS Placement*

Cisco FirePOWER is a next-generation IPS (NGIPS). There are two options in which you can deploy Cisco FirePOWER:

- As a service module in ASA
- As a standalone appliance

You can deploy Cisco FirePOWER IPS as a service module in Cisco ASA. This module is also known as ASA SFR. Cisco ASA with FirePOWER Services provides

- Precise application visibility and control (AVC). More than 3000 application-layer and risk-based controls can invoke tailored IPS threat-detection policies to improve security effectiveness.

- Highly effective threat prevention and a full contextual awareness of users, infrastructure, applications, and content to help you detect multivector threats and automate the defense response.

- Reputation- and category-based URL filtering. This filtering provides comprehensive alerting and control over suspect web traffic. It enforces policies on hundreds of millions of URLs in more than 80 categories.

- Advanced malware protection. Effective breach detection with low total cost of ownership (TCO) offers protection value. Discover, understand, and stop malware and emerging threats missed by other security layers.

You can implement this module when ASA is in single- or multiple-context mode, and in router or transparent mode. The module has a basic command-line interface (CLI) for initial configuration and troubleshooting. You configure the security policy with FireSIGHT Management Center, which can be hosted on a separate FireSIGHT Management Center appliance or as a virtual appliance running on VMware server. The module can be a hardware module (on the ASA 5585-X only) or a software module. The hardware module has separate management and console ports.

You can deploy the module in two modes (see Figure 23-16):

- **Inline mode:** The traffic is sent to the firewall, and all checks are executed on the firewall before traffic is forwarded to the ASA FirePOWER module. The module inspects the traffic. After dropping undesired traffic and taking any other actions that are applied by the policy, traffic is returned to the ASA for further processing.

- **Monitor-only mode:** A copy of the traffic is sent to the device, but it is not returned to the ASA. The module applies security policy to the traffic, and you are able to see what the device would have done to the traffic if operating in inline mode.

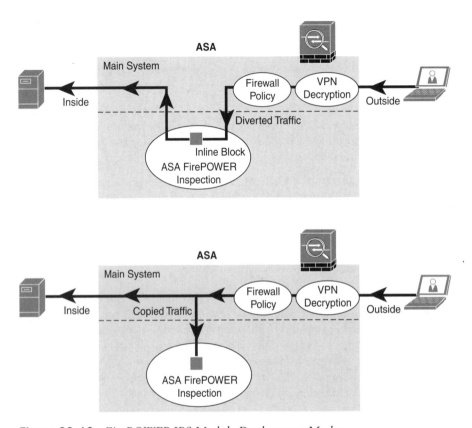

Figure 23-16 *FirePOWER IPS Module Deployment Modes*

> **Note** You cannot configure both monitor-only mode and normal inline mode at the same time on the ASA. Only one type of security policy is allowed. In multiple-context mode, you cannot configure monitor-only mode for some contexts and regular inline mode for the others.

When you deploy a standalone Cisco FirePOWER IPS appliance, you can implement the device in either passive or inline mode. In the passive deployment, you deploy the system out of band from the flow of network traffic. In an inline deployment, you configure the system transparently on a network segment by binding two ports together.

In a passive IPS deployment, the IPS monitors traffic flowing across a network using a switch SPAN or mirror port, as shown in Figure 23-16. The SPAN or mirror port sends a copy of the traffic from other ports on the switch. It allows visibility of the traffic without being on the traffic path, which means that this deployment does not affect the traffic itself. The weakness of such a deployment is that the IPS can take only limited actions on malicious traffic. The IPS cannot provide blocking or traffic shaping, for example. The IPS does not send traffic on SPAN or mirror ports.

In inline IPS deployment, you deploy the IPS transparently between two network segments by binding two ports together. It means that the IPS is on the traffic path, as shown in Figure 23-17. When you deploy the IPS in inline mode, the IPS is able to block or shape traffic, attacks, and other malicious traffic. Inline interfaces receive all traffic and must also transmit the traffic on the other interface. The IPS applies configured security policy to the traffic.

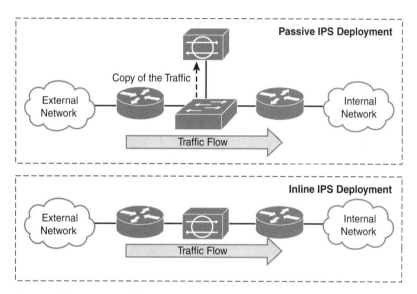

Figure 23-17 *Standalone Cisco FirePOWER IPS Deployment Modes*

You can configure interfaces on an IPS device in inline mode as switched interfaces or as routed interfaces. In switched interfaces, the appliance provides packet switching between two or more networks, whereas in routed mode, IPS is seen as a routed hop. You must assign IP addresses on each interface, and packet-forwarding decisions are done according to the destination address. When you implement devices in routed mode, you must define static routes or implement a routing protocol to provide routing information.

Case Study 4: Building a Secure Campus Edge Design (Internet and Extranet Connectivity)

Enterprises usually want to focus on their core business. They often outsource some activities to their partners. To efficiently cooperate with partners, enterprises often need some data exchange. Many security challenges exist when enterprises expose parts of the network to their partners. This case focuses on extranet challenges and solutions.

Upon completing this case study, you will be able to

- Explain campus edge design on a case study.
- Identify the challenges of connecting external partners.

- Identify connectivity options.
- Explain extranet topology using the remote LAN model.
- Explain extranet topology using the interconnect model.
- Describe security and multitenant segmentation.

Campus Edge

You work as a network architect, and you have received the task to redesign the Campus Edge network for a medium-sized company.

The new Campus Edge network must have the following characteristics:

- **Provide connectivity to and from the Internet:** You will be hosting public services in your DMZ network. These services would have to be accessed from the Internet on your own public address space. You also need to provide Internet access for internal users and services.

- **Enforce a security policy for network traffic between the internal network, DMZ networks, and the Internet:** The headquarters and remote-site networks are internal zones, and the Internet is considered an external zone. The DMZ networks at the Internet edge fall somewhere in between the internal and external classification. The design must support the following security capabilities:
    - Hide internal network addresses by using NAT
    - Permit internal network access to the Internet
    - Permit internal network access to DMZ networks
    - Permit Internet access to DMZ networks
    - Block all other traffic

- **Provide resilient Internet access:** A Campus Edge network needs to be tolerant of the most commonly observed failure types:
    - In the event of hardware failure, the system must provide failover from active to standby units.
    - The Campus Edge network must reroute traffic from the primary ISP to the secondary in case of failure.

- **Detect and block inbound attacks to the Internet services in the DMZ:** Your new Campus Edge must detect and block attacks to your public services that are located in the DMZ. Monitoring for and blocking network-based attacks improve the reliability and performance of an organization's web presence and keep resources available for partners and clients.

Case Study 4: Building a Secure Campus Edge Design (Internet and Extranet Connectivity)

- **Detect malicious traffic on the internal networks:** Monitoring and detecting worms, viruses, and other types of malware are essential to maintaining a high-performing network. You must prevent your network from becoming the source of attacks.

Your first step is to design a network for connecting to the Internet. Your goal is to create a resilient design with a primary and a backup Internet connection. If the Internet access via the primary link is lost, the design will automatically fail over to the secondary link. To implement the resilient design, you will deploy two routers. Each router will be connected to one ISP. Edge routers are connected to the enterprise network through outside switches.

You have provider-independent IP address space. To announce your prefix, you need BGP routing at your edge network. You have agreed with both service providers to establish BGP sessions with the provider routers. As you know from Chapter 5, "Border Gateway Protocol Design," this option enables you to announce your prefix to the rest of the Internet. In this scenario, both ISPs are sending only the default route to your edge router through EBGP. You have also established the internal BGP between both edge routers, as illustrated in Figure 23-18. In addition, it is recommended that you consider establishing a direct IBGP session between the edge routers. As you learned from Chapter 5, this IBGP session will help ensure that both routers are always fully converged in the event of one ISP link or an EBGP peering session failing.

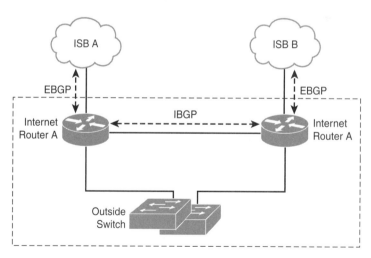

Figure 23-18 *Internet Connectivity at the Campus Edge*

The next step is to add a layer of network security to the Internet connectivity by connecting firewalls to the Campus Edge network. Because one of the design requirements is to have a resilient Internet access design, you will need to implement two firewalls. The firewalls will be configured in an active/standby mode for high availability. Thus, in case of any firewall hardware failure, the impact to the Internet access will be minimal. The firewalls will be implemented in routed mode because at the Internet edge you may need to use the firewall to perform some tasks that require this mode, such as

Network Address Translation (NAT) or VPN tunnel termination. You will connect both firewalls using the Multichassis EtherChannel (MEC) connectivity model. The advantage of such a connection is that traffic will be load-balanced between links. This design will also offer a resilient solution for cases in which one of the links fails.

You will use your own public address space for the outside network. This solution will remove the need for NAT features on the edge routers. Therefore, you do not need any routes to the RFC 1918 address space in the outside segment.

You will use Open Shortest Path First (OSPF) to distribute the default route to the firewalls from the edge routers. To implement such a solution, you need to add your internal interfaces of the edge routers to the OSPF process. You will also need to add outside interfaces of the firewalls to the OSPF process, as illustrated in Figure 23-19. You will announce only the default route that is received through BGP to the edge routers. To prevent equal-multipath routing, as it is not desirable in this case, you need to announce the default route from the secondary edge router with the worse metric. With OSPF, you will receive a resilient solution with fast failover to the secondary provider in case of failure.

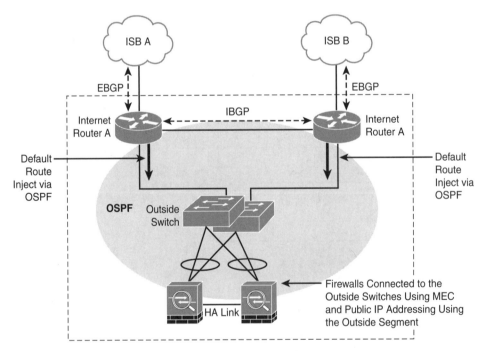

Figure 23-19 *Routing Between Internet Edge Routers and the Firewalls*

As part of the Campus Edge design, you have several public services that need to be accessed from the Internet. The traffic is tightly restricted between DMZ to the other parts of the network. To connect the DMZ to the Campus Edge network, you will deploy

Case Study 4: Building a Secure Campus Edge Design (Internet and Extranet Connectivity)

a pair of switches. You will connect firewalls to those switches by using EtherChannel to provide high availability. The DMZ servers will also be connected to these switches, as shown in Figure 23-20.

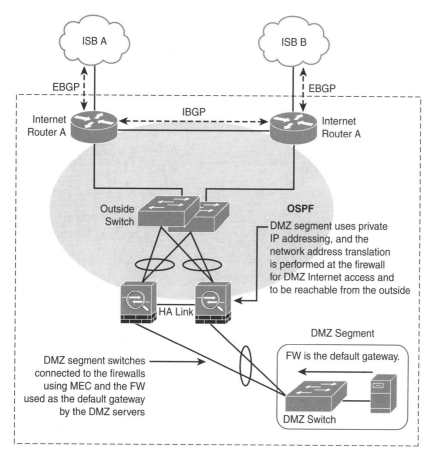

Figure 23-20 *DMZ Connectivity*

You will use private address space for the servers in the DMZ. You will then perform Network Address Translation on the firewall to enable access to the services from the Internet. The solution with NAT will offer more flexibility because internal DMZ addressing is hidden from the public Internet. You can, for example, change the IP address of the servers in the DMZ network, and you need to change only the NAT setting on the firewall. The DMZ servers will have the default route to the DMZ interfaces.

To provide connectivity to the internal network, you will connect Campus Edge firewalls to the distribution layer of the internal network, and you should also use Multichassis EtherChannel to provide an optimized level of resiliency.

Chapter 23: Designing Firewall and IPS Solutions

From a Layer 3 routing design point of view, you should implement the default route on the distribution layer switches that will point to the Campus Edge firewalls. Also, you need to implement static routes to the RFC 1918 address space of the internal network, on the firewalls. Those routes will point to the distribution layer switches. The firewalls will offer NAT services to the internal hosts (see Figure 23-21).

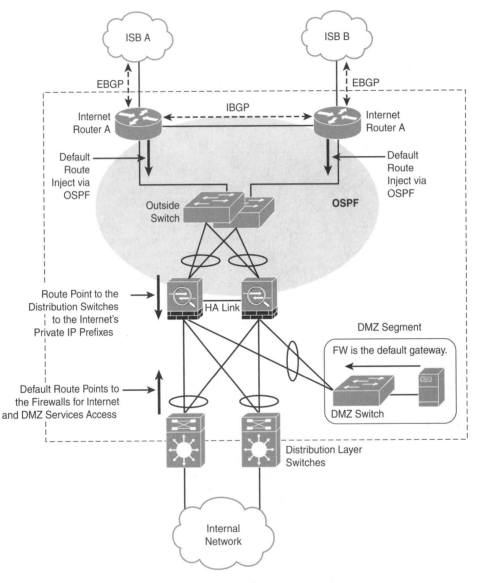

Figure 23-21 *Connectivity to the Internal Network*

You want to minimize the impact of the network intrusions; therefore, you will deploy IPS. The IPS technology complements the firewall and inspects traffic that is permitted by the firewall policy. You will use the service modules in the firewalls for an IPS solution (such as Cisco FirePOWER IPS as a service module in Cisco ASA). IPS services that are integrated into the firewall rely on the firewalls for high-availability services. The firewalls in the Internet edge are deployed in an active/standby configuration. If the primary firewall fails, the secondary firewall will take over all firewall operations. The IPS module in the secondary firewall will take care of traffic inspection.

You need to tell your firewalls which traffic will be forwarded through the IPS module. You will redirect all traffic to your public services in DMZ through IPS. You will also inspect traffic from your internal traffic to the Internet. You do not want your network to become a source of attacks to other public systems (see Figure 23-22).

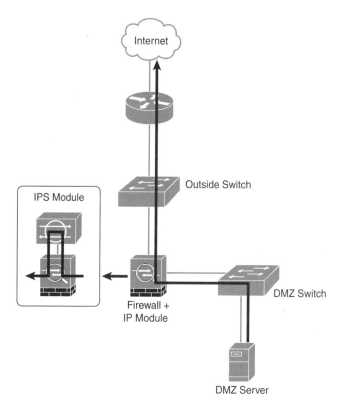

Figure 23-22 *Adding IPS Service Modules to the Campus Edge Firewalls*

From an application-layer security point of view, you should also consider implementing a web security policy. In this scenario, you will use Cisco Web Security Appliance (WSA) to implement a security policy for web browsing. The WSA offers a combination of web usage controls with category- and reputation-based control, URL filtering, malware filtering, and data protection. From a design point of view, you can connect the Cisco

WSA on the inside network to the distribution layer switches or connect it to the DMZ switch. The latter option provides more scalable design because the WSA can service multiple distribution blocks of the internal network, as shown in Figure 23-23. In this scenario, you will use explicit proxy deployment, in which you must tell the client application to use a web proxy. With such a configuration, the client application will send all requests for the Internet to the web proxy. The web proxy will then forward traffic to the Internet. You will need to perform NAT on the firewall for all requests to the Internet.

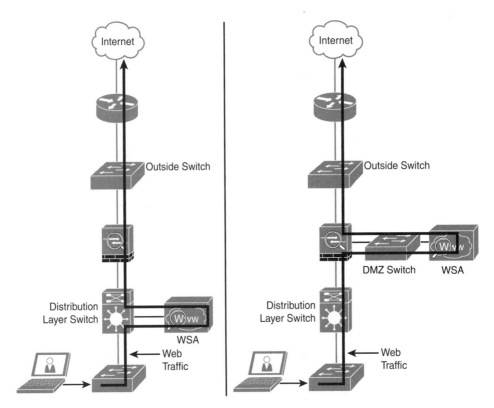

Figure 23-23 *Adding Internet Proxy Service to the Campus Edge*

To provide high availability, you will deploy two WSA appliances. You will need to configure your client applications to use a backup proxy server if the primary proxy server fails.

Connecting External Partners

The strategy of the enterprises is usually to focus on the core business and outsource some tasks to outside partners. If the enterprise wants to successfully outsource ongoing functions, it needs secure and affordable connectivity between its own network and partner sites.

The goal of the extranet is to provide secure access to internal resources. One of the options is to duplicate all the resources that partners need and to place them in a secure network that is connected to the Internet. This option is not always possible because you can have an extensive resource base, which can lead to high cost and complexity. The alternative is to build separate and secure managed network access for each partner.

There are three possible scenarios for extranet access:

- The partner accesses the enterprise network.
- The enterprise accesses the partner network.
- Reciprocal network access occurs between the partner and enterprise.

Challenges of Connecting External Partners

When you want to build a separate extranet network, you must design your network with security in mind. You need to protect your resources from security threats such as intruders and viruses. You must also protect the partners from security threats that can source from your network. Usually, you do not want to forward traffic from one to the other. Therefore, you must provide an extranet design that offers traffic separation from each partner.

The extranet design must be affordable. If you have an enterprise that has partners all over the world, the extranet connection can be expensive if you need dedicated links. Therefore, you must consider the cost of the links when designing the extranet.

Extranet Topology: Remote LAN Model

A remote LAN model is one of the extranet topologies. The other is the interconnect model. The remote LAN model is supported on different transport technologies.

As shown in Figure 23-24, the remote LAN model is an extension of the enterprise network at the partner site. When you are deploying the remote LAN model, you implement a managed router into the partner network. This router usually terminates the transport connectivity from the enterprise network. The router is often connected to one or more managed switches. The enterprise can also provide the PCs and printers that are installed at the partner site.

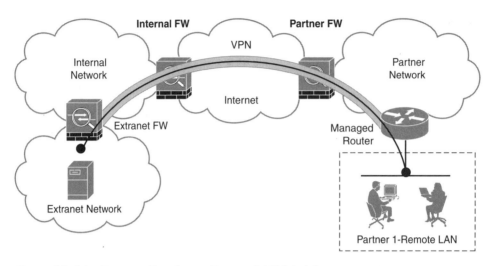

Figure 23-24 *Extranet Topology—Remote LAN Model*

The remote LAN model can support either a leased-line connectivity or site-to-site VPN connectivity. The advantage of using a leased line for extranet connectivity is that the service provider often offers quality of service (QoS) and a service-level agreement (SLA). On the other hand, VPN connectivity can greatly reduce the cost of extranet connectivity. It can also accelerate implementation and is also appropriate for short-term extranet connectivity. From a security design point of view, you must take into account a few challenges when designing such a connectivity model, including physical security with regard to the network devices placed at the partner site, access ports and Layer 2 security, and AAA consideration for network devices.

Extranet Topology: Interconnect Model

In addition to the remote LAN model, you can implement an extranet using the interconnect model. The interconnect model is supported on leased-line or VPN connections.

In the interconnect model (see Figure 23-25), a partner connects through its own corporate LAN. You can establish a VPN connection over the Internet, or you can implement a leased-line connection between your network and the partner's network. When you are using the interconnect model, it is important to implement a firewall at both ends. The firewall protects resources from each other. The advantage of using the interconnect model is that partners can connect from any desktop on their LANs. Also, from a security point of view, this option offers more controlled demarcation between the partner network and the enterprise network, which leads to better security control.

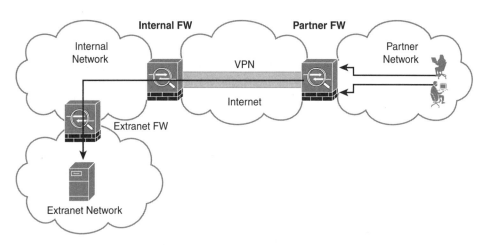

Figure 23-25 *Extranet Topology—Interconnect Model*

One of the biggest challenges is how you can handle the overlapping IP addresses. You can implement NAT to perform address translation before sending a packet over the VPN or leased-line connection.

Extranet: Security and Multitenant Segmentation

One of the biggest challenges when working with extranets is security. Usually, you cannot control perimeter security of your partners.

When you interconnect with a partner and you open your network to the partner, your network is exposed to potential security threats. If the partner does not offer adequate security in its own network, you actually open a backdoor into your environment. Some of the potential risks that you should mitigate include DoS attacks, spreading of viruses and worms, and hop-off threats. A partner also may not inform you when employees leave the partner's company. The problem lies in the fact that these employees can still have access to your resources, even if they are not authorized anymore.

To address these challenges, you should take care of legal measures, access restrictions, and security enforcement.

To implement legal measures, you can have your partners sign several agreements. For example, a partner can sign a nondisclosure agreement, which obliges the partner not to expose your internal information. You can also have your partner sign an agreement that demands expected user behavior and security policies that the partner is expected to enforce.

Access restrictions include the following:

- **Firewall permissions:** You should limit access from the partner's site to your organization's network by setting the machine-to-machine access policy at the protocol level on the firewall. This restriction will allow minimal traffic into your network from the partner. You can also limit the traffic that is allowed from your organization to the partner or leave this task to the partner to implement an incoming security policy.

- **Web proxy:** You can limit traffic on the firewall only by host and port. A partner can use any service on that port and host. You can, for example, use reverse proxies to limit access to only specific sites on that host and port.

- **Sandbox infrastructures:** Sandbox infrastructures can protect you against hopping off a host that the partners are authorized to access to one that they are not. To implement this solution, you allow partners to access the host for which they are authorized, but that host is restricted from initiating traffic to other hosts or networks.

- **Authentication and authorization:** You can implement authentication and authorization services at the host and application layers. The challenge is how to monitor which partner employees are still authorized to access to the resources.

To enforce extranet security, you can use a combination of intrusion detection systems, occasional physical audits of partner environments, and periodic access reviews to ensure that your partners still need access to the same hosts and services.

Summary

- The most common architectures of the firewall system are single-tier and two-tier architectures.
- Implement the firewall in routed or transparent mode.
- Cisco offers two options for firewall virtualization:
  - Multicontext mode to virtualize a physical firewall appliance
  - VSG, ASA 1000 V, and ASAv virtual firewalls
- Server-server traffic:
  - Try to keep it in a Layer 2 domain.
  - Use virtual appliances to keep the traffic in virtualized server layer.
- Deploy interface-level and device-level high availability on the firewall.
- Deploy IPS in monitoring or inline mode.
- Provide high availability for IPS management platforms and IPS device-level high availability.

- Security and affordability are the main goals when building an extranet.
- Two typical extranet topologies are
    - Remote LAN model
    - Interconnect model
- There is a three-pronged approach to addressing security challenges:
    - Legal measures
    - Access restrictions
    - Security enforcement

Review Questions

After answering the following questions, please refer to Appendix A, "Answers to Review Questions," for the answers.

1. Which is the best description of a two-tier firewall architecture?
    a. The firewall system is implemented with internal and external firewalls in a chain.
    b. The architecture decreases complexity in comparison to a single-tier architecture.
    c. A DMZ is typically located on the inside network.
    d. It is the most common firewall architecture.

2. Which of the following are true about a firewall in transparent mode? (Select three.)
    a. The firewall acts as a routing hop.
    b. The firewall acts like a "bump in the wire."
    c. Forwarding is based on IP addresses.
    d. Forwarding is based on MAC addresses.
    e. No routing is needed to forward data traffic.
    f. A routing protocol or static routing must be implemented.

3. Which of the following describes IPS in inline mode?
    a. IPS receives only a copy of the data traffic.
    b. Data traffic is forwarded through IPS.
    c. IPS changes source IP addresses.
    d. IPS can only send alerts but cannot filter the traffic.

4. Which is usually the most expensive and offers a more flexible security extranet connectivity option?
    a. Leased line
    b. Site-to-Site VPN
    c. User-based VPN
    d. GRE tunnel

5. Which extranet model utilizes managed equipment at the partner site?
   a. Remote LAN model
   b. Interconnect model
   c. Internet edge model
   d. WAN connectivity model

6. Which action is not included in a three-pronged approach to address security challenges?
   a. Legal measures
   b. Access restriction
   c. Equipment rental
   d. Security enforcement

7. Which two of the following are common IPS deployment architectures?
   a. Inline mode
   b. Outside zone
   c. Inside zone
   d. Monitoring mode

8. Connect each firewall type with the proper description.

Firewall Type	Description
IOS Firewall	Software-only firewall running in a hypervisor
ASA	Firewall that can be deployed as an interface-based firewall or as a zone-based firewall
ASA in multicontext mode	Dedicated firewall enabling a highly scalable, high-performance, high-availability, and fully featured deployment
Virtual firewall	Virtualized firewall running on a single physical ASA appliance

Chapter 24

IP Multicast Security

Upon completing this chapter, you will be able to

- Identify the challenges with IP multicast security
- Identify problems in the multicast network
- Describe multicast network security
- Describe network element security
- Describe how to secure a multicast network edge
- Describe how to secure Auto-RP and BSR
- Explain how to secure an internal multicast network
- Describe multicast sender controls
- Describe multicast receiver controls
- Describe multicast admission controls
- Explain how to secure MSDP

On an abstract level, any multicast deployment can be subject to security threats. When designing for security, you must be aware of the specific threats that could compromise security. You must also be aware of the associated risks or how relevant those threats are for a particular system. Different systems will always be exposed to different threats. Therefore, you need to perform risk management separately for each system. There are no universal recipes for security. If that were the case, you could build secure networks easily, based on templates. This chapter explains the issues and challenges with IP multicast security and how to enable security solutions.

Multicast Security Challenges

Many security challenges must be addressed in IP multicast deployments. Some of them are generic and apply to any network- or IP-based communications. Others are specific to multicast implementations. When identifying security challenges, security administrators should consider the system as a whole. They should look for potential vulnerabilities at various layers of the Open Systems Interconnections (OSI) model and in all the implemented IP multicast mechanisms.

Following are the most common security challenges:

- Compromise of the infrastructure:
  - Router break-in
  - Tampered IP routing
  - Disabused denial of service (DDoS) against network resources
- Compromise of multicast signaling:
  - Protocol-Independent Multicast (PIM)
  - Multiprotocol BGP (MP-BGP)
  - Multicast Source Discovery Protocol (MSDP)
  - Auto-Rendezvous Point (Auto-RP)
  - Bootstrap Router (BSR)
  - Internet Group Management Protocol (IPv4)/Multicast Listener Discovery (IPv6) (IGMP/MLD)

Problems in the Multicast Network

When a multicast server is misconfigured or an attack originates from a malicious host, serious network issues can result. For example, in the scenario shown in Figure 24-1, in a multicast-enabled environment, a server misconfiguration can cause serious network issues. Technically, these issues occur because even if the routers support large multicast routing tables, they may run out of memory and this will lead to a serious network issue. However, if the network operator considered simple protection mechanisms would have prevented this. The subsequent sections in this chapter will discuss the different possible mechanism and use cases to secure such environment.

Note In Figure 24-1, it is assumed that there is a large number of multicast receivers in order to introduce such issues/concerns.

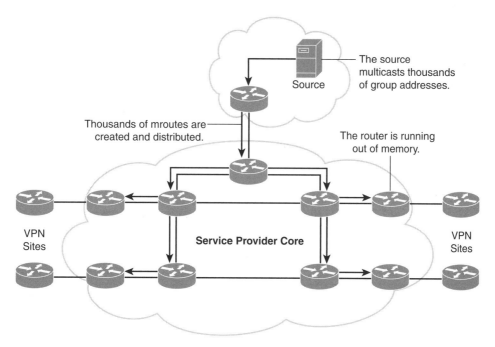

Figure 24-1 *Security Concerns in a Multicast Environment*

Multicast Network Security Considerations

In general, to secure a multicast network, you must consider the following three important areas:

- Securing network elements
- Securing the network at the edge
- Handling PIM and internal security

The subsequent sections discuss each of these areas in more detail.

As a network architect or designer, you should always look at the big picture and overall solution and not focus only on a certain element. For instance, in many cases, multiple protection methods can be deployed to protect a single vulnerability of an IP multicast solution. Having many measures increases overall security through the defense-in-depth concept, in which the protection methods complement and reinforce one another. The protection mechanisms have various approaches and can focus on the infrastructure, the overlay VPN, or the admission control capabilities. For example, the following methods are infrastructure-based:

- **Router hardening:** This mechanism includes enhanced password security, unused services disablement, and control-plane protection.
- **Access control to the network:** This mechanism includes ACLs and Unicast Reverse Path Forwarding (uRPF).
- **Quality of service (QoS):** This mechanism involves congestion avoidance.

In contrast, VPN-based services aim at providing privacy, integrity, and authenticity to the multicast signaling and traffic streams, especially to sensitive data. Admission control, however, focuses on controlling the receivers that are allowed to join multicast groups and source registration attempts. It also includes filtering techniques that, for example, prevent DoS attacks that are based on spoofing RP addresses. An example of such a filter is the **ip pim rp-announce-filter rp-list** *ACL* [**group-list** *ACL*] command that is configured on mapping agents in the Auto-RP implementation.

Network Element Security

Security is not a point feature. It is an intrinsic part of every network design. As such, security must be considered at every point in the network. It is of paramount importance that each network element is appropriately secured.

As shown in Figure 24-2, one possible attack scenario, applicable to any technology, is the subversion of a router by an intruder. When intruders have control of a router, they can run several different attack scenarios, including eavesdropping, spoofing, and active protocol attacks. Each network element must therefore be appropriately secured against any form of basic attack, as well as against specific multicast attacks.

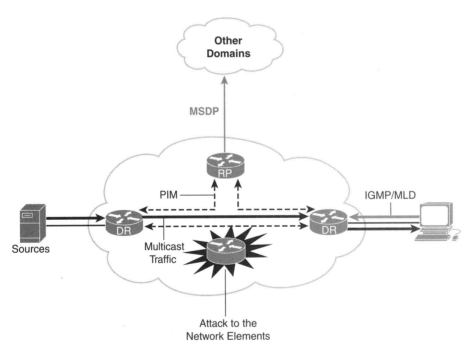

Figure 24-2 *Multicast Network Element Security*

Before taking specific measures to secure routers and other network elements, such as switches, against specific multicast attack forms, you must deploy basic security. These cautionary measures apply to routers, switches, and any other element on the path.

For routers, these steps are recommended for fundamental security:

Step 1. Secure router remote access.

Step 2. Disable unneeded servers/services.

Step 3. Configure basic access lists.

Step 4. Enable logging.

Step 5. Secure management access.

Step 6. Enable authentication, authorization, and accounting (AAA).

Step 7. Configure traffic filtering.

Step 8. Enable routing security.

Step 9. Perform router maintenance and testing.

The following are two common and effective protection capabilities available in different Cisco software releases that help to prevent or mitigate the impact of certain network targeted attacks:

- **Receive access control lists (ACLs):** Filter traffic that is destined to the control plane of a router. This global filter is applied to all received packets, or in other words, to all packets that are sent to any address owned by the router. This group includes all configured unicast addresses of the router and the multicast groups to which the router is listening. This filter can be useful to restrict these packets:

    - Unicast packets that are addressed to one of the router interface addresses
    - IP broadcast packets
    - Packets for joined IP multicast traffic
    - Packets for link-local scope groups

- **Control-plane policing (CoPP):** The evolution of rACLs. CoPP will police only traffic that is destined to the router. You must take care when configuring rACLs and CoPP in a live network. Because both features filter all traffic to the control plane, all required control and management plane protocols must be explicitly permitted. The list of required protocols is therefore large. It is easy to overlook less obvious protocols such as Network Time Protocol (NTP) or Terminal Access Controller Access Control System (TACACS). As such, all rACL and CoPP configurations should be tested in a lab before deployment. Furthermore, initial deployments should start with a permit policy only. This precaution enables you to check with ACL hit counters for any unexpected hits.

In a multicast environment, the required multicast protocols based on the design requirements, such as PIM, MSDP, IGMP, and so on, must be permitted in rACL and CoPP configurations for the multicast environment to function properly. The first packet in a multicast stream where PIM Sparse Mode (PIM-SM) is being used is also a control-plane packet, even though, strictly speaking, it is data-plane traffic. It is used as a control-plane packet because, as the first packet, it creates the multicast state, which is a control-plane function. Therefore, it is important to permit relevant multicast groups in rACL and CoPP. In CoPP, these groups can be rate limited.

In addition, disabling unneeded services is an important aspect in device-level security. For instance, the Session Announcement Protocol (SAP) is a traditional protocol that dates from the days of the multicast backbone. Its messages indicate directory information about multicast content that might be available now or in the future. Because these messages can cause a DoS against router CPU and memory resources, it is recommended that you disable this feature.

Similarly, Multicast Information Protocol (mrinfo) is an existing protocol that provides information that now is better retrieved via SNMP. Completely filtering mrinfo is recommended. Furthermore, all the other considerations discussed in Chapter 22, "Designing Enterprise Infrastructure Security," about securing and controlling the data plane and control plane such as routing security (for both unicast and multicast) are key for securing any multicast environment. For example, you should ensure the routing table (global or VRF routing table) should be stable and not overwhelmed with a large number of unwanted or misleading routes that can lead to traffic blackholing or overutilizing the device hardware resources (memory and CPU).

Security at the Network Edge

Figure 24-3 shows a typical multicast-enabled network that needs to be secured at the edge.

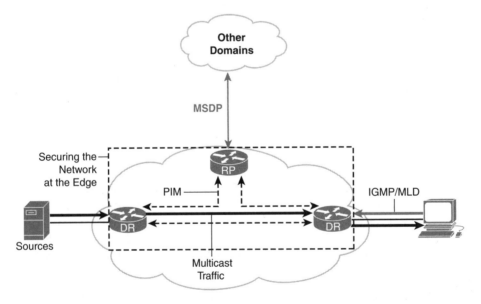

Figure 24-3 *Multicast Network Edge Security*

To secure multicast at the network edge, you need first to control multicast operation at the network edge. By considering ACL, you can disable all operations for multicast groups. If packets appear for any of the denied groups, they are dropped in all control protocols. These protocols include PIM, IGMP, MLD, and MSDP. The packets are also dropped on the data plane. Therefore, no IGMP or MLD cache entries, PIM, multicast routing information base (MRIB), or multicast forwarding information base (MFIB) states are ever created for these group ranges. All data packets are immediately dropped.

The recommendation (best practice) is to deploy the following two commands on all routers in the network, when and where available, so that all multicast traffic originating outside the network is controlled. These commands affect the data plane and the control plane because they limit all multicast operations at the data plane and permit only groups you define in the ACL. Also, ensure that the ACL should contain the allowed (S, G) or (*, G) groups and deny groups that are not in use:

```
router(config)# ip|ipv6 multicast group-range ACL
router(config)# ip multicast boundary ACL [filter-autorp]
```

In addition, in an interdomain environment, secure the data plane by using the **multicast boundary** command. The multicast boundary ensures that multicast traffic is accepted only for defined groups and potential sources.

As discussed earlier in this chapter, like unicast routing, securing multicast control protocols such as PIM is a vital aspect to consider when you need to have a reliable and secure multicast network. As you know from Chapter 21, "Rendezvous Point Distribution Solutions," both Auto-RP and BSR help to provide a mechanism in which viable group-to-RP mappings can be formed and propagated across the PIM routers in a PIM/multicast domain. MSDP, however, is more commonly used to achieve the same thing between different multicast domains. The following sections discuss the security aspects of these protocols at the network edge.

Securing Auto-RP and BSR

Auto-RP, which is a protocol developed by Cisco, serves the same purpose as the PIMv2 BSR mechanism. Auto-RP was developed before BSR and only supports IPv4. BSR supports IPv4 and IPv6. The mapping agent in the Auto-RP approach serves the same function as the bootstrap router in the BSR approach. In BSR, messages from the candidate RP are unicast to the bootstrap router. In Auto-RP, messages are sent via multicast to the mapping agent, enabling easier boundary filtering.

As shown in Figure 24-4, two attackers introduce malicious candidate-RP-announce packets and candidate-RP-discovery packets. Figure 24-4 also shows where Auto-RP must be blocked to filter out malicious candidate-RP-announce packets and candidate-RP-discovery packets.

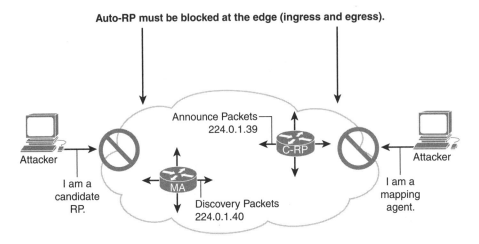

Figure 24-4 *Securing Auto-RP*

In Cisco IOS software, the forwarding of Auto-RP and BSR packets is always enabled and currently not configurable. This default can present a particular security exposure for Auto-RP.

Auto-RP, even though it is a mechanism for PIM-SM RP announcement and discovery, does not use PIM packets. Auto-RP instead uses UDP packets with multicast addresses. Auto-RP uses these two packet types:

- **Candidate-RP announce packets:** These packets are multicast to all mapping agents using an IANA-reserved well-known address (224.0.1.39).

- **Candidate-RP discovery packets:** These packets are multicast to all PIM routers using an IANA-reserved well-known address (224.0.1.40).

Each of these packet types is intended to be flooded through the network. Both 224.0.1.39 and 224.0.1.40 are forwarded in PIM Dense Mode (PIM-DM) to avoid having to know the RP for a group when that group is used to distribute RP information. This is the only recommended use of PIM-DM.

In Cisco IOS XR Software, Auto-RP messages flood the reverse path forwarding (RPF) information for an RP hop by hop from neighbor to neighbor. Therefore, you do not need to create a PIM-DM mroute state to support Auto-RP in Cisco IOS XR Software. Actually, Cisco IOS XR software does not support PIM-DM at all.

Similarly, BSR messages need to be blocked at the ingress and egress of the multicast domain, as illustrated in Figure 24-5, where BSR must be blocked to filter out malicious BSR messages. No access list is necessary because BSR messages are forwarded hop by hop via link-local multicast.

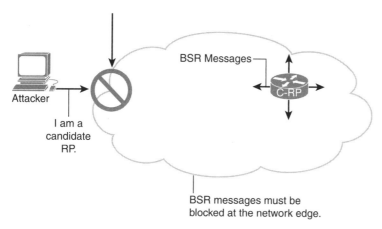

Figure 24-5 *Securing BSR*

MSDP Security

MSDP is the IPv4 protocol that allows a source in one domain to be announced to a receiver in another domain via their respective rendezvous points. MSDP is specified in RFC 3618.

As illustrated in Figure 24-6, MSDP works by forwarding information about active sources between PIM domains. If a source becomes active in one domain, MSDP ensures that all peer domains learn about this new source. This notification allows receivers in other domains to rapidly make contact with this new source if it happens to be sending to a group. Therefore, to have a layer of security in such environment, you need to consider interdomain filtering with MSDP.

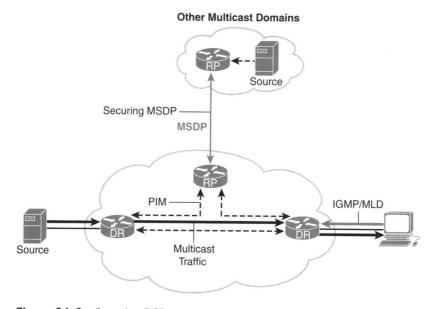

Figure 24-6 *Securing BSR*

For instance, when an ISP acts as a PIM-SM transit provider, it is only supporting MSDP peering with neighbors. Also, it is only accepting (S, G)—not (*, G) —traffic on the border routers. In an interdomain environment, two basic security measures can be taken:

- Securing the data plane, using the **multicast boundary** command. This action ensures that multicast traffic is accepted only for defined groups (and potentially sources).

- Securing the MSDP interdomain control-plane traffic. This activity consists of several separate security measures, including MSDP content control, state limitation, and neighbor authentication.

Furthermore, practically, to provide optimal secure communication for an interdomain scenario, you should consider securing both the unicast control plane (most commonly BGP) and the multicast control plane (commonly MSDP). Table 24-1 compares the different features both of these protocols offer that you can use for securing the control plane.

Table 24-1 *MSDP and BGP Features Comparison*

	BGP	**MSDP**
Peer authentication	MD5	MD5
Limit state, globally	maximum-prefix	ip multicast route-limit
Limit state, per neighbor	neighbor peer maximum-prefix n	ip msdp sa-limit peer n
Prefix filtering	Prefix filter lists	ip msdp sa-filter [in|out]
Check first autonomous system (AS)	enforce-first-AS	—
Check AS path	AS path filter	—
Limit attack horizon	TTL security	—

PIM and Internal Multicast Security

To establish PIM neighbors, a PIM router must receive PIM hellos. PIM neighbors are pivotal in the election of DRs; in the DR failover process; and in the sending and accepting of PIM join, prune, and assert messages. The following are some multicast features and capabilities that can be used for hardening the internal multicast security

- Rate-limiting PIM register messages are sent from the first-hop router to the RP:

    `router(config)# `**`ip|ipv6 pim accept-register list`** *ACL*

- Filtering of the PIM register messages on the RP:

    `ip|ipv6 pim accept-register list` *ACL*

- Interface-based PIM neighbor filtering:

    `router(config-if)# `**`ip pim neighbor filter`** *ACL*

Multicast Sender Control

IP multicast senders, as depicted in Figure 24-7, whether PCs or video servers, are sometimes not under the same administrative control as the network. Therefore, from the view of the network operator, the sender is mostly treated as untrusted. Given the powerful capabilities of PCs and servers, and their complex security settings—which are often incomplete—the senders pose a substantial threat against any network, including multicast.

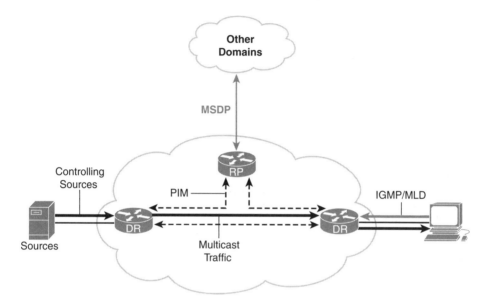

Figure 24-7 *IP Multicast Sender*

Multicast senders' threats can take many forms, including the following:

- **Layer 2 attacks:** There are a wide range of attack forms on Layer 2 to carry out eavesdropping, masquerading, or DoS attacks. These threats apply to unicast and multicast networks.

- **Attacks with multicast traffic:** As described previously, it is difficult to conduct attacks with multicast traffic because the first-hop router will not forward IP multicast traffic unless there is a listener for the group. However, the first hop can be attacked in various ways with multicast packets:

    - An attacker can flood a segment with multicast packets, overutilizing the available bandwidth and creating a DoS condition. This threat is known as a network saturation attack.

- An intruder can flood the first-hop router with multicast packets, creating too much state and, so, a DoS attack condition. This threat is known as a multicast state attack.
- A sender could attempt to become the PIM DR, sending PIM hellos. In such cases, no traffic would forward to or from the LAN.
- Election packets for a BIDIR-PIM DF could be spoofed. In such cases, no traffic would forward to or from the LAN.
- A sender could spoof Auto-RP discovery or BSR bootstrap messages. Spoofing would effectively announce a fake RP, and bring down or disrupt a PIM-SM or bidirectional service.
- A sender could source unicast attacks, such as PIM source register or register-stop messages. Or it could send BSR-announce packets and announce a fake BSR.
- A sender can send to any valid multicast group, unless this activity is filtered. If source address spoofing is not prevented at the edge, the sender can use the source IP address of a legitimate sender and override content in parts of the network.
- Intruders can also perform multicast attacks against control-plane protocols. Several protocols that are not associated with multicast, such as OSPF and DHCP, use multicast packets. These packets can be used to attack these protocols.

- **Masquerading:** There are several attack forms by which a sender can pretend to be another sender. Source IP spoofing is one such attack form.
- **Theft of service:** Unless senders are controlled, attackers can use the multicast service illegitimately from the sender side.

In addition, hosts should never send or receive PIM packets. If they do, they are likely attempting an attack. Following are the different features that are used when protecting a multicast-enabled network from malicious sources (see Figure 24-8):

- Use the **ip multicast boundary** command to configure an administratively scoped boundary on an interface to filter multicast group addresses in the range that is defined by the access-list argument.

Multicast Network Security Considerations

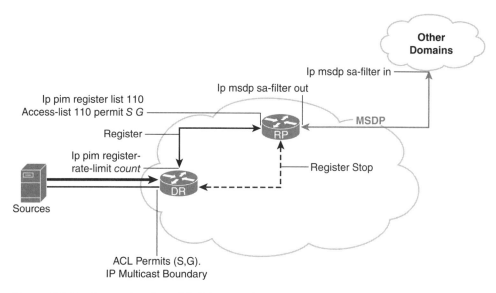

Figure 24-8 *Protection from Malicious Multicast Sources*

- Use the **ip pim register-rate-limit** command to limit the number of register messages that the designated router (DR) will allow for each (S, G) entry. Enabling this command will limit the load on the DR and the Rendezvous Point (RP) at the expense of dropping those register messages that exceed the set limit. Receivers may experience data packet loss within the first second in which register messages are sent from bursty sources.

- Use the **ip pim accept-register** command to prevent unauthorized sources from registering with the RP. If an unauthorized source sends a register message to the RP, the RP will immediately send back a register-stop message.

- Use the **ip msdp sa-filter** command to filter SA messages to or from the specified MSDP peer.

Multicast Receiver Controls

Attacks can originate from multicast receivers, where you need to impose a level of control (see Figure 24-9). Any receiver sending an IGMP/MLD report will typically create a state on the last-hop router. There is no equivalent mechanism in unicast. Receiver attacks can take three forms:

- A multicast receiver can attempt to join a flow without authorization and try to receive content it is not permitted to receive.

- A multicast receiver can potentially overload available network bandwidth by joining too many groups or channels. This sort of attack becomes a shared-bandwidth attack against other potential receivers of content.

- A multicast receiver can attempt to launch an attack against routers or switches. Many IGMP reports can be generated, which can create a large amount of multicast tree state and potentially overload router capacity. This overload can result in an increase in the multicast convergence time or in a DoS on the router.

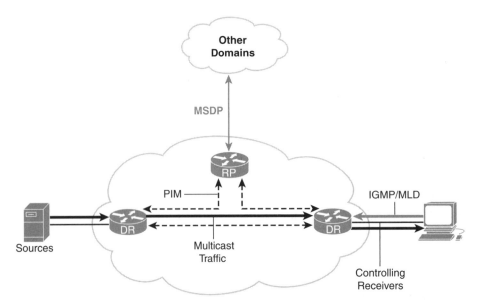

Figure 24-9 *Controlling Malicious Traffic from Multicast Receivers*

Most receiver issues fall into the domain of controlling the IGMP/MLD receiver protocol interactions. When filtering IGMP or MLD packets, you should consider the following:

- IPv4: IGMP is an IPv4 protocol type.
- IPv6: MLD is carried in ICMPv6 protocol type packets.

The IGMP process is enabled by default as soon as IP is enabled. IGMP packets also carry the following protocols, which means that all these protocols are enabled whenever IP is enabled:

- **PIMv1:** The first version of PIM, PIMv1 is always enabled in Cisco IOS software for migration purposes. Current deployments all use PIMv2.
- **Mrinfo:** Cisco IOS software inherited this UNIX command to display multicast neighbors. Cisco recommends the use of SNMP instead of the **mrinfo** command.
- **DVMRP:** A traditional dense mode distance vector protocol, the Distance Vector Multicast Routing Protocol (DVMRP) has limited scaling characteristics. Cisco IOS SOFTWARE support for DVMRP is being retired.
- **Mtrace:** This protocol is the multicast equivalent of unicast traceroute and is a useful tool.

Unicast IGMP packets should always be filtered because these are most likely attack packets and not valid IGMP protocol packets. Unicast IGMP packets accommodate unidirectional links and other exception conditions.

In particular, hosts should never send IGMP queries because a query sent with a lower IGMP version can cause all hosts that receive this query to revert to the lower version. In the presence of IGMPv3 and SSM hosts, this reversion can attack the SSM streams. In the case of IGMPv2, this condition can result in longer leave latencies.

If a nonredundant LAN with a single IGMP query is present, the router needs to drop IGMP queries that are received. If a redundant or common passive LAN exists, a switch capable of IGMP snooping is required. Two specific features can help in this case:

- Router guard
- IGMP minimum version command

Multicast Admission Controls

Access control delivers a yes or no answer for certain flows, independently of the state of the network. Admission control, by contrast, limits the number of resources that senders or receivers can use, assuming that they passed the access control mechanisms. Various devices are available to help with admission control in a multicast environment.

At the receiver-side router, there is the possibility to limit the number of IGMP groups joined both globally and per interface. The three main possibilities for admission control are as follows:

- **IGMP/MLD state limits (global and per interface):** It is recommended that this limit is always configured per interface and also globally. In each case, the limit refers to counts of entries in the IGMP cache.
- **Per-interface mroute limit:** Enabling per-interface mroute state limits is a more generic form of admission control. It not only limits the IGMP and PIM state on an outgoing interface, but also provides a way of limiting the state on incoming interfaces.
- **Bandwidth limits:** You can make a further subdivision of access bandwidth between multiple content providers.

Summary

- IP multicast must be protected against privacy, integrity, and availability violations.
- Basic security must be deployed on routers, switches, and any other element on the IP multicast path. Also ensure the state containment in the network and that CPU utilization is controlled.
- To mitigate attacks to the network edge, use the **ip multicast group-range** and **ip multicast boundary** commands.

- To mitigate attacks to the internal multicast-enabled network with PIM, use the **ip pim register-rate-limit, ip | ipv6 pim accept-register list, ip pim neighbor filter**, and **ip pim rp-announce-filter** commands.
- Multicast security issues originating at the sender can be mitigated with unicast security mechanisms.
- Receiver issues can be controlled with the IGMP and MLD protocols.
- Admission control limits the number of resources that a sender or receiver can use.
- MSDP security consists of MSDP content control, state limitation, and neighbor authentication.

Review Questions

After answering the following questions, refer to Appendix A, "Answers to Review Questions," for the answers.

1. Which general router security steps are needed before securing IP multicast elements? (Select four.)
    a. Physical security
    b. Strong passwords
    c. Secure protocols
    d. AAA
    e. ACL containing multicast-allowed (S, G) or (*, G) entries
    f. ACL denying groups not in use
    g. Interface-based PIM neighbor filtering

2. Which unicast features are recommended for securing a multicast-enabled network on the source side? (Select three.)
    a. ACLs
    b. AAA
    c. uRPF
    d. HTTPS
    e. Strong passwords
    f. Physical security

3. True or False? Access control delivers a yes or no answer for certain flows, independently of the state of the network.
    a. True
    b. False

4. True or False? When you are designing a secure IP multicast network, it is not a must to secure the unicast routing; however, it is desirable to secure both.
    a. True
    b. False

Chapter 25

Designing Network Access Control Solutions

Upon completing this chapter, you will be able to

- Provide an overview of IEEE 802.1X-based access control
- Identify IEEE 802.1X authorization options
- Describe 802.1X phased deployment
- Describe the EAP authentication framework
- Describe native 802.1X supplicants and compare them with AnyConnect
- Describe Cisco TrustSec technology

The threat of a network service disruption by unauthorized sources grows when technology becomes more important in business processes. It is critical for organizations to protect access to the network. Protection can reduce the probability of intrusions from threats such as viruses and worms, as well as unauthorized access. Technologies such as 802.1X can be implemented to perform network access control.

IEEE 802.1X Overview

IEEE 802.1X is an industry standard that is used to provide authentication-based port access control and authorization. With the IEEE 802.1X port-based authentication, network devices have the following roles (see Figure 25-1):

- **Supplicant:** This role is an agent or service running on the device that requests access to the network. It responds to requests from the switch.

Figure 25-1 *802.1X Device Roles*

- **Authenticator:** Network devices such as LAN switches and wireless LAN controllers act as authenticators. This device controls physical access to the network based on the authentication status of the client. Authenticator requests identify information from the client, verify the information with authentication servers, and relay the response from authentication servers to the client.

- **Authentication server:** This role performs the actual authentication of the client. The authentication server validates the identity of the client and notifies the authenticator whether the client is authorized to access the network. Because the authenticator acts as a proxy, the authentication service is transparent to the client.

In addition, with 802.1X, two possible methods are mainly used for authentication:

- Digital certificate
- Username and password

Therefore, considering 802.1X offers the following benefits specifically on wired networks:

- **Visibility:** 802.1X provides greater visibility into the network because the authentication process provides a way to link a username with an IP address, MAC address, switch, and port. This visibility is useful for security audits, network forensics, network use statistics, and troubleshooting.

- **Security:** 802.1X is the strongest method for authentication and should be used for managed assets that support an 802.1X supplicant. 802.1X acts at Layer 2 in the network, enabling you to control network access at the access edge.

- **Identity-based services:** 802.1X enables you to leverage an authenticated identity to dynamically deliver customized services. For example, a user might be authorized into a specific VLAN or assigned a unique access list that grants appropriate access for that user.

- **Transparency:** In many cases, 802.1X can be deployed in a way that is transparent to the end user.

- **User and device authentication:** 802.1X can be used to authenticate devices and users.

Although 802.1X enables unparalleled visibility and security, your design must address the following limitations:

- **Legacy or non-802.1X-capable endpoints:** By default, 802.1X provides no network access to endpoints that cannot authenticate because they do not support 802.1X or do not have a supplicant such as a legacy printer. Alternative mechanisms such as MAC Authentication Bypass (MAB), in which a device is authenticated based on the MAC address, or Web Authentication must be provided for these endpoints.

- **Delay:** By default, 802.1X allows no access before authentication. Endpoints that need immediate network access must be capable of performing 802.1X at or near bootup/link-up time, or alternative mechanisms must be used to grant the necessary access in a timely manner.

> **Note** As mentioned previously, there are always endpoints that require network connectivity but do not or cannot support 802.1X; they include network printers, badge readers, legacy servers, and PXE boot machines. Some provision must be made for these endpoints. Cisco provides features to accommodate non-802.1X endpoints, including MAB, Web Authentication, and Guest VLAN. These features provide fallback mechanisms when there is no 802.1X supplicant. After an 802.1X timeout on a port, the port can move to an authorized state if MAB or Web Authentication succeeds, or if the Guest VLAN is configured. Judicious application of these features is required for a successful 802.1X deployment. The flow chart in Figure 25-2 shows the interactions of these fallback mechanisms.

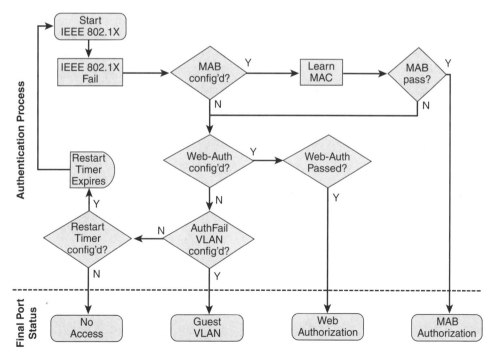

Figure 25-2 *Fallback Mechanisms of 802.1X Authentication*

802.1X uses the following protocols:

- **Extensible Authentication Protocol (EAP):** This is the message format and framework defined by RFC 4187; it provides a way for the supplicant and the authenticator to negotiate an authentication method (the EAP method). In other words, the EAP framework provides a transport for authentication parameters.

- **EAP method:** This protocol defines the authentication method—that is, the credential type and how it is submitted from the supplicant to the authentication server using the EAP framework. (EAP methods are covered in a later section.)

- **EAP over LAN (EAPOL):** This encapsulation method is defined by 802.1X for the transport of the EAP from the supplicant to the switch (supplicant and authenticator) over IEEE 802 networks. EAPOL is a Layer 2 protocol.

- **Remote Authentication Dial-In User Service (RADIUS):** This is the de facto standard for communication between the switch (authenticator) and the authentication server. The switch extracts the EAP payload from the Layer 2 EAPOL frame and encapsulates the payload inside a Layer 7 RADIUS packet.

The supplicant or the authenticator can initiate the authentication. The authenticator initiates authentication when the link state changes from down to up, or periodically as long as the port remains up and unauthenticated.

The authenticator sends an EAP request or identity frame to the client to request its identity. Upon receipt of the frame, the supplicant responds with an EAP response or identity frame. However, if during bootup, the supplicant does not receive an EAP request or identity frame from the authenticator, the supplicant can initiate authentication by sending an EAPOL start frame. It prompts the authenticator to request the identity of the client.

When the supplicant provides its identity, the authenticator begins its role as the intermediary and passes EAP frames between the supplicant and the authentication server until authentication succeeds or fails. If the authentication succeeds, the authenticator port is authorized, as illustrated in Figure 25-3.

The specific exchange of EAP frames depends on the authentication method that is used.

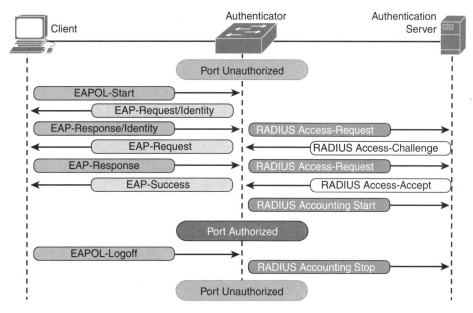

Figure 25-3 *802.1X Message Flow*

Extensible Authentication Protocol

An IEEE standard for port-based network access control uses the EAP to authenticate users who wish to access the network.

EAP messages are exchanged between a supplicant and an authentication server. The EAP messages are directly encapsulated in the LAN protocol between a supplicant and an authenticator using the EAPOL encapsulation. They are encapsulated in the RADIUS protocol between an authenticator and authentication server. The authenticator acts like a proxy between a supplicant and an authentication server and does not actively participate in the communication. Instead, it waits for the decision of the authentication server, which is communicated to it natively over the RADIUS protocol.

EAP provides two-way authentication between the client and the authentication server. Many authentication methods (some of them hybrid) are possible, and they support many types of credentials. The main advantage of EAP is that it is extensible to implement almost any authentication processes.

The two types of EAP architectures are as follows (see Figure 25-4):

- **Nontunnel EAP:** In nontunnel EAP architecture, a single session exists between the supplicant and the authentication server. The supplicant sends its identity in clear text to the authentication server. The next step is the exchange of messages, which authenticates the authentication server to the user and the user to the authentication servers.

■ **Tunneled EAP:** In tunneled EAP architecture, the outer EAP encapsulates an inner EAP. The outer EAP provides the server with authentication and a cryptographically secure tunnel for the inner EAP method to run in.

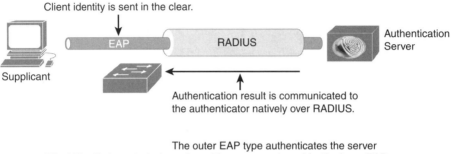

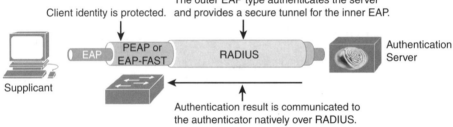

Figure 25-4 *EAP Architectures*

EAP has many variations that use different classes of authentication protocols and support different credentials. The most common EAP methods or types are described in Table 25-1.

Table 25-1 *EAP Types*

EAP Type	Mode	Authentication protocol	Supported credentials	When to use
EAP-MD5	Nontunnel	Challenge response with hashing	Passwords to the client authentication; no server authentication	Avoid using it. Vulnerable to man-in-the-middle attacks.
EAP-MS-CHAPv2	Nontunnel	Challenge response with hashing	Password for the client and the server authentication	Use in Active Directory environments.
EAP-TLS	Nontunnel	Challenge response with public keys	Certificates for client and server authentication	Use with client-side certificates.

EAP Type	Mode	Authentication protocol	Supported credentials	When to use
EAP-GTC	Nontunnel	Cleartext transfer of passwords	Passwords or OTPs for client authentication	Use in the OTP environment.
EAP-FAST	Tunneled	Challenge-response with symmetric cryptography	Passwords or OTPs for client, and passwords for server authentication	Use to support plain passwords as client and server credentials.
PEAP	Tunneled	Challenge response with public key cryptography	Certificate server-side authentication; other credentials inside PEAP-tunneled protocols	Use to tunnel other inner EAP variations: EAP-MS-CHAPv2 or EAP-GTC.

EAP allows user or machine authentication. Traditional machine and user authentication works by treating the machine and user as two separate and independent entities. User authentication is performed when the user logs on. When the user logs off, machine authentication is performed. All common supplicants, such as AnyConnect or Windows native supplicant, support these two authentication options.

A more advanced option is to use EAP chaining. It supports machine and user authentication inside a single outer Transport Layer Security (TLS) tunnel. It enables you to combine the results of the machine and user authentication into a single overall authentication result. You can, for example, assign greater privileges to users who connect to the network using corporate-managed computers.

EAP chaining was first implemented in Extensible Authentication Protocol–Flexible Authentication via Secure Tunneling (EAP-FASTv2), which is a Cisco solution. The Internet Engineering Task Force (IETF) is working on a similar solution, which is called Tunnel Extensible Authentication Protocol (TEAP).

802.1X Supplicants

The Cisco AnyConnect Secure Mobility client, depicted in Figure 25-5, is modular software that includes modules for VPN, network access, web security, and others. The module that is used to provide services for network access is called the Network Access Manager.

Figure 25-5 *Cisco AnyConnect Secure Mobility Client*

The Network Access Manager provides Layer 2 device management and authentication for access to both wired and wireless networks. It enables organizations to deploy a single 802.1X authentication framework to access both wired and wireless networks. You can also manage user and device identity and network access protocols.

The Network Access Manager supports the following EAP methods:

- EAP-TLS

- PEAP with support for the EAP-TLS, EAP-MS-CHAPv2, and EAP-GTC inner methods

- EAP-FAST with support for the EAP-TLC, EAP-MS-CHAPv2, and EAP-GTC inner methods

- EAP-TTLS with support for the PAP, CHAP, MS-CHAP, MS-CHAPv2, EAP-MD5, and EAP-MS-CHAPv2 inner methods

To combine user and machine authentication in one authentication result, the Network Access Manager supports EAP-Chaining (EAP-FASTv2). In this mode, you can differentiate the access based on enterprise and nonenterprise assets. The Network Access Manager is supported only on Windows in Cisco AnyConnect client version 4.0.

You can also use native 802.1X supplicant in Windows. Windows offers separate supplicants for wired and wireless access. Native supplicants support all the most common EAP methods like PEAP, EAP-FAST, and others. EAP-Chaining is currently not supported.

IEEE 802.1X Phased Deployment

IEEE 802.1X can be implemented using a phased deployment model that allows for limited impact on network access while introducing authentication and authorization. In the phased approach, network administrators can gain visibility into who will succeed and who will fail, determine the reason for failure, and remediate the problem before enabling a stronger enforcement mode.

The following are the three modes of phased deployments (see Figure 25-6):

- Monitor
- Low impact
- Closed

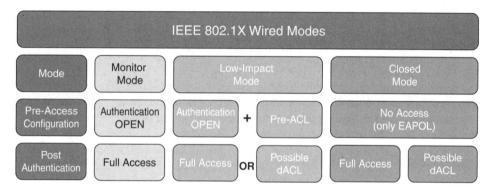

Figure 25-6 *802.1X Deployment Modes Comparison*

The phase deployment starts with a monitoring mode and then shifts to either a low-impact mode or a closed mode. The monitoring mode allows deployment of the authentication methods without any effect on the user or endpoint when accessing the network. The monitoring mode is enabled using 802.1X with open access and multiauth mode. The open-access feature allows you to provide unrestricted access to all traffic, even though authentication is enabled.

With the low-impact mode, security is enhanced by adding an ingress access control list (ACL) to the 802.1X-enabled ports. These ports are configured in the open mode. The ACL controls which traffic is allowed for unauthenticated hosts. For example, you can allow the use of DHCP or DNS and access to the Internet, while blocking access to the internal resources. When a port is authenticated, you can apply the appropriate authorization policy.

The default behavior on the Cisco switchport that is configured for 802.1X is the closed mode, where only EAPOL traffic is allowed until the authentication process completes. When authentication is completed, you can apply the appropriate authorization policy.

Cisco TrustSec

End users use many types of devices, including laptops, smartphones, and tablets, to connect to the network wired, wirelessly, and remotely through VPN. With bring your own device (BYOD) access, the devices can be personal or corporate owned. Every enterprise has policies that dictate who can access what applications and databases, when, and how. Traditionally, IT manages the policy either by introducing appliances at points in the campus where users connect or by manually configuring all the access switches. Appliances incur additional capital and operational expenses, whereas manual configuration of the switches requires maintenance of every switch. Moreover, the network can carry traffic using Ethernet, IPv4, IPv6, or other technologies, so the configuration must keep up with changes in technology, which leads to higher operational complexity and costs.

Cisco TrustSec simplifies the provisioning and management of secure access to network services and applications. Compared to access control mechanisms that are based on network topology, Cisco TrustSec defines policies using logical policy groupings. For that reason, secure access is consistently maintained even as resources are moved in mobile and virtualized networks.

In fact, Cisco TrustSec, as an intelligent access control solution, mitigates security risks by providing comprehensive visibility into who and what is connecting across the entire network infrastructure, and exceptional control over what and where they can go. In addition to combining standards-based identity and enforcement models, such as IEEE 802.1X and VLAN control, the TrustSec system also includes advanced identity and enforcement capabilities such as flexible authentication, downloadable access control lists (dACL), Security Group Tagging (SGT), device profiling, posture assessments, and more.

Profiling Service

The Profiling Service is one of the Cisco TrustSec advanced identity and enforcement capabilities that provides dynamic detection and classification of endpoints connected to the network. Using MAC addresses as unique identifiers, the Cisco Identity Services Engine (ISE) collects various attributes for each network endpoint to build an internal endpoint database. The classification process matches the collected attributes to prebuilt or user-defined conditions, which are then correlated with an extensive library of profiles. As depicted in Figure 25-7, these profiles include a wide range of device types, including mobile clients (iPads, Android tablets, BlackBerry phones, and so on), desktop operating systems (for example, Windows, Mac OS X, Linux, and others), and numerous nonuser systems such as printers, phones, cameras, and game consoles.

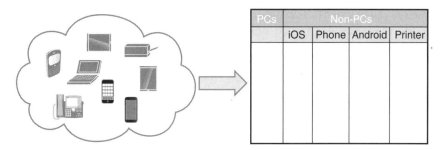

- In today's networks, it is important to know what devices connect to the network.
- The Cisco ISE Profiler as part of Cisco TrustSec solution is responsible for endpoint detection and classification.

Figure 25-7 *Device Profiling*

Once classified, endpoints can be authorized to the network and granted access based on their profile. For example, endpoints that match the IP phone profile can be placed into a voice VLAN using MAC Authentication and Bypass (MAB) as the authentication method. Another example is to provide differentiated network access to users based on the device used. For example, employees can get full access when accessing the network from their corporate workstation but be granted limited network access when accessing the network from their personal iPhone.

Note Cisco TrustSec is a solution specific to Cisco devices. Also, the Cisco Identity Services Engine (ISE) is a component of Cisco's Borderless Networking and the company's TrustSec product line. ISE is a network administration product that enables the creation and enforcement of security and access policies for endpoint devices connected to the company's routers and switches.

Security Group Tag

Part of the Cisco TrustSec architecture, Cisco Security Group Tag (SGT) is a technology that overcomes the shortcomings of the traditional approaches to policy administration. When a user connects to the network and tries to access an application, the Cisco access switch automatically profiles the user and finds out the user's ID, device being used, location, and time of access. The switch then tags all traffic coming from the user's device based on the IT policy for the user's profile. The tag is a numerical value and is either manually assigned to the access switches or automatically administered through the Cisco Identity Services Engine (ISE) application. If Cisco ISE is used, it transmits the tag information to all the supported Cisco devices in the network (centralized configuration and provisioning).

Cisco TrustSec classifies traffic based on the contextual identity of the endpoint versus its IP address. This means that a Cisco TrustSec Policy Security Group Tag (SGT) is assigned to an endpoint typically based on that endpoint's user, device, and location attributes (predefined profiling). The SGT denotes the endpoint access entitlements, and all traffic from the endpoint will carry the SGT information. Switches, routers, and firewalls use SGT to make forwarding decisions that are based on a security policy.

The features that are associated with SGTs on the network devices can be broken into three categories:

- Classification
- Transport
- Enforcement

Classification is the assignment of SGT to an IP address, which can be accomplished either dynamically or statically. Dynamic classification is typically performed at the access layer and can be done using a network access control solution such as 802.1X. The SGT is assigned through authorization of the endpoint. Static classification is typically used in the data center and is configured on the switch to which servers are attached. Options for static classification include the mapping of IP address, VLAN, or port to an SGT.

Security group mappings follow the traffic through the network, which can be accomplished either through inline tagging or the Security Group Tag Exchange Protocol (SXP). With inline tagging, the SGT is embedded in the Ethernet frame header. Because not all network devices support inline tagging, SXP can be used to transport SGT mappings across such devices.

Enforcement is implementing a permit or deny policy decision that is based on the source and destination SGTs. It can be accomplished with security group access control lists (SGACL) on switching platforms and Security Group Firewall (SGFW) on routing and firewall platforms, as illustrated in Figure 25-8.

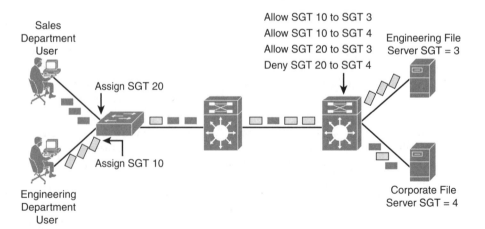

Figure 25-8 *Policy Enforcement Using SGACL*

For example, in the scenario illustrated in Figure 25-9, the IT security team set up an access policy in the Cisco Identity Services Engine (ISE) stating that the marketing group cannot access the financial application. When a marketing person connects a laptop or tablet to the network, ISE uses Active Directory credentials to authenticate the user. ISE then assigns a tag, say, 20 for the marketing group. The access switch and wireless LAN controller (WLC) receive tag 20 from the ISE and add it to every packet coming from the user's device. The packet traverses the network with tag 20. If the user attempts to connect to the financial application/database, which only allows a tag of 10, the access switch connected to the server will deny the request. If the marketing user switches the role to finance, that user's user group will change based on Active Directory, and the application can be accessed without IT having to program all the access switches. The entire authentication and enforcement process is automatic. Similarly, in this example, the financial application has been given the SGT value 30, which is blocked at the users' distribution layer (VSS) from communicating with marketing users' subnets (wired and wireless) to also prevent any traffic flow sourced from this application.

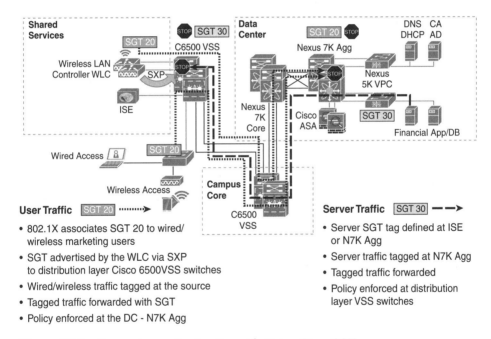

Figure 25-9 *Secure Access Design Example Using Cisco SGT*

> **Note** In Figure 25-9, the wireless traffic from the access point will be tunneled back to the WLC, and from the WLC the traffic from wireless users will enter the LAN using the respective VLAN/subnet to reach other networks. Therefore, the SGT is assigned at the WLC for the wireless users.

> **Note** Because SGT assignments can denote business roles and functions, Cisco TrustSec controls can be defined in terms of business needs and not underlying networking detail. For example, the business or the enterprise security policy may dictate that any personal devices such as tablets or smartphones used by the employees should be restricted to access the internal mail server and the Internet only, even though the users use their corporate credentials to log in to the network from these devices. If the Cisco TrustSec is used for SGT and profiling, this goal can be achieved and maintained in a centralized and efficient manner without introducing any operational complexity.

Case Study: Authorization Options

The enterprise campus network consists of several access switches that are located in several buildings. Users often migrate from building to building, and you are responsible for updating VLAN memberships for the client devices. Because many migrations occur every day, much of your daily activity includes moving users from one VLAN to another. You are thinking about how to automate this activity.

The campus network is implemented as a three-level architecture. Access layer switches are Layer 2 switches. Inter-VLAN routing is done in the aggregation layer. Users are segmented in different VLANs based on their role in the company. Firewall policy is implemented in accordance to the VLAN membership, which means that every VLAN has a specific IP subnet. Firewall rules are implemented based on these subnets.

You have already implemented 802.1X access control on all access switches in the campus network. When a client is successfully authenticated, it is assigned to the VLAN that is configured on the specific port. Therefore, you have to manually change the port VLAN membership if the client moves from one location to the other. You are wondering whether there is a way to implement automatization in this process.

You came up with a solution to implement a dynamic VLAN assignment. Because you have already implemented 802.1X with RADIUS authentication, you can easily extend your 802.1X deployment to support authorization. To perform dynamic VLAN assignment, the RADIUS server must return the VLAN attribute in the Access-Accept message (refer to Figure 25-7).

With the VLAN assignment, the authentication server can associate a VLAN with a particular user or group, and instruct the switch to dynamically assign the authenticated user into that VLAN. This method can easily provide strong access control and auditing within the enterprise network.

The dynamic VLAN assignment is the easiest way to enforce and segment endpoints, because standards support this method. But, on the other hand, VLAN assignment can result in subnet change, which is usually not communicated to the endpoints. You also need to enforce the VLAN-to-VLAN security policy. It can be costly when you add more VLANs.

Besides assigning appropriate VLANs for users that can successfully authenticate with the authentication server, dynamic VLAN assignment can also be used to assign VLANs for users who fail the authentication. The advantage of using authentication-server-assigned VLANs for failed authentication is that VLAN assignment will be centrally logged in the AAA system.

You can also dynamically assign a VLAN based on the configuration of a switch:

- **Guest VLAN:** Guest VLAN assignment can be used locally on the switch for users who do not have the 802.1X supplicant. You can offer limited network access to such users.

- **Restricted VLAN:** You can configure restricted VLANs for users who have the supplicant but fail the authentication process. A restricted VLAN allows users who do not have valid credentials on an authentication server to access a limited set of services.

- **Default VLAN:** The default VLAN is the VLAN that is configured on the port. When a client successfully authenticates to the server and the authentication server does not assign a dynamic VLAN, the default VLAN is retained on the port.

- **Critical VLAN:** A critical VLAN is the VLAN that is applied to the 802.1X-enabled interface if the authentication server is unavailable.

You also want to extend this solution to limit the access for the external contractors that support the internal IT team. You want to dynamically assign access restrictions to only allow access to the resources that a specific contractor needs.

You want to implement a simple solution that is also manageable. You are thinking of creating a per-contractor VLAN and then limiting access to the systems on the SVI interface for that VLAN. But you come to the conclusion that this solution is not scalable. You decide that a better solution is to use downloadable ACLs.

The downloadable ACLs allow you to enable per-user ACLs on the RADIUS server. When a user is authenticated on the 802.1X port, the RADIUS sends ACL attributes to the switch. The switch applies the attributes to the 802.1X port during the user session (see Figure 25-10). The switch removes the per-user ACL configuration when the session is over if authentication fails or if a link-down condition occurs.

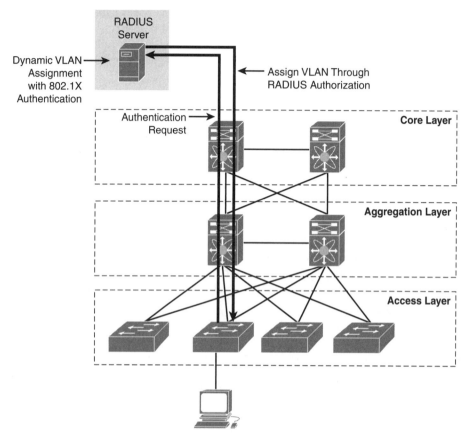

Figure 25-10 *Dynamic VLAN Assignment*

Downloadable ACLs are a more flexible way of blocking the traffic from the source to certain destinations. Because all ACLs are configured on the RADIUS server centrally, there is no need to change ACLs on a local switch. But when you are implementing ACLs, you must be careful because ACLs consume ternary content-addressable memory (TCAM) space on the switch.

You have implemented this solution. The RADIUS server is responsible for assigning a common VLAN for all contractors. Each contractor has an ACL applied on the RADIUS server, which is downloaded when the contractor is successfully authenticated to the network.

> **Note** Consider a Cisco TrustSec solution in this case study, such as adding SGT, which will leverage the existing design to support more complex and dynamic access polices no matter how the user is connected to the network (wired or wireless). In addition, profiling services will add an additional layer of access control and visibility to the types of devices used to access the network and provide the ability to assign different access polices based on the used device.

Summary

- IEEE 802.1X provides authentication-based port access control and authorization.
- EAP is a protocol for authentication in IEEE 802.1X.
- You can assign VLAN or downloadable ACLs through IEEE 802.1X authorization.
- You should use phased deployment mode for limited impact on network access.
- Cisco AnyConnect can act as an IEEE 802.1X supplicant.
- Cisco TrustSec enforces policy based on contextual identity of the endpoint.

Review Questions

After answering the following questions, please refer to Appendix A, "Answers to Review Questions," for the answers.

1. Which is the recommended first step when deploying 802.1X?
    a. Monitor mode
    b. Closed mode
    c. High-impact mode
    d. Low-impact mode

2. Match the 802.1X VLAN types with their proper descriptions.

802.1X VLAN Types	Description
Guest VLAN	Assigned to users or devices that do not have the 802.1X supplicant
Critical VLAN	Assigned to users or devices that fail the authentication process
Restricted VLAN	VLAN that is configured on the port and is assigned to users or devices that successfully authenticate
Default VLAN	Assigned to a port when the authentication server is unavailable

3. Which of the following describes EAP chaining?
   a. Uses separate EAP procedures for user and machine authentication.
   b. Allows authentication only with username and password.
   c. Uses two EAP exchanges inside the same TLS outer tunnel.
   d. First implemented in EAP-TLS.

4. What alternatives can be used for clients that do not support 802.X authentication? (Select two.)
   a. Web-authentication
   b. Public certificate
   c. Shared key
   d. MAB
   e. VPN client with user and password

5. A large enterprise with several departments needs to have the flexibility to restrict users' access to data center applications based on the department the users belong to. Which one of the following access control approaches or mechanisms would you suggest this organization to use without introducing operational complexity?
   a. Infrastructure access control lists (iACL) at the access switches
   b. Separate VLAN and VRF per department
   c. Cisco ISE + SGT
   d. iACL at the DC firewall

Chapter 26

Design Case Studies

This chapter walks you through some sample design scenarios that focus on specific design case study domains in the enterprise. The goal is to help you understand how to identify design requirements and how to apply the design concepts and technology solutions discussed in this book. This chapter covers the following design scenarios:

- **Design Enterprise Connectivity:** The aim of this design scenario is to learn how to take into consideration customer requirements and then design an enterprise network as a result of the customer's migration plans from RIPv2 to OSPF.

- **Design Enterprise BGP Network with Internet Connectivity:** The aim of this design scenario is to learn how to take into consideration customer requirements and how to design an enterprise network based on a BGP that suits those requirements.

- **Design Enterprise IPv6 Network:** The aim of this design scenario is to learn how to take into consideration customer requirements and then design an IPv6 enterprise network that suits the requirements.

- **Design Enterprise Data Center Connectivity:** The aim of this design scenario is to learn how to take into consideration customer requirements and then design a data center network that suits the requirements.

- **Design Resilient Enterprise WAN:** The aim of this design scenario is to learn how to take into consideration customer requirements and then design a modern and resilient WAN connectivity that suits the different customer requirements.

- **Design Secure Enterprise Network:** The aim of this design scenario is to learn how to take into consideration customer security requirements to build a secure IP network design by dividing the network into multiple logical zones and apply the appropriate security polices based on the design requirements.

- **Design QoS in Enterprise Network:** The aim of this design scenario is to learn how to take into consideration customer requirements by identifying the different types of applications used across the network and their criticality to the business and then how to design end-to-end quality-of-service strategies and polices to meet these requirements.

Case Study 1: Design Enterprise Connectivity

You are working for an IT company, and your customer, ROBASISI Acoustics Ltd., has hired you to design the expansion of its network and at the same time to migrate its network from RIPv2 to OSPF. This large enterprise company has many branches with primary and redundant links. Recently, after it connected many more branches to the network, intermittent network failures and slow convergence started to occur.

Detailed Requirements and Expectations

The customer's network connects a large number of branches in a classic hub-and-spoke topology. Each branch has a primary link and a backup link to the company's headquarters (HQ). All primary links are metro Ethernet with a separate interface for each branch location. The backup links are implemented via a separate physical infrastructure that uses GRE tunnels across the public Internet. Most branches are implemented using similar equipment and topology except branch 3, which has an EIGRP cloud that is a legacy solution from a past merger. Mutual redistribution between RIPv2 and EIGRP takes place at that point. The customer does not want to migrate the EIGRP part of the network; it should be left in its current form.

The customer informs you that extended downtime in the EIGRP cloud during the migration is not an issue. Apart from the EIGRP segment, the network is operating using RIPv2 as the IGP. However, the RIPv2 network was designed and implemented poorly. Therefore, the customer is not happy with the routing protocol's performance and wants to migrate the network to another protocol. As the network has been growing lately, the customer has experienced more intermittent network failures and slow convergence times at times of primary link failures. By assessing the situation, you notice that even though the branches' IP routes can be summarized, they are not summarized at the moment. In addition, the customer is planning the rollout of a new VoIP service, and this service will require the network performance, mainly the convergence times, to improve significantly.

Because the network consists of devices from several vendors, the customer is considering a migration to a standards-based link-state protocol that has wide vendor support and good documentation. The customer is relying on your expertise to choose the protocol and implement the migration with the least possible downtime. Note that some of the routers in branches are low-end routers and might not support service-provider–oriented routing protocols. Finally, the customer does not want to use BGP because it would need to buy expensive licenses for existing routers. Figure 26-1 illustrates the current WAN and routing design.

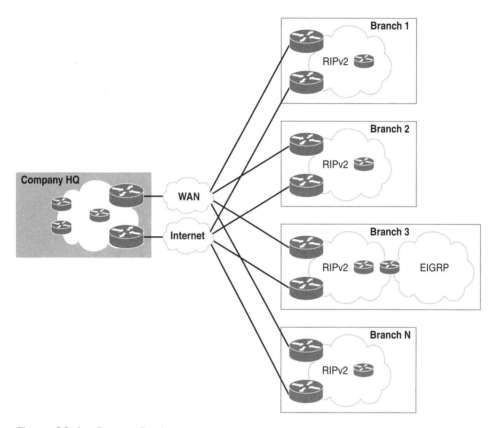

Figure 26-1 *Current Design*

Design Analysis and Task List

Based on the information provided, you must consider the following primary points across all the design stages:

- The customer has a hub-and-spoke network, where spokes have redundant connectivity to the hub.
- A small part of the network runs EIGRP. The hub-and-spoke part of the network runs RIPv2. The customer wants you to replace the routing protocol:
  - It must not be proprietary.
  - It must provide fast convergence.
  - It must have good documentation for enterprise deployments.
  - It must not be BGP because of licensing concerns.

The main required tasks are as follows:

- Select a replacement routing protocol for RIPv2.
- Design for the new routing protocol.
- Plan and design the migration from the old to the new routing.

Selecting a Replacement Routing Protocol

Based on the brief analysis in the preceding section, logically the first question you would ask yourself as a network designer is: "Which interior routing protocol will you recommend to the customer, as a replacement for RIPv2, given the customer's requirements?" Answers might be

- BGP, because it is standards-based even though it is not an IGP.
- EIGRP, because EIGRP is already in the network (note that EIGRP is defined in IETF RFC 7867).
- OSPF, because it is standards-based.
- IS-IS, because it is a link-state protocol.

After you consider the customer's requirements and the topology, you should base your design on OSPF because

- It is standards-based.
- It is a link-state protocol with fast convergence.
- It is proven in the field and well documented.
- It works well between devices of different vendors.
- It is supported in lower-end routers in the customer's network, so the migration does not require extra cost in hardware.

BGP is out of the question because the customer's current equipment does not support BGP and buying extra licenses would be expensive. Although EIGRP is now published as an RFC (RFC 7868), EIGRP is not commonly implemented yet in non-Cisco platforms. IS-IS fulfills most requirements, but you rule it out because it is used mainly in service provider environments and the support availability and install base in the enterprise segment are not as good as with OSPF. Also, in this scenario, there is backup path over a GRE tunnel, and IS-IS is not supported to run over IP tunnels.

Designing for the New Routing Protocol

After selecting OSPF as the IGP, you need to think about how you will design OSPF in a network. You must consider the customer's requirements, such as providing scalable design and fast convergence and supporting the current connectivity model (for example, connectivity of branch 3 to the EIGRP domain).

When designing a link-state routing protocol with multiple areas, ideally you should start with the backbone area design. Therefore, you should ask the following questions:

- Which routers should participate in the backbone area? Only HQ devices? Branch devices? Only border devices? All routers in HQ and border devices in branches?

- After deciding which devices should participate in the backbone area, how will you ensure that backup links are less desirable than the primary links? (Sometimes you need to think ahead using the design requirements; for instance, the answer to this question may influence your OSPF backbone area design choice in the preceding question.)

Although technically all the suggested OSPF backbone area design options are possible, the most optimal ones in this particular scenario are as follows (see Figure 26-2):

- All routers in the HQ and border routers in branches are part of the backbone area. This option provides scalable and modular OSPF design in which you can later summarize the branch routes, and it offers a good level of fault isolation. However, because the HQ routers are part of the backbone area, any change in any of the branches (such as link flapping) will be propagated to all the HQ routers, which may lead to reduced stability when the network grows in size.

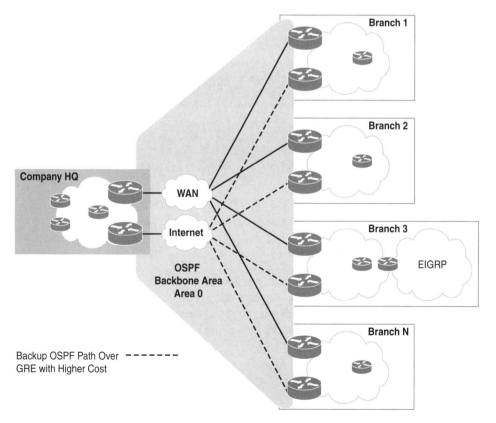

Figure 26-2 *OSPF Backbone Area Design*

- All border devices are part of backbone area. This option offers more optimized design compared to the preceding one with regard to the level of fault isolation and design stability. Therefore, this option will be selected in this design scenario.
    - OSPF places interfaces in areas, so the HQ and branch border routers will place interfaces only facing the WAN in area 0.
    - You should include area 0 links from both primary and backup routers.

In addition, to ensure that the backup links are always less preferred than the primary links, you must define a higher OSPF link cost for backup links so that the GRE tunnels will appear more costly to OSPF.

OSPF Design Optimization

After the decision is made to place the WAN interfaces of all border routers to participate in the OSPF backbone area (area 0), each branch/spoke will be placed in its own area for the following reasons:

- To provide a more stable, scalable design, area 0 must not grow to such a scale to include each branch LAN and too many devices.
- More optimized route advertisement as summarization can be applied at area border nodes.

> **Note** In large-scale networks, you can group branches; however, you do not want too many (for example, 20 to 50 branches) in a single OSPF area.

Now, you need to decide what type of area will you implement for the branches. Should it be one of the following?

- Stubby
- Totally stubby
- Normal area
- Not-so-stubby area (NSSA)

Because the branches in this scenario do not have any other exit but the hub, it is safe and advisable to deploy each branch network as a totally stubby area. With this design (see Figure 26-3), each branch router will receive only the default route from the backbone (border routers of the branch).

Case Study 1: Design Enterprise Connectivity 783

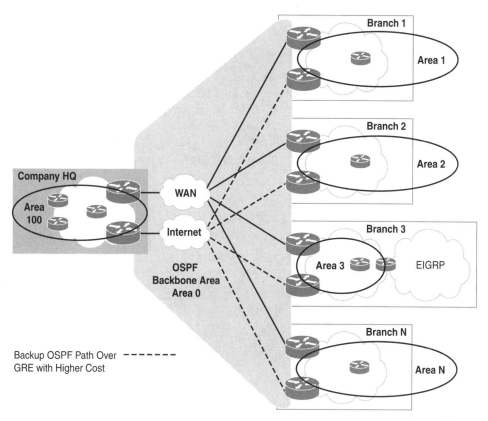

Figure 26-3 *OSPF Area Design: Branches*

Note In each branch, ensure that the border routers are interconnected over a dedicated link that is part of area 0 (no summarization) to avoid sending some packets over the backup path (see Figure 26-4).

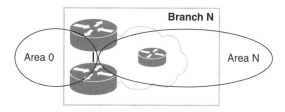

Figure 26-4 *Border Routers Interconnect Without Summarization*

On the other hand, "branch 3" in this scenario has a slightly different layout. Therefore, if you configure branch 3 (area 3) as totally stubby like the other branches, how will you inform the core about the EIGRP networks (external routes)?

As discussed in Chapter 3, "OSPF Design," regular stubby areas cannot advertise external routes into the backbone. Consequently, area 3 will be configured as a totally not-so-stubby area (NSSA), as shown in Figure 26-5. With this design, area 3 will be able to

- Receive the default route only into the area.
- Advertise external routes redistributed from EIGRP to the backbone.

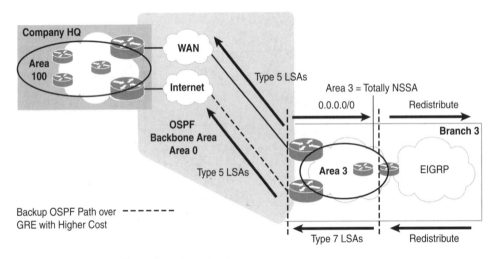

Figure 26-5 *Branch 3 OSPF Area Design*

At this stage, you should start looking into how to optimize this design further. Route summarization helps to achieve a more simplified routing design with better stability and scalability. In this scenario, at which points should you apply OSPF route summarization, taking into consideration the final state of the OSPF area design? Within the backbone? Within areas? At area borders?

OSPF summarization in an area is not an option because it is a link-state protocol; therefore, you should use the following OSPF route summarization approach in this scenario (see Figure 26-6):

- You should perform summarization at the area borders, where the stub areas of the branches and the normal area of the HQ will advertise a summary into the backbone.
- You should perform summarization at the ASBR if there is a large number of summarizable routes received from the external network.

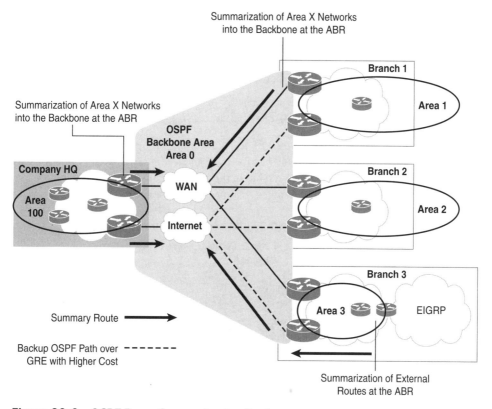

Figure 26-6 *OSPF Route Summarization Design*

Planning and Designing the Migration from the Old to the New Routing

After you complete the targeted design of the new protocol (OSPF), it's time to start with the migration and implementation plans. Typically, when migrating RIPv2 to OSPF, the first question you should ask is, "Will you implement a gradual migration or a cut-over?" You also need to ask the following questions:

- Should area 0 or the stub areas be deployed first?
- Should branches be migrated one by one or cut over after everything is configured?
- Should route redistribution be used between OSPF and RIPv2?

In addition, in any routing migration scenario, you must consider the administrative distance (AD) of each routing protocol and how they will impact the migration. It is almost always gradual (phased) migration that is recommended to minimize downtime and reduce risks. You can use the following steps in this scenario (see Figure 26-7):

Step 1. Configure area 0.

Step 2. Configure redistribution between OSPF and RIPv2 on both hub routers.

Step 3. Configure OSPF at stub areas one by one, while verifying routes and connectivity. Repeat until area N is done.

Because of lower AD of OSPF (OSPF 110, RIP 120), both protocols coexisting as OSPF routes will always be preferred over RIPv2 for any route learned over both protocols. This approach is commonly referred to as a "ship in the night" because route redistribution between the two protocols is not required.

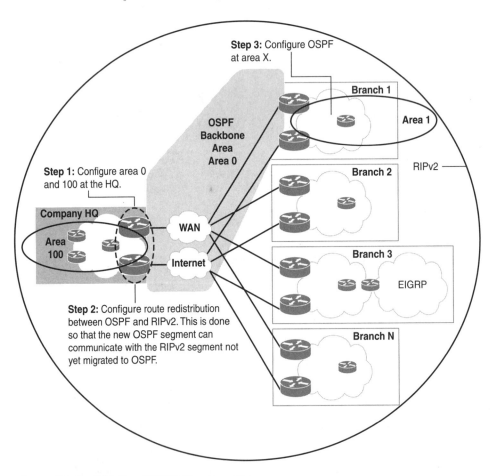

Figure 26-7 *RIPv2 to OSPF Migration Steps*

With this approach, as soon as a branch migrates to OSPF, the prefixes of that branch will not be seen in the rest of the RIPv2 network (because of lower OSPF AD). To maintain reachability during the migration routes, redistribution should be done at both hub routers in a way that OSPF routes will be redistributed into RIPv2 only. (The purpose is for OSPF segments to be able to communicate with RIPv2 segments not yet migrated.)

As shown in Figure 26-8, when branch 1 migrates to OSPF, the prefixes of branch 1 will not be seen in the rest of the RIPv2 network—until redistribution from OSPF to RIPv2 happens. However, in this scenario, mutual redistribution will not be required because OSPF-migrated branches will have a default route to the hubs that hold the complete routing information.

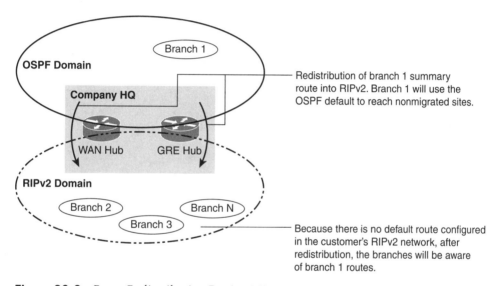

Figure 26-8 *Route Redistribution During Migration*

RIPv2 can be completely removed from configurations of all routers after all branches have been migrated to OSPF. All routes in the routing tables of all routers will be OSPF routes because of the lower AD of OSPF. Because RIPv2 does not play an active role at this point, there are no relevant RIP routes in the routing tables; therefore, shutting it down will not influence the routing tables of the routers.

Scaling the Design

While the network keeps growing, with this design the WAN hub routers at the company HQ will maintain many adjacencies, mainly with the branch routers. What will you recommend to the customer if the number of adjacencies becomes a burden to the hub routers and the network operation suffers as a result?

Excessive backbone growth can cause issues in any network; however, the number of adjacencies on a single router can be a problem that manifests itself a lot sooner and needs to be addressed. Because area 0 design is not easy to change in this scenario, adding extra hub routers is the best solution to lower or maintain the number of adjacencies per router. Other area 0 routers and branch routers are not at risk of a high adjacency number because they each will have only a handful of neighbors.

Splitting the load across multiple hub routers will help the overall OSPF operation, as illustrated in Figure 26-9.

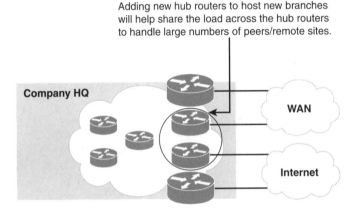

Figure 26-9 *Scaling the Design*

Another possible option here is to migrate the WAN to an MPLS Layer 3 VPN provider in which the WAN edge router (CE), including hub routers, will have a single routing session with the provider (PE) router. However, this may be a more expensive WAN option.

Case Study 2: Design Enterprise BGP Network with Internet Connectivity

PILE Forensic Accounting Ltd. has hired you to design a network expansion of its network. This large enterprise recently expanded to multiple worldwide markets. The company's new network will span over multiple continents and regions. You will also need to redesign Internet access to allow the overseas branches to use a local Internet breakout if it is more economical to do so. The cost of WAN links used to interconnect different regions can be very high, so you should design the network to accommodate strict policies on the conditions in which some links will be preferred to others.

Detailed Requirements and Expectations

The customer has indicated that the data center that is situated at the current company headquarters will not be able to sustain the traffic from the new markets, so it wishes to build another data center abroad. The new data center will need to be deployed in

Europe, and communication between the two data centers will have to be established. All branches, regardless of location, will have to access services that are located at the HQ data center.

PILE Forensic Accounting has three regional centers: one is located in North America (with two main sites), one in Europe, and one in Asia. All regional centers connect to several small branches of their own. The small branches that connect to the regional center will only require default routing to the regional centers they connect to. The regional centers already have an IGP running in their respective networks. The three North American sites run OSPF, and the European and Asian sites run EIGRP (see Figure 26-10a).

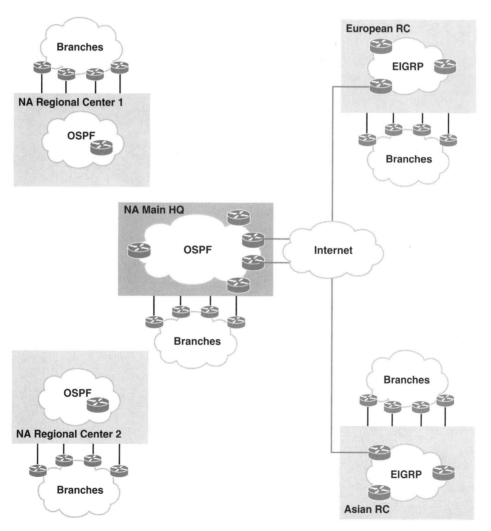

Figure 26-10a *PILE Forensic Accounting Ltd. Routing Topology*

790   Chapter 26: Design Case Studies

The following link requirements have been set by the customer (see Figure 26-10b):

- North American regional centers and the main headquarters should form a triangle between the three edge routers.
- The links between RC1 and the main headquarters and between RC1 and RC2 will be 10 Gbps.
- The link between RC2 and the main headquarters will be 100 Mbps.
- Traffic to and from RC2 should use faster links when communicating with the rest of the network.
- The main headquarters will connect to the European RC and Asian RC with 1 Gbps links. The European and Asian RCs will be connected with one 100 Mbps link.

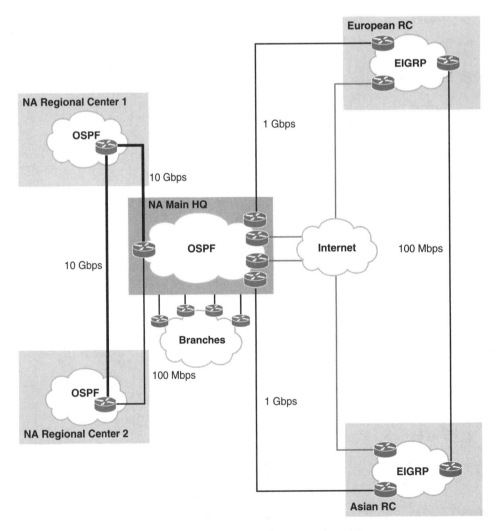

Figure 26-10b *PILE Forensic Accounting Ltd. New Links*

The customer has strict requirements on how different regional centers should access different services with regards to the location. Before you apply any policy, you will have to devise a means of tagging the corporate routes and Internet-sourced routes with different tags. The European and Asian devices should communicate via the main headquarters, and the link between Europe and Asia will be used as backup. Additionally, North American RC2 devices and Asian HQ devices should not be allowed to communicate.

Internet access should be implemented in several different regional centers as follows:

- The main headquarters should be multihomed to two independent local ISPs.
- The European RC will be single-homed and use private ASN.
- The Asian RC will be single-homed and use private ASN.

The customer requires that the clients at North American RCs and the main HQ primarily access the Internet through the main HQ. The main HQ's ISP1 connection should be active for all traffic, and the connection to ISP2 should be active only in case of ISP1 failure. North American RCs should receive only the default route to be able to reach the Internet. However, in case Internet connectivity completely fails at the main headquarters, the Internet traffic from North America should be routed via the remaining European and Asian Internet links in order of priority—first the European, then the Asian link. At every Internet exit point, there will be Network Address Translation (NAT) to the respective public IP range. RCs will only announce their own prefixes to the Internet.

European and Asian RCs should use their own Internet breakout and serve each other as a backup path for Internet traffic in case of local failure. In the event of failure of Internet links at both RCs, they will use the main HQ's Internet access.

Design Analysis and Task List

Based on the information provided, you must consider the following primary points:

- A company with networks in North America, Europe, and Asia has hired you to design its routing.
- WAN link costs have driven the customer to require strict traffic flow policies across its network.

The main required tasks are to do the following:

- Discuss routing choices.
- Decide on the number of ASNs, types of BGP sessions, the BGP community scheme, and the type of public IP addressing.
- Design routing polices between the customer's international sites and policies to access the Internet that meet the customer's requirements.

Choosing the Routing Protocol

Based on the information provided, which routing protocol will you use in your consolidated topology: OSPF only, EIGRP only, both EIGRP and OSPF, or BGP on top of any existing IGP?

The use of EGP is warranted because of the diversity of the current network setup, which consists of "islands" using different IGPs. Taking into account that the customer expects the network to grow rapidly on a global scale and considering the strict policy requirements given by the customer, the use of BGP, which has very powerful policy capabilities, is a clear choice. Also, BGP is already needed at the Internet edge.

It would take a lot of effort to merge the networks under a single IGP domain, but even then the granular policy features that are provided by EBGP would be hard to achieve in an IGP-only network. There would be a complex redistribution in place, and route filtering and control could prove to be a considerable administrative effort. Scaling is another factor to be considered. The number of nodes in the future could be a limiting factor when using IGP in a network of this scale. BGP on top of existing IGPs presents advantages, including

- No need to merge different IGP domains.
- No need for complex IGP redistribution and filtering.
- Summarization possible.
- BGP already needed at the Internet edge.

BGP powerful policy capabilities offer

- Precise control between autonomous systems.
- Prefix filtering and path selection.
- Complete control over what you advertise and receive.
- Policy changes that can be applied on the fly.

Choosing the Autonomous System Numbers

In a scenario like this one, the following questions are the most logical ones that you would ask regarding BGP ASN design strategy:

- How many ASNs should there be?
- Would you consider private ASN, public ASN, or a mix for the following sites?
    - Main HQ
    - European RC
    - Asian RC (the answer for this region is already known: "single-homed and using private ASN")

- Should you include the two North American RCs and the HQ in one BGP autonomous system or use three separate AS numbers?
- Do you require any special policy between RCs?
- Will you use BGP at branch locations?

The network design will contain five different AS numbers. If the customer adds more RCs in the future, it will need more AS numbers. Each regional center should use a different AS number because this configuration will enable you to define a precise BGP policy at the edge of each autonomous system. You should not configure branches with BGP; instead you should use only IGP because the branches will use default routing to the RC.

The following summarizes BGP ASN design (see Figure 26-11):

- Public ASN on main HQ.
- Private ASN on European and Asian RC.
    - Local ISPs support private ASNs.
- Every North America RC should be a separate BGP ASN:
    - EBGP policy enforcement.
    - Consistency with other RCs.
    - Easier deployment of future RCs.
- Branches will not use BGP:
    - They are stub regions.
    - IGP will propagate the default route.

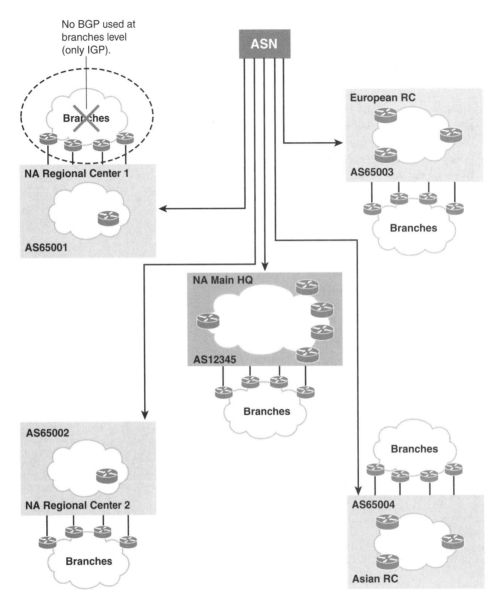

Figure 26-11 *PILE Forensic BG ASNs Design*

BGP Connectivity

You need to decide for the BGP sessions design and BGP community values allocation to form the foundation of the BGP communication in this scenario that ultimately will facilitate the creation of BGP policies (networkwide) to steer the traffic and control the communications as required.

BGP Sessions

After you decide the BGP ASN design strategy, the next step is to form BGP sessions between the different peers across the network. To do so, answer these questions:

- Where will you establish EBGP sessions?
- Where will you establish IBGP sessions?
- Do you need route reflectors?
    - Per autonomous system or globally for all autonomous systems?
- What are the criteria for deploying route reflectors?

As you learned in Chapter 5, "Border Gateway Protocol Design," you should implement IBGP sessions within every autonomous system between all routers in full mesh if there is no use of route reflectors or confederation. If you use route reflectors, you need to implement IBGP between all clients and route reflectors. IBGP is used internally only. EBGP sessions will be established between the pairs of edge routers belonging to different autonomous systems. Therefore, the following basic BGP session design logic will be used (see Figure 26-12):

- EBGP sessions are established between routers in different autonomous systems.
- IBGP sessions are established between routers inside an autonomous system.

For IBGP design within each autonomous system, as a rule of thumb, you can use route reflectors if there are more than four routers at one location. For the main HQ, you will use route reflectors because there will probably be more than four routers in total. If you use route reflectors, you should use two for redundancy. You will position them centrally in the path of the traffic. Other RCs might not need to use route reflectors for now but could use them in the future.

Note You still can position the route reflectors out of path. However, you need to keep in mind the possibility of suboptimal routing in an environment with MPLS because the route reflector will send the best route to its clients from its point of view to the topology that may not be the optimal path to the RR-client.

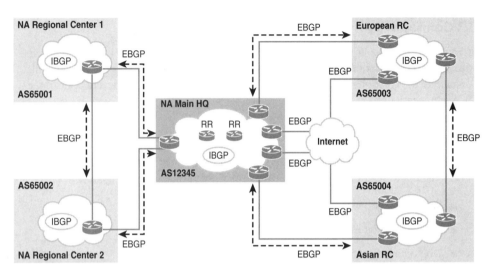

Figure 26-12 *BGP Sessions*

BGP Communities

In a scenario like this one, where complex BGP polices are required, considering a structured and simple BGP community values allocation helps to simplify BGP policy design.

- How will you tag your enterprise routes?
    - Per location-based tags?
- How will you tag the routes received from the Internet?
    - Will you receive only default routes from all ISPs?
- How is it good to separate your corporate routes from the public ones?

Because the BGP communities will be used for tagging routes, if you want to apply policies at various points in the network, you should create a scheme that will clearly mark the routes that are originated by your enterprise as opposed to the routes received from the Internet. An example of a community scheme that you can use is in the form of 12345:RC_AS. By this logic, all routes that are originated by AS 12345 will be tagged as 12345:12345, all routes that are originated by AS 65001 will be tagged as 12345:65001, and so on. Routes that are received from the Internet (a default route in this case) will be tagged as ISP_AS:0 (see Figure 26-13).

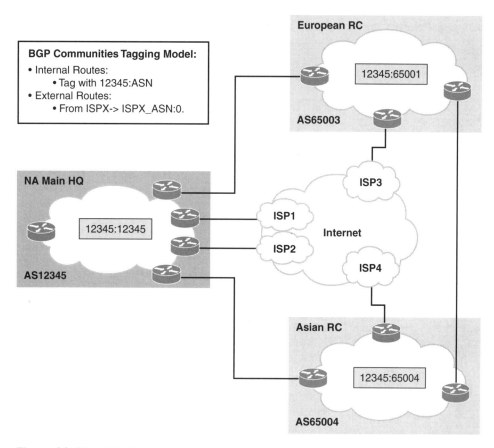

Figure 26-13 *BGP Communities*

Routing Policy

Based on the information and design requirements provided, several routing polices can be enforced to either steer traffic over certain paths or to restrict communication between specific locations. For simplicity, this section discusses the requirements and solutions of internal routing polices based on the geographical location; then it discusses the Internet routing polices.

Routing Policy in North American Sites

The first traffic engineering requirement that you need to consider with the BGP policy design is to force traffic from RC2 to the main HQ through the fast 10 Gbps links via RC1 in both directions (see Figure 26-14).

798 Chapter 26: Design Case Studies

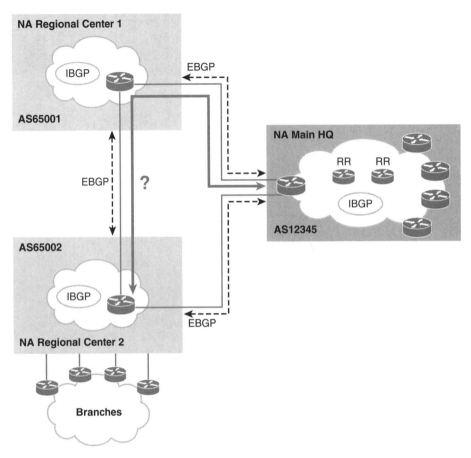

Figure 26-14 *How to Steer Traffic Between RC2 and HQ*

How can you achieve this effect with BGP policies? How is the policy applied? Is it in the ingress or egress direction? What about local preference, weight, and AS-path prepend? Where is it achieved: the Main HQ, RC1, or RC2? Technically, you can achieve the desired effect (traffic routing as specified) in several ways (see Figure 26-15):

- **Option 1:** If you influence the policy at the main HQ, you will configure the main HQ router facing RC1 and RC2 in the following way:
    - Assign a higher local preference to routes originated at RC2 AS, received from the RC1 peer.
    - AS-path prepend two times to all prefixes when sending to the RC2 peer.

- **Option 2:** If you want to apply the policy at the RC2 router, you will configure it in the following way:
    - Assign a higher local preference to all routes received from the RC1 peer.
    - AS-path prepend two times all prefixes when sending to the main HQ peer.

Case Study 2: Design Enterprise BGP Network with Internet Connectivity 799

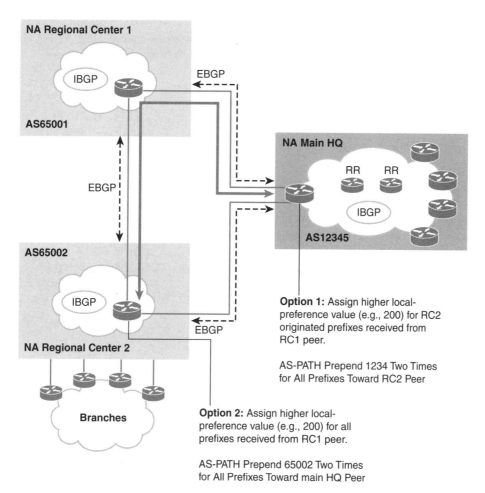

Figure 26-15 *BGP Policies to Steer Traffic Between RC2 and HQ*

Routing Policy in European and Asian Sites

As part of the region design requirements, you need to design a BGP policy in a way that ensures traffic routing always prefers the path via the main HQ. Before suggesting the design, you should think about the following:

- Which path will be preferred by default? Why?
- What tools should be used and where?

As shown in Figure 26-16, the easiest way to influence this behavior is to adjust the policy at the direct peering point between European and Asian RCs. To achieve this objective, you will have to make the direct path seem more distant than the path via the main HQ. You can achieve this behavior by AS-path prepending. On the European RC, on the router peering with Asian RC, you can prepend local AS two times for all routes that are originated by the local AS. You should perform a similar configuration on the Asian-side router. You can use communities to match locally originated prefixes for AS-path prepending.

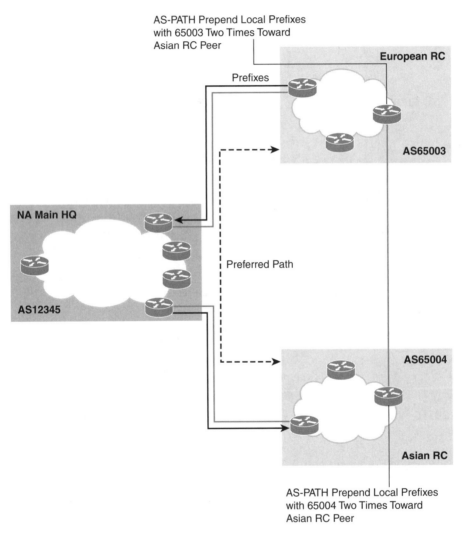

Figure 26-16 *BGP Policies to Steer Traffic over the HQ*

During the design, the customer expresses an interest to do load sharing across the available paths between these two regions (as a new requirement). How will the policy change if you wanted to load-share between the two paths?

To load-share between the direct path and the main HQ path, you should selectively prepend the AS-path on the Asian and European HQs. You can select half of the local prefixes for which you will do the AS-path prepend and leave the other half unchanged. The traffic for the prepended prefixes will go via the main HQ, while the traffic for the unchanged prefixes will follow the direct path between RCs. In addition, path redundancy still exists for all prefixes in case of any link failure (see Figure 26-17).

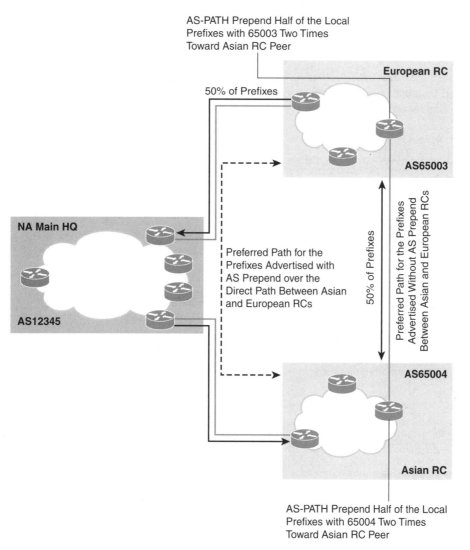

Figure 26-17 *BGP Policies for Load Sharing*

One of the BGP policy design restrictions involves restricting the communication between North American RC2 and Asian RC (including their branches). So how can this effect be achieved? First, you should think of the following questions:

- Which BGP policy tool will you use?
- How will you select prefixes?
- Where will you apply the policy?

As you know with BGP, any policy design can be achieved in different ways; the decision on which is to use is always a matter of which choice is less complicated and meets all the requirements. In this scenario, the simplest and most dynamic way to achieve the aforementioned restriction requirement is to drop prefixes based on communities at the AS edge (see Figure 26-18):

- Match prefixes by community and drop.
- Apply the policy to several points in the inbound direction.

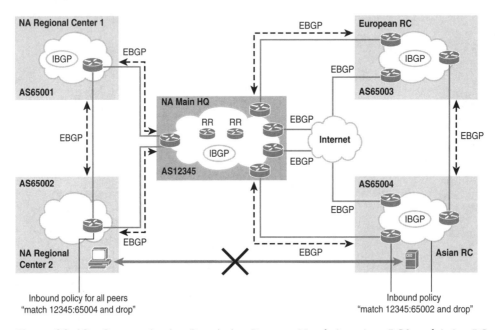

Figure 26-18 *Communication Restriction Between North American RC2 and Asian RC*

Internet Routing

This section discusses considerations regarding the design of the IP connectivity and BGP policy to meet Internet routing requirements.

Public IP Space Selection

The nature of the scenario (a network with different internal connectives across the different locations) should drive you to ask the following questions when you start thinking of how to achieve the Internet connectivity that meets the design requirements:

- What type of public IP address space to access the Internet (provider-independent [PI] or provider-assigned [PA]) will you require for the following?
    - Main HQ
    - European RC
    - Asian RC
- Can you use provider-independent space everywhere?
- What would change your mind about European and Asian RC IP-type selection?

For basic Internet connectivity, typically you should use NAT at every exit point. Because you will have two connections to two different ISPs at the main HQ, you will have to request and use a provider-independent range of IP addresses.

For the European and Asian RCs, you can use a provider-assigned IP address range (see Figure 26-19). However, you could also use a provider-independent range at those RCs so that you are ready if, in the future, you want to connect another ISP. In that case, you will also require a public ASN for European and Asian RCs. Therefore, it would require more administrative work beforehand to secure the PI address ranges and the public ASN.

804 Chapter 26: Design Case Studies

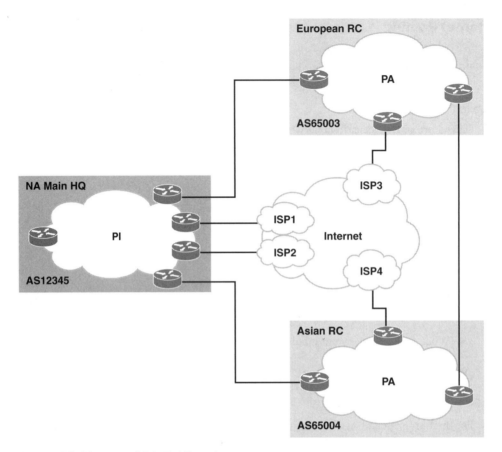

Figure 26-19 *PI and PA IP Allocation*

Main HQ Multihoming

Based on the provided information, the customer requires ISP1 to be the primary Internet provider. Before considering any BGP policy design, as a network designer, you should answer the following questions:

- Where will you use local preference and where will you use AS-path prepending?
- Would you consider any other tools?
- What will you announce to ISPs? What should you never announce?

Note Do not forget to consider BGP policy in *both* directions!

To make the ISP1 path better as an exit point from your network for all traffic, you should assign a better local preference for all prefixes received from ISP1 (or reduce the local preference for all prefixes received from ISP2; for example, you might set it to 90, which is less than the default value in Cisco IOS). This design will ensure that all traffic leaves your autonomous system via ISP1, and the traffic will be sent via ISP2 only in case of failure.

For incoming traffic, the mechanisms are different. You will AS-path prepend your provider-independent address space several times when announcing to ISP2. Even though you can never absolutely control the incoming traffic path, this configuration will make the return path via ISP1 the better path in most cases (see Figure 26-20). In addition, you should announce only your provider-independent address space to both ISPs and filter all other prefixes. This configuration will ensure that your autonomous system does not become a transit AS for other traffic that does not belong to you.

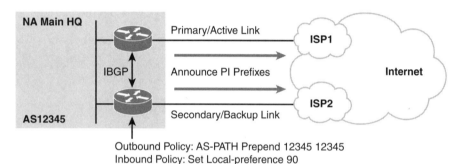

Figure 26-20 *HQ Internet Multihoming BGP Policy*

Default Routing

A complex situation is created when there are multiple exit points to the Internet because the default route is received through three sources: the main HQ, European RC, and Asian RC. The question here is how you will prioritize different default routes from three sources in each location. Is there a preference for the closest exit? What BGP mechanism will you use? What points are best suited to enforce policy? What will North American RC1 and RC2 use for default routing?

The best way to control routing in this scenario is to use the community tags that you can assign to the different default routes at different points and then apply the desired action for the BGP policy at different points in the network. Consequently, each region will set the highest local preference to its own default route prefix and then a lower one for the next in line, with the lowest local preference to the least desirable default route based on the assigned BGP community tag to the default route. Local preference is set at the ISP edge. When receiving 0/0, it will be assigned the highest local preference. The routers on the edge of ASNs will assign local preference to routes coming from other ASNs and set the local preference accordingly, but as a rule, it will be lower than that of the local default route. NA RC1 and RC2 will receive and use whatever 0/0 is preferred at the main HQ at the moment. In any case, they will always send traffic to the main HQ because there is no direct way to access the Internet locally (see Figure 26-21). The following policies will be applied on the border routers in the inbound direction:

- Main HQ:
    - Prefer local exit (ISP1 and then ISP2): set Local Preference to 200,100.
    - European RC exit: set Local Preference to 90.
    - Asian RC exit: set Local Preference to 80.
- European RC:
    - Prefer local exit ISP3: set default Local Preference to 100.
    - Asian RC exit: set Local Preference to 90.
    - Main HQ exit: set Local Preference to 80.
- Asian RC:
    - Prefer local exit ISP4: set default Local Preference to 100.
    - European RC exit: set Local Preference to 90.
    - Main HQ exit: set Local Preference to 80.

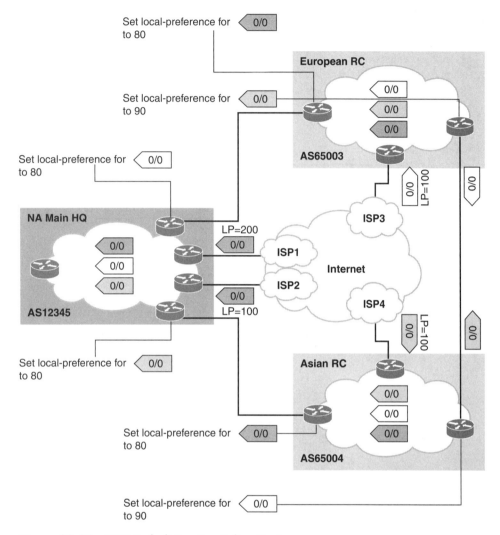

Figure 26-21 *BGP Default Routing Policy Design*

Case Study 3: Design Enterprise IPv6 Network

You are working for an IT company, and your customer, SHOOKY Breweries Ltd., has hired you to prepare the network for IPv6 support. The CEO of the company is focusing on growth of the business from the Asia Pacific region, where IPv4 connectivity is scarce and new partner companies may have IPv6 only to access corporate resources. The CEO requires the infrastructure to enable partners to access the business portals regardless of the Internet protocol version that is used. You are tasked with choosing the deployment method and implementing the changes on the existing infrastructure to be ready for partners to connect at later stages.

Detailed Requirements and Expectations

The SHOOKY Breweries Ltd. network consists of a headquarters office with 200 employees and two branch offices with 15 employees. The branch offices are connected via secure tunnels using IP connectivity that is offered by the local service provider (see Figure 26-22). All supporting infrastructure is located at the headquarters office (WWW, Mail, CRM, and so on) to which branch offices have access.

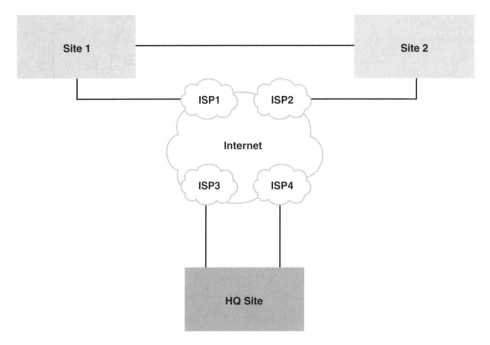

Figure 26-22 *SHOOKY Breweries Ltd Topology*

The HQ LAN has IPv4 connectivity to two service providers using a PI prefix and advertising it via BGP to both service providers. Both branch offices have a single link to the local service provider and are using IPsec over GRE to connect to the headquarters. The routing protocol that is used to advertise internal subnets is OSPF. Each branch office is designed to support a local breakout to the Internet.

The service provider at the Site 1 branch allows native IPv6 connectivity, but the Site 2 branch service provider offers only IPv4 connectivity because this service provider has not yet completed IPv6 implementation. The headquarters connects to two ISPs that both offer native IPv6 connectivity.

Headquarters has its own firewall solution that is configured to allow access to the DMZ externally and limit access to the internal network. Branch offices also employ local firewalls but do not have any DMZ servers. Firewalls also serve as termination points for telecommuters connecting to the company network through SSL VPN.

The customer initially requires an assessment of the existing infrastructure and the capability to support the new protocol. Depending on the assessment results, you will need to resolve the situation with minimum cost and choose the deployment method.

Existing DNS servers currently resolve A and PTR records. A dedicated DHCP server is used to assign addresses to clients in the headquarters. Branch routers act as DHCP servers for their local clients. Also, DHCP provisions a DNS server to hosts and TFTP address to IP phones.

Design Analysis and Task List

Based on the information provides, your primary design goal is to transition the current network design to be IPv6 enabled to support both IPv4 and IPv6 communication.

To achieve this goal, you must address the following required tasks:

- Choose the type of IPv6 address space.
- Decide how you will connect the branches to the headquarters.
- Decide on the IPv6 deployment model.
- Decide on IPv6 addressing.
- Decide on IPv6 address provisioning.
- Design communication between branches.
- Create a migration plan.
- Discuss network management for the IPv6 network.

Choosing the IP Address Type for the HQ

Logically, the first thing that you need to consider is which IPv6 address space type you will choose for the headquarters. Should it be provider assigned or provider independent?

Because the HQ is multihomed to two different ISPs, consider the PI prefix and advertise it through BGP. This is the best practice design because it offers multihoming and failover. Plus, it is a robust, tested design that is parallel to IPv4, and the customer can use one prefix to address hosts (see Figure 26-23).

> **Note** RIR Regional Internet Registries (RIR) manage, distribute, and register Internet number resources (IPv4 and IPv6 addresses and Autonomous System numbers) within their respective regions. The European IP Networks RIPE forum is open to all parties with an interest in the technical development of the Internet. The community's objective is to ensure that the administrative and technical coordination necessary to maintain and develop the Internet continues. It is not a standards body like the Internet Engineering Task Force (IETF). (See https://en.wikipedia.org/wiki/RIPE.)

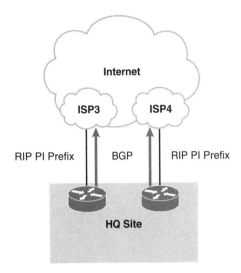

Figure 26-23 *HQ Connectivity*

The existing IPv4 WAN design at the headquarters is based on the PI allocation from the regional registrar and advertised to connected ISPs. This allows the customer prefix to be advertised globally and ensures resiliency in case of the failure of a single service provider.

The most recommended design for guaranteeing resiliency and multihoming capabilities is to replicate the IPv4 WAN design. When applying for a PI prefix with your regional registrar, you will receive a default prefix of /48. It will allow you to deploy up to 65,536 VLANs in your network.

The downside of the PI advertisement is that the upstream service providers are required to advertise your prefix and are not capable of /32 summarization; this leads to an excessive increase in the global routing table.

Connecting the Branch Sites

After you decide which IP address type you need to consider for the HQ, the second design consideration for which you need to make a decision is how the remote branches will communicate with the HQ site over IPv6. Consider that the ISP connected to branch site 1 supports IPv6, whereas the ISP connected to branch site 2 does not support IPv6. Given these facts, how should the connectivity be formed? Should you use tunneling, no tunneling, PI, or PA?

When connecting sites over an IPv4 network, you typically use tunnels for two reasons: to extend private IP address connectivity over the public IPv4 network and to satisfy security requirements. When connecting sites with native IPv6 connectivity, you do not require tunnels to achieve connectivity.

The use of global unicast prefixes (PA or PI) allows for end-to-end connectivity without translation or tunneling. IPsec tunnels may be implemented between sites only to achieve confidentiality.

The Site 1 branch connects to an ISP that offers both IPv4 and IPv6 natively, which allows you to implement dual stack on WAN. The service provider will allocate a PA prefix in the range of /48 or /56; as a result, you can address the Site 1 LAN. This type of design will allow for local breakout to the Internet without NAT.

For Site 1, native connectivity can be used with ISP1 using the PA address space because

- Single-homing requires no PI.
- ISP1 PA space is globally routable, so there is no need for a tunnel.

Note Based on the information provided, there are currently no security requirements that would dictate the use of tunnels to ensure confidentiality.

As you know, the Site 2 branch cannot connect its external interface natively because the service provider does not yet support IPv6. In this case, you need to interconnect the Site 2 branch to the headquarters by using a tunneling mechanism.

Several tunneling mechanisms exist; however, to allow the exchange of routing updates between the sites, you should use a tunneling mechanism supporting multicast (such as GRE or IPsec/GRE if demanded by security policies).

Therefore, for Site 2, you will use IPv4 connectivity offered by ISP2 to establish an IPv6-in-IPv4 tunnel to the headquarters using the following design attributes:

- No requirement for multihoming.
- Using a /56 subnet from headquarter PI to address LAN.
- Access to IPv6 Internet only through HQ.

Figure 26-24 shows the connectivity model of remote branch Sites 1 and 2.

You should configure your firewalls to allow communication with the allocated IP prefixes for any of the remote branch sites, on the headquarters firewall, and vice versa.

Chapter 26: Design Case Studies

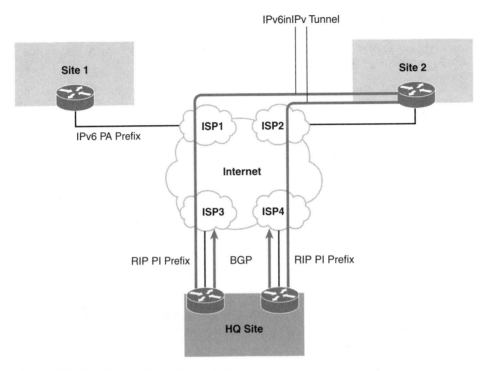

Figure 26-24 *Remote Sites Connectivity*

Deployment Model

As discussed throughout this book, the available models of integrating/transitioning to IPv6 include

- Dual stack
- Tunneling
- Translation
- Hybrid (combination of above)

Avoiding transition mechanisms where not required should direct you to choose dual stack in LAN and WAN. An assessment phase is necessary before deployment of dual stack to avoid any possible show stoppers. The result of the network assessment will give you insight into which components need attention before deployment.

Network areas where native IPv6 is not viable, like the Site 2 WAN connection, will require you to implement a transition mechanism, such as tunneling. You will also require translation mechanisms (NAT64) in the DMZ for migration of the IPv4 application that does not support IPv6 natively (see Figure 26-25).

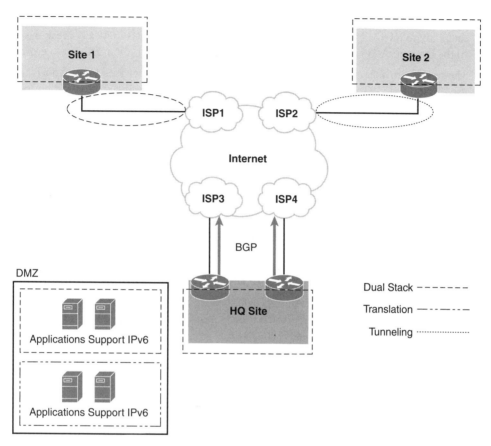

Figure 26-25 *Deployment Model*

Addressing

After choosing the IP addressing types to be used over the Internet and the deployment model to enable IPv6, you need to start designing the addressing scheme for the internal networks and DMZ.

The headquarters will receive its prefix from the regional registrar in the form /48. The /48 can be split up into smaller segments for different parts of the network. Other appliances should be connected either directly to the collapsed core switches or to access fabric extenders, depending on the expected traffic patterns and port availability. Following are some sample allocations for HQ:

- **LAN:** /56 allowing for 256 VLANs
- **DMZ:** /56 allowing for 256 VLANs
- **Network Devices:** /64 allowing you summarize all loopback and management interfaces
- **Site 2:** /56 allowing for 256 VLANs

814 Chapter 26: Design Case Studies

Because the Site 1 branch can receive a PA prefix from its service provider, you can use the prefix to internally address the hosts. It allows your Site 1 hosts to locally break out to the Internet. A /56 is sufficient to handle multiple VLANs with enough room to grow.

The service provider at Site 2 does not offer native IPv6 connectivity, so you need to use a dedicated /56 from the headquarters PI prefix and route the IPv6 traffic to the headquarters through a tunnel and then forward it to the Internet.

Address Provisioning

After deciding on the addressing scheme, you need to think about how you will implement provisioning of addresses to hosts both in the headquarters and in the branches. What protocols will you use, and where will you implement them?

The customer's environment demands support for additional information (DNS, TFTP, and so on) when provisioning addresses. In its latest releases, SLAAC allows only DNS information to be passed to hosts, so you need to use DHCPv6. You will place a dedicated DHCPv6 server to provision IPv6 addresses at the headquarters. By setting the managed flag, you allow hosts to query the DHCPv6 server for a prefix.

The branch offices currently do not implement a dedicated DHCPv6 server, so you will implement the functionality on the WAN routers. Both Site 1 and Site 2 will have the same type of implementation (see Figure 26-26).

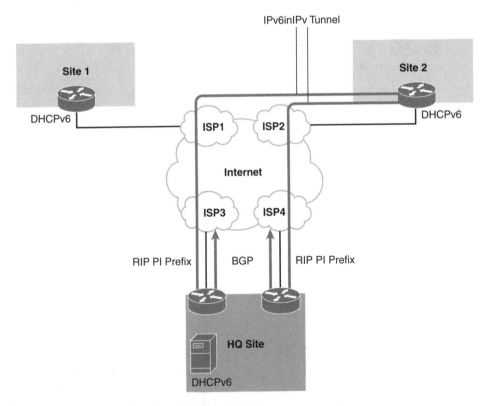

Figure 26-26 *DHCPv6 Deployment Model*

Communication Between Branches

When branches need to communicate directly using IPv6, you can implement a hub-and-spoke model or configure dedicated tunnels for direct access between branches. Because the Site 2 branch does not have native IPv6 connectivity, the only available model is to use a hub-and-spoke approach, which will force the traffic through the headquarters and then be routed to the other branch.

You may change this approach in the future when the Site 2 branch obtains native IPv6 connectivity from the ISP, and you will be able to build direct IPv6 tunnels. If direct communication between the branches is necessary, you can consider DMVPN. This option will support a larger number of spokes/branches along with the capability to automatically provision spoke-to-spoke tunnels. In other words, your decision is made based on the availability of native IPv6 communication:

- Native if possible
- Tunnel if necessary

Application and Service Migration

Starting with the application's migration to operate with IPv6, how will you approach the migration of applications to support IPv6? A network-readiness assessment is crucial and includes

- Operating system support
- Application support

Application migration is also important:

- The application supports IPv6.
- The application needs to be rewritten, and source code is available.
- The application needs to be rewritten, and source code is not available.

The network-readiness assessment must include the evaluation of network devices, services, and applications. Large software vendors either support IPv6 with their software, or they have it defined in their road map. An upgrade or installation of such applications to the IPv6-compatible version is therefore suggested.

Custom applications, however, require you to perform a detailed inspection of the code and fix hard-coded calls to the protocol stack. In situations in which access to the source code is not available, you may consider a full rewrite of the application.

When legacy applications are stuck supporting only IPv4 or a quick migration is expected, you can implement a translation mechanism on a network level. IPv4 applications can be presented as IPv6 nodes through translation mechanisms such as

NAT64 or SLB64. Furthermore, which network services would you migrate immediately and why? The final goal is to have a full dual-stacked infrastructure including

- Network devices
- Services
- Applications

One of the most important network services is DNS. By configuring your DNS to provide AAAA and PTR records, you have started the migration path. With early IPv6 DNS deployment, you will gain early experience, before the production deployment.

The transport of AAAA records to end hosts can be implemented over both IPv4 and IPv6. It is, however, recommended that you keep the initial transport of AAAA over IPv4 both on the external and internal DNS because it provides reliability and robustness of a tested IPv4 network while you test your DNS infrastructure.

Add transport of AAAA over IPv6 only when the LAN and WAN migrations are tested and prepared to avoid application timeouts when falling back to IPv4.

Last but not least, after the applications and services migration to IPv6, does it make sense to immediately implement management over IPv6 and why?

Most management protocols are supported over IPv6:

- SSH
- Telnet
- SNMP
- NTP

Although many of management protocols have been ported to IPv6 (SNMP, SSH, Telnet), it is very likely that management applications have limited capabilities that are connected to the new protocol stack. The management solution that is based on IPv6 might not provide any additional business value to your company. At this moment, then, it is recommended that you keep management of devices on IPv4 until IPv6-based management solutions gain feature parity and stability.

Case Study 4: Design Enterprise Data Center Connectivity

You are working for an IT company, and your customer, KOLLMANN Insurance Company Inc., has hired you to design its new data centers. Facing the expansion of its business and the introduction of new online insurance services, the company has decided not to expand its old mainframe and physical server–based data centers. To serve the dynamic and ever-growing needs of its current and future business, the company wants to build two highly efficient, scalable, virtualized data centers. They will serve as a pilot for multiple similar data centers around the continent that the company plans to build as the business growth will require it. You are tasked with designing both data center networks, while your colleague Tine will design the compute and storage parts.

Detailed Requirements and Expectations

A floor at the KOLLMANN Insurance Company Inc. HQ and a floor in its regional branch have been dedicated and will be refurbished to data center requirements. The customer wants both data centers to be similar to each other to simplify operations and allow for seamless disaster recovery. The existing enterprise network is present in both buildings. The distance between the sites is around 500 miles.

The customer would like the data center network connected to the existing enterprise LAN at both locations. Changed by past network failures, customer policies dictate a maximum fault isolation between the existing enterprise LAN and the data center network. However, the customer is already running a high-speed WAN, connecting HQ and all branches, and would like to avoid purchasing additional WAN connections if possible.

Based on the customer's requirements, your colleague Tine estimates that each data center will host a mix of 50 rack-mountable and blade servers of different vendors, mostly running a set of virtualization solutions from different vendors. The number of servers is expected to double in the near future, so the data center network must be easily expandable to accommodate that need. Resiliency standards demand that no server should rely on a single network path. According to Tine, around 500 VLANs are required at the data center launch, with possible two or three times expansion in the near future. Servers should have 10 Gbps connectivity. According to Tine, the total traffic flow through the data center should be no more than 100 Gbps, with possible expansion in the future. In addition, the customer prefers to have the design based on the multitier model to comply with its enterprise standards.

The primary storage protocol that is used in the new data centers is FCoE. Two FCoE storage arrays will be present in each data center. Planned applications are very sensitive to storage latency, demanding excellent storage network performance. Storage data will be asynchronously replicated between the data centers for disaster recovery. The storage vendor synchronization protocol runs over the IP protocol.

The customer is very security conscious, and company policies demand strict security measures. The data center network should be multitenant. Security policies demand firewall and IPS/IDS inspection between all communicating devices in the data center. The firewall and IPS/IDS solutions are being determined by your colleague Andrew, who works closely with the application team. Load-balancer selection is handled by another team. All that you need to do is to place these devices in your network. Customer security engineers are currently against using virtual security solutions, such as virtual firewalls. Andrew, however, is presenting to them the advantages of virtualized firewalls in a virtualized server infrastructure, so you should allow your topology to be expanded with virtual firewalls and other security appliances if this capability will be required in the near future.

The application team demands a Layer 2 interconnection between the data centers. The team members are aware of the Layer 2 DCI drawbacks, but they cannot avoid them at this point.

Design Analysis and Task List

Based on the information provided, the customer is building two highly efficient, scalable, virtualized data centers, serving as a pilot for multiple similar data centers to meet business growth requirements. You are tasked with designing both data center networks while your colleague will design the compute and storage parts.

To achieve this goal, you must perform the following required tasks:

- Create a high-level design for the data center per the customer's requirements, taking into consideration the scalability, performance, and systems virtualization aspects.
- Design a Data Center Interconnect.
- Create a bill of materials.

Selecting the Data Center Architecture and Connectivity Model

The first step in such a design is typically to select the suitable data center network (DCN) architecture. For example, you may select the multitier versus spine-leaf (Clos) architecture. Although the Clos architecture offers more optimized and simplified design to support modern data center networks with systems and applications virtualization, in this case study, the customer needs to comply with its enterprise standards, so the multitier DCN architecture is a must.

Consequently, how many and which layers will you use in your topology? Will you use a two-tier or three-tier topology?

Customer fault isolation requirements dictate a separation of data center Layer 2 domains from the enterprise LAN already present at each of the locations. The data center network should thus be built around its own core that is connected to the LAN core with Layer 3 connections. Because the servers demand a relatively small number of physical connections, a separate aggregation is not required. All the functions of the aggregation layer can be performed by core switches, thus forming a collapsed core layer.

Customer requirements state that around 50 rack-mountable and blade servers will be present at each data center. Even with the expected expansion of physical servers, a single pair of data center switches, such as the Cisco Nexus series, can provide the required throughput and the number of required 10 Gbps ports. However, to simplify cabling, you should add more access switches or fabric extenders, forming a ToR design.

Taking the preceding requirements into consideration, will you use Layer 2 switches, multilayer switches, data center switches, or fabric extenders to connect the servers to the data center network?

FCoE requirements eliminate the possibility to use simple Layer 2 switches in the access layer, reducing the total cost. You need to make a choice between multilayer switches, data center switches, and fabric extenders. The customer requires FCoE support and lossless Ethernet extensions, ruling out normal multilayer switches. Fabric extenders in the access layer eliminate the need for STP between access and collapsed core layers, bring all functions of a collapsed core switch to the access layer, and simplify the management of the network—all that at a fraction of the cost of data center switches (see Figure 26-27).

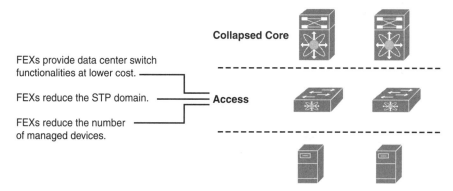

Figure 26-27 *DCN High-level Architecture*

DCN Detailed Connectivity

After choosing the DCN architectures, you need to decide how you will wire the servers and the chosen layers of the data center networks.

Collapsed core switches should be bundled with vPC. To provide path redundancy, you can connect every physical server to a pair of fabric extenders (dual-homed servers), connect every FEX to a pair of collapsed core switches, or use a combination of both. Any combination is possible and provides a degree of redundancy for the LAN traffic. However, FCoE best practices require FCoE traffic from a single logical FC adapter to land on a single data center switch. When fabric extenders are dual-homed, every FEX can be associated with only one data center fabric for FCoE forwarding. Figure 26-28 illustrates the selected connectivity model.

820 Chapter 26: Design Case Studies

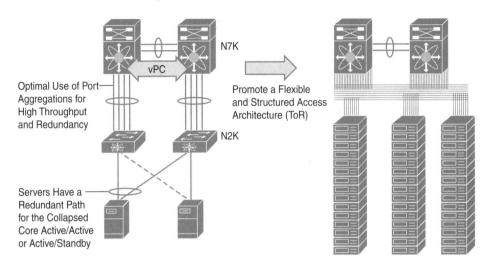

Figure 26-28 *DCN Connectivity Model*

You implement redundancy by dual-homing servers to a pair of fabric extenders.

> **Note** Network topologies rely on implementation capabilities. Data center switches evolve with lightning speed, so topologies not possible today might be recommended in the near future.

The next logical step is to think about where to position the boundary between Layer 2 and Layer 3 in this design:

- Do you need Layer 2 or Layer 3 connectivity with enterprise LAN?
- Where will you perform Inter-VLAN routing?

In this design scenario, the customer requires a Layer 2 data center domain to be separated from the enterprise LAN; thus, Layer 3 is brought to the collapsed core layer. You have chosen the two-tier topology with fabric extenders, so the boundary between Layer 2 and Layer 3 can only be placed at the collapsed core layer, as shown in Figure 26-29.

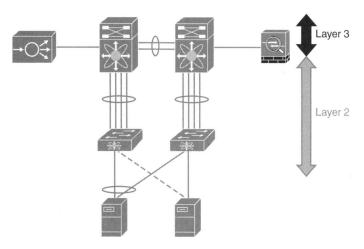

Figure 26-29 *Positioning of the Layer 2 and Layer 3 Boundary*

Connecting Network Appliances

In addition to the design of the DCN switches, you need to think about how to connect the other required network devices such as firewalls and storage in way that should integrate seamlessly with the design you selected.

First, start with the firewalls and load balancers. Where should they be positioned based on the selected design model?

- Place it in the north-south traffic path.
- Place it in the east-west traffic path.

Because this design is based on the two-tier architecture, both the east-west and north-south traffic flows will pass through the collapsed core. In addition, the inter-VLAN function is performed at this layer. Also, because most of the north-south traffic and a decent amount of the east-west traffic will flow through firewalls, you should connect them directly into the collapsed core switches. This way, you avoid congestion on the oversubscribed links between the collapsed core and access layer. You should also connect load balancers to the collapsed core, for reasons similar to those shown in Figure 26-29.

Note The connectivity of the firewall and load balancer in Figure 26-29 is only meant to show which layer these devices should connect to in this design. The actual physical links' connectivity can vary (Layer 2 link versus Layer 3/routed). Also, the firewall design, such as ASA clustering, can change the way you physically connect the firewall links.

Other appliances should be connected either directly to the collapsed core switches or to access fabric extenders, depending on the expected traffic patterns, bandwidth capacity, and port availability.

Similarly, where will you connect the storage?

- To the collapsed core layer
- To the access layer

FCoE storage traffic has a typical east-west traffic pattern. To reduce traffic on the oversubscribed links between the collapsed core and access layers, you should connect the FCoE storage devices directly to the collapsed core switches, as shown in Figure 26-30.

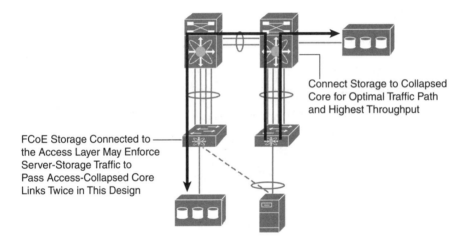

Figure 26-30 *Connecting the Storage to the DCN*

Asynchronous storage replication procedures can be performed between the data centers across the existing IP network and require no special consideration.

Data Center Interconnect

After completing the DCN foundational design, how will you interconnect the data centers? And which network device series do you need to support the chosen DCI technology?

An IP network is already established between the customer sites. Unfortunately, some of the customer services require Layer 2 DCI between the data centers. Layer 2 DCI technology selection includes the following features:

- Dark fiber/DWDM
    - The long distance excludes the dark fiber option.
- EoMPLSoGRE
    - Complex configuration (multiple pseudowires for multiple sites)
    - Additional layers (MPLS, GRE)
- VPLSoGRE
    - Additional layers (MPLS, GRE)
    - Increase the size of Layer 2 flooding domain
- OTV
    - Best match

Finding the collapsed core switch pair leaves you to choose between two Cisco data center switches: the Cisco Nexus 5000 series and Cisco Nexus 7000 series. In this case, look at the feature support matrix. Only the Nexus 7000 series provides OTV support.

Data Center Network Virtualization Design

Based on the design requirements, which multitenancy mechanisms will you implement? Where will you implement them? And will you use contexts? If so, how many and where?

You will use VRF-Lite to separate Layer 3 traffic that is northbound from your collapsed core switches and VLANs to separate Layer 2 traffic southbound from the collapsed core.

The customer is security conscious, so you will use device contexts on the collapsed core switches to provide more isolation. You should start with four basic contexts on the Nexus 7000 series:

- Layer 2 context (includes all southbound ports)
- Layer 3 context (includes all northbound ports)
- OTV context (includes OTV endpoints)
- FCoE context (includes FCoE ports)

Contexts provide total isolation, so to extend the Layer 2 domain across the OTV DCI, you need to interconnect the Layer 2 and OTV contexts with physical cables. FCoE context is an exception. The same ports are used to carry Layer 2 and FCoE traffic.

A physical port that carries both types of traffic can be a member of both contexts (FcoE and Layer 2), while the fabric takes care of logical isolation of both traffic types.

- Did the customer request overlay networks?
- Do you believe that, based on customer requirements, overlay networks solve any of the problems?
- Can the overlay networks be added to the proposed design later?

However, in this design, the decision was made not to include overlay networks because

- It has not been requested by the customer.
- Current requirements can be fulfilled with classic mechanisms, such as VLANs.

Nevertheless, your topology creates a solid foundation for overlay networks if the customer decides to use it in the future.

Last but not least, based on the design requirements, you could also consider the implementation of virtual switches and firewalls in the environment:

- Did the customer request virtual switches and firewalls?
- Do you believe that, based on customer requirements, virtual switches and firewalls solve any of the problems?
- Can virtual switches and firewalls be added to the proposed design later?

You have decided not to include virtual switches and firewalls because

- The customer has not requested them.
- Current application requirements do not advocate the use of virtual network devices.
- You advise the customer to use virtual network devices for multitiered applications with strong east-west traffic to reduce traffic on FEX links.
- The topology creates a solid foundation for virtual network devices should the customer be convinced to use them.

> **Note** You could advise the customer to use virtual network devices for multitiered applications with strong east-west traffic to reduce traffic load on the FEX links.

Figure 26-31 illustrates the final proposed design of the interconnected data centers.

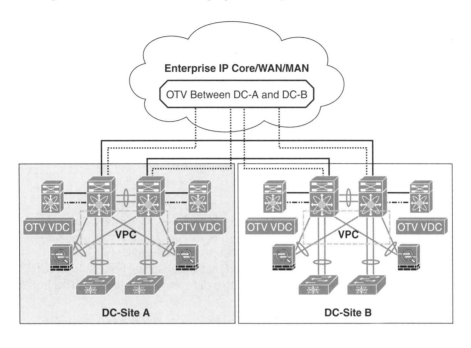

Figure 26-31 *Final DCN Design*

Case Study 5: Design Resilient Enterprise WAN

You were recently contacted by the IT manager from TINC Garbage Disposal, who received a recommendation regarding your work from one of your existing customers. The company has successfully grown in recent years and opened several new branch offices. Now it plans to refresh and consolidate the WAN part of the network, and it is looking for your help. To get started, you already received a list of initial expectations together with some background info.

Detailed Requirements and Expectations

The customer is looking forward to consolidation of its existing WAN connections. The company wants to move from several different WAN technologies to a unified solution that would be applicable to all its branches. Currently, it is satisfied using Cisco routers, but if there are no applicable vendor-specific benefits, the customer prefers the use of open standards and protocols.

The customer has more than 200 branch offices in all major cities, and further growth of the network is currently not expected.

Because the business relies on a centralized infrastructure that is positioned in the HQ, the customer is looking for a reliable solution where a single fault does not bring down services.

It plans to connect each site with a primary and a redundant link. For larger branches, it plans to use two routers per office, each terminating one WAN link. For smaller locations, a single router will be used, terminating both WAN links. The desired convergence in the event of a link failure occurs within tens of seconds.

Due to a larger security incident at one of the company's major competitors on the market, the company board of directors has recently approved a larger investment into network security. As a result of this ongoing security project, branch traffic will be segmented into different security zones. Connectivity between the zones will be controlled centrally at the HQ by a corporate firewall. It has already been coordinated between different departments in the company that the new WAN solution will support such segmentation.

TINC Garbage Disposal needs your help to come up with a suitable solution and to help it select suitable WAN connections for branches.

Design Analysis and Task List

Based on the information provided, you know the following:

- There are 200+ branch offices, but further network growth is not expected.
- The customer currently uses Cisco equipment. Proprietary protocols should be used if applicable benefits are delivered.
- The business relies on a centralized infrastructure.
- A single fault should not bring down the company's services.
- Two WAN links are planned for each branch.
- There are larger branch offices with two WAN routers and smaller offices with a single router.
- The branch LAN is segmented into isolated security zones.
- A WAN must support traffic segmentation; connectivity between zones is controlled by a centralized firewall.
- The customer is looking for a unified solution for branch connectivity and needs your help.

However, there is a lot of information missing if you want to get the whole picture. Following are some examples of questions that you should ask the customer:

- Should sites be interconnected with Layer 2 or Layer 3 connectivity?
- Is there a need to encrypt traffic between the sites?
- Is there any need to enable multicast over the WAN?
- How reliable must be primary and secondary links?
- What kind of branch traffic needs to be isolated? How many isolated zones must the WAN support?
- Is it important that more zones of isolated traffic can be added easily?

Following are the answers provided by the customer to your preceding questions:

- Should sites be interconnected with Layer 2 or Layer 3 connectivity?
    - *Layer 3 connectivity is the preferred option to improve network resiliency.*
- Is there a need to encrypt traffic between the sites?
    - *Yes, traffic should be encrypted to ensure privacy.*
- Is there any need to enable multicast over the WAN?
    - *Not required over the WAN.*
- How reliable must be primary and secondary links?
    - *Primary links must be offered with SLA, whereas secondary links can work on a best effort basis.*
- What kind of branch traffic needs to be isolated? How many isolated zones must the WAN support?
    - *Each branch currently supports three types of isolated traffic: production network, guest network, and video surveillance network. Traffic is isolated using individual VRFs for each traffic type.*
- Is it important that more zones of isolated traffic can be added easily?
    - *Yes, adding an extra isolated zone should be fairly easy without major network changes.*

Tasks include

- Help the customer choose WAN links for the branch offices.
- Analyze requirements for overlay VPN.
- Prepare a high-level design proposal for WAN redesign

Selecting WAN Links

The offers that were received from two SPs are shown in Table 26-1.

Table 26-1 *WAN: Service Providers' Offerings*

Service Provider	Type	SLA available	Price[*]
ISP A	VPWS	Yes	$$$
ISP A	MPLS Layer 3 VPN	Yes	$$$
ISP A	Internet	No	$
ISP B	VPLS	Yes	$$$$
ISP B	Internet	No	$

[*] The $ represents pricing/cost weight; the more $, the higher the price/cost.

The customer clarified that it would like to connect branch offices with two links. The primary link should come with an SLA, whereas for the backup link, best effort service is acceptable. The customer also has no need to connect branch offices with Layer 2 connections. Layer 3 connectivity is preferred because it offers better resiliency.

When selecting the primary and secondary link, you should try to select two independent service offerings. Otherwise, your secondary connection could easily go over the same infrastructure and be prone to the same incidents. In general, picking the secondary service from a different service provider is a step in the right direction. However, if redundancy plays a very important role, you should get more clarifications about the infrastructure that the service providers use.

The best fit for your customer in this scenario is MPLS Layer 3 VPN from ISP A with available SLA, and Internet connectivity from ISP B, which will serve as a backup connection.

WAN Overlay

After you select the WAN links, the solution will be operating over two different connectivity models (MPLS L3VPN and public Internet). Thus, the question here is, Is there a need for an extra overlay VPN to interconnect the sites shown in Figure 26-32? If yes, which technology would you recommend to the customer?

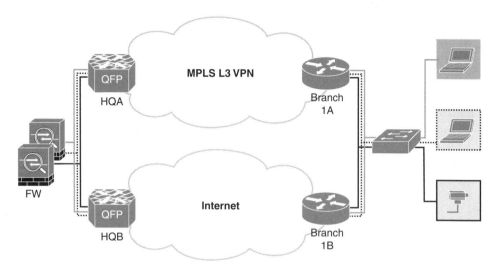

Figure 26-32 *The Need for a VPN Overlay*

In other words, is there a need for an enterprise-managed VPN over the SP MPLS Layer 3 VPN?

The customer requested that you secure communication between locations. Because service providers cannot be trusted, you need to encrypt communication between locations. The need for encryption is applicable to both the primary and secondary WAN link. Several different options are available to encrypt the traffic between locations. However, the selection of technology influences not only the security perspective, but also the overall WAN design, its routing, and the convergence options.

Two reasonable overlay VPN technologies for the described scenario are GRE over IPsec and DMVPN.

Both options have some benefits and drawbacks. Because the customer does not expect larger network growth in the future and does not need spoke-to-spoke communication, GRE over IPsec is the preferred solution. As an additional benefit, GRE over IPsec also fulfills the customer preference to use public standards and protocols within the solution. The solution will work also with all other potential vendors who support standard protocols.

Last but not least, primary router Branch1A connects to the MPLS Layer 3 VPN WAN service, which provides connectivity with the HQA router. Because data must be protected, GRE over IPsec is configured between routers. To simplify configuration tasks and reduce the amount of needed configuration on the HQ site, the use of dynamic IPsec crypto maps is suggested. Once a secure tunnel is established, routers set up a GRE point-to-point tunnel, which provides support for dynamic routing protocols. To support communication of isolated traffic, MPLS is enabled on tunnel interfaces, establishing a label-switched path between the HQ and the branch router. LSP enables processing of traffic that is based on assigned labels, which correspond to different VRFs defined for isolated traffic groups. MP-BGP, which is established between routers, exchanges routing and label allocation information. MP-BGP also offers you all common BGP features that are used to manipulate best-path selection, which enables you to easily implement customer path preferences.

Default BGP timers are rather slow, which is acceptable for large networks like the Internet, where stability is preferred over very quick convergence. However, in this scenario, you will need to improve convergence to meet customer expectations. With GRE tunnels, you can use keepalives, which detect link issues and reflect the status of the interface accordingly. But keep in mind that a change of the interface status influences only EBGP neighbor sessions, while IBGP does not react to it. Another option to achieve faster convergence is to optimize BGP timers.

Figure 26-33 illustrates the final proposed WAN solution

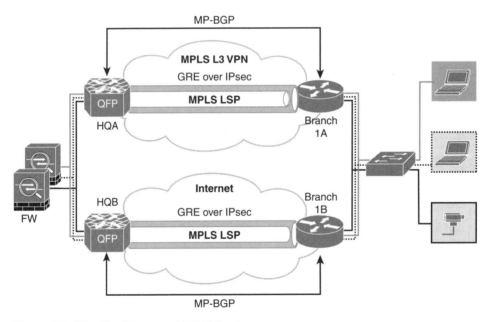

Figure 26-33 *Final Proposed WAN Design*

Case Study 6: Design Secure Enterprise Network

You are working for an IT company, and your customer, SHISKO Groceries Ltd., has hired you to design security for its network. Facing the expansion of its business and the introduction of new branches, the company has decided to expand its network beyond the original site and to implement new services. To allow for optimal security in its environment, the customer has requested an overhaul of its existing and new locations. You are tasked with designing an overall scenario of securing the customer locations.

Detailed Requirements and Expectations

The current customer network is composed of a single site, with multiple users connected to a core switch, and a single Internet gateway, providing basic routing and NAT functionality. During the expansion, the customer wishes to expand its network by adding two new remote branches, with users at both locations.

At the main location, the customer wishes to add a few public-facing web servers and back-end database servers for its e-commerce business, which will be separated from the internal network. Due to security concerns, the customer wishes to create separation between public-facing and back-end servers, as well as between all servers and user networks.

All the network devices on customer networks must be protected against unauthorized access, and anyone connecting to the devices must be notified about the legal consequences of unauthorized access. Authorized administrators can access the network devices from the management section of the customer network, and a detailed audit of their actions must be maintained. The customer wishes to maintain a centralized database of administrators, allowing for easy password changes and user account management.

The customer wishes to use Cisco Catalyst switches for user and physical server connectivity, while maintaining the same level of access control for virtualized servers. All user connections must be mutually authenticated using certificates. Server network access should also be authenticated, using the servers' MAC addresses. Because the customer is already using a remote-access SSL VPN agent to access its environment remotely, it wants to expand the platform to endpoint network authentication also.

All users in the customer environment will use dynamically assigned IP addresses, using the DHCP protocol. Customer switches must be configured to allow IP address assignment only from authorized DHCP servers, and to disallow access from devices with spoofed or static IP addresses.

The customer wishes to maintain a stable switching topology, even if a user connects a hub or another switch to the existing devices. Customer switches must be configured to prevent unauthorized networking device connections.

To combat blended threats and provide an insight into connection and security events within the environment, the customer wishes to deploy next-generation firewalls on all its locations. In addition to routing and Layer 3/4 traffic inspection, the firewalls must also provide advanced network analysis using in-line intrusion prevention mechanisms, URL filtering, and network-based advanced malware protection. All the firewalls must be managed from the main location, and the management environment must also provide detailed insight into detected and blocked threats within the customer environment. The firewall deployment at the main location must allow for a single-device failure while maintaining uninterrupted connectivity. At the same time, no redundancy is required for remote locations.

As the customer's virtual environment continues to grow, the company would like to introduce security features into that sphere also. It does not wish to modify the network settings of existing servers and virtual switches but would like to perform traffic filtering between virtual servers.

Security Domains and Zone Design

Based on the information provided and security separation requirements, which security zones will the new customer network contain? And what will you use for main separation points between the security zones?

The customer network consists of three locations: the main and two remote locations. There are users at all three locations, while the main location also houses the servers, both Internet-facing and back-end ones. In addition, a management network is required for the administrators. So, altogether you should have three separate security domains (see Figure 26-34):

- Remote location 1
- Remote location 2
- Main site, which consists of the following zones:
    - Public servers at the main location
    - Back-end servers at the main location
    - Main location
    - Management subnet

Because the firewalls will be used for routing and filtering, they will provide segmentation between the security zones at the main location.

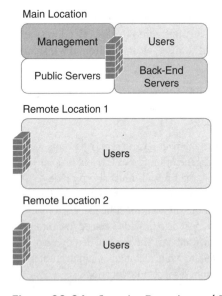

Figure 26-34 *Security Domains and Zones*

Infrastructure and Network Access Security

Which security mechanisms can you deploy to secure the networking infrastructure?

- Interface ACLs
- Management traffic restrictions
- Banners
- Access authentication, authorization, and audit
- Data confidentiality

The requirements state that the network devices will be accessible only from the management network on the main location. Also, access is required over secure management protocols, such as SSH, HTTPS, and SNMPv3, for device management. You can use interface access lists and per device access controls, such as VTY access lists on switches and SSH/Telnet/HTTP restrictions on the firewalls.

After selecting the desired protocols for management access, you need to think about how you can achieve the following access security mechanisms:

- Centralized authentication
- Centralized authorization
- Centralized accounting/auditing

Centralized admin authentication, authorization, and command accounting can be provided by an access server, such as Cisco ACS. The TACACS+ protocol would be used on all network devices to achieve this purpose. Nevertheless, both RADIUS and TACACS+ can be used for admin access authentication (considering Cisco ISE provides the flexibility to centralize the management and provisioning of these activities, as illustrated in Figure 26-35).

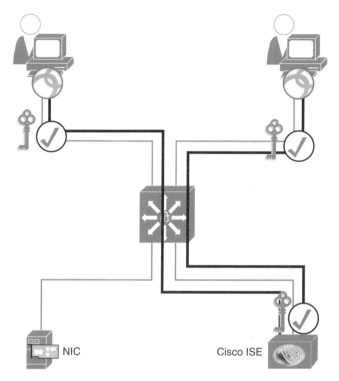

Figure 26-35 *Network Access Control*

The other aspect that you need to consider is the access security of the users and servers. Before making any design decision, you should obtain and analyze the answers to the following questions:

- Which mechanism will you use for user and server network access authentication?
- Which protocols will you use for user and which for server authentication?
- Which software components are involved in user authentication?

The customer should implement the 802.1X protocol for both user and server network access authentication. The users will be authenticated using EAP-TLS, while the servers will be authenticated using MAC Authentication Bypass (MAB).

Because the customer already uses the Cisco Anyconnect client for SSL VPN connections, it can extend the client by installing the Network Access Manager module that is used for 802.1X authentication.

Layer 2 Security Considerations

Based on the customer design requirements, which mechanisms will you use for Layer 2 security on customer switches?

Because the customer uses DHCP for user IP address assignment, DHCP snooping and ARP Inspection can be used as security mechanisms. To prevent unauthorized switches from being connected to the network, the customer can use the Spanning-Tree BPDUGuard functionality. To prevent network topology changes, the customer can use the Spanning-Tree RootGuard functionality.

Main and Remote Location Firewalling

To meet the customer requirements with regard to deploying next-generation firewalls, which firewalling solution can you use at the main and remote locations? Also, which redundancy mechanism can you use at the main location?

You should deploy Cisco ASA with FirePower services at all locations. You should also deploy an HA pair (active-standby) at the main location and standalone firewalls at remote locations. You should use the FirePower IPS, AMP, and URL licenses on all firewalls, and the FireSight Management Center for the FirePower services management.

On the other hand, for the virtualized firewalling requirements, you can deploy an ASAv in transparent mode to allow for traffic filtering without any addressing and routing changes.

Case Study 7: Design QoS in the Enterprise Network

You are the head network engineer in the networking company FOKSI Data Ltd. The general manager of the company has given you the task of drastically improving user experience with voice and video applications. The employees are complaining that at certain times of the day voice communication is degraded and video conference calls are of poor quality. The general manager of the company has explicitly told you that the company does not have the money to invest in better equipment or more money to spend on a better MPLS/VPN service.

Detailed Requirements and Expectations

In the past six months, several employees have been complaining about increased delay in internal communication and business-critical traffic. A frequent remark was that voice is choppy and video quality is low. Business-critical traffic was often described as unresponsive when branch office users wanted to communicate with servers that are located at the headquarters. Employee complaints were reported mostly in times of peak traffic, but you do not have any information regarding which traffic type is using most of the bandwidth in peak times.

Your company has implemented IP telephony and several collaboration solutions including video conferencing. Business-critical applications include SAP, Citrix, and the Oracle database. E-mail is also considered a critical traffic type that requires prioritization. Figure 26-36 illustrates the FOKSI Data Ltd network topology.

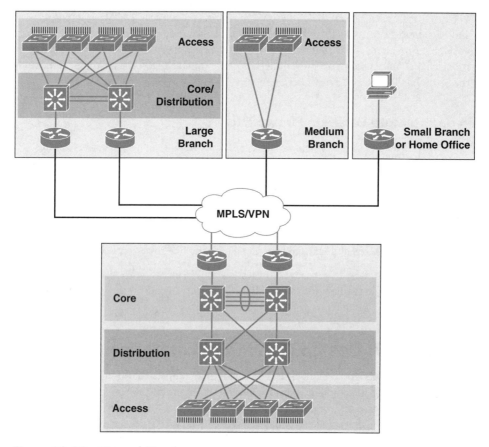

Figure 26-36 *Network Topology*

Your company is a multinational corporation with over 50 branch offices in 20 countries worldwide. The headquarters, which is located in Germany, hosts more than 500 employees. The branch offices range from 5 to 50 employees, depending on the size of the branch itself.

The headquarters implements a LAN in the form of a three-layer architecture. Medium-size branch offices implement a collapsed core architecture. Small offices have a flat architecture, employing a single router.

To communicate between the branches, your company is leasing a Layer 3 MPLS/VPN service from a large service provider that implements SLAs for each location.

Traffic Discovery and Analysis

Analysis and inspection of production traffic are often challenging. To correctly analyze the data, you need to obtain statistical data at the appropriate time frames to understand the traffic patterns.

The following are different options to collect and analyze data within a network, each with different pros and cons:

- Dedicated deep-packet inspection devices are often expensive because they offer line-rate deep-packet inspection on customized hardware and real-time policy control and reporting capabilities. Because the general manager of your company made it clear that spending additional money is not an option, using dedicated packet inspection devices is probably not an option for this project. You would normally implement a dedicated deep-packet inspection device between the core and distribution layers. Dedicated inspection devices are deployed inline.

- *NBAR2* is a classification engine that recognizes and classifies a wide variety of protocols and applications. NBAR2 can be enabled on Cisco IOS devices. The protocol discovery feature provides real-time statistics on applications currently running on the network. It provides per interface, per protocol, and bidirectional statistics (bit rate, packet counts, and byte counts).

- *NetFlow*, which is a feature that was introduced on Cisco routers, provides the ability to collect IP network traffic as it enters or exits an interface. By analyzing the data that is provided by NetFlow, a network administrator can determine the source and destination of traffic, class of service, and the causes of congestion, for example. Cisco Flexible NetFlow is a method for configuring NetFlow and not a new version of NetFlow. NBAR2 can also use NetFlow instead of protocol discovery. This way, you will get real-time statistics of applications running in your network. However, this will also use up a lot of resources.

- Open-source sniffing solutions involve enabling SPAN functionality on Layer 2 switches and redirecting traffic to a PC that is used as a sniffer. An example of such an open-source solution is Wireshark.

In any situation, the analysis and inspection of traffic is a temporary process used only for discovery and should be disabled after you get a good understanding of the traffic flows.

QoS Design Model

The discovery phase confirms the traffic types shown in Table 26-2. Based on the requirements, one of the possible solutions is a six-class QoS model with the associated per hop behavior.

Table 26-2 *Traffic Types*

Name	Traffic	PHB
Voice	Voice	EF
Video	Video conferencing	AF4
Network	OSPF	CS6
Critical	SAP, Citrix, Oracle	AF2
Best Effort	Browsing, E-mail	DF
Scavenger	Social websites, Torrents	CS1

You may design a more intricate model involving eight or more classes. In that case, however, make sure that the deployed QoS model is not too complicated and resolves the business requirements. Your QoS design should also take into consideration your service provider's MPLS QoS model.

QoS Trust Boundary

You should deploy the trust boundary at the level of the trusted endpoint where the hosts directly connect to a device that implements classification and marking (IP Phone, access switch). Depending on the size and design of the LAN, the trust boundary may be located at different points, including the following:

- Headquarters:
    - Optimal trust boundary: IP Phone or access switch
    - Suboptimal trust boundary: Distribution switch
- Large branch office:
    - Optimal trust boundary: IP Phone or access switch
    - Suboptimal trust boundary: Collapsed core/distribution
- Medium branch office:
    - Optimal trust boundary: IP Phone or access switch
    - Suboptimal trust boundary: WAN router
- Small branch or home office:
    - Optimal trust boundary: WAN router

Congestion Management

When you design QoS, it is critical to look at the points that link high-bandwidth links to lower-bandwidth links. This is typically at the WAN routers. Therefore, you need to think of what queueing mechanisms you need to implement on the WAN routers to guarantee that business-critical traffic is prioritized.

Voice and video traffic have specific delay and jitter requirements to be able to provide a good user experience; thus, a requirement for a low-latency mechanism is present. The remaining classes need to be prioritized based on DSCP markings.

Low Latency Queue adds a strict-priority queue to the class-based weighted fair queuing (CBWFQ) subsystem (see Figure 26-37). It is used for delay-sensitive traffic with strict requirements regarding delay and jitter. CBWFQ will be used for the non-delay-sensitive traffic by guaranteeing a percentage of the bandwidth per class. To avoid congestion of the incoming traffic, you use a congestion avoidance mechanism to randomly drop traffic as the queue fills up to capacity.

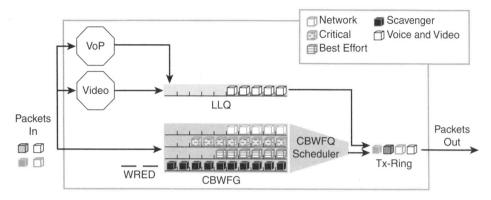

Figure 26-37 *QoS Queuing*

Scavenger Traffic Considerations

You can treat scavenger-type traffic in multiple ways, depending on your security policy and business requirements:

- **Dropping:** By using NBAR2, you can selectively mark traffic that is not allowed in the enterprise network during business hours and instruct the queueing mechanisms to drop the marked traffic.

- **Degrading:** Scavenger traffic is marked using NBAR2, and the queuing mechanisms assign a low amount of bandwidth to the scavenger traffic, which allows the protocols to be used but does not affect business-critical traffic.

Note If scavenger traffic is uncontrolled, it can considerably degrade the usable bandwidth for voice and business-critical applications to the level of being severely degraded or unusable.

MPLS WAN DiffServ Tunneling

RFC 3270 defines three distinct modes of MPLS DiffServ tunneling:

- Uniform mode
- Short-pipe mode
- Pipe mode

You should use short-pipe mode because the company and service provider are in different DiffServ domains. This mode is useful when the service provider wants to enforce its own QoS policy, but the customer requests that its own QoS policy be preserved through the MPLS network. Re-marking in the MPLS cloud is limited to the MPLS EXP, and the inner DSCP value is left intact (see Figure 26-38).

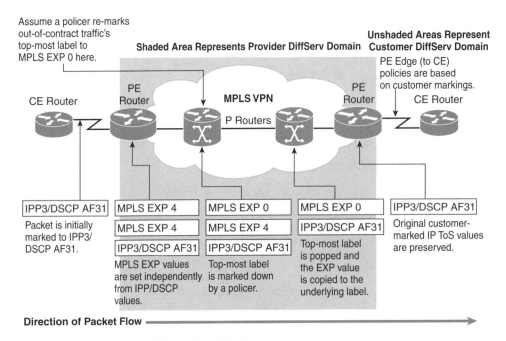

Figure 26-38 *MPLS DiffServ: Pipe Mode*

Figure 26-39 depicts the final solution based on the QoS design discussed in this section.

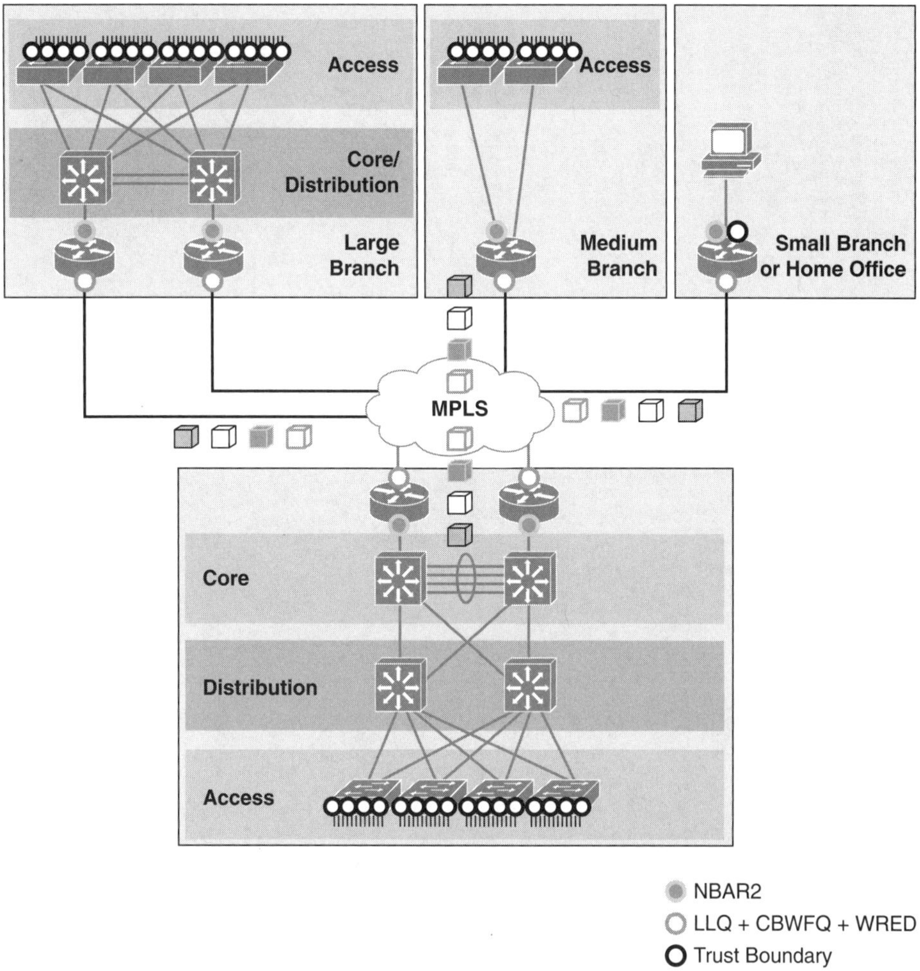

Figure 26-39 *Final QoS Design*

Appendix A

Answers to Review Questions

Chapter 1
1. C
2. D
3. B, D
4. C, D
5. A, C
6. C
7. C
8. B, C

Chapter 2
1. B, C
2. C
3. A, F, G
4. C
5. A, C

Chapter 3
1. D, E
2. D

3. A, C, F
4. A, C
5. A, C
6. A, D

Chapter 4

1. A, B
2. D, E
3. A, C
4. A, E
5. A, D
6. A, B
7. A, C
8. C
9. C, D
10. B, C

Chapter 5

1. A, E
2. D, E
3. B, C
4. A, D
5. A, D
6.

no-advertise	Do not advertise routes to any peer.
no-export	Do not advertise routes to real EBGP peers.
no-export-subconfed	Do not advertise routes outside of local AS.
no-peer	Re-advertise conditionally.

7. D
8. D
9. A

Chapter 6

1. C, D
2. C
3. D
4. C, D
5. B
6. A

Chapter 7

1. C, D
2. A, B
3. B
4. A

Chapter 8

1. C
2.

Component	Description
Provider network	MPLS forwarding backbone
Customer network	Customer-controlled domain
PE router	Router on the edge of provider cloud
P router	Router in the core of the provider network
CE router	Router on the edge of the customer network

3. A, C, E
4. C
5. B
6. A
7. C
8. C
9. C
10. B

Chapter 9

1. C, D
2.
DMVPN Phase 1	It does not allow spoke-to-spoke tunnels.
DMVPN Phase 2	It allows spoke-to-spoke tunnels, but you need full reachability.
DMVPN Phase 3	It allows spoke-to-spoke tunnels, and you can send only the default route to the spokes.

3. B, E
4. D
5. A
6. C
7. **Internet Key Exchange (IKE)** provides key management to IPsec.

   Authentication Header (AH) defines user traffic encapsulation that provides data integrity, data origin authentication, and protection against replay to user traffic.

   Encapsulating Security Payload (ESP) defines user traffic encapsulation that provides data integrity, data origin authentication, protection against replays, and confidentiality to user traffic.

8. C, D

Chapter 10

1.
DMVPN Only	Design model use only Internet VPN as transport.
Dual DMVPN	Design model uses two Internet connections.
DMVPN Backup Shared	Design model uses the Internet as a secondary link and implements the VPN hub on an existing MPLS router.
DMVPN Backup Dedicated	Design model uses the Internet as a secondary link and implements the VPN hub on a dedicated router.

2. A
3. A
4. D
5. B, C, D

6. B
7.

TID	fVRF and DMVPN
IPC	PfR
AO	WAAS and Akamai Connect
SC	ZFW, NAT, CWS

8. A

Chapter 11

1.

Access Layer Designs/Technologies	Properties
Top of Rack	Reduces cabling, expands STP topology
End of Row	Simplifies STP topology, requires extensive cabling
Fabric Extenders	Reduces STP topology, does not allow local switching

2.

DC Design Model	Attributes
Two-tier	Limited scalability
Three-tier	Scalable; however, STP reduces the overall solution efficiency
Three-tiers with vPC	Scalable and offers nonblocking solution

3. A, B
4. B, D
5. B, C

Chapter 12

1. D
2. B, C

3.

Technology	Description
VRF-Lite	Provides Layer 3 separation without the need for MPLS.
VDC	Provides data, control, and management plane separation.
VLAN	Provides Layer 2 separation.
VRF	Provides Layer 3 separation in conjunction with MPLS.

4. C
5. B
6. B
7. A, C
8. A, B

Chapter 13

1. A, C
2. B, C
3.

ACI Object	Description
EPG	Provides a mean of grouping endpoints based on a certain common communication requirement or application attribute.
Contract	Allows or denies communication between EPGs.
NAP	Contains EPGs and contracts for a given application or service that can be applied to the ACI fabric.
Context	Represents a private network and is equivalent to VRF

4. B
5. B
6. A, C
7. B
8. C

Chapter 14

1. B

2.

DCI Technology	Description
Dark Fiber	Limited range, used to build DWDM networks
VPLS	Supports connection of multiple sites. SP managed VPN.
OTV	Transports Layer 2 over Layer 3 network. Has control plane protocol and does not use data plane flooding for address learning.
EoMPLSoGRE	Uses pseudowires, enterprise-managed VPN over Layer 3 network

3. D

4.

Data Center Flows	Description
Inter-DC	Flows across the DCI.
North–south	Enters or exits the data center and typically flows between the clients that are located outside the data center and servers in the data center.
East–west	Flows between the servers or devices in the data center and does not leave the data center

5. A, E

6.

DCI Technology	Design Requirements
DWDM Dark Fiber	Interconnects two data canters only with the capability to provide separate 10 Gbps for transport for storage replication (FC) and separate 10 Gbps for Layer 2 DCI traffic over single physical link.
P2P AToMoGRE	Interconnects two data centers only over IP transport.
OTV	Provides a LAN extension between multiple data center sites.
Layer 3 DCI + LISP	Provides active-active DC design, provides VM mobility; each DC has its IP range; DCI must used for data replication and VM migration traffic only.

7. A, C

8. B, D

Chapter 15

1. B
2. A
3. A, B, C
4. A
5. A, B
6. C
7. B
8. C

Chapter 16

1. C
2.

VoIP Telephony	EF
Call Signaling	CS1
Network Control	CS6
Real-time interactive	CS4
Transactional Data	AF21

3. A
4. D
5. B, C

Chapter 17

1. A
2. C
3. D

4.

High-performance trading architecture	Minimal QoS requirements.
Big data architecture	Requirements similar to campus network requirements
Virtualized multiservice architectures	Not only application traffic classes, but also class of customer service needs to be identified

  5. C, D
  6. B
  7. D
  8. B

Chapter 18

  1. E
  2.

Short pipe mode	On PE egress, the customer QoS policy is implied.
Pipe mode	On PE egress, the service provider QoS policy is implied.
Uniform mode	The customer and service provider share the same DiffServ domain.

  3. A, E

Chapter 19

  1. A, C
  2. D
  3. A

Chapter 20

  1. E
  2. A
  3. A
  4. B
  5. B, D

6. A, B
7. C
8. B, D
9. B
10. C

Chapter 21

1. C
2. B, D
3. C, D
4. A
5. C

Chapter 22

1. C
2.

Enterprise Module	Description
Enterprise campus	Provides network access to users and devices
Enterprise Internet edge	Provides connectivity to the Internet
Enterprise branch	Provides connectivity to users and devices at the remote locations
Enterprise WAN edge	Aggregates links from the branch offices
Intranet data center	Serves applications and stores data
Enterprise core	High-speed infrastructure that connects all other modules

3. C, E, F
4.

Management Access	Description
Log and account for all users	Record all accesses and actions that are performed by the connected user
Present legal notification	Notify users of the security policy enforcement

Authorize actions	Restrict the actions and views that are permitted by particular user
Restrict device accessibility	Limit the permitted methods and scope of IP addresses to connect to the device
Ensure the confidentiality of data	Use encryption algorithms for storing and transferring sensitive data
Authenticate access	Allow access only to the users who are allowed access

5. B
6. B, C
7. A, C

Chapter 23

1. A
2. B, D, E
3. B
4. A
5. A
6. C
7. A, D
8.

Firewall Type	Description
IOS Firewall	Firewall that can be deployed as an interface-based firewall or as a zone-based firewall
ASA	Dedicated firewall enabling a highly scalable, high-performance, high-availability, and fully featured deployment
ASA in multicontext mode	Virtualized firewall running on single physical ASA appliance
Virtual firewall	Software-only firewall running in a hypervisor

Chapter 24

1. A, B, C, D
2. A, B, C
3. A
4. B

Chapter 25

1. A
2.

802.1X VLAN Types	Description
Guest VLAN	Assigned to users or devices that do not have 802.1X supplicant
Critical VLAN	Assigned to a port when the authentication server is unavailable
Restricted VLAN	Assigned to users or devices that fail the authentication process
Default VLAN	VLAN that is configured on the port and is assigned to users or devices that successfully authenticate

3. C
4. A, D
5. C

Appendix B

References

1. "Enterprise Campus 3.0 Architecture: Overview and Framework," http://www.cisco.com
2. "Borderless Campus 1.0 Design Guide," http://www.cisco.com
3. "Campus Network for High Availability Design Guide," http://www.cisco.com
4. "Network Virtualization for the Campus," http://www.cisco.com
5. "Is Cisco Application Centric Infrastructure an SDN Technology?," http://www.cisco.com/c/en/us/solutions/collateral/data-center-virtualization/application-centric-infrastructure/white-paper-c11-733456.html
6. "VXLAN Overview: Cisco Nexus 9000 Series Switches," http://www.cisco.com
7. VXLAN Network with MP-BGP EVPN Control Plane Design Guide," http://www.cisco.com
8. "Cisco Application Centric Infrastructure (ACI) - Endpoint Groups (EPG) Usage and Design," http://www.cisco.com
9. "OSPF Design Guide," http://www.cisco.com
10. "Intermediate System-to-Intermediate System Protocol," http://www.cisco.com/en/US/products/ps6599/products_white_paper09186a00800a3e6f.shtml#wp39006
11. "BGP Case Studies," http://www.cisco.com
12. "Border Gateway Protocol" http://docwiki.cisco.com/wiki/Border_Gateway_Protocol
13. "BGP Named Community Lists" http://www.cisco.com/c/en/us/td/docs/ios/12_2s/feature/guide/fsbgpncl.html
14. "Enterprise IPv6 Transition Strategy using the Locator/ID Separation Protocol," http://www.cisco.com

15. "Understanding and Using RPL," https://supportforums.cisco.com/document/88676/asr9000xr-understanding-and-using-rpl-route-policy-language

16. "Design zone for WAN and remote sites," http://www.cisco.com/c/en/us/solutions/enterprise/design-zone-branch-wan/index.html

17. "Design Zone for Data Centers," http://www.cisco.com/c/en/us/solutions/enterprise/design-zone-data-centers/index.html

18. "Cisco Data Center Design Summary," http://www.cisco.com/c/dam/en/us/td/docs/solutions/CVD/Aug2014/DataCenterDesignSummary-AUG14.pdf

19. "Cisco Virtualized Multi-Tenant Data Center Design Guide," http://www.cisco.com/c/dam/en/us/td/docs/solutions/Enterprise/Data_Center/DC_Infra2_5/DCI_SRND.pdf

20. "Scale Data Centers with Cisco FabricPath," http://www.cisco.com/c/en/us/products/collateral/switches/nexus-7000-series-switches/white_paper_c11-605488.html

21. "Cisco Application Centric Infrastructure Design Guide," http://www.cisco.com

22. "Understanding VRF-lite," http://www.cisco.com/c/en/us/td/docs/switches/lan/catalyst4500/12-2/25ew/configuration/guide/conf/vrf.html

23. "Technical Overview of Virtual Device Contexts," http://www.cisco.com/c/en/us/products/collateral/switches/nexus-7000-10-slot-switch/White_Paper_Tech_Overview_Virtual_Device_Contexts.html

24. "Data Center Interconnect: Layer 2 Extension Between Remote Data Centers," http://www.cisco.com/c/en/us/products/collateral/data-center-virtualization/data-center-interconnect/white_paper_c11_493718.html

25. "Cisco Application Centric Infrastructure (ACI) - Endpoint Groups (EPG) Usage and Design," http://www.cisco.com/c/en/us/solutions/collateral/data-center-virtualization/application-centric-infrastructure/white-paper-c11-731630.html

26. "Technology Comparison: OTV and VPLS as Enablers of LAN Extensions," http://www.cisco.com/c/en/us/products/collateral/switches/nexus-7000-series-switches/white_paper_c11-574984.html

27. "OTV Technology Introduction and Deployment Considerations," http://www.cisco.com/c/en/us/td/docs/solutions/Enterprise/Data_Center/DCI/whitepaper/DCI3_OTV_Intro/DCI_1.html

28. "Cisco Design Zone for Data Center," http://www.cisco.com/c/en/us/solutions/enterprise/design-zone-data-centers/index.html

29. "Cisco Design Zone for Security," http://www.cisco.com/c/en/us/solutions/enterprise/design-zone-security/index.html

30. "Cisco TrustSec for Policy-Defined Segmentation," http://www.cisco.com

31. "Enterprise QoS Solution Reference Network Design Guide," http://www.cisco.com

32. "Deploying High Availability in Campus," http://www.cisco.com

Index

Numbers

3G/4G VPN design models, 335
4-class QoS strategy model, 561–562
6RD (6 Rapid Deployment), IPv6, 210–211
6RD border relay, 210
6RD prefix, 211
6RD-capable router, 210
8-class 1P1Q3T egress queueing, 581–588
8-class 1P1Q3T ingress queueing, 580–581
8-class QoS strategy model, 562–563
12-class QoS strategy model, 564–565
/40 prefix, 197
/48 prefix, 198
/56 prefix, 198
802.1p, QoS (quality of service), 517–519
802.1Q, 27
 QoS (quality of service), 517–519
802.1X, 759–763
 message flow, 763
 phased deployment, 767
 supplicants, 765–766

Symbols

*, G (star comma G), 644, 645
 PIM-SM (Protocol-Independent Multicast—Sparse Mode), 653

A

ABR placement, hub-and-spoke design, OSPF (Open Shortest Path First), 89–90
access control lists (ACLs), 702
access coverage, WAN connections, 232
access layer, enterprise campus design, 4–5
access management, enterprise WAN, 367–368
access restrictions, 740
access-distribution block, enterprise campus design, 13–15

ACI (Application-Centric Infrastructure), 431
 ANP (application network profile), 449, 459–460
 application design, 459–460
 architecture, 434
  APIC (Application Policy Infrastructure Controller), 434–437
  fabric, 437–440
 characteristics, 432
 EPG (endpoint groups), 450–453
 external Layer 2 connections and networks, 461–465
 fabric access policies, 454–455
 integration and migration connectivity options, 471–473
 network virtualization overlays, 441–446
 networking limitations, 432–434
 route propagation inside ACI fabric, 468–470
 routing, 465
  border leaves, 467–468
  first-hop layer 3 default gateway, 465–466
 STP-based layer LANs, 464–465
 tenants, 456–459
ACI APIC cluster, 440
ACI fabric
 connecting to external Layer 3 domains, 470–471
 route propagation, 468–470
ACI policy model, application design, 447–450
ACLs (access control lists), 702
acquiring IPv6 prefixes, 197–198
active passive failover mode, ASA firewall, 722

active/active mode, firewalls, 722
adaptive security appliance (ASA), 696
Adaptive Security Virtual Appliance (ASAv), 713–714
additive keyword, 177
Address Family Translation (AFT, 206
address provisioning, 814
addressing
 enterprise IPv6 networks case study, 813–814
 IS-IS (Intermediate System-to-Intermediate System), 114–116
addressing services, IPv6, 220–221
adjacencies, IS-IS (Intermediate System-to-Intermediate System), 108–109, 120
adjacent neighbors, OSPF (Open Shortest Path First), 76–77
AF (Assured Forwarding), 561
AF drop probability, 521
AF PHB, 521
AF profiles, 546
AFT (Address Family Translation), 206
aggregation layer deployment model, DCI (Data Center Interconnect), 499
aggressive mode, IKE (Internet Key Exchange), 279
AH (Authentication Header), 278
algorithms, token bucket algorithms, 529–531
analysis and task list
 enterprise BGP network with Internet connectivity case study, 791
 enterprise data center connectivity case study, 818

architecture 859

enterprise IPv6 networks case study, 809

resilient enterprise WANs case study, 826–827

analyzing enterprise connectivity, 779–780

ANP (application network profile), 449

    ACI (Application-Centric Infrastructure), 459–460

anti-replay window sizing, 630

Any Transport over MPLS over GRE (AToMoGRE), DCI (Data Center Interconnect), 497–498

Anycast RP, 681

    examples, 682–683

    MSDP (Multicast Source Discovery Protocol), 683

AnyConnect Secure Mobility Client, 623, 765–766

APIC (Application Policy Infrastructure Controller), 357–358, 434–437, 439

APIC-EM (Application Policy Infrastructure Controller Enterprise Module), 357–358, 368–370

    design, 370–371

application adaptation, IPv6, 223

application design

    ACI (Application-Centric Infrastructure), 459–460

    ACI policy model, 447–450

application migration, enterprise IPv6 networks case study, 815–816

application network profile (ANP), 449

application optimization, WAN, 356–357

Application Policy Infrastructure (APIC), 357–358

application support, IPv6, 222–223

    application adaptation, 223

    application workarounds, 223–224

application tiers, separating, 714–716

Application Visibility Control (AVC), 357

application workarounds, IPv6, 223–224

Application-Centric Infrastructure. *See* ACI (Application-Centric Infrastructure)

application-specific integrated circuits (ASIC), 554

architecture

    ACI (Application-Centric Infrastructure), 434

        APIC (Application Policy Infrastructure Controller), 434–437

        fabric, 437–440

    big data architecture, data center QoS, 596

    EAP (Extensible Authentication Protocol), 763–764

    firewalls, 709–712

    FlexVPN, 315

    hierarchical architecture, IS-IS (Intermediate System-to-Intermediate System), 105–106

    HPT (high-performance trading), data center QoS, 595

    IPS (intrusion prevention system), 726–729

    modular network architecture, 691–695

        zones, 695

    MPLS VPNs, 234–236

    multilayer architectures, EIGRP (Enhanced Interior Gateway Routing Protocol), 53–56

new network architecture, 397–398
ONE (Open Network Environment) architecture, 435
provider edge (PE) routers, 237–238
  route distinguishers, 238–239
  route target (RT), 240–241
three-layer hierarchy architecture, EIGRP (Enhanced Interior Gateway Routing Protocol), 57–59
three-tier data center network architecture, 380–381
two-layer hierarchy architecture, EIGRP (Enhanced Interior Gateway Routing Protocol), 56–57
two-tier data center network architecture, 378–380
virtualized multiservice architectures, 596–597

area, OSPF (Open Shortest Path First)
number of areas per ABR, 81–82
numbers of routers in an area, 80–81
routing information, 78–80

area design
IS-IS (Intermediate System-to-Intermediate System), 113
OSPF (Open Shortest Path First), 82–83, 112–113

ARP inspection, 702

AS (autonomous systems), EIGRP (Enhanced Interior Gateway Routing Protocol), 50–52
multiple autonomous system drivers, 53

AS (autonomous systems) number
EIGRP (Enhanced Interior Gateway Routing Protocol), 243–244
PE-CE routing protocol, 242–243

ASA (adaptive security appliance), 696, 712
FirePOWER services, 727

ASA 1000V, 714

ASA clustering, 723

ASA firewall active/passive failover mode, 722

ASA SFR, 726–727

ASAv (Adaptive Security Virtual Appliance), 713–714

ASBRs (autonomous system border routers), 79

Asian sites, routing policies, 799–802

ASIC (application-specific integrated circuits), 554

as-override, 254

assessment phase, IPv6, 196

asymmetric routing versus symmetric routing, IS-IS (Intermediate System-to-Intermediate System), 129–132

asymmetrical routing issues, GLBP (Gateway Load Balancing Protocol), 34

ATM WAN design, 344–346

AToMoGRE (Any Transport over MPLS over GRE), 497–498

attacks
multicast traffic, 753
preventing, 703

attributes, BGP (Border Gateway Protocol)
extended community attributes, 241–242
path attributes, 150

authentication, 740

Authentication Header (AH), 278

authentication servers, 760

authenticators, 760

authorization, 740
authorization options case study, 772–775
autonomous system border routers (ASBRs), 79
autonomous system numbers, choosing, 792–794
autonomous systems. *See* AS (autonomous systems)
Auto-RP, 667, 668–669
    candidate RPs, 670
    case studies, 670–674
    mapping agents, 670
    multicast network edge security, 749–751
    operations, 671–674
    routers, 670
    scope problems, 674–676
AVC (Application Visibility Control), 357
A-VPLS (Advanced VPLS), 496

B

backdoor links between customer sites, PE-CE routing protocol
    BGP (Border Gateway Protocol), 254–255
    EIGRP (Enhanced Interior Gateway Routing Protocol), 245–247
    OSPF (Open Shortest Path First), 250–251
backoff messages, DF election messages, 660
backoff timers, 94
bandwidth allocation, 558–559
bandwidth keyword, 539
baseline network policy enforcement, 701–702
baseline switching security, 702
bestpath as-path multipath-relax, 183
BFD (bidirectional forwarding detection), EIGRP (Enhanced Interior Gateway Routing Protocol), 70–71
BFD echo, 71
BGP (Border Gateway Protocol), 146
    case studies, 172–177
    communities, 169–170
        named communities, 171
        planning for, 171–172
        well-known BGP communities, 170–171
    confederations, 155–156
        versus route reflectors, 157
    dual-homing, 178
    extended community attributes, 241–242
    load-sharing design, 177
        single-homing versus multi-homing, 177–178
    loop prevention, 148–149
    multihoming, 178
    overview, 146–147
    path attributes, 150
    path selection, 150–151
    PE-CE routing protocol, 252–254
        backdoor links between customer sites, 254–255
    peer-forwarding rules, 158
    route reflectors, 153–155
        congruence of physical and logical networks, 165–167
        hierarchical route reflector design, 167–168
        loop prevention, 162–165
        network design issues, 169

redundancy, 159–160

route reflector cluster-ID, 161–162

route reflector clusters, 160–161

split-horizon rule, 158–159

single-homed, multiple links, 178–180

speaker types, 147–148

split-horizon rule, 148–149

traffic engineering techniques, 352–353

TTL Security Check, 700

bgp always-compare-med, 151

BGP ASN design, 792–794

bgp bestpath med missing-as-worst, 151

BGP communities, 796–797

BGP connectivity

BGP communities, 796–797

BGP sessions, 795–796

BGP Originator-ID attribute, 162

BGP sessions, 795–796

bidirectional forwarding detection (BFD), EIGRP (Enhanced Interior Gateway Routing Protocol), 70–71

BIDIR-PIM (bidirectional PIM), 657, 754

DF election, 658–659

DF election messages, 660

PIM modifications, 658

big data architecture, data center QoS, 596

black holes, route summarization, EIGRP (Enhanced Interior Gateway Routing Protocol), 61–63

bootstrap router (BSR), 667

Border Gateway Protocol. *See* BGP (Border Gateway Protocol)

border leaf devices, 439

border leaves, ACI (Application-Centric Infrastructure), 467–468

boundaries, trust states and, 570–573

branch border routers, 366

branch master controller, 366

branch offices, remote-site WAN design, 346–348

branch sites, connecting, 810–812

bridge domains, tenants, ACI (Application-Centric Infrastructure), 456–457

broadcast links, IS-IS (Intermediate System-to-Intermediate System), 119

BSR (bootstrap router), 667

multicast network edge security, 749–751

PIMv2, 676–677

PIMv2 BSR, 678

securing, 751

buffering, 535

buffers, QoS (quality of service), 569–570

building a secure campus edge design (Internet and extranet connectivity) case study, 729–740

bursts, QoS (quality of service), 569–570

C

Campus Edge network, 730–736

characteristics, 730–731

DMZs (demilitarized zones), 732–733

firewalls, 731–735

internal networks, connecting, 733–734
Internet, connecting, 731
campus network virtualization, 16–23
path isolation, 19–23
VLAN assignment, 17–18
VRF (virtual routing and forwarding), 18
campus QoS, 568
design examples, 576–588
candidate RPs, 676–677
Auto-RP, 670
PIMv2 BSR, 677–678
candidate-RP announce packets, 750
candidate-RP discovery packets, 750
capabilities, FlexVPN, 315
case studies
authorization options, 772–775
Auto-RP operation, 670–674
building a secure campus edge design (Internet and extranet connectivity), 729–740
dark fiber DCI, 490–494
DC QoS application, 599–601
design enterprise BGP network with Internet connectivity, 788
  analysis and task list, 791
  BGP connectivity, 795–797
  choosing autonomous system numbers, 792–794
  choosing routing protocols, 792
  Internet routing, 803–807
  requirements and expectations, 788–791
  routing policies, 797–802
design enterprise connectivity, 778
  analysis and task list, 779–780
  designing for new routing protocols, 780–782
  migrating from old to new routing, 785–787
  OSPF design optimization, 782–785
  requirements and expectations, 778–779
  scaling, 787–788
  selecting replacement routing protocols, 780
design enterprise data center connectivity, 816–817
  analysis and task list, 818
  connecting network appliances, 821–822
  data center interconnect, 822–823
  data center network virtualization design, 823–825
  DCN detailed connectivity, 819–821
  requirements and expectations, 817–818
  selecting architecture and connectivity model, 818–819
design enterprise IPv6 network, 807
  addressing, 813–814
  analysis and task list, 809
  application and service migration, 815–816
  choosing IP address types for HQ, 809–810
  communication between branches, 815
  connecting branch sites, 810–812

deployment models, 812
requirements and expectations, 808–809
design QoS in the enterprise network, 835
congestion management, 838–839
MPLS WAN DiffServ tunneling, 839–841
QoS design model, 837–838
QoS trust boundary, 838
requirements and expectations, 835–836
scavenger traffic, 839
traffic discovery and analysis, 836–837
design resilient enterprise WANs, 825
analysis and task list, 826–827
requirements and expectations, 825–826
selecting WAN links, 828
WAN overlays, 828–830
design secure enterprise networks, 830
firewalls, 835
infrastructure and network access security, 833–834
Layer 2, 834–835
requirements and expectations, 831
security domains and zone design, 832
designing enterprisewide BGP policies using BGP communities, 172–177
DF election, 660–662
EIGRP DMVPN, 295–302
firewall high availability, 720–725

implementing firewalls in a data center, 717–720
MPLS VPN routing propagation, 255–258
MPLS/VPN over GRE/DMVPN, 304–312
MSDP operations, 684–686
multitenant data centers, 425–426
redundancy and connectivity, 343–354
RPF check fails and succeeds, 641–642
separation of application tiers, 714–716
small data centers (connecting servers to an enterprise LAN), 376–378
three-tier data center network architecture, 380–381
two-tier data center network architecture, 378–380
virtualized multiservice architectures, 596–597
Catalyst switches, 554, 571, 574
CBWFQ (class-based weighted fair queueing), 536, 538–541, 591
WAN/branch edge, 592
cellular connectivity, 335
CGA (cryptographically generated access), 222
challenges of SDN (software-defined networking), 419–421
characteristics
ACI (Application-Centric Infrastructure), 432
Campus Edge network, 730–731
DiffServ, 516
ECN (explicit congestion notification), 550
IntServ (Integrated Services), 516

IS-IS (Intermediate System-to-Intermediate System), 103–104, 110–112

OSPF (Open Shortest Path First), 110–112

PIM-SM (Protocol-Independent Multicast—Sparse Mode), 645

SDN controller characteristics, 418

SSM (source-specific multicast), 654

traffic policing, 529

traffic shaping, 529

choke points

EIGRP (Enhanced Interior Gateway Routing Protocol), 54

summarization and, 55–56

choosing

autonomous system numbers, 792–794

WAN connections, 230–233

CIR (committed information rate), 530

Cisco AnyConnect Secure Mobility client, 765–766

Cisco Application-Centric Infrastructure. *See* ACI (Application-Centric Infrastructure)

Cisco ASA 5500-X Series Next-Generation Firewall, 696

Cisco ASA 5506-X, 696

Cisco ASA 5512-X, 696

Cisco ASA 5555-X, 696

Cisco FabricPath, 402–407

Cisco FirePOWER, NGIPS (next-generation IPS), 696, 726–727

Cisco Identity Services Engine (ISE), 768

Cisco IOS, encryption, 623–625

Cisco IOS XR software, 750

Cisco modular network architecture, 691–695

Cisco next-generation security, 696

Cisco Security Group Tag (SGT), 769–772

Cisco TrustSec, 768

Profiling Service, 768–769

SGT (Security Group Tag), 769–772

Cisco Web Security Appliance (WSA), 735–736

cLACP (Cluster Link Aggregation Control Protocol), 724

class-based weighted fair queueing (CBWFQ), 536, 538–541

classification, QoS (quality of service), order of operations, 623–625

classification and marking, QoS (quality of service)

design principles, 554–555

Layer 2 marking, 517–519

Layer 2.5 marking: MPLS experimental bits, 524

Layer 3 marking: DSCP per-hop behaviors, 520–523

Layer 3 marking: IP type of service, 519–520

Layer 7: NBAR/NBAR2, 526–527

mapping markings between OSI layers, 524–525

traffic policing and shaping, 527–529, 532

classification/marking/policing QoS model, 573–574

classifications and marking tools, QoS (quality of service), 516–517

client-server traffic, 479

CLNP (Connectionless Network Protocol), 102
CLNS (Connectionless Network Service), 102
Cluster ID, 164–165
Cluster Link Aggregation Control Protocol (cLACP), 724
Cluster-List attribute, 163
committed information rate (CIR), 530
communication between branches, enterprise IPv6 networks case study, 815
communities, BGP (Border Gateway Protocol), 169–170, 796–797
  named communities, 171
  planning for, 171–172
  well-known BGP communities, 170–171
comparing
  802.1X deployment modes, 767
  control planes and data planes, 414–415
  DMVPN (Dynamic Multipoint VPN)
    and GET VPN, 629
    phases, 302
  EF and AF profiles, 546
  enterprise campus access-distribution design models, 45
  IntServ and DiffServ, 514–516
  MSDP and BGP features, 752
  point-to-point GRE and multipoint GRE, 276–277
  QoS design drivers and considerations based on the PIN, 602
  RP deployments, 667
  traffic shaping and traffic policing, 529

  virtual firewall models, 714
  VPLS and VPWS, 266–267
complete sequence numbers (CSNP), 123–124
confederations, BGP (Border Gateway Protocol), 155–156
  versus BGP route reflectors, 157
configuration blocks, FlexVPN, 315–316
congestion avoidance, 541, 575
congestion management, QoS in the enterprise network case study, 838–839
congruence of physical and logical networks, route reflectors, BGP (Border Gateway Protocol), 165–167
connecting
  ACI fabric to external Layer 3 domains, 470–471
  ACI to outside Layer 2 domains, 462–465
  branch sites, 810–812
  external partners, 737
  internal networks, Campus Edge network, 733–734
  Internet, Campus Edge network, 731
  network appliances, 821–822
  servers to enterprise LANs, 376–378
Connectionless Network Protocol (CLNP), 102
Connectionless Network Service. See CLNS (Connectionless Network Service)
connectivity, case studies, redundancy and connectivity, 343–354
connectivity model, MPLS VPNs, 606
content and application security, 695

contracts, 449
control plane, 697
control plane optimization, VXLAN (virtual extensible LAN), 413–414
control plane policing (CoPP), 747
control plane protection, 697
control plane security, 414–415
   IPv6, 224
convergence
   EtherChannel convergence, 28
   OSPF (Open Shortest Path First), 93
      event detection, 94
      event processing, 96–97
      event propagation, 94–96
   WAN connections, 231
CoPP (control plane policing), 747
core layer, enterprise campus design, 6–7
core layer deployment model, DCI (Data Center Interconnect), 499
CQ (custom queueing), 536
critical VLANs, 773
cryptographically generated access (CGA), 222
CSNP (complete sequence number), 123–124
custom queueing (CQ), 536
customer edge (CE) routers, 235
customer-managed Layer 2 DCI deployment models, 497
   aggregation layer deployment model, 499
   Any Transport over MPLS over GRE (AToMoGRE), 497–498
   core layer deployment model, 499
   limitations of, 501

   overlay transport virtualization DCI, 501–506
   separate DCI layer deployment model, 500
CWDM, 490

D

dark fiber DCI, 490–494
data center briding toolset, 597–598
Data Center Interconnect. *See* DCI (Data Center Interconnect)
data center network virtualization design, 823–825
data center QoS
   big data architecture, 596
   data center briding toolset, 597–598
   DC QoS application case study, 599–601
   HPT (high-performance trading), 595
   overview, 594
   virtualized multiservice architectures, 596–597
data center traffic flows
   DCI (Data Center Interconnect). *See* DCI (Data Center Interconnect)
   traffic flow directions, 478–479
   traffic flow types, 479–482
data centers
   case studies, implementing firewalls in a data center, 717–720
   end of row versus top of rack design, 383–384
   fabric extenders, 385–388
   high availability, 388–392
   interconnecting, 822–823
   inter-VLAN routing, 381–383
   modern data centers. *See* modern data centers

868 data centers

new network architecture, 397–398
NIC teaming, 392–393
small data centers (connecting servers to an enterprise LAN), 376–378
three-tier data center network architecture, 380–381
two-tier data center network architecture, 378–380

data flow, IS-IS (Intermediate System-to-Intermediate System), 118–119

data plane, 414–415, 697

data plane protection, 697

Database Overload Protection, OSPF (Open Shortest Path First), 97–98

DC QoS application, 599–601

DCB (Data Center Bridging) toolset, 597–598

DCI (Data Center Interconnect), 482–483

customer-managed Layer 2 DCI deployment models, 497
  aggregation layer deployment model, 499
  Any Transport over MPLS over GRE (AToMoGRE), 497–498
  core layer deployment model, 499
  limitations of, 501
  overlay transport virtualization DCI, 501–506
  separate DCI layer deployment model, 500
dark fiber DCI, 490–494
IP address mobility, 484–490
Layer 3, 507–509
LISP (locator/ID separation protocol), 487–489

overlay networks, 507
pseudowire DCI, 495
virtual private LAN service DCI, 496

DCN connectivity, enterprise data center connectivity, 819–821

DCN connectivity model, 820

decision process, IS-IS (Intermediate System-to-Intermediate System), 119

default forwarding (DF), 558

default routing, 805–807

default VLANs, 773

delays, jitter and latency, WAN QoS, 590–591

demilitarized zones (DMZs), 710

dense mode protocols, 642

deployment

IPv6, 194–195
  assessment phase, 196
  discovery phase, 196
  implementation and optimization phases, 197
  planning and design phase, 196–197
PfRv3, 366–367
phased deployment, 802.1X, 767

deployment models

DHCPv6 deployment model, 814
DMVPN (Dynamic Multipoint VPN), 285
enterprise IPv6 networks, case study, 812

design

APIC-EM (Application Policy Infrastructure Controller Enterprise Module), 370–371
campus QoS, examples, 576–588
IPv6, 194–195

assessment phase, 196
discovery phase, 196
implementation and optimization phases, 197
planning and design phase, 196–197
link aggregation of EtherChannel interface, 575–576

designated forwarder (DF), BIDIR-PIM (bidirectional PIM), 658

designing
enterprise BGP network with Internet connectivity, 788
  analysis and task list, 791
  BGP connectivity, 795–797
  choosing autonomous system numbers, 792–794
  choosing routing protocols, 792
  Internet routing, 803–807
  requirements and expectations, 788–791
  routing policies, 797–802
enterprise connectivity, 778
  analysis and task list, 779–780
  designing for new routing protocols, 780–782
  migrating from old to new routing, 785–787
  OSPF design optimization, 782–785
  requirements and expectations, 778–779
  scaling, 787–788
  selecting replacement routing protocols, 780
enterprise data center connectivity, 816–817
  analysis and task list, 818
  connecting network appliances, 821–822
  data center interconnect, 822–823
  data center network virtualization design, 823–825
  DCN detailed connectivity, 819–821
  requirements and expectations, 817–818
  selecting architecture and connectivity model, 818–819
enterprise IPv6 networks, 807
  addressing, 813–814
  analysis and task list, 809
  application and service migration, 815–816
  choosing IP address types for HQ, 809–810
  communication between branches, 815
  connecting branch sites, 810–812
  deployment models, 812
  requirements and expectations, 808–809
infrastructure protection, 696–697
for new routing protocols, 780–782
QoS in the enterprise network case study, 835
  congestion management, 838–839
  MPLS WAN DiffServ tunneling, 839–841
  QoS design model, 837–838
  QoS trust boundary, 838
  requirements and expectations, 835–836
  scavenger traffic, 839
  traffic discovery and analysis, 836–837

870   designing

resilient enterprise WANs, 825
   analysis and task list, 826–827
   requirements and expectations, 825–826
   selecting WAN links, 828
   WAN overlays, 828–830
secure enterprise networks, 830
   firewalls, 835
   infrastructure and network access security, 833–834
   Layer 2 security considerations, 834–835
   requirements and expectations, 831
   security domains and zone design, 832
device profiling, 769
device resiliency, 24
device-level virtualization, separation, 424–425
DF (default forwarding), 558
DF (designated forwarder), BIDIR-PIM (bidirectional PIM), 658
   DF election, 658–659
   DF election messages, 660
DF election, case studies, 660–662
DF election messages, BIDIR-PIM (bidirectional PIM), 660
DHCP snooping, 702
DHCPv6, 220
DHCPv6 deployment model, 814
DiffServ (Differentiated Services), 515–516
discovery phase, IPv6, deployment and design, 196
Distance Vector Multicast Routing Protocol (DVMRP), 756

distribution layer, enterprise campus design, 5–6
distribution-to-distribution interconnect
   multitier access model, 37–41
   routed access model, 41–42
   virtual switch model, 43–44
distribution-to-distribution link design, 36–37
DMVPN (Dynamic Multipoint VPN), 621
   benefits of, 286
   EIGRP (Enhanced Interior Gateway Routing Protocol), 69
   limitations of, 287
   overview, 283–287
   Phase 1, 287–289
      EIGRP, 295–297
   Phase 2, 289–292
      EIGRP, 297–299
   Phase 3, 292–295
      EIGRP, 299–301
   QoS (quality of service), 626–628
   redundancy, 302–304
   VPN WAN design models, 331–333
DMZs (demilitarized zones), 710
   Campus Edge network, 732–733
DNS64, IPv6, 206–208
domains, IS-IS (Intermediate System-to-Intermediate System), 104
drop probability, 543
   DSCP, 522
dropping design principles, QoS (quality of service), 557–558
dropping modes, RED (random early detection), 543–544
dropping recommendations, QoS (quality of service), 574–575

dropping tools, DSCP-based WRED, 541–546
DSCP (Differentiated Services Code Point)
  drop probability, 522
  IP precedence mapping, 523
  markings, 555
DSCP MPLS EXP bits, 611
DSCP-based WRED, 541–546
DS-Lite, IPv6, 211–212
dual domains, 104
dual IS-IS, 104–105
dual stack, IPv6, 205–206
dual-bucket policing, 532–533
dual-homed to one ISP using a single local edge router, 180–181
dual-homed to one ISP using multiple edge routers, 182–183
dual-homing, 178
dual-rate metering. *See* policing tools
Dual-Stack Lite, IPv6, 211–212
dual-stack security, IPv6, 225
DVMRP (Distance Vector Multicast Routing Protocol), 756
DVTI (Dynamic VTI), IPsec and, 283
DWDM, 490
Dynamic Multipoint VPN. *See* DMVPN (Dynamic Multipoint VPN)
dynamic trust states, 572–573
dynamic VLAN assignments, 772–774
Dynamic VTI (DVTI), IPsec and, 283

E

EAP (Extensible Authentication Protocol), 762, 763–765
  types of, 764–765
EAP chaining, 765
EAP method, 762
EAP over LAN (EAPOL), 762
EAP-Chaining, 766
EAP-FASTv2 (Extensible Authentication Protocol-Flexible Authentication via Secure Tunneling), 765
EAPOL (EAP over LAN), 762, 763
east-west traffic, 478
  securing, 716–717
eBGP (external BGP), 151
ebgp multihop, 179
ECN (explicit congestion notification), 520, 547–550
  characteristics, 550
  operations, 549
  WRED, 548–549
e-commerce, 693
edge routers
  dual-homed to one ISP using a single local edge router, 180–181
  dual-homed to one ISP using multiple edge routers, 182–183
  multihoming with two ISPs using a single local edge router, 183–186
  multihoming with two ISPs using multiple local edge routers, 186–188
EF PHB, 521
EF profiles, 546
EF traffic, 546
EFC (Ethernet Flow Control), 598
EGP (Exterior Gateway Protocol), 146
egress tunnel router (ETR), 213
EIGRP (Enhanced Interior Gateway Routing Protocol), 49–50
  AS (autonomous systems), 50–52
  BFD (bidirectional forwarding detection), 70–71

DMVPN (Dynamic Multipoint VPN)
Phase 1, 295–297
Phase 2, 297–299
Phase 3, 299–301
scaling, 69
fast convergence design, 70
GR (graceful restart), 71–72
hub-and-spoke design, 60–61
scalability optimization, 65–68
summarization challenges, 61–65
multilayer architectures, 53–56
multiple autonomous system drivers, 53
with multiple autonomous systems, 50–52
PE-CE routing protocol, 241–242
backdoor links between customer sites, 245–247
different AS number, 243–244
same AS number, 242–243
some sites only, 244–245
queries, 52–53
scalable EIGRP design, 50
stub leaking, 67–68
three-layer hierarchy architecture, 57–59
two-layer hierarchy architecture, 56–57
EIGRP DMVPN, case study, 295–302
election
DF election, BIDIR-PIM (bidirectional PIM), 658–659
DF election case study, 660–662
DF election messages, BIDIR-PIM (bidirectional PIM), 660
encapsulating security payload (ESP), 278

end of row versus top of rack design, 383–384
endpoint groups (EPG), 449
Enhanced Interior Gateway Routing Protocol. See EIGRP (Enhanced Interior Gateway Routing Protocol)
enhanced VXLAN (eVXLAN), 443–444
enterprise BGP network with Internet connectivity, designing, 788
analysis and task list, 791
BGP connectivity, 795–797
choosing autonomous system numbers, 792–794
choosing routing protocols, 792
Internet routing, 803–807
requirements and expectations, 788–791
routing policies, 797–802
enterprise branch, 692
enterprise campus, 692
enterprise campus access-distribution design models, comparing, 45
enterprise campus design, 2–3
distribution-to-distribution link design, 36–37
flexibility, 15–16
campus network virtualization, 16–23
hierarchies, 3
access layer, 4–5
core layer, 6–7
distribution layer, 5–6
three-tier layer model, 9–10
two-tier layer model, 8–9
high-availability enterprise campus. See high-availability enterprise campus
modularity, 10

access-distribution block, 13–15
OSPF (Open Shortest Path First), 10–12
resiliency, 23
enterprise connectivity, designing, 778
  analysis and task list, 779–780
  designing for new routing protocols, 780–782
  migrating from old to new routing, 785–787
  OSPF design optimization, 782–785
  requirements and expectations, 778–779
  scaling, 787–788
  selecting replacement routing protocols, 780
enterprise core, 692
enterprise data center connectivity, designing, 816–817
  analysis and task list, 818
  connecting network appliances, 821–822
  data center interconnect, 822–823
  data center network virtualization design, 823–825
  DCN detailed connectivity, 819–821
  requirements and expectations, 817–818
  selecting architecture and connectivity model, 818–819
enterprise Internet edge, 692
enterprise IPv6 networks, designing, 807
  addressing, 813–814
  analysis and task list, 809
  application and service migration, 815–816
  choosing IP address types for HQ, 809–810
  communication between branches, 815
  connecting branch sites, 810–812
  deployment models, 812
  requirements and expectations, 808–809
enterprise LANs, connecting servers to, 376–378
enterprise routing, WAN, 236–237
enterprise WAN, access management, 367–368
enterprise WAN edge, 692
enterprise-managed VPNs, 272
  case studies
    EIGRP DMVPN, 295–302
    MPLS/VPN over GRE/DMVPN, 304–312
  DMVPN (Dynamic Multipoint VPN)
    overview, 283–287
    Phase 1, 287–289
    Phase 2, 289–292
    Phase 3, 292–295
  GRE (generic routing encapsulation), 273–275
  IPsec, 278–280
  overview, 272–273
EoMPLS, 497–498
EoR (End of Row) design, 383–384
EPG (endpoint groups), 449
  ACI (Application-Centric Infrastructure), 450–453
  extending, 462–463
equal-cost multipath routing, 724
ESP (encapsulating security payload), 278
EtherChannel, link aggregation of EtherChannel interface, 575–576
EtherChannel convergence, 28

Ethernet, 480–481, 721
Ethernet Flow Control (EFC), 598
ETR (egress tunnel router), 213
European sites, routing policies, 799–802
event detection, OSPF (Open Shortest Path First), 94
event processing, OSPF (Open Shortest Path First), 96–97
event propagation, OSPF (Open Shortest Path First), 94–96
eVXLAN (enhanced VXLAN), 443–444
explicity congestion notification (ECN), 520
extended community attributes, BGP (Border Gateway Protocol), 241–242
Extensible Authentication Protocol (EAP), 762, 763–765
Extensible Authentication Protocol-Flexible Authentication via Secure Tunneling (EAP-FASTv2), 765
Exterior Gateway Protocol (EGP), 146
external Layer 2 connections and networks, ACI (Application-Centric Infrastructure), 461–465
external Layer 3 domains, connecting, ACI fabric, 470–471
external partners, connecting, 737
extranet topology
   interconnect model, 738–739
   remote LAN model, 737–738
extranets, security, 739–740

F

fabric
   ACI (Application-Centric Infrastructure), 437–440
   ACI fabric
      connecting to external Layer 3 domains, 470–471
      route propagation, 468–469
fabric access policies, ACI (Application-Centric Infrastructure), 454–455
fabric extenders, 385–388
FabricPath, 402–407
fair-queue keyword, 539
fair-queueing, 537–538
fast convergence design, EIGRP (Enhanced Interior Gateway Routing Protocol), 70
FCoE (Fibre Channel over Ethernet), 597–598
FCoE Initialization Protocol (FIP), 388
FEX (fabric extenders), 385–388
FHR (first-hop routers), 637, 644
FHRP (First-Hop Redundancy Protocol), 31–35
   remote-site LANs, 342–343
Fibre Channel over Ethernet (FCoE), 597–598
FIP (FCoE Initialization Protocol), 388
FirePOWER, 726–727
FirePOWER IPS appliance, 728
FirePOWER IPS deployment modes, 728–729
FirePOWER IPS module deployment modes, 728
FireSIGHT Management Center, 727
firewall clustering, 722–723
firewall modes, 719–720
firewall permissions, 740
firewall placement, in DC networks, 718
firewall virtualization, 712–714

firewalls, 695
  architecture, 709–712
  ASA (adaptive security appliance), 712
  Campus Edge network, 731–735
  case studies, separation of application tiers, 714–716
  DMZs (demilitarized zones), 710
  high availability, 720–725
  implementing in data centers, case studies, 717–720
  IOS firewalls, 712
  nonredundant firewall connectivity design, 721
  routed mode, 719
  secure enterprise networks, 835
  single-tier firewalls, 710
  transparent mode, 719
  two-tier firewall, 710
  virtualization, 712–714
first-hop layer 3 default gateway, ACI (Application-Centric Infrastructure), 465–466
First-Hop Redundancy Protocol. *See* FHRP (First-Hop Redundancy Protocol)
first-hop router (FHR), 644
first-hop routers (FHR), 637
first-in, first-out queueing, 535
flat IS-IS routing design, 134–135
flexibility, enterprise campus design, 15–16
  campus network virtualization, 16–23
FlexVPN, 314
  architecture, 315
  capabilities, 315
  configuration blocks, 315–316

flooding, LSPs (link state packets), IS-IS (Intermediate System-to-Intermediate System), 122–123
flooding problems, PIMv2 BSR, 678–679
flooding reduction, OSPF (Open Shortest Path First), 97
forward process, IS-IS (Intermediate System-to-Intermediate System), 119
forwarding, MPLS VPNs, 258–259
front door virtual routing and forwarding (fVRF), 338
full drop (tail drop), 544
full-mesh design
  IS-IS (Intermediate System-to-Intermediate System), 133–134
  OSPF (Open Shortest Path First), 87–88
fully meshed MPLS VPN QoS, 608–609
fVRF (front door virtual routing and forwarding), 338
  IWAN Hybrid design model, 360

G

Gateway Load Balancing Protocol. *See* GLBP (Gateway Load Balancing Protocol)
generic routing encapsulation (GRE), 208
GET VPN, 317–320, 621
  QoS (quality of service), 629–630
GLBP (Gateway Load Balancing Protocol), 31–35
global synchronization, 541
GM (group member) router, 629
GR (graceful restart), EIGRP, 71–72

GRE (generic routing encapsulation), 208
    comparing point-to-point GRE and multipoint GRE, 276–277
    DMVPN (Dynamic Multipoint VPN), case studies, 304–312
    IPsec, 280–281, 622–623
    multipoint GRE (mGRE), 275–276
    overview, 273–275
group member (GM) router, 629
group-to-RP m mapping, 670–674
guest VLANs, 773

H

Head of Line (HOL), 598
hierarchal IS-IS design, 135–136
hierarchical architecture, IS-IS (Intermediate System-to-Intermediate System), 105–106
hierarchical route reflector design, BGP (Border Gateway Protocol), 167–168
hierarchies
    enterprise campus design, 3
        access layer, 4–5
        core layer, 6–7
        distribution layer, 5–6
        three-tier layer model, 9–10
        two-tier layer model, 8–9
    OSPF (Open Shortest Path First), 84–85
high availability
    data centers, 388–392
    firewalls, 720–725
    high-availability enterprise campus, 23–24
    distribution-to-distribution interconnect
        multitier access model, 37–41
        routed access model, 41–42
        with virtual swi, 43–44
    FHRP (First-Hop Redundancy Protocol), 31–35
    link aggregation, 28–31
    overview, 44–46
    trunking, 27
    VLAN design, 24–26
high-performance trading (HPT), data center QoS, 595
HOL (Head of Line), 598
hold-interval, 95
hop-by-hop easy virtual network (EVN) based, 20
hop-by-hop VRF-lite based, 19
Hot Standby Router Protocol. *See* HSRP (Hot Standby Router Protocol)
HPT (high-performance trading), data center QoS, 595
HQ, choosing IP address types for, 809–810
HSRP (Hot Standby Router Protocol), 31
hub border router, 365
hub mast controller (MC), 365
hub-and-spoke design
    DMVPN (Dynamic Multipoint VPN), 285
    EIGRP (Enhanced Interior Gateway Routing Protocol), 60–61
        scalability optimization, 65–68
        summarization challenges, 61–65
    NBMA hub-and-spoke, IS-IS (Intermediate System-to-Intermediate System), 132–133
    OSPF (Open Shortest Path First), 88

ABR placement, 89–90
network types, 92–93
number of areas, 91
H-VPLS, 263–264

I

iBGP, 148
  scalability limitations, 152
  scalability solutions, 152–153
    confederations, 155–156
    route reflectors, 153–155
Identity Services Engine (ISE), 768
IEEE 802.1X, 759–763
  message flow, 763
  phased deployment, 767
  supplicants, 765–766
IETF (Internet Engineering Task Force), 31
IGMP, multicast receiver controls, 755–757
IGMP membership report, 646–647
IGMPv3, SSM (source-specific multicast), 655
IIF (incoming interface), 653
IIH PDUs, 117–118
IIHs, IS-IS (Intermediate System-to-Intermediate System), 121–122
IKE (Internet Key Exchange), 278
  phases of, 278–279
IKE GDOI (Group Domain of Interpretation), 317–318
IKEv2, FlexVPN, 316
implementation and optimization phases, IPv6, 197
implementing, firewalls in a data center, 717–720

incoming interface (IIF), 653
information data flow, IS-IS (Intermediate System-to-Intermediate System), 118–119
infrastructure
  network infrastructure devices, resiliency and survivability, 700–701
  routing infrastructure, security, 699–700
  secure enterprise networks, designing, 833–834
  switching infrastructure, 702–703
infrastructure device access, 698–699
infrastructure devices, LISP (locator/ID separation protocol), 213–216
infrastructure protection, 695
  designing, 696–697
ingress traffic filtering, 702
ingress tunnel router (ITR), 213
inline mode, 727
inside zone, IPS (intrusion prevention system), 726
integrated IS-IS, 104–105
  for IPv6, 138–141
Integrated Services. *See* IntServ
integration options, ACI (Application-Centric Infrastructure), 471–473
intelligent path control, WAN, 356
Intelligent WAN. *See* IWAN (Intelligent WAN)
Intelligent WAN (IWAN), 354–355
inter-AS MPLS VPN, WAN connections, 232
interconnect model, 738–739
interconnecting, data centers, 822–823

inter-DC traffic, 478
interdomain, 639
interface-based PIM neighbor filtering, 752
Intermediate System-to-Intermediate System. *See* IS-IS (Intermediate System-to-Intermediate System)
internal multicast security
  multicast admission controls, 757
  multicast receiver controls, 755–757
  multicast sender control, 753–755
  PIM (Protocol-Independent Multicast), 752
internal networks, connecting, Campus Edge network, 733–734
Internet
  connecting, Campus Edge network, 731
  remote sites, using local Internet, 337–339
Internet Engineering Task Force (IETF), 31
Internet Key Exchange (IKE), 278
  phases of, 278–279
internet keyword, 171
Internet routing
  default routing, 805–807
  multihoming, 804–805
  public IP space selection, 803–804
Inter-Switch Link (ISL), 27
inter-VLAN routing, 381–383
intradomain, 639
intranet data center, 692
intrusion prevention system. *See* IPS (intrusion prevention system)
IntServ (Integrated Services), 514–515, 516
IOS encryption, order of operations, 623–625

IOS firewalls, 712
IOS XR software, 750
IP address mobility, 484–490
IP address types, choosing for HQ, 809–810
IP ECN, 547–550
IP gateway redundancy, VSS (virtual switching system), 35–36
ip msdp sa-filter, 755
IP multicast, 633–634
  how it works, 634–635
  multicast forwarding and RPF check, 639–641
  multicast groups, 635–636
  multicast networks, 638
  multicast protocols, 638–639, 642–644
  PIM-SM (Protocol-Independent Multicast—Sparse Mode). *See* PIM-SM (Protocol-Independent Multicast—Sparse Mode)
  security, 743
    challenges of, 744
  SSM (source-specific multicast). *See* SSM (source-specific multicast)
ip multicast boundary, 754
IP multicast service model, 636–637
IP packet DiffServ DS field, 522
ip pim accept-register, 755
ip pim register-rate-limit, 755
ip pim rp-announce-filter rp-list, 746
IP precedence mapping, DSCP, 523
IP RTP priority queueing, 536
IP source guard, 702
IP spoofing protection, 702
ip tcp adjust mss [size]626
IP type of service, QoS (quality of service), 519–520

IP-in-IP (IPIP), 208
IPIP (IP-in-IP), 208
IPS (intrusion prevention system), 696
  architecture, 726–729
  security, 695
IPsec, 278–280, 284
  DVTI (Dynamic VTI), 283
  GRE (generic routing encapsulation), 622–623
  GRE (generic routing encapsulation) and, 280–281
  VTI (virtual tunnel interface) and, 281–282
IPsec SA anti-replay, 630
IPsec VPNs
  modes, 621–623
  QoS (quality of service), 619–620
    MTU (maximum transmission unit), 625–626
    use cases, 621
IPv4 addresses, 194
IPv6, 194
  6RD (6 Rapid Deployment), 210–211
  application support, 222–223
    application adaptation, 223
    application workarounds, 223–224
  control plane security, 224
  deployment and design, 194–195
    assessment phase, 196
    discovery phase, 196
    implementation and optimization phases, 197
    planning and design phase, 196–197
  DNS64, 206–208
  dual stack, 205–206

Dual-Stack Lite, 211–212
dual-stack security, 225
integrated IS-IS, 138–141
link layer security, 221–222
manual tunnels, 208–209
migration
  acquiring IPv6 prefixes, 197–198
  transition mechanisms, 203–205
  where to start, 199–200
migration models
  IPv6 islands, 200–201
  IPv6 WAN, 201–203
multihoming, 226
NAT64, 206–208
transition mechanisms, 216–217
tunnel brokers, 209
tunneling security, 225–226
IPv6 embedded RP, 679–681
IPv6 islands, 200–201
IPv6 services, 219–220
  addressing services, 220–221
  name services, 220
  security services, 221
IPv6 WAN, 201–203
ISE (Identity Services Engine), 768, 771
IS-IS (Intermediate System-to-Intermediate System), 87, 102, 141–142
  addressing, 114–116
  adjacencies, 108–109, 120
  characteristics, 103–104, 110–112
  domains, 104
  flat routing design, 134–135
  hierarchal IS-IS design, 135–136

hierarchical architecture, 105–106
information data flow, 118–119
integrated IS-IS, 104–105
    for IPv6, 138–141
level 1/level 2 LSPs, 121–122
link state packets flooding, 122–123
LSDB synchronization, 123–124
network types, 119
OSPF versus, 110–112
    area design, 112–113
overview, 102–103
packets, 117
protocol operations, 119–121
route summarization, 136–138
router and link types, 106–108
routing, 125–126
    asymmetric versus symmetric, 129–132
    full-mesh design, 133–134
    NBMA hub-and-spoke, 132–133
    route leaking, 126–129
single topology restrictions, 138–139

IS-IS PDUs, 117
ISL (Inter-Switch Link), 27
ITR (ingress tunnel router), 213
IWAN (Intelligent WAN), 354–355
    AVC (Application Visibility Control), 357
    PfR (Performance Routing), 356
    PfRv3, 363–366
    secure connectivity, 357
IWAN design, 358–359
IWAN Hybrid design model, 361
IWAN Hybrid WAN design model, 359
IWAN WAN aggregation (hub) designs, 359

J

jitter, WAN QoS, 590–591

K

keywords
    additive, 177
    bandwidth, 539
    fair-queue, 539
    internet, 171
KS (key server), 629

L

L3Out, connecting ACI fabric to external Layer 3 domains, 470–471
LAN segments, 703
LANs, remote-site LANs, 339–343
latency, WAN QoS, 590–591
Layer 2 attacks, 753
Layer 2 connections and networks, ACI (Application-Centric Infrastructure), 461–465
Layer 2 DCI:LISP based, 488
Layer 2 hub-and-spoke WAN QoS design model, 607
Layer 2 marking, QoS (quality of service), 517–519
Layer 2 MPLS VPN, 259
Layer 2 outside connections, ACI (Application-Centric Infrastructure), 463–464
Layer 2 private WAN QoS, 607
Layer 2 switch networks with STP, 703
Layer 2 VPN provisioning models, 497

Layer 2 WAN design models, 329–331

Layer 2.5 marking: MPLS experimental bits, QoS (quality of service), 524

Layer 3 DCI, 507–509

Layer 3 marking: DSCP per-hop behaviors, QoS (quality of service), 520–523

Layer 3 marking: IP type of service, QoS (quality of service), 519–520

Layer 3 MPLS VPNs, 233–234

Layer 3 separation with VRF-Lite, 423–424

Layer 7: NBAR/NBAR2, QoS (quality of service), 526–527

leaf nodes, ACI (Application-Centric Infrastructure), 467

leaf switches, 401, 439

level 1 router, IS-IS (Intermediate System-to-Intermediate System), 107

level 1/level 2 LSPs, IS-IS (Intermediate System-to-Intermediate System), 121–122

level 1/level 2 router, IS-IS (Intermediate System-to-Intermediate System), 107

level 2 router, IS-IS (Intermediate System-to-Intermediate System), 107

limitations of
  ACI (Application-Centric Infrastructure), networking limitations, 432–434
  current networking technology, 398–399
  customer-managed Layer 2 DCI deployment models, 501

link aggregation, high-availability enterprise campus, 28–31

link aggregation of EtherChannel interface, QoS (quality of service), 575–576

Link Layer Discovery Protocol (LLDP), 464

link layer security, IPv6, 221–222

link types, IS-IS (Intermediate System-to-Intermediate System), 106–108

Link-State Database Overload Protection, OSPF (Open Shortest Path First), 97–98

link-state routing protocols, designing, 781

LISP (Locator/ID Separation Protocol), 212–216

LISP (locator/ID separation protocol), DCI (Data Center Interconnect), 487–489

LISP infrastructure devices, 213–216

LISP site edge devices, 213

LLDP (Link Layer Discovery Protocol), 464

LLQ (low-latency queueing), 536, 540, 591

load balancing
  enterprise routing, WAN, 237
  EtherChannel, 575

load-sharing design, BGP (Border Gateway Protocol), 177
  single-homing versus multihoming, 177–178

Locator/ID Separation Protocol (LISP), 212–216

loop prevention
  BGP (Border Gateway Protocol), 148–149
  route reflectors, BGP (Border Gateway Protocol), 162–165

low-latency queueing (LLQ), 536, 540

LSA throttling timers, 96
LSDB synchronization, IS-IS (Intermediate System-to-Intermediate System), 123–124
LSPs (link state packets), IS-IS, 121–123
  flooding, IS-IS (Intermediate System-to-Intermediate System), 122–123

M

MAB (MAC Authentication and Bypass), 769
main HQ multihoming, Internet routing, 803–804
main mode, IKE (Internet Key Exchange), 279
managed CE service, WAN connections, 232
managed VPNs, 230
management, WAN, 357–358
management access, securing, to infrastructure devices, 698–699
management network, 693
management plane, 697
management plane protection, 697
management restricted zones, 695
manual tunnels, IPv6, 208–209
mapping QoS markings between OSI layers, 524–525
mapping agents, Auto-RP, 670
Map-Resolver (MR), 214
Map-Server (MS), 213–214
mark probability denominator, 543
markings
  DSCP (Differentiated Services Code Point), 555
  mapping QoS markings between OSI layers, 524–525
masquerading, 754

maximum threshold, 543
maximum transmission unit (MTU), 80
max-interval, 95
MCP (Mis-Cabling Protocol), 464
MEC (Multichassis EtherChannel), 30
message flow, 802.1X, 763
messages, DF election messages, 660
mGRE (multipoint GRE), 275–276, 284
  versus point-to-point GRE, 276–277
microsegementation, overlay networks, 427–428
migrating
  from old to new routing, designing enterprise connectivity, 785–787
  from RIPv2 to OSPF, 785
migration, IPv6
  acquiring IPv6 prefixes, 197–198
  transition mechanisms, 203–205
  where to start, 199–200
migration models
  IPv6 islands, 200–201
  IPv6 WAN, 201–203
migration options, ACI (Application-Centric Infrastructure), 471–473
minimum threshold, 543
Mis-Cabling Protocol (MCP), 464
mobility, IP address mobility, 484–490
models
  3G/4G VPN design models, 335
  ACI policy model, 447–450
  classification/marking/policing QoS model, 573–574
  customer-managed Layer 2 DCI deployment models. *See* customer-managed Layer 2 DCI deployment models
  DCN connectivity model, 820

deployment models
  DMVPN (Dynamic Multipoint VPN), 285
  enterprise IPv6 networks case study, 812
enterprise campus access-distribution design models, comparing, 45
interconnect model, 738–739
IP multicast service model, 636–637
IWAN Hybrid design model, 361
Layer 2 hub-and-spoke WAN QoS design model, 607
migration models
  IPv6 islands, 200–201
  IPv6 WAN, 201–203
MPLS VPNs connectivity model, 606
network-centric security model, 715
QoS (quality of service), 12-class QoS strategy model, 564–565
QoS design model, 837–838
QoS strategy models, 560–561
  4-class QoS strategy model, 561–562
  8-class QoS strategy model, 562–563
remote LAN model, 737–738
three-tier layer model, enterprise campus design, 9–10
three-tiered e-commerce application functional model, 714
two-tier layer model, enterprise campus design, 8–9

modern data centers, 400
  microsegementation, with overlay networks, 427–428
  multitenant data centers, 422
    secure tenant separation, 422–425
  network overlays, 402
    Cisco FabricPath, 402–407
    VXLAN (virtual extensible LAN), 407–408
  SDN (software-defined networking), 414–416
    benefits of, 416–417
    challenges of, 419–421
    nontraditional SDN, 421
    requirements, 419
    selection criteria, 417–418
  spine-leaf topologies, 400–401
  VTEP (VXLAN tunnel endpoint), 408–411

modes
  active/active mode, 722
  ASA firewall active/passive failover mode, 722
  FirePOWER IPS deployment modes, 728–729
  firewall modes, 719–720
  inline mode, 727
  IPsec VPNs, 621–623
  monitor-only mode, 727

modular enterprise campus with OSPF, 10–12

modular network architecture, 691–695
  security zones, 695

modularity, enterprise campus design, 10
  access-distribution block, 13–15
  OSPF (Open Shortest Path First), 10–12

modules, 692–693

monitor-only mode, 727

MP-BGP (Multiprotocol BGP), 468–470, 639

MP-BGP EVPN (Multiprotocol Border Gateway Protocol Ethernet Virtual Private Network), 413–414
MPLS (Multiprotocol Label Switching), 230
   Layer 3 MPLS VPNs, 233–234
   MPLS VPNs, architecture, 234–236
   MPLS DiffServ tunneling modes, 609–611
   MPLS EXP, 612–613
   MPLS headers, 524
   MPLS Layer 3 WAN design models, 326–329
   MPLS uniform DiffServ tunneling mode, 612
MPLS VPNs
   architecture, 234–236
   connectivity model, 606
   forwarding, 258–259
   fully meshed MPLS VPN QoS, 608–609
   Layer 2 MPLS VPN, 259
   QoS (quality of service), 605–607
      MPLS DiffServ tunneling modes, 609–611
      pipe tunneling mode, 614–615
      role mapping, 616
      sample roles, 615–617
      short-pipe tunneling mode, 612–614
      uniform tunneling mode, 612
   routing propagation, 255–258
MPLS WAN DiffServ tunneling, QoS in the enterprise network case study, 839–841
MQC, 536
MR (Map-Resolver), 214
mrinfo, 756
MS (Map-Server), 213–214
MSDP (Multicast Source Discovery Protocol), 639, 654
   multicast network edge security, 751–752
   neighbor relationships, 683
   operations, 684–686
   RP (Rendezvous Point), 683
mtrace, 756
MTU (maximum transmission unit), 80
   QoS (quality of service), 625–626
   WAN connections, 232
multicast. *See also* IP multicast, security challenges, 744
multicast admission controls, 757
multicast boundary, 749, 752
multicast distribution trees, 642
multicast distribution trees identification, 644–645
multicast forwarding, 645
   RPF check, 639–641
multicast groups, 635–636
Multicast Information Protocol, 748
multicast network edge, security, 748–749
   Auto-RP and BSR, 749–751
   MSDP (Multicast Source Discovery Protocol), 751–752
multicast networks, 638
   network element security, 746–748
   problems in, 744–745
   security considerations, 745–746
multicast protocols, 638–639, 642–644
multicast receiver controls, 755–757
multicast rekeying, 318–319
multicast routing protocols, 642

multicast routing tables, PIM-SM (Protocol-Independent Multicast—Sparse Mode), 652–653
multicast sender control, 753–755
Multichassis EtherChannel (MEC), 30
multicontext mode, firewall virtualization, 712
multihoming, 178
   Internet routing, 804–805
   IPv6, 226
   versus single-homing, BGP (Border Gateway Protocol), 177–178
   with two ISPs using a single local edge router, 183–186
   with two ISPs using multiple local edge routers, 186–188
multihop GRE tunneling based, 21
multihop MPLS core based, 22–23
multi-hypervisor-ready fabric, 445
multilayer architectures, EIGRP (Enhanced Interior Gateway Routing Protocol), 53–56
multiple autonomous system drivers, EIGRP (Enhanced Interior Gateway Routing Protocol), 53
multiple autonomous systems, EIGRP. *See* AS (autonomous systems)
multipoint GRE (mGRE), 275–276, 284
   versus point-to-point GRE, 276–277
multipology IS-IS, for IPv6, 140–141
Multiprotocol BGP (MP-BGP), 468–469
Multiprotocol Border Gateway Protocol Ethernet Virtual Private Network (MP-BGP EVPN), 413–414
Multiprotocol Label Switching. *See* MPLS (Multiprotocol Label Switching)
Multiprotocol Label Switching Virtual Private Networks. *See* MPLS VPNs
multitenant data centers, 422
   case studies, 425–426
   secure tenant separation, 422–425
multitenant segmentation, extranets, 739–740
multitier, access-distribution block, 13
multitier access model, distribution-to-distribution interconnect, 37–41
multitier data center designs
   data center high availability, 388–392
   end of row versus top of rack design, 383–384
   fabric extenders, 385–388
   inter-VLAN routing, 381–383
   NIC teaming, 392–393
   small data centers (connecting servers to an enterprise LAN), 376–378
   two-tier data center network architecture, 378–380

N

name services, IPv6, 220
named communities, BGP (Border Gateway Protocol), 171
NAT64, IPv6, 206–208
NBAR (Network-Based Application Recognition), 526–527
NBAR2 (next-generation NBAR), 526–527, 837
NBMA hub-and-spoke, IS-IS (Intermediate System-to-Intermediate System), 132–133
neighbor relationships, MSDP (Multicast Source Discovery Protocol), 683

NetFlow, 837
network access control
   authorization options case study, 772–775
   Cisco TrustSec, 768
      Profiling Service, 768–769
      SGT (Security Group Tag), 769–772
   EAP (Extensible Authentication Protocol), 763–765
   IEEE 802.1X, 759–763
   secure enterprise networks, 833–834
Network Access Manager, 766
network and security management, 695
network appliances, connecting, 821–822
network bgp router, 151
network design issues, route reflectors, BGP (Border Gateway Protocol), 169
network element security, 746–748
network infrastructure devices, resiliency and survivability, 700–701
network interface controller teaming, 392–393
Network Layer 2 separation, 423
Network Layer 3 separation, 422
network overlays, modern data centers, 402
   Cisco FabricPath, 402–407
   VXLAN (virtual extensible LAN), 407–408
network policy enforcement, 701–702
network resiliency, 24
network security zoning, 690–691

network separation, multitenant data centers, 422–423
network service access points (NSAPs), 102
network services separation, 423
network targeted attacks, security, 747
network types
   hub-and-spoke design, OSPF (Open Shortest Path First), 92–93
   IS-IS (Intermediate System-to-Intermediate System), 119
network virtualization overlays, ACI (Application-Centric Infrastructure), 441–446
Network-Based Application Recognition (NBAR), 526–527
network-centric security model, 715
networking limitations, ACI (Application-Centric Infrastructure), 432–434
networking technology, limitations of, 398–399
networks
   multicast networks
      problems in, 744–745
      security considerations, 745–746
   overlay networks, microsegementation, 427–428
new network architecture, data centers, 397–398
next-generation IPS (NGIPS), Cisco FirePOWER, 726–727
next-generation NBAR (NBAR2), 526–527
next-generation security, 696
next-generation WAN (NGWAN), 354–355

Nexus ACI fabric software, 440
Nexus switches, ACI fabric mode, 439
NGIPS (next-generation IPS), Cisco FirePOWER, 726–727
NGWAN (next-generation WAN), 354–355
NHRP, 284
   DMVPN (Dynamic Multipoint VPN), Phase 2, 290
NIC teaming, 392–393
no drop, 543
no next-hop-self, 298
no-advertise, 170
no-export, 170
no-export-subconfed, 170
nonclients, 155
nonredundant firewall connectivity design, 721
non-RR clients, 155
nonstop forwarding (NSF), EIGRP (Enhanced Interior Gateway Routing Protocol), 71–72
nontraditional SDN, 421
nontunnel EAP, 763
no-peer, 171
North American sites, routing policies, 797–799
north-south traffic, 478
NSAPs (network service access points), 102
NSF (nonstop forwarding), EIGRP (Enhanced Interior Gateway Routing Protocol), 71–72
number of areas, hub-and-spoke design, OSPF (Open Shortest Path First), 91
number of areas per ABR, OSPF (Open Shortest Path First), 81–82
numbers of routers in an area, OSPF (Open Shortest Path First), 80–81

O

offer message, DF election messages, 660
OILs (outgoing interface lists), 639
ONE (Open Network Environment) architecture, 435
ONF (Open Networking Foundation), 398
   OpenFlow, 415–416
Open Network Environment (ONE) architecture, 435
Open Networking Foundation (ONF), 398
Open Shortest Path First. *See* OSPF (Open Shortest Path First)
OpenFlow, ONF (Open Networking Foundation), 415–416
open-source sniffing solutions, 837
operational resiliency, 24
operations
   Auto-RP, 671–674
   MSDP (Multicast Source Discovery Protocol), 684–686
   PfR (Performance Routing), 362–363
operations zone, 694
order of operations, QoS (quality of service), 623–625
OSI layers, mapping QoS markings, 524–525
OSPF (Open Shortest Path First), 75
   adjacent neighbors, 76–77
   area design, 82–83
   characteristics, 110–112
   convergence, 93
      event detection, 94
      event processing, 96–97
      event propagation, 94–96
   design optimization, 782–785

DMVPN (Dynamic Multipoint VPN), 289
flooding reduction, 97
full-mesh design, 87–88
hierarchies, 84–85
hub-and-spoke design, 88
   ABR placement, 89–90
   network types, 92–93
   number of areas, 91
IS-IS versus, 110–112
   area design, 112–113
Link-State Database Overload Protection, 97–98
migrating from RIPv2, 785
modularity, enterprise campus design, 10–12
number of areas per ABR, 81–82
numbers of routers in an area, 80–81
PE-CE routing protocol, 247–250
   backdoor links between customer sites, 250–251
   route summarization, 251–252
routing information in the area and routed domain, 78–80
scalability design, 76
sham links, 250–251
summarization, 85–86

OSPF backbone area design, 781–782

OTV (overlay transport virtualization), DCI (Data Center Interconnect), 501–506

outgoing interface lists (OILs), 639

outside zone, IPS (intrusion prevention system), 726

overlay networks
   ACI network virtualization overlays, 441–446

   DCI (Data Center Interconnect), 507
   microsegementation, 427–428

overlay transport virtualization DCI, 501–506

overlay transport virtualization (OTV), DCI (Data Center Interconnect), 501–506

oversubscription, 380

P

P routers, 235
PA (Provider-Assigned) prefixes, 197–198
PaaS (platform as a service), 596
packet dropping, 547
packets, IS-IS (Intermediate System-to-Intermediate System), 117
PAgP (Port Aggregation Protocol), 28, 30
partial SNP. *See* PSNPs
partner and extranet modules, 693
pass messages, DF election messages, 660
passive interfaces, 700
path attributes, BGP (Border Gateway Protocol), 150
path isolation, campus network virtualization, 19–23
path selection, BGP (Border Gateway Protocol), 150–151
PAUSE frame, 598
PBR (policy-based routing), 724
PDUs, 117
PE (provider edge) routers, architecture, 237–238
   route distinguishers, 238–239
   route target (RT), 240–241
peak information rate (PIR), 533

PE-CE routing protocol, 241
  BGP (Border Gateway Protocol), 252–254
    backdoor links between customer sites, 254–255
  EIGRP (Enhanced Interior Gateway Routing Protocol), 241–242
    backdoor links between customer sites, 245–247
    different AS number, 243–244
    same AS number, 242–243
    some sites only, 244–245
  OSPF (Open Shortest Path First), 247–250
    backdoor links between customer sites, 250–251
    route summarization, 251–252
peer-forwarding rules, BGP (Border Gateway Protocol), 158
performance, platform performance, WAN QoS, 589–590
per-hop behavior (PHB)
  Layer 3 marking, 520–523
  queue design principles, 558–559
Pervasive SVI, 465–466
PFC (Priority-based Flow Control), 598
PfR (Performance Routing), 361–362
  IWAN (Intelligent WAN), 356
  operations, 362–363
PfRv3
  design and deployment, 366–367
  IWAN (Intelligent WAN), 363–366
Phase 1, DMVPN (Dynamic Multipoint VPN), 287–289
  EIGRP (Enhanced Interior Gateway Routing Protocol), 295–297
Phase 2, DMVPN (Dynamic Multipoint VPN), 289–292
  EIGRP (Enhanced Interior Gateway Routing Protocol), 297–299
Phase 3, DMVPN (Dynamic Multipoint VPN), 292–295
  EIGRP (Enhanced Interior Gateway Routing Protocol), 299–301
phased deployment, 802.1X, 767
phases of IKE (Internet Key Exchange), 278–279
PHB (per-hop behavior), Layer 3 marking, 520–523
PHB-DSCP bit mapping, 520
PI (Provider-Independent) prefixes, 197–198
PILE Forensic Accounting, enterprise BGP network with Internet connectivity case study. *See* enterprise BGP network with Internet connectivity
PIM (Protocol-Independent Multicast), 637
  BIDIR-PIM (bidirectional PIM), 658
  internal multicast security, 752
    multicast admission controls, 757
    multicast receiver controls, 755–757
PIM source-specific multicast (PIM-SSM), 646
PIM-DM (PIM Dense Mode), 750
PIM-SM (Protocol-Independent Multicast—Sparse Mode), 645–646
  (S, G), 653–654
  *, G (star comma G), 653
  bidirectional PIM (BIDIR-PIM), 657
  characteristics, 645
  IP multicast, 645–646
  multicast routing tables, 652–653
  receiver joins PIM-SM shared tree, 646–647

RP registration, 647–648
SPT switchover, 649–652
SSM (source-specific multicast). *See* SSM (source-specific multicast)
PIM-SM SPT switchover, 668
PIM-SSM (PIM source-specific multicast), 646
PIMv1, 756
PIMv2 BSR, 676–677
   BSR (bootstrap router), 678
   candidate RPs, 677–678
   flooding problems, 678–679
   routers, 678
PIMv6, 646
PIN (Places-in-the-Network), 568
   internal multicast security, multicast sender control, 753–755
pipe mode, MPLS DiffServ tunneling modes, 610
pipe tunneling mode, MPLS VPNs, 614–615
PIR (peak information rate), 533
placement of, RP (Rendezvous Point), 667–668
Places-in-the-Network (PIN), 568
planning and design phase, IPv6, 196–197
platform performance, WAN QoS, 589–590
PoE (Power over Ethernet), 378
point-to-point GRE versus mGRE, 276–277
point-to-point links, IS-IS (Intermediate System-to-Intermediate System), 119
policies, ACI fabric access policies, 454–455
policing and remarking design principles, QoS (quality of service), 556

policing tools
   single-rate three-color marker, 532–533
   two-rate three-color marker, 533–535
policing traffic, 527–529, 532
policy-based centralized control, 418
policy-based routing (PBR), 724
Port Aggregation Protocol (PAgP), 28
port extenders, 385–388
Power over Ethernet (PoE), 378
PQ (priority queueing), 535
PQ-WFQ, 536
prefixes
   6RD prefix, 211
   acquiring IPv6 prefixes, 197–198
prefix-suppression, 79
preventing, attacks, 703
priority command, 540
priority queueing (PQ), 535
Priority-based Flow Control (PFC), 598
problems, in multicast networks, 744–745
Profiling Service, 768–769
protocol operations, IS-IS (Intermediate System-to-Intermediate System), 119–121
Protocol-Independent Multicast (PIM), 637
Protocol-Independent Multicast—Sparse Mode. *See* PIM-SM (Protocol-Independent Multicast—Sparse Mode)
protocols
   BGP. *See* BGP (Border Gateway Protocol)
   EAP (Extensible Authentication Protocol), 762, 763–765

EGP (Exterior Gateway Protocol), 146

EIGRP. *See* EIGRP (Enhanced Interior Gateway Routing Protocol)

FHRP (First-Hop Redundancy Protocol), 31–35

FIP (FCoE Initialization Protocol), 388

GLBP (Gateway Load Balancing Protocol), 31–35

HSRP (Hot Standby Router Protocol), 31

IS-IS. *See* IS-IS (Intermediate System-to-Intermediate System)

LISP (Locator/ID Separation Protocol), 212–216

LLDP (Link Layer Discovery Protocol), 464

MCP (Mis-Cabling Protocol), 464

MPLS (Multiprotocol Label Switching), 230

Multicast Information Protocol, 748

multicast protocols, 638–639, 642–644

PAgP (Port Aggregation Protocol), 28, 30

PE-CE routing protocol, 241

    BGP (Border Gateway Protocol), 252–254

    EIGRP (Enhanced Interior Gateway Routing Protocol), 241–242

    OSPF (Open Shortest Path First), 247–250

routing protocol authentication mechanisms, 699

SAP (Session Announcement Protocol), 748

SXP (Security Group Tag Exchange Protocol), 770

VRRP (Virtual Router Redundancy Protocol), 31

provider (P) networks, 235

provider edge (PE) routers, 235

  architecture, 237–238

    route distinguishers, 238–239

    route target (RT), 240–241

Provider-Assigned (PA) prefixes, 197–198

provider-assigned approach, IPv6 WAN, 201

Provider-Independent (PI) prefixes, 197–198

provider-independent approach, IPv6 WAN, 201–202

Proxy Tunnel Router (PxTR), 214

pseudowire DCI, 495

PSNPs (partial number packets), 123–124

public access zones, 690, 694

public IP space selection, Internet routing, 803–804

public zones, 690, 694

pure IP domain, 104

pure ISO domain, 104

PxTR (Proxy Tunnel Router), 214

Q

QoS (quality of service), 514, 745

  buffers, 569–570

  bursts, 569–570

  campus QoS

    design examples, 576–588

    overview, 568

  classification, order of operations, 623–625

  classification and marking

892 QoS (quality of service)

  classification and marking tools, 516–517
  Layer 2 marking, 517–519
  Layer 2.5 marking: MPLS experimental bits, 524
  Layer 3 marking: DSCP per-hop behaviors, 520–523
  Layer 3 marking: IP type of service, 519–520
  Layer 7: NBAR/NBAR2, 526–527
  mapping markings between OSI layers, 524–525
  traffic policing and shaping, 527–529, 532
 classification and marking design principles, 554–555
 classification/marking/policing QoS model, 573–574
 classifications and marking tools, 516–517
 data center QoS, 594
  big data architecture, 596
  DC QoS application case study, 599–601
  HPT (high-performance trading), 595
 DMVPN (Dynamic Multipoint VPN), 626–628
 dropping design principles, 557–558
 dropping tools, DSCP-based WRED, 541–546
 GETVPN, 629–630
 IP ECN, 547–550
 IPsec VPN, 619–620
  MTU (maximum transmission unit), 625–626
  use cases, 621
 Layer 2 private WAN QoS, 607

  link aggregation of EtherChannel interface, 575–576
 MPLS VPNs, 605–607
  fully meshed MPLS VPN QoS, 608–609
  MPLS DiffServ tunneling models, 609–611
  pipe tunneling mode, 614–615
  sample roles, 615–617
  short-pipe tunneling mode, 612–614
  uniform tunneling mode, 612
 overview, 553–554
 per-hop behavior queue design principles, 558–559
 policing and remarking design principles, 556
 policing tools, 532–533
 queueing
  CBWFQ (class-based weighted fair queueing), 538–541
  fair-queuing, 537–538
  Tx-Ring, 536–537
 queueing design principles, 557
 queueing tools, 535–536
 queueing/dropping recommendations, 574–575
 RFC 4594, 559–560
 token bucket algorithms, 529–531
 traffic descriptors, 516–517
 traffic policing, 527–529
 traffic shaping, 527–529
 trust boundary, QoS in the enterprise network case study, 838
 trust states, boundaries and, 570–573
 video, 568–569
 VoIP (voice over IP), 568–569

WAN connections, 231
WAN QoS. *See* WAN QoS
QoS design model, 837–838
QoS in the enterprise network case study, 835
   designing
      congestion management, 838–839
      MPLS WAN DiffServ tunneling, 839–841
      QoS design model, 837–838
      QoS trust boundary, 838
      requirements and expectations, 835–836
      scavenger traffic, 839
      traffic discovery and analysis, 836–837
QoS strategy models, 560–561
   4-class QoS strategy model, 561–562
   8-class QoS strategy model, 562–563
   12-class QoS strategy model, 564–565
quality of service (QoS). *See* QoS (quality of service), WAN connections, 231
queries, EIGRP (Enhanced Interior Gateway Routing Protocol), 52–53
queueing, 535
   8-class 1P1Q3T egress queueing, 581–588
   8-class 1P1Q3T ingress queueing, 580–581
   CBWFQ (class-based weighted fair queueing), 538–541
   fair-queueing, 537–538
   Tx-Ring, 536–537
   WAN QoS, 591–592

queueing design principles, QoS (quality of service), 557
queueing recommendations, QoS (quality of service), 574–575
queueing tools, 535–536

R

RA spoofing, 222
rACLs (receive access control lists), 747
RADIUS (Remote Authentication Dial-In User Service), 762, 763
random drop, 544
random early detection (RED), 542
   dropping modes, 543–544
rate-limiting PIM register messages, 752
receive access control lists (rACLs), 747
receive process, IS-IS (Intermediate System-to-Intermediate System), 118
receiver joins PIM-SM shared tree, 646–647
Recovery Point Objective (RPO), 482
Recovery Time Objective (RTO), 482
RED (random early detection), 542
   dropping modes, 543–544
redundancy
   case studies, redundancy and connectivity, 343–354
   DMVPN (Dynamic Multipoint VPN), 302–304
Regional Internet Registries (RIR), 809
regional offices WAN design, 348–351
rekeying options, 318–319

Remote Authentication Dial-In User Service (RADIUS), 762, 763
remote LAN model, 737–738
remote sites
    local Internet, 337–339
    WAN, 324–326
remote VPN solutions, 272
remote VTEP discovery, 411–413
    tenant address learning, 411–413
remote-site LANs, 339–343
remote-site WAN design, 346–348
Rendezvous Point. *See* RP (Rendezvous Point)
replacement routing protocols, selecting, 780
requirements
    enterprise BGP network with Internet connectivity case study, 788–791
    for enterprise connectivity, 778–779
    enterprise data center connectivity design, 817–818
    enterprise IPv6 networks case study, 808–809
    QoS in the enterprise network case study, 835–836
    resilient enterprise WANs case study, 825–826
    for SDN, 419
    secure enterprise networks case study, 831
resiliency
    enterprise campus design, 23
    high-availability enterprise campus, 23–24
    network infrastructure devices, 700–701
    VPLS (Virtual Private LAN Service), 265–266

resilient enterprise WANs, designing, 825
    analysis and task list, 826–827
    requirements and expectations, 825–826
    selecting WAN links, 828
    WAN overlays, 828–830
REST, 422
restricted VLANs, 773
restricted zones, 690, 694
reverse path forwarding (RPF), 635
RFC 791, 523
RFC 2474, 523
RFC 2597, 556
RFC 3168, 547
RFC 3171, 636
RFC 3956, 679
RFC 4594, 559–560
RIPv2, migrating to OSPF, 785
RIR (Regional Internet Registries), 809
role mapping, MPLS VPNs, 616
route distinguishers, provider edge (PE) routers, 238–239
route filtering, 224
route leaking, IS-IS (Intermediate System-to-Intermediate System), 126–129
route reflector clients, 155
route reflector cluster-ID, BGP (Border Gateway Protocol), 161–162
route reflector clusters, BGP (Border Gateway Protocol), 160–161
route reflectors, BGP (Border Gateway Protocol), 153–155
    versus confederations, 157

congruence of physical and logical networks, 165–167
hierarchical route reflector design, 167–168
loop prevention, 162–165
network design issues, 169
redundancy, 159–160
route reflector cluster-ID, 161–162
route reflector clusters, 160–161
split-horizon rule, 158–159

route summarization
black holes, EIGRP (Enhanced Interior Gateway Routing Protocol), 61–63
IS-IS (Intermediate System-to-Intermediate System), 136–138
OSPF (Open Shortest Path First), PE-CE routing protocol, 251–252
suboptimal routing, EIGRP (Enhanced Interior Gateway Routing Protocol), 63–65

route target (RT), provider edge (PE) routers, 240–241
routed access, access-distribution block, 14–15
routed access model, distribution-to-distribution interconnect, 41–42
routed domains, OSPF (Open Shortest Path First), 78–80
routed mode, firewalls, 719
router hardening, 745
router types, IS-IS (Intermediate System-to-Intermediate System), 106–108
routers
Auto-RP, 670
customer edge (CE) routers, 235
P routers, 235
PIMv2 BSR, 678
provider edge (PE) routers, 235

routing
ACI (Application-Centric Infrastructure), 465
  border leaves, 467–468
  first-hop layer 3 default gateway, 465–466
default routing, 805–807
enterprise routing, WAN, 236–237
Internet routing, 803–807
inter-VLAN routing, 381–383
IS-IS (Intermediate System-to-Intermediate System), 125–126
  asymmetric versus symmetric, 129–132
  flat IS-IS routing design, 134–135
  full-mesh design, 133–134
  NBMA hub-and-spoke, 132–133
  route leaking, 126–129

routing information, area and routed domain, OSPF (Open Shortest Path First), 78–80
routing infrastructure, security, 699–700
routing policies
Asian sites, 799–802
enterprise BGP network with Internet connectivity, case study, 797–802
European sites, 799–802
North American sites, 797–799

routing policy language (RPL), 169
routing propagation, MPLS VPNs, 255–258

routing protocol authentication mechanisms, 699

routing protocols, choosing, for enterprise BGP network with Internet connectivity design, 792

RP (Rendezvous Point), 665
- Anycast RP, 681
  - *examples, 682–683*
- Auto-RP, 668–669
  - *candidate RPs, 670*
  - *case studies, 670–674*
  - *mapping agents, 670*
  - *routers, 670*
  - *scope problems, 674–676*
- candidate RPs, 676–677
- IPv6 embedded RP, 679–681
- MSDP (Multicast Source Discovery Protocol), 683
  - *neighbor relationships, 683*
  - *operations case study, 684–686*
- PIMv2 BSR, 676–677
  - *BSR (bootstrap router), 678*
  - *candidate RPs, 677–678*
  - *flooding problems, 678–679*
  - *routers, 678*
- placement of, 667–668

RP (Rendezvous Point) discovery, 665–667

RP deployments, comparing, 667

RP registration, PIM-SM (Protocol-Independent Multicast—Sparse Mode), 647–648

RPF (reverse path forwarding), 635

RPF check
- case studies, 641–642
- multicast forwarding, 639–641

RPL (routing policy language), 169

RPO (Recovery Point Objective), 482

RT (route target), provider edge (PE) routers, 240–241

RTO (Recovery Time Objective), 482

S

(S, G)
- PIM-SM (Protocol-Independent Multicast—Sparse Mode), 653–654
- PIM-SM SPT switchover, 649–652

SA (Security Association), 278

sandbox infrastructures, 740

SAP (Session Announcement Protocol), 748

scalability
- iBGP, 152–153
  - *confederations, 155–156*
- VPLS (Virtual Private LAN Service), 263–265
- WAN connections, 231

scalability design, OSPF (Open Shortest Path First), 76

scalability optimization
- DMVPN (Dynamic Multipoint VPN), EIGRP (Enhanced Interior Gateway Routing Protocol), 69
- hub-and-spoke design, EIGRP (Enhanced Interior Gateway Routing Protocol), 65–68

scalable EIGRP design, 50

scalable passive monitoring, PfRv3, 364

scaling, enterprise connectivity design, 787–788

scavenger traffic, QoS in the enterprise network case study, 839

scheduling, 535
- WFQ (weighted fair queueing), 537–538

scope problems, Auto-RP, 674–676
SDN (software-defined networking), 398, 414–416
   benefits of, 416–417
   challenges of, 419–421
   nontraditional SDN, 421
   requirements, 419
   security, 703–704
   selection criteria, 417–418
SDN controller characteristics, 418
SDWAN (software-defined WAN), 354–355
secure connectivity, WAN, 357
secure enterprise networks, designing, 830
   firewalls, 835
   infrastructure and network access security, 833–834
   Layer 2 security, 834–835
   requirements and expectations, 831
   security domains and zone design, 832
secure neighbor discovery (SeND), 222
secure network access, 695
secure network design, 695
Secure Sockets Layer (SSL) VPN, 312–313
Secure Sockets Layer virtual private network (SLL VPN), 221
secure tenant separation, multitenant data centers, 422–425
securing
   BSR (bootstrap router), 751
   east-west traffic, 716–717
   management access, to infrastructure devices, 698–699

security
   control plane security, IPv6, 224
   dual-stack security, IPv6, 225
   extranets, 739–740
   firewalls. *See* firewalls
   infrastructure device access, 698–699
   internal multicast security, 752
   IP multicast, 743
      challenges of, 744
   link layer security, IPv6, 221–222
   multicast network edge, 748–749
      Auto-RP and BSR, 749–751
      MSDP (Multicast Source Discovery Protocol), 751–752
   multicast networks, 745–746
   network element security, 746–748
   network infrastructure devices, resiliency and survivability, 700–701
   network policy enforcement, 701–702
   network security zoning, 690–691
   next-generation security, 696
   routing infrastructure, 699–700
   SDN (software-defined networking), 703–704
   switching infrastructure, 702–703
   tunneling security, IPv6, 225–226
Security Association (SA), 278
security domains, designing, 832
security group access control lists (SGACL), 770
Security Group Tag Exchange Protocol (SXP), 770
Security Group Tag (SGT), 769–772
security services, IPv6, 221

security zones, modular network architecture, 695

segmentation, multitenant segmentation, extranets, 739–740

selecting
- data center architecture and connectivity model, 818–819
- replacement routing protocols, 780
- WAN links, 828

selection criteria, SDN (software-defined networking), 417–418

SeND (secure neighbor discovery), 222

send-community, 169–170

separate DCI layer deployment model, 500

separating, application tiers, 714–716

sequence number packets (SNPs), 123

server-server traffic, 480

service graphs, 459

service migration, enterprise IPv6 networks case study, 815–816

service provider-managed VPNs230

service-level agreement (SLA), WAN connections, 231

Session Announcement Protocol (SAP), 748

SGACL (security group access control lists), 770

SGT (Security Group Tag), 769–772

sham links, OSPF (Open Shortest Path First), 250–251

shaping traffic, 527–529, 532
- WAN QoS, 592–593

shared distribution trees, 643–644

shared trees, 642, 643–644

shortest path trees (SPT), 637

short-pipe mode, MPLS DiffServ tunneling modes, 610

short-pipe tunneling mode, MPLS VPNs, 612–614

show ip community-list, 171

show ip pim rp mapping, 671

SIA (stuck in active), 52

simple demarcation, 329

single topology restrictions, IS-IS (Intermediate System-to-Intermediate System), 138–139

single-homed, multiple links, BGP (Border Gateway Protocol), 178–180

single-homing, versus multihoming, BGP (Border Gateway Protocol), 177–178

single-rate three-color marker, 532–533

single-tier firewalls, architecture, 710

site-to-site VPN solutions, 272–273

SLA (service-level agreement), WAN connections, 231

SLAAC (Stateless Address Autoconfiguration), 221

SLL VPN (Secure Sockets Layer virtual private network), 221

small data centers (connecting servers to an enterprise LAN), connecting servers to an enterprise LAN, 376–378

smart probing, 364

SNPs (sequence number packets), 123

software-defined networking (SDN), 398, 414–416
- benefits of, 416–417
- challenges of, 419–421
- nontraditional SDN, 421
- requirements, 419
- selection criteria, 417–418

software-defined WAN (SDWAN), 354–355
solution manageability, 355
source distribution trees, 643
source-rooted trees, 642
source-specific multicast. *See* SSM (source-specific multicast)
source-specific multicast mode, 655
spanned EtherChannel, 724
sparse mode protocols, 642
speaker types, BGP (Border Gateway Protocol), 147–148
SPF-Hold, 96
SPF-Max, 96
SPF-Start, 96
spince switches, 439
spine switches, 401
spine-leaf topologies, modern data centers, 400–401
split brain, 485
split-horizon rule, BGP (Border Gateway Protocol), 148–149
   route reflectors, 158–159
spoke-to-spoke, DMVPN (Dynamic Multipoint VPN), 285
SP-provided VPN services, 230
SPT (shortest path trees), 637
SPT switchover, PIM-SM (Protocol-Independent Multicast—Sparse Mode), 649–652
SSL (Secure Sockets Layer) VPN, 312–313
SSM (source-specific multicast), 654–656
   characteristics, 654
SSM out-of-band source directory, 656
stages of PfRv2, 363
start-interval, 94

Stateless Address Autoconfiguration (SLAAC), 221
storage traffic, 480–482
STP blocking links, GLBP (Gateway Load Balancing Protocol), 35
STP-based layer LANs, ACI (Application-Centric Infrastructure), 464–465
stub leaking, EIGRP (Enhanced Interior Gateway Routing Protocol), 67–68
stuck in active (SIA), 52
suboptimal bandwidth utilization, 541–542
suboptimal routing, route summarization, EIGRP (Enhanced Interior Gateway Routing Protocol), 63–65
summarization
   choke points and, 55–56
   hub-and-spoke design, EIGRP (Enhanced Interior Gateway Routing Protocol), 61–65
   OSPF (Open Shortest Path First), 85–86
   route summarization, IS-IS (Intermediate System-to-Intermediate System), 136–138
supplicants, 759
   802.1X, 765–766
supported traffic, WAN connections, 232
survivability, network infrastructure devices, 700–701
SVI (switched virtual interface), 468
switched virtual interface (SVI), 468
switching infrastructure, 702–703
SXP (Security Group Tag Exchange Protocol), 770

symmetric routing versus asymmetric routing, IS-IS (Intermediate System-to-Intermediate System), 129–132

synchronization, LSDB synchronization, IS-IS (Intermediate System-to-Intermediate System), 123–124

T

TACACS+ 833

tail drop, 544

task lists, enterprise connectivity, 779–780

TCP windowing, 547

TDM (time-division multiplexing), 530

TEAP (Tunnel Extensible Authentication Protocol), 765

teleworker, 693

tenant address learning, remote VTEP discovery, 411–413

tenant separation
- device-level virtualization, 424–425
- multitenant data centers, 422–425

tenants
- ACI (Application-Centric Infrastructure), 456–459
- multitenant data centers, 422

TEP (tunnel endpoint), 441

theft of service, 754

three-layer hierarchy architecture, EIGRP (Enhanced Interior Gateway Routing Protocol), 57–59

three-tier data center network architecture, 380–381

three-tier layer model, enterprise campus design, 9–10

three-tiered e-commerce application functional model, 714

TID (Transport-Independent Design), 356

time-division multiplexing (TDM), 530

TLVs (type, length, value, 103

token bucket algorithms, 529–531

tools
- dropping tools, DSCP-based WRED, 541–546
- policing tools. See policing tools
- queueing tools, 535–536

topology depths, 54

ToR (Top of Rack) design, 383–384

traffic
- east-west traffic, 716–717
- scavenger traffic, 839

traffic descriptors, QoS (quality of service), 516–517

traffic discovery, QoS in the enterprise network case study, 836–837

traffic engineering techniques, 351–354

traffic filtering, Layer 2 segments, 703

traffic flow directions, 478–479

traffic flow types, 479–482

traffic policing
- ECN (explicit congestion notification), 547–550
- QoS (quality of service), 527–529

traffic shaping, QoS (quality of service), 527–529

traffic trombone, 487

trail drop, 547

transit border router, 366

transit link, remote-site LANs, 343
transit master controller, 365
transition mechanisms
    IPv6, 216–217
    IPv6 migration, 203–205
transparent mode, firewalls, 719
transport mode, IPsec VPN, 621
transport options
    for remote sites using local Internet, 338–339
    remote sites using local Internet, 350–351
Transport-Independent Design (TID), 356
trunked demarcation, 329
trunking, high-availability enterprise campus, 27
trust CoS, 571
trust DSCP, 571
trust states
    boundaries and, 570–573
    dynamic trust states, 572–573
TrustSec, 768
    Profiling Service, 768–769
    SGT (Security Group Tag), 769–772
TTL Security Check, 7006
tunnel broker approach, 202
tunnel brokers, IPv6, 209
Tunnel Extensible Authentication Protocol (TEAP), 765
tunnel mode, IPsec VPN, 621
tunneled EAP, 764
tunneling modes, MPLS DiffServ tunneling modes, 609–611
tunneling security, IPv6, 225–226
tunnels, manual tunnels, IPv6, 208–209
tuples, 103

two-layer hierarchy architecture, EIGRP (Enhanced Interior Gateway Routing Protocol), 56–57
two-rate three-color marker, 533–535
two-tier data center network architecture, 378–380
two-tier firewall, architecture, 710
two-tier layer model, enterprise campus design, 8–9
Tx-Ring, 536–537, 591

U

unicast, 635
unicast rekeying, 318
unicast reverse pack forwarding (uRPF), 702
uniform mode, MPLS DiffServ tunneling modes, 610
uniform tunneling mode, MPLS VPNs, 612
untrusted, 571
update process, IS-IS (Intermediate System-to-Intermediate System), 118
uRPF (unicast reverse pack forwarding), 702

V

VDCs (virtual device contexts), 424–425
video, QoS (quality of service), 568–569
virtual device contexts (VDCs), 424–425
virtual extensible LAN (VXLAN), 407–408
virtual firewalls, 712

Virtual MAC (vMAC), 489
virtual machines (VMs), 716–717
virtual network interface cards (vNICs), 715–716
Virtual Network Management Center (VNMC), 713
virtual private LAN service DCI, 496
Virtual Private LAN Service (VPLS), 259, 261–263, 265–266
   scalability, 263–265
Virtual Private Wire Service (VPWS), 259–261
Virtual Router Redundancy Protocol (VRRP), 31
virtual routing and forwarding. *See* VRF (virtual routing and forwarding)
Virtual Security Gateway (VSG), 713
virtual switch model, distribution-to-distribution interconnect, 43–44
virtual switch (switch clustering), access-distribution block, 13–14
virtual switching system (VSS), IP gateway redundancy, 35–36
virtual tunnel interface (VTI), IPsec and, 281–282
virtualization
   campus network virtualization, 16–23
   device-level virtualization, 424–425
virtualized firewalls, 712–714
virtualized multiservice architectures, 596–597
Virtualized Multiservice Data Centers (VMDC), 596–597
VLAN assignment
   campus network virtualization, 17–18
   dynamic VLAN assignments, 772–774

VLAN design, high-availability enterprise campus, 24–26
vMAC (Virtual MAC), 489
VMDC (Virtualized Multiservice Data Centers), 596–597
VMs (virtual machines), 716–717
vNICs (virtual network interface cards), 715–716
VNMC (Virtual Network Management Center), 713
voice traffic, QoS (quality of service), 568–569
VoIP (voice over IP), QoS (quality of service), 568–569
vPC, 388–392
   firewall routing, 725
VPLS (Virtual Private LAN Service), 259, 261–263
   DCI (Data Center Interconnect), 496
   resiliency, 265–266
   scalability, 263–265
   versus VPWS, 266–267
VPN use cases, QoS (quality of service), 621
VPN WAN design models, 331–335
VPNs (virtual private networks)
   enterprise-managed VPNs. *See* enterprise-managed VPNs
   FlexVPN, 314
      architecture, 315
      capabilities, 315
      configuration blocks, 315–316
   GETVPN, 317–320
   Layer 3 MPLS VPNs, 233–234
   managed VPNs, 230
   MPLS VPNs, architecture, 234–236
   security, 695

service provider-managed VPNs230
SSL (Secure Sockets Layer) VPN, 312–313
VPWS (Virtual Private Wire Service), 259–261
versus VPLS, 266–267
VRF (virtual routing and forwarding)
  campus network virtualization, 18
  firewalls, 712
VRF-Lite, Layer 3 separation, 423–424
VRRP (Virtual Router Redundancy Protocol), 31
VSG (Virtual Security Gateway), 713, 714
VSS (virtual switching system), IP gateway redundancy, 35–36
VTEP (VXLAN tunnel endpoint), 408–411, 441
VTI (virtual tunnel interface), IPsec and, 281–282
VXLAN (virtual extensible LAN), 407–408
  control plane optimization, 413–414
  overlay networks, microsegementation, 427–428
  remote VTEP discovery, 411–413
  VTEP (VXLAN tunnel endpoint), 408–411
VXLAN tunnel endpoint (VTEP), 408–411

W

WAN (Wide Area Network)
  3G/4G VPN design models, 335
  application optimization, 356–357
  case studies, redundancy and connectivity, 343–354

  enterprise routing, 236–237
  intelligent path control, 356
  IWAN (Intelligent WAN), 354–355
  Layer 2 WAN design models, 329–331
  management, 357–358
  MPLS Layer 3 WAN design models, 326–329
  NGWAN (next-generation WAN), 354–355
  regional offices WAN design, 348–351
  remote sites, local Internet, 337–339
  remote-site LANs, 339–343
  remote-site WAN design, 346–348
  SDWAN (software-defined WAN), 354–355
  secure connectivity, 357
  TID (Transport-Independent Design), 356
  traffic engineering techniques, 351–354
  VPN WAN design models, 331–335
WAN aggregation, 325–326, 327
WAN connections, choosing, 230–233
WAN links, selecting, 828
WAN overlays, resilient enterprise WANs case study, 828–830
WAN QoS
  examples, 593–594
  latency and jitter, 590–591
  overview, 588–589
  platform performance, 589–590
  queueing, 591–592
  shaping traffic, 592–593
WAN remote sites, overview, 324–326

WAN remote-site design models, 328

WAN remote-site transport options, 325–326

WAN/branch edge, 588–589
- CBWFQ (class-based weighted fair queueing), 592

WAN/VPN QoS design, 593

WDM, 490

web proxy, 740

Web Security Appliance (WSA), 735–736

weighted fair queueing (WFQ), 536

well-known BGP communities, 170–171

WFQ (weighted fair queueing), 536, 537–538

winner messages, DF election messages, 660

wired networks, 802.1X, 760

wireless LAN controller (WLC), 771

WLC (wireless LAN controller), 771

WRED, 544–546, 547, 591
- dropping design principles, 557–558
- ECN (explicit congestion notification), 548–549

WSA (Web Security Appliance), 735–736

X-Y-Z

zone interface points, 690

zones
- designing, 832
- EIGRP (Enhanced Interior Gateway Routing Protocol), 54
- modular network architecture, 695

zoning, 690–691

Exclusive Offer – 40% OFF

Cisco Press Video Training

livelessons▶

ciscopress.com/video

Use coupon code **CPVIDEO40** during checkout.

Video Instruction from Technology Experts

Advance Your Skills

Get started with fundamentals, become an expert, or get certified.

Train Anywhere

Train anywhere, at your own pace, on any device.

Learn

Learn from trusted author trainers published by Cisco Press.

Try Our Popular Video Training for FREE!

ciscopress.com/video

Explore hundreds of **FREE** video lessons from our growing library of Complete Video Courses, LiveLessons, networking talks, and workshops.

Cisco Press

ciscopress.com/video

ALWAYS LEARNING — PEARSON

The Cisco Learning Network
The IT Community that helps you get Cisco Certified.

Be a Part of the Community | Prepare for Success | Interact with Professionals | Mentor, Share, Achieve

Join over 1 Million Members on the Cisco Learning Network, featuring powerful study resources like IT Training Videos, Study Groups and Certification Exam Topics.

Connect with us on social media at:
cs.co/LearningatCisco-About

ciscolearningnetwork.com

REGISTER YOUR PRODUCT at CiscoPress.com/register
Access Additional Benefits and SAVE 35% on Your Next Purchase

- Download available product updates.
- Access bonus material when applicable.
- Receive exclusive offers on new editions and related products.
  (Just check the box to hear from us when setting up your account.)
- Get a coupon for 35% for your next purchase, valid for 30 days.
  Your code will be available in your Cisco Press cart. (You will also find it in the Manage Codes section of your account page.)

Registration benefits vary by product. Benefits will be listed on your account page under Registered Products.

CiscoPress.com – Learning Solutions for Self-Paced Study, Enterprise, and the Classroom
Cisco Press is the Cisco Systems authorized book publisher of Cisco networking technology, Cisco certification self-study, and Cisco Networking Academy Program materials.

At **CiscoPress.com** you can
- Shop our books, eBooks, software, and video training.
- Take advantage of our special offers and promotions (ciscopress.com/promotions).
- Sign up for special offers and content newsletters (ciscopress.com/newsletters).
- Read free articles, exam profiles, and blogs by information technology experts.
- Access thousands of free chapters and video lessons.

Connect with Cisco Press – Visit CiscoPress.com/community
Learn about Cisco Press community events and programs.

Cisco Press